RAVEN

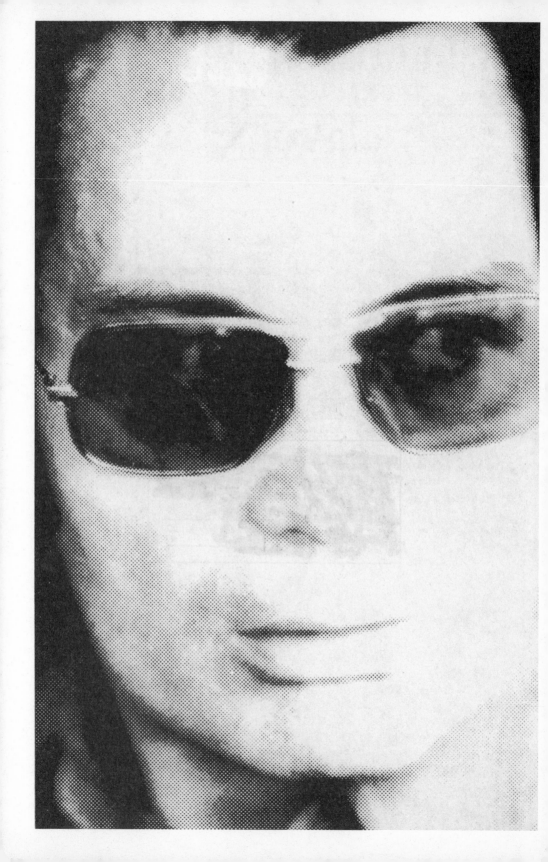

TIM REITERMAN
with JOHN JACOBS

RAVEN

THE UNTOLD STORY OF THE REV. JIM JONES AND HIS PEOPLE

JEREMY P. TARCHER/PENGUIN
a member of Penguin Group (USA) Inc.
New York

JEREMY P. TARCHER/PENGUIN

Published by the Penguin Group

Penguin Group (USA) Inc., 375 Hudson Street, New York, New York 10014, USA • Penguin Group
(Canada), 90 Eglinton Avenue East, Suite 700, Toronto, Ontario M4P 2Y3, Canada (a division of
Pearson Canada Inc.) • Penguin Books Ltd, 80 Strand, London WC2R 0RL, England •
Penguin Ireland, 25 St Stephen's Green, Dublin 2, Ireland (a division of Penguin Books Ltd) •
Penguin Group (Australia), 250 Camberwell Road, Camberwell, Victoria 3124, Australia
(a division of Pearson Australia Group Pty Ltd) • Penguin Books India Pvt Ltd, 11 Community
Centre, Panchsheel Park, New Delhi–110 017, India • Penguin Group (NZ), 67 Apollo Drive,
Rosedale, North Shore 0632, New Zealand (a division of Pearson New Zealand Ltd) • Penguin Books
(South Africa) (Pty) Ltd, 24 Sturdee Avenue, Rosebank, Johannesburg 2196, South Africa

Penguin Books Ltd, Registered Offices: 80 Strand, London WC2R 0RL, England

Originally published in 1982 by E. P. Dutton, Inc.
Introduction copyright © 2008 by Tim Reiterman
Copyright © 1982 by Tim Reiterman

Most Tarcher/Penguin books are available at special quantity discounts for bulk purchase for sales
promotions, premiums, fund-raising, and educational needs. Special books or book excerpts also can
be created to fit specific needs. For details, write Penguin Group (USA) Inc. Special Markets,
375 Hudson Street, New York, NY 10014.

Library of Congress Cataloging-in-Publication Data

Reiterman, Tim.
Raven : the untold story of the Rev. Jim Jones and his people /
Tim Reiterman with John Jacobs.
p.   cm.
Originally published : New York : Dutton, © 1982. With new pref. by the author.
ISBN 978-1-58542-678-2
1. Peoples Temple.   2. Jones, Jim, 1931–1978.   I. Jacobs, John, 1950–2000.   II. Title.
BP605.P46R44   2008   2008027271
289.9—dc22

Printed in the United States of America
9   10

While the author has made every effort to provide accurate telephone numbers and Internet addresses at the time of
publication, neither the publisher nor the author assumes any responsibility for errors, or for changes that occur after
publication. Further, the publisher does not have any control over and does not assume any responsibility for author or
third-party websites or their content.

The cover and title page photo of Jim Jones was taken
by San Francisco Examiner *photographer*
Greg Robinson
a few hours before he was shot and killed,
by Peoples Temple gunmen.

This book is dedicated to Greg,
our colleague and friend, and to the memory of
NBC newsmen Don Harris and Bob Brown,
Representative Leo Ryan,
and the hundreds of other victims in Guyana.

*"Prophet!" said I, "thing of evil!—
Prophet still, if bird or devil!"*

EDGAR ALLAN POE

*"I come with the black hair of a raven.
I come as God Socialist!"*

JIM JONES

PREFACE TO THE
TARCHER/PENGUIN EDITION

Three decades have passed since more than nine hundred Americans suffered horrible deaths in the jungle of the impoverished South American country of Guyana. The events in Jonestown on November 18, 1978, orchestrated by a charismatic preacher named Jim Jones and triggered by the slaying of a United States congressman on a nearby airstrip, have long ago moved from worldwide headlines to the pages of history. Yet fascination with the final days of Jonestown and the life of Jones has persisted over the years.

One of the most shocking and baffling events of the last century, the demise of Peoples Temple has been chronicled in books, movies, documentaries, plays, scholarly studies, and countless television retrospectives. The images of an American tragedy on foreign soil—poisoned punch squirted down the throats of infants, families locked in final embrace, mounds of bodies bloated in the tropical heat—have endured in print, photos, video footage, and memory.

Jonestown has come to symbolize unfathomable depravity, the outermost limits of what human beings can visit on each other and themselves, the ultimate power of a leader over his followers. Although complex and elusive, the reasons for the collapse of the Temple's utopian dream into a hellish nightmare have been reduced again and again to a simplistic interpretation: A Svengali led his compliant, even robotic, flock to mass suicide. But Peoples Temple was more than a creation of one man's vision. The Temple was a product of its time and the search for alternative religions and social relevance in the post–civil rights and post–Vietnam eras. Its story also speaks to the timeless yearnings of the human spirit for a sense of belonging, to be part of something larger than ourselves.

Above the wooden, thronelike chair from which Jones lorded over his people hung a sign that said: "Those who do not remember the past are condemned to repeat it." However, remembering the past is one thing, understanding it quite another. And this volume endeavors to do both, while piercing the many myths that have shrouded the truth about Jones, his followers, and the remote agricultural settlement that bore his name.

It is particularly important to put to rest enduring misconceptions and to grasp the forces that drove the temple inexorably toward its end:

- Jones was not a good man gone bad, as many believed. The seeds of madness, violence, and cruelty had grown in him since his childhood in Indiana. And he later filled his followers with his own paranoia and built psychological walls that kept them from the outside world and within his control.

- Although Jones borrowed ideas from unconventional religious groups, the Temple did not spring from New Age or Eastern religions but from Christianity in America's heartland. It was sanctioned by a mainstream denomination, and his major religious inspiration was Pentecostal hucksterism, with its tradition of faked healings and other "miracles."

- Jones, who called himself a socialist God, was not a pure ideologue but also was a pragmatic chameleon driven by his weaknesses and his personal needs for family, acceptance, and power.

- Rather than social misfits, Jones's followers generally were decent, hardworking, socially conscious people, some highly educated, who were drawn to the interracial church. Many wanted to help their fellow man and serve God, not embrace a self-proclaimed deity on earth.

- When the poor and troubled came together at the Temple with those who wanted to help such people, they formed a family-like bond that for many was as strong as their loyalty to Jones.

- Peoples Temple was not merely a cultlike organization that stripped away individuality; it also was a church, a social movement, and a political organization that energized its members, did some good works and won Jones public appointments in Indiana and later California. But Jones perverted his church's social goals by aggrandizing himself and preaching that the ends justified the means.

- Good and evil coexisted in Jones, and he hid the sickness within him from most of his members. The trusted ones who knew at least part of the truth were so committed or compromised that they rationalized whatever he did.

- Jones did not act alone in seizing the psyches, belongings, and lives of his followers. He had accomplices among elected officials who looked the other way rather than look more deeply into an organization that provided troops to further their political agendas. Meanwhile, government agencies and some news media were unwilling or unable to take on Jones despite telltale signs that he was exploiting and abusing followers and breaking laws.

- On one level, Jonestown was justifiably a source of pride, a community carved out of the jungle by mostly urban people. But this place they called the Promised Land began its ominous decline and ultimately imploded after Jones settled there for good.

- Finally, although many share responsibility for the death spiral of the Temple, Jones's own actions dictated the catastrophic outcome. What happened in Jonestown amounted to mass murder, not mass suicide. Jones put all the pieces in place for a last act of self-destruction, then gave the order to kill the children first, sealing everyone's fate.

Today the scene of the carnage is but a haunting memory. By the tenth anniversary of the tragedy, the sprawling settlement had been reduced to a yellowish green scar on the dark forest landscape and to pieces of rusted machinery. The jungle had reclaimed land where fruit trees and rows of cassava and vegetables once were tended by young and old alike. Rain, rot, and wildfire had wiped out what was not already looted from the metal-roofed buildings. But what remains is one abiding and cautionary truth: People who surrender their worldly resources, their offspring, and the most basic decisions in their lives to a man, a cause, and an organization do so at their peril.

This new edition of *Raven* is completed without the presence of my coauthor, John Jacobs, a dear friend and widely respected journalist who died in 2000 and whose talents and contributions made this book possible.

—Tim Reiterman
2008

CONTENTS

Preface and Acknowledgments

The narrative that follows is a work of fact. Given the often-erroneous accounts that have proliferated since the demise of Peoples Temple, it seemed to us of utmost importance to ensure the veracity of the only complete history of Jim Jones and his movement. The task became more compelling because events following the November 18, 1978, tragedy indicated there never would be a comprehensive impartial official investigation into its roots and causes, nor a study of Jim Jones's personality. In some ways, we present this book as that missing investigation.

In order to penetrate the myths and misconceptions surrounding the Temple and Jones, we have adopted two methodologies. In most cases, the two-source rule was applied; indeed in most cases more than two sources provided confirmation, or the information was corroborated by Temple documentation. In cases when by necessity only a single source existed and the information seemed important, we relied upon documentation, other sources and/or our own accumulated knowledge to weigh our source's words and confirm or dismiss them. Cross-checking became somewhat easier as we came to know the real Jim Jones. And we believe the reader, too, will find the threads of his personality running consistently through the book.

In several cases, we have relied heavily on one person's perspective to provide personal motivation or atmosphere. This vehicle is used even-handedly, and the perspective is clearly indicated, if not in the text, then in the "Notes and Sources" at the back of the book. This section provides a record of sources and documentation, and also clarifies peripheral questions or addresses directly some of the misinformation published about Jones. The notes are not all-inclusive; this book is the distillation of hundreds of voices, thousands of documents and years of work—so exhaustive documentation was prohibitive.

No matter how thorough our research, re-creating dialogue presented us with a tricky problem. It was necessary, particularly in the early Indiana period, to rely on memories of events years earlier. Our rules have been the following: all short dialogues in the text are quoted verbatim from interviews with identified firsthand witnesses or from their writings and recorded recollections; all protracted monologues and dialogues come from tapes and reliable transcripts. Still, we have not simply accepted tapes and written documents at their face value but have confirmed their contents, where possible, and have evaluated them critically in light of other research.

The research spanned not just the three years since the tragic end, but also the previous year and a half of Tim Reiterman's investigation. Reiterman is the primary author and the only first-person narrator, yet the book essentially has been a collaboration between two writers, each with his own strengths. Reiterman, having worked longer on the Temple story, was closer to many of the defectors, politicians, Concerned Relatives and others who figured prominently in the Temple's last years. In addition to filling out the California period, he did the basic research on the Indiana and Brazil periods. John Jacobs went to Guyana immediately after the holocaust and established contacts within the government, the diplomatic community, the religious community and opposition party. He also became acquainted with Jones's son, Stephan, and with many Temple loyalists and defectors. The authors' stateside interviews with these sources, Jacobs's own return trips to Guyana and his trip to Washington to review nine hundred tape recordings recovered at Jonestown provided a solid basis for writing about the church's South American period. The entire text has gone through numerous revisions, and the final interpretation/presentation of events represents our consensus.

This book would not have been possible without the contributions of others. First there are Peoples Temple loyalists and defectors, friends and family of Jim Jones, members of the Concerned Relatives, elected officials and law enforcement investigators, and others who gave so much of their time. By allowing themselves to be interviewed, in some cases for dozens of hours, they helped us understand Jones, his church and its people. In addition to the numerous sources listed in the chapter notes, the authors wish to extend special thanks to the *San Francisco Examiner*,

Jones's son Stephan and Jones's boyhood friend Donald Foreman for making available photographs that complete this work.

Only with the support and assistance of the staff and management of the *San Francisco Examiner* did this book become possible. We want to convey our appreciation especially to Assistant Managing Editor Jim Willse, Managing Editor Dave Halvorsen, former publisher Reg Murphy, former Assistant Managing Editor Ed Orloff, photo editor Eric Meskauskas and to photographer Paul Glines who beautifully reprinted photos, and to writers Nancy Dooley, James A. Finefrock and Peter H. King whose reporting proved invaluable.

In a sense, this book belongs not only to us but also to our editor Paul De Angelis, who helped shape it from conception to completion and constantly provoked new ideas. His talents and encouragement helped maintain the momentum of the project for the many long months, and his critical judgment challenged us to keep improving and honing down a massive manuscript. Our thanks also go to others at Dutton, including Roxanne Henderson, Bill Whitehead, and Leslie Wells, who took the time to read the manuscript and offer suggestions.

Our appreciation also goes to our agents Elizabeth Pomada and Michael Larsen, to Professor Alex Greenfeld of the Graduate School of Journalism, University of California at Berkeley; to copy editor Millie Owen, production editor Elisa Petrini, to typist Shirley Sulat and to Leonie Jacobs, who did important transcribing work for us. Thanks are also extended to Dick Reynolds of the *Richmond Palladium Item*, to Peter Carey of the *San Jose Mercury News*, and to Carey Winfrey, Wallace Turner and Joseph B. Treaster of the *New York Times*. And we deeply appreciate the cooperation of the law offices of Charles Garry, and of Pat Richartz.

Finally, we are indebted to our families and friends for bearing with us and indeed encouraging us during the months of reporting, writing and editing—and most of all, for listening and sharing our excitement at each juncture of this project.

—The Authors

Peoples Temple: The Principals

THE JONESES
Lynetta
Jim
Marceline
Stephan
Agnes
Stephanie
Lew
Suzanne   } adopted
Jimmy
Tim Tupper
Johnny Brown

THE FOUR PASTORS
Russell Winberg
Jack Beam
Archie Ijames
Ross Case

OTHER OLD-TIMERS
The Cordells
The Parkses
The Cartmells
The Beikmans
The Cobbs
The Swinneys
The Touchettes

STAFF
Patty Cartmell
Carolyn Moore Layton
Sharon Amos
Linda Dunn
Christine Lucientes
Sandy Bradshaw
Grace Stoen
Maria Katsaris
Teri Buford
Debbie Layton Blakey

SPECIAL AIDES OR ASSISTANTS
(ALL ON PLANNING COMMISSION
AT ONE TIME)
Tim Stoen
Gene Chaikin

The Mertles (the Millses)
Dick and Harriet Tropp
Joyce Shaw Houston
Bob Houston
Mike Prokes
The Carter brothers
Larry Schacht
Annie Moore
Paula Adams
Karen Tow Layton

CALIFORNIA SECURITY
Marvin Swinney
Wayne Pietila
Jim Cobb
Chris Lewis
Jim McElvane

JONESTOWN SECURITY
(BESIDES JONES'S SON)
Lee Ingram
Al Simon
Johnny Brown

THE EIGHT REVOLUTIONARIES
Jim Cobb
Mickey Touchette
Wayne Pietila
Terri Cobb
John Biddulph
Vera Ingram
Lena Flowers
Tom Podgorski

SOME OF THE "TROOPS,"
BLACK AND WHITE
The Olivers
The Bogues
The Edwardses
The Kices
The Slys
Birdie Marable
Leon Broussard
Le Flora Townes

RAVEN

Prologue

One afternoon near the end of 1976, a month or so after Bob Houston had been found dead along the tracks at the Southern Pacific railroad yards in the Potrero Hill area of San Francisco, his father pulled me aside. Sammy Houston—a wiry, jocular photographer who was a popular character around the San Francisco Associated Press office—did not come to me first as a friend. He wanted to confide in someone, and he thought I might be interested in investigating the death someday. Perhaps I also reminded him of his son: we were about the same age; we had both gone to Berkeley in the 1960s.

Sammy's real name was Robert, like his son's, but everyone called him Sammy because he came from Texas and was related to the general, Sam Houston. At the ballpark he was easy to spot, with his voluminous bag of cameras, and a hat with red feathers in the band. Around the office he was a bit of a cut-up. Yet things had changed since his son's death. Sammy looked ten years older.

He was not coming to me for sympathy, but because of the mysteries in his son Bob's death. Bob had been working two jobs at the time: days as a youth counselor, nights on the railroad, where he was nicknamed "Sleeping Dog" because he napped when things were slow. But Sam could not believe Bob had fallen asleep that night: it had been too chilly to nap outside, and he should have been rested after several days of vacation. Nor did it look like an accident: Bob was not careless, and his glove and lantern had been found neatly positioned on the train car. The father grimaced when he talked about his son's death; the train wheels had mutilated the body terribly.

1

A church run by a faith healer named Jim Jones figured in the mystery. Bob and his wife Phyllis had joined Jones's Peoples Temple some seven years before, shortly after Bob finished his courses at San Francisco State. Sam did not understand how a college-educated young man had fallen for a faith healer—although Sam admitted that the church had been known as a progressive, socially oriented organization.

While his son was in the church, Sam had seen little of Bob, his wife Phyllis or their daughters. There was a hint of friction between the Houstons and their daughter-in-law, perhaps because of problems in the marriage. In any case, Phyllis and Bob were later divorced, and Bob remarried. His second wife, Joyce Shaw, also was a follower of Jones.

The situation sounded complicated: the first and second wives both devoted their lives to the church; the two daughters by the first marriage lived with the son and his second wife; everyone was loyal to the church above all else. Furthermore, Bob had been donating all his income to the church for years.

Sam poured out more and more details in the course of several sessions. "What's really bothering me is this," he said one day in November. Sliding several letters out of an envelope, he explained that his second daughter-in-law had been writing recently. "I'll just let you read them," he said.

A little uncomfortable, I breezed through the first pages. The tone was one of deep concern. These were not hastily scrawled notes, but a strangely loving epistle from a widow to in-laws whom she hardly knew except for abbreviated and awkward family encounters. Begun as a sort of "briefing" of the Houstons, the letters had turned ominous.

Joyce Shaw told how she and Bob had lived together in a communal church framework devoted to social justice and community work. Peoples Temple was much more than just church on Sunday, she noted; it was a life commitment. In the final analysis, Joyce Shaw explained, that meant that church goals justified whatever means it took to realize them. In the process, the dream was crushed. Joyce had left Peoples Temple shortly before Bob's death.

Although she lacked evidence of Temple involvement in Bob's death, she believed he might well have been murdered. In fact, the church maintained that Bob had resigned from the Temple the morning of his death. "There are several interpretations of this. One is that Jim Jones who supposedly has a lot of supernatural power could not admit that a member of his 'inner 100' was killed." She implied that Jones made up the story of Houston's untimely defection. "The other [interpretation] is that anyone who tries to leave the church will die."

Joyce Shaw did not stop there with her disclosures. She wrote of disciplinary "boxing matches" and mandatory confessions to false crimes. She said the Temple, as a test of loyalty and perhaps more, required them to sign false confessions and blank pieces of paper that could be used any way the church wished. "One thing I need to tell you," she said in her

November 27, 1976, letter. "I, Bob and *every* person who was on the Planning Commission or church board wrote and signed documents to the effect that we had sexually abused our children. Yes, incredible but true.

"Sam, if I hadn't heard these insensitive people had gone to [relatives] with their filthy lies, I never would have burdened you with all of this mess. . . ."

Reading this, I was as baffled as Sam. Were these things true? Were church members capable of killing? What kind of a humanitarian organization would demand such perverse self-incrimination?

As I read on, it became apparent that the church had a hook into Sam Houston. Joyce Shaw warned the Houstons not to allow his two granddaughters ever to go to the church's South American jungle project, because, she said, it was a fraud and Jones was evil. "Legally, I am powerless to do anything. You and Nadyne, as their grandparents, are the only ones. . . ."

Having lost his only son under unclear circumstances, Sam now had found out that his son's church seemed willing to do literally anything to keep his two grandchildren under its sway. And yet with his son dead, how could Sam prevent them from going to South America, if their mother remained loyal to the church, hostile to the grandparents?

"I don't know what to do or what to believe," Sam told me. "Tim, I'm afraid if I do anything, they'll keep the girls from me," he said. "At my son's funeral, we asked Phyllis if she and the girls would please come sit with the family. One of the Temple members shook her head—it was like the Gestapo."

"It seems someone should look into this," I ventured to Sam. "But without doing some checking, I can't be sure there's a story."

"Now's not the time for a story," Sam stressed. "They'd think I put you up to it. And I'm afraid, Tim. I'm afraid they'll keep my granddaughters away from me. I want to do what I can do for them," Sam stressed. His voice turned metallic with determination, and his face hardened at the thought of his son's death.

Every so often, Sam Houston would update me on his depressing bout with a situation he could neither control nor fully understand. Each contact with his lawyer, each letter or phone call from his daughter-in-law, was related for a while, but nothing got resolved. His son was dead; his granddaughters were out of his grasp. Helplessness gnawed at him, and his misery showed. His co-workers were saddened that a good man was obsessed with something beyond changing. I too cautioned him not to let the problem consume him. But how could you tell a man to shove aside his son's mysterious death and forget the future of his granddaughters?

Two years later, on November 20, 1978, I lay wounded in a hospital bed on the guarded VIP floor of Malcolm Grow Medical Center at Andrews Air Force Base near Washington, D.C. With an intravenous tube in me, with a bullet hole through my left forearm and lead imbedded in my wrist, I had spent a virtually sleepless night, writing stories longhand and dictating them by phone to my employer, the *San Francisco Examiner*. FBI agents hung around waiting to interview me, because they knew little about events in Guyana two days earlier and virtually nothing about Peoples Temple. The phone in my room kept ringing until the switchboard cut off the calls, then the messages came in notes. News media of all sorts wanted to talk with me, and some offered money for an interview. A publisher assured me that I could sign a quickie book contract within twenty-four hours if I wanted. Everyone, it seemed, wanted to hear the bloody details of the airport ambush of U.S. Representative Leo Ryan's party, to know the final body count in Jonestown.

With my dead colleague Greg Robinson's cameras in a box nearby, with my bloodstained and muddied clothing in the hospital laundry, I asked myself how those first conversations with Sammy Houston sucked me into a whirlpool of events that almost cost me my life, how my investigation of Peoples Temple over the past eighteen months had led to my own victimization at the hands of Jim Jones as he brought down his movement in a final act that took the lives of more than nine hundred human beings, including Sam's granddaughters.

In those days after the holocaust, I decided two things. I would not speak about the Temple until I understood what had happened. And I would not write an "instant book" to capitalize on the worldwide interest without adding any perspective.

By the same token, there were factors that made me hesitant to undertake a long-term research and writing project on the Temple. As with other survivors, the subject naturally depressed me—many times I relived those days in Guyana minute by minute. The experience left me torn by conflicting emotions—helpless outrage over the brutal airstrip murders; grief for those who died in Jonestown, especially the children; guilt that somehow my presence had contributed to the terrible outcome; a desire to be rid of the subject once and for all, as well as the need to get to the bottom of the story; and a measure of fear of the unknown, because the unthinkable had happened once before.

Several months later, after being contacted by E. P. Dutton, I decided to write a history of the church. My primary goal was somehow to express the humanity of the members—including Jones; to make them into real people for the first time. In print, they had been treated as insensitively as their bodies were handled after the holocaust; as worthlessly ignorant victims of a conniving minister-turned-madman. I knew from talking with defectors and from meeting Jones and his followers in Jonestown that the preacher had an incredibly raveled personality, that the Temple attracted a variety of basically good people. And I recoiled when outsiders took the attitude that they or their children would never be crazy or vulnerable enough to join such an organization. Such complacency is self-delusion, for the lessons of Jonestown, while hard for some to accept, raise fundamental issues about this country—about the failure

of institutions, including the churches; the growth of nontraditional religions; the importance of the nuclear family; the depth of racism; the rise
of the Right; the methods of distributing economic resources; the suscep-
tibility of the political system to manipulation by well organized groups;
and the treatment of our unwanted children, elderly and poor.

Peoples Temple was—as many communes, cults, churches and social movements are—an alternative to the established social order, a nation unto itself. The Temple I knew was not populated by masochists and
half-wits, so it followed that the members who gave years of labor, life
savings, homes, children and, in some cases, their own lives had been
getting something in return. I wanted to capture the lure of the Temple,
to convey the thinking and personalities of not just disgruntled defectors
but also of the heartbroken loyalists with something positive to preserve
and remember—and to unmask the real Jim Jones. And I wanted to
humanize them all to get at the truth, to make the ending comprehensible.

To get through the walls erected by Jones and into the minds of
Jones's people, my coauthor John Jacobs and I would conduct more than
eight hundred interviews—of Temple members, ex-members, relatives,
officials and others—and review tens of thousands of pages of documents,
hundreds of hours of tape recordings, film and videotape.

There was no easy or simple explanation of the Peoples Temple
tragedy. It was necessary to explore the life of Jim Jones and of his
organization from birth to death, to trace both the rise and the fall.
Though the pages that follow fall naturally into two halves—the story of
the coalescence of a personality and group, then the degeneration of that
same personality and group—it would be well to remember that in truth
both aspects of Jones's personality, the positive and the negative, coexisted.

From the very beginning.

PART ONE

HELLBENT

I took a piece of plastic clay
And idly fashioned it one day,
And as my fingers pressed it still,
It molded, yielding to my will.

I came again when days were past,
The bit of clay was firm at last,
The form I gave it, still it wore,
And I could change that form no more.

A far more precious thing than clay,
I gently shaped from day to day,
And molded with my fumbling art,
A young child's soft and yielding heart.

I came again when years were gone,
And it was a man I looked upon,
Who such godlike nature bore
That men could change it—*NEVERMORE.*

LYNETTA JONES[1]

O N E

A Scruffy Start

There was more than the usual anticipation that spring as hardwood groves burst into green and plows cut ribbons across the sandy loam fields in east central Indiana. As in other years, the fertile farmland would yield many tons of grain and tomatoes. This year, however—1931—was one of the cruelest of the Great Depression. Farms and livelihoods were being ravaged by forces more sinister than any midwestern twister. Just two years after the Crash of 1929, the country's economy was spiraling downward, taking tens of thousands of mortgaged farms with it. Farm prices were caving in. Foreclosure notices were being tacked on fenceposts and county courthouses. These were the bitterest of times. Yet in the countryside, one could momentarily forget. . . .

One day in the spring of 1931, a road crew shoveled its way up Arba Pike toward the half-dozen houses that made up the settlement of Crete. The laborers paused to take note of another sign of spring; on the front porch of a white two-story house on a knoll overlooking hundreds of acres of gently rolling fields sat a tiny dark-haired woman of about twenty-eight. She was basking in the warm sun, cradling a round-faced, black-haired baby boy. The infant had been born to Lynetta Jones and her husband, James Thurman Jones, on the thirteenth day of May that year. They had named him James Warren Jones and they called him "Jimmy."

Despite the classic mother-and-child image seen by the workers, motherhood was an ambivalent state of affairs for Lynetta Jones. For years before her marriage, Lynetta's steel trap of a mind had been locked on the notion that she would neither marry nor bear a child. Instead she would pursue a business career, perhaps breaking new ground for women; she would give free rein to her individuality and ambition, without the drag of a husband or a child. But personal tragedy evidently had altered the course of this would-be businesswoman.[2]

Born near Princeton, Indiana, Lynetta was the oldest child of Jesse and Mary Putnam. Lynetta grew into a rather odd combination of fanciful dreamer and aggressively ambitious achiever. Full of imagination, she felt almost as much kinship with animals as people; she even looked upon snakes as her friends. She evidently picked up her ambition from her father's foster father, a businessman named Lewis Parker, who became her paternal role model when her father died.

Parker had acquired his wealth in lumber mills in southern Indiana, but when the timber ran out, he turned with less success to grain specula-tion. Lynetta respected him because he blended business acumen with a big heart—and she blamed his financial downfall on his generosity and humanitarianism.

Extraordinarily headstrong and frugal, Lynetta aspired to follow in Lewis Parker's footsteps. She attended Jonesboro Agricultural College in Arkansas for two years before dropping out in 1921. A few years later, she enrolled at Lockyear Business College in Evansville, Indiana, where she also stayed for two years. Then, in 1925, her mother died of typhoid fever. Somehow this death reversed Lynetta's thinking about marriage and motherhood.

Even before Lynetta's engagement to a Hoosier road-construction worker named James T. Jones, she resolved that she would bear a single child, a boy, and he would resemble the most admirable man she knew— Lewis Parker. Although in doing so she denied a part of herself, Lynetta married James T. Jones in the late 1920s. He was sixteen years her senior.

Several years later, after her own bout with typhoid, she became pregnant. The baby boy, though he had Lewis Parker's brown eyes, did not quite measure up to her other expectations. From his looks, the olive-complexioned child might have been a conglomeration of every nationality in the world. His eyes were slanted, almost Oriental, his face round, his hair shiny, black and straight like an Indian's. She thought he resembled most a baby Eskimo, and an ugly one at that.

When money threatened to run out, the Joneses were forced to sell their farmland, and the Depression overwhelmed them. James T. Jones dropped in tears to the living room carpet and beat the floor with his fists. "I gone as far as I can go," he cried. Bending over his body, Lynetta comforted her husband. "You cry, my love," she said with gentle determi-nation. "But I'll whip this if it's the last thing I ever do."

James T. Jones was a native Hoosier with family ties to nearby Lynn, a community of about nine hundred where his father was living out his final years. His family were Quakers, with a reputation for intelligence and decency. Though there was a black sheep in the family—an alcoholic who would eventually jump to his death from a bridge in nearby Richmond—most of the children had done well for themselves. James T. Jones was also known as a good man, but his life had taken a sad turn.

A road-construction foreman before going to France to fight in World War I, he had returned home with lungs scarred by mustard gas. With no more than a grade school education and cursed with bad health, the forty-five-year-old Jones had become a semicripple in the land of the work ethic. He collected government checks, and when his coughing spells subsided and his strength was up, he still worked on the railroads or bent his back on horse-assisted highway construction crews. In an area of small farms of sixty to eighty acres, he and his wife worked for wages.

By 1934, the Jones family had picked up and moved several miles to Lynn, about eighty miles east and slightly north of Indianapolis. They were not the only ones arriving in financial straits. Farmers who had forfeited their land to banks and mortgage companies were resettling in town. They hoped to get jobs in a casket factory or to take advantage of seasonal work at the tomato cannery or to join car pools to factories in Richmond sixteen miles away, Winchester ten miles away, or Muncie thirty-two miles away.

In 1934—as today—Lynn was a drowsy, comfortable town. People there did little more than earn a living, raise children, attend church on Sunday and cultivate vegetables in small gardens. In that sort of conservative midwestern town, Prohibition had had little impact. Even after repeal of the Eighteenth Amendment in 1933, not a single bar popped up. The menfolk generally drove across the Ohio line, eight miles away, to buy liquor. Dancing was prohibited at the high school as immoral. A total population of less than a thousand sustained a half-dozen churches, most on Church Street. Porch-sitters lolled on their swings and rockers on hot summer days, sipping lemonade. There were no blacks to speak of, few Catholics—and no reason for the Knights of the Ku Klux Klan to raise their sinister white-sheeted ranks there. Crime was rare.[3]

The landless people in town sat at the low end of the economic scale. Above them were the owners and managers of businesses along Main Street—Chenoweth dry goods, Citizen's Bank, the barbershop and the rest. Also comfortably situated were retired farmers who had surrendered backbreaking work to their children and had chosen to live out their years with town conveniences and Lynn's meager social amenities —the pool hall–card parlor, the croquet courts, high school athletic events and music recitals, and an occasional Main Street parade or outdoor picture show on one of the side streets.

The town was not marred by any slums as such, but the prominent people occupied larger homes along Sherman Street, known as "Millionaire Street" among the less fortunate. The Jones house, on the other hand, was located at the south edge of town in one of the scruffiest sections. Behind its outhouse ran the railroad tracks.

Moving to town hardly eased the Joneses' financial condition. Mr.

Jones, with high cheekbones, average height and gaunt build, would always suffer from his premature infirmity. He was a gray, brooding man whose stints at work and periodic stays in Veterans Administration hospitals were mere interruptions in his forlorn routine: each morning at about nine-thirty or ten, he shuffled the one and a half blocks downtown to the pool hall–card parlor on Main Street. A smile rarely crossed his face; he was too preoccupied with his next breath. People made allowances because he was a war victim, yet he was so retiring that after a while most people did not bother to say hello.

By contrast, Lynetta steamed through town like a little locomotive, puffing on a hand-rolled cigarette, clouds of smoke in her wake. The skinny and undernourished-looking woman with a pretty face and flat black hair that stirred rumors of Indian blood literally wore the pants in the family. And while she was personable enough, her appearance, her feistiness and her habits caused some of the proper town ladies to raise their eyebrows. She seemed loud, foul-mouthed and manly to some. Rarely did she wear a dress. Her language was colorful. She drank beer at home and made no attempt to hide her smoking. Ladies were supposed to hang up their coveralls when they came to town. But those were Lynetta's work clothes, and work was about all she had time to do.

Though far from the only working mother in town, Lynetta was a different breed. She was educated and earthy, independent in her ideas, ambitious and frugal, eccentric. She considered herself a humanitarian and thought her husband's family bigoted. In those days, she was better schooled than most men—not to mention women—in Lynn. Her ambitions were frustrated by her marriage and by where she lived. She had been trained for business and finance, but she had to take the only jobs available: mostly seasonal work in canneries, and later, factory jobs in Richmond, where she observed firsthand the dreary lot of the workers. Unions eventually became her cause, and she did some organizing, though it could have cost her job. By the late 1940s she would be regarded as a troublemaker by other workers and plant management.[4]

Despite the tedium of her routine, Lynetta found time to dream, to read, to write—and to pass on her verbal skills to her son. In her grandest dreams, Lynetta Jones would have become a professional writer in the Mark Twain mold. But self-expression was a luxury for which she had little time in the years of the Depression.

Being the breadwinner absorbed so much energy that her homemaking suffered. But that, after all, was secondary. What Lynetta wanted was for her son to be a success, not a slave to the rich. She was determined that life would not be a disappointment to him. From her earnings, she scrimped and saved a few dollars for Jimmy's college education. The price exacted on the mother-son relationship was great, however. While Jimmy was left with others or by himself, she boarded a Richmond-bound bus each morning, put in a day's unsatisfying work, then returned by bus in the evening to put together a dinner for her family. There was little prospect of change, not till Jimmy grew up.[5]

If there was an afternoon Cincinnati Reds baseball game, her husband reemerged from the card room and made his ponderous journey back to the gray two-story house. He would collapse into a wooden rocker facing the lone living room window, with shades pulled low. In the near-darkness, he would rock and hum and listen to the Reds on a crackly old crystal radio set. Lynetta sometimes tried to fire his spirit, but he would have none of it.

As though the infant sensed he would be on his own soon, Jimmy learned to walk very early, using a red wooden cart the way some children use the supportive hands of their parents. One day when Lynetta was at work and Jimmy was playing by the railroad tracks behind his house, he was nearly mowed down by a passing train; his cart went riding out of Lynn on the cowcatcher. When his neighbor Mrs. Kennedy, who was a religious woman, heard about it, she took Jimmy's escape as a sign of the Lord's grace.[6]

Even before he was toilet-trained, Jimmy would toddle around unsupervised with a dirty face and bare bottom. At times, he was seen walking around unattended with dried excrement on his bottom. Mrs. Kennedy or other neighbors cleaned him up a little, sometimes clucking about what a neglectful mother Lynetta was.

Jimmy's nudity was perhaps his first attention-getting device. Once he did it in front of cattle drivers, with his mother chasing him. Another time, he marched into a church bottomless, accompanied by a troop of dogs, and presented the minister with a bouquet of flowers.

Animals provided security to the isolated little boy who wandered like a stray pup. To entertain himself, he played with his dogs and cats and the neighbors' dogs, adopting animals right and left, even picking up sacks of kittens thrown out of cars. In fact, so many dogs tagged along with Jimmy that his mother wondered if she could spank him without being bowled over by them. He could go nowhere without them, just as he later could not travel without an entourage of people.

Not long after he began to talk and walk, Jimmy Jones discovered deficiencies in his life. He learned that he was different from other children: his mother did not care for him during the day, his father did not work, and his parents did not attend church, or share a bed. And he began to yearn for something seemingly beyond his reach—conventional family life according to the norms of Lynn.

Jimmy's earliest glimpses of community standards may have come from Myrtle Kennedy, the Joneses' neighbor. During the day, Mrs. Kennedy's house, across the way from the Joneses on Grant Street, often served as his house and she was for all purposes his surrogate mother.

Mrs. Kennedy was also Jimmy's spiritual mother. What Myrtle Kennedy saw underneath the grime was a sweet little boy, affectionate, smart as a whip and precocious with words. Mrs. Kennedy had set about saving Jimmy's soul right from the outset. When he was old enough to understand, she spent hours rocking on the porch telling him about the affairs of God and man. On Sundays, she and her handyman husband would walk Jim to the nearby Nazarene church, where he joined the respectable people for an hour. The Kennedys made sure he went to Sunday school, and they took him to revival meetings before he was old enough to go to the public school.

Lynetta did not mind entrusting Jim's religious upbringing to Mrs. Kennedy. The two were fond of each other, though Mrs. Kennedy disapproved of some of Lynetta's sinful habits, and Lynetta sometimes teased her with occasionally colorful language.

By the time he was four, Jim became friends with another four-year-old, Donald Foreman, who lived with his family across Main Street. Sometimes the boys would drop by the car garage, a stone's throw away from the Jones house. There the local men—"the loafers," Lynetta called them—congregated, a few working on cars, but most just passing the time with breezy conversation and a cold soft drink.

Jim Jones went there for soda pop. He seldom had spending money, but he knew how to get what he wanted. Don, the fair-haired, fair-skinned son of a railroad worker, would hang back as Jim did his routine. Holding out nickels, the middle-aged men would ask Jim to say a few words for them. Jimmy would cut loose with a stream of cussing that would delight them to the point of knee-slapping. He called them dirty bastards, sons of bitches and other epithets that would have given Mrs. Kennedy heart failure. The sight of a little boy spouting foul language struck the men as so hilarious that they kept paying. It soon became a routine. Two or three times a week Jimmy Jones cussed for his soda, exhilarated at the power of his own voice.

One morning in the fall of 1937, Jim fell into step with his friend Don as he came up the block. They turned up the unpaved alleyway behind the Main Street stores. Bursting with curiosity and anticipation, they were on the way to their first day of school—the first grade at Lynn Elementary. Over the years, they would make the same hike hundreds of times, sometimes playing with tin cans and rocks as they went.

Both Jim and Don quickly developed into good students, receiving mostly *B*s in a tough grading system. In his early school years, Jim was sometimes a discipline problem, often talking in class without permission. His deportment improved as he fell in love with the printed word. He was a fanatical reader. By third or fourth grade, he spent his spare time behind the glass doors of the school library, devouring volumes intended for seventh and eighth graders. He lugged home several books a night in a strap slung over his shoulder. The books were not for show: his inquisitive mind required tremendous amounts of fuel.

Jim was an unusual sort of loner. On the surface, he did not seem to lack confidence. He was outspoken in class, sure of himself and his ideas. Yet he did not blend in, physically or otherwise. A noticeably handsome little boy with Asiatic eyes, a dark complexion and straight blue-black hair—raven hair, as he would say later—he was conspicuous in a town of fair-haired children, many of German extraction. Like the other students, Jim also was of European extraction, partly Welsh, though he later would claim Indian blood, sometimes attributing it to his mother, other times to his father.

In contrast to his toddling days, now he groomed himself impeccably. Cleanliness became an obsession. He was very proud of his hair, his dominant physical feature. He kept every strand in place, and sometimes in public, even while talking to people, he would sweep a comb across his head. He bathed regularly in the back porch washroom at home. He kept his clothes exceptionally clean and well pressed, and his shoes polished, a habit that would remain with him for life.

Even as a schoolboy, Jim Jones avoided any situation which would dirty him or cause him to sweat. He shunned physical activity, and instead concentrated on cerebral games and pursuits. As other kids scuffled and played tag or horsed around on playground equipment, he often positioned himself to one side, watching. The other children could not understand his standoffish behavior and his smug, almost condescending defiance. Most did not bother with him; a few bullied him, though he could shout up a storm. It took great provocation to get Jim to defend himself physically, yet he found conflict somehow fascinating, and was always around for the schoolyard tussles. Some teachers mistakenly thought he was instigating trouble.

Jim Jones already was playing several roles, a talent he would polish over the years. In the company of Myrtle Kennedy, he was an innocent. At school, he was a playground recluse and a sometimes mischievous high achiever and bookworm. At the car garage, and on the streets, he was a holy terror. And in his small circle of neighborhood friends, he was a roguish little natural leader.

It was outside the institutional framework, in a vacuum of authority where Jim could make his own rules, that he first felt confidence and some power. Outside school, he could control the same playmates who intimidated him at school. He structured the environment to suit himself, using a certain knack that, when full-blown in adulthood, could rightly be called genius. He learned at a very early age how to attract playmates, keep them entertained and maintain a hold on them. To accomplish it, he shifted modes, from playmate and companion to dominator, pushing his authority then backing off.

After school, Jim and Don sometimes drifted down Main Street, where Jim often stung the ears of adults with his random curses, shouted at passersby to see how they reacted.

Sometimes, Don and a handful of other children were drawn to Jim's home. They would troop along the driveway to the left of the Jones house, past the side garden, past the small barn to a small wire enclosure near the back porch. Jim kept all manner of creatures—rabbits, chickens, ducks, a goat and more—confined in the pen, with a small wooden shed for shelter. The shadeless ground was barren—browsed and pecked clean except for the dung.

Some children loved to come to his little menagerie. It was a novelty for town kids, because most families did not keep farm animals. Jim spent many hours talking to his animals, training them and playing with them. He took care of his aversion to dirty tasks by enlisting his visitors to do his chores for him. Like Tom Sawyer, he convinced them that feeding and cleaning was just another form of play. If the kids tired of the "fun," he scolded them impatiently.

Don never could figure out why Jim wanted animals if he did not enjoy caring for them. The lack of shade, grass and open space seemed inhumane. "Why do you want so many different things and kinds?"

"I just want them," Jim replied.

"Why not build a better place for 'em?"

Jim was not interested in that. The animals were in part a drawing card, like a roadside gas station zoo of creatures whose imprisonment was the price of the pleasure of others.

Eccentricity was almost an inherited trait. The gap between the ages of his parents set Jim apart. His father's age and infirmity meant he missed most common father-son activities, physical or otherwise. A further disquieting note must have been the apparent suicide of Jim's uncle Bill, a drunkard who was living with the Jones family when he plunged from Richmond's G-Street Bridge.[7]

By her frequent absences and by her direct and indirect influence, Lynetta was the dominant force in young Jim's development. Along with her canny aggressiveness, she passed on to the child a general irreverence toward the world; and a certain self-righteousness and grandiosity that allowed him to see himself as an independent spirit proudly pushing against the prevailing flows of society. Along with a certain sensitivity, she gave him a mission—a sense of wrongs to be corrected, a feeling of persecution, a resolve to fight back for his mother and himself.[8]

Most important, Jim inherited a set of family circumstances that reminded him that life had cheated him. He felt deprived by birthright of a loving, close-knit family—something he would crave for the rest of his life. Nothing seemed to lure the Joneses outside as a family—not parades, carnivals or picture shows. The pain of being alone, of being an outcast, of being "different" from the other children, ripped at him whether he was visiting his friends or was in school or church.

Jimmy internalized the shame and pain, and probably first spoke openly of it a year before his death: "I was ready to kill by the end of the third grade. I mean, I was so fucking aggressive and hostile, I was ready to kill. Nobody give me any love, any understanding. In those days a parent was supposed to go with a child to school functions . . . There was some kind of school performance, and everybody's fucking parent was there but mine. I'm standing there. Alone. Always was alone."[9]

In the late afternoon, when stoves all over Lynn were fired up, and the smells of cooking filled kitchens, the Jones house would be dark, the stove dead cold. Then Lynetta would arrive home with groceries and start preparing the evening meal. Sometimes she allowed Jim to invite his friend Don for dinner. There was no dessert. Neither parent ate with the boys. While her husband rocked in the living room, Lynetta put her elbows on the kitchen table, lit a cigarette, pulled over an ashtray and worked on a cup of coffee. She encouraged Jim to study, to put in his hours with his books at the kitchen table each night. "Don't be a nothing like your dad," she harped. "You have to make something of your life and be somebody. Work at it. Nobody's gonna help you." Her words must have been within earshot of the silent man in the next room.

"Big Jim"—as the soft-spoken Mr. Jones was called to avoid confusion with his son—had found two marks of distinction amid all the burdens of his life: his strawberry patch produced some of the biggest berries in Lynn; and the town authorities had presented him with a gun and given him the quasi-official title of Night Marshal. This glorified night watchman who patrolled the business district on foot did not inspire much admiration, not even in his own son. To little Jim, his father was a bitter and cynical man, engrossed in pain and debilitating self-pity.

While most other children in Lynn worshiped with their parents, Jim began a solitary quest for a church that would embrace him. For a while, he attended services with the Kennedys, but soon he experimented, drifting in and out of churches as he drifted around town. His pursuit of an independent spiritual path was not systematic, though at first he attended churches closest to his home. He was seen in the pews of the Quaker church, where he heard antiwar views; in the staid Methodist church; in the very popular Christian church; and in the Nazarene church attended by the Kennedys. Then he made his way out Highway 36 to the Gospel Tabernacle church at the west end of town.

Gospel Tabernacle had started out as a storefront service for a few faithful, but the congregation had mushroomed. Now worshipers by the hundreds gathered in a solid-looking church made of glazed tan building blocks. Still, it was not a proper or dignified house of God in the eyes of many townspeople. This Pentecostal church was considered radical; its members were called Holy Rollers for their rather gymnastic, almost orgiastic, services complete with boisterous healings and people babbling in tongues. Those in less demonstrative denominations thought it a lowbrow phenomenon of self-delusion, or worse. For example, when Myrtle Kennedy learned that the "tongues people" had gotten a grip on Jimmy, she rushed off some prayers to God, asking that he be steered away from certain corruption.[10]

Lynetta Jones admittedly paid little mind to Jim's religious upbringing. But even she became alarmed when she found that her son, then ten at most, was being groomed as a child evangelist by a fanatically Pentecostal woman minister. Jim would bring flowers to the woman when she was sick. In turn the woman would invite him out to the country to her farm where he could play with animals and talk about the Lord. It did not take long for the woman to discover Jimmy's verbal gifts, his mind-boggling ability to throw out more well formed words per minute than most people from Lynn could read. So the cherub-faced boy who used to cuss for nickels was placed in the pulpit, where he addressed congregations in Lynn and in nearby towns. A handsome child who could read the Bible with aplomb and speak eloquently about God was—and always has been—a great crowd pleaser.

Lynetta figured that the Holy Rollers were trying to make a buck for themselves by exploiting her son. She was neither overjoyed with his ministerial bent nor pleased by his attraction to the Pentecostal woman. But she let it slide until Jim began having what she called "night terrors." The boy broke into heavy sweats in his sleep and experienced frightening dreams, particularly of a horrible snake; these were first signs of a life-long pattern of insomnia.

A local doctor proved little help, so Lynetta did some detective work on her own. Suspecting that the snake nightmare might have been provoked by talk of the biblical serpent, she accepted a long-standing invitation to attend the Holy Roller church services, and was suitably distressed. The next time the woman minister came to visit, Lynetta threw her out of the house in a fury.

The boy's sleep became less fitful, but Jimmy's religious inclinations did not fade away. Lynetta peered into the loft of the small barn in back of the house one day and saw him preaching to other children from behind a small altar. The ministry was not exactly the future she had in mind for her son. But she got a kick out of seeing him communicating the Word to even the progeny of some of the town's social elite. It seemed harmless to her, just as it did when Jimmy used a savage tongue and hawkish eyes to order other children around. Better a leader than a servant, she thought. She had tolerated enough exploitation already in the canneries and the factories: it was time an underdog stood tall in the world.

From the barnwood rafters and bare walls, to the single window and wooden floors, the loft was Jimmy's domain. He made the rules; he decided how the time was spent. It was his church, classroom, carnival show, laboratory. No one could exclude him or make him uncomfortable, no one could bully him or call him names behind his back.

The loft was furnished as simply as the Jones house, with a couple of small tables on which Jim draped white sheets. He set out candles, and most often several books were stacked on the main table. Behind it he enthroned himself on the only chair, and motioned to places on the wooden floor. Usually about four children took seats, but the gatherings increased to eight and sometimes a dozen for special occasions. All were boys.

For an hour, two hours and more, Jim Jones kept his young audience attentive and sometimes enthralled—though teachers at school were hard-pressed to achieve the same results. He read to them from the Bible and addressed the lessons of life, usually without fire and brimstone. He entertained them with his vocabulary, his gestures, his theatrical manner. It was fun to watch him speak. Jimmy read to them from school books and books borrowed from the library. Every so often he would stop and talk extemporaneously—though he jotted things down, he never spoke from notes. He solicited comment from his playmates, yet no one ever stood in for him. They allowed him to scold them. It was clear that he was doing their work for them, digesting the material, distilling it, presenting it. Jim was particularly pleased when they were inquisitive; it showed that they were paying attention. Sometimes he helped them with homework.

Jimmy seemed to sense that monotony was the surest way to lose his following. Through either design or his own changing interests, he varied the activities. In winter it was a challenge to attract children to an unheated barn, yet some tromped through the snow to the loft. In summer, when the poorly ventilated loft was hot as an oven, Jimmy made a bowl of lemonade or a sweet punchlike drink to attract them. Spring and fall were his best seasons and his longest sessions. Some kids became so engrossed that their parents had to come and fetch them after dark.

He maintained his animals as an attraction. His pride and joy were what he called his carrier pigeons—eight or ten run-of-the-mill mongrel pigeons with leg bands. He would place messages on little pieces of paper that fit inside the bands. Some pigeons would fly out and others would fly in. It was all very mysterious; he kept mum about their secret missions.

"Where are you sending them?" Don would ask.

"I've got a place for them. They'll be back," Jim would say confidently. He never divulged who—if anyone—was at the other end of the line. He loved intrigue.

Jim's pigeons, like some of his other animals, were not in the bloom of health. When an animal died, Jim held a ceremony. Last rites for God's creatures were solemn occasions. Jim conducted them for birds, a chicken and even a rat. Once he had everyone seated and sufficiently expectant in the loft, he let down the trap door, gently. Everything was done with flair and polished precision, as though rehearsed. He put out all the candles except the one on his little altar. The children, most eight to eleven years old, craned to see as he wrapped the body of the deceased in a shroud and placed the remains in a little cardboard or wooden box. He poured oil on the cloth before closing the coffin lid and leading a reverent funeral procession outside for the burial.

The ritualistic aspects of the funerals did not appeal to some children, who found them unsettling. But there were more attractive scientific aspects to Jim's loft entertainment as well. With World War II under way, Jim Jones's parents had given him a children's medical kit with a microscope. Soon medicine absorbed his energies. Jim invited kids over for science shows. Arriving, they would find the microscope set on a table, already focused. The guests were permitted to stand over it and look through the lens, though Jim would not permit them to make adjustments or select the slides from a small box. He magnified all manner of insects, worms and bugs to the proportions of hairy monsters. It was riveting.

Sometimes the kids looked at smears of blood from Jim's various animals. Jim used a small kitchen knife to draw a little from the legs of chickens, ducks, goats and others. He made it seem clinical, not cruel. It was for science, after all. He also tried to transfuse a little blood between different species to see what would happen. Once he tried to graft the leg of a chicken onto a duck with string. The poor duck waddled around with three legs until the experiment clearly had failed.

Jimmy hated to be outdone in his own realm. He usually ensured his superiority by claiming positions of authority or special powers in their make-believe games. At one time, for instance, the password to enter the loft was "Heil Hitler." Jim would stand above the trap door with his hair combed straight to the side like the Führer's, admitting his playmates. He acted like an adult, and sometimes a lord and master.

Some of the boys, including George Fudge, spent a few weekend nights camping in the Jones barn. During these slumber parties, Jim delighted in frightening them. Jim Jones kept talking into the middle of the night, outlasting his audience. In sometimes macabre performances, he would shine a flashlight beneath his chin or wear a white sheet as he talked of his mysterious powers and laughed in a weird high-pitched cackle. Taking a chicken or a rabbit and placing it on a table, he would claim that he could make the animal be still, stand up or sit down. When the animals seemed to obey his commands, he called attention to his powers. Sometimes he would move his hands over animals and claim to heal them.

At times it was easier to get into Jim's loft than out of it. Late one afternoon, he asked Don and another boy up to the loft to help him with a building project. Once they were settled, he said he needed to go downstairs to look for something. When the trap door shut, the two boys heard the metal latch bolt rammed home. They looked to each other. "I think he's locked us in." They dashed to the front window and looked out. Down on the ground in the driveway was Jim Jones. His head was turned upward, his squinting eyes fixed on them, as he smiled his tight, mischievous smile.

The more the two captives banged on the window and hollered, the more Jim smiled. Eventually he turned and went inside his house. His two friends spent the better part of the night trapped.

After this incident, Mrs. Foreman tried to discourage Don from spending so much time with Jim Jones. She did not push too hard, however, because Jim seemed good-natured and good-hearted, charitable even to the disheveled tramps who rode the rails into town and curled up at night in the coal bins. Located near the railroad, the Jones house was a likely place for bums to go begging, and it was a good choice. Jimmy did not hesitate to gather food for them in a paper sack, and Lynetta helped them too. She taught her son that bums were as good as other people. Even at this early age, compassion and empathy coexisted with some unkind tendencies.

T W O

Breaking Away

Jim Jones was maturing earlier than most other boys his age. As the first signs of puberty appeared—Jim was only eleven or twelve—a disturbing series of incidents took place that further fractured his relations with his peers and other townspeople.

The sap was rising in this precocious, unconventional youngster, adding a new urgency to his behavior. While other boys discovered sports, Jim turned to spiritual things. Gradually estranged, he felt his few friends slipping away from his grasp. In reaction he often made himself outlandish, rebellious, demanding, though as he matured he made at least a superficial compromise by moderating or concealing his eccentricities.

The first attempt at overt control had been the locking of his friends into the barn. Don Foreman had been bothered by Jim's domineering behavior, but it would take many more such incidents before Don— like others who were simultaneously attracted and repelled by Jim— would part company with him. Though at school he often felt pity for Jim, Don remained fascinated by him outside the classroom. Young Jim was years ahead of his peers. He was studious, full of ideas and things to do, seemingly sure of his direction

Jim shared very few adolescent rites with his boyhood friends, except for "pissing contests," in which four to eight boys would line up alongside a barn and try to see who could shoot highest up the wall. The other boys were impressed with the size of Jim's genitals, and his sexual maturity. Also Jim, by pinching the end of his penis to build up pressure, could nearly get the spray over the peak of the roof. Jim's superiority became such a foregone conclusion that some kids quit trying to beat him.[11]

Pissing contests were soon a thing of the past, however. As the other boys attained puberty and became athletic, Jim became isolated. He refused to go fishing in a creek or swimming in the string of flooded gravel pits outside town, refused to join them when they swiped a few cigarettes and some beer from their parents and sneaked off to enjoy the illicit pleasure. To Jim, such activities were either a waste of valuable time or immoral. He had once more resumed his odyssey through the churches, this time conscious of a greater purpose.

He still longed for a family, brotherhood, a sense of inclusiveness. But now he was also on a quest for a truly religious experience, for the ecstasy of spiritual fulfillment. As before, his search would touch every church in Lynn. His friends, and even his mother, had trouble keeping track of which church he was attending.

For a while, Jim's flowering interest in religion was no barrier to his friendships. Though religion frequently cropped up in his conversation, and the Bible became one of the books he slung over his shoulder each school day, he did not force his beliefs on others. In fact, churchgoing was a group activity in his circle of friends. They went to the Methodist church, which Don and a number of other playmates attended. They went to the Quakers, and to the Christian church. Then it was Jim's turn to be host.

One midweek evening, Jim and Don walked out Highway 36 to the Gospel Tabernacle church. At the door, Don stopped, but Jim entered, taking a place near the rear. From a window, Don could see his friend carrying on with the others, waving his arms, making loud overtures and entreaties to the heavens. Don turned and walked away. He could not abide that sort of radical church.

The Pentecostalists were Jim's favorites. He could appreciate the Quakers and Methodists; he had known the Nazarene church since he was a toddler. He would often walk into services at the Christian church (Disciples of Christ), with which he would someday affiliate. But the Gospel Tabernacle church—the one with the shabby reputation, the one on the outskirts of town, the one frowned upon by the "respectable"—suited him best. In that setting of warmth and freedom of emotion where people hugged and praised Christ, Jim Jones experienced the delicious taste of acceptance for the first time in his life. The spiritual bond inspired him to think of being a preacher someday. The people were his people—the rejects. The church drew less from the old stock of Lynn than from the southerners of Kentucky and Tennessee—"hillbillies," as some uncharitably referred to them—who came to the area to work in World War II–spawned industry and stayed.

While Don fell victim to "Hoosier hysteria," as basketball was affectionately dubbed, Jim pored over his Bible. Not once did Jim join neighborhood boys who played hours and hours on Don's homemade court, shooting at a standard attached to his uncle's barn, alongside a cornfield. Don nonetheless spent time with Jim. After all, they had been friends too long to allow sports to stand in the way.

In junior high Jim's father gave him a BB gun for plinking cans and shooting birds. Jim usually ignored the little rifle. One humid summer day however, while he and Don were chatting aimlessly, shirtless, near the loft, Jim pointed the barrel at Don's midsection and shot him. A tiny trickle of blood formed; the BB was imbedded in his skin. As Don picked out the tiny copper sphere, a sick smile came over Jim's face. When pressed to explain, Jim said, "I just wondered whether you could stand it."

Don was furious, yet a few months later, in late fall, he and Jim started off on a rabbit hunt together: Jim had finally agreed to participate in one of Don's pastimes. Don loaned him a .22-caliber rifle and armed himself with a .410 gauge shotgun. While leading the way through a cornfield, Don noticed that Jim was carrying the rifle unsafely, pointing it at Don's legs. The third time that Don turned and asked Jim to point it elsewhere, Jim issued his own warning:

"I've been thinking about demanding that you stop walking," said Jim.

"What do you mean?"

"If you take one more step, I'll shoot you."

With that, the .22 discharged and a bullet tore through the toe of one of Don's shoes, narrowly missing his foot.

Even before these incidents, which Don never talked about with others, Jim Jones was becoming an oddity around town. Toward the end of junior high school, he had begun evangelizing his neighbors, wrapped —like Mahatma Gandhi or some Eastern ascetic—in a full-length white sheet. In fact the sheet resembled the one he wore up in the loft when he was healing sick chickens and rabbits. At times, he wore these robes over his street clothes and leather oxfords when he hiked out to the Pentecostal church, a white apparition moving west on the dusty shoulder of Highway 36.

Sometimes after school Jim would throw on his holy robes and stride downtown. With a big black Bible pressed against his heart, he beckoned to pedestrians, halting some, offering salvation, paraphrasing from the Bible, pleading with them to allow the Holy Spirit into their hearts. But the Main Street of Lynn was not prime missionary territory, and Jim's reputation impeded him: some recalled his cussing, and others disapproved of his parents. Most ignored him.

Jim Jones took action against them too, or at least against his father. Since he was a little boy, he had hated the town pool hall. Now, with his jaw set and his white robes fluttering, he would storm down Main Street. Usually he would halt at the threshold of the pool parlor, shouting toward the card players in back: "You're all going to hell!" One day he kept right on going past the lunch counter stools and the displays of candy and tobacco goods. Planting his feet near his father, he threatened, "You'll all go to hell if you stay here." Mr. Jones, who had no breath to waste, said succinctly, "I'll be home shortly." Jim could only retreat.[12]

When Jim Jones entered high school, there never was any question that he was college material. His IQ was placed at 115 to 118. He always ranked at the top of his class in public speaking, and his grades were among the best five or six in a class of about forty. He was a voracious reader with the ability to digest great volumes of ideas. He spent hours at the new public library. He took elective courses such as algebra, geometry and physics. In the classroom, he held himself up as an intellectual and insisted that his ideas were correct. Most of the time he was right. He was brighter, better informed and better read than virtually all of his peers and some of his teachers.

Young Jones stayed preoccupied with religion, medicine, current events and world figures. He and Don had started ninth grade in 1945, the year Nagasaki and Hiroshima were bombed, and Jim read extensively about the war and about the men influencing history—Mahatma Gandhi, Joseph Stalin, Karl Marx and, most of all, Adolf Hitler. He did not take these figures lightly; he studied each as one would study a model, an idol or an opponent, assessing strengths and weaknesses, accomplishments and failures. The personalities and power of Stalin and Hitler particularly intrigued him: he respected the Russian's new social order and the Machiavellian abilities and oratory of Hitler, though he did not endorse his goals.

Though young Jim eagerly compared different political systems, he did not espouse any radical ideas. He showed no particular interest in the plight of black Americans, nor any strong identification with the poorest children at school. He was attracted to boys and girls like himself, the excellent students with drive, those preparing for college, those most likely to break out of the farming town, to become professionals.

Along with Jim's expanded literary horizons had come a growing sophistication about social situations. Evidently Jim began to realize that he would never gain acceptance unless he moved a little closer to the mainstream than he had been in his eccentric junior high days. Though he remained intensely religious and carried a Bible everywhere, his sheet soon became the relic of an adolescent religious crisis. Jones was smart enough to recognize that holding controversial views was one thing, but wearing bizarre costumes and violating the norm hurt his efforts. It was an early lesson in compromise—and concealment.

Adopting the trappings of normalcy made sense from another standpoint too. Jim was interested in the opposite sex. He took care to make the most of his dark good looks. He always wore slacks and leather shoes, never coveralls or sneakers, and though he had no telephone or car, he did his best. He was fond of Barbara H., a doctor's daughter, and like every other boy in class, he had a crush on Marilyn K., who was outgoing, pretty and involved in school activities. Perhaps most of all, he liked Sara Lou Harlan, the adopted daughter of a respected dentist. She was a slender young lady with dark soulful eyes, heavy eyebrows and an olive complexion as smooth as Jim's. Every Sunday she attended the Christian church. Her parents would not allow her to date, but they would invite her classmates home. Jim walked her around town now and then, and at least once went to her house. Afterward, he told Don that it had been a wonderful evening, with her parents graciously serving a nice dinner and Sara playing the piano for him.[13]

In the meantime, he and Don had moved in incompatible directions. Their contact had become sporadic, and Don did not even bother to invite Jim fishing anymore. One day in their sophomore year, Jim spotted Don and three other basketball fanatics dribbling and shooting at the hoop on the barn. Jim strode over and proposed that all of them sit down and read the Bible. When they refused, he attempted to stop the game by positioning himself in the middle of the court and grabbing for the ball. Don ordered him to leave, but Jim would not budge. Don shoved; Jim moved as if he were going to slug Don. But as he lunged, Don swung. His fist connected solidly with Jim's face, knocking him into the adjoining cornfield. Dazed and disbelieving, he sat there among the dried corn stalks. A little blood seeped from the corner of his mouth.

Don had completely lost touch with Jim. Their eleventh grade class picture captured their relationship in black and white. Don and Jim were positioned at opposite ends of the composition, Jim well groomed and posing formally, Don playing the young athlete, with his hair combed back and a small rakish curl on his forehead. To Don's right posed some of the prettiest girls, several in pleated skirts, bobby socks and white and brown saddle shoes. Behind Don stood his coach and adviser, with a crew cut, arms folded across a burly chest.

Probably the coach could not have been less interested in Jim Jones's future. On the other hand, his Latin teacher, Violet Myers, could not help but notice him. He sat directly in front of her desk in that class of about fourteen, and he had a propensity for argument. His shouting matches sometimes led to scuffles on the school grounds. As one of the students told Mrs. Myers: "He's hellbent for doing what he pleases."

Despite his occasional rudeness, Jim managed to impress Mrs. Myers with his creative use of English. Once when Jim was bothered by something Mrs. Myers said, he asked pointedly, "On what do you *bias* your opinion?" She thought his little twist of language so clever that she borrowed it in the future.

The only time Jim's religious views caused any friction was during study of the gods and goddesses of early Roman times. Jim felt compelled to make a pitch for his own Christian views, and became dogmatic. Mrs. Myers had to cut him off; religion was a potentially explosive subject in Lynn.

Outside the classroom, other students did not so much exclude or reject Jim as ignore him. Even his old buddies felt they could not invite him on their backroads beer runs. On the few occasions Jim joined other students for parties or get-togethers, he would not dance. Dancing, drinking and playing cards were sinful.

Although his religious expression had taken on a more conventional tenor, and Jim now preached in neat street clothes, the people of Lynn still would not listen to him. Finally, he began hitchhiking to Richmond, the industrial city to the south, where he worked part-time in a hospital and sometimes preached on the streets to anyone who would pause for a while. Some did, so he kept going back.

He held his ministry on the north side of Richmond, down by the railroad tracks in a predominantly black residential and industrial area. His pulpit was the intersection of two streets, with a tavern on each corner —watering spots for the workers.

His raven hair combed in place and his clothes straightened, Jim cut a mature and respectable figure. Despite his smooth face and boyish features, he hardly looked like a sixteen-year-old from a farming hamlet. His manly stature made him difficult to ignore as he stopped virtually everyone who strolled by or groped out of the bars. "Get out of the way," many would snap, brushing past the nonstop talker. Some shoved, but he persisted. Some resented his presence, but gradually hostility turned to tolerance.

Once he had drawn four or five adults with his brazen technique, Jim strode to the lamppost, where he had placed a rolled-up blanket and his jacket. He unfurled the blanket on the ground before him. Inside was his Bible. Using it as a prop, he raised his voice and preached a mixture of Christianity and equality of all men under God. Jim had no reason to address racial issues when he preached in virtually all-white Lynn. But here, in a town that was one-fifth black, where the blacks were confined almost exclusively to the extreme northern and southern neighborhoods, something needed to be said about race and poverty. As he stood on that street corner waving the Good Book, he stressed the need for brotherhood and tied the message to the written word of God. In less than an hour, he would collect a small crowd of twenty-five to thirty people, about half black and half white. In his blanket were the coins he needed to keep his mission moving.[14]

Toward the end of his junior year, Jim Jones told his friend George Fudge that he was moving to Richmond with his mother. He said his parents were separating, and that his mother was dating "Shorty" Beverly, a slightly built mechanic whose marriage had fallen apart. He too was moving to Richmond.

In all probability Jim was embarrassed by his parents' breakup. In explaining the move to Don Foreman, he said he was moving because Richmond High had a superior curriculum which would help him get into a university.

Jim asked Don to supper one evening that spring. They had not visited for a long time, having drifted even farther apart after their fight. Don still felt somewhat guilty about the fight and did not want to part on unpleasant terms.

Answering the door, young Jim seemed glad to see his friend and invited him inside. His father—"Big Jim"—was settled in his rocker, the .45 pistol swinging on the back of the chair, the way it had when Don used to ask, "How the Reds doin'?" and the old man replied either "Doin' good" or "Doin' bad."

The meal took place in the kitchen as usual, the boys eating alone. Lynetta moved in and out, serving sandwiches. Jim and Don updated each other on their activities, and Jim broached the subject of Don's motorcycle. Don had already heard through the grapevine that Jim disapproved of the black Harley Davidson he had bought himself. Even the town barber knew about Jim's objections.

Jim now explained in person how concerned he was over Don's safety: motorcycles were dangerous, he warned. He also probed Don's reasons for buying what was an obvious status symbol. In almost the same breath, he said he would appreciate a ride to Richmond if Don was ever going that way.

When dusk approached, Don started to get up to leave. Two or three times, Jim persuaded him to stay longer. Don lingered. Finally, he announced firmly that he had to get home to do chores before dark.

"Stay a bit," Jim said. He had adopted an insistent tone. Don stood there a moment while Jim pressured him to stay, then at last he walked out of the kitchen door to the darkened living room. Mr. Jones was in his chair, humming and rocking and listening to the radio. Don said good-bye.

As Don continued across the room to the front door, Jim passed behind his father. Don stepped outside, and Jim, pausing a minute behind his father's chair, followed his friend. The light was fading as Don stepped onto the wooden porch boards and turned. He walked to the end of the porch, stepped down and turned again, following the walkway toward the sidewalk. He glanced back. Jim stood in the doorway, one hand hanging down alongside his leg. His fingers were clasped around the plastic handle of his father's big black pistol.

"I really don't want you to go," Jim said. He dropped the words with tremendous weight, as though their friendship hung in the balance. Don said he had to leave.

He proceeded down the walkway at an unbothered pace as Jim pursued him. When he had just about reached the sidewalk, Don heard a command: "Just stop. Or I'll shoot ya." Don had never heard such a tone of voice from Jim. The disappointment in it was raw. Jim commanded his friend to stop, to return.

"Just stop, or I'll shoot ya," said Jim.

"Jim, I'm going home." Suddenly, Don was worried. He pivoted ninety degrees and headed down the tree-lined sidewalk. Some fifty feet behind him, on the porch, Jim leveled the pistol in his direction. Almost instantaneously, an explosion went off, and a three-inch chunk of bark went flying from a tree Don had just passed. A horrible ear-ringing noise hit him like a blast of icy wind and set his legs in motion.

He lit out for the cover of a row of shrubs along the driveway. When he was out of sight, he peered back through the greenery. Jim was staring from the porch, the gun dangling at his side.

THREE

Marceline

The girl that I marry
Will have to be
As soft and as pink
As a nursery. . . .

Every Memorial Day weekend Main Street, or U.S. 40 by another name, was clogged by motorists en route to the Indy 500. But tourism was only one part of the bustling economy of this solid industrial city of 45,000; Richmond, Indiana, was the economic, social and cultural center for farming towns throughout the area. People from miles around would come for a basketball game, a movie, the theater, a good meal or drinks in the cocktail lounge of the Leland Hotel.

It was not a homogeneous place. There were extremes of wealth: an elite white area called Reeveston, a black slum called Northside, and all the neat, middle-class white neighborhoods west of the Whitewater River. Wayne County itself was rockbound Republican, but Richmond's political leadership varied. In the late 1940s, it too was Republican, and one of its City Council members was Walter Baldwin.

A Richmond native with an office job at International Harvester, Baldwin harbored no great political ambitions. But when the Republican party asked him to run, he responded to the call, and he won. The Baldwins lived comfortably on the west side of town in a century-old two-story white farmhouse that had belonged to Mr. Baldwin's father. In that solid Christian home, Walter and Charlotte Baldwin had raised three girls: Marceline, Eloise and Sharon. Life revolved about family and church. Evenings were spent around the radio nibbling popcorn and listening to programs such as "Fibber McGee and Molly," or playing cards with Grandma Lamb, who lived with them. Sundays they all strolled down the street to the Methodist church. The family cultivated their natural vocal talents. The parents often went church to church singing spiritual duets. Marceline's lilting voice became an asset in the church choir as she grew, and she performed, with Eloise on piano, at the annual minstrel shows.

Marceline was a gentle, warmly expressive girl; she knew how to make people feel good about themselves. Even as a teen-ager, she had a way of looking at her little sister Sharon with an expression that bespoke worlds of love. Twelve years older than Sharon, Marceline became almost a second mother to her. But despite her soft manner, she was not afraid to stand up for what she believed, and she could speak her mind.

By example, the Baldwins had planted in all their girls a strong tolerance, a trusting, almost naïve attitude toward the world. Marceline's parents, in large part for Christian reasons, were not inclined to think or speak evil of others. To their daughters, they stressed the importance of seeing things from the perspective of others, of seeing life as grays rather than as black and white, of trying to see the best in people.

Pretty as she was, with a thin five-foot-seven figure, light reddish curls, finely drawn features and a movie starlet's mouth, Marceline was content to stay at home on Saturday nights with her family. She took life seriously and had experienced her share of difficulties. Rheumatoid arthritis gave her terrible backaches. And she had to work hard for her *B*s and a few *C*s, though she had strong ambitions.

Her grades would have earned her admission to a university, but rather than heap a financial burden on her parents, she decided to enter nursing school through a federally funded World War II program. Marceline did not view nursing as a bridge to marriage, but as a means of helping people. She put her first stipend check into clothing for a fatherless family of eight children. She bought a new coat for her mother.

The nurses' three-story brick residence at Reid Memorial Hospital resembled a college dormitory. The girls lived in pairs and even had to answer to a house mother, who enforced rules designed to preserve the academic environment and Christian morality. The regime was rigorous from mandatory morning chapel meetings to 10:30 P.M. "lights out." Naturally, dating was much on the minds of the young women, and to some the rules were mere obstacles to fun. Marceline, however, was not one of those girls who took cocktails at the Leland Hotel or disappeared for the night—or was willing to give up her career and principles for a man. She refused to sleep with a local young man who wanted her to become a housewife while he went on to college and career. And she lost him.

In summer of 1946 Marceline got a new roommate, a Richmond native, named Evelyn Eadler, and they became good friends. The two young women had no car and little money, but they did everything together, sharing confidences and simple pleasures. Marceline sometimes read the Bible to her. To escape the hospital environment, they would walk downtown for a nickel cup of coffee at the railroad station restaurant.

In the last year or so of her nurse's training, Marceline began talking to Evelyn about a handsome young orderly who had helped her one day with a particularly grim task. A pregnant woman had died of trichinosis. The orderly on call, a handsome fellow named Jim Jones, had seemed visibly touched as they prepared the body for the undertaker. His sensitivity and concern, especially for the suffering of the woman's family, instantly attracted Marceline.

Through their work, the two became better acquainted. Soon they were dating. Jim was like a breath of fresh air compared to most men. He was compassionate and gentle and principled, but seemingly humble. As he pursued her with flattering diligence, her respect for him grew. Here was a serious young man who spoke so much of truth, honesty, of helping others, who so confidently presented his analysis of social issues and world events. How could she not admire a young man who said he had been a star on his high school basketball team but quit because the coach slurred black opponents? How could there possibly be a more compatible man for her?

More than most young men, Jim Jones knew how to sell himself while courting. Already he was an actor and even a con man. He had cultivated the knack not only for perceiving what people wanted to hear but also for saying it in an appealing way with a performer's timing. His reading and his experiences at home and on the streets of Lynn and Richmond schooled him well in human nature and provided him with a reservoir of information, insights and anecdotes. And if none of those fit a given situation, he possessed the self-assurance, imagination and theatrical ability to fabricate, fantasize or bend a thought or a story to suit his needs. And in Richmond his storytelling knew even fewer constraints because here he was virtually unknown. Around the hospital, there was no advantage to presenting himself as a would-be preacher; instead he emphasized his medical interests and general humanitarian aims.

Physical attraction aside, Marceline could not help but be drawn to the pure energy of young Jones. What she saw was a contagious personality trumpeting a wonderful dream, not fully drawn, of making a better world. Something about his presence—his musical voice, his chesty posture, his gaze, his unquestionably sincere manner, his dark hair and dazzling mind—made a believer of Marceline Baldwin. In part, she believed in his potential for greatness; in part, she went on faith that he and she together possessed the power to serve mankind. Already, Jim Jones had appointed himself a sort of ambassador of positive thinking. Like his mother, he believed he could do anything if he put his mind to it. He spoke often of pulling himself up "by the bootstraps." He promised, in effect, a ready answer to aimlessness and inspired Marceline by presenting himself as a living example of his own message—humanitarianism mixed with ambition. The extreme contrast between his background and Marceline's worked to his advantage. He could and did claim a more informed understanding of the downtrodden. He knew how to stir up guilt and use it to channel people in his own direction. Marceline—perhaps the first to witness Jim Jones as social critic—already was sensitive to the poor. But she found that Jim heightened her awareness of social inequalities and problems by pointing out the failings of the system, including the churches.

As she fell in love with Jim, Marceline began confiding her feelings to her roommate—and Evelyn reinforced them. Jim was very congenial whenever he paused at Evelyn's nursing station to chat, and he did not seem to mind when Evelyn tagged along with him and Marceline on walks to downtown Richmond for coffee or a movie. After all, Jim came across to practically everyone as a pleasant, well-mannered fellow. He was good to the patients and popular among them, and *that* was the litmus test in the hospital.

One day in summer of 1948, between their junior and senior years of high school, Jim's old friend Don came to work at the hospital. Jim had asked him whether he would be interested in filling in as an orderly. Don hesitated because he really wanted to keep his distance from Jim after the shooting incident. But he needed the money, and Jim said there were lots of pretty nurses, so he applied.

Don had assumed he would be an orderly like Jim, an equal, and could go his own way. But he found himself acting as Jim's flunky. On the pretense of training, Jim had established a boss-employee relationship from the first day.

Jim had been working part time or full time for two years. He knew his way around the hospital, from the main building on the hillside to the student nurses quarters at the end of the L-shaped tunnel. Jim looked and acted the part of an important and efficient young man. He wore a spanking clean white coat, like a doctor, and took pains to keep it clean. His medical vocabulary was impressive; he knew the proper medical terms for common ailments. He had mastered the orderly's routine, and knew how to impress the nurses, doctors and administrators.

Jim was not working at the hospital simply for monetary reasons —he could have earned more than his $30 weekly salary in a factory. The world of medicine had intrigued Jones since the day he was given that microscope. Bodily functions fascinated him. Witnessing healings as a boy, he could not help but wonder about the relationship between the body and the mind. Also, the hospital was like a community unto itself, crisp and clean, with neatly defined structures, and it appealed to his sense of order. In fact, he was thinking about a possible career in hospital administration. He could visualize himself running a place where people were healed, where he would oversee an institution in the traditionally prestigious health profession. He could satisfy his needs for leadership and could help ease human suffering while earning a good salary. Moreover, his mother could swallow a medical career more readily than a life of preaching. Already it seemed that Jim's interest in religion was flagging. He started spending less time with his Bible.

Like the little taskmaster from Lynn, Jim hovered over Don, directing him step by step through each procedure. Jim stayed clean because Don did the physical work. Don resented Jim's behavior, and at home in Lynn he griped to his parents. But at Reid, he was the outsider, the newcomer, so he accepted his travails in silence there.

Not all was slavery under Jim Jones. An important fringe benefit of working at the hospital were the dozens of student nurses, most a cut above the Lynn girls in appearance and maturity. And, since virtually all the doctors were married, many nursing students were willing to date younger men, even high school boys. Don went out with a couple of blond nurses and Jim's interest in girls seemed to be on the rise too. That summer—around the time Jim came to know Marceline and Evelyn—he told Don that he was taking out from three to five young nurses.

The handsome young orderly had such a solid rapport with nurses that they collaborated with him in his pranks. At the hospital, Jim seemed happier and more comfortable than he ever had been in Lynn, and he relaxed enough to show a sense of humor. Not surprisingly, he delighted in turning the tables on his old friend Don, the athlete who had once knocked him on his duff, someone who could expose his past.

Since childhood Jim had known that Don did not like the dark. While at the hospital, he had listened to Don's confession of squeamishness about some hospital procedures. Jim promptly assigned Don to sweep the long, dimly lit tunnel that connected the hospital with the nursing quarters. The predawn cleanup seldom was uneventful. Once Don was sweeping a dark corner and came upon a human head, and another time someone threw a limb at him from behind a door. These artificial body parts were training aids for the nurses, but the episodes were nerve-racking nevertheless.

"Let's go get George ready," Jim told Don one morning. The two orderlies proceeded to strip George, a man suffering from elephantiasis of the scrotum, in preparation for his bath. Jim then found some reason to coax him into a hall just as the nurses gathered for their morning briefing. George stepped out into the hall stark naked, his huge scrotum hanging almost to the floor. The nurses screamed and hollered.

The first time Don was called to the operating room during an emergency surgery, Jim met him at the door. "They have something for you to burn in the incinerator." The object, longer than a loaf of bread, was wrapped in newspapers. With his arms out, his palms up and his heart in his mouth, Don received the garbage. Jim disappeared, but not before ordering Don to stay with his charge until it was totally burned.

On the elevator the paper soaked through, clung and became translucent. Don could see that he was holding someone's gangrenous leg.

Somehow, he survived the elevator ride and the walk to the incinerator. He tossed it inside and dutifully waited while his stomach did contortions. The leg was halfway consumed by flame, stinking as only burning human flesh can, when Jim arrived. "You can sit here with me until it's completely burned," he said.

After Jim blocked the door to the autopsy room until Don had cleaned up every last bloody tool and gory bit of flesh, Don decided to call it quits. He left the hospital, never to return. It was over between him and Jim Jones.

The first victim had escaped.

By fall of that year, 1948, Marceline was in a quandary over young Jim and needed to confide in her friend Evelyn. She was crazy about Jim, and respected him. She used the word "good" to describe his character. But there was a problem: their relationship was getting deeper, approaching a crossroads, and Jim's age bothered her. Evelyn was startled to learn that Jim was almost four years younger and only starting his senior year in high school. He looked and acted much more mature.

Beyond young love, Jim Jones was facing other changes in the fall of 1948. After a whirlwind stay of several months at Richmond High, he had decided to move on to Indiana University at mid-term. He would be leaving his mother's second-story apartment on Main Street in Richmond; he would be leaving his sweetheart's hometown.

In November, Jim Jones collected his last paycheck at Reid Hospital. Though he had continued putting in long hours there while finishing his senior year, he graduated from Richmond High—early and with honors—in winter of 1948–49. It did not matter that he missed the euphoria of the last days of high school. At Richmond High, he had been more of an outsider than ever. His classmates hardly knew him—young Jones had presented himself more as a candidate for hospital administrator than as a friend. Next to a handsome picture that he would use for years to come, the yearbook carried this superficial, mildly mocking tribute: "Jim's six-syllable medical vocabulary astounds us all."

His courtship had reached a critical stage. The previous March, Marceline had taken the step of introducing her beau to her parents. She chose her graduation from nursing school as the occasion, and this probably tended to magnify the age factor. The Baldwins were a little concerned that a darkly handsome high school boy was sweeping their trusting daughter off her feet with his aggressive courtship; with flowers, candy, visits and phone calls. On the other hand, they always had trusted Marceline's judgment, and she never had failed them.

In the space of a few visits, Jim nearly became part of the family. He treated Marci's parents respectfully, but was not afraid to express his opinions. He eased their apprehensions when he mentioned he was active in a church in Lynn, though he did not say he had dabbled in "tongues." Jim showed special attention to Grandma Lamb, who was in her eighties, and became a big brother to little Sharon, who was bedridden with rheumatic fever. In turn the family included Jim in their 1948 Christmas ritual. When the tree was trimmed and the lights turned on, Jim was genuinely dazzled. "It's the most beautiful thing I've seen in my life!" he exclaimed, confiding sadly that his family had never bothered with Christmas trees.

As a more formal introduction to their family, the Baldwins invited Jim and Marceline to a dinner with relatives. Rather than dressing up for the occasion, Jim strutted into their house wearing a defiant demeanor, and what had to be his oldest clothes. It was embarrassingly obvious that he felt inferior and thought Marceline's family uppity. Jim had misread the Baldwins; they were a hardworking, unpretentious middle-class household, not the snobby rich. The Baldwins overlooked Jim's rudeness. And when Marceline later apologized, they acted as though nothing had been amiss.

When he arrived in Bloomington that January, Jim Jones received a university-required typhoid shot and immediately took ill. While other students bundled themselves against the cold, he sprawled across the lower bunk bed in a cinder-block dormitory near the sorry-looking creek known as Jordan River. His hair was disheveled, his face clammy. His body quaked with chills.

As he lay there, his new roommate, an eighteen-year-old named Ken Lemmons, showed up and expressed surprise that Jim was on his bed, the prized lower bunk. But Jim had a ready answer. For the time being, he said, he was too ill to move. And over the course of a couple of hours, he explained that he never would be able to take the upper bunk because he had an overwhelming fear of heights. Out of compassion, the easygoing Lemmons did not press the issue. The episode—one of the earliest signs of Jim's hypochondria—also was a classic example of his manipulation.

Of all dormitories on the stately Bloomington campus, that was probably the worst possible assignment for a sixteen-year-old small-town boy starting mid-year. Many of the dorm residents—war veterans on the GI bill—were well into their twenties. Other residents included upper classmen from wealthy families well on their way to graduate school and careers. Again the outsider, the newcomer, Jim Jones had walked in on an established social order, a happy, sometimes chaotic place held together by 1950s-style chumminess and pranksterism. The "guys" would head out in groups to burger joints, or go drinking or girl-watching.

On his dresser at college in Bloomington, Jim displayed a picture of Marceline. His roommate was surprised to learn that this handsome, obviously somewhat older woman was planning to marry Jim in June. What did this mature woman see in an Indiana University freshman just short of seventeen who made so much of his tender age and spoke of pulling himself up "by his bootstraps"?

From the start of school, Jim had been preoccupied with his impending marriage, his future and school. Initially fellow students had taken him for a whiz kid. But Jim's study habits were shoddy, and he spent as much time expounding his personal philosophy as studying. When his ideas were challenged, he spouted preacherly rhetoric.

Jim Jones kept a Bible in his desk at college and read it regularly, and sometimes talked of going to Bible school. Lemmons, who had been attending Disciples of Christ churches all his life, found Jim's religious views incongruous and his knowledge of scripture full of holes. On one occasion Jim might bend the Bible to support his own unorthodox views, and on another he might recite dogma in the most rigid of terms. His tendencies were secular and social, his rhetoric primitive and evangelistic. Jim dominated conversations and was intolerant of his roommate's ideas. Lemmons tried to get a rise out of him by asking pointed questions and introducing Hinduism, Judaism, Catholicism and Eastern Orthodox theology into their conversations. The older student was interested in the ecumenical church movement, but the small-town boy named Jones seemed blind to sophisticated points of theology. When Lemmons asked a question such as, "How do you know Jesus Christ and God are synonymous?," Jim would simply quote scripture.

Rather than become close to others in the dorm, Jim withdrew; he disliked their immaturity, their indulgent, sinful lifestyle. While the jovial dorm crew raised hell, he sat alone in the lounge, or in his room with the door open so he could hear what was going on. At least once, after a three-day firecracker skirmish, he stood up and lambasted their immaturity. He had worked hard to finance his education; his dormmates, the professionals of tomorrow, were frivolously squandering their opportunity. It disgusted him.

Jim took sanctuary from the dormitory each weekend. He rode the bus to visit Marceline in Richmond, and sometimes she drove him back to school. He never dated anyone but her; and, while they were apart, they had long affectionate phone conversations. In those months of planning their wedding and their lives together, she was both mother and fiancée to him. They established a joint bank account, and she helped support him.

Jim Jones referred to his prim bride-to-be with the utmost respect. To his dormmate he painted his first erotic experience—supposedly with another woman—as a trauma. He said that, while he worked briefly at a state mental hospital with Marceline, a female patient had attacked and almost raped him. Implicit in his account was a twin boast: that he was virile, and that he was sexually attractive to other women. He would repeat such boasts, obsessively, over the years.

An uneasy truce reigned in the room, though Ken and Jim occasionally had verbal jousts over religion and study habits. Then, late one night a month or so before Jim's wedding, while Ken was asleep in his upper bunk he was awakened by a sharp pain in the middle of his back. He presumed it was a loose wire in his bed, until he started to hear hissing noises, and felt a push beneath his mattress.

A prick brought him into a sitting position. He peered over the edge of the bed. Jim's arm was extended, and he was working a long hatpin in and out of the mattress.

"What in hell's wrong with you?" Ken shouted, leaping to the floor. He was frightened. It did not seem a simple prank; Jim had not even cracked a smile. Ken immediately went to the counselor to complain.

The date was Sunday, June 12, 1949. On that perfect Indiana spring day, two wedding parties gathered at the Baldwin family home. Marceline and her nineteen-year-old sister Eloise were dressed in white gowns of identical material but different design. Jim and Eloise's fiancé, Dale Klingman, looked dashing in their matching white dinner jackets. Each bride had her own attendants. Little Sharon was a flower girl. Marceline's nursing school roommate, Evelyn, served as her maid of honor.

Though happy for their two oldest daughters, the Baldwins fretted that Eloise was too young to take such a step, and that Marceline's groom was too immature. Yet those last minute doubts fell away when the wedding party moved on to Trinity United Methodist Church, site of Marceline's parents' own wedding a quarter century earlier and only five doors from their home. On this day, it was filled to capacity, with the mayor and City Council members among the guests.

It was a straightforward ceremony, but doubled. When Eloise and Dale were pronounced married, Dale kissed his bride suavely. When Jim and Marceline were wed, however, he grabbed her in a bear hug and let her have a breathtaking kiss. The family members smiled at Jim's boyish enthusiasm. His inexperience was evident.

The Joneses fell immediately into the hyperkinetic lifestyle that would dominate their marriage. Without so much as a honeymoon weekend, they took up residence in Bloomington. Their first home, located across the street from the hospital where Marceline worked and not far from the I.U. campus where Jim attended summer school, was one room, aptly known as a "convenience apartment." For his part, Jim continued his education and looked for part-time jobs. Marceline took courses in nursing education at the university and worked nights in surgery at the hospital in town. She sacrificed to help pay for Jim's schooling, believing he some day would make a mark, perhaps as a hospital administrator or a lawyer, certainly helping the disadvantaged.

Perhaps Jim sensed his bride's need to maintain her close family ties, because, time permitting, they made the hundred-mile drive to Richmond to see relatives and friends. Jim loved to burst into his in-laws' home, calling, "Grandma! Sharon! I'll take you to the movies tonight!" And he and Marceline would load Grandma, who was in her eighties, and

Sharon, who was wheelchair-bound, into the car and take them out on the town.

Jim's relationship with little Sharon was special. He treated her as a little sister, and she, in turn, looked up to him as a big brother, respected him for his compassion and intellect. He told her what was happening in the world and what was wrong with it. Minorities were mistreated, he said, and hypocritical churches contributed to the problem with their segregated congregations. When no one else was around, not even Marceline, he used to sing George Gershwin's "It Ain't Necessarily So," to Sharon, especially the line "The things that you're liable/To read in the Bible,/It ain't necessarily so. . . ." It seemed to the little girl that her brother-in-law must be losing sight of his God.

Back at the Jones apartment in Bloomington, Jim's irreverence took on stronger manifestations. Always unorthodox, Jim now even dropped his evangelistic mouthings. His views became a source of friction with his bride. While Jim expressed atheistic views, Marceline clung to her Methodist faith. Jim's sacrilegious talk hurt her badly. But Jim could not be silent, could not allow his wife to nurture religious delusions like those that he had cast off gradually when he left his hometown and was exposed to suffering. He felt duty bound to tell her what he had discovered intellectually: that there was no God. He knew it from hospital experiences, from seeing the poor on city streets; no merciful God would allow so much earthly suffering. And no churches could serve mankind if they hypocritically screened people according to skin color.[15]

Despite Jim's attitudes, Marceline continued to practice her religion. She knelt down at night to pray, as she had all her life. Her praying infuriated him; he said he could not stand to see his wife kneeling before an imaginary deity. Finally, he demanded that she stop praying altogether. When she resisted, he threatened petulantly to throw himself out the window, to put his death on her conscience. Whether Jim meant his childish threat or was bluffing, it deeply troubled Marceline. Jim had demanded that she deny her faith and accept his will in its place.

Because they loved each other, because Marceline was willing to bend and forgive, the religious conflict was shoved aside most of the time. In any case, they must have been distracted by financial pressures. Despite their simple lifestyle, the Joneses were forced to move into a trailer outside Bloomington. Jim was even posing as an art class model at the university to pick up extra money. When Marceline's parents and Sharon came to visit, there also were signs that he was undergoing a sort of youthful identity crisis, reaching out for new ideas and feeling renewed antagonism toward his in-laws.

He told Marceline's family how impressed he was with a campus speech by Eleanor Roosevelt, who was sensitive to the plight of American blacks. On at least one occasion, he made sympathetic statements about communism—this during the Korean war. It was ridiculous that people treated communism like a disease, Jim said, authoritatively. Later Jones would claim he had been an avid communist since childhood.[16] If so, there is no evidence he ever presented himself as such. Nevertheless, Jim's somewhat admiring defenses of communism disturbed little Sharon. She fantasized that any day the FBI might bang on the door of her house because of her brother-in-law's controversial views.

Once, after a few hours' visit with Jim and Marceline, the Baldwins found that their car would not start; the repairman was certain someone had tampered deliberately with the engine. Though the Baldwins were never suspicious people, they shared a gut feeling that Jim had done some sabotage under the hood. The suspicion deepened after two other odd incidents in that first year of the marriage.

A similar hostility manifested itself another evening when Jim began reading Marceline a newspaper story about a horrible automobile accident while she was cooking dinner. Going down the list of the dead, he ticked off the name of one of her dearest friends. Stricken, Marceline burst into anguished tears while Jim watched her, stolidly, measuring her love for her friend. Finally, he admitted he was kidding. Marceline was probably horrified at the time, though later she would minimize Jim's cruelty and even almost laugh it off. At the time, this and other incidents evidently were eclipsed by love. Jim wanted Marceline's love whole. Friends were rivals, and so was family. In his insecurity, Jones needed to constantly test others' loyalty, sometimes sadistically.

Marceline, out of love and trust, usually submitted. She dreamed of someday having children with Jim, raising a family like her parents'. Overall, Jim seemed to be the most decent man she had met. His kindness and his age allowed her to dismiss the disturbing elements in his personality, perhaps to write them off as youthful rebellion.

In 1950, for instance, Jim responded in characteristic fashion to the plight of one of Marceline's cousins. Ten-year-old Ronnie Baldwin, placed in an unfamiliar foster home because of his father's premature death and his mother's incapacity, had been suffering severe stomachaches. Alerted to the symptoms by Ronnie's brother at the Baldwins' home, Jim and Marceline jumped into the car, fetched Ronnie, and raced to Reid Hospital with him. As they had guessed, Ronnie's appendix had ruptured. The emergency surgery probably saved his life.

Ronnie soon became the Joneses' first foundling. Through him they could put into practice their talk of helping the weak and disadvantaged, and prepare themselves for parenthood. The summer of 1951 was an opportune time to bring Ronnie into their household. The boy, of course, was between school terms, as was Jim. After completing his third semester at Bloomington, Jones had shifted his emphasis from business to social sciences and was pondering a career in law. So the three of them moved to Indianapolis, where Jim could continue his studies at the I.U. campus there and enter I.U. Law School as an undergraduate if he wished. In fact, Jim did everything else but study in Indianapolis.

Events in the fifteen months Ronnie Baldwin spent with the

Joneses came exceedingly fast. Life was a whirlwind of jobs, ventures, near-nightly outings. Driven by a worrisome force, Jim Jones led an almost nomadic existence, searching for the proper direction in his life, no longer certain that higher education would provide the answer.

The Joneses first lived in an apartment behind a Shriners Temple. But their stay in the downtown area apartment ended quickly, because they acquired too many pets. Keeping a menagerie was nothing new to Jim, but in addition to the standard pets, he graduated to more intelligent life, a chimpanzee. The chimp, however, died mysteriously of strychnine poisoning—the first of a string of poisonings in Jim's life. Blaming the death on a neighbor, he replaced the chimp with a monkey when he purchased a house on the north side of town.

Probably the move increased the financial strain. Deferring law school, Jim worked a number of unsatisfying jobs, often more than one at a time.[17] As a night watchman, he slept during the day, though rarely a full eight hours. Like his father in Lynn, he seemed proud of the gun he carried—and once fired it, loaded with blanks, in the house. Remarkably, he almost could do without sleep.

Although Marceline wished for a family of her own, Jim insisted that she work too. In fact, he bought a typewriter and taught her to type so she could get a school nurse job. She also worked in the children's ward of the hospital, and together they operated a short order café next to a factory.

Though the Joneses pushed themselves to near exhaustion, they did not neglect their young charge or begrudge him anything. They treated Ronnie like their own son, and had him call them "Mom" and "Dad." Because he was small for his age, they immediately put him on vitamins. They bought him a Pomeranian dog, a bicycle, nice clothes. They even paid for tap-dancing lessons at one of the best dancing studios in Indianapolis, although Jim had holes in his shoes and Marceline washed out her single uniform every night.

In return for their sacrifice, they expected the best of Ronnie—they pushed him to get better than average grades, and they punished him when he did something wrong. Ronnie learned about his cousin Marceline's righteous anger once when she spanked him furiously for forgetting to feed the animals—dog, monkey, coatimundi and hamster. When the boy threatened back with his fist, Marceline suddenly restrained herself. Perhaps she had overreacted, she admitted. They talked out the problem, and as a sign of understanding, she treated him to an ice cream cone. "We won't tell Jimmy about this," she said. It was a role she would play in the coming years: the good and gentle wife of her more wrathful husband.

Jim had promoted himself consciously as a replacement father to Ronnie, but Jim's overbearing personality made Ronnie wary. Jim, who never had much of a paternal role model, emphasized moral leadership rather than companionship. At the dinner table and in the car, Jim, though only about twenty, philosophized and jabbered nonstop. Communism is not so bad, he said, and black people are just like you and me. Jim tried to indoctrinate the boy through these lectures and by deeds, as when he helped out some poor immigrants in the neighborhood. Jim showed no interest in Ronnie's religious upbringing and omitted grace at meals, but he wanted to make sure that the boy knew the facts of life. To supplement his rather explicit lectures, he gave the boy books; as a result Ronnie had a better sex education than his school pals.

The Joneses always delighted in their pets. The three of them laughed to tears when the monkey learned to open the window, then escaped, ransacked a kitchen next door and eluded everyone for a few days, until the fire department knocked him out of a tree with a high-pressure hose. Despite such antics, Ronnie feared the monkey—because Jim had trained the animal to attack on command. Once or twice when Jim let out an odd noise and pointed at Ronnie, the monkey would leap after the boy as he scampered to safety atop the bathtub. As the monkey held Ronnie at bay, Jim chortled until Marceline, watching with mounting concern, called a stop to the "game."

Such episodes passed quickly—at least for Marceline. Unkind one minute, Jim could turn almost saintly the next. He could counsel and expound on the most serious subjects, then suddenly behave like a mischievous little boy.

The Joneses had few friends, but they seldom stayed home. When not working, sleeping or eating, they would hop into the car and cruise around the city, talking, looking at people, noting changes in the neighborhoods. Usually, Jim drove. But once, with Marceline protesting, Jim gave the boy the wheel, until they nearly got in an accident.

Jim took Ronnie along to movies—particularly those on the bomb —and to political lectures he attended. During a meeting at a churchlike auditorium, it seemed communism was being discussed. At one point, someone came up and whispered something in Jim's ear. Hurriedly, they slipped outside. FBI men evidently were keeping the place under surveillance. Maintaining his composure, Jim bade "Good evening" to one of the G-men and kept walking.

The family packed up and went on summer vacations in their old Lincoln. The first summer, they spent a week at Indian Lake resort in Ohio. One day, while Marceline rested at the cottage, Jim and Ronnie rented a motorboat and stopped in the middle of the lake for a swim. While Ronnie still was in the water, Jim climbed into the boat and restarted the motor. Ronnie hung onto the side while Jim towed him in circles. "Let go," Jim said. Ronnie refused; Jim insisted. "No," cried out Ronnie—he was afraid he would be sliced up by the propeller. Jim dragged around the frightened boy until a lake patrol official motored out to them and chewed out Jim for endangering the boy.

In a similar incident on the family's second vacation, the three of them were standing along the river about a quarter mile above Niagara

Falls. The water swept by them toward the deafening cataract. Jim instructed Ronnie to wade into the swift current, promising to hold him at arm's length. Petrified, Ronnie did not wish to go. Jim persisted, reassuring the boy, but Ronnie refused again. Jim insisted even after the boy broke into tears, but Marceline did not intervene. Finally, unhappily, Ronnie surrendered. The powerful current frightened him, yet Jim held on tight.

On the way home from Niagara Falls, the old Lincoln took them through Canada, then south through the Great Lakes region. It was most likely on this trip or shortly after it that Jim saw a document that would have a pivotal effect on their lives. Marceline had found it difficult to refute Jim's criticisms of organized religions, yet on this day she convinced him to come to a Methodist church with her. On a bulletin board, Jim Jones found and read with interest a document that underscored the social relevance of the church.

In 1952, the Methodist social creed answered Marceline Jones's prayers for a resolution to her biggest marital conflict. The five-page creed espoused goals that the Joneses supported: abatement of poverty; a form of security for the aged; collective bargaining; free speech; prison reform; jobs for all. And most significantly, the creed declared, in the decade before the civil rights movement, "We stand for the rights of racial groups. . . ." Although Jones could not bring himself publicly to embrace communism at the height of the McCarthy years, he believed that collective action was the only way, and he knew that he wanted to lead rather than follow. Until now the proper vehicle had not come along.

In April of 1952, during Ronnie Baldwin's first tap-dancing recital, Marceline leaned over and announced to her mother that Jim was entering the ministry. The entire family was shocked: Jim had seemed to be trying every direction but the ministry. Little Sharon assumed that Jim had a lightning-bolt religious experience; she knew nothing of his childhood evangelism. Explaining his plans, Jim mentioned only that the Methodist social creed had figured heavily in his decision; it showed that organized religion was, after all, compatible with social goals.

Through the ministry, young Jones could synthesize his own ideas, his personal needs and his talents. Given his earlier experience and speaking abilities, the ministry would allow him, finally, to excel. It would fulfill his personal need to lead people and would provide a forum, not to say a cover, for his controversial views.

Characteristically, Jim took action at once. By June 1952, less than two months after his decision, he had accepted a position as student pastor at Somerset Methodist Church in the predominately poor white southside section of Indianapolis. During this on-the-job apprenticeship, he took a correspondence course to acquire standing in the Methodist Conference and fitfully continued his college education, attending occasional classes at I.U. extension school. And for the third time in about a year, the family moved, this time to a tiny bungalow near the church.

For his first sermon, Jim Jones simply pointed out moral lessons taken from the Bible, much as he had done in the loft in Lynn. His liberal colors were showing. He spoke against discrimination and about "living Christianity." He no longer rejected the ecumenical stance taken by his college roommate three years earlier; he adopted it as his own, using it to attract people from various religious faiths.

At the same time, Jim's real interests led him out of the white neighborhoods. On the sly, he took Ronnie to various black churches around Indianapolis, where together they experienced the same emotional brand of religion that had captivated Jim as a boy. During this church-hopping, which resembled his experimentation in Lynn, Jim made some friends among black people. He brought them home to socialize—a rarity in those times—and invited them to his own church services, which was not always welcomed by white members.

Though Ronnie was already known around church as the student preacher's son, Jim and Marceline wanted to make it official. They met a few times with a social worker to begin procedures, but Ronnie feared Jim and resisted the idea of adoption. Jim tried to convince him that he had nowhere else to go, even claiming, falsely, that Ronnie's mother did not love him, that she had contributed nothing to his support, and that she was a terrible person.

Young Jones's divide-and-conquer tactics boomeranged. In early September of 1952, while Ronnie was in Richmond attending a brother's wedding, the boy spoke at length with his mother. He came back to Indianapolis convinced not only that his mother loved him and would take care of him, but also that Jim was lying. When Jim tried to get the boy to sign the adoption papers, Ronnie withheld consent. All that night, Jim argued and cajoled, to no avail. Though very upset, Marceline could not stop the scene; she disagreed with Jim's threatening methods but wanted to keep Ronnie.

Ronnie, having toughed out one of the worst nights of his life, was put aboard a plane for Richmond the next morning. A short time later, the mere sight of Jim at a Baldwin family reunion sent Ronnie jumping fences to avoid him. In fact Jim did not give up until two further attempts to convince the boy to return proved fruitless.

This incredible persistence would become characteristic; the pattern of constant testing, repetition and dividing those around him from their loved ones would mark virtually all of his attempts to keep his foundlings and followers. If young Jones fought so tirelessly to keep Ronnie, it is not hard to imagine the emotional appeals to Marceline whenever she threatened—even if not openly—to leave him. Nothing could wound Jim Jones as much as abandonment, and at this stage of his life he needed no one more than Marceline.

During the first two years of their marriage, she had seriously considered divorcing him. The accumulation of incidents, the oppression of domination and control, the possessiveness became too much for her.

Although she did not confide her unhappiness to her family at the time, the marriage had not shaped up as she had hoped. She wanted a full partnership, not a subordinate's position. She wanted children, and she did not necessarily want to work. The problems in the marriage left her terribly torn. She loved Jim but cherished her individuality. She respected his gentleness and compassion but already feared his temper, his verbal explosions and his fierce teeth-gritting expressions. She shared and admired his good intentions but disliked some of his methods. Apparently she, like many who came later, focused her attention on Jim's good qualities and hoped tomorrow would be better.

The thought of divorce must have caused Marceline tremendous pain. Divorce would have stigmatized her; she had been brought up to believe that marriage was a lifetime proposition. It probably was easier to suffer a little longer, especially with such a hopeful development as his calling to God's work.

FOUR

The Calling

From the little shacks in hamlets with names like Martinsville, to the storefront churches and splendid cathedrals of Indianapolis, the promise of Christianity drew the people. On the radio, religion was debated and discussed like politics. Legions of clerics served all strata of people, in backwater towns, in baronial houses of worship with fancy parsonages or on the "revival meeting" circuit. A few spread the word over the airwaves, for the price of radio time. Yet among the patchwork of Protestant churches in the Hoosier state, perhaps the most critical distinction turned not on dogma, nor on historical tradition, but upon color. With few exceptions, blacks and whites did not share church pews.

More than a few remnants of racism plagued the automotive city where the Ku Klux Klan had paraded openly in the 1920s, and in the state where they once played political kingmaker. Occasionally a cross burned or blacks were harassed for stepping out of place. Black people did not wander casually into certain outlying towns or even some Indianapolis neighborhoods. In 1950, the Indianapolis schools were segregated, some businesses allowed whites only, neighborhoods were divided along racial lines and blacks were barred de facto from holding certain jobs.

Though working in a white area of the city, Jim Jones did what he could to knock down racial and religious barriers. The Methodist student preacher launched a campaign to build a $20,000 recreation center for children of all faiths, to be run by an interdenominational board.

His efforts earned him a feature article in the *Richmond Palladium Item* in March 1953. The story—relating how Jim as a child brought home a tramp—probably was the first of hundreds of stories about the do-gooder preacher.

Another newspaper piece pictured him with several young supporters of his recreation project, all of them white. "Our boys and girls here are in desperate need of a recreation center setup," Jones said. "The parents realize the need, but funds in this neck of the woods are scarce. . . ." What Jim Jones described was a little ecumenical movement created around the need for supervised recreation. "Our congregation numbers over 100, with 35 active members. Non-members began coming here for convenience sake. . . ."

Jones wanted to increase his numbers and take inclusiveness even further, by racially integrating his congregation. In visiting black churches, he concluded that Pentecostalism would help him on both scores. Unlike the old-guard Methodists, white Pentecostalists, with their healings and emotional services, were somewhat inclined to accept blacks of similar persuasion, and vice versa. Furthermore, Pentecostal churches and evangelists drew far and away the biggest crowds.

To prepare himself, Jones spent countless hours in healing services, tent meetings and revivals, studying the methods of the best evangelical preachers. His attitude was: "If they can do it, I can too." Although his first healing attempts were a waste of energy, he kept working on his technique. If only he too could attract the tremendous crowds that flocked to healers, he would put them and their money to good use. Helping the disadvantaged was foremost in his mind, but under that was a personal need to be admired, loved and lauded by the crowds.

There is a certain magic in faith healing, more so than in discernment. A preacher can "discern" something about the past or present of a subject, using trickery, intuition or a quick eye. Success is a direct result of his ability. But with healing, success hinges heavily upon the faith of the sufferer.

Jim had not struck upon the proper formula until he and Marceline attended a Columbus, Indiana, church convention. There, a fellow minister, a little old white-haired lady in a print dress and white socks, introduced Rev. Jones to the congregation with this prophecy: "I perceive that you are a Prophet that shall go around the world. . . . And tonight you will begin your ministry." Marceline, the skeptical nurse and a Methodist, became uncomfortable, thinking that Jim would surely fall flat on his face.

Jones did not know what to do. Fitful and about to break out in hives, he mounted the pulpit. When he went to address the group, his mouth would not open. He closed his eyes, probably wishing he could drop dead. Then it began. All manner of thoughts flew through his mind; he called out people as fast as his tongue would allow. Soon the people streamed toward him, to be touched in the name of the Lord. To Marceline's utter amazement, her husband's touch made these people fall down, praising Jesus. The gathering broke out in screaming and hollering; the noise, the energy of the crowd seemed to shake the building. Marceline stood there in awe, proud that the man she loved had been blessed with such a gift.

Word traveled fast among the faithful. So many people arrived for the second night's meeting in Columbus that the audience overflowed. Jim called out names and clamped his eyelids shut, belting out words, laying his hands on heads and bodies. The emotional level rose to a near-frenzy as Jim poured out his seemingly endless incantation. Later, he would confess to mixed emotions during the sessions: he was happy that the juices finally had flowed, but the intensity of healing drained him. He thought he could not stand to do it again, yet he could not stop. The feeling of power and control—the adulation—must have overwhelmed him, regardless of whether he actually believed that the Holy Spirit was working miracles through him.

The Columbus, Indiana, performance was only a beginning. His truly public debut came in 1953 in Detroit. Hundreds of Protestant ministers had assembled at Bethesda Missionary Temple for an interdenominational missionary seminar. In that conventioneers' atmosphere, amid some of the Midwest's most adept and inspirational preachers, Jim Jones hoped to formally establish the reputation and record of his gift ministry. It was such a distinguished gathering, however, that he had not been scheduled as a speaker.

The event proceeded as expected with sermons and prayers, singing and lecturing. As Jim watched a Los Angeles evangelist "discern" the aches and pains of various people in the crowd, he became confident that he could do better. The tension and pent-up frustration built until he broke out in hives, his eyes puffy, his lips swollen. A woman organizer who noticed him told him he should go ahead and express his ministry; so Jim took the pulpit unscheduled.

"I'm a Methodist," Jones opened. "And I've come into the realization of the Holy Spirit." He was handsome, if slightly overweight, with baby fat padding his prominent cheekbones. His lips were taut; he clearly was frightened. Standing behind the pulpit, he seemed to focus every muscle, every nerve, every bit of energy into his thought. He started calling out to those in the audience. He called out names of people. He called out their phone numbers. He called out items in their purses or elsewhere on their persons. He spoke about their past illnesses and present ailments, and he prayed fervently, demonstratively, for them.

By the time he was through, Jones had upstaged the featured evangelist, and the organizers were seriously upset.

But not all were skeptical of the young upstart. Among those in the church that day were Rev. Edwin Wilson and his wife Audrey, from

Elmwood Temple in Cincinnati, Ohio. The Wilsons viewed Jones's gift ministry as one of the most dynamic they had witnessed. The accuracy and precision of his clairvoyance impressed them, and they were certain that the Holy Spirit was acting through him. Outside the church, the couple approached Jim Jones and soon found a common ground in their youth, openness to new ideas and Methodist background. Both, Wilson felt, were attuned to the Holy Spirit and believed that God worked wonders on earth. They exchanged phone numbers and would soon begin a friendship that included guest preaching at each other's church in Indianapolis and Cincinnati.

Positive feedback came from other conference participants who lived closer to home. Several Pentecostalists from Indianapolis's Laurel Street Tabernacle told Jim that he could easily break into the special fraternity of popular healers.

Unbeknownst even to Marceline, Jones had assured continuation of his "gift"—as he would admit later—by taking little notes and gathering bits of intelligence about the people he planned to call out. He had not yet openly avowed the philosophy "the ends justify the means," but he practiced it.

Jones wanted to integrate the Methodist church with his newfound friends, the Pentecostalists and the blacks. But he doubted that the Methodists, especially the older ones, would accept the changes, and he soon realized he was unlikely to draw very many blacks to the relatively unhospitable environment of Beech Grove. On his drives around town with Ronnie and Marceline and on his visits to various churches, Jim had sized up the suitability of various neighborhoods for a racially mixed church of his own. And he must have realized his best bet lay in the middle-class neighborhoods just north of downtown that were then being integrated.

He would need money first, however. Jones always needed money, not only because of his grand plans, but also because he had dreaded poverty and insolvency since his childhood. On his self-made treadmill, he preached at least two days a week and worked various jobs. He even imported little monkeys from South America and sold them door to door for $29 each. Riding his bicycle around southside Indianapolis with a cage of monkeys, he was such a comical sight that kids threw rocks at him. But with his glib solicitations and cute merchandise, he often got his foot in the door. Some of those who listened to his monkey business pitch started attending his services. Jim already had learned to economize on his actions.

The monkeys brought unexpected and probably unwelcomed publicity. On April 10, 1954, the *Indianapolis Star* ran a front-page story about the bureaucratic flap precipitated by young Jones's refusal to claim an air shipment of monkeys because many were sick or had died en route.

Although the monkeys enterprise was beginning to stink up the little Jones house on Villa Street, other problems weighed more heavily on Marceline. Jim had become so preoccupied with his work, ambitions and successes that she was relegated to secondary status. It was not that she did not share her husband's social goals. But she often wished to spend more time at home, to deepen her relationship with Jim, to have children. However, when she argued, Jim's assertiveness usually wore her down, and his will prevailed. Each month their home life strayed further from the sort of conventional family for which Marceline longed.

First, Jim insisted that she work to maximize their income. The domestic duties were turned over to a middle-aged woman named Ozzie, a live-in cook and housekeeper who did her best to keep Jim on the straight and narrow scripturewise, to no avail. In the next year, the Jones household ballooned into Jim's first extended family with the addition of Goldie, a big-boned eighteen-year-old blond woman whom the Joneses helped point toward a career in nursing, and of Esther Mueller, a lonely and very religious middle-aged white woman who would remain with the family until the end.

In about 1954, a child came into their lives, as Ronnie had—partially through chance, partially through their initiative. One day, after Jim had preached a sermon at Somerset, an unkempt girl of about nine in ragged clothes wandered up to the church door with a handful of violets. Handing them to the young minister, she said with a terrible stutter, "I love you." The poor little girl immediately stole the heart of Jim Jones, who no doubt recalled how he, half-naked, had presented flowers to a preacher in Lynn. The girl's neglectful mother was willing to let the Joneses adopt her. So Agnes Jones joined the household and, with speech therapy, lost her stutter.

Although Agnes brightened Marceline's life, her marriage depressed her. She would often break into tears in front of others but refused to confide her troubles. Once she hinted at the problem when she advised her sister Sharon, then about fifteen, "If you get married, don't marry a man who's domineering."

While Marceline felt trapped, frustrated and unappreciated, Rev. Jones spread his wings, reveling in his youthful attractiveness, his budding career and his ability to make things happen. At his most optimistic, energetic and grandiose, he felt—and claimed—that he could walk through walls, that his mind could conquer matter. Miracles aside, his fortunes were on the rise, and he sensed success. Already, he had enjoyed the taste of the matinee idol syndrome common among handsome and talented young preachers. He would come home and pointedly tell Marceline that women were flirting with him on the streets.

At about this time, Jim Jones left Somerset and rented a small building at Hoyt and Randolph streets in a racially mixed area. "Community Unity," he christened it. Brotherhood was the theme, "Holy Rolling" the style.

Rev. Russell Winberg from the Laurel Street Tabernacle decided to take a look at the young preacher whose reputation was spreading.

Winberg, a printer by trade and rather sluggish when off the pulpit, could thunder with the best of them when he was booming the Word and shouting down the devil. He came to Jones's church one afternoon, in the spirit of fellowship and perhaps out of a little curiosity about the new competition. A respectable-size crowd of about 150 filled the church that day. After some preliminary hymns, prayers and offerings, the people came forward to be blessed and, Christ willing, to be healed. Jones downplayed his healing gift to some elderly women who wanted physical remedies but not the social message; being a glorified doctor was not his ambition.

Nevertheless, Edith Cordell, another visitor from Laurel Street Tabernacle, came to Jones with her arthritis. Rev. Jones directed her to draw some water at a small sink near the pulpit platform, then drink it. She tasted it: "Oh, my, it's sweet. It's wine!" The demon of pain fled her body. A miracle. "Hallelujah! Praise God!" Instantly, Rev. Winberg believed; he had never witnessed anything to compare to this facile duplication of Jesus' miracle at the marriage feast, with a healing for good measure.

On the wings of such wondrous events, the crowds burgeoned beyond the limits of the little church. Officials at Laurel Street invited Jones to come to the larger Pentecostal church, where Rev. Winberg was associate minister. Jones brought his own people along, as he always would do. Like the little boy who hauled his pets everywhere, he kept his religious flock together; their familiar faces and the strength of their numbers helped dispel his own insecurity and create the proper atmosphere for his miraculous sleight of hand.

It was common practice for guest ministers to conduct revival meetings by invitation at other churches. But this temporary visit almost turned into a permanent post—in fact, the Laurel Street congregation responded so enthusiastically to Jones's magic that he won over some of them in 1954. Among these was Loretta Stewart, a sixteen-year-old girl who had become disenchanted with Christianity. This particular Sunday night, she was torn between going to the revival or rounding up her girl friends for a dance in a nearby park. Because she loved the spirit of revivals and never had missed one, she decided to see the first of a series being offered by Jim Jones. As usual, she took a front pew where her fine singing voice could be heard clearly. This night was different somehow: she sensed that something extraordinary was going to happen, and she wanted to witness it.

When time came for demonstrations of divine love, she leaned forward in her seat as Jim prophetically called out a first-time visitor from an old-fashioned Methodist church. He informed the man, named Gilbert, that he had cancer and ordered him to the restroom. Gilbert emerged to testify that he had passed a bloody cancerous growth from his bowels. In all her revivals, Loretta never had witnessed such a miracle.

While other healers called out phone or social security numbers, or pinpointed long-standing illnesses in their congregations, even sometimes relieving psychosomatic ailments, Jones's bloody cancer extractions were a real advancement of the art. It took more than dramatic choreography and his nearly photographic memory to palm off animal innards as malignant tumors; it required a quick hand, a knack for concealment, a calculating mind and, most of all, a willingness to deceive. Jones shared the truth about this "benevolent" deception—his means to a worthwhile end—with no one at first, not even with Marceline, although she sometimes collected the passed cancers in a paper bag.

For some time it appeared that Jim Jones, on the basis of his remarkable feats and charismatic speaking abilities, would take over the Laurel Street church itself. The aging pastor was planning to retire and needed an inspirational young replacement. Rev. Jones was invited back on numerous occasions and drew tremendous crowds. But in the end, the church board voted down the move to hire him because members feared his aggressive recruiting of blacks. "Wherever I have a church, *all* people will be welcome," he said. With that, he walked away from Laurel Street for good; about a hundred people, almost half of the congregation, followed him. It was his first major public stand for principle and his first successful theft of church members.

By 1956, Jones had stopped renting the little "Community Unity" building and had put a down payment on a nicer church at Fifteenth and North New Jersey in a racially mixed inner-city neighborhood. The little church, which he called "Wings of Deliverance," constituted a real step up in the world. It had stained glass, arched windows, a steeply peaked roof and a red brick parsonage next door. Having acquired a congregation and a solid church building, Rev. Jones then further dignified his brand of religious work by referring to it as a "movement."

The core of his congregation came directly from Laurel Street. Among them were Loretta Stewart, who became an organ player, her mother Mable, who became a church nursing home supervisor, plus several members of Edith Cordell's family. Rev. Russell Winberg, seeing that he too had no chance to take over the Laurel Street pastorship, assumed a position as Jones's associate pastor and brought along his wife Wilma, the other half of his ministerial team. The idealistic young couple, who had met while attending an Assemblies of God Bible school in Texas, were among the strongest fundamentalist Christians in Jones's church. But perhaps the most important newcomer was Jack Beam, a husky pharmaceutical company maintenance man.

Beam had devoted tremendous amounts of time to the Laurel Street church, doing odd jobs there and serving on the church board. The jovial, shrewd and extremely loyal man hit it off with Jim Jones, and gave him the same single-minded dedication. Through all sorts of trials and to the very end, Jack Beam would remain a true friend and important aide.

Most Laurel Street defectors tagged along for the same reason that many would initially follow Jones over the years—his healings. This fact trapped Jones: to maintain the hold on such people, he was forced to continue healing, carrying the entire load of deception on his own. In Jones's frenzied rise, amid overflow crowds and a chaotic barrage of words, he hardly had time enough to try to understand the phenomenon buoying up his career. But he marveled sometimes at how a faked healing could stimulate seemingly genuine healings. Though drugged by a stupendous sense of power, he kept a degree of skepticism about his miracle cures. In fact, he often wondered to himself about how long they lasted or whether people really were ill in the first place. Jones was not above convincing someone that he had a disease in order to "cure" the nonexistent ailment.

Wider recognition would help him expand Wings of Deliverance into the movement he almost immediately renamed "Peoples Temple." Jones did not care where he harvested his people. He brought his congregation around to black churches for exchange services and tried to recruit whenever he could. Once he went to a spiritualist state convention where his revelations were accepted as clairvoyant. Eventually, he drew nearly twenty spiritualists to Peoples Temple, one of them Edith Parks, the middle-aged matriarch of a growing family that would follow Jones almost anywhere.

Jim Jones had realized that the ministry amounted to a numbers equation. More people produced money and projects, and those in turn equaled more accomplishments and notoriety. For Jim Jones, the key to breaking into that circle of success seemed to be people, not dollars. He did not inherit a ready-made congregation with a big church and fat offerings, as some young preachers did. He was not bankrolled by a wealthy denomination. Fittingly, Jim Jones took the hard road, alone and with no outside support. But along the way, he grasped an important lesson: an image could serve as well as or better than reality. Religious people, with their eyes and minds on the heavens, and their hearts open, were more susceptible to a con job and sleight of hand than most people.

Creating an image meant creating publicity, and that meant a bold move. Soon after the move to his new church, he organized a mammoth religious convention to take place June 11 through June 15, 1956, in a cavernous Indianapolis hall called Cadle Tabernacle. To draw the crowds, Jim needed a religious headliner, and so he arranged to share the pulpit with Rev. William Branham, a healing evangelist and religious author as highly revered by some as Oral Roberts or Billy Graham.

As a prelude to the event, the *Herald of Faith*, a Christian newsletter out of Chicago, provided Jones a forum in its May 1956 issue. In his eloquent and almost biblical prose, Jones disguised his agnosticism—or atheism—and hid the fact that he was using religion for social goals. But he subtly revealed the role of religion in his own escape from poverty.

"Christianity, like a watch, needs to be wound if it is to start running. The Word states that, 'He that hungereth and thirsteth after righteousness shall be filled.' We cannot progress with God until we see if there is something to answer our quest for truth. Is there any divine response to man's yearning for a transformed life? Is progress merely a lifting of one's self 'by his own bootstraps'? Is what we hear from heaven but the echo of our own pleading cry?"

Some eleven thousand Christians attended opening day of the convention, to see Branham and twenty-five-year-old Jim Jones. Though Branham was known from Chicago to the Carolinas, his ministry was not particularly strong among blacks, but Jones's was becoming so. Blacks constituted about a fifth of the congregation that day. Many came to see Jim Jones in the afternoon preliminary service, then stayed around for the climactic nighttime session with the great healer Branham, a quietly charismatic, balding man in his mid-forties.

Though Jones was much more boisterous in his delivery and prayers than Branham, both preachers followed much the same Pentecostal procedure, relying heavily on numbers—addresses, social security, telephone and insurance policy numbers—all facts any good private detective could dig up. Like fortune-tellers, they told people about their past and future lives. Branham even told people what their doctor had said on the last visit. All this discernment was designed to build faith to that peak when "healing" was possible. The prayer lines stretched from the rear of the auditorium to the stage and across it. Individuals came forward in turn for a private consultation with Jones or Branham. As the preacher laid hands on the person and prayed aloud, the energy climbed. In the pews, the faithful lifted their hearts and minds in prayer. Feverish, some uttered cries of ecstasy, or pleaded to Jesus for a miracle. Some "fell out" before the preacher could even touch them. But usually the preacher appeared to give them a good shove on the forehead at the conclusion of the prayer, and that, their own inclination and whatever power came from the Holy Spirit sent them toppling backward, their hands up in surrender to the heavens. Some crumpled softly to the floor, but many keeled over, stiff as boards; it was fortunate that sturdy young men stood by to catch them and lay them down gently. "Hallelujah! Praise the Lord," the people cried as their brethren experienced the Holy Spirit. All around the auditorium people raised their voices in thanks. If all went well, bodies spilled down the aisles like an upset pile of cordwood. Some people touched by the Holy Spirit were supine, twitching, eyelids aflutter, their mouths spasmodically opening and closing, like fishes on land. Some popped to their feet almost immediately, smiling, disheveled but refreshed; their neighbors hugged them as they returned to their seats. Others stayed entranced on the floor—seemingly forgotten by everyone—for minutes and sometimes hours.

By evangelical standards, the more people who "fell out," the better. Branham not only enjoyed one of the best averages around, but he also could get people to fall out of their seats when he was on stage; he

could reach them without touching them. And sometimes virtually everyone on whom he placed his hands dropped over. Jim Jones the novice could
not rival Branham's percentages.

The exposure proved invaluable to Jones. One person introduced to
the Peoples Temple pastor by the event was a lanky black man in his
mid-forties named Archie Ijames. Ijames had come to hear William Branham, but he was just the man Jim Jones needed. Jones had been experiencing difficulty making blacks believe he was sincere about racial brotherhood; Ijames could help bring them into the fold.

When Jones later contacted him personally by phone as part of a
citywide effort to recruit blacks, Ijames at first declined to come to Temple
services. But then he and his family began listening to Jones's paid radio
show each Sunday night. The message of the Living Gospel jibed with
Ijames's personal philosophy; the humility and honesty of the preacher
struck him. "I don't know everything and I don't pretend to have all the
answers," Jones said. "But I'm doing the very best that I know. . . . Come,
and let's get together." The following Sunday the Ijames family went to
a new, larger Peoples Temple church, a former synagogue at Tenth and
Delaware streets, near downtown Indianapolis.

It did not take Jones long to realize that he had found a black man
to stand by his side. For his part, Ijames had discovered an organization
which could resolve his own conflicts over race and religion.

Born into a North Carolina farming family in 1913, Archie Ijames
had quit school at sixteen when his father, a schoolteacher and sharecropper, died. His poor but proud Methodist family took religion seriously,
kept holy the Sabbath, and taught its seven children never to swear. At
seventeen, Archie had a religious experience that led him to affiliate with
the Church of God, Body of Christ. But over the years religion eventually
proved ineffective against the racial problems confronted by Archie and
his wife Rosie, also from a sharecropper's family. Though he attended
Bible school and served as a pastor of a church until the mid-1940s, Ijames
quit organized religion altogether after he moved to Indiana. He became
disgusted with churches after getting an insider's view of a very un-
Christian power struggle.

When he met Jim Jones, Ijames considered himself an independent
thinker and called himself a universalist; he too wanted to break down
barriers between people. Recently he had seen little hope for doing it
through a church. But he was heartened by Jones's efforts to fully integrate Peoples Temple by increasing black representation from about 15
percent to 50.

Jones made Ijames feel needed and wanted. The church invited
Ijames's two oldest daughters to join the choir, and accommodated the
family's long-standing religious practice by promising never to ask them
to work on their Sabbath, Saturday. Soon it shaped up as a church for life.
"The day will come, Brother Jones, when I'll find people with whom I can

share my life one hundred percent," Ijames said. Replied Jones, "Well, if you don't find it here, you won't find it anywhere in the world."

The quest for brotherhood, however, did not rank highest on the list of attractions for most who came to Peoples Temple. It frustrated Jones that so many people gravitated to the church wanting only miracles. "Grand Central Station" he called it, with a touch of bitterness. Too many people came to be healed, then left without hearing the social message. But gradually Jones managed to perfect a sort of bait and switch technique; some of those who came initially for the healings would stay for the social commitment.

The presence of Archie Ijames on the pulpit as associate pastor served as a reminder of that message, and helped convince many blacks that Jones was a true integrationist. As for the white fundamentalists, they could always look up at the reassuring long white face of Rev. Winberg. The two sat along with Jack Beam in nice padded chairs. This little team shared the preliminary duties, opening the service, leading singing and prayers, introducing Jones.

The services were scheduled for Sunday mornings and a weekday evening and followed—as they always would—the revivalist format familiar to Jones and to most of the people. Yet the young minister maintained his tolerant ecumenical tenor. People stood and testified about their experiences, joys and troubles, all in the spirit of brotherhood. Some spoke in tongues and others interpreted. Jones, though he thought it gibberish, participated to make the "tongues people" feel welcome. He simply faked it.

In a warm-up, the husky preacher usually sang a couple of songs, his chest swelling, his lungs booming out traditional hymns. The crowd joined in, swaying, waving their arms in the air. Then without notes, he sermonized for hours, about brotherhood, the failure of organized religion to address social injustice, the problems of the poor. To make his points, he was as apt to throw in something from that day's newspaper as he was to quote the Bible.

In a climate of love, a line formed down the center aisle for the finale, the healings. At his invitation, people would come forward and gather around him like children. On one day in 1957, Jones spotted a seven-year-old black boy named Jim Cobb hiding in the crowd. The boy had cried when his mother, Christine Cobb, had coaxed him, almost dragging him, to the cluster of people around the pulpit.

Christine Cobb, a steelworker's wife, had abandoned her neighborhood Baptist church to go across town to Peoples Temple. Her neighbors were baffled—they had not experienced the warm and friendly atmosphere that so attracted her, and were not impressed when she told them about the psychic powers of Jones, who could tell her about a recurring dream she often had.

As the others around young Jim moaned and shouted, young Jim

Cobb hunched down shyly. Yet the white man, wending his way through the crowd, stopped dead in front of him.

The air pulsed with excitement as Rev. Jones looked down at the boy. Jim Cobb stood there with a lump in his throat as the preacher wrinkled his forehead and bore his eyes into him. Then the minister put his right hand on Jim's head, and his left fell onto his ear. "You have an ear problem, my son," he declared softly.

Jim Cobb was startled. How did this man know about the ear surgery and his dizzy spells?

"Your ear will be fine, my son," the preacher assured him as though he could foresee the future. As Jim's mother cried out thanks to Christ, Rev. Jones started to walk away, then turned. "You're going to be a leader someday," he told the boy with a smile.

As things turned out, Jones was only half right. Jim Cobb would need another ear operation five years later; but he *would* become a leader someday—a youth leader in Jones's church. As he grew older, Jim Cobb would realize that Peoples Temple promised something very rare in Indianapolis. From his earliest years in the ghetto, racial disharmony had been an ugly reality to him. So he reveled in the pervasive feeling of brotherhood in the huge congregation. And he respected the courage and frank uncompromising language of Rev. Jones: "We are an interracial group. And if anyone doesn't like that, you don't have to give your money."

The rhetoric was substantiated by human service projects that yielded some positive publicity in 1957. On January 4, the now-defunct *Indianapolis News* reported that Jones had made the human relations honor roll of the weekly black newspaper, the *Indianapolis Recorder*.

Jones wanted the church to exemplify egalitarianism, to shelter the needy, to provide a family for the lonely. Stray animals and people were taken in. He ordered everyone to wear casual clothes to church one Easter Sunday, so no one would feel out of place or inferior. He rounded up black kids in the neighborhood and took them to the zoo for a picnic. The church opened a soup kitchen for the poor and skid row characters in February 1960, and soon expanded its social services with missionary ardor. Peoples Temple gave away canned goods or paid the rent for some indigent, provided free clothing at a job placement center and delivered coal to poor people who otherwise could not heat their homes.

Jim Jones inspired it all. Often he reached into his own pocket to help street beggars and the needy. But before he gave a substantial sum to anyone, he had his aides investigate to make sure the person deserved it. If Jones saw a need, he tried to fill it. A benevolent opportunist, efficient, savvy, businesslike, he was the sort of preacher who could convince the owners of the synagogue he bought to loan the money interest-free if it were repaid within a year—and who would satisfy the debt one day early.

Human services aside, Jim Jones was not fashioning an ordinary church. Step by step, he demanded more of his people than most Christian churches. His always escalating demands would cause some followers to drop by the wayside, but in the long run would tighten his organization. As part of a systematic binding process, he attempted to keep his members with the Temple "family" on Christmas and Thanksgiving, rather than with blood relatives. It was the earliest sign that he someday would ask members to forsake their families. He wanted his congregation to look upon him and the Temple as the most important part of their lives; indeed he hoped they all would dedicate their lives to the Temple and its goals, as he had. Total commitment, he realized, would maximize the contribution of each individual member. And total dependency would ensure continued commitment. Consequently, as he issued his call to humanitarianism, he offered a deal: if you donate your material possessions, I will meet all your needs. Summoning up passages from the Bible, he urged his people toward a form of socialism he called religious communalism.

Archie Ijames was among the first to commit his life to Temple work. When the free restaurant opened in 1960, the response was overwhelming: the Temple served eighteen meals on the first day, one hundred on the second. Asked to help out, Ijames, a carpenter by trade, quit all outside work and dedicated himself to hustling food for the poor. Charity was not a novelty to him and Rosie; even before meeting Jones, they had distributed scrounged and scavenged foodstuffs to the needy. Now, adapting their methods to the Temple program, Ijames stretched the $25 weekly food program budget into meals for several hundred poor people. He and his wife bought overripe produce dirt cheap or found free edible food at railroad freight yards and unloading areas. They convinced butchers to discount their prices for a small payoff, and to give them Saturday's meat that would spoil over the weekend.

Thanks to such enterprising efforts, the Temple soup kitchen dished up an average of about 2,800 meals a month. Transients lined up outside the church basement, sometimes at 7:30 A.M., anxious for a hot lunch served by Temple volunteers. Most guests were white, many were alcoholics, and all were down on their luck. They came for the food, not the proselytizing. Yet Winberg and some others preached and counseled about the evils of alcohol and tobacco. Along with working-class degenerates, now and then a former professional on the skids would pass through the food lines. Once a former doctor from Colorado interrupted his free meal to put a splint on a bum's broken leg.

The soup kitchen rules were simple: no drinking, smoking or fighting. Belligerent drunks came and went, but people generally behaved, especially during the cold Indiana winters. Sometimes the peace, however, was disturbed by chief cook Rheaviana Beam, Jack Beam's tall and attractive wife. She could do wonderful things with food, but she acquired a reputation for moodiness and fits of temper. She drove some other church members to distraction, and many steered clear of her. But Archie Ijames broke through to her one day, and found that in her private world, Rheaviana felt unappreciated and insecure, unloved. An emotional and philosophical man, he voiced respect for her tireless work helping others, in spite of her temperamental nature. "We're inclined to see personality [alone]," he told her in the kitchen. "But God is bigger than personality. He sees those doing the work. And I see you doing the job."

She turned to face him, tears flowing down her cheeks. "You don't know how much that means to me. You just can't know." Each sensed that something special had happened; they had revealed themselves to each other, and expressed the sort of love that Peoples Temple fostered: a love of common cause, an appreciation of your fellowman. In the Temple climate, a black man and a white woman could love each other as friends, as brother and sister, without sexual byplay, family ties or marriage. That always would prove one of the strongest attractions.

Such touching moments of communication moved Archie Ijames. By increments, he made the Temple his religion—and changed his lifestyle to meet its needs. One day his wife asked him, "If you're working seven days a week at the restaurant, what about the Sabbath?" He retorted, "I'll make my church down there with the poor and disenfranchised." Sabbath or not, the Ijameses would feed the needy. This was the beginning; the distinction between their lives and church life was disappearing.

The home life and church life of the Joneses already had merged beyond separation. When they found one of the Temple members unhappy and covered with bedsores in a nursing home, they brought the woman to their large white duplex on North College near Twenty-fourth Street. Marceline converted her own house into a nursing home, with help from Jim, and, while working an outside nursing job, brought the home up to state standards. Though capacity was twenty-four patients, the integrated nursing home sometimes exceeded that number because it was clean and inexpensive; when the nursing inspector came, extra patients were secreted next door in a church member's house.

The first home belonged to the Joneses, but a second opened as a church enterprise. Both were profitable and required full-time management. So when Marceline's father took early retirement at fifty-five, he and his wife moved to Indianapolis to help out. They wound up running the homes and living with Jim and Marceline at 2327 North Broadway in a big brown house.

Although Marceline was happy with the nursing homes, she seemed depressed at times. She confided some of her misgivings to her parents: Jim thrived on all the attention he received from his congregation —so much so that he had transformed their house into a quasi-commune. Though Marceline craved privacy, Jim had brought about a dozen people into their home, including at one point his own mother, who worked as a correctional officer at a state women's prison. They were Temple members, foundlings and friends; and by their cohabitation they formalized the commingling of their religious and personal lives.

With Jim playing pastor, confessor and counselor, the house was turned over to church-related matters, personal problem solving and, sometimes, to chaos. People came and went, making demands twenty-four hours a day. But young Rev. Jones was enamored of his enlarged family for personal, political and psychological reasons.

He took in people who needed and admired him, who were willing to let him guide their lives by direction and example. At home, on a small scale, he experimented with communalism, already convinced of its virtues as a unifying force, a concentrator of his power and an economizing tool. Yet years would pass before the political climate, the times and the place would allow him to put his prototype into full-scale practice.

FIVE

New Directions

With the determination of the little boy experimenting with churches in Lynn, Jim Jones searched for methods and recruiting grounds that would enlarge and tighten his organization. While he pursued the conventional goals of an aggressive fundamentalist preacher—money and members— he also moved in new directions: toward cultlike control of his people and toward communism under the guise of Christian communalism. Jones was a driven young man. He beat the roads of Indiana and Ohio several days a week, often bringing along a few carloads of his followers. And when he was not visiting and recruiting in places such as Cincinnati and Columbus, Indiana, and South Charleston, he tried to increase his numbers in Indianapolis and to generate income to pay for Temple facilities and new programs.

With his extended family, he always had an ear to bend, someone with whom to share an idea or new plan. And he ran his assistants ragged with all his motoring and noisy marathon services which sometimes went to 5:00 A.M., to the chagrin of the church's neighbors. Jones would not hesitate to wake his assistants with an assignment or a brainstorm in the middle of the night; he seemed to think that because he did not want to sleep or was in the throes of insomnia that no one else was entitled to sleep either. His dynamo mind ran day and night, with sometimes no more feedback than the television, no more company than a book. One way or another, all his problems—petty and awesome—and all his thoughts were channeled into the growth of his fledgling movement. Yet even dynamos and zealots sometimes exhaust their energies, and Jones did too, with increasing frequency. Eventually his problems would become so serious that Marceline would ask their minister friend, Rev. Wilson, and his wife Audrey to pray for Jim.

Jones's expansion attempts were those of an impatient and aggressive man. While on a quest for new organizational techniques in the late 1950s, he had read extensively about Father Divine, spiritual father of the gigantic Peace Mission movement. In typically direct fashion, Jim Jones drove to Philadelphia to meet the black cult leader in person. He invited Rev. Wilson along.

Jones hoped to learn something from a sharecropper's son who had become a self-proclaimed "Dean of the Universe," god to tens of thousands of followers and lord of a religious empire worth millions of dollars. But most of all, Jones hoped to acquire Divine's throne; he was acutely aware that the elderly evangelist soon would be departing this earth.

Father Divine had climbed a long, somewhat zany ladder to deification. Born sometime between 1860 and 1880 as George Baker in Savannah River country, he had decided to turn preacher when he tired of handyman's work in Baltimore. In 1914, Baker—arrested and booked as "John Doe, alias God"—was found to be of unsound mind and evicted from Georgia. The next year, however, he turned up in Harlem with a dozen followers. Divine's next arrest provided him with his first bona fide miracle: four days after having sentenced "God" to a year in prison and a $5,000 fine for being "a public nuisance," the judge dropped dead. Informed of the heart attack, Divine nodded forlornly: "I hated to do it."

The legend spread. By 1936, authorities estimated that his New York-based movement was making $10,000 a week from dozens of business concerns including apartments, restaurants, cleaning shops and two newspapers. In the 1940s, while headquartered in the City of Brotherly Love, the movement picked up momentum and incalculable amounts of money. Divine purchased hotels, or "Heavens," around the country's largest cities and filled them with followers whose names reflected the philosophy of peace, love and docility.

In 1946, the "Heavens" quaked when Divine, then between fifty-five and seventy-five years old and bald-headed, married a twenty-one-year-old blond Canadian stenographer named Edna Ritchings. He eventually silenced murmurings of dissent with a revelation: his late wife, a black woman named Penninah, had approved the marriage and entered the white woman's body.

Divine—who seldom appeared publicly except to dispel recurring rumors of his demise—reigned from a nineteenth-century mansion on the seventy-three-acre Woodmont estate. It was there that he received Rev. Jones.

The visit went harmoniously because the two men shared concerns about segregation and overpopulation. Divine even invited Jones to deliver a sermon to his followers, and the Mission photographers took photos of the Indiana preacher for an article in Divine's newspaper, *The New Day*. Jones noticed another favorable sign: Divine was too old to preach, and instead played tape recordings of sermons from his more robust years. The visit ended with expressions of hope for future fellowship.

On the drive back to the Midwest, Jones's enthusiasm for Divine upset his traveling companion; Rev. Wilson did not believe Divine was God, and it seemed stupid and scripturally unsound to advocate celibacy as the cult leader did.

But Jones had more than a flirtation with Divine's ideas in mind. Back in Indianapolis, the preacher lavished praise on the man and his mission. Privately, he confided to his aides a long-range plan: he would succeed Divine, if only Mother Divine would stay out of the way, he said.

Jones prepared for his inheritance by studying tape recordings of Divine's sermons. He examined more of Divine's writings. He instructed Russell Winberg, the printer, to run off copies of a religious tract defending Jones's acceptance of the controversial evangelist, and largely praising him. And he encouraged his aides and congregation to not only give all to Peoples Temple, but also to refrain from sex, in keeping with Divine's teachings—and only to adopt children.

Some of his own followers became extremely upset when he lauded Father Divine. The religious tract scandalized other preachers who criticized the Temple for supporting a pretender to the throne of God. Then, during the Joneses' supposed life of celibacy, Marceline turned up pregnant—and Jim had to swallow his pride and announce it to the bemused congregation.

After the initial visits to Father Divine, not-so-subtle changes crept into Jim's theology and behavior. Troubling as they were to his family and closest aides, these trends could not be attributed to the black evangelist's influence, as many attempted to do.

One day Mrs. Baldwin rebuked Jim gently when he came flying down the stairs, Bible in hand, declaring: "Mom, this Bible has got to be torn down! It's full of inconsistencies, and our churches are failing to carry out the great commandment to feed the widows and children and take care of the needy. 'The letter killeth, but the Spirit giveth life!' "

"Jim," she said patiently, "that Bible is very precious to me, but I do believe the Holy Spirit makes it alive in our hearts."

Jim had started reading his Bible again with great intensity, picking it apart with the vigor of a crusader; the list of inconsistencies he compiled would serve him for years. When he began speaking publicly about such things, however, he touched off a firestorm. After all, he was assailing the Word of God, the foundation of belief for Bible-oriented Christians. Many could not tolerate such blasphemy and deserted. More important, those remaining behind were compromised; by allowing Jones to ridicule the Gospel, these fundamentalists had surrendered part of themselves to him.

One Sunday in 1959, twenty-eight-year-old Jim Jones tested them with a fiery sermon in his Delaware Street church. The evangelical rhetoric leaped from subject to subject, as Jones guided his congregation along an emotional journey, from despair at the threat of damnation to ecstasy at the promise of redemption. His voice, his dramatic timing, with exhausting climaxes followed by an almost conversational lull, carried the crowd from one feverish crescendo to another. Into his evangelism, Jones wove themes that indicated the long-range direction of Peoples Temple, and he projected a kind of "us against them" view of the world, enunciated in terms of those who would enter God's kingdom and those who would not.

There was another tone as well—that of the petulant, egotistical man impatient with the inattentive, pleased when he had the audience firmly within his control. "You ready to go home?" he would shout at one point, mockingly secure in his own power. "Too bad!" At another moment, he warned his listeners to wake up for the healings coming. "Either you endure sound doctrine when I preach it," he threatened, "or you don't hear it."

Then at one point, readopting his pose of humility, he apologized for rambling. Yet upon examination, even Jones's vagaries possess an uncanny internal logic.

"You need to wash somebody's feet today, most of you," Jones thundered from his pulpit. "Not some little grandma you love, but someone you don't like at all. I'll never forget one old lady in our church. She was so starchy. She said, 'I'm not going to wash feet.' Finally, we talked her into washing feet, the feet of a friend, and the friend wouldn't let her. . . .

"And that poor old lady just sat there and sat there, and the blackest Negro woman in my church—she hated 'em, she hated 'em so bad she couldn't stand 'em—the blackest, ugliest, dirtiest Negro woman in our church"—the crowd laughed—"came up and sat down and said, 'Wash my feet.' " There was more laughter. "And she washed the feet and she got her victory.

"I didn't speak that to reflect on race. We got a principal and a doctor and a dentist in my church who are Negro. My best and most intelligent people and some of my most forthright of our constituency are Negro—about ten percent—and by far the ten percent of our Negro population got more intelligence than our so-called white people. But in our church we don't call 'em white or Negro. We call 'em by name."

Jim Jones paused for a moment to gather momentum for the next burst. Then, with his voice, he transported his listeners to a streetcorner. There he was, he told them, at the corner of Market and Alabama ministering to a drunk. The moral: Jim Jones cares about everyone; he is not a hypocritical Christian.

Having aroused their admiration, Jones now challenged his people to do the same, to dedicate everything to the cause. He reminded the congregation of the early days of Christianity, and he drew parallels between Christ's apostles—who had forsaken their belongings to live communally—and the Temple's ministers.

"I'm not *the* pastor. There are four pastors and we get along beautifully. I'm so thankful for just a little bit of it, that touch, that togetherness, that creates a fellowship in the heart. And we need it. It speaks for itself."

He picked up the volume, suddenly, to roughly quote the Bible: "And they *sold* their possessions and goods and imparted them to every man as every man had need." And he boomed a challenge: "Now what are you gonna do with that? Any opinion? *No,* I didn't think so.

"It's true and it's pitiful. Communism has *sold* itself to the possession of the group mind. Only one thing's gonna counter communism. It has its Messiah. It has its Bible. It has its tomes. And the *only* thing that's gonna stop it . . . is for us to sell what we have and impart them to every man that has need."

Here was Jones's proposal: to fight communism with communalism.

"God for some time has been putting it upon our hearts to sell what we have and give it to the corporate community of our church," he went on. "Our Temple now is starting our restaurant, a mission that will feed people without cost. Running a grocery and no charge for food. We're asking people to give as God blesses them. No charge for anything because God is free and everything He has is free. It's been provided. Our aged home, the nicest in the state of Indiana, has been established on the basis of from each according to his ability to each according to his need."

Had there been another closet Marxist in the audience that night, surely he would not have missed that most famous of lines from Karl Marx's 1875 "Critique of the Gotha Program." But Jones, though borrowing from Marx, played upon the fact that his Christian audience would recall the similarities in the Acts of the Apostles, 4:34–35: "There was not a needy person among them, for as many as were possessors of lands or houses sold them and brought the proceeds of what was sold and laid at the apostles' feet; and distribution was made to each as any had need."

That biblical passage eventually would allow Jones to call Christ the first communist. In the meantime, it allowed him to use religion to bring people to communalism—the best way to keep them in his organization—and ultimately to communism.

He went on. "I know if there weren't a few people healed here every week . . . or a different person called out by discernment, I know some of you wouldn't come to hear me preach. . . . Some of you don't like to hear this tonight. But you better get ready to hear a lot more of it . . . We needed it. *Amen."*

Jones concluded his hour-and-a-half sermon with music and a prayer, then spoke in tongues to keep the hard-core Pentecostalists happy. "In the name of the Son of God, Hallelujah! Mura muca shukado da mucada mucada. . . . Blessed be the name of the Lord."

It was a remarkable performance. Yet Jim Jones could not convert fundamentalist Christian midwestern capitalists into communists overnight. Apparently unable to convince enough Indianapolis blacks to devote themselves entirely, and communally, to Peoples Temple, he looked elsewhere for recruits. He had been watching the Cuban revolutionary struggle with great interest since Fidel Castro's overthrow of Batista in January 1959. Reasoning that many black Cubans probably were eager to escape economic chaos and austerity following the revolution, he seized on an idea: he could speed up his plan to build a communal organization in the United States by recruiting Cuban blacks to live in Indiana.

Arriving in Cuba in early 1960, Jones first staked out the Havana Hilton in search of a translator. Looking like a camera-toting tourist, he called out a friendly hello to a black man. The man, Carlos Foster, was a Cuban of Jamaican descent and was receptive to Jones's overtures. Jones introduced himself as an evangelical minister and part-time nightclub singer; he offered Foster $24 a day and promised to send him and his family to the United States if he would help with the recruitment plan. Foster wanted to join his fiancée in the United States, so agreed to act as a sort of executive confidant for Jones.

Jones took the Cuban to a hotel room and spent a week, from 7:00 A.M. to 8:00 P.M., briefing him, talking endlessly, even sending out for meals through room service. The plan was to bring forty Cuban black families to America, to work on communal farms financed by his Indiana congregation. (This same idea—of displaced agricultural laborers in an ideal interracial environment—would emerge, years later, as Jonestown.)

After the briefings, Jones and Foster went into the slum areas of Havana and interviewed dozens of families. Once they had collected the names and addresses of fifteen that were receptive to the plan, Jones headed home, but before leaving Cuba, he told Foster to carry on until he had gathered names of an additional twenty-five families.

Back in the States, Jones revealed little of his plan, depicting his stay more as tourism than church business. He showed off photos of Cuba, taken in February 1960, which depicted new educational and medical facilities built by the Castro government and a sugarcane mill. One picture—a gruesome shot of the mangled body of a pilot in some plane wreckage—indicated that Jones witnessed the pirate bombings of the cane fields. Jones told his friends that he had met with some Cuban leaders, though the bearded man in fatigues standing beside Jones in a snapshot was too short to be Castro.

Four months later, Jones sponsored Carlos Foster's trip to Indianapolis: alone, without the families. The black Cuban mostly stayed indoors at the Jones home because Jones had cautioned him that white middle-class neighbors might lynch him if he left the house alone. Jones's plan—which would have cost far more than Peoples Temple could afford —was not actively pursued. Meanwhile, Foster felt like a virtual prisoner; Jones would not allow him to find a job, although he compelled him to take part in church services. Winberg thought that Jones's Cuban friend had no interest at all in the Temple, and he was right. After two months, Foster left to see his fiancée in New York, and Jones never heard from him again.

In the meantime, Jones had been encouraging members of his congregation to adopt children, especially young orphans in war-ravaged Korea. The Joneses themselves set the example. In October of 1958, they traveled to California to bring home two orphans. Everyone in the Jones household fell in love instantly with four-year-old Stepha-nie, her beautiful face and black bangs; and they gave extra affection to Chioke, a two-year-old renamed Lew Eric, who needed medical attention for malnutrition.

The children were both a blessing and a curse for Marceline. They made it easier for her to accept Jim's preoccupation with his work and the couple's lack of privacy; finally, she had little ones to love. But they—and the child in her womb—also would bring tremendous obligations and would make it much more difficult to ever leave her husband. Jim still tried to dominate her, and when they argued, his temper sometimes turned physical. Once, in fact, he kicked her in the stomach, making her fear for her unborn child.

Tragedy struck the Joneses not long after the adoptions. On May 11, 1959, Stephanie wanted to go to Cincinnati for her father's church exchange service at Rev. Wilson's Elmwood Temple. This one time Marce-line, in her eighth month of pregnancy, stayed at home. During the service in Cincinnati, Mable Stewart asked for a song. Jones later would recall leading the chorus:

"On up the road
Far in the distance
I saw a light shining in the night. . . .
Then I knew. . . ."

As they often did when Jim Jones was in the pulpit, services ran late at Elmwood Temple. Afterward the Temple contingent divided up into various cars. Stephanie hopped into Mrs. Stewart's car. The other passengers were a ten-year-old boy and four adult church workers. On a wide open stretch of U.S. 421, Mrs. Stewart appeared to pull out to pass a station wagon with only 100 feet of passing space. A high-speed, head-on collision wiped out six lives, including Stephanie's.

Jim Jones raced to the scene. "It's a little hard to understand these things," he told the Associated Press in a tremulous voice. "Those people were like my flesh and blood."

Of Stephanie, he said, "She was an exceptional child. Already she could speak perfect English. At least we have the consolation of knowing she received more love in those few months than in her entire life before."

But he pulled his emotions together enough to say that he would go on with his regular Sunday evening radio sermon and to reveal that he had had a premonition about the Saturday night tragedy.

"For some strange reason, I told them that some of our people will never be back. I don't know what made me say it."

Earlier, Jim Jones apparently had tampered with his in-laws' car. Years later, he would say that he made his prophecies come true—and he would prophesy malfunctions in the cars of members of his congregation. And, over the years, he would anguish again and again in public over the deaths of the six. The cause of the collision remained a mystery.

As Marceline grieved the loss, her mind strayed to a statement Stephanie made one day while having her hair brushed: "I wish [my friend] Oboki had a mother and dad like I have." The day Stephanie was buried, Mother's Day, the Joneses called the orphanage in Seoul to ask if there was a girl named Oboki. A cable soon confirmed that there was, and that she and Stephanie had been fast friends. Immediately, the family set up plans for adopting the child.

Meanwhile, Marceline's pregnancy came to term, and she was driven to the hospital. Her mother and Jim kept the watch, anxious and excited, typical expectant grandmother and father. The baby finally arrived on June 1, 1959, in a difficult breach birth. It was a boy of seven pounds, with Jim's dark hair and Marceline's fine facial features. They named him Stephan Gandhi Jones after the Indian leader. Though Jim was proud, no one could have been prouder than the mother: as the pink-faced baby was placed in Marceline's arms for the first time, she saw in her mind the image of a tall, handsome American Indian warrior, throwing a spear.

Before the Jones household's elation over the birth had faded, six-year-old Oboki, renamed Suzanne, arrived from the Korean orphanage. Then the Joneses decided to take an even bigger humanitarian step by adopting a black infant. Marceline's mother thought the move might well lead to trouble, not just from outsiders but from jealousy between the black child and Stephan, who was about the same age. "For Stephan's sake," Mrs. Baldwin asked her daughter, "I wonder if you should adopt this black boy."

"Mother," came the reply, "I am doing it for Stephan's sake, so he won't grow up with prejudices."

Within several months, the Jones family had adopted a black baby and accorded him the honor of his new father's name—James Warren

Jones, Jr. The song that Marceline began to sing at services captured her own love for the child and the tenor of the Temple:

> *"Black Baby, black baby, as you grow up*
> *I want you to drink from the plenty cup*
> *I want you to speak up clear and loud*
> *I want you to stand tall and proud*
> *My little black baby. . . ."*

While Jones made his family a living example of integration, he sought to exploit his "rainbow family" for his own purposes. In the summer of 1959, shortly after Stephen was born and before Marceline had fully recovered, Jones announced another trip to Philadelphia to see Father Divine. Neither Marceline nor her mother, who went along to care for the baby, believed in Divine's pretensions to divinity; they went because Jim wanted company. Marceline appeared unhappy and weak; her mother diagnosed it as postbirth depression, but Marceline conceivably might have been disturbed by her husband's fascination with the evangelist or by larger problems.

In Philadelphia, the Temple contingent was accorded the finest hospitality Father Divine could offer, accommodations in one of his downtown hotels. In the care of his docile followers, they toured the spectacular Woodmont mansion, its opulent rooms and the pastoral grounds. They attended great feasts called Holy Communion, with several kinds of salads, bread, roasts, vegetables, even several desserts. Father Divine presided from the head of the table with beautiful Mother Divine; his taped sermons ran during the meals. Afterward, the men and women left the banquet halls by separate exits.

The Jones party met privately with Father and Mother Divine. Never one for subtlety, Jones broached an important subject for the first time; he conveyed his readiness to assume the leadership of the Peace Mission movement if Divine should decide to lay down his body. Divine, said to be immortal, did not take the invitation seriously. On the other hand, Mother Divine, his designated successor, did not appreciate Jones's intrusions. Her mistrust only deepened when Marceline confided stories of Jones's earlier atheism.

It was on another such visit that Mrs. Wilson learned of one of Jim Jones's fears. While the minister stood on the balcony of one of the Peace Mission hotels, looking out over Philadelphia, Mrs. Wilson—who had a playful streak—did an impetuous thing; she touched Jones as though she were going to shove him. He panicked, fearfully backing away from her. Mrs. Wilson tried to apologize. But Jim shouted, "You really wanted to do that! You did!" He accused her of trying to murder him. Then, probably to explain his own overreaction, he confessed a fear of heights—the same explanation he had used in college to secure the lower bunk.

Between visits to Father Divine, Jones curried his favor through letters and phone calls. He introduced Divine's hymns to Peoples Temple and told his aides he intended to take over the evangelist's movement upon his death. In his grandiose view, he saw nothing illogical in assuming that Father Divine would bequeath the fruits of over four decades of evangelizing to his Indiana pen pal.

Jones tried every imaginable shortcut to the building of a large integrated congregation—the trip to Cuba, his visits to Divine, even a pitch to the Black Muslims. Jones was willing to work with anyone willing to work with him—and to swipe people along the way. When he traveled to Chicago to ask the Honorable Elijah Muhammad for cooperation, he was not allowed inside the Muslim mosque because he was white. Jones protested that he had given his own name to an adopted black son, but the Muslims remained unimpressed.

S I X

The Crusader Collapses

Integrationist white preachers were scarce in the Midwest during the early civil rights movement. But Jones was by no means alone. One other, thirty-two-year-old Ross Case, integrated his churches, intended to adopt a child of black or mixed blood and thought it intolerable that the Sunday morning church service was the most segregated hour in America. Racial tolerance and religion had gone hand in hand for Case since he was a boy in Independence, Missouri, where he felt a strong calling to the ministry and a strong aversion to the bigotry there. Then, as a college-educated young minister in the Christian church, Disciples of Christ, Case and his wife Luella combined their marriage and his ministry with a commitment to racial equality.

In August 1959, while attending a two-week spiritual camp in southern Indiana, the Cases became friendly with a young black woman who told them about a truly interracial church in Indianapolis. The following Sunday the couple drove to Indianapolis to see for themselves. They walked in on a lawn party in the backyard of the Jones house on Broadway. Everyone was milling about, socializing, nibbling food from a table, drinking punch—except for a cheeky raven-haired young man in a chair. This presiding figure wrote checks and carried on two or three conversations with people around him. Instantly Case was impressed with the agile mind and commanding presence of Jim Jones—yet he could not know that the same energetic personality, while promoting his own deification, was racing toward a nervous breakdown.

The meeting with Jones and his three assistants—Archie Ijames, Jack Beam and Russell Winberg—made Case ecstatic. The Temple leaders endorsed his efforts to integrate his own church in Mason City, Illinois. Here at last he had found an entire staff that shared his integrationist sentiments.

There were other areas of compatibility, too. Though Case's denomination rejected Pentecostalism at this time, he had begun to believe in the Pentecostal experience, the power of the Holy Spirit to work miracles on earth. Communalism also posed no problem: the Cases had investigated an integrated religious commune in Americus, Georgia, and found it attractive. Further, Case was comforted by the apparent biblical orientation of the Temple ministers, who cited scriptural passages to support their integrationist views.

Jones and his assistants wanted Case to join Peoples Temple immediately. Case indicated that after he fulfilled his prior commitments in Mason City, he would welcome an opportunity to join the Temple team. And before he left, Temple leaders sought his advice about a matter currently under discussion in the church: whether Case's denomination, the Disciples of Christ, would accept the Temple as an affiliate. "You might try it," came the reply.

While Case returned to Mason City, the Temple made its application to Disciples of Christ and was accepted into the denomination in 1960, before Jones was ordained as a minister. The denomination leadership respected the Temple, believing its programs for the downtrodden exemplified Christianity in action. Jones himself was unique among ministers —an attractive character with quiet charisma and entrepreneurial instincts. A. Dale Fiers, who would become president of Disciples of Christ in 1964, had grasped Jones's potential while listening to him on the Temple's Sunday night radio show. He told colleagues at the time, "Here is a man who can accomplish great good. But he also has the kind of power and gifts that could go off the deep end."

Jones first had become interested in Disciples of Christ when Ijames showed him newspaper articles indicating that the Indianapolis-based Disciples of Christ would tolerate all political views—and that the denomination respected local autonomy, asking only that a congregation have baptism and take communion every Sunday. Jones immediately pressed for the alliance, telling his congregation, "If you take my advice, you will [join] too, because it will be for your protection." Benefits of affiliation would show themselves over the years. Chief among them was the mantle of legitimacy afforded by membership in a 1.5 million- to 2 million-member denomination, and, on the material side, an umbrella tax exemption. Membership would also provide a curtain over the Temple's political drift.

Ross Case finally teamed up with Jones in August of 1961. In the previous year, in periodic phone conversations from Mason City, Case had discovered that Pastor Jones was inclined to make theological blunders. For instance, Jones had got himself in hot water with his aides and the congregation by denying the virgin birth—and had to reverse himself. Case thought, rather naïvely, that he, as an ordained college-educated minister well versed in the Bible, could provide Jones with guidance. However, in his several months on the pulpit platform with Jones, Case would find that the pastor's troubles did not always originate with honest mistakes. Meantime, Case was excited to take a post with an organization now aligned with his own denomination and headed by a preacher who had become a minor public figure in Indianapolis.

In 1960, conservative Democratic Mayor Charles Boswell had made available $7,000 to fund the city Human Rights Commission directorship. Advertising the job mostly by word of mouth, the selection committee heard from few applicants in the next eighteen months—in fact, only one. In the job interview at City Hall, the committee—a rabbi, a black judge and a priest—appraised Jim Jones without doing a background check. They were not aware of his healings, although they had seen his name on the religious page of the newspaper and knew him as an advocate of the poor and blacks. Jones came across as an articulate and humane "eager beaver" social worker, though he put off the priest a little by flaunting his fundamentalist Protestantism.

The committee recommended their only candidate to the mayor, who made the appointment because the post had to be filled. The mayor instructed Jones to keep a low profile, to proceed diplomatically and to avoid inflaming the racial climate—or antagonizing the business community.

Almost immediately Jones garnered more press coverage than Mayor Boswell had hoped. In his craving for publicity, Jones exploited his public appointment and used it to feed both his career and his social goals, as well as to document the myths about his personal history. Shortly after his February 1961 appointment, an article described the twenty-nine-year-old Jones "as Hoosier as punkin pie," from a "lily-white town where Negroes were not allowed to remain after sundown." No doubt Jones had provided the old canard about redneck towns. Jones also supplied a personal anecdote: "He once walked out of a Bloomington barber shop with his hair half cut because a Negro patron was refused service. Incidentally it was a Negro shop." Two weeks later, Jones was back in print. A local paper reported, no doubt courtesy of Jones, that the human rights director had persuaded three local restaurants to stop discriminating against blacks; the paper printed as fact Jones's claim that he arranged for dozens of his friends to eat at the newly integrated restaurants to offset any loss of bigoted clientele.

Through his position, Jones gained access to new forums for his views—on radio and television and in public appearances. He capitalized on the highly newsworthy topic of race relations—and increased his own visibility tenfold. He even traded in his 1949 Ford for a used black Cadillac limousine (to take old ladies to church, he said). Jones made himself a public personality and integrationist by lifestyle, often using a picture of his "rainbow family" as a prop. He demonstrated an aptitude for the catchy quote. "The Negro wants to be our brother in privilege, not our brother-in-law," he reassured his white audience.

After less than two months on the job, the mayor and some commissioners ordered Jones to slow down on his "journalistic efforts." Jones, they thought, showed a counterproductive appetite for publicity in a delicate area. But with a crusader's bent, he continued to shout his principles, often with rhetoric more militant than his actions.

One night, Ross Case accompanied Jones to a meeting of civil rights groups, including the NAACP and the Urban League. At this time, the South was boiling, and these local leaders wanted to discuss the tenor of their own struggle against discrimination. At the outset, everyone seemed to favor a conciliatory approach, which would bring less danger of backlash. Then Jones took the microphone, for what people felt would be an endorsement of the city's behind-the-scenes tactics. Instead, the new human rights director built up into a long harangue about the evils of racism and the centuries of abuse of blacks. He urged his listeners to be aggressive and militant, to struggle and fight. As if from his own pulpit, Jones marched the audience along to the cadence of his voice. At the climax, he screamed, *"Let my people go!"* The gathering responded with a deafening outburst of applause, as if they had just heard Dr. Martin Luther King, Jr., himself.

Jones's public position was a source of real pride within the Temple; after all, not every church in Indianapolis could boast a pastor who made the headlines. Naturally, Jones's assistants felt a part of something larger than a church—a nationwide fight for social justice. In their common cause the Temple ministers established a camaraderie and shared responsibility for running the church. No one disputed Jones's dominant role; his fundamentalist Christian aides did not threaten his leadership in any way; their humanitarian aims, thinking and personalities either meshed with Jones—or could be molded to his programs. The church revolved around him, yet he kept them happy, with his public and private praise and flattery, with titles and responsibilities, with a sense of mission. As with each member, Jones made his assistants feel important, letting each share in the aura of his success.

As fellow crusaders and friends, they grew close, intertwining their social, religious and personal lives. They asked favors of each other, and called each other "Brother." When Jones was occupied with human rights business, he did not hesitate to call on Wilma Winberg to write school papers for him, or on Ross Case to take class notes at Butler University, where Jim was a senior in the night school division. His aides did not begrudge their time; he had inspired them to make great personal sacrifices to keep the church expanding.

Russell Winberg—though he kept more to himself and though the others considered him less staunchly committed to social goals—nonetheless filled an important function. Aside from Jones, he probably had the most effective Pentecostal preaching manner—and he enjoyed a small following of white fundamentalists from Laurel Street.

Crew-cut Ross Case, though schooled in the intricacies and snares of the Bible, lacked the showmanship to hold the attention of the Holy Roller types. His highly structured sermons, in the tradition of the Disciples of Christ, relied on a fine storytelling ability rather than on the emotionalism and rhythms of the Pentecostalists.

Jones always assigned Archie Ijames, the only black ever in the pulpit, a highly visible if not always significant role. Articulate and expressive, Ijames was a great asset, a sensitive and emotional man whose eyes would water at the thought of something spiritually beautiful. Perhaps more so than the others, he represented a living symbol of the Temple; this well-meaning hard worker would rather improve church property than build his own house; he would treat outsiders with no less caring than his own family. Whenever he was called upon, he would preach in his fast-talking style. He began to realize that Jones was using him as a figurehead black but accepted the role.

Though Jack Beam possessed neither the education of Ross Case nor the style of Russell Winberg—nor the sincere manner of Archie Ijames—Jones gave him a key role and let him preach in his bombastic shouting style. In return, Beam—who could be as jolly as he was fiercely righteous—gave Jones absolute loyalty. Beam, the model of a "joiner," enjoyed the light cast on him by Jim Jones's rising star. The thickly built, hardworking Hoosier would turn over his last dollar to a friend like Jones.

In their fellowship, Jones, Ijames, Beam and Case became as close as brothers. They talked for hours on end about the church, race relations, the Bible and practical Christianity. Sometimes they dined together with their wives, and the Cases once attended an outdoor concert with the Joneses. The true fraternizing occurred among the men alone, often in a car, driving aimlessly, as Jones liked to do, or heading to a service someplace. After they had dispensed with church business, the conversation would drift—or be steered by Jones—to cult leaders, particularly Father Divine or Daddy Grace, a black San Francisco evangelist who opined publicly that Divine had died in 1957 and who himself passed away in 1960. They also talked of sex. With his sometimes coarse humor and natural ability to evoke laughter, Jack Beam played court jester to Jones. Ijames, Beam's boon companion, philosophized but steered away from expletives, and Ross Case, the new arrival, found himself embarrassed when Jones started to speak more openly about sex; he was the sort who would spell out the word "screw" rather than speak it. Though ill at ease, the four were drawn to the subject almost like schoolboys comparing notes. They talked about how they had resisted the temptation of extramarital sex. Another time Jones agreed with an assistant who confessed that he felt dirty following sex with his wife. And Case was flabbergasted when, as the foursome's car passed the house of a sweet, white-haired lady who always embraced her guests, Jones mocked: "You know what she really needs? Someone to throw her down on the bed and screw her."

Peculiar statements by Jones hardly distracted the Temple ministers from their social work. In May of 1961, the city's human rights director spread the message of integration on foot. After the homes of two black families had been painted with swastikas and racial tensions were high, Jones walked door to door in the Butler-Tarkington area, comforting blacks and telling whites not to sell their homes and trigger a white flight. "Instead of running away, integrate." Adopting a conciliatory tone, Jones blamed juveniles outside the neighborhood for the vandalism. The minister's campaign for brotherhood got results: community leaders and about twenty students from Butler University lent support to the blacks and helped repair their homes; the white neighborhood association asked blacks to join.

Jones went around town like a hired gun, taking on any injustice called to his attention. Sometimes he put the Temple's human resources to work for him, such as the time a black man complained that a lunch counter had barred him. Jones set up a plan: on the appointed day, Ross Case and Russell Winberg were seated at the counter when the black man sat down and tried to order a meal. "You mean you want a lunch to go?" the waitress said. "Or do you want to be served out back?"

"No, I want to be served here," the black man insisted.

"We don't serve Negroes."

Having witnessed the crime, Case filled out a police report and indicated his willingness to testify against the owner. The manager knuckled under and started serving blacks.

The minister integrated a downtown movie theater and placed blacks in jobs with previously all-white establishments. Though he used behind-the-scenes persuasion, conservative white businessmen in the downtown area complained to city officials, maintaining they had the right to choose their own clientele.

By summer of 1961, the attacks on Jones had taken a different tone. Perhaps Jones's publicity and his actions had antagonized bigots. Perhaps Jones exaggerated—and even orchestrated—opposition to his efforts in order to make his integration crusade more dramatic and courageous, or to justify his own fears of being attacked. Perhaps it was a combination of these things. He went to the newspapers and told of hate letters and phone threats—over seventy-five crank calls. "They seem to fluctuate in direct proportion to the importance of the race problems we handle," he told the *Indianapolis Times.* "I've only been getting about four letters a day and haven't had a call for a week now. When we had the incidents of vandalism to Negro homes on the North Side, I got a dozen letters a day and the telephone rang around the clock." As in the future, the culprits eluded everyone. Authorities could not trace any letters turned over by Jones, not even the blatantly bogus antiblack letters sent to integrationists over Jones's signature.

Jones invited controversy by writing letters to American Nazi leaders and leaking the responses to the press. One leader whom he had challenged to a debate declined the invitation, saying, "It does not surprise me that an integrationist would attempt to annihilate his opponents with love. The trouble with all your beliefs is that they are unnatural." It would not be the last Nazi hate mail he would publicize; the letters always appeared when Jones was being criticized by more moderate forces. By implication, he tried to portray those who opposed him as Nazi-like—and by so doing, cause them to back off.

At this time, the Jones family commune and the Temple itself took on a siege mentality. Unknown parties painted a swastika on the church door, placed a stick of dynamite in the church coal pile, threw a dead cat at the Jones house, made call after threatening phone call. A woman spit on Marceline as she carried her black adopted child, Jimmy, Jr. The accumulation of these incidents stirred a climate of fear felt even by little Stephan. During one especially tense period, Lynetta Jones accidentally blasted a hole in a closet floor with a shotgun.

There seemed to be no denying some incidents, especially the spitting incident. But others came with such frequency and under such strange circumstances that the Winbergs—and once, Marceline—began to wonder. For instance there was the time Jones found glass in his food at a Sunday afternoon potluck dinner. Jones jumped up from his plate of chicken, crying that someone had planned to kill him. Jones's ruckus put everyone but Winberg into a lather; he had served the food and seen nothing in it. Over the years glass would appear in Jim Jones's food again and again.

The Winbergs also doubted the validity of two bomb scares that had prompted church evacuations. They thought that Jones, prone to exaggeration as he was, overstated the harassment. But the couple themselves began receiving crank calls every night at two or three o'clock. They got so fed up with this sick "breather" who would say nothing that they hired a lawyer who planned to put a trace on the line. When the Winbergs told Jones about their little trap, his face turned crimson and he said quickly, "I wouldn't do that if I were you." The crank calls stopped abruptly.

Marceline also suspected her husband of generating some of the attacks. One evening, as they visited with some of Marceline's friends, a crash startled them all. The others found Jim alone in a room, with a broken window and a rock on the floor. One of his racist enemies had tried to injure him, he said. But his hosts noticed that the window glass had broken outward and accused Jim of shattering the glass himself. Marceline backed up her husband's indignant denials, though it cost her a friendship. But deep down, as she later told her son Stephan, she knew that Jones had staged the attack. He seemed to need to prove to those around him that he was not overreacting, paranoid or crazy—that, indeed, people *were* out to get him.

As she grew more worried about disturbing changes in Jim, Marceline confided in their friends Rev. Edwin and Audrey Wilson. By degrees, her domineering husband was himself becoming dominated by his fears and worries. The Wilsons, she thought, might prove a stabilizing influence. Edwin and Audrey Wilson knew of Jim's absorption in his ministry and his insensitivity to his wife's needs. They knew he was foundering among Christian beliefs, agnosticism and leftist political views, openly admitting his struggles with his own mind and with the world. Then, little by little, he also exposed the Wilsons to the fearful facets chiseled into his personality.

From the start of their friendship in the 1950s, Jones had seemed far too insecure for a promising young preacher whose hands and voice supposedly directed the power of the Holy Spirit. When he came to visit their Cincinnati church, Jim sometimes broke out in hives, evidently from the strain of his healings. Putting aside the demands and postures of leadership, Jones revealed his frailties. In private, Jones presented not the certitude of a visionary, but rather insecurity and an inferiority complex. Although he seemingly had psychic powers such as foretelling license numbers of cars and reading playing cards by touch, Jim doubted himself, just as he doubted the existence of an Almighty. Negativism and undercurrents of paranoia swept him. Rev. Wilson, a survivor of the Battle of the Bulge, recognized the pattern of fear. No single phobia, no single set of circumstances, provoked Jim's overreactions. Incapable of identifying his enemy, Jones was equally incapable of surmounting it. The fears lingered or returned quickly, assaulting him again and again. He submitted to them—and they became a part of him, like a chronic injury. When he could not shake them, he used them to his advantage or tried to get others to share them, so he would not face them alone, so others would not think him cowardly or excessively fearful—or mentally ill.

No one in the position of Jim Jones would want to admit he was losing control of himself. But fears were getting the better of him. Confidants like the Wilsons saw the dark shadows as they passed, some rapidly, others painfully slowly. One night, he would be consumed by fear of being murdered for his racial views. Another he would be paralyzed with worry that he was dying. Other times he would be afraid of flying in airplanes or scared of heights. The Bomb terrified him constantly.

His fears pushed him to overreaction, which someday would become his most dangerous trait. Once when Jim's leg cramped while he was swimming in a lake, he panicked, screaming desperately for help though his wife and friends had a secure grip on him. Perhaps he remembered Ronnie Baldwin in a similar situation.

His worst attacks came for some reason at his own home on Broadway in Indianapolis. On a few occasions, he actually keeled over while emotionally discussing some problem or even while just watching television during stressful times. Thus began a lifetime pattern of collapses, at least some of which were faked.

Marceline became a veteran of the routine. Jones would gasp, throw back his head and seem to black out. Always she jumped into action, fetching a hypodermic needle and injecting Jim's arm with what she called vitamin B_{12}. To others she explained that Jim had anemia from a past case of hepatitis. Slowly, Jones would come out of his deep sleep. While recovering, he would complain of extreme sensitivity to sound; the slightest noise amplified in his head like clashing tin pans.[18]

Jones acted unembarrassed by his collapses, which lasted only minutes. He would simply say that he hoped to get over the problem soon. But the real source and nature of the problem remained obscure; sometimes he blamed his liver, sometimes he blamed it on "cancer."

Faithfully, Marceline provided comfort when he took ill. Internalizing her own emotional suffering, she treated Jim like a fragile child and assumed the role of both mother and nurse. As a nurse, she certainly knew that Jim's troubles were not entirely physical. But out of love and loyalty, she became the first person to help conceal Jones's crumbling psyche from a curious outside world.

In counterpoint to these insecurities, Jones began to build a cult around his own personality. He had seized on the notion of using a tangible personality on which to base the faith of his followers. Wrapped up in that notion was a philosophy that cut a fine line between atheism—the belief in no God—and a religious view Jones expressed in his earliest tracts—that God is simply the force of goodness and love in each person. In claiming to be the ultimate receptacle of good qualities, Jones began to promote himself as a fountain of faith. Subtly he encouraged his rank and file to see him in Christlike and Godlike terms. Though his aides complained privately, Jones rationalized that his people needed the false illusion of his deification in order to dedicate themselves totally to the Temple's worthwhile goals. Only decades later—in Jonestown, when he had an unbreakable hold on hundreds of people—would he drop most pretenses of being God himself.

Jones's assistants—in Indiana and later—never challenged the self-aggrandizing tendencies of their leader. By not publicly opposing them, they gave tacit endorsement. The early members of his inner circle were not far, for instance, from accepting Jones as a prophet with a special pipeline to God, although Jim's actions seemed to show he was not God Almighty. Ross Case, for one, reasoned that if Jones were God, his Bible knowledge would not have been so sloppy.

Case was operating under an illusion of his own—that Jones's controversial utterances were accidental results of deficiencies in his theological education or mere errors of judgment. Jones ran into most trouble with his congregation when he tore into scripture's contradictions, or espoused communism without disguising it. During a late 1961 sermon, Jones preached directly in favor of communism, causing one member to stand in defense of free enterprise. Jones handled the objection with poise, hearing the man out. But Rev. Case—who deplored communism as "forced and atheistic"—felt embarrassment for Jones; Jim should have employed a better choice of words, perhaps communalism rather than communism, he thought. To avoid division, Jones would not use the term "communism" so openly again for years.

Although most Temple members remained unwilling to forfeit their material possessions, the congregation probably did not object to the principles of voluntary Christian communal experience, or even a classless society. For instance Archie Ijames, a strong anticommunist, saw merit in living communally. But even this extremely loyal man nearly abandoned the Temple when Jones first expressed a philosophy of total pragmatism, namely, that the ends justify the means.

Ijames's moment of decision arrived when Jones and Beam defended the right of a Temple woman to lie about a trip she had taken. Ijames was outraged. "I never thought I would be with a group of people who would lie and justify it." Jones managed to restrain Ijames from leaving long enough to cite a passage in which Paul says, "If by any means. . . ." Eventually Ijames retracted his decision, because he felt the good in the Temple outweighed the bad. The Temple represented his best opportunity to live his principles.

Jones was an enigma to his closest aides. He was their inspiration and curse, their strength and weakness. With his help, they would blind themselves to his failings, minimize or rationalize his emotional storms. In fall of 1961, as their leader became more paranoid and worried, they observed a number of his collapses; once he fell down some steps at the church. Jones called these recurring seizures heart attacks. He may have been faking them, using them to hide the fact that he was suffering a mental breakdown. He may have managed to hide this breakdown even from his physician, Dr. E. Paul Thomas, who had been treating him for an ulcer brought on by stress.

Upset and fearful about racial harassment, Jones had been calling the black doctor to complain about attacks against him. Finally, in October, the human rights director was hospitalized for a week; this hospital stay was described to the public as a checkup. In fact, the real and imagined harassment had left Jones distraught and had aggravated his ulcer condition. Dr. Thomas prescribed treatment and rest but noted no evidence of psychotic behavior or withdrawal from reality.

While hospitalized, Jones continued to garner publicity as human rights director. "The Rev. Jones 'Integrates' Hospital While a Patient," read the headline in the weekly black newspaper, the *Indianapolis Re-*

corder, on October 7, 1961. In actuality, Jones had wound up in a black ward by mistake; officials had assumed that any patient of a black doctor would himself be black. Jones refused attempts to move him to a white ward, and proceeded—in a symbolic but rather peculiar gesture—to make the beds and empty the bedpans of his fellow black patients. To his credit, this incident pressured hospital officials to desegregate the wards. The episode, with embellishments, became Temple lore.

Mounting pressures from the human rights post, his vicious cycle of fears, the Temple's organizational demands and his own internal difficulties proved too great a burden for Jones. He needed an escape from his own labyrinth. Yet inside the Temple, where he had begun to exalt himself, he could not admit his frailties. He had to find some other excuse to get away. . . .

During a service one day, Ijames and Case were sitting on the pulpit platform quietly discussing a certain type of tree that had been dropping a tremendous number of seeds around town that autumn. Case speculated that the species was making an extra effort to ensure survival during a long and difficult winter. He wondered aloud: was God preparing the trees for some great natural disaster or tragedy?

Jones overheard snatches of the conversation. On taking the microphone, he dramatically revealed an "ancient prophecy." He proclaimed that something terrible was bound to happen when seeds proliferated as they were now. Case was disgusted; he thought that Jones had filched his story and messed it up in the telling. But almost certainly Jones had calculated the distortion. He kept building on it during the fall, pumping the faith and gullibility of his aides to provide himself a pretext for an escape.

In October 1961, Jones apparently was "hearing" what he had told Ijames were voices from extraterrestrial beings. One day as he strode into the house and started up the stairway, he had wheeled around suddenly, holding his eyes. He had seen a big flash of light, he told his people: a vision of a nuclear explosion in Chicago that burned down within miles of Indianapolis. Indianapolis too would come under attack. To religious people, this vision of apocalypse summoned up terrible images of hell on earth, of the judgment day, of fear. Coming from Jim Jones, one who had healed and revealed so expertly in the past, the warning assumed prophetic proportions.

Shortly after the "vision," the church custodian came up to Case and confided, "Brother Case, did you know that Jim had a vision of Indianapolis in great holocaust?"

Case fell for Jones's vision. Thinking the interracial church must be preserved, he said, "It would seem to me that it would be a course of wisdom to move the church to a position of safety." Case began to promote a move to another area, and got Ijames's endorsement for the plan. Though Jones had started the whole thing, he acted at first as though he did not take the idea very seriously. He quipped once from the pulpit—while shooting a grin at his two assistants—that there were "two boys" who wanted to "run away to a safer place." Adroitly he had shifted blame for his "escape" on to others.

Within days, Jones took a walk with Case. The pastor seemed pensive. "Ross, you know that idea about relocating the church? I think we ought to do that. I think we'll move a hundred at first, and bring the rest later."

On what would become a two-year sojourn, Jones traveled far and wide. He briefly visited Georgetown, British Guiana, on the northeast shoulder of South America. Jones did some healing and attracted some news media attention, but not much. He made page seven of the *Guiana Graphic* by accusing churches—and thieving American missionaries and evangelists—of being largely responsible for the spread of communism. Entering politically volatile South America, he seemed to want to put himself on the record as an anticommunist. To compatriots back home, he reported that a communist in Guiana had told him, "If all Christians were like you, I wouldn't have become a communist." And he stated, enigmatically, without advocating it: "If we go to Guiana, a man can have two wives."

Jones later took off alone in a plane for Hawaii later, ostensibly to scout for a new site for Peoples Temple. But he also could get a much-needed rest, far from most of his responsibilities; he had resigned as human rights director and had turned over his pastorship to Russell Winberg, on a temporary basis. Yet he brought along his emotional problems, and large questions about his future and the future of his church.

In Honolulu, Jones explored a job as a university chaplain. Though he did not like the job requirements, he decided to stay on the island for a while anyway, and sent for his family. First, his wife, his mother and the children, except for Jimmy, joined him. Then the Baldwins followed with the adopted black child. It amounted to a family vacation, since Hawaii was a poor choice as a long-term haven. It was an expensive place to resettle; and with its explosive history—Pearl Harbor—and military installations, it was probably a more likely target for nuclear warfare than Indianapolis. During the couple of months in the islands, Jones seemed to decide that his sabbatical would be a long one. He signed over his power of attorney to his mother, so that she could oversee the family's financial interests and keep a measure of control of church finances in Indiana. He did not want to lose his church, his life's work, yet he was not certain he wanted ever to return to Indiana.

In January 1962, *Esquire* magazine published an article listing the nine safest places in the world to escape thermonuclear blasts and fallout—a timely article in that era of backyard fallout shelters. The article's advice was not lost on Jones. Soon he was heading for the southern hemisphere, which was less vulnerable to fallout because of atmospheric and political factors. The family planned to go to Belo Horizonte, an inland Brazilian city of 600,000.

On a stopover in California, Jones called Ijames and asked him to come to Mexico City to brief him on recent developments in the Indiana church. Jones had intended that Ijames keep close tabs on Winberg, the acting pastor and treasurer. In Mexico City, Ijames reported that Winberg was turning the Temple into a more traditional Pentecostal church—and might have a takeover in mind. He said Winberg brought in outside evangelists, and his wife Wilma reemphasized the Bible in teaching at the church school. Winberg had been thwarted thus far because Ijames had moved in and taken control of the youth group—and now the young people were resisting any deemphasis of social goals. But Ijames cautioned that he could not hold the fort forever. He wanted his pastor to return.

SEVEN

Asylum

He was a little man of about five feet seven, well knit at about 140 pounds. But he prided himself on his fierceness of spirit, developed in part during a difficult childhood in the Roaring Twenties in the wilds of Chicago. In his west side neighborhood, he learned to steal whiskey, shoot craps, play poker. Called "Halfpint" because of the whiskey bottle in his back pocket, he and his buddies idolized gangsters and battled other gangs of kids. After a few months in a juvenile home, Halfpint hopped trains, hoboing around the country. By his twentieth birthday, he had lost all control over his drinking.

Then, after brushes with some good Christians and a vision of Jesus, he converted. One day, the Lord spoke to him as he passed a church; inside he found a young blond woman praying. They married eventually, and Edward Malmin went on to Aimee Semple McPherson's Los Angeles theological seminary, and to an Assemblies of God school in Costa Mesa, California.

In 1958, a Japanese immigrant ship carried Rev. Malmin, his wife Judy, a son Mark, and a teen-age daughter Bonnie to Brazil. On orders from God, the balding and bespectacled minister had journeyed there to bring Christ to the Brazilian interior, about a hundred miles east of Paraguay. There, in widely scattered areas, the hearty missionaries set up several churches and established an orphanage. Then after three and a half years, Rev. Malmin brought his family to Belo Horizonte—a city with a large missionary colony—to raise more money for missionary work.

Belo Horizonte had been built at the turn of the century as the first of Brazil's synthetic cities, part of the industrial triangle formed by Belo, Rio and São Paulo. With steel mills on the outskirts and skyscrapers downtown, Belo blended old and new architecture and swaths of greenery. Despite the language barrier, the city's size, prosperity and bustling charm made the transition easier for many North American visitors.

One day early in 1962, Rev. Malmin stopped by the post office, where a clerk asked him to return a parcel left on a table by an American customer. The American, who was just across the room, spoke only English and the clerk spoke only Portuguese. Malmin carried the parcel over to a robust-looking man in his early thirties. Courteously thanking the missionary, the stranger introduced himself as Jim Jones, an Indiana preacher in Brazil for a rest. Malmin invited Jones to bring his family to dinner. So began an unforgettable relationship.

At first, Malmin could not understand the young minister's deep feelings of persecution. But after various get-togethers with Jones's "rainbow family," the anxieties made a little more sense. Jones said that, back in Indiana, people shot at him and put poison in his food. Marceline told of the times people shouted "nigger lover" at her and spat upon her and her black baby. Rev. Jones explained that such pressures drove him toward a complete emotional and mental breakdown.

The Joneses, after a brief stay in a Belo hotel, had rented a modest three-bedroom home with a veranda in the suburb of San Antonio. While Jim did advance work for the Indiana congregation, he tried to put his thoughts and emotions in order. He was in a tortured state of mind. During the day, he would tend to business in town and each night would take long thoughtful walks. He appeared wracked with indecision. He did not know what direction to take his life, his family, his church. As a thirty-year-old man with responsibilities, he entered a more serious phase of his life, the years when he could make a mark on the world. Yet he was lost, adrift in a new land, an unfamiliar setting, a preacher who could not preach because he did not speak the language.[19]

Distraught, he sought out advice from his mother-in-law, who had flown down for a six-week visit in early 1962. Once he confessed, "Mom, I don't know what to do. Should I give up the struggle for the poor and needy and black people? It seems that I put my family through so much."

When the Joneses first came to the Malmin home for dinner, Malmin's teen-age daughter Bonnie stayed in her room, avoiding the guests until the meal was ready. The pretty young lady who affected sexiness and adopted Brigitte Bardot as a role model knew all too well the condescend-

ing attitudes of white missionaries; some were scandalized that she
wanted to marry her Brazilian boy friend. She presumed the new missionary family would be no different, but this time Bonnie was surprised. She
found the Jones children of all colors delightful, their parents refresh-
ingly free of racial prejudices and judgmental moral attitudes. They did
not even blink at mention of Bonnie's Brazilian boy friend.

In the ensuing days, Bonnie gravitated toward the Joneses, in part
because she was skirmishing with her parents over dress and dating
habits. The somewhat rebellious girl was happy to be exposed to new
thoughts and new people. She took the children on outings to the park
across from the post office. She helped the family get settled in the country, translating for them and providing a practical education about Brazil.
Finally, Bonnie got her parents' permission to move in with the Joneses
for several months—until September, when she would enter Bible school
in Minnesota.

The Joneses lived simply, supported almost exclusively by the Indiana church and nursing homes. Instead of meat, they relied on rice and
beans as staples. They seldom entertained guests. Jim and Marceline
showered love on the children. Marceline would bathe the three boys
together, standing back to admire them, one black, one white, one yellow,
all splashing. The whole family helped toilet-train Jimmy, applauding his
successes.

The parents always impressed upon their children the gap between
the rich and the poor, and taught them to appreciate their relative comfort. Each night, Marceline made a huge pot of rice to dish out to a dozen
or so children who lined up along the curb. She served the poor the same
evening meal as the family. To Bonnie, this was further evidence that the
Joneses were humanitarians, unlike the sanctimonious missionaries who
warned that feeding stray children was like feeding stray cats.

In her admiration and affection for the couple, Bonnie began to
consider the Joneses temporary adoptive parents. Selfless Marceline, who
tied her hair in a ponytail and seldom left the house, replaced Bardot as
Bonnie's idol. Despite the age difference they became companions, win-
dowshopping, buying groceries together, taking in movies, going to the
beauty parlor. At home, they sometimes played around girlishly, dancing
the Charleston to a tinny transistor radio. Bonnie, looking ahead to the
day when she would marry, found Marceline's devotion to Jim absolutely
inspiring—Marceline always excitedly awaited her husband's return
home after his day-long outings downtown, and when it rained, she invariably rushed to the bus stop with an umbrella to meet him.

Bonnie idolized Jim too. His talk of the hypocrisy of organized
religion rang true to her, and she could understand his apparent difficulty
integrating religious beliefs and social activism. As a young rebel, she
appreciated his courageous defense of unfortunates and outcasts.

Troubled though not usually morose, Jones studied and thought, trying to map out his life. Often he read for almost the entire day, studying, analyzing the news which Bonnie translated from Brazilian newspapers. At this time, the Brazilian political picture was taking some leftward turns, though Jones worried about the military and the right wing. Before President Janio Quadros resigned in 1961, he had moved closer to Fidel Castro and to the Soviet Union. His leftist vice-president, João Goulart, had succeeded him after twelve days of instability and a brief military coup.

A few preoccupations emerged in Jones's daily routine. He remained obsessed with the prospect of nuclear war, and with the balance of world power. He read everything available about military hardware. He ranted about the Bomb whenever he saw a pointed shape, such as a church steeple, that resembled a missile. "Man is out to destroy himself," he would say.

Researching Belo as a resettlement site occupied much of his time. Jones studied the local economy, the availability of land and the general receptiveness to racial minorities. Though severely hampered by language barriers, he would journey downtown on many days and introduce himself to government officials.

Jones repeated to neighbors his standard tale about racism in the United States and garnished his life's story with some untruths. He described himself as an ex-Marine who had fought for his country and said he currently worked in a laundromat in a nearby town. And he piqued their curiosity when he sometimes left his home at night with a dark-skinned woman and came back late. Perhaps the woman was the family's Brazilian housekeeper; or perhaps she had responded to an ad Jones had placed in a journal called *Estado de Minas* (State of Mines) asking that people come to his home for spiritual guidance. Jones apparently was interested in testing the religious waters, in finding how receptive the native population would be to his ministry.

Jones frequently aired concerns about the world situation during visits with Rev. Malmin. He sought out Malmin, then forty-six, as an older minister with more experience in Brazil. Jones loved to bring his family to the Malmin place, which he once considered buying for a Temple sanctuary. While the children played inside and the wives talked or cooked, Jones and Malmin usually chatted on the veranda, drinking lemonade under a cool canopy of leaves. There, Jones let a self-censored version of his troubles pour out. He professed to trust Malmin—he even claimed the Holy Spirit had informed him of Malmin's trustworthiness. But after sizing up Malmin's rather conservative views, Jones naturally was selective and guarded, though he did talk quite frankly about his nervous breakdown. The Indiana preacher put his psychological problems in the context of persecution by Indiana bigots and the attempts on his life.

It seemed to Malmin that the integrationist probably had a subconscious need for the very conflict that terrified him. Malmin was also troubled by Jones's tendency to constantly invoke the Holy Spirit, so much so that he finally warned: "Demons can transmit voices [too] on the wavelength of ESP."

When Jones brought up matters that perplexed him, Malmin would supply biblical references as answers. At first, Malmin was reluctant to instruct a minister who had swayed crowds and built a large church. But Jim Jones showed little insight into the Bible and seemed to gratefully accept Malmin's sincere and direct counsel. Probably some of his seemingly naïve questions were designed to test Malmin, to determine safe topics for discussion. He talked only casually about the apostolic communal lifestyle and never of Castro or Marx. He never assailed the churches but acknowledged wistfully sometimes: "I wish I had your faith."

Malmin sought to bring him closer to the Protestant community in Belo and invited him to his own Sunday church services. When Jones attended, he often sat in the last row, seeming uncomfortable and detached, as Malmin preached and occasionally attempted to exorcise evil from some practitioners of the voodoolike cultism abounding in Brazil. The Malmins tried to involve the Joneses in their social life, too, by inviting them to monthly missionary gatherings at their home. But Jim seemed stiff and awkward around his fellow ministers, and they found him odd and unapproachable.

After each contact with Jones, the Malmins began to experience a strange sensation. They felt unclean, as though they had sustained some spiritual contamination. One day in particular, as they left the Joneses and got back to their car, they felt the power of darkness come over them; they held hands and prayed to break the spell, to get back the "clean" feeling.

Marceline, for all her Charleston dancing, lived with the same old problems in Brazil. Even her subconscious told her that she would never get the family life she wanted: in a recurring dream, the face of Jack Beam intruded, parting her and Jim.

The dream was not unrelated to reality. At the time, Jack Beam was preparing to leave Indiana with his family, as the second stage of the migration to a safe place. Beam had first to sell their house and obtain his passport. By telegram Jones directed Beam to falsify his passport application, to say the Disciples of Christ were sponsoring the family's missionary work with impoverished Brazilian children. In fact, Beam, like Jones, had no training at all to be a sanctioned Disciples of Christ missionary.

When Jack, Rheaviana and their two children joined the Joneses in Brazil in October 1962, the poverty devastated them. Saddened, they could hardly believe the numbers of children starving and dying of intestinal diseases in hovels with no sanitation. They helped the Joneses buy clothing for children and set up a food program for two hundred of them. Seeing seven-year-old beggars and children eating garbage day after day, they recognized their own impotence in fighting the poverty. It pained them to be using up church resources for themselves when there was not enough money for the needy. Like Jones, Beam found it nearly impossible to make a living in the country, especially without speaking Portuguese. In June 1963, Jack became tired of "freeloading," as he called it, of being supported by Jones and the Temple. There seemed to be no future for the church in Brazil. The Beams headed home as Jones abandoned the mass migration plan.

By mid-1963, the Joneses had packed up and moved from Belo Horizonte to Rio de Janeiro. The change in scenery and social conditions from the inland industrial town to the magnificent port city was striking. Uncharacteristically, the Jones family wound up living in one of Rio's most prestigious neighborhoods, in a rented seventh-story apartment three blocks from Copacabana Beach. Jones later would say that the family's days sunbathing and swimming among the bronzed bodies at the sandy beach were perhaps the closest thing to freedom from worry in his experience. As a part-time English instructor at a university, he had put the family on a firmer financial base. Problems, if only for a short time, could be forgotten.

Soon the Joneses began working with the poor who lived on tier after tier of shanties in the steep ravines and cliffs behind the city. While living among the rich, the Joneses fed children at an orphanage and in these hillside *favellas*. They asked for more and more money from Indiana, but in Jones's absence the church had fallen into debt and could not meet its own operating costs, let alone finance the pastor's missionary work.

The financial squeeze gave rise to a new legend. Jones, frustrated that he could not wring more money out of Indiana, was soon looking elsewhere. According to his probably apocryphal story, Jones turned gigolo in order to save "his" orphans from starvation: a diplomat's wife, while visiting the orphanage, took a shine to Jones and offered to donate $5,000 to the orphanage if he would give her three days of sexual bliss. Loathsome or not, the deal was the only sure way to provide for the hungry children, so Jones went through with it, having asked for permission, of course, from Marceline. True or not, Jones would repeat this parable to thousands of followers over the next two decades. It probably is the first and most dramatic demonstration of the Jones maxim—the ends justify the means—and also gives a glimpse of Jones's changing sexual mores.

In Rio, Jones became more and more distraught over the major question confronting him from the day he arrived in Brazil: Do I return to the United States or not? His flight to Brazil had been no escape at all. Jones almost certainly was tugged by guilt for having left the civil rights struggle at an important time and by new fears that he would lose all he had worked to build in Indiana. Also, history itself was catching up with his phobias—the Cuban missile crisis in October 1962 must have stimulated new spasms of fear. Finally his religious interests took a bizarre turn that both harkened back to past interest in spiritualism and Father Divine, and signaled his future drift toward deification.

Jones explored some of the Brazilian cults, as Marceline later would tell Bonnie Malmin. Macumba, a voodoolike religion practiced by millions of South Americans, could not have escaped his attention. Certainly he noticed the lighted candles on the beach at night, and the Macumba women, with their heads wrapped, with statues before them, vending candles in front of Rio's churches. Macumba, an amalgam of West African religions, South American Indian spiritualism and Christian names, had the mystique of magic. And although its adherents included all classes and colors of Brazilians, the descendants of African slaves most strongly embraced it, and it was considered a lower-class phenomenon, like Pentecostalism in the United States.

Jones probably found some rather obvious similarities in the dynamics of Macumba and Peoples Temple. Historically, Macumba contained an element of benevolent deception and pragmatism; so their masters would not put a stop to their rituals, slaves had pretended to pray to Christian saints while actually praying to their African gods. Macumba also provided a powerful extended family to protect the true believer, to wash away feelings of abandonment and loneliness, to simplify the complex world. Like Holy Rollers surrendering to the Holy Spirit, Macumba followers became entranced, and sometimes fell, with their limbs trembling. They came forward to give testimonies or to ask for help. And sometimes, like a Pentecostal preacher with a gift ministry, the Macumba leaders issued warnings and prophecies. Like Jones, these leaders gave credit to the spiritual forces when illness or death befell congregation members. And as one of them, Maria-Jose, "The Mother of Gods" of a popular Rio congregation, summed up: "What you feel is more important than what you think. . . . As long as your God is with you, you have nothing to fear. But you must be careful not to offend him. . . ."

In Rio, Jones displayed some renewed willingness to claim powers in the realm of the occult, though he preferred to call it ESP. During one visit, he called the Malmins to the window of his apartment and pointed below to three women waiting on a bench for a bus. "Would you like to see how I can make one of them get up?" he asked. "I'll make the middle one. . . ." The women in the middle stood. "I'll make her sit down." And sit she did. "And she'll get up again." He went through the routine several times as though he were pulling a marionette's strings. The feat left the Malmins flabbergasted. In fact Jones had managed similar stunts with chickens as a boy in Lynn, and he was certainly capable of paying off a woman to stand up and sit down a few times at a bus stop.

That same year, the Malmins decided to end their Brazil ministry and return to the United States. During a day-long flight layover in Rio, they killed time with the Jones family. To hear Jones tell it, their visit and their intended return to the States were great coincidences. He had just received another of his messages from the Holy Spirit—this one telling him that Rev. Malmin should go to Indianapolis to act as caretaker of the Temple until Jones could return. The young minister confessed he was not yet equal to the task himself: coping with racists, nuclear war, failing finances and a mutiny by his stand-in pastor would give him another breakdown, he maintained.

"Let me pray about this," Malmin said. "If this is God's will, I am willing to do it." He promised to go to Indianapolis, look over the situation, consult the Lord and render a decision. As Malmin prayed later, the words of scripture leaped out at him. "And being found in human form, he humbled himself and became obedient unto death, even death on a cross." Malmin interpreted these words from Philippians 2:8 as confirmation; he would have to humble himself to accept an unpalatable project.

A mountain of bills, a chilly group of ministers and a somewhat resentful congregation greeted him in Indianapolis. Jim Jones had neglected to prepare the Peoples Temple for his arrival; not even the assistant pastors had been alerted that Malmin was coming. Jones had sent Malmin, with his rather conservative Assemblies of God background, to be an administrator, not a stand-in leader. He wanted Malmin to put the church on a secure financial footing again; after two years without Jones—in an environment full of dissent and suspicions—the Temple's congregation and revenues had shrunk, and the phone and utilities companies were ready to cut off service unless the bills were paid.

But through no fault of his own, Malmin's arrival added to existing tensions over Winberg's pastorship and over the financial problems created by Jones's absence and his demands for money in Brazil. Because of the way Malmin was installed, Winberg felt unwanted and wounded. Both he and his wife left, taking two or three dozen members with them. And resentment lingered among both the remaining social-service-oriented ministers and the congregation over the intrusion of the outsider with such a conventional religious approach.

In that downward spiral of deterioration, only about seventy-five to a hundred Temple members now remained in a church where services once had drawn upwards of two thousand people. However, Malmin soon discovered one cause for hope. People around town appreciated the ongoing humanitarian works by the Temple. Newspaper stories about the financial plight of the Temple brought crucial donations from other churches and from the Disciples of Christ.

While Malmin restored the church to a semblance of financial solvency, Jones put a constant strain on their relationship, meddling by telephone from Brazil, asking his mother in Indiana to promote his private financial interests while pumping Malmin for church financial information. The parishioners constantly looked to Brazil for guidance. The prying and the dual leadership system irritated Malmin. Less than six months after his arrival, he put Jones on notice; the situation was intolerable, and he was bailing out.

At this juncture, Ijames—who had battled with Winberg and who saw Malmin as little improvement—wrote Jones: "If you're not coming back, I wish you'd let me know because I've had just about all I can take.

Brotherhood isn't going to survive here [without you] and I'm not going to stay without it."

Within a week, the Baldwins received a cable from Brazil: the Jones family was returning.

During his two years' asylum in Brazil, Jim Jones had observed from afar one of the most significant transition periods in U.S. racial history—from nonviolent to militant. Jones—a moderate by the new standards—had not charged toward the Rio airport, eager to take on the challenges of a changing America. Indeed, he had always collapsed whenever someone introduced the subject of returning. As he escaped this admittedly painful, nonproductive period in his life, he still lacked a sense of direction.

When the plane touched down at Indianapolis airport in December 1963, more than fifty of Jones's followers turned out to welcome the family home from their sabbatical. For Jones, the homecoming presented an entirely new set of challenges. Winberg was out of the way. Malmin had squared away most of the fiscal difficulties. But there was a congregation to motivate, building to do—and that seemed awesome to the troubled preacher. Jones confessed his insecurity to Malmin, saying nervously that he did not know whether he could meet the task. Malmin encouraged him to have confidence and promised to stay on so the transition would be smooth.

The older minister also resumed his role as counselor. Jones asked him to point out any personality flaws or traits indicating mental illness or emotional instability. Yet every time Malmin did point out something, Jones would rationalize his own behavior. On home turf again, Jones exhibited peculiarities that had been largely hidden in Brazil. He deceived and manipulated people; he showed some signs of tyranny; he encouraged his congregation's adoration.

The combination of domination and submission, criticism and adulation, was not accidental; Malmin could see that Jones was establishing himself as an oracle. Whenever someone took a position contrary to his, Jones would take the extraordinary step of criticizing the person from the pulpit, of accusing the person of going against God. To support his contention, the minister would say the Holy Spirit told him this or that. And to validate his claim, Jones would perform some bit of psychic phenomena such as revealing a social security number.

Perhaps sensing Malmin's dismay, Jones became increasingly inhibited around the older minister who knew so much about his emotional problems. Jones blatantly sent him out of the church during services on minor errands and business, which probably served a threefold purpose. Jones could do or say whatever he wished—he could heal cancer or encourage adoration. He also made Malmin into a sort of errand boy, reducing him in the eyes of the congregation. And finally, he was telling Malmin, unsubtly, to go for good.

Jones passed the same message one afternoon in early 1964 when the two of them climbed onto the Temple roof to find where some doves had been entering the upper windows and dirtying the church. As they stood alone on the roof, high above the ground, about seven feet apart, Malmin looked at Jones's eyes and had a flash of cognition. He thought: Jim Jones wants to throw me off the roof to my death. Almost instantly, Malmin, a good forty pounds lighter, braced himself for any shove; he prepared to take Jones with him over the edge if need be. As though sensing this, Jones relaxed, seeming to banish the thought. Without a word, the tension between them subsided.

Such things always are subject to misinterpretation—but years later, Jones himself would allude to the incident in terms of his desire to throw an interloping minister from a building.[20] And shortly after the rooftop incident, Jones came to Malmin and said, "I am deeply concerned about you. I had a dream. I saw a man jump out of a car and go down a hill, and it was a self-destructive act. And he was committing suicide, rolling down the hill. The face was not distinguishable, but deep inside, I knew it was you." Having read some Freud, Malmin recognized Jones's death wish for him. The older minister left the Temple as soon as he could, a month or so after Jones's return.

PART TWO

THE CHOSEN PEOPLE

*October is a fun time
When time grows short
When the leaves fall down
And the witches are flying around,
When the night grows dark,
And the moon goes out.*

JUDY HOUSTON, *1973*

E I G H T

The Prophet

By 1964, no conventional minister—no Malmin or Winberg—could have displaced Jim Jones inside Peoples Temple. No one else could have met the expectations of a congregation conditioned by Jones's miraculous hoaxes and social evangelism, especially not after he began coaxing them toward accepting his divinity. Trusting no one, Jones jealously guarded his life's work, taking calculated measures to preserve his position even during his absence.

By naming Russell Winberg acting pastor when he left, Jones had deliberately split the church: Winberg was unacceptable to the social activists, as Malmin would later be. In any case, Winberg's position was more titular than anything else, even if a handful of members preferred him to Jones. Jones left the Temple's moneymaking concerns—the care homes—in charge of his in-laws, and church properties in the hands of his mother. And he commanded Winberg to send every dime of revenue, from collections and elsewhere, to South America. Jones had stacked the hierarchy with loyalists such as Archie Ijames, who wasted no time in embroiling the church in a divisive controversy.

The controversy, like many Temple incidents, bordered on the bizarre. The Ijameses, a black family, had wished to adopt a white daughter. Blacks adopting whites was rare enough, but, in this case, the prospective adoptee was a young married woman with a child of her own. Her name was Becky Beikman; she was married to an illiterate ex-Marine named Chuck Beikman.

When Becky, in threadbare old clothes, had come to the Temple to ask for food, Rosie Ijames saw to her needs; and she and Archie took her into their own home.

The Ijameses took pity on this young woman who was to outward appearances what they considered "poor white trash." The couple treated her with kindness and loved her like a daughter, and she responded. "You're more of a mom and dad to me than my own mom and dad," she told them one day. Then a revolutionary idea seized Ijames: it was racist for the Temple to encourage white members to adopt minority children and not to encourage blacks to adopt white children. After some research, he found only a couple of precedents, including the case of one wealthy black dentist thwarted in attempts to adopt a white child. Ijames decided nonetheless to go ahead.

When the Ijameses filed a petition to adopt Becky, all hell broke loose inside and outside the Temple. Church members and Becky's family opposed it vociferously; outsiders made crank phone calls. Some accused Ijames and Becky of promiscuity and dishonorable motives, calling the black preacher everything from a crackpot to a pervert. Once Becky's relatives tried to have her taken by force from the Ijameses.

Gossip around church took on the heated and pious tone of a crusade. Neither side yielded; both supported their positions with the Bible and reported prophecies and revelations from God. Becky's husband Chuck inflamed the controversy by telling other members that Ijames had been "getting chummy" with Becky. Helpless and frustrated, Winberg decried the adoption as nonsense, but Ijames remained firm. "God has laid this upon my heart and I can't let it go," he proclaimed. The climax came when Temple leadership set up a committee to hear testimony for two days. Virtually all adamantly opposed the adoption; some quoted the commandment: "Thou shalt not covet thy neighbor's wife." Young Harold Cordell, an influential member and an ardent Jones supporter, spoke in favor of the adoption, to no avail. Ross Case finally told Ijames: "This thing about being interracial is experimental in Indianapolis and if it fails here, people will always say 'Peoples Temple tried it and look what happened to them.'

"Let it go," he pleaded.

The rest of the committee sided with Case, and Ijames backed off. Still, the controversy had further kept Winberg off balance until Jones could give him a rude shove out the door in June 1963. That month a sequence of events touched off by Jones seemed to dash all hopes that the four ministers ever would be reunited. First, the exiled pastor dispatched Malmin to take over the church and gave no advance notice. Next, Ross Case, sensing a showdown coming, decided to leave Indiana—and to strike out for the nuclear "safe zone" of Eureka, California, a few hundred miles north of San Francisco. Then Jack Beam came back from Brazil with disheartening news about Jones's missionary labors. Instead of staying around Indiana to help put the church back in order, he was heading for Hayward, California. He said he was joining relatives in that suburb across the bay from San Francisco. But Beam was actually following orders from Jones to scout California for a possible relocation site.

When Jim Jones himself resumed his place in the pulpit a few months later, he discovered he could not recapture times past. At first, he tried to regain his old momentum; the cash flow improved almost immediately, and by New Year's he had summoned up his old Pentecostal rhythms. But soon his paranoia about nuclear holocaust, his self-adulation and his attacks on the Bible escalated to the point of counterproductivity. Without the forum and the legitimacy of his human rights post, he was perceived simply as a controversial preacher chipping away at the written foundation of Christianity and elevating himself on an altar. Inside the church, having laid the groundwork through Bible-criticism and "miracles," he now accepted the mantle of Jesus Christ. Humility gave way to insecurity and fear, which in turn fed his hunger for reinforcement, prestige, power. Rather than working through the emotional problems that had caused him to flee to Brazil, he surrendered to them.

Step by step Jones was leading his people to the conclusion that he was a prophet. They had seen him Christlike feeding the hungry, clothing the naked, inspiring compassionate deeds; they had witnessed his miraculous feats through the Holy Spirit. The people trusted him and stood in awe of him; they compromised themselves by accepting his destruction of the Bible.

The first time Jones referred to himself as more than a man, Archie Ijames tried to protest, though privately. "Brother Jones, you shouldn't let it be happening. They'll say we're just another cult." As so often happened, it was another member, not Jones, who answered the criticism, with these words: "He's the only God you'll ever see."

Jones's defender was a heavyset white woman named Patty Cartmell. Though Ijames did not know it yet, Jones had taken this earthy and fanatical woman into his confidence; he recruited her to gather information for his revelations, by spying and subterfuge. She helped him with his cheap magician's tricks, perhaps out of love, or belief in Jones. When Patty Cartmell said, "He's the only God you'll ever see," she did not necessarily mean that Jones was a heavenly God; she meant that there was no God except the force of goodness and love in each person. And she would believe to the end that Jim Jones was filled with more love than any living being.

As in Lynn, Jim Jones ran into more difficulty outside his safely encapsulated sphere of control. Outside the church, he needed to be circumspect, but was not. Rather than continue the religious message Ijames had been delivering on WIBC radio during his absence, Jones adopted a purely social message combined with detailed criticism of the Bible. In one brochure Jones billed himself as an apostle: "I am causing untold thousands to believe in the Jesus of ancient history by the great miracles of healings, prophecies and discernment I perform in His Name."

Jones seemingly misjudged how far he could go without being labeled a heretic. His radio shows aroused such consternation in the Christian community that radio WIBC took him off the air. Though Jones told confidants that the station had silenced him because of complaints from listeners, he claimed to the *Indianapolis News* on April 17, 1965, that outside harassment—including anonymous phone callers who told his children he was a "devil, an anti-Christ"—had caused him to drop the show.

At this same time, Jones believed that ministers were spreading a rumor that he had been committed to an insane asylum during his two-year absence. He also apparently believed that the Internal Revenue Service was investigating him, though it was not. These concerns, coupled with the religious community furor over his statements and the Temple's somewhat retarded condition, did not bode well for the church's future in Indiana.

By the end of 1964, Jones started to make scouting trips to California to see how his two former assistants, Jack Beam and Ross Case, were faring. Early in 1965, he and Marceline settled on a westward move. Despite certain inherent risks in uprooting the church, the move could prove personally therapeutic and bring tremendous organizational benefits.

The move to California represented far more than a search for a haven from nuclear holocaust and racism. Jones also envisioned a unifying experience; he was already interrogating members to test their loyalty, and squelching dissenters. A change of location would be an acid test. Removing his people from their midwestern roots, having them sell their homes and quit their jobs, would make them more dependent, and thus more receptive to total commitment.[21]

Jones chose a time and a place—California in the 1960s—where change and conflict abounded; yet the locale was in a pastoral place, not entirely unlike his own Indiana farm country. Such a redneck area would hardly welcome with open arms an integrated group of communalists, but this alienation would isolate his people and tie them yet closer to him. The place he chose could feed his conflicting needs for escape and ongoing conflict.

Even the dream he shared with his people was wrought in the darkness of his paranoia, tinged with love and a strange melancholy that would bear no antidote other than an entire world that was free, and happy. But first Jones had to convince his people to leave Indiana when, in fact, only he needed to leave; he had to persuade them that it was in *their* interests to flee with him. One Sunday, in a touching display of emotion, Jim informed the Indianapolis congregation of his plans. With nostalgia and sadness, he sang the song "September." He went around the church and touched each member lovingly. He seemed truly to care. He took pains to reconvey the danger of nuclear holocaust. The world conflagration would come July 15, 1967, he said, and only those in nuclear safe zones would be spared in that terrible blast and fallout. He set up a moment of truth: Were they with him or not?[22]

Jones wanted others to adopt his apocalyptic vision. In his grand castle of paranoia, justifiable concerns about thermonuclear war exploded into a doomsday scenario. He, like some latter-day Moses, would lead the people to the Promised Land to live interracially. Yet there was no way to separate the warped world view from his idealized vision and his social conscience, nor the real threats from his paranoia, his benevolence from his cruelty, his genius from his madness. Jones was a puzzle within a fragile puzzle. For some, the beautiful sides of Jim Jones, his charisma, his childlike frailties, his charity, justified the migration across the continent.

> The safest place in the United States is Eureka, California, a landlocked port of nearly 30,000 people 283 miles north of San Francisco and more than 100 miles north of the nearest target. . . . It is west of the Sierras and upwind from every target in the United States.
>
> *Esquire*
> January 1962

The Cases had auctioned or given away almost everything they owned, paring down their belongings to clothes, a refrigerator, books, a Ping-Pong table and not much more. After writing away for California teaching credentials, they had piled into a rented plane with Archie Ijames's son Norman, a pilot. In charting routes over the 10,000-foot Sierra Nevada, Norman determined that he could not fly directly to Eureka, but needed to pass over the mountain range farther south, and land first in Ukiah. That met Case's approval, because he recalled that the nuclear "safe zone" described in the *Esquire* story had included Ukiah as a southern boundary. Case decided to start applying for teaching positions in each city from Ukiah northward. Fortuitously, the school superintendent in Ukiah offered him a job. The Cases put their money into a tract home in a relatively new neighborhood and dug a backyard fallout shelter. As they went about the business of small-town living, time stretched the distance from Indiana.

Now and then, the Cases made the trip south to the Bay Area to visit their old friends, the Beams, in Hayward. And once Beam phoned Case and invited him down to Hayward for a reunion of the old Temple ministers, including Jones. During that gathering, it became clear that nuclear annihilation remained on Jim's mind.

"Jack, you must go to bed every night with nightmares thinking about nuclear bombs that could fall on this place," Jones said. Hayward was not only outside the safe zone but dangerously near the many military installations around the bay. Case's new hometown, on the other hand, held immediate appeal for Jones. When Case invited him up to

Ukiah for a visit, Jones readily accepted. The area seemed safe from fallout, and there were plenty of job possibilities.

Since the Gold Rush, Mendocino County's timber had bound it to the San Francisco Bay Area one hundred miles to the south. Recently the county's vineyards had become a major producer of California wines, but even in Ukiah, a city of 10,000 surrounded by vineyards and pear orchards, the lumber industry held sway. Masonite, Louisiana Pacific and other companies operated big mills there. Also, as a county seat, Ukiah enjoyed economic benefits and public-sector jobs out of proportion to its size.

Jones used the invitation to Ukiah as much to test his former assistant as to evaluate the city. Jones knew Case's traditionalism might clash with his own self-deification, that Ukiah might prove too small for both of them. While being escorted around town and later in Case's home, Jones picked the brain of his former assistant. In the process, Jones dropped several comments about his own philosophical drift. For instance, Jones once asked, "Would they go for any Hindu or Buddhist teachings in Ukiah?"

A little lost for words, Case said, "I don't think so."

Though Case took him literally, Jones, in mentioning Eastern religions, was alluding to an increasingly eclectic theology that provided stepping stones to self-deification.[23] And during a drive down School Street, Jones declared pointedly, in discussing the unfortunate fate of an Indiana member who had failed to heed one of his warnings: "People must learn to obey their spiritual leaders."

Rankled, Case criticized Jones. "You take too much control over people," he said.

"I've thought about that," Jones responded with patronizing sincerity. "And I've talked about it with my psychiatrist. He said I can't release them too fast from their dependency or they'll have psychological problems." Jones's mention of a psychiatrist, if he indeed was seeing one this early, came as a surprise to Case.

Not having gleaned enough from Case face to face, Jones had others continue the testing.

Harold Cordell, who had stood up for Archie Ijames in the adoption fight, did the first bit of probing. He, his brother Rick and a few other family members were part of the Temple advance team sent to California to make sure housing, food and jobs were ready for the settlers.

On February 18, 1965, Harold Cordell, then a professional accountant, wrote Case six pages of praise for Jim Jones and criticism of the Bible. The disconcerting letter immediately confirmed Case's suspicions about Jones's religious plunge. It questioned the Bible's story of creation, and expressed the opinion that demons cast out by Jesus were probably germs. "Many think God spoke to these 'prophets' and 'disciples' of past history, but that he has never spoken since," Cordell wrote. "I know this to be untrue. I know he has always had a man speaking his will through the ages and does have at least one that I know today, namely Jim Jones. He is a prophet of the first degree whose prophecies always come true to the minute detail. . . ."

In a postscript, Cordell cautioned against misconstruing his praise of Jones, saying, "He is a man as Jesus was."

Though the adoring words revolted Case, he played coy when Jack Beam visited him a few days later; he suspected Beam was there as Jones's agent to monitor his reaction to the letter. When Beam asked Case to read the letter aloud, Case did so as though it did not faze him in the least. But later that month, when a group of four Temple men, including Beam and Archie Ijames, came to the area to make arrangements, Case revealed himself. He called Beam and Ijames into the kitchen, where he again read the letter aloud, critically this time, and asked his two friends whether they agreed with Cordell's sentiments. Beam kept interrupting until Ijames said, "Quiet down. Brother Ross has a problem with this letter."

"That's funny," Beam said. "I told Jim that he didn't have any problems with that letter at all."

After hearing the letter, Ijames maintained that the time for dissent in the Temple had ended, that the will of Jones was paramount.

Case then posed the gut question: "Are you still a Christian?"

"I am not," Ijames said. "I'm a universalist."

Traumatized and disappointed, Case told his old friend, a man he had called his brother, that he could never subordinate his mind to the commands of a minister who pretended to be a prophet. He quit Peoples Temple at that moment: it was February 24, 1965.

The rift had widened too far. Case was through with Jim Jones, or so he thought. Had Case been left behind in Indiana like Winberg, he would have been nothing more than another orthodox Christian sifted out of the changing Temple. But Case had the misfortune to be living in the path of Jim Jones.

NINE

Rural Eden

In July 1965, as schools let out for summer vacation, the Indiana congregation prepared to push west. Dozens had turned deaf ears on Winberg and other skeptics who thought they were mad to abandon their Indiana homes for what promised to be a nomadic life governed by a capricious preacher. They said good-bye to friends, loved ones and neighbors; they packed their cars, pickup trucks and moving vans, then headed west in a big caravan led by a car carrying Jones, his mother and his housekeeper Esther Mueller, along with a sick dog and her puppies. Marceline Jones had traveled to California earlier with Stephan and Jimmy, Jr.

The contingent bumped along with everything they owned piled high, looking like refugees from the Dust Bowl days, imagining what lay ahead in the Promised Land. One can only imagine the awesome responsibility Jones felt as he looked over those dozens of exhausted and expectant travelers strung out behind him. They had altered their life course to follow him across the continent, toward uncertainty. They placed their faith in a troubled man who had told them they might need to change the name of their church, in case Indiana racists tracked them to California. Jim Jones no longer was running alone.

Jones had asked a great deal of his people. Some were unwilling to uproot their families; many considered church a weekend ritual, a weekly investment in the hereafter. Others, like Christine Cobb, the mother of the little black child with the ear problem, held back because her husband, a nonmember, declined to forfeit twenty-two years of seniority and good pay to follow a "Prophet of God." The migration split families too, with some members joining the exodus, others taking their chances with the mushroom cloud.

That summer, about 140 Hoosiers poured into Ukiah. The Beams arrived too, from Hayward. Soon word spread around town that an Indiana preacher had transplanted his entire church into this small town. For those who did not hear about the Temple through the grapevine, the *Ukiah Daily Journal* carried an admiring story headlined "Ukiah Welcomes New Citizens to Community." It was a very good public relations kickoff, and took on added significance because the editor's wife, Kathy Hunter, had written it.

Despite the hospitable welcome, Jones apparently had some misgivings about the extent of the racial tolerance—he told Hunter that his adopted son was of "Negro, Caucasian and Indian heritage." Few blacks lived in Ukiah, and some white people preferred to keep it that way. A few black church members, among them Archie Ijames, experienced discrimination when they tried to buy or rent homes. Still, the church members settled their families in the area and found or made jobs.

As with his followers, the immediate task for Jones was finding a job. His family could not survive simply on offerings, because members were struggling with financial problems of their own and Jones had no drawing power in his new home. As Jones had hoped, Marceline lined up a social worker's position at Mendocino State Hospital, which would become one of the Temple's best sources of jobs. And Jones, with his education degree from Butler University and a California teaching credential, landed various jobs as a schoolteacher.. He substituted at first, generally in hamlets outside Ukiah proper, such as Redwood Valley, where his family lived, and Potter Valley. Then he taught sixth graders at rural Boonville, a forty-five-minute commute. By the fall of 1966, the polite, well groomed teacher, who had initially received good ratings from his superiors, had become a controversial adult-school teacher in Ukiah. He taught only one course each semester, and was paid five dollars an hour for six hours a week of teaching. Yet his classes in American history and government drew over fifty students each, making them among the most popular classes. Unbeknownst to officials at the time, Jones's popularity was guaranteed, since Jones encouraged his church members—Ijames and Beam among them—to attend to get their high school diplomas.

In addition to his own salary and educational benefits to his members, the teaching job provided Jones with some standing in the community and provided a forum for his views—and to some extent, for indoctrination and recruiting. Discarding the textbooks, he instead moderated discussions, liberally sprinkled with humor and his own attacks on the U.S. government and overpopulation. Speaking of unwanted babies, he went so far as to say the Catholic church opposed abortion because it wanted to rule the world, and he advocated masturbation as a substitute for sex, describing his own technique. Some students thought that Jones promoted socialism in an oblique way. A number of students complained to the administration.

When Jones suspected the school administration had begun spying on him, he posted Temple members at the doors and locked the windows even on warm nights. Having protected himself against eavesdroppers, he went on quasi-Marxist diatribes, lectured on religion and even demonstrated bits of his "extrasensory perception." Using reverse psychology, he said he would not allow any students to join the Temple, since he did not want to be accused of recruiting in the classroom. Yet almost a dozen students were converted.

With Christine Lucientes, his first move was a harmless compliment about her gaudy flower-print dress. Jones's attention cheered her up. Then he made several revelations about her and her family, tidbits that she thought were family secrets. A short time later, a church member carried a message from Jones to the young woman: stop hitchhiking. Shortly thereafter, she saw the wisdom of the warning. Juvenile authorities started taking unchaperoned young girls into custody for hitchhiking.

After that, Chris Lucientes was prepared for an invitation to the Temple services. Shyly, she took a seat in the rear of a rented church and, somewhat confused, watched and listened as Jones called out people and made revelations. One by one, the people came to be blessed by Jones, touched by his gentle hands. As one Temple chronicler wrote, "She had the impression that he was only a servant standing there. One would be hard put, she thought, to read collusion, or any kind of chicanery into these holy proceedings, for looking into their eyes, even the most hardened sophisticate must confess that these men and women—and above all

Jim—are honest and earnest and for real." Thus Chris Lucientes was enlisted for life.[24]

Another Jones student, named Wanda Kice, decided to attend a Temple service at Church of the Golden Rule, a communal-style organization engaged in fellowship with the Temple. She was surprised to find many adult school classmates there listening to Jones preach. She too would join, and would bring in her husband and children.

The Golden Rule church in Willits presented a rare opportunity for Jones. The organization had declined from a peak of seven hundred members throughout the Far West to a mere two hundred in California alone. Still, the church was wealthy, endowed with over 16,000 acres, including Ridgewood Ranch lands, once home to the great racehorse Seabiscuit. Somewhat isolated in their utopian community, they ran a farm and a dairy, attended church services every morning, and did unto others as they would have others do unto them.

So, when Jones professed interest in starting an apostolic community of his own, they received him warmly. They allowed the Temple to use their schoolhouse for meetings until Jones could find a church of his own. During the summer of 1966, the Temple moved a piano to the Golden Rule school and started to hold services there.

Like the early visits to Father Divine, the relationship between the organizations was harmonious at first, with swimming for the children and communal dinners. But it soon became apparent that Jones had designs on the Golden Rule. Some Golden Rule members were drawn to the vibrant young faith healer who spoke of injustice in America and black oppression. Then the Temple tried to recruit more. That violation of the "Rule" made elders suspicious of Jones's motives when he made a gradual merger move. The church board voted down the merger proposal, partly because the Temple revolved around the worship of Jones's personality.[25]

Homeless again, the Temple packed away its piano. During the fair-weather seasons, Jones conducted services in the Swinney family's yard, claiming to use his powers to make occasional rains stop. But when winter ushered in the heavy rains, he gathered his people in his own garage—as he had in his boyhood loft—and preached to them from a chair while they sat shoulder-to-shoulder on the concrete, like children at his feet.

The Temple had become an extended family for those who had traveled west. At last, Jones had penetrated the barrier of blood relationships—and brought a sizable number through it. As father to them all, a living standard of love, Jones made the rounds to their homes in the hills and hollows, chatting, enjoying their company, listening, showing concern for their well-being and understanding for their problems. As a friend and counselor, he listened as no man could listen, with dark eyes mirroring understanding, empathy and love. Without sounding preachy, he talked about the need to help and love one another. He would break up a fight between two children, then sit down on the ground with them for a couple of hours to convey the message. No problem or concern was too small to bring to his attention; he took on a remarkable burden of caring, while demanding little in return. Only with apology in his voice would he ask members to do things for their church. "Darling, I hate to ask you this. . . ." People did not mind helping someone work on his car, or harvest grapes or dig a septic tank. They were loving one another and loving Jim Jones.

While recruiting proceeded slowly, cautiously, by invitation only in Ukiah and the surrounding areas, the Temple settlers coaxed some of their former Indiana cohorts into joining them in the West Coast paradise of open spaces, vineyards and orchards. After a barrage of phone calls and letters, and two years of haggling with her husband, Christine Cobb gave him an ultimatum in 1967. "I'm going," she said. "If you want to go, you can."

James Cobb, Sr., acceded to his wife's urgings, though it meant that the experienced steelworker would end up changing truck tires and doing maintenance work at menial wages. His oldest son, James Cobb, Jr., stayed behind temporarily in Indianapolis so he could finish the season with his high school baseball team. A decade earlier, he had been the little boy with the ear problem. Now he was seventeen, eyeing college athletic scholarships and a possible pro baseball career.

After his team was edged in state playoffs, young Cobb turned his thoughts westward. Using money from his precious coin collections, he paid for his own food on the cross-country bus trip. He reached San Francisco dreaming, as he had since the age of twelve, of walking into the San Francisco Giants training camp as an unknown eighteen-year-old and taking his place alongside the likes of Willie Mays. But having passed over the Golden Gate Bridge and threaded north through Marin County and out into miles of open farmland, he soon realized that Ukiah was indeed the "boondocks," as his high school coaches had warned him.

Worse blows were yet to come. Even a cursory look around town told him that Ukiah was as white as the whitest sections of his hometown —and inside the Temple there was not a single young black man with his interests. Still, everyone tried to make him feel welcome. Temple teenagers took him and his sister on a tour of the town. Though the escorts talked more about the war in Vietnam than baseball, he could not help but like them. Within a few days of his arrival, his newfound friends threw a church welcoming party in his honor. Though basically shy, Jim Cobb, at Jones's insistence, taught the dozen or so Temple teen-agers big-city dances.

"Maybe this place is all right after all," Cobb told himself. His heart, not his skin color, mattered in this large family where everyone seemed committed to racial equality. In the context of Jones's church, perhaps he could nurture the spirit of compassion and giving; he always knew it was inside himself, but did not know how to tap it.

"Self-sacrifice" held more appeal in the abstract than in practice. As defined by Jones, it pried Cobb away from his first love, athletics. In sermons on the evils of competition, Jones railed about brutality in sport. "If you got hurt, then you would be dumped. The coach doesn't really care about you." Jones used competitive sports as a metaphor for the capitalist system and inhumanity. So that none of his listeners would suspect that his antisport message was in part personal bitterness dating to childhood experience, Jones bragged of his own athletic prowess, claiming falsely that Butler University had awarded him an athletic scholarship.

Much of what Jones said made sense to Jim Cobb, but the lure was too strong. He played football while Jones preached his antisport message. Jones reluctantly let him play basketball too, and young Cobb won printed accolades. Then it was spring, time for *his* favorite sport. But, knowing that Jones frowned on baseball and worrying that someone would catch him, Jim Cobb could not concentrate properly in spring training. Finally, Jones brought young Cobb before the congregation: "Well, you played football, and that's a savage game. . . . Then you played basketball. Okay, there's nothing wrong with that. But *baseball!* Now, what are you going to do with your life?" Though it hurt him to do it, Jim Cobb, burdened by guilt, quit the team.

Jones chose an ideal area for building a closed community. Most Temple members lived isolated outside the city in a number of unincorporated bedroom communities tucked in valleys formed by the Russian River. Potter Valley and Redwood Valley shared both a timeless ambience of Americana and a conservative guarded attitude, especially toward the long-haired city people.

Redwood Valley, home to many Temple members and to Jones himself, lay nestled in modest pine- and oak-studded hills. With small vineyards, orchards and pastures, and only one lumber concern, Redwood Valley got light traffic even along its main road with its 1950s vintage food market, one tavern, car garage, barbershop. There was little population pressure—yet the old-timers who held bull sessions every afternoon in the volunteer fire department still longed for the days when everyone knew everyone on a first-name basis.

The arrival of Jones and his interracial flock in Redwood Valley aroused more curiosity than alarm at first. The Jones family took up residence less than a mile from the center of town in a roomy house with a cinder-block foundation and a view of surrounding hills. Rows of grape vines stretched from the house to the main road, a hundred yards or so away. A tributary of the Russian River cut across the back of the property.

In that idyllic setting, life inside the Jones household at first approximated the harmonious image promoted in the Temple services and in the community. The Joneses raised their children in a secure, homey atmosphere. They had love, affection, stability—and father and mother figures who embraced one another in front of their children. Marceline enjoyed relieving Esther in the kitchen and making fried chicken. Jim roughhoused with his children on the lawn. When the weather warmed up, the family took outings together, for a swim and a picnic lunch. At clear Cold Creek, they shot white water rapids on inner tubes; Jim liked to sit on his easy chair on a little island while the family dogs fussed over him.

Stephan Jones preferred Lake Mendocino because they sometimes ran into other Temple members there. Sometimes they played football; even the Jones children themselves had enough bodies to organize a game, though their father never played.

Things began to spoil their fun, however. One day, a few teen-agers were stoning waterfowl. The Jones family gave chase, and the minister collared one boy, shaking him furiously and lecturing him. Stephan was proud.

Another time, rednecks at the lake shouted "nigger" and "nigger lover" at church members. It was a discouraging awakening for people who had wanted to escape Indiana bigotry. So Jones and his followers decided they could tear out some of the vineyards in front of the pastor's house and construct their own pool. For these midwesterners, a private pool for the children exceeded all their dreams. But Jones had taught his people the lesson that his mother instilled in him: they could do anything if only they channeled their spirit. With a borrowed tractor and hand tools, they attacked the sandy earth with the same decisiveness and dedication that would mark the Temple for years.

Once the pool, with heater and diving board, was finished, it seemed silly for the Temple to go begging for space for services in the Grange Hall and elsewhere. The Temple commissioned an architect to build a church directly over the pool. They hired a construction company for the major work, and Archie Ijames, himself a carpenter, directed a crew of Temple volunteers to complete the job. Religious people did not always make the best laborers and carpenters, however; they came late, left early, kept one eye on the clock and half their mind on the dinner table. Even the hard workers had to be waltzed through their tasks, step by step. And even then, the church wasted a fair amount of time rectifying blunders—windows put in upside down, wall panels hung incorrectly.

When it was completed, Ijames's headache subsided. Those who had contributed their labor and money took great pride in the modern redwood building with its peaked roof. Their monument to collective action—a church with a swimming pool inside—became a curiosity around town. Yet it suited the Temple's needs perfectly; they even installed an institutional kitchen where they could heat and serve their potluck dinners. And as an ornamental touch, plastic stained-glass-style windows

with an inspirational Temple logo—a sunburst and the dove of peace—
were added above the pulpit in the front and the pool in the rear. Jones
had planned ahead with this imposing physical plant; it was large enough
to accommodate every man, woman and child in the valley. Someday he
would fill it.

The nearby two-story shake-roofed parsonage became an extension of the church. The house drummed with activity day and night. As
the family dined in a spacious yellow kitchen, Jones often read the paper
and took phone calls. But he still kept track of everyone, managing to
convince the children that he used the powers of ESP to detect the food
hidden beneath their plates, to discern when they were lying to him.

After dinner, the family usually retired to the living room. Across
from the cinder-block fireplace, Jones liked to stretch out in his leathery
recliner chair to read and watch television. His family joined him in watching the news and his favorite show, "Hogan's Heroes," a situation comedy
about American soldiers in a Nazi prison camp.

The Joneses retired to separate bedrooms at the rear of the main
floor, with a bathroom separating them. On the right was Jones's room,
furnished as sparely as a college dormitory. On his bookshelves, he kept
the Bible and books about religions; books on Hitler, Lenin, Marx and
revolution; books on nuclear war and organized crime; books about psychology and mind control. In a closet to the right of his bed, he stowed
a shotgun. In a vanity, he stored his medicines.

With windows overlooking the vineyards, Marceline's room felt
more spacious and sunny. The children and older women—Esther and
Lynetta—lived upstairs in more crowded quarters. The children wanted
for little; they had a record player, athletic equipment and bicycles. Like
other church children, they dressed neatly with short hair; Jim Jones
wanted his people to look and act like doers, not hippies.

Although the "rainbow family" symbolized the Temple's brotherhood, a sibling rivalry developed, as Mrs. Baldwin had once predicted.
Stephan, the only natural child, felt that his brothers and sisters resented
him, and perhaps he resented some of them. He believed church members
considered him a brat while they adored his brother Jimmy. Friction
erupted sometimes into teasing and fighting. Jimmy taunted Stephan as
"white trash," and Stephan called Jimmy a "nigger." When Jimmy tattled
on Stephan for using that taboo word, Stephan would be reprimanded or
spanked. Their parents tried to put a stop to it, but emotions were not as
easily legislated in a family as in a church.

Home life was often idyllic for the children. Diversions abounded
in that Huck Finn-like setting. A church member built a treehouse for
them near the creek. The kids all swung on a rope from a thick tree limb.
And among the grape vines, they played cowboys and Indians, war games
and hide and seek.

Reverence for life, all life, was taught in the Jones household,
primarily by Lynetta. As with Jim, something about her attracted ani-

mals. Dogs and cats would frisk about her when she walked to the berry patch or nap at her feet while she sat dragging on a hand-rolled cigarette by the camellias at the back porch—the only place Jones permitted her to smoke in his house. Although she was an activist of sorts who worked with a local senior citizens group and the Red Cross, Lynetta was a little bit of an embarrassment to Jones; he had to explain her drinking, by saying she drank beer on doctor's orders. To explain her absence in church, he said that she had donated heavily.

Many of Lynetta's attitudes rubbed off on Stephan. Though many boys grew up with BB guns, he did not hunt. When the creek lost its water in late summer, he scrambled down the bank with a bucket and tried to save the fish. His major chores involved the care of dogs, cats and farm animals. His favorite pet was a mongrel named Husky, but there was also a monkey named Leo, plus two family nags—Tubby and his cantankerous offspring Sonny. Sonny's blackguard reputation was enhanced considerably when he tossed Jones off on his head. The pastor's survival was declared a "miracle" at church; later he would claim someone drugged the horse in an assassination plot.

The Jones children enjoyed special status in the church. In turn, they were expected to set a model of brotherhood, as sons and daughters of a man revered as prophet or God. Stephan resented sharing his father with Temple children who hung all over him and called him "Father." Jim Jones was *his* father, as Stephan sometimes reminded his playmates in no uncertain terms.

From his youngest days, Stephan could remember the crackling energy of Temple services, even ones in Indiana where people climbed through the windows and craned over each other to see the miracle worker who simply was his dad. In Ukiah, he tired of the repetitive marathon sessions. He, his friends and brothers would sneak away from services whenever possible; they would go play somewhere else or climb on the church roof and drop pebbles on the unsuspecting. But the hours of church tedium were more often than not part of the family routine. The children, like others in the church, were given duties. Stephan was named a microphone boy, one of those who hustled a microphone to worshipers so they might make a testimonial to Jones or ask a question. His arms ached and his dedicated expression faded into a grimace whenever he held the mike for the long-winded. And that irreverence infuriated his father.

Escaping was no easy matter. Even if the children had homework to do, they were kept inside the church. Tables were set up around the wrought-iron pool railing, and the children were forced to study with the tempting odor of chlorine under their noses. And there were other distractions too. One night as Jones claimed to communicate with the departed, an eerie howl came out of a vent that ran across the church center beam. Some of the children may have been frightened, but Stephan knew the identity of the "lost spirit"—Patty Cartmell's daughter Tricia—and how she climbed up there. As Jones's son, he would be privy to many secrets.

TEN

A Dream of Love

It was not merely that he was handsome in a clean-cut way, nor that he had the manner and appearance of someone who would succeed, nor that his apartment showed good taste and breeding, nor even that he seemed to project goodness. There was a measure of fate involved in their meeting. She and a friend had been hiking along the Lower Great Highway, parallel to the dunes of San Francisco's Ocean Beach, singing to themselves, "Hey ho, nobody home, eat nor drink nor money have I none, Yet I will be me-er-er-ry. . . ." Suddenly she stopped in front of a garden; she could not help exclaiming how beautiful it was and calling out a compliment to the apparent owner, a good-looking young man standing on the porch. Though a girl friend stood beside him, he was struck by the beauty of the dark-haired young woman in a lavender blouse. At first sight, there was some indefinable chemistry drawing Tim and Grace together; months later chance again would give them the opportunity to meet.

Grace Lucy Grech, a slender, dark-eyed young woman whose brown complexion blended the best of her Mexican and Maltese heritage, was the youngest of four in a family of survivors. She had grown up conscious of the arduous economic journey her parents had traveled, both before and after her birth. Her mother—a native of Guadalajara—came to the United States, married a butcher and ended up working as a seamstress in San Francisco's Apparel City garment industry.

The family had lived on a hill above Farmer's Market, where Grace picked up a few cuss words and a mild South of Market Street twang. Then her family stepped up to a better neighborhood, the Sunset-Parkside District out toward the ocean. In that white working-class neighborhood and around Catholic churches, Grace was made to feel inferior over her dark skin and she soon identified with unpopular kids. In her junior year in high school she suffered rejection by her longtime boy friend and was emotionally devastated. Yet with characteristic energy and a positive attitude, Grace Grech immersed herself in school activities at Lincoln High. She was elected vice-president of her eleventh grade class. And in her senior year, she made basketball cheerleader. Though her grades— Bs and Cs—would have qualified her for college admission someplace, she was not really encouraged. When she told her parents about college hopes, they suggested that she go to night school. So she put in eight-hour days downtown as a secretary and attended San Francisco City College at night.

In the fall of 1969, an energetic co-worker coaxed her to march one Saturday against overpopulation and pollution. Grace hardly qualified as an activist, but these were not the most controversial issues of the day. The protest terminated at Civic Center, opposite the City Hall dome. Amid a scatter of countercultural booths, a rally got under way. While her friend Susan went off for literature, Grace tried to listen to the speakers, but a thirtyish man with horn-rimmed glasses interrupted her. "Hi," he said. She took one look at him and thought to herself: Why do strange men think they're doing me a favor trying to pick me up? Grace largely ignored the fellow; neither realized they had seen each other before, near the ocean.

When Susan returned, she and the talkative stranger hit it off. His name was Tim Stoen; he said he was in private law practice nearby; he had taken a break from work to attend the nearby rally. He mentioned he was planning to run for Congress as, of all things, a liberal Republican.

When Susan left, Stoen hung around, trying to break through Grace's coolness. Finally he invited her for a Coke. Having nothing better to do, she went along to a cafeteria near Hastings Law School, then to Stoen's law offices. His framed diplomas—from Wheaton College in Illinois, from Stanford Law School—put her at ease.

As he told her about himself, Stoen mentioned that he lived in Berkeley. She said she had never seen the Harvard of the West—though she had lived in the Bay Area all of her life—and on the spot he invited her to visit. When they got to his car, she could see why he had kept alluding to it in their conversations. Soon they were whizzing across the Bay Bridge in the stylish new burgundy Porsche Targa.

In Berkeley, the young lawyer showed her around Telegraph Avenue with its boutiques and street gypsies. As they passed one store, he said, "This is where I bought my crystal." At another, he said, "I buy my clothes here." Several people called Tim's name as they walked.

The little tour impressed her less than the furnishings in his South of Campus apartment. She feasted on his art books—exquisitely photographed and printed volumes of fine paintings and objects like nothing she had ever seen. She craved "culture."

Before too long, other people trickled in, and when a handful had arrived, Grace asked, a touch embarrassed: "You having a party?"

"No. I just tell my friends they're always welcome."

These people from First Presbyterian Church, where Stoen belonged to a social action group, tried to draw Grace into their boring shop talk about religion and religious projects, but the nineteen-year-old kept her nose buried in the art books. Later, when the others left, Stoen turned down the lights and put on gentle music. Grace stiffened: how prudent had it been to go home with a worldly thirty-two-year-old bachelor? But rather than having to fend off his hands, she was entertained. He read poetry to her, treated her with respect and kindness, and took no liberties. Instead of dropping her off at a seedy bus station, he drove her home.

Grace, like a lot of urban teen-agers, was a little toughened around the edges, but she had a soft heart and was not beyond naïveté. Although she could see through Stoen's obvious efforts to impress her, she was flattered by his attention. She felt herself falling for this lawyer a dozen years her senior. After a couple of dates, she knew he was special. He was the first person to value her highly, to take enough interest in her to read to her, to teach her. In their Pygmalion romance, Stoen tried to shape Grace as he had shaped himself. For all his breeding, Timothy Oliver Stoen lacked the street smarts of Grace. The child of religious, middle-class parents from Littleton, Colorado, he had been reared with money, attention and recognition. He was blessed with a good mind, and he used it with Protestant perseverance. He had gone through high school and college as a scholar, athlete and devout Christian. He even joined Campus Crusade for Christ. During a year in England on a Rotary Foundation scholarship, he went behind the Berlin wall with a missionary spirit. "The first thing that I noticed was the blank expression on the faces of everyone," Stoen told the Rotary Club upon his return to Littleton. "You could tell they were just waiting for the day when they might have some freedom...."

Stoen did not switch modes of idealism—from small-town conservative to urban liberal—until after he graduated from Stanford Law School and gained admittance to the California Bar in 1964. For almost a year he worked in an Oakland real estate office, then he joined the Mendocino County prosecutor's office in Ukiah. In 1967 he left with the intention of doing legal aid work for flower children in San Francisco's Haight-Ashbury. Instead Stoen's charitable instincts took him across the bay to Alameda County, where he adapted his ultrareligious world view to the leftist political climate. He wore a beard and rationalized the purchase of his Porsche as a useful status symbol in the ghetto. He was as ambitious as ever. While representing some black militants—apparently none of note—the young Republican lawyer seriously considered running for the U.S. Congress on an ecology platform. The Democrats, he reasoned, should not get all the liberals by default.

Stoen had first encountered Peoples Temple in Mendocino County in 1967 when, on someone's advice, he had called on the Temple to help renovate the local legal aid offices. Two dozen cheerful and industrious Temple members showed up the following Sunday morning. And Stoen soon was sending people to the Temple for drug and marriage counseling.

The church's good deeds and Jones's character overwhelmed the young attorney, and caused him to revise his definition of religion. For Stoen the clincher was seeing Jones with his sleeves rolled up, scrubbing a toilet in a Temple building. Over the next two years, even while he lived in Berkeley, Stoen drew closer to the Temple. He and Jones became personal friends, and Stoen would drive to Redwood Valley for services, sometimes bringing along friends and girl friends.

At that stage of his life, activist Christianity presented the perfect resolution of Stoen's fundamentalist background and his political and social liberalization. Jones was selling precisely that. With each visit, Stoen became more taken with Jones's broad knowledge of current events, the activism of the ministry, the climate of love and perhaps the church's political potential. He also witnessed a faith healing by Jones, who was then the foreman of the county grand jury. Stoen rationalized the healings, attributing them to the power of love. In any case, the hocus-pocus was eclipsed by the political line, against racial hatred, poverty and the Vietnam war. At the end of 1969—the year Berkeley became a war zone over Peoples Park and Third World student rights—Tim Stoen began to integrate his personal life and his church life.

Smitten as she was, Grace Grech was taken aback when Tim Stoen asked her to meet his friend the "healer." Both her inner-city savvy and her Catholic upbringing were offended by such claims. Nevertheless she climbed into the Porsche for that first two-hour drive to Redwood Valley.

She wanted the time with Tim, not the religion. Yet she could not help but feel warmth among the varied interracial congregation that sang hymns about brotherhood and embraced one another. She wondered about the man who pulled together this spectrum of humanity. "Is Jim Jones good-looking?"

"Not really," Tim said. "He's okay."

Hearing that, she mistakenly assumed that the man in the pulpit spewing fire with a socialistic fervor was Jones. Then Jack Beam gave way and a very handsome man with hair as black and shiny as coal tar bounded onto the blue-carpeted platform. Applause reverberated from the white linoleum floors to the skylights, as though a rock star had taken the stage. Quieting them with his gentle hand motions, Jim Jones invited his people to greet their neighbors. Everyone hugged. Grace saw at once that Jones emphasized the real world, not the Bible and moldy, pious phrases. Instead of preaching, he unfolded a Sunday newspaper and led a discussion of current events.

Despite those initial positive impressions, Grace Grech could not swallow the hokum that followed. Jones called out names, telling people about their lives. He made prophecies. Then, in ritualistic fashion, he called up a woman said to have cancer and sent her to the bathroom. When she reemerged, Jones claimed that a malignant tumor had been passed from her bowels—and that she now was cured. Grace was as shocked by Tim's acceptance of the "miracle" as by the display itself.

She also found Jones's money pitch repugnant, all too similar to the squeeze Catholic priests put on their parishioners. And when the services ended, and the adults were conducting a business meeting, she was appalled to see that children were left to fall asleep on the cold floors.

Unbeknownst to Grace, the Temple had been putting the rush on Tim for some time.

In the final push, Jones sent college students Jim Cobb and Mike Cartmell—then two leaders of the church youth group—to visit Stoen at his Berkeley apartment. Cobb and Cartmell were amazed to discover that Stoen was more than willing to cast off his bachelor pad, fancy car and potentially lucrative private practice for a struggling church in the sticks. He wrote Jones a letter on January 9, 1970, as he prepared to join the Temple:

> Dear Jim,
>   Mike Cartmell suggested I write and formally ask certain questions in my mind as I plan to move to Ukiah.
>   First what factors should one employ in purchasing a car—new vs. old, big vs. small, American vs. foreign?
>   Second, what factors in buying clothes?
>   Third, what type of furniture? Should it be sturdy but as unpretentious as possible ... ? Or is it okay to have nice furniture if shared ... ?
>   Fourth, what about possessions like books and records ... an expensive stereo system ... expensive paintings, art books? What do [I] do with them?
>   Fifth, is it best for us to completely refrain from alcohol, including a glass of wine before bed? Is it harmful to an antimaterialist lifestyle for us to ... [go to] nightclubs?
>   I hope you won't be offended by these questions, Jim, for I know the mere fact I ask them shows how important these aspects of materiality are to me. I have, however, decided to live up to the standards of the communal Christian church as set forth in Acts [of the Apostles] ... to donate everything I have. ... I can no longer be the same person, seeking power and pleasure, as I have blueprinted myself to be. ...
>
>   Sincerely,
>   Tim Stoen
>
> P.S. In your opinion, could I do more good for the church by becoming Assistant District Attorney (civil) or by becoming Directing Attorney of Legal Services? Please advise.

In the end Stoen rejoined the district attorney's office in Ukiah, in the civil division, as county counsel. In a way, it was a circular move for the ambitious attorney. He not only advanced his career little, he also undertook a major image change on behalf of the Temple. People who remembered him in the mid-sixties as a rather hip, bearded legal aid attorney were surprised to see him in three-piece suits. As an ambassador of Jim Jones, Stoen had adopted a straight-arrow image.

A short time after his letter to Jones, Stoen asked Grace to share his life. "Are you willing," he asked, "to give one year of your life for a good cause? . . . And after that, I'll be running for [Congress]. Would you be willing to campaign and be a politician's wife?" Stoen evidently felt confident enough of Grace's devotion to attach conditions to their marriage. She was willing to accept him on his terms. She appreciated him for nurturing her, for telling her what a decent and interesting person she was, for helping her with her vocabulary. When he proposed, she did not agree to commit her life to socialism or a church. Emotionally myopic, she saw only Tim Stoen when she promised a year of her life to the Temple. The time would fly, she thought. They had years ahead, and someday would have a home and children of their own.

From the start, however, the man she loved seemed to place a higher priority on pleasing the Temple than her. Grace's parents had wanted a Catholic wedding; Jones insisted it would be a Temple wedding and Stoen acquiesced. The bride-to-be had wanted an elaborate traditional ceremony, one to remember, but knew the Temple would frown on that.

Though not storybook material, the wedding did turn out to be a gala affair by Temple standards. Jones had decided it was an ideal way to introduce the church to Tim Stoen's many friends in the legal community and among local political bigwigs. More than three hundred people watched Grace and Tim exchange vows on June 27, 1970, in the Redwood Valley church. With Jones officiating, the couple read vows tailored to their relationship. Tim's words imparted a Christian yet mildly socialistic tone: "This is what life is all about—to share, for that is love and that is joy. . . ." Stoen talked of his marriage to Grace in terms of the need to reduce the gap between the haves and have-nots, and the need for peace among nations.

With the Temple band playing, young and old dancing, the newlyweds cut their cake and toasted their marriage with nonalcoholic punch. Some of the church hurried outside to ride Sonny and Tubby. For the adults, the wedding was more than just a good time. The marriage of the country's new assistant district attorney amounted to a social event in Ukiah and warranted local newspaper coverage.

The couple took a one-night honeymoon at the quaint old Mendocino Hotel on the bluffs of the Pacific. Tim promised Grace that she did not have to work, that she could get the college education she had always wanted. They embarked on marriage full of optimism.

Grace Stoen's education began at home, in their little rented house on Road E near the Temple. Each night, they talked and read to each other, learning together; they read Guy de Maupassant's short stories,

Paul Ehrlich's *The Population Bomb* and Eldridge Cleaver's *Soul on Ice.* Tim sent Grace to piano lessons so they both could play. And they took ceramics and first-aid classes together.

While Jones allowed the Stoens a richer, more comfortable life than he allowed other members, he pushed the lawyer toward greater commitment. The minister was aware of the lawyer's materialism. But he allowed the couple to keep their books, stereo and nice furnishings. The public rationale was that it was only fitting for the county counsel's home to be adequately outfitted. More important, Jones wanted the couple happy so he would not lose Stoen's talents. Therefore, he increased the burdens gradually.

Initially, the Stoens went to the church just once a week, in addition to mass birthday parties (for everyone with a birthday that month). At the behest of Jones, Stoen set up a church legal clinic to help with divorces, criminal cases, welfare problems and other legal matters. He played church lawyer after services, and showed an amazing capacity for work. He also gave Jones legal advice.

Stoen was enamored of the principle, "The greatest good for the greatest number of people," and soon it kept him away from home with increasing frequency. The Temple's human service organization needed him. He viewed the Temple as a model for a utopian community to be emulated throughout the world. His idealism was fulfilled by the church's love and respect for the aged and weak, the caring for the children and needy—all within the political context. The onetime anticommunist who had been horrified by the Berlin wall was venturing behind an even more insurmountable organizational wall.

Within a year of joining, Stoen wrote a required essay, purging himself of negative stereotypes he previously had associated with socialism. "Until two months ago," he began, then rewrote, "Until I turned of age, socialism was for me a very unnerving word. . . . So imbued am I by the Rotary luncheon speeches praising free enterprise and condemning socialism as mutually exclusive and slavery-invoking, that it's been the greatest deterrent to a full acceptance of the values held by Peoples Temple. . . .

"Socialism . . . sees the individual as existing on behalf of the community. . . . He is not an elitist. . . . Economically, he resents the accumulation of money into the hands of an unresponsive elite (capitalists). . . .

"The socialist wants the means of production nationalized. . . . He wants the wealth of the country redistributed so that everyone has his basic needs met. . . ."

Stoen had become a true believer. But it was more than an eclectic definition of socialism that inspired his commitment. The intellectual side of him took comfort in the pastor's personal makeup. A naïve Bible-pounder could never have drawn a Tim Stoen. Jones was a perceptive, pragmatic diamond-in-the-rough, a little crude in language and manners, yet boundlessly compassionate. He possessed the qualities Stoen admired, particularly the rhetorical skill to engage crowds and cajole politicians. But Stoen saw Jones in Christian terms too—as nearly the Second Coming, the greatest miracle worker and healer since Christ.

E L E V E N

Children of the Sixties

An air of revolution hung over Berkeley. The long siege raged on, and the scars of past battles could be seen everywhere. Along Telegraph Avenue, just south of the University of California campus, the Bank of America had bricked up its windows. Some stores had been "trashed" so often that no one would sell them glass insurance. Slogans emblazoned the sides of buildings and the plywood over broken windows. Nearby, "Peoples Park" dried up behind chain-link fencing erected by the authorities. On campus, political rallies were an almost daily occurrence. Che, Mao and Ho Chi Minh were heroes, while Reagan, Johnson and Nixon were abominated.

Yet in the years since the 1964 Free Speech Movement, protests had not attracted all of the 27,500 U.C. students. On most days, the majority hiked to classes, sometimes through tear gas, while hundreds of their contemporaries attended rallies, marched or skirmished with police.

In the fall of 1964, while Mario Savio entreated his fellow students to throw their bodies on the university machinery to stop it, other students poured into Memorial Stadium Saturdays to watch the Golden Bears throw their bodies against gridiron rivals. At half time, the Cal Marching Band charged like an army onto the field, strutting in blue uniforms, flying gold braid. With their regimentation and rolling drums, band members were considered the epitome of the politically uninvolved, a throwback to the traditions of the 1950s.

The student director of the band that fall, a tall, dark-haired junior named Bob Houston, fit the stereotype. He was studious, not a protester or boat rocker. And he was a fine musician. In addition to baritone horn, he played piano, trumpet and guitar. Though conservative in style and manner, and never particularly assertive, he impressed his peers with his musical talents, his positive attitude and his dedication.

Out of uniform and off the stands, Bob Houston was just another anonymous face from the band, another young white liberal middle-class kid lugging his books through Sather Gate, perhaps interested in the protests but otherwise occupied. Actually, Bob Houston was an unusually busy student—for besides rolling up good grades, he was a husband, father, railroad worker and high school music instructor.

Bob had married his high school sweetheart, a tall brunette named Phyllis Tuttle. She was the daughter of Bob's Boy Scout troop leader. It had been their first romance, and it culminated in elopement in 1962. Within two years, Phyllis and Bob were parents of two daughters. The marriage, considered premature by both sets of parents, was not trouble-free. The family lived in married student housing during the Free Speech Movement and the early years of antiwar and antidraft protests. Often Bob would walk to campus, attend a full day of lectures, practice with the band, then ride his motorcycle across the bay to San Francisco, where he worked in the Southern Pacific railroad yards. Phyllis resented Bob's absences and felt stifled being a housewife. When she was depressed, she would ignore the housework. Bob would come home drained and find the house in turmoil. They would argue; the babies would cry.

The couple had married too young and in the wrong circumstances, but they survived the first difficult years. Bob graduated in 1966 with a degree in education. Hoping to teach music someday, he enrolled that year at San Francisco State University and began work toward his teaching credentials. He and his family moved to an apartment on Lincoln Way, across the street from Golden Gate Park. The nearby Haight-Ashbury district was bubbling over with young hippies and acid rock. In the park, free concerts were thrown by groups such as the Jefferson Airplane and Grateful Dead. Though not captivated by them, Bob and Phyllis were tolerant of the new trends. To friends they seemed happy-go-lucky, non-judgmental. They loved music of all kinds, from classical to popular; and they played records often or entertained each other on piano or violin. Their common goal was Bob's teaching credential; it would give them mobility, a better life and happiness. But it also meant hard work. While studying at State, Bob continued to work in the railroad yards.

The Southern Pacific railroad yards were a familiar landmark near the Potrero Hill area of San Francisco. For generations, kids had flattened pennies on the tracks there. It was a relaxed place to work, especially night shifts, a sort of endless parking lot, with switchmen and lanterns and a glittering panorama of the downtown skyline. Trains here were usually pulled from track to track at the speed of a lame dog. Bob Houston liked the job because the salary was good. He could catch up on his sleep during slow periods, and he could pick his own hours.

In the mid-1960s, no neighborhood of Berkeley had been entirely insulated from political fury, not even the bucolic hills north of campus. Up there, in a brown-shingled house with a bay view, a tennis court and a swimming pool, lived biochemist Laurence Layton with his wife Lisa and their four children. The two older children were on their way to science careers. Teen-ager Larry had been quickly drawn into the hip scene and antiwar movement, while his vivacious younger sister, Deborah, was still in grade school.

The family history reflected the turmoil of the twentieth-century world. Lisa Phillips Layton, the daughter of a prominent Jewish family form Hamburg, had played with Rothschilds and Berensons as a child. In 1935, the year an uncle of hers won the Nobel Prize, she escaped her native Germany just before her parents were taken off to the concentration camps. She fled to the United States. At Penn State she tutored a brilliant young biochemist named Laurence Layton. And soon they fell in love and married. Layton, a Quaker from a once prominent West Virginia family, began climbing the ladder of professional success. Yet this very achievement provoked a series of arguments between him and his wife.

Lisa Layton had been attracted to her husband's Quaker beliefs because they embodied her own pacifism and contempt for affluence. But, as Layton moved from one university to another during the 1950s, he was often asked to work in war-related areas, even helping develop various kinds of nerve gas, missiles and satellites. Lisa, whose mother had committed suicide after surviving the death camps in Nazi Germany, insisted that her husband get out of weapons research altogether. Finally, in 1957 the family moved to Berkeley, where Layton's studies at the Department of Agriculture laboratory attracted international attention.

In California, the family seemed to have everything—wealth, fame, education, intelligence. They attended a Quaker church in Berkeley. Lisa and the children, however, developed a guilty conscience over their personal good fortune.

Larry, a slight pale-looking boy with feelings of inferiority, had been a manageable little child who entertained himself in his playpen. As the third born, he did not get as much attention as his older siblings. While his older brother and sister followed their father into the sciences, the humanities attracted Larry. After a rather anonymous four years at Berkeley High School, where he was a member of the Young Democrats club, Larry did what was expected of him—he went on to college, at the University of California at Davis, near Sacramento. At this time Davis was considered a safe harbor for the politically naïve. But Larry was not one of these. A loner whose beard and heavy brow made him look older, whose sandals gave him a bohemian air, Larry Layton did not fit in. His vocal antiwar politics and dogmatic manner grated on most of the others in his dorm. He hung out mainly with another Berkeley High graduate, and they sometimes laughed together about the political neanderthals in their dorm.

In 1966, when Vietnam teach-ins, draft counseling and draft card burning came to the Central Valley campus, Larry Layton regularly attended rallies against the war. One day, he watched a draft card burning with a young woman named Carolyn Moore, daughter of the Methodist minister on campus. Unlike Layton, Carolyn Moore almost inherited a tradition of activism; her father had helped down-and-outers in the San Francisco Tenderloin and participated in civil rights and antiwar protests. Although she took her politics equally seriously, she had a fun-loving side —and had drawn a bead on her life's goals. She made the dean's list, had studied French for a year in Bordeaux and was working hard toward her secondary teaching credential.

The petite young woman, who even looked French with her dark hair in a twist, fell in love with Larry Layton. Her humor and need to verbalize softened his almost withdrawn personality. Her certainty about her teaching career contrasted with his lack of personal direction and seeming inability to put himself fully to work. Her parents, Barbara and Rev. John Moore, attributed his problems, his personal weakness, to his use of drugs, though they otherwise found him to be pleasant.

In 1967, Carolyn and Larry were married. While Larry continued undergraduate studies, Carolyn worked to support them both and to finish a fifth year of college for her credential. By 1968, she was ready for her first teaching job. Larry, who was trying to slip through the Selective Service with a religious deferment for his Quaker background, needed an alternative service job as a conscientious objector. They began looking. . . .

When the first hippies and long-haired college graduates and dropouts showed up in Mendocino County searching for land, houses to rent and jobs, the locals welcomed them about as readily as a flash flood. They were viewed as outsiders, deviants, invaders, the very people then-Governor Ronald Reagan had taken to task for tearing up the campuses. The last place the locals wanted them was in the educational system, where they could infect the local children with their ideas.

The Potter Valley school system was decidedly provincial. Outsiders were always suspect and were sized up carefully, especially the two new teachers who appeared on the first day of school in 1968. One was Carolyn Moore Layton, who taught French and modern dance. The other was a music teacher from Berkeley, a tall austere man with long sideburns.

At Potter Valley, Bob Houston finally earned his grade school nickname, "The Little Professor." The former University of California band leader's first teaching assignment proved immensely satisfying, though he had sacrificed a great deal to get his credential and though his teaching load was heavy. In addition to economics and civics, he taught classroom music, gave instrumental instruction and supervised the school chorus and band.

As much as he enjoyed children and his work, the teaching climate did not suit him entirely. Even Bob Houston, with barely shaggy hair and a reserved manner, found himself unfairly classified as a hippie. He began to feel vulnerable, defensive and lonely.

That year, a woman teacher who wore her dark hair in braids and played guitar had some brushes with the school administration; it seemed that some parents objected to her innovative grade school teaching techniques. Bob Houston identified with her and came to her defense, which did not endear him to the administration. He thought it cost him renewal of his teaching contract. But by taking this stand, Houston had changed the direction of his life.

His courage had attracted the attention of the other new teacher, Carolyn Layton. They commiserated in the hallways. Their world views were similar, and each seemed sensitized to the poor, the disadvantaged, the maligned. When the Laytons joined an unusual church in Redwood Valley, Carolyn mentioned it to Bob, who had attended church all his life and had shown particular interest in the liberal Episcopal policies of the late California Bishop James Pike. The church described by Carolyn Layton seemed to offer Houston a solution—it was an organization with humanistic values and relevance to the times. This church did not suffer from the reactionary malaise that touched almost every institution in the rural area. And it was unusual in another respect; membership was by invitation only.

When Carolyn Layton asked Bob to bring his family to a Peoples Temple barbecue, he was flattered. It was about the most hospitable invitation he had received in that area. Also, he and Phyllis had been bound too closely to their home, and needed some outside activities to revive their stagnant marriage. In their reclusive existence alongside Highway 20, Phyllis's frustrations over their premature marriage and parenthood had intensified. Bereft of real friends, she felt imprisoned by her children and by a husband insensitive to her needs. She was an excellent candidate for a women's liberation group.

The barbecue at Peoples Temple provided the Houstons, including the little girls, with the most fun since their move from San Francisco. Rather than being frozen out, as in Potter Valley, they were welcomed warmly to what seemed like a pleasant and vibrant country church with a swimming pool and open space, horses and other animals for the children. The church offered camaraderie: brothers for Bob, sisters for Phyllis and playmates for their two daughters. Bob particularly appreciated the interracial aspects. He immediately took a liking to Jones's two longtime assistants—philosophical Archie Ijames and wise-cracking Jack Beam. Phyllis welcomed the outlet; she met other young women frustrated by the role of housewife and mother.

The Houstons, the Laytons and other refugees of the 1960s knew little of the church's history, although they heard that Jim Jones had been harassed in Indiana. They were seduced by the mix of big-city blacks and whites—mostly midwestern fundamentalists and Ukiah locals—and by Jones himself, who seemed a combination of Martin Luther King, Jr., Billy Graham and Mario Savio. Rev. Jones avoided the piety that kept many people away from religious institutions; he talked about social issues more often than he quoted the Bible, and called his religion apostolic socialism—"apostolic" for the church-oriented, "socialism" for those with social goals and political objectives. He issued warnings of impending disasters while simultaneously providing an ingenious plan for the survival of his chosen people: they would store provisions—water and food-stuffs—in a deep cave where they could weather the blast and fallout of nuclear war. These white children of the sixties were shown only the compassionate facets of Jim Jones's personality, and on that basis, they allowed the church to annex larger and larger portions of their lives.

Other members began calling on Bob Houston for help with projects, and he seldom turned them down. He always had enjoyed structural group activities. But he had not learned that Jones would tap and drain his spirit of self-sacrifice, would take whatever he was willing to give. Soon he was playing in the Temple band and helping out with Temple publications. He donated his income as a music therapist at Mendocino State Hospital to the Temple. And in return he and his family were given comradeship and a church apartment in a ranch-style complex that housed a Temple-owned laundromat and other church facilities.

The church effectively cut them off from their families, though the Bay Area was only two house away by car. Once, however, in 1969, Phyllis's family drove up to Redwood Valley to visit, primarily so her brother, Tom, could introduce his fiancée.

Inadvertently, Phyllis's relatives had intruded on the Temple's increasingly closed community, and Phyllis, through her brusque and decidedly cold manner, told them so. Her brother and father were hurt by her attitude, appalled by the filthy condition of her sparsely furnished living quarters, which reeked of dog feces. When they asked Phyllis about the absence of furnishings, she said they had all been donated to the church. So had her 1960 Valiant. The church had everything.

In the short space of six months, the church had become their family, their landlord, their life.

TWELVE

Family Affair

My Mother
is different from any other
In her smile
Once in awhile
She's as quiet as a mouse
When she cleans the house
The rest of the time
Watch out
Her eyes are like the moon
Just risen in June
And I love her
Because she's different from any other.

STEPHAN JONES, 1971

Through the years of her marriage, Marceline Jones tended to cry often, but kept her troubles to herself. Her family realized that the problems revolved around her husband, but the nature eluded the Baldwins until the late 1960s. When Marceline's sisters visited her in 1968, they found that Jones had moderated his message of love. He preached about physical love as well as emotional love—and encouraged his members to cast aside selfish, exclusive relationships and share their love with others. In essence, he urged his congregation to have sex with different people, married or not, young or old, beautiful or ugly. He talked about the uplifting and unifying experience of free love.

Though disturbed by the changes in the church and her brother-in-law, Sharon felt helpless to do anything. She broached the subject one night before dinner with her friends from Indiana, Harold and Loretta Cordell. But Loretta defended Jones, and they quarreled. Jim Jones somehow had conditioned churchgoing fundamentalist Christians to embrace free love and free sex. Sharon could not bring herself to confront Marceline about the matter, yet she was tempted to ask Jim. One evening as they talked alone in the parsonage living room, she came close to challeng-

119

ing the preacher she had once considered a big brother. Yet Jones's domineering, confident personality muffled her.

As Jim Jones became more than a minister, his idyllic country church changed by increments into an instrument of his personal goals, a mirror of his turmoil. On occasion, he wrestled with the children on the lawn or shot baskets with the boys on the sideyard court. But the fun—the carefree times when he strolled around the sunny parking lot after services, chatting and joking with Temple people—vanished. He was too busy; for the sake of the organization, he had begun to lose sight of the people, even his own family.

The flourishing church occupied Jim Jones day and night. Dinnertime phone calls increased in frequency, and the preacher often chatted with local politicos and church leaders while his family ate. Only rarely did Jones pack his family in the Toyota for a family outing. They sometimes dined at modest restaurants where the frugal preacher tipped little but loaded his kids' pockets with free mustard and ketchup packages. As always, moviegoing remained a true family production, though Jones—feeling some guilt over pleasures he encouraged his followers to forgo—now pretended he went only for the sake of his family.

The "rainbow family"—Jones's living symbol of brotherhood—was cracking. Jealousy and rivalry kept the children at odds. As the natural son, and the only white, Stephan was often at the center of spats. But he nonetheless took pride in his blood lines, when his mother called him her "little Indian," when people compared him to his father.

Stephan loved his dad and bragged about him. But the hoopla and ecstatic yelling in church offended the boy. Stephan savored the quiet times, their intimate moments together, when he knew his father loved him more than anyone else.

One night, after a particularly bad day at school, Stephan dropped face down on his bed and cried, overcome with persecution feelings, self-doubt and confusion. His fifth grade teacher had accused him of being nasty to other children. His father heard him, walked in and sat down beside him. "What's the matter?"

"She said I was crazy. Maybe I am crazy," he sobbed.

"What time is it?" his father asked him. When Stephan told him the time, Jones noted that their watches were only a minute or so apart. "See?" Jones said. "You're not crazy."

With his arms around him, his father lay with Stephan on the bed until the boy pretended to drop off to sleep. Falling for the act, Jones got up and tiptoed carefully out the door. Before he was gone, Stephan called softly, "Good night, Dad."

Jones turned and smiled. "You little shit," he said good-naturedly.

Those few minutes of tenderness reinforced Stephan's belief in a psychic link between his father and him, a telepathic system that allowed them to peer into each other's minds. His father was truly a great man, he thought, and they were a special pair. Jones used to tell him, "There are only two people, you and I, in this world. There is nobody else like us. We are unique. We're very close genetically."

When Stephan was nine or ten, Marceline's chronic back problems temporarily worsened to the point that she could not work. In terrible pain, she was confined to bed and placed in traction. While she lay helplessly on her back, Carolyn Layton, the dark-haired French teacher, began taking the Jones children on outings, with their father's blessings. Though she acted reserved and inhibited around them, Carolyn tried to get Stephan, Lew and Jimmy to enjoy themselves. Even the young boys sensed something lurking in her mind that prevented her from loosening up. She began to telegraph messages with decreasing subtlety. Finding that circumspect hints about a relationship between her and their father did not work, she sat them down in a little park in Willits one day for a heart-to-heart talk. But she could not spit out blunt enough words. She was very close to their father, she said. The boys did not catch her meaning.

Jones had started to bring his natural son on drives up Highway 20, through the mountainous country, toward Potter Valley. They arrived alone at the little cabin Carolyn Layton—now separated from her husband Larry—shared with a couple from the Temple. The picturesque drive suited Stephan, and he liked the rustic cabin, though it lacked a TV. Carolyn fussed over him and tried to make him feel at home. She seemed a nice lady, and intelligent; but he could not figure out why she pampered him or why they visited this place.

At bedtime, she made up a sofa bed for Stephan in the living room. She and Jones drifted into her bedroom. With his head practically against the wall, Stephan could not help eavesdropping. He could hear conversation, and when the talking stopped, he heard noises—movement, panting, sounds of passion. In the middle of it all, he heard Carolyn reciting poetry and singing. Stephan did not know exactly what was transpiring behind the wall, but he understood that his father and Carolyn had a secret, illicit relationship. The mysterious physical act of sex did not concern him as much as his father's betrayal of his mother. The boy knew fathers, especially his father, were not supposed to behave that way. He sensed that telling his mother would hurt her too much; so he buried it within himself and did not even tell his brothers or sister.

One day while talking to his bed-bound mother in her room, he found there was no reason to keep his secret any longer. In bed, strapped in a traction contraption, she languished in deep emotional pain. Having nowhere else to turn, she confided in her "little Indian." She said that his father had told her about his liaisons with Carolyn. Stephan could not believe his father would confess something so cruelly—not until his mother gave him a telltale detail. Carolyn, she said, quoted poetry and sang at the most intimate of moments.

As his mother cried, Stephan cried too. Confusion and disappointment overwhelmed him. In his pain, he blamed his mother first, thinking: how could such a great man have gone astray unless his wife somehow caused it? Maybe it was true, as his father bellowed from time to time:

"Your mother, she's a beautiful woman, but she always manipulates guilt." Stephan was bewildered. "Why are you doing this?" he thought resentfully about his mother. "Why are you breaking up my family?" He could not look at it in the open: the bond of the "rainbow family" had fractured like glass in the sun. He ran out, hurt and in tears.

When Carolyn Layton's parents learned that she and Larry had separated a short time after joining the Temple, it surprised them little. Though their increasingly remote daughter provided no real explanation for the separation, they attributed it to Larry's problems—perhaps drugs or his overall weak character. Perhaps Carolyn had tired of carrying the heavy load in the relationship. Because of their isolation from their daughter, Rev. and Mrs. John Moore really could not have imagined the role of the minister.

Carolyn's absence on Christmas and Thanksgiving holidays had disturbed the Moore family, because such events always had provided a special family unity. It was painful—particularly for Carolyn's younger sister Annie, who someday would find herself in a similar situation—to see Carolyn wedded to Temple ideology and to Jones's personality. The Temple had replaced the family. Still the Moores kept open lines of communication and resisted temptations to criticize, both because they feared forcing Carolyn to make a choice and because they endorsed in principle the Temple's humanitarian aims.

Larry Layton's family knew even less of the collapsed marriage. He had not written or accepted phone calls from his family since joining the Temple; he had eliminated his kin from his life. They remained unaware of his marital difficulties, of his drug rehabilitation inside the Temple. The almost unfathomable extent of his loyalty to Jones would not become known to them for years, and then, in a new tangle, more Laytons would join him.

Shortly after Marceline's confidences to Stephan, her sister Sharon phoned the Jones house long distance from Texas. Jones would not allow Sharon to speak with the invalid: Marceline was in a very bad way. He told Sharon not to worry and assured her he would not send Marceline to an insane asylum. Sharon fell into the trap; frightened by the implications of Jones's disavowal, she encouraged him to get Marceline professional help. Through trickery, Jones got Marceline's own sister to endorse psychiatric treatment that could help him later commit his wife to an institution.

Marceline, stranded in bed with her husband philandering and plotting behind her back, needed allies, not a psychoanalyst. Jones realized she would turn to her parents for help, so he got to them first. Reaching Mrs. Baldwin on the phone, he first explained Marceline's illness, saying she had a herniated disk and would need to remain in traction for some time. This did not surprise Mrs. Baldwin, because Marceline's job entailed much driving and that aggravated her back problem.

But Marceline had more than a physical problem, Jones went on. "Marceline's been tearful and depressed. As much as I hate to, I think we're going to have to put her in an institution."

Mrs. Baldwin was shocked—Marceline previously had always accepted physical ailments without ever becoming preoccupied with herself. "What's wrong, Jim? Tell me."

"I suppose I might as well tell you that a young schoolteacher in the church has an attraction for me, and I for her. She claims she was my wife in a former life. It's very difficult for me under the circumstances."

"Jim, we're coming right away," Mrs. Baldwin said excitedly. For the first time Mrs. Baldwin genuinely feared what Jones might do to her daughter. This was not the same minor, ill-concealed animosity Jones had shown years earlier. She could read between the lines well enough to see that he wanted Marceline out of the way.

After four straight days of driving from Indiana, the Baldwins pulled into Redwood Valley. Marceline was still in traction, still in an emotional state. At a church service before the Baldwins really had a chance to talk to their daughter, Jim took them aside and told stories designed to convince them Marceline had suffered a breakdown. She had tried to take her own life, he said, as several church members confirmed.

But Jones's plan backfired. In private talks with Marceline, the Baldwins found no signs of insanity or suicidal tendencies. She had been badly wounded by her husband's infidelity. In a frank session, Marceline told her parents that their son-in-law had demanded she accept his philandering, that even during their visit he was brazenly sneaking away every evening, ostensibly heading to meetings but actually spending the night with Carolyn. Her parents resolved that they would not allow Marceline to be committed. Jim, sensing he would meet too much resistance, never raised the matter again.

Though he could not put Marceline away, Jones tried to restrict and define her role in the family, and replace her with Carolyn. In one breath he told the children Marceline was an insane and impossible wife, and in the next he praised Carolyn's beauty and human understanding. He tried to substitute his mistress for Marceline on everything from weekend outings to vacations. Again, the rationale was suicide, only now it was Carolyn who was threatening to take her own life if she could not have Jim.

Jones had projected suicidal tendencies onto his followers for some time. During this crisis, he aimed his projection onto those closest to him, his wife and mistress. But Marceline knew this emotional blackmail all too well. Though she still loved him, the agony was too much. She decided, as she had almost decided in the first two years of their marriage, that divorce was the only answer. She recognized that she could not change Jim—and that he was out to destroy her. She resolved to escape, taking the children with her. Divorce papers could be filed later.

She enlisted cooperation from an unexpected quarter. Lynetta, who did not condone Jim's affair, agreed to help with the getaway plans. Everything was set for the escape, but one of the children leaked the plan to their father.

Ever the strategist, Jones blocked his wife's path with the one obstacle she could not ignore—the children. Gathering them together in private, he outlined the situation in his own terms, feeding them the line about their mother's emotional problems, undermining her and coaching them. "Your mother's going to ask you if you want to go with her," he told the children. "You're going to say no. Your mother loves you, but that's not the best thing for you." He portrayed himself as the upholder of the family bond; he knew that if he could keep the children from leaving, Marceline would abandon her plan. Under no circumstances would she abandon her kids. Her motherly instincts would outweigh her need to escape, he knew.

Then Jones executed the second stage of his divide-and-conquer strategy. When their mother was about to leave, the children were gathered in one room. Marceline entered, crying. "I'm leaving," she explained. "I'm leaving your father and I'm leaving here. And I want you children to come with me. Will you come with me?" To her surprise, the children appeared unresponsive. Surmising they did not want to choose between mother and father, she assured them, "I won't keep you from your father. You can see your father as much as you want."

Nothing seemed to work. As the children watched her plead, red-eyed, tearful, distraught, it was not difficult for them to see the correctness of their father's admonitions and warnings: their mother *was* crazy, she was falling apart. Under the circumstances, there was no alternative to following Jones's orders, to making the decision that would hold the family together. "No," they told Marceline. They would not budge.

At this point, Jones stepped in as conciliator and cajoled Marceline into staying. The children aside, she would have found it difficult to wrest herself away; she loved Jim as a leader, a husband and a lover. She forgave him and forgave him again, compromising herself as she accepted one aberration after another.

But Jim Jones, like a hardened piece of clay, did not change. He not only kept seeing Carolyn as a mistress; he chipped away at Marceline's standing, alternately praising her and running her down in front of the children and church members. In his frustration and guilt over his affair, he would throw angry fits and become so hostile that she threatened again to leave; then he would beg her to stay, telling her she was the only one he loved. Sometimes he threatened to harm her and the children if they deserted him.

Stephan Jones loved his mother too much not to be affected by his father's infidelity and violent railings against her. His initial confusion turned to certainty that blame lay with his father. Disillusionment and hostility set in; his mother's pain became his own. As the little boy listened to his mother's confidences, he provided what comfort he could; through their conversations, they formed a rare relationship. He assumed part of her burden and formed an alliance with her, one that would strain his young psyche but last until the end.

While Jones succumbed to his own desires and psychological needs, he lost the respect of his son Stephan by degrees. The boy saw and heard enough to know his father was breaking his own rules and making up others to suit his needs. In a church that ballyhooed its drug rehabilitation work, Jones was shooting himself with what supposedly was vitamin B_{12}, just as Marceline had injected him after his collapses in Indiana. After the shots, the preacher, curiously enough, could not converse; he became almost incoherent. Once, after taking an "insulin" shot, Jones screamed and carried on until Marceline came to the rescue.[26] He reportedly had begun abusing drugs, taking stimulants, pain-killers and tranquilizers to suit his mood and purpose. Marceline became concerned about this new source of friction and psychological problems. It came to a head once when she grabbed the stash from his medicine chest and, while Jones struggled with her, flushed his drugs down the toilet.

Within a year or so, the emotional clouds enveloped Stephan Jones, and darkened. He felt hostility for his father, a man supposedly above reproach. He wondered whether he himself was crazy, out of step with the world. Finding a supply of Quaalude tranquilizers among his father's drugs, he swallowed them one by one until they seemed to take effect. He took thirteen in all. Then, instead of quietly lying down and ending it all, he went to his mother and asked, "How many is an overdose of Quaaludes?"

"Why do you want to know that?"

"Well . . ." he hesitated.

"Just a couple."

He left the room, without confessing what he had done. Moments later he had second thoughts. He told Tim Tupper Jones, a friend who recently had been adopted into the family, "You better tell Mom I just took an overdose of Quaaludes."

Marceline charged into the room. Bringing him to his feet, she made him walk around and filled him with cold coffee. He woke up two days later in a hospital, still unhappy, still confused and in need of help and a resolution of his family problems.

Yet Jones, the model of compassion, either could not or would not recognize his own son's dilemma. Rather than spend more time with him, Jones enlisted an older Temple member, Mike Touchette, as his playmate.

THIRTEEN

Golden Boy

By 1968, the Temple had been granted standing under the Disciples' Northern California-Nevada region. And, as in Indiana, the Temple soon capitalized upon its denominational affiliation. In newsletters, letters to officials and dignitaries and in various applications, the Temple almost automatically identified itself as part of the "1.5-million-member" church. Sometimes the reference was so vague as to leave the impression that Jones himself headed the huge nationwide group, which had numbered J. Edgar Hoover and Lyndon Johnson among its members. Without permission the Temple had inserted laudatory statements from Disciples' officials on leaflets and flyers announcing Jones's miracle healing services across the land. A further advantage to affiliation, of course, involved taxes: federal and state tax exemptions and breaks on local property tax assessments.

The Disciples never impeded the Temple, even though Jones ignored even the minimal requirements of the mother church, such as regular holy communion and baptism. Jones, like Father Divine, administered holy communion in the form of church dinners. He baptized people in the Temple swimming pool "in the holy name of Socialism."

Even if they had uncovered his sacrilegious practices, the Disciples could have done little, for the denomination lacked procedures for examining local congregations and the power to expel them. Moreover, ordination in Disciples' churches historically had been left in the hands of the local congregation, and training requirements were minimal. Over the years, Jones manufactured ministers as the need arose, some with little or no ministerial expertise. There were exceptions, however; Tim Stoen and Guy Young, a Temple member who was also a probation officer in Contra Costa County, both had educations from church-related institutions. They applied for and got official ministerial standing within the denomination proper. And Stoen would go on to become a member of the Disciples of Christ's regional board, practically assuring the Temple's continued protection.

From the perspective of the Disciples, Peoples Temple, headed by a respected Ukiah figure, had become an important asset. It was one of the largest and most generous Disciples churches in the country. The church's donations kept apace of its lengthening membership rolls. Additional infusions of funds arrived periodically, often coinciding with Temple crises. As Temple membership shot up from a reported 86 in 1966 to 300 in 1969 to 2,570 in 1973, donations to the Disciples went from zero to $13,775.

Tim Stoen handled most Temple liaison work with the Disciples. In addition to being church board chairman and church attorney, Stoen— religious and righteous-sounding—projected the correct image. Stoen played a similar role as secret agent, adviser and ambassador for Jones in the larger community. His primary task as church attorney was to keep the church on the safe side of the line between legality and illegality. Being attached to the district attorney's office did not hurt. He could keep Jones briefed if a case arose involving a Temple member. And his very presence in the D.A.'s office would tend to discourage people, including Temple members, from filing complaints against Jones's church.

Temple members were employed throughout the local and county government in Ukiah, but none, including Pastor Jones, was as highly visible and as widely respected as Tim Stoen. The lawyer came into almost daily contact with the most powerful people in the county; through his job, he knew the district attorney, the judges, the newspaper editor, county supervisors, police, school officials, state and county agency heads and others. Stoen provided a living example of the humane philosophy of Peoples Temple. People who knew little of Jim Jones thought well of the Temple because of Stoen and other hard-working, sincere members. The erudite and articulate attorney made the proper contacts, was active in the Rotary Club and Republican party. His effusive praise of his leader and organization could not simply be written off.

Whether chatting in the grocery store or among his employees, the Mendocino County Board of Supervisors, Stoen came across strongly as a true believer. Some, like county welfare chief Dennis Denny, thought it remarkable that such an analytical man could adopt such outlandish religious beliefs. Stoen dumbfounded Denny once by telling him Rev. Jones had healed himself instantly after being shot point-blank with a pistol. As an eyewitness, Stoen offered proof: "Jim took the bullet and held it up and dropped it, and it went 'plink.' " And at that, Denny shot him a skeptical eye, and said sarcastically, "Tim . . . it went *plink?*"

Stoen could not check his zeal even in political settings, when talking to other active Republicans or attending receptions for statewide campaigners such as then-California Attorney General Evelle Younger. Local Republican Central Committee leader Marge Boynton, though fond of Stoen, once remarked at a planning seminar, "It sounds like you think Jim is God." Stoen replied, "I guess I think he is."

On at least one occasion, Stoen made it quite clear where his allegiance would fall if his two commitments came into conflict. During a session of the Board of Supervisors, Stoen's secretary rushed in to hand him a note—welfare chief Dennis Denny and an investigator had gone to Jones's house asking him questions about some apparently stolen agricultural commodities seen on a Temple-owned truck. Without any explanation, Stoen took off from the meeting, leaving them without their county counsel.

The next day, in explaining his disappearance to Supervisor Al Barbero, Stoen stated: "I took the job on the condition that if anything came up, I worked for the church first."

Indeed, the cause consumed his day. He rose often at 4:00 A.M. to study history and other subjects he would need to know cold if his ambitions and the church's were to be realized. Life was a string of appointments and phone calls, all tightly scheduled. He accounted for every minute of his day on paper—shaving and showering, eating, sleeping, exercising. He expected great things of himself, and he compartmentalized his life to maximize his efficiency.

Stoen's accomplishments were astonishing. Yet with such demands upon him, even Stoen had to sacrifice something. He neglected his young bride. As commitment to the Temple hardened into obsession, he devoted less and less time and energy to the woman with whom he promised to share life. When she complained or became saddened by his absences and outside interests, Tim encouraged her to suppress her selfish feelings so as to become a good Temple member.

According to most external indicators, their marriage went well. They lived in a comfortable wood frame house in Ukiah. The home—with its furniture, television, stereo, art books and literature—was more important to Grace than Tim, because she could not take for granted the bourgeois trappings he had known all his life. Having heard Jones's harangues, she realized that her personal desires conflicted with Temple teachings. But, after all, she herself never had volunteered for the people's vanguard.

Though Jones personally conceded a nice home to the Stoens to keep them happy, other members resented their privileges, and the Stoens were accused of elitism. Grace—who wore tasteful clothes and kept her shoulder-length black hair long after Temple women clipped theirs short as an ego reducer—faced the charges of narcissism. Though she felt their disapproval, she did not want to surrender what she had wanted all her life. It was almost as bad as being white in a church where Jones harped about the evils inflicted upon blacks.

The Stoen house was never turned into a Temple commune. It was never overrun with stray dogs, cats and people. The Stoens boarded no more than three outsiders at a time, and most were children of church members. Jones knew that Grace needed to play lady of the house, and adults would upset that. Most boarders were too young to provide her with any companionship during Tim's frequent absences, until blond, pert Jeanette Kerns arrived from Florida in the summer of 1971. . . .

Kerns, a spunky ex-surfer and daughter of a Temple member, had been coaxed into quitting her job and coming to California to live in what sounded like Christian church-run college dormitories. Jones did not want her to be hit too abruptly with cultural shock, so he sent her to the Stoens with orders to keep her contented. The arrangement worked well, because Jeanette and Grace genuinely enjoyed their companionship and soon found common interests. Neither was imbued with the Temple's spirit of self-deprivation.

The two young women took shopping jaunts to downtown Ukiah, or sneaked away to Lake Mendocino to sunbathe and swim. They exchanged gossip, chatted about Grace's youth in San Francisco, Jeanette's days as a Florida beach girl. The latest fashions did not escape them, though they sat for hours hearing Jones rave about the virtues of frugality, of buying secondhand garments. The women exchanged "good dirt" about church people; they talked about who was sleeping with whom and ridiculed the pompous members who flaunted their loyalty and bowed and scraped around Jones family members. They groused about going to choir lessons and made fun of the Pentecostal pantomime, mocking the way people shouted "Hallelujah" and "Thank the Lord."

Yet when Jim Jones called or stopped by the Stoen household, it was a special event. Even Grace, unenthusiastic as she was, changed her tune. While Tim was at work and Jeanette was staying there, he phoned now and then and talked to Grace during the day. And he came by to have dinner a couple of times with the Stoens. Grace treated him with great respect, waiting on him hand and foot.

Though Grace had begun to admire this handsome and energetic young minister who did so much for others, she was put off by those who adored him. To her, Jim Jones was a human being, a good man no more above reproach than anyone else, at least not in private. She prided herself on her ability to maintain her dignity when talking with him, her readiness to correct him if he slipped or if she disagreed. Perhaps Jones sensed her need to be treated equally, as one human being to another. He accepted her criticism, but slowly he built her respect for him and his goals. He wanted her as a follower, in part because it would keep Tim in the fold. Someday he would claim that he had given her "special attention" to keep her loyal.

How Jones divided, conquered and bound the couple to the church provides a case study of his manipulative techniques:

During the first year or so of Stoen's membership, Jones built him up tremendously, entrusting him with great responsibilities, singing his praises and encouraging other members to like him. And he gave Stoen, as he would with some other key members, a "reward." Jones complained that too many women were demanding his love, attention and sexual favors. He asked Stoen to help relieve that drain upon him by becoming intimate with a woman of low self-esteem. For Stoen, whose taste always ran to the beauty-queen type, Jones selected rather homely Sharon Amos. After all, this was supposed to be a self-sacrifice.

Jones then let Stoen's wife know in various ways about her husband's philandering, never mentioning, of course, his own role in the liaison. Although Jones created friction between Grace and Tim, they loved each other and wanted to stay married at first.

Around this time, in summer of 1971, while Tim and Grace were living and sleeping together, she became pregnant. This only brought new conflicts. One Wednesday night meeting in July 1971, Grace got a preview of the criticism she might expect for carrying the baby to term. Already upset with her husband's extramarital activity, she suffered a cutting remark from none other than Sharon Amos, who said pointedly that people who contribute to the overpopulation problem should pay all childbirth costs. Though her peers pressured her to get an abortion, Grace wanted to keep the baby.

The day following the meeting, she confronted her husband. She accused him of infidelity, of chasing other women in the church. Crying, she said her pride had been hurt, that people laughed at her. Stoen argued feebly that he merely wanted to help women who needed affection based on respect. The three women in whom he had shown an interest were not beauties, he pointed out. Tearfully accusing him of using her, of letting her cook, clean and wash, Grace criticized him for not making the time to take her to breakfast or to spend even a few minutes with her, though he made time for other women. She said she could not go on living with him.

That afternoon as Stoen drove Grace to her doctor in Santa Rosa, she proceeded to cross-examine Tim about Jones's role in his contacts with other women. "Did Jim ask you to get involved with Linda [Sharon] Amos?" she asked at one point.

Stoen covered for Jones, apparently not sensing his pastor's manipulation, and still mystified as to how Grace had gleaned her information. Instead of exchanging confidences with her, he played spy on his own marriage. The following day he sent a four-page handwritten letter to Jones, detailing the above and warning him: "Be careful. My wife is about to ask you some loaded questions." What was most important, Tim said, was that Grace not leave either him or the church. With that, Stoen·closed the circle for Jones. An even greater measure of his loyalty would soon be tapped.[27]

It was 3:30 A.M. on January 25, 1972. Grace Stoen's water broke. She and Tim climbed into the car and drove through a heavy rain south on U.S. Highway 101 to Santa Rosa Memorial Hospital. While Grace measured contractions in a labor room, Tim went to provide information for the admission forms. Grace signed the forms and checked her wedding ring for safekeeping at 5:10 A.M. She was twenty-one, her husband thirty-four. It was a great comfort to have him at her side during the hours of waiting in the labor room. The time crept past, the day dawned, and late in the morning, she finally had dilated enough to go to the delivery room. At first the nurse evicted Tim, but the doctor asked, "Where's the father? Get him in here. He's the best person to have here. She needs him." At 11:25 A.M., Tim signed a release form absolving the hospital of responsibility if he passed out or injured himself during the birth. The delivery was difficult. Almost three hours later, at 2:16 P.M., a tiny head with matted black hair squeezed out of Grace's body. Tim was electrified. He later would describe the birth of John Victor Stoen as the greatest moment of his life.

This squirming little being would, through no fault of his own, become a critical factor in determining the fate of a thousand people. One of these people, the Reverend Jim Jones, was at that moment bemoaning to one of his lovers that he could not claim John Stoen as his own.

Owing to her rough labor, Grace was confined to bed. Visits were restricted to relatives. When Jones came to visit a few days later, nurses stopped him, but he bulled ahead, saying, "I've come all the way from Ukiah. I'm her minister." Grace vouched for him, and the nurses made an exception. It was his only visit; he had stopped off en route to San Francisco.

When the hospital released Grace, Tim signed a promissory note for $325. When the infant came home, Stoen acted like an obnoxiously proud father, doting over the baby, helping with the bottles and diapers.

On February 1, 1972, a week after the birth, the Stoens received a copy of the birth certificate from the health department. It listed the mother as Grace, the father as Tim Stoen. Grace had provided the information and signed the legal document.

On February 6, 1972, a week after filing of the birth certificate, Mendocino County Assistant District Attorney Timothy Oliver Stoen signed a contradictory piece of paper which, whether a truthful statement or not, exhibited phenomenal trust in Jim Jones:

"I, Timothy Oliver Stoen, hereby acknowledge that in April 1971, I entreated my beloved pastor, James W. Jones, to sire a child by my wife, Grace Lucy (Grech) Stoen, who had previously, at my insistence, reluctantly but graciously consented thereto. James W. Jones agreed to do so, reluctantly, after I explained that I very much wished to raise a child, but was unable after extensive attempts, to sire one myself. My reason for requesting James W. Jones to do this is that I wanted my child to be fathered, if not by me, by the most compassionate, honest, and courageous human being the world contains.

"The child, John Victor Stoen, was born on January 25, 1972. I am privileged beyond words to have the responsibility for caring for him, and I undertake this task humbly with the steadfast hope that said child will become a devoted follower of Jesus Christ, and be instrumental in bringing God's kingdom here on earth, as has been his wonderful natural father.

"I declare under penalty of perjury that the foregoing is true and correct."

The document also bore the signature of Marceline Jones as witness. Marceline believed that Jones was the father, that Grace was one of the women making sexual demands on her husband. Later, she would cover for him further, saying she had granted Jim permission in advance to impregnate Grace.

Stoen later would say he assumed the document was going into a safe. He did not tell Grace he signed it, although the statement, in effect, bound the child to Jones and the church for life. The circle was drawn, with the entire Stoen family inside its boundaries.

FOURTEEN

On the Road

The Temple spread like ivy, through families in Ukiah and beyond, putting down roots wherever it touched ground. In the space of just a couple of years in the early 1970s, Temple membership and assets multiplied several times over as the church combined its old recruiting patterns among poor, blacks and the uneducated with assistance from an elite of college-educated, middle-class whites. In collecting people and money coast to coast, Jones dictated the formula with the master's touch of a traveling evangelist. His past experience—from the religious convention shared with William Branham to the door-to-door recruiting of blacks in Indiana —had taught him essential steps in the recruitment process. Follow-up was as important as an impressive initial contact; then it was necessary to get potential recruits involved at once.

However, as the Temple grew and recruited nationwide, even the hard-driving Jones could not be omnipresent, could not make personal visits to every home, could not take the time to counsel everyone personally and ask them to join. Instead he used his people as salesmen. And the Temple relied increasingly on a sort of subscription list of all who attended a Temple service, knew a Temple member or belonged to a church "fellowshiping" with the Temple. Prospective and active Temple members were mailed newsletters.

Though little more than mimeographed flyers primarily designed to announce Temple services and events, the newsletters also functioned as a recruiting tool and a written record of Temple history and lore. They carried portions of Jones's sermons and reported church acquisitions and expansion plans, as any church bulletin would. But Temple publications reflected an urgency, issuing warnings about emergencies and impending crises, ballyhooing the bizarre and the miraculous—and tossed these ingredients together with folksy humanitarian concern and reverence for life. The church bulletins touted nonviolence along with euphemisms for socialism—such as "apostolic social justice." The Temple presented a largely religious façade; no one would yet catch Jim Jones promoting socialism in writing.

In fact, Jones honestly did fear exposure and attack for his ideas. But the line between fabrication and truth, between real and imagined threats, ran a crooked course. Under the influence of paranoia and drugs, his mind leaped to fearful conclusions, bypassing judgment and reason. His sickness magnified problems: he anticipated not just one reaction to an action, but many. If he were exposed as a socialist, he believed a sort of domino effect would destroy him and his church—the friendly Republican power structure disowning him, Disciples of Christ stripping away his church status, the Internal Revenue Service moving in, the news media attacking, redneck vigilantes bringing up the rear. Such fears dogged him everywhere. His paranoia and his grandiosity nourished each other. He told his followers that only effective crusaders need fear being attacked. If he were not under attack from someone somewhere, his self-importance suffered, and he needed to create his own bogeyman, or to provoke natural enemies, as he apparently did with the Nazis in Indiana.

As in the Midwest, Jones wielded fear like a club, prophesying bombs, earthquakes, fascist revolutions, plus fires in homes, auto accidents, deaths and injuries to the unfaithful. In pleading for members, he combined a foreboding sort of hucksterism along with a promise of salvation. "Attention," shrieked the first line of a newsletter in 1970. "This one time, you need to read every word of what may be your last communication with us unless we hear from you. Vital prophecies about people and events herein. Your future depends upon it." To such twentieth-century fire and brimstone, Jones added the true message: social justice is our primary concern. Contribute to the cause. Join us if you want to catch the freedom train.

Jones adjusted his rhetoric to make the Temple more palatable to his targets. "Living the Acts of the Apostles" was his euphemism for Christian communalism—or Temple-style communism—but the newsletters implied a nonpolitical orientation. In 1970, the newsletters did not even take stands on current issues such as the war in Vietnam or the civil rights record of the Nixon administration. That year, with only 1,500 people on the mailing list, with the Temple chartering buses and exploring expansion to San Francisco, the Temple presented little in the way of a coherent identity.

A year later, a well-coordinated nationwide recruiting drive was under way, still relying most heavily on the healings. In 1971, the newsletters heralded recruiting efforts in San Francisco and bus trips to Los Angeles and big cities in the Pacific Northwest, the Midwest and the East Coast. The church purchased its first few buses, and Jones kept up a superhuman road schedule, leading several services during each of his stops, often two a day. In the course of this all-out effort, newsletter mailings catapulted from 6,000 to 36,000. By late 1971, the voice of Jim Jones could be heard on radio broadcasts over much of the United States, Canada and Mexico. The Temple had purchased time on religious stations in California, Washington, Ohio and other places.

Jim Jones always played the headliner's role, but his supporting cast of young white crusaders increased the scope of his ministry. Their writing and language skills immediately improved the newsletters; their social skills and appearance helped create a favorable public image.

In relying heavily on them, Jones attached a higher priority to building a strong organization than in making it a model of integration. Falling victim to his impatience, he reinforced the racism of the larger society. Because many whites came to the Temple with educational advantages and social skills, the pragmatic preacher drew a disproportionate number into his inner circle. His white elite in turn attracted even more well-educated whites, many of them from the Bay Area. . . .

When the first warm spring days arrived in May of 1970, Joyce Cable Shaw was sunbathing in the garden of her Upper Market Street apartment in San Francisco. Her snowy Samoyed puppy frolicked around her. As she puffed on a marijuana cigarette, sipped a cold beer, read a book on astrology, Shaw felt good about herself. She earned a decent salary as a psychological tester at the University of California, and had a busy social life. Her biggest worry was deciding whether to buy a Volkswagen van. In fact, she had dropped her analyst the previous afternoon because she no longer needed one.

When the phone rang, it was a girl friend, another astrology buff. "How 'bout coming with me tonight to hear a good man talk?" she asked. Shaw did not have a date that Saturday night, so she agreed to go along, out of curiosity.

When Joyce Shaw entered the rented auditorium on Geary Street with her friend, she was immediately approached for what turned out to be the equivalent of a sorority rush. The welcomer was Linda (Sharon) Amos. Seeing Shaw's semihip garb of wire-rimmed glasses, poncho, and Levi's, Amos told of her own artistic interests, her attempts at a professional dancing career, her dabbling in the North Beach beatnik scene. Learning that Joyce was divorced, she talked about her own failed relationships, her marriage to a "male chauvinist" who provided her with a daughter and little else, her live-in arrangement with a black man who gave her two more children. The Temple, she said, had lifted her out of her depression, made her feel useful. Much of what Amos said registered with Shaw; her own rather hedonistic life, though running smoothly, lacked something.

When Jim Jones strode onto the stage, a rush of energy rippled through the audience and a peculiar feeling of déjà vu flashed over Shaw. As the preacher spoke of guilt and injustice and euphemistically of socialism, Shaw's instincts pulled her in opposite directions. The power of Jones's presence was undeniable, but ambiguous—as if he were either very good or very evil.

That night Shaw reached no conclusions, despite Jones's manipulations. The preacher, calling out a little black woman sitting next to Shaw, claimed to have healed her of a stroke. As proof, he asked Shaw to take the woman's hand. The woman gripped with what appeared to be normal strength—and Shaw reported that to the congregation, thus confirming the "miracle" healing. Perhaps a healing had occurred, thought Shaw. She believed in metaphysics and psychosomatic healings. In any case she shared the joy of those Jones claimed to heal.

Looking around the auditorium, evaluating the people, Shaw asked herself whether the organization held anything for her. As her eyes roamed, she spotted a tall dark-haired young man, with pale complexion, glasses and severe features, a member of the church band. Their eyes may have met for a moment. She found him handsome. He looked like her type of person, a college graduate from her generation.

By the end of May 1970, Joyce Shaw felt twinges of dissatisfaction with her job, her nine-to-five routine, the life of a single working woman in the city. With her new VW van and her puppy, she contemplated moving back to the country. But the first time she attended a Temple

Jim Jones as a toddler in Lynn, Indiana, around 1933. The earliest known portrait. COURTESY STEPHAN JONES.

Jim Jones around 1934, most likely with the family home in the background. COURTESY STEPHAN JONES.

Jim Jones, nine, with playmate and pet at his home in Lynn, 1940. COURTESY STEPHAN JONES.

*Jim Jones posing with
a guitar, approximately
1940.* COURTESY STEPHAN
JONES.

Lynetta Jones. COURTESY
STEPHAN JONES.

Jim Jones's sixth grade class, 1942. Jones is fourth from the left on the bottom row. Note that he is attempting to shine a hand mirror into the camera to ruin the portrait.

Jones's eleventh grade class, 1947. Jones is fourth from the left on the top row. Boyhood friend Don Foreman is on far right in the front row. PHOTOS COURTESY DON FOREMAN.

Jim Jones as he looked when he first began preaching on streetcorners in Richmond, 1946–47. COURTESY STEPHAN JONES.

Marceline Baldwin as a student nurse, soon to be Jim Jones's wife. COURTESY STEPHAN JONES.

Jim Jones at graduation from Richmond High, 1948. COURTESY STEPHAN JONES.

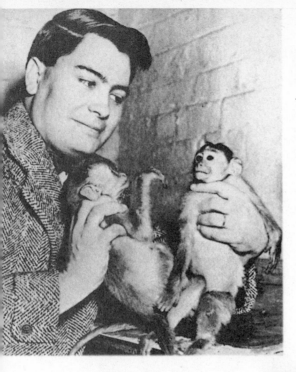

Jim Jones, the twenty-four-year-old minister, selling monkeys door to door, around 1955, to raise money for his fledgling Peoples Temple. COURTESY *San Francisco Examiner*, REPRINTED FROM *Indianapolis Star News*.

Marceline Jones in June 1959, shortly after the birth of her only biological son, Stephan Gandhi Jones.

Stephan and Jimmy Jones, Jr., doing the twist in Belo Horizonte, Brazil, around 1963. PHOTOS COURTESY STEPHAN JONES.

Jim Jones and Stephan, most likely in Indianapolis in 1964. COURTESY STEPHAN JONES.

Associate minister Archie Ijames. PEOPLES TEMPLE FILES.

Associate Minister Jack Beam. PEOPLES TEMPLE FILES.

*Peoples Temple Christian Church in Redwood Valley. The swimming pool was in
the right-hand portion of the building; the Jones family residence was to the rear
of the church.* PEOPLES TEMPLE FILES.

*A communal meal served in the parking lot behind the church, most likely in the
early 1970s. Note Peoples Temple buses in the background.* PEOPLES TEMPLE FILES.

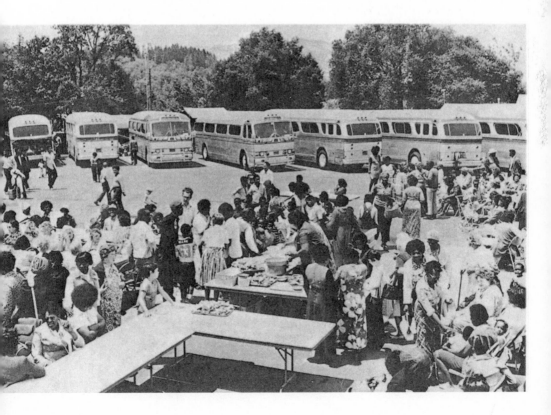

Peoples Temple members streaming up steps of the Capitol in Washington, D.C., during one of the church's cross-country bus "vacation" trips in the mid-1970s. On such trips, the Temple recruited, raised funds and lobbied congressmen. PEOPLES TEMPLE FILES.

The Peoples Temple choir posing for a group photo in front of a pond, mid-1970s. PEOPLES TEMPLE FILES.

Jim and Marceline Jones and son Lew relaxing on a sandbar on a tributary of the Russian River outside Ukiah in August 1966. COURTESY STEPHAN JONES.

A February 1967 portrait of the Jones family in their Redwood Valley home, with Christmas stockings still on the fireplace. COURTESY STEPHAN JONES.

Jimmy Jones and Stephan Jones in junior high school. PHOTOS COURTESY STEPHAN JONES.

Carolyn Moore Layton with Kimo, her three-year-old son by Jones. COURTESY *San Francisco Examiner.*

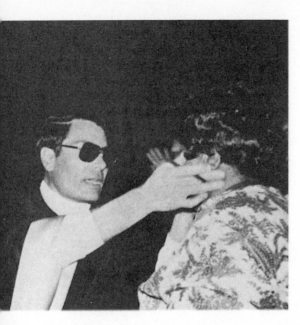

Pastor Jones "healing" an unidentified woman in the Redwood Valley church, September 1972. PEOPLES TEMPLE FILES.

Jones posing for a church photographer, probably in Redwood Valley in the early-mid-1970s. Such photos were sold to members as devotional objects to protect them against a variety of ills. PEOPLES TEMPLE FILES.

Grace Gretch Stoen. GORDON STONE, *San Francisco Examiner.*

Tim Stoen in front of the San Francisco Temple on Geary Boulevard. JUDITH CALSON, *San Francisco Examiner.*

Associated Press photographer Sammy Houston posing in front of portraits of his son, Temple member Bob Houston, who died mysteriously while still in the church, and Bob Houston's daughters, Judy and Patricia Houston. COURTESY *San Francisco Examiner.*

Group portrait around 1973–74, of Grace Stoen, Tim Stoen, Jim Jones and unidentified man holding toddler John Victor Stoen. COURTESY STEPHAN JONES.

Left to right: unidentified child, Bob Houston, Joyce Shaw (holding another unidentified child), and in front Judy Houston (holding doll) and Patricia (holding camera). ROBERT H. "SAMMY" HOUSTON.

Jones on the podium during the early-mid-1970s, filling vials with what is apparently holy oil or water to be sold to visitors.

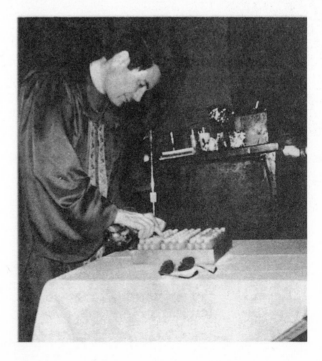

Peoples Temple Church in Los Angeles, at Alvarado and Hoover streets. PEOPLES TEM-
PLE FILES.

service in Redwood Valley, she felt her metal folding chair get harder and harder. When she heard a rooster crow, something dawned on her: she had grown up in Ohio less than a hundred miles from Jim Jones's hometown—these Temple people were primarily transplanted midwesterners, the very type of people she had wanted to escape.

Shaw had been reared in New Carlisle, Ohio, in a socially prominent family. Though conservative by background, Methodist by upbringing, she had kept an open mind about religion and experimented with a pacifistic church. She had attended Miami University of Ohio, married a Hungarian and, before their divorce, become an anticommunist. She had supported Hubert Humphrey for president in 1968 and marched against the war in Vietnam.

When Shaw came to Peoples Temple that spring day in 1970, she still was groping for a framework for her life. Her misgivings about the midwesterners and their rural parochialism soon gave way as she discovered the beauty of the Temple's caring atmosphere. She started to like the homey Hoosiers such as Rheaviana Beam. She could relate to a handful of college-educated people such as Amos. And Jim Jones seemed to live up to his billing as a great humanitarian.

On her birthday, New Year's Eve of 1971, she faced a choice. Should she go to Winterland auditorium in San Francisco for a rock concert or should she drive to Redwood Valley for one of the Temple's monthly birthday parties? When she arrived at the Temple, she found that the church was inaugurating a new practice, issuing membership cards for admission to services. The membership requirements seemed minimal to Shaw, similar to tithing in other churches—donating 25 percent of her income, and agreeing to request the church's permission before taking a vacation. When Shaw enlisted, Jones instructed her to secure a job in the Ukiah area before moving north, evidently so she would not burden the church financially.

Soon she was hired as an eligibility worker at the county welfare department where Sharon Amos and a few other members worked, and she moved into a rented house. Her place needed painting, but before she could tackle the job, a church member called. "Joyce. We really need you. You have to come and work on 'files.' " Obediently she went to alphabetize names and addresses of those who attended meetings, for a master list used to mail newsletters and to solicit donations. It so happened that the tall man she had noticed at her first service also was assigned to work on the files. She knew little about him, except that his name was Bob Houston and he had two lovely daughters. They had chatted once outside church. She thought him pleasant, good-hearted, intelligent. When she looked at him, she thought of a stern Calvinistic minister with a stiff clerical collar and a personality to match. But he spoke her language and knew what was going on in the world. He was not one of those blindly ignorant followers, orgiastically waving his arms, adoring Jim Jones. The social service work and the humanistic values excited him.

It soon became apparent to Shaw that all was not harmony in the Houston household. In a criticism session in front of the church, members accused Houston, falsely, of flirting with another man's wife. The charge gave Jones a convenient bridge to a full airing of the couple's problems. Phyllis was put on the hot seat, too, as the pastor dissected their sex lives and the state of their marriage. When Bob and Phyllis acknowledged that they had not slept together for a year, Jones sent out their daughters to clear the way for the personal questions. "Do you think about sex?" he asked. And Houston replied, "All the time."

Phyllis proclaimed that she did not like her husband or the sexual demands he put on her. Assuming the role of Solomon, Jones asked her: "What are you going to do? How do you feel about Bob interacting with someone else?"

"I don't care, but I don't want it to be blatant," she replied. The couple would stay married in name only, for the sake of the daughters. Agreeing that the arrangement was preferable to divorce, Jones granted each permission to establish extramarital relationships.

Shortly after this unconventional ministerial counseling, Joyce and Bob were driving home together from their work at the church when the inevitable happened. They had been sitting together in the car talking, and one thing led to another. Like good Temple members, they went to Jones for sanction. He approved the affair, merely cautioning discretion.

Late that year, Bob moved out of the family apartment and into a cottage at Mendocino State Hospital, where he worked as a music therapist. He and Shaw announced their wish to live together. Jones gave his blessing—yet only a few weeks later, as though to reinforce his control over their love lives, he withdrew permission. He did not do so directly; he used the newly formed church council, a group of so-called counselors who advised church members with problems and helped enforce Temple policies. The council decreed that the Houstons would have to start living together again for the sake of the community—and presumably the children. Though the council said Joyce and Bob could continue to see each other, Houston was annoyed. Shaw was livid. But every time she objected, members of the council cut her off.

Bob Houston moved back home. He and Phyllis wasted no affection on each other. They lived under constant stress, a dresser jammed between their beds. While Phyllis found a Temple boy friend of her own, Bob's affair with Joyce went on, time and energy permitting.

Like other couples in the Temple, they became as attached to the church as to each other. They undertook tasks with the enthusiasm of new converts, happy to be made an integral part of the organization so quickly. A word from Jones, the hint of a suggestion, might send them off to do his bidding.

When the church had matured beyond the mimeographed bulletin stage, Jones mentioned the need for a magazine. Eagerly Bob Houston, Joyce Shaw, a peace movement veteran named Garry Lambrev and others threw themselves into the project. Houston and Shaw spent more time together, working late in the Redwood Valley publication office, taking long drives to Fort Bragg on the coast to borrow a typesetting machine, or to San Francisco to moonlight on a printing press. Through innovation and long hours, the group turned out the first issue of *The Living Word* in July of 1972. When Jones saw the slick tabloid-sized newspaper, filled with photo features and testimonies, he beamed. "This is really good."

Within a short time, the Temple would purchase its own presses, set up a corporate publishing entity called Valley Enterprises and make some of its college graduates, including Joyce Shaw, full-time publications workers. They would sleep and eat sporadically, work around the clock and fight deadlines and Jones's eccentricities. They bit their tongues when Jones ordered them to destroy ten thousand copies because he thought the word "vivisection" would offend some people, though it was applied to the Temple's rescue of a chimpanzee named Mr. Muggs. (Actually, the chimp had been bought in a pet store.) The publications crew would excitedly inaugurate the *Peoples Forum* newspaper in fall of 1973, and watch it grow to a circulation of tens of thousands, distributed to many neighborhoods in San Francisco. Jones's grand plan would be to compete as a third major daily newspaper in the city to the south. But that was in the future. First, he needed more bodies.

Jones always said that religious people made the best members because they were the most easily conditioned to self-sacrifice, devotion and discipline. From the churches of America, he wrested most of his people. For several reasons, the majority of these were blacks. As a group, blacks were traditionally religious. Blacks had suffered more than other racial groups and were more receptive to an egalitarian message. And, like a number of white Protestants, young blacks were seeking "relevance," activism, even militancy in their churches.

Jones's recruiting patterns reflected his emphasis on blacks. The church canvassed poor and working-class neighborhoods in San Francisco with leaflets, inviting the public to services at rented and borrowed auditoriums and halls.[28] The invitations proclaimed the miracles of Jones and, in alarmist terms, tied the Temple's future presence in San Francisco to their funding appeal. As part of the come-on, newsletters invited the city folk to bring their children on Bay boat cruises or to Redwood Valley for picnics, swimming and horseback riding. Prospective members were asked whether they wanted Jones to establish a church outright in the Bay Area, to join the leadership of an established church or to accept an existing pastorship, as though one had been offered.

The Temple used two buildings on Geary Boulevard in the mainly black Western Addition–Fillmore area. When meetings were held at Benjamin Franklin Jr. High School, a top aide to then-Mayor Joseph Alioto greased the skids with school officials. Crowds in the hundreds wedged into the auditorium. Some meetings lasted so long that the Temple provided box lunches. The Temple arranged other services at the Way Auditorium and across town in Bayview-Hunters Point at the Old Opera House. And Jones tried to borrow facilities from other ministers.

Ironically enough, it was the 1968 assassination of Dr. Martin Luther King, Jr., that presented Jones with his first opportunity to steal black members from established San Francisco churches. When racial feelings heated up following King's murder, Rev. George L. Bedford, black pastor of Macedonia Missionary Baptist Church, invited members of Caucasian churches to come and worship. Jones brought about fifteen of his Temple members to services and asked Bedford for permission to continue the fellowship. Next time, Jones showed up with busloads of members from Ukiah, about 150 in all. The Temple and Macedonia began a Christian exchange program, rotating services between Redwood Valley and San Francisco. The generous Bedford put up Jones at the downtown Hilton Hotel one time and opened his own home to Jones another time. Once, at Jones's request, he put up a married couple and two young white women—all Temple members—at his home.

At the third service at Macedonia, Jones went into a healing performance, using one of Bedford's members as a subject. When the member emerged from the restroom and Temple aides displayed a red blob of "cancer" supposedly passed from the rectum, dozens of Bedford's members watched in awe. Unimpressed, Bedford resolved to stay away from Jones after that. But the damage had been done.

Temple members had been taking down the names and addresses of Macedonia members—even in Bedford's vestibule. Surreptitiously the Temple contacted Bedford's members and invited them to Temple services. At these services, Jones condemned the "mercenary" Baptists and portrayed himself as an antimaterialistic friend of the poor, a minister who banned fur coats and stoles, and who did not demand a dime of anyone. In the worst affront, Jones alleged that Bedford had tried to seduce the two young white women who spent the night at his house.

Though the allegation was patently false, Bedford and his wife Estelle—who had been with him that night—swallowed their outrage. They never confronted Jones; they believed justice would be served, if not in this life, then the next. In the meantime Jones, on the basis of such lies and manufactured miracles, enticed away many of Bedford's congregation members. Some eventually found their way back; still, an estimated 150 to 200 of Bedford's people joined the Temple for life.

Jones committed "sheep stealing" on other black congregations in San Francisco, though not always so brazenly. Several other black ministers lost substantial numbers of members to Peoples Temple too. Jones viewed these practitioners of what he called "the opiate of the masses" as Temple enemies; indeed he made them so. To measure the extent of their antagonism, he had top aides pose as pollsters and newspaper reporters and call the ministers to ask what they thought about Peoples Temple. To try to intimidate his apparent enemies, he arranged anony-

mous phone threats, in which the language was ambiguous enough for a
legal out if anyone were caught. At least one minister, Rev. Hannibal
Williams, reported to police a death threat that he believed had originated
within the Temple.

In their complaints about Jones, the black ministers could not avoid
the appearance of jealousy of a white preacher who had been pulling
members out of the pews of black churches. Some of their own community
leaders brushed aside their grievances about the Temple breaking up
families and fleecing Christians of property, businesses and income. By
strategically selecting his friends in the black community, by building an
image as an activist church leader, by infiltrating the Council of Churches,
Jones left the traditional black ministers with little recourse. They could
not deter the Temple aggression without sounding petty or racist. Those
who dared fight him were intimidated one way or another. The approach
typified Jones; he conquered those he could conquer, and befriended,
deceived or compromised those he could not.

For his most ambitious raiding attempt ever, Jones loaded his followers aboard their fleet of buses one day in 1971 and rolled them day and
night toward the City of Brotherly Love.

In late July, more than two hundred Temple members piled out of
the buses at the late Father Divine's Woodmont estate. Many had never
seen such splendor. The thirty-two-room mansion was set like a gemstone
amid formal gardens, fountains and lakes on a high point of land overlooking the Schuylkill River. Compared to the Redwood Valley church, Woodmont qualified as an empire, the epitome of the materialism Jones attacked from the pulpit.

The Temple members had been housed at the Peace Mission's
downtown hotels, where all had proceeded harmoniously until they aggressively began to stalk the buildings, jotting down the names of Mother
Divine's followers. The longer they stayed, the bolder they became.

When the Temple contingent arrived at Woodmont for a tour of the
shrine housing Father Divine's body, Jones executed stage two of his
assault. Through sculptured bronze doors, the visitors entered a burial
chamber with 24-karat gold tiles on granite walls. Two bronze angels
spread their wings atop a limestone sarcophagus: the resting place for the
millionaire god. Jones and his hostess paused to read a gold-inlaid inscrip-
tion memorializing the words of Divine: ". . . Father coming to the country
that is supposed to be the country of the free. . . ." Jones sarcastically
repeated, *"Supposed* to be the country of the free." This irreverence
offended Mother Divine, but she let it pass. Then, as the others cleared
out, Jones informed Mother Divine that his five-foot-ten white body was
in fact the reincarnation of the cherubicly black Father Divine. Jones was
staking his claim to the Kingdom of Peace.

Mother Divine, a gentle and pretty blond woman of forty-five,
handled the matter delicately. "Well," she conceded. "Father *is* supposed

to be in every one of us." When Jones twice insisted that he was Father Divine in a new body, Mother Divine informed him, "No one can take Father's place. . . . You're no more [special] than anyone else."

That night, during a banquet in the Crystal Ballroom of the Divine Lorraine Hotel, as Peace Mission people sang praises of Father Divine, Temple members raised their arms and swayed in rapture, channeling their adoration directly at Jones. Mother Divine sat horrified. Temple member after Temple member stood to give testimonies to Jones. These little spiels were so ludicrous that Temple members had chortled among themselves during rehearsal. Still, the Temple gained control of the banquet. Finally, Jones arose and, puffing himself up, declared, "Father Divine has conferred his mantle on me. We are from the same celestial plane and are messengers. His spirit has come to rest in my body."

Feeling like an outsider in her own church, Mother Divine was beside herself. Vibrations told her this man not only was making a false claim to be Father Divine, but was in fact the "other fellow"—the Devil. Anger seized her followers. She told Jones, privately, that he should leave in the interest of peace. The Temple contingent departed abruptly, without violence, but also without its coup.

Though no longer welcome, Jones did not bow to defeat or abandon his idea. After the return trip to California, he began a new campaign. He told Temple members that Mother Divine had rejected him only because he refused to have sex with her. She had torn open her blouse, he said, and thrown herself upon Father Divine's sarcophagus, pleading, begging for him—but he would not stoop to it. (Actually, he and Mother Divine were never even alone together.)

The Temple then wrote letters to those whose names were procured in Philadelphia, impugning Mother Divine's purity and repeating Jones's claims. In June of 1972, several nearly empty Temple buses returned to Philadelphia; room had been left for Peace Mission defectors. Temple recruiters invaded Peace Mission hotels and restaurants with armloads of leaflets. Confrontations between the two pacifistic groups sometimes became physical. One woman slapped someone. Some Temple recruiters got doused with water. Having been tossed out of the Peace Mission establishments, the Temple contingent took to the buses and circled the blocks. Leaning out windows, they shouted through megaphones: "Welcome. This is Peoples Temple. The pastor is Jim Jones, the great humanitarian. We are leaving on Sunday at three P.M. You're invited to Redwood Valley."

As membership thefts go, the Temple invasion was petty. Only some dozen Peace Mission members climbed onto Temple buses for California. Jones gained no more than a handful of sweet old ladies who would need housing in Temple nursing homes. Further, to make the defections stick, he needed to substantiate his claim to be a renovated Father Divine. To make them feel welcome, he had the Temple choir learn Peace Mission songs, with appropriate substitutions of his name for Divine's. And he had his followers call him "Father," and Marceline "Mother."

As a further accommodation, the Temple held banquets, though with more of a California potluck flavor than the Woodmont touch. At one, many elderly former followers of Divine were seated together. Suddenly, without warning, Jones hollered at Jack Beam's wife. "Rheaviana, you lied to me! Drop dead!" Rheaviana Beam fell to the linoleum floor.

A young black man leaped up, saying, "I can't believe this." Jones flashed angry eyes at him. "You too!" A second body toppled to the floor. When a white man leaped up to protest, Jones yelled, "You too!" Same effect.

The old ladies were petrified. Father Divine had never dropped anyone dead, except maybe the judge who sent him to jail. However, Jones soon showed his forgiveness. He resurrected the "dead" one by one, and each issued a warning to the crowd, lest the message be lost on them. Said Rheaviana Beam: "You better believe Father. You should never tell a lie because he will strike you down."

In return for housing in care homes, the Peace Mission people gave the Temple everything they owned, including their shares in Mission properties in Pennsylvania, New York and New Jersey. Temple attorneys actually drew up papers transferring title to the Temple, but Jones ran into a legal tangle: Father Divine had set up joint tenancy for all property. Many members owned only minuscule shares of each mission property, and upon their deaths, the shares reverted to the mission. There was no value in pressing the claim. It was the final disappointment for Jones. His instant dynasty had been denied him.

PART THREE

THE HEAVENLY EMPIRE

Campaigns have been launched promoting kindness [to animals], and yet we have among us those who painstakingly wrap the lethal dose in tempting tidbits. . . .

LYNETTA JONES
"The Poisoner"

FIFTEEN

The Hair of the Raven

It was Sunday morning in 1971, shortly before eleven o'clock. Clouds of dust billowed over the Temple parking lot as car after car pulled off Road E. Soon the metal folding chairs were filled. The microphones were in place, the long cords in order. The musicians fussed with their instruments, then an impatient hush exploded into applause as Jim Jones took the stage wearing satiny red robes over a white turtleneck sweater. A swath of hair angled across his forehead. Sunglasses with fashionable dark wire-rims masked his eyes. He took a position behind the pulpit where a high barstool-like padded seat made him appear to be standing.

Upon receiving the proper cue, Loretta Cordell, plain-looking and pinched-faced, dipped her head in an imaginary downbeat and started to pound on the organ. Others played guitars and wind instruments. Bob Houston, with his trombone, stood tall among them.

With his arms keeping time, Jones led the singing, his baritone voice rising and falling to the tune "Amen."

"We live and die for free-eee-dom.

We live and die for free-eee-dom!"

Then a sweet chorus, dominated by women and children:

"Free-eee-dom. *Free-eee-dom. Free-dom.*"

Peoples Temple was becoming a nation unto itself. It could claim its own president for life, its own unique mix of people, its own institutions, its creeds and liturgy, its dietary and sexual practices, its justice and educational systems. Jim Jones had fashioned his Temple with input from many: Jesus Christ, Karl Marx, Father Divine, Joseph Stalin, Adolf Hitler, Mahatma Gandhi, Martin Luther King, Jr., and Fidel Castro; also Lynetta

Jones, Myrtle Kennedy, Marceline Baldwin, and a Pentecostal lady from Lynn, Indiana. For Peoples Temple was in essence a reflection of what he thought best.

The church and many of its people had been bonded permanently to an extraordinary man who was a victim of his own experience. He swallowed whole his environment and personal history, and spit out bits of it every time he spoke. His single greatest ache was the loneliness and lack of acceptance he felt as a child. It was no great mystery why communism and communalism appealed to Jim Jones. People were his labor of love, his hedge against loneliness, and ultimately against history.

From the pulpit, Jones bombarded his people with almost impressionistic messages. Because the catch words of love, brotherhood, unity and equality defied challenge, his contradictory messages defied analysis. Sexual and family identities were dashed. "Break down the barriers," Jones cried. "Lose your ego. Become selfless. Don't establish superficial relationships on the outside." As he kept track of the personal lives of hundreds of members, he not only showed them he cared for each of his "children," he also located the wedge that would alienate them from family and society. They confessed to each other, and criticized each other openly, purging old values. They lived together, worked together in love, and when it was in the interest of the Temple, informed on each other.

The exhilaration of having a family and a cause that could save the world kept them going around the clock, giving until they were spent. But it was Jones's personal magic—above all the black magic, webs of ideas and disguised threats—that weaned people from their pasts and tied them to the Temple's future.

Total commitment was demanded piece by piece. As he declared in a 1970 newsletter: "One must not worship things. Treat heat and cold alike. Pain and blessing are just alike. . . . Have firm convictions. Don't vacillate!" Only thoughts existed and mattered, he said. "If your mind is negative in attitude . . . it will produce disease and likewise if positive, there is a great deal of information to indicate that one can almost obtain eternal youth, the cessation of cellular death. . . ."

Jones promised essentially eternal life and protection. And he buttressed his promise with the concept of reincarnation. It helped explain the deification of Jones, the presence of a God-force in his body. It also allowed him to borrow from the auras of great historical and religious figures—pharaohs, Christ, Buddha, Lenin among them—and claim to be their reincarnation. But most significantly, he used the concept to comfort those members who might have to suffer and give their bodies for the cause. Death was not final, he told them. And in so convincing them, he grasped control of individual lives that went qualitatively beyond that of any world leader in history.

"We live and die for free-eee-dom," they sang.
"Free-eee-dom. *Free-eee-dom. Free-dom.*"

"No more poverty!" Jones shouted, then led the chorus again. He talked over the singing, through the singing, directing them, bringing them down the home stretch so he could speak:

"I'm here to show you as a sample and example that you can bring yourself up with your own bootstraps," he began to approving shouts.

"And you can become your own God!" he promised. "Not in condescension but in resurrection and upliftment from whatever economic condition, injustice or racism or servitude which you have had to endure. Within *you* rest the keys of deliverance.

"We ask for no condescending saviors," he went on, criticizing Father Divine, "that has been pawned off on every breast. And I, God that came from earth of earth, this dust of this toils and fields, hardships of labor, from the lowest of economic positions, from the misery of poverty near the railroad tracks, I came to show you that the only God you need is within you."

"Yeah," they cried, the male voices overpowering. "Right!!"

"None other!" Jones repeated. "That's my purpose in being here. When that transition comes, there shall be no need for Gods, any other kind of ideology. Religion, the opiate of the people, shall be removed from the consciousness of mankind. There shall no longer be any need for anything religious when freedom comes."

"Yeah." They nodded heads and waved hands, revived. They were with him every step of the way.

"I came in the power of God in religion. . . . All the power you said God had, I have. [I've] come to make one final dissolution, one final elimination of all religious feeling. Until I have eradicated it from the face of the earth, I will do all the miracles you said your God would do and never did." His voice quickened. "I shall heal you of all the diseases, [provide the cures] that you prayed for that never happened. . . ."

Pausing, he reminded them all how he warned a woman and saved her from fire, how he had had a crippled woman dancing around the room. As he addressed his people, he scanned the faces before him, hundreds of them, his son Stephan in his shirt and tie nearby with the microphones, the rest of his family, his faithful friends Jack Beam and Archie Ijames, Grace Stoen with her arms folded over her bulging abdomen, Bob Houston peering through his black-rimmed glasses, and many more. Even through his glasses, Jones's gaze could be felt, through the force of his presence and the voice, that tool that kept them in their hard metal seats when their backs ached, their legs went numb and their bladders and bowels threatened to burst.

"I see some," he said raising his voice, "are not aware what God is. The only thing that brings perfect freedom, justice and equality, perfect love in all its beauty and holiness is socialism. *Socialism!*"

A roar of assent echoed through the church and out the louvered windows opened to pick up a cross-draft. Their hands and voices pushed him onward:

"I have taken myself a body, the same one that walked on the [ancient] plains . . . of whom Solomon said his hair was as black as a raven, and he would shave as Isaiah said, 7:20, with a razor. I *come* shaved with a razor! I *come* with the black hair of a raven! I come as God socialist!"

The shouts—"All right. *All right.* Yeah"—drowned him out.

Proceeding more deliberately now, as if clarifying a point, he said, "I shall show you, from time to time, proofs of that, so that you will have no further need of religion because the highest authority tells you. I come to you doing all the things you have ever imagined God to do and you have never seen done. . . .

"It's beautiful to know God is a socialist worker. He is one of the people. He is all that you have desired, all the freedom, justice, all the sensitivity in minds.

"And I must say it's a great effort to be God."

There was not a single snicker from the audience.

For his first miracle of the day, Jones called out a man named John to convince people that nothing, no matter how seemingly insignificant, is lost in the consciousness of a socialist worker God. "My brother John came to me last week," he said gesturing to the black man. "You were concerned that something was lost. He lost it miles and miles away. Well, my spirit retrieved it for you today."

Then, to hoots and howls, Jones held out an object. John came for his miraculously recovered credit card. "God damn!" another man shouted in amazement.

With organ music and people keeping time with their hands, Jones shouted over them like some Bible thumper, urging people not to hate because it boomerangs, decrying loopholes that let the rich escape taxes, calling for freedom from the bondage of the aristocratic rich. Then, in frantic and seemingly incoherent fashion, Jones railed about the theft of the Bill of Rights, the spread of social disease, drug abuse by eight- and nine-year-olds and drug pushing to fourth graders even here, in rural Redwood Valley. No heavenly God could cope with those things, could he? He reminded them of his own miracles and parapsychology—and social goals—all in one breathless rush.

"If you don't need a God, fine. But if you need a God, I'm going to nose out that God. He's a false god. I'll put the right concept in your life.

"You understand the mystery? If you don't have a God and you're already believing that you have to build a society to eliminate poverty, racism and injustice and war, I will not bother you.

"But," he exclaimed, "if you're holding onto that sky God, I'll nose him out, ten lengths every time!!!

"Will you tell me you believe in God out there?" he shrieked in anger at imaginary doubters. "So what? What's your sky God ever done? Two out of three nations in the world are hungry. Misery in every one of your homes. . . ." His voice rose to a crescendo: "The only happiness you've found is when you've come to this earth God!"

Waiting for their cries to die down, he went on. "When you came to your socialist worker father, some of you never knew the fulfillment of happiness, you never knew that anyone cared. Your children were in difficulties. No one came to the jails. You prayed to your sky God and he never heard your prayers. You asked and begged and pleaded in your suffering, and he never gave you any food. He never gave you a bed, and He never provided a *home.* But *I, Your socialist worker God,* have given you *all* these things."

Then, in a display of power, as though to demonstrate that no harm would befall blasphemers, he slammed a black Bible to the floor. There were cheers. "No fears of doing that," he said, almost out of breath. "Say what you feel. Tap all the resources of energy within you!

"No, it's not sacred. You won't die if. . . ." He flung the book down again. "If you drop it. You won't die if you stand on it." He put both feet on the book, the toes of his shoes hanging over the edge, and tottered a little.

His audience delighted in the performance, reveled in his rebelliousness; they too were above the Bible that had guided the lives of so many of them. "You won't die if you jump up and down on it."

Jones calmed himself purposefully. "I talk pretty loud. Hope I didn't strain your ears."

They laughed and spoke in unison, "All right."

He told them, "I want you to realize that *you* must be the scripture, that any other scripture other than you and the word that I am now imparting is idolatry."

"Yeah!" They were with him again. He urged and they urged back. They were one.

"I know where I am going. I know what I believe. And I know what I'm doing," Jones hollered, straining for a peak. "And I've got a principle that will carry me on if the world passes away.

"When your world has failed you, I'll be standing," he murmured, braking himself, savoring each word as if it were being handed down from the Almighty. "Because I am freedom. I am peace. I am justice. . . . I AM GOD!!!!"

They went wild, cheering, cheering, cheering.

"See socialism as God in me," he told them. "Look upon me harmoniously. Every service I've said that socialism has a higher dimension than the three dimensions. You don't have to worry about that God up there," he told those who still believed in a heavenly Being. *"I* can heal your back when your spine's wasting away and your doctor says you can't be helped, and I cure it. *You're free! You're free of God! I want you to penalize that old God up there!"* He was ranting now, shouting at the heavens, challenging.

"If you're all-powerful, *send* one of your magic wands," he mocked. *"Send* your electric lightning. *Send* your thunder. Let it rain!"

He stopped to give God a chance to perform. Nothing happened. The people chortled.

That contest won, Jones took it one step further. "When I was laying on springs with no covers, and the rain was pouring through the roof of my old ramshackle house, and they told me to pray to God . . . there was no God that came. The rain kept pouring. I had a beam of consciousness. I said there shouldn't be any poor; there shouldn't be any private property."

The pain of poverty and disadvantage flowed from his voice; a matter-of-fact righteousness, vengeance, swelled his chest. "Every time I take a drive in the country, and I see 'Private Property—No Trespassing,' I take those signs down." Approving laughter all around. "When I want to trespass, I just trespass. Because they *robbed* the people to get it! They took it from my people, the Indians! They came and shot down our babies! Raped our mothers!" His words boomed like cannon fire. "They took our babies and stripped off the scalps!"

He jumped from Indians to the preciousness of children of mixed races, to sex. "It's come up that there have been bisexual and homosexual patterns [among church members]," he said. "And we got somebody coming in that won't tell the facts. And they say . . . I am a great lover. Now I know what you told me." He pauses, and there is silence. One by one, he points them out with his index finger, one cluck of his tongue for each. He was making their admissions for them, those homosexuals, latent and otherwise.

Raising his volume preacherly and righteously, he said, "There can be nothing going on in the bedroom, until mankind is liberated! There's no freedom in that bedroom! I've come to one of you! I've come to all of you! As I said, you'd all be happier to admit it."

"Right," a woman called out.

"Right," a man called out. "Right" came a whole chorus of voices.

SIXTEEN

Wiring the Town

This little nation's dealings with the outside world were characterized by paranoia, pragmatism and, always, concealment of the Temple's inner workings. For self-protection, Jones emphasized a good public image and warm relations with the news media and law enforcement officials. The

Temple wanted to be seen as a purely do-gooder church with social services. But Jones's need for secrecy conflicted with his desire for power and notoriety.

In relatively conservative Mendocino County, the church as a matter of strategy broke into the Republican power structure. It did the same in San Francisco with a liberal Democratic administration. Jones built peace treaties and alliances across the political spectrum, and called in political debts with the aggression of a backroom power broker. He knew how to woo politicians and public officials, and how to push a bureaucrat, but he also usually knew when to back off. His clever knack for taking the offensive while pleading persecution proved effective. However, his judgment remained flawed by overreaction and, as his power grew, by overkill.

In a hostile environment, a strong political base became a necessity. In the rural area of Ukiah–Redwood Valley, Jones for the first time realized that his relatively modest numbers of people, if utilized properly, could bring a measure of power to his church.

To build a positive image, Jones required his people to be well groomed and clean cut, to register to vote and to be model citizens. Many joined the PTA. The Temple also undertook good works with a fervor that defeated their supposed desire for anonymity. Home-baked cakes and candy were packed and delivered to politicians, government officials and just about anyone else whose good will was sought. Sometimes a cake would just appear on a person's doorstep with a friendly note, incidentally praising Jim Jones. A death in the family, a family crisis, a personal success—anything would fetch cakes and cookies from Peoples Temple. It became a joke around town that if you had not received a cake from Peoples Temple, something had to be wrong with you.

The timing of the gifts was uncanny. Supervisor Al Barbero received a cake the moment he came home from the hospital, though he had not told a soul his discharge date. There was, of course, a logical explanation. Several Temple members, including Walter and Patty Cartmell, worked at the town's only answering service. Church members had access to all the ambulance calls in town; and after hours, the service took calls for a number of Ukiah doctors. Messages for almost a hundred accounts —many the most prominent people in town—were dutifully logged. Temple members could use the service as they wished, not only for "good works," but presumably for Jones's revelations as well.

Jones was never one to underestimate the power of a well-aimed letter. He would direct letter-writing campaigns from the pulpit in the early days of Ukiah, and later, with the addition of college-educated zealots, the process became more streamlined and institutionalized. Thousands were routinely mailed under the direction of Dick Tropp, an English professor at Santa Rosa Community College. The church determined the targets of the letter campaigns and the approaches to take; sample letters were provided for guidance. In 1970, for instance, members were asked to write Congressmen about a host of laws regarding civil liberties. Those involved would gather about once a week and, with a variety of stationery, envelopes, typewriters and pens, each cranked out dozens of letters. Sometimes they borrowed names from telephone books, taking a last name from one person and a first name from another. Often they wrote letters simply praising public figures, tailoring the letters to their political leanings. A right-winger most likely would receive a law-and-order letter, a progressive an antiwar letter.

In order to get more than bland form responses, the Temple sent multiple letters, some with small gifts such as candy. And often Jones would write. The goal was to get a personal response praising the Temple. These were kept behind plastic in a thick binder; and excerpts were reproduced in Temple public relations literature. Apparent endorsements from public figures in Ukiah, San Francisco, statewide and nationally were employed to impress other public officials of potential assistance.

Typical of the responses was one from then-Governor Ronald Reagan, whom Jones would deplore for shutting down Mendocino State Hospital, thus putting a number of Temple members out of work:

> *Dear Pastor Jones:*
> *I just wanted to take a moment to express my appreciation to the members of your congregation for their many good letters regarding the roses I recently delivered to the wife of one of our servicemen. . . .*

One of the most prized letters came from FBI Director J. Edgar Hoover thanking the Temple for candy at Christmastime. The Temple used donations to stimulate letters from law officials too. Then-San Francisco Police Chief Alfred Nelder thanked Jones for $50 for the family of a slain officer. Ukiah Police Chief Donn Saulsbury thanked "Jim" for $225 donated to the city police reserves for gear. The Temple collected letters from newspaper columnists, including the late Drew Pearson and his successor Jack Anderson, as well as an impressive lineup of politicians, from President Richard Nixon to congressmen all over the nation.

At a grass-roots level and in the chambers of bureaucracy, the Temple's most effective public relations instruments were the people themselves. The Ukiah area was saturated with church members, especially in government offices. Among other places, members landed jobs in the sheriff's office, where Phyllis Houston was a dispatcher, and in the Probation Department, where Sandy Bradshaw was a deputy probation officer. Members found jobs in the private sector too, several dozen of them in the big lumber mills. Their co-workers heard rumors about heavy tithing and queer goings-on at the Temple. But Temple members tended to be good workers, though they sometimes would be exhausted and less than productive after bus trips and late meetings. Co-workers of Temple members at the mills sometimes would stumble upon them curled up in quiet places, sneaking some shuteye.

Jones and his top aides used personal contacts to build a reputation among influential people in town. They touched all bases, from the most liberal judges to the most conservative political dabblers, such as John Birch Society leader Walter Heady. The friendship of Heady and Jones was based largely upon personality. Heady's raspy declarations and iron-clad conviction—regardless of his right-wing beliefs—impressed Jones; here was an enemy with whom he could hit it off as a human being. Heady visited the Jones household, and Jones ordered a church newsletter article about Heady and his wife. Jones even invited Heady to make presentations and show Bircher films at the Redwood Valley and San Francisco churches under the justification of "knowing your enemy."

Jones and Heady seldom talked about Richard Nixon because they agreed that presidents were puppets of "big government." Yet in his rambling phone conversations with Marge Boynton, head of the Republican Central Committee, Jones let her know that as a registered Republican he was supporting Nixon for president. Marge Boynton knew of Tim Stoen's Republican party and Rotary Club work, and she met other Temple members who helped with local antidrug programs and the Heart Fund. Some church members did volunteer work for the Republicans, and one, a popular schoolteacher named Jean Brown, sat on the Republican Central Committee.

Boynton first encountered Jim Jones through her husband, a children's dentist to whom the Temple sent so many patients that Marceline reserved a block of three to four hours office time each week.

The case that most deeply touched the dentist involved a fourteen-year-old runaway who supposedly had been peddling her body. The Temple picked up the stray one weekend, then brought her to the dentist first thing Monday morning because her teeth were rotting. Six sessions later, all paid for by the Temple, she had been transformed into a proper young lady.

The Temple's good deeds likewise impressed Sheriff Reno Bartolomie, who noticed that Temple kids from broken homes and probation departments stayed out of trouble. And he admired the church for weaning people from drugs in a county where marijuana was fast becoming one of the biggest cash crops. To enhance its image and help the prisoners, the church donated almost $400 for a stereo-radio for county jail inmates. Stoen became a political supporter of the sheriff—and Bartolomie and Jones became friendly, if not friends.

The Temple found the relationship beneficial. At least two members, including Stoen, became reserve deputies and received concealed weapons permits. Then Stoen asked the sheriff for at least a dozen and perhaps as many as twenty additional gun permits so Temple members could guard large sums of money collected at services. The Temple was granted a handful.

The relationship with Bartolomie was amicable, so the Temple supported him for reelection in June 1974. But they were not sure he was going to win, so they supported his opponent, Tom Jondahl, as well. The strategy proved prudent. Jondahl, police chief of Fort Bragg on the coast, upset the longtime sheriff and took office the following year.

Jones and Stoen also established a good rapport with the *Ukiah Daily Journal.* Jones had made a point of inviting Managing Editor George Hunter and his reporter wife Kathy to his home when the Temple first came to town. The Temple showed particular attention to Kathy Hunter, and she in turn wrote favorable stories about the church. The reporter had ongoing health problems, including back pains that drove her to alcohol. Whenever she was hospitalized, the Temple sent her cakes and get-well cards. And while others in town sometimes dismissed her as an eccentric or a crackpot, Jones seemed to treat her with respect—though he called her a drunk behind her back. For every unsavory rumor about the Temple, George Hunter got a friendly phone call from the church, or a helpful news briefing from county counsel Tim Stoen. The grapevine always had the Temple fixing a widow's broken fence or mowing someone's lawn; and there was scuttlebutt too about some racial incident or harassment.

To Hunter, the Temple was not entirely unlike other churches. For example, it advertised its Sunday services in the *Journal.* But Jones took a more active interest in politics than most ministers. Before each election, Jones would call the editor and ask him which candidates deserved the vote of Temple members. Usually, Hunter would laugh and say, "Look over the field, and make up your own mind." Still, Jones never missed a flattering election eve call.

In political circles, it was common knowledge that the church voted as a block, a fact since substantiated by a check of precinct records. Temple members made political contributions; the church bought tickets to Republican fund raisers. When the voting age was reduced to eighteen, the Temple drew up a list of newly eligible voters so the Republican party could register them. And despite all the Republican flag-waving, Jones would support Democrats, too, and some of his members were registered as Democrats.[29]

Marge Boynton figured the Temple controlled two hundred to three hundred votes in one area alone. Anyone could see that a few hundred votes could have a very substantial impact on the outcome of a first supervisorial district election with 2,500 to 3,000 voters.

From his pulpit, Jones would discuss the various candidates and issues and, nominally, solicit the congregation's reaction. "Do we want to vote for . . . ?" he would ask, then shake his head no or nod yes, or point his thumbs up or down, afraid to verbalize his choice in case he was being taped. To be sure that his message was executed, he had church secretaries phone members on election eve. At the next service, everyone was required to bring a polling place receipt showing they had cast their ballot.

One of the biggest potential trouble spots for the Temple was the county Social Services Department, the agency responsible for overseeing the Temple care homes. Dennis Denny, the director of social services, was not impressed by the church's do-good reputation and was wary of the presence of five to eight Temple members in his own agency. He had come from Orange County in 1969 with experience in jousting with religious organizations and cult groups that tried to exploit or defraud the welfare system. And it did not take him long to conclude that Jones had settled in Ukiah in large part because of the Mendocino Plan, a nationally known program designed to get mental hospital patients into local board-and-care homes. Denny estimated that through about ten care homes with up to fifteen patients each, Jones had a tremendous revenue source, plus a new source of recruits. He frankly warned Jones not to abuse the system.

By and large, Jones's people seemed to abide by the rules. The Temple-run homes were clean, and when Denny's inspectors showed up unannounced, they found everyone in the homes to be eligible for aid. They did not know that the operators were required by written agreement to turn over all extra money to the Temple—and that some were squeezing every last dime out of the homes. Denny believed that he was staying on top of the Temple situation, in part through a Temple member on his staff, Sharon Amos. Seemingly playing double agent, she leaked him information. For instance, when Mendocino State Hospital was closed down in 1972 and church members lost jobs there, Amos told him about top-level Temple meetings to figure out ways to recoup the resulting loss of income. The solution was simple: with state aid, the Temple would set up foster homes housing orphans or problem children imported from the San Francisco Bay Area. Soon, as planned, probation offices from all over California were sending children to the Temple, bypassing Denny. The welfare director told the Temple that they had to license their foster homes. After twenty-four months of being stalled, he threatened prosecution. The Temple then circumvented the law by securing "guardianships" for the children, obviating the need for foster home licensing.

Several other problems put Denny at odds with the Temple. In one, a Temple child was beaten by a Temple member with a cat-o'-nine-tails of copper wires. There also were reports of patients at Temple homes being herded to church services. And Denny got a call from a woman who said that her brother had been "abducted" from a Temple care home and farmed out to a Pasadena convalescent hospital. The church invariably backed off, but Denny began getting late night and early morning phone calls from Jones. In defense, the minister took the offense; he attempted to make Denny feel guilty for impeding good works. Once, however, he said in a 2:00 A.M. call, "Do you know what God does to those who destroy his humanitarian efforts?"

"I'm taking that as a personal threat against my body," Denny said, and reported it to the authorities. Nothing came of it.

SEVENTEEN

The System at Work

In just a few years, Jones had mastered the trick of being all things to all people. The church population had climbed from about 150 settlers to perhaps as many as 3,000 members by the mid-1970s. The racial makeup shifted from mostly white in the early California years to predominantly black because the Temple, as always, built its following on the· revival circuit, and that circuit, in California's urban centers, was more black than white.

Most California recruits were people of little education who sought to ease the aches of a hard life or to smooth the transition to the hereafter. The largest numbers of people and funds came from the black neighborhoods of San Francisco and Los Angeles, but the Temple also established outposts in Fresno and other cities in the white Central Valley, California's version of the Midwest. The people came for the healings, the charisma of Jones and, to a lesser extent, the interracial experience and activist religion. Black or white, they were largely working class, people with no earthly hopes beyond a decent job, a family, perhaps eventually owning a home. Only a minority were on welfare, and a substantial portion had marketable skills or small businesses of their own.

These people, 70 to 80 percent of them black, constituted the Temple rank and file, "the troops," as they became known by outsiders in Jones's political heyday. They set up the chairs for the meetings and filled the offering boxes. They brought in thousands of dollars in the form of donations, tithes, signed-over government checks and property, personal savings and possessions that could be converted to cash at flea markets or church-owned secondhand stores.

Such people were the lifeblood of the Temple—its primary source of sustenance and the proof of its espoused social aim of lifting burdens from oppressed peoples. Most made the leap from Christianity to Jones's quasi-socialism in part because they were responding to the form rather than the substance of his services, in part because they were exposed to political reeducation. Yet despite all Jones's talk of integration and brotherhood, his condemnation of elitism, very few of these people were elevated to the church hierarchy.

To mobilize a smooth-running organization, Jones surrounded himself with several dozen mostly white, privileged young people in their twenties and thirties. He relied increasingly upon them because they were effective. They brought him skills in law, accounting, nursing, teaching, music and administration. They carried out public relations and financial duties and more mundane chores while bringing in good salaries from outside jobs. He, in turn, bestowed responsibilities, and power and personal attention on them.

The most trusted of the trusted around Jones were those guarding his secrets. Information was the measure of an individual's power in the Temple, and the most sensitive information was distributed on a need-to-know basis. Since the Indiana days, Jones had been relying quite heavily on Patty Cartmell, a portly mother with a coarse wit that made her an ideal partner for Jack Beam in raucous church skits. She always stayed close to Jones on the buses or in services, yet she was more than the simple bundle of loyalty she often appeared to be.

Her true role had remained a secret until the early 1970s when Jones established a hierarchy in his socialistic model—from planning commission (p.c.) to church council of guidance counselors to "staff." Staff was at the top, under the direction of Cartmell. This select group undertook sensitive missions for Jones. Intelligence, resourcefulness, absolute loyalty and unquestioning obedience were their qualifications. At peak, only eight to ten members achieved such status. All were women, all were white. Virtually all were college-educated.

One of the earliest arrivals was Sandy Bradshaw. In 1970 she was working for Head Start in the Western Addition of San Francisco and living with a black man named Lee Ingram. Both were New Yorkers, Lee from Bedford-Stuyvesant, Sandy from Syracuse. Sandy, at twenty-four, considered herself a socialist and an atheist, though she had been raised a Methodist. She first rejected God at the age of seven when she wrote a nasty letter criticizing Him for letting her dog die. When a woman at work told her about the Temple healings, she shut her ears. But she listened closely to an account of Jones's all-night drug counseling sessions. That was worth a trip to Redwood Valley.

Then she was impressed with the church's detoxification program and its attempts to feed and help the poor. She also responded favorably to Jones, who exuded warmth and compassion while remaining uncompromising. He did not sugarcoat. "If you don't like it, leave," he said in effect.

The stumbling block for Bradshaw was the very idea of joining a church, but she and Ingram gave it a try. Almost immediately, they took a major step at Jones's request—they married. As an interracial couple, they would be highly visible in Ukiah, and living together without legal sanction would be undesirable.

Sandy's dedication soon attracted Jones's attention. While working at Juvenile Hall with Patty Cartmell, she often covered while Cartmell was occupied with Temple business. Jones could think of no better way of immersing this new recruit in the church than by asking her to join the staff. She accepted the honor.

Her baptism involved cloak-and-dagger work. The explanation: though Jim could do all the revelations and healings on his own, they sapped such tremendous energy that for years, Cartmell had collected information to give his powers a respite and save him from self-destruction. Now, with the church expanding, she needed help.

On their first outing together, Cartmell and Bradshaw visited a house in Pittsburg, California. Their task was to weasel their way into the home of a person who had written Jones and would be attending a service; they would try to collect as much information as possible about the furnishings, the interior spaces, the residents, their health, their family background, their friends—anything that could be gleaned by total strangers in a few minutes of snooping around or asking questions under other pretenses.

Bradshaw mistakenly assumed she would simply observe her partner at work. When the door of the Pittsburg house opened, Cartmell, without the slightest warning, said, "Can we get a drink, please? My friend's pregnant." Caught off guard with her hands in her coat pockets, Bradshaw quickly pushed the material into a bulge in front, and the two went about their intelligence-gathering.

By that time, Carolyn Layton already was helping Cartmell gather "supplemental information" for Jones's miracles. Still others would be added to the inner circle and assigned various geographic jurisdictions and duties. Among them were Sharon Amos, who worked at the Social Services Department, Cartmell's daughter Trish, Christine Lucientes and Teri Buford, a Navy-brat-turned-pacifist.

To be on staff, these women necessarily acclimated themselves to the philosophy: "The ends justify the means." Their jobs were not pleasant. They had to accept, in essence, what some organizations call "heavenly deception." Only by keeping their attention and their ethics riveted to the greater good—the advancement of Peoples Temple and the principles espoused by Jim Jones—could they have brought themselves to help deceive so many people. Only by surrendering moral reservations could they lure poor black people to the church and help strip them of their possessions in the name of liberating or saving them. The rationalizations were fed to them directly and indirectly by Jones. Because of the intensely secretive nature of their work, they had no opportunity to explore it with outsiders. And they could not trust each other.

Probably more so than any other members, the staff was isolated. Scorned as elitists in an egalitarian organization, they were seen as·a villainous secret police. Sometimes they were blamed for the unpopular deeds and policies of Jones, which is just what he wanted.

Because they could do tremendous damage if they turned on him, Jones selected them carefully. He praised them and sometimes flattered them. Their biggest reward was trust—getting to know him, to see his frailties, to love him in spite of them. He also made love to some and convinced more than one that she alone would have absorbed his attentions were it not for the needs of the organization.

In the eyes of the rank and file, staff members were treated to special privileges. For instance, their special membership cards allowed them to enter the church without a body search or inspection of their ever-present suitcases. They had a special locked room for their files. Some members thought them snobbish and standoffish, too closemouthed about their precious duties, too close to Jim. Members begrudged them their cars and freedom of movement. And some blacks resented the rapid rise of college-educated whites, especially bossy or bitchy women.

The resentment cut both ways. Staff members felt they were doing the unglamorous, exhausting and dangerous tasks. Bradshaw and perhaps some others believed that men were excluded from staff because they would not do the humiliating dirty work. They saw themselves as unsung heroines, commandos in the people's army, armed with wiles and disguises.

A few were afraid to conduct nighttime garbage raids. But the rest, dressed in dark clothing, scaled backyard fences, often in black neighborhoods such as the Fillmore District in San Francisco and Watts near Los Angeles. Avoiding watchdogs, they would make their way to the garbage cans of church members or potential members, then sift through decaying vegetables, Kotex, dirty diapers, dog feces—everything imaginable— looking for information. Eating habits could be discerned from discarded cartons and cans. Phone bills would lead to friends and relatives, as would used envelopes. Old credit cards, canceled checks, papers and discarded letters all helped. It was risky. If caught by the police, a staffer was on her own. Certainly, she would not point the finger at Jones or confess to her true mission. Once Patty Cartmell, taken into custody disguised as a black woman, won release with the outlandish story that she was sneaking over to her black boy friend's house.

Jones wanted particulars, not generalized or easily obtained information such as the description of a home exterior. To serve his purposes, the details could not have emanated from public records, not even close friends, but only from divine revelation. So staff members gained entry to a house through some ruse, often in disguise, in case they were seen later at a meeting. A visit to the bathroom might lead to the medicine cabinet and a wealth of personal health data—prescriptions, doctors' names, ailments, hygiene, dates. Such medical evidence could be further supplemented by a book of personal phone numbers, grabbed on the way there and copied down inside, in privacy. The reports Jones ultimately received were typed on cards containing the name, address, race, political background and an assessment of the person's intelligence plus assorted "revelation" material. Despite such obvious fakery, most staff members were true believers, convinced that Jones did indeed possess great powers.

Some believed Jones could rub his hands over the briefing cards and pick up the information. Bradshaw saw him time and time again correct mistakes on the cards, made by his staff in gathering information or typing —mistakes he seemingly could not have picked up without some "psychic" powers. They believed in Jones although they knew the cancers were being palmed by nurses who went into bathrooms with these aging men and women and put fingers down their throats or got them to "bear down" over a toilet. They knew because they had gone to market for the chicken livers. And they knew that the blood which poured out of Jones's palms, like the stigmata of Christ, would heal nothing, although the faithful daubed it on their failing eyes, their arthritic wrists, their clogged-up hearts. Staff knew because they had provided him with blood from their own arms.

Through clever use of theatrical makeup, young white women could be healed as elderly black women—or as crippled old white women. One night in Seattle, Jones called out an old white Swedish lady in a wheelchair. It was revealed that she had been crippled for years, ever since she saw her husband and children killed in a car wreck. Jim summoned all his energy while his kindly voice caressed her. He coaxed her. She strained with her atrophied legs and pushed with her arms. Her fat cheeks bulged, and sweat seeped from her wrinkled skin. With hundreds urging her on and Jim Jones leading the cheers, she came up, a little at a time. That daring lady fought every weak fiber in her body—and in the space of five minutes, five excruciatingly tense minutes, managed to get to her feet—and walk.

Linda Dunn hated herself for it, and was petrified. Yet she did it, with help from old Salvation Army clothing and shoes, the Kleenex in her cheeks, the wig, and dried egg whites wrinkling her skin, the leg padding and the face powder, the artificial quaver in her voice.

The planning commission was not conceived as a secret society. It was the official church governing board in what always would be described as a democratic organization with collective decisionmaking. But commission membership also was a symbol of status and a measure of trustworthiness, because it was the central institution in an incestuous family.

Since the Temple was everything to them, members were consumed by a desire for information about church operations and the activities of their "brothers" and "sisters." As he brought fifty, one hundred and more of his members into the p.c., Jones was able to chart everyone's attitudes, job performance, economic situation, family, love lives. He enlisted his members to inform on each other and divulge private things about themselves through criticism sessions, written assignments, questionnaires and reports. Gossip and tattling were refined into art forms.

Jones appointed some to p.c. because they were jealous that other seemingly less worthy members were honored. Spouses sometimes were brought into the group to keep an eye on spouses already in p.c. Jones used p.c. to reward those who were assets, or who might be wavering in commitment. Some were named for reasons known only to Jones. The composition was largely white, more women than men. And a p.c. developed within the p.c., dominated by staff and some men, such as Tim Stoen.

Meetings convened during the week at various locations in Redwood Valley—often in the claustrophobic surroundings of the "Loft," an A-framed area under the peak of the laundromat complex roof. The meetings ran as long as or longer than services, sometimes until dawn. Some were so intense that Jones would get on a tear and would not stop speaking even to urinate; instead he would use a bucket while someone held a towel in front of him.

Hours and hours were spent discussing the people in the church, from their work habits to their sex lives. Meetings also covered less intimate matters—organizing and expanding the church, purchasing buses and other equipment, upcoming events, travel, projects and political difficulties in the community. Everything was talked about—from getting Mrs. Smith's rent paid, to upcoming elections, to flirtations, to guardianships, to the legality of selling guns collected from members. Debate went on interminably. Sometimes Jones would say nothing at all until the others settled on a decision. Then he would offer his opinion, stating his reasons so convincingly that the others could see their own faulty reasoning.

Jones probably devoted more time to catharsis than business. Gradually, pseudopsychotherapy sessions were installed as a regular fixture. The weaknesses of certain individuals—often their sexual interests and practices—were explored in unsparing fashion. Jones often targeted the victims and orchestrated punishments through his surrogates. It was necessary to strip away ego to become a good collectivist, he said. Sessions started with verbal sniping, slipped into verbal brutality that brought people to tears, and gradually plunged into the sphere of physical violence. The residual effects of the larger society needed to be ripped away like dead skin, maintained Jones. It took repetition and confrontation to crush ego problems and jealousy games, to excise the ugly scar tissue of racism and sexism, agism, classism, and to replace it with the healthy muscle of equalitarianism.

In early 1973, Jones approached Mike Touchette, a college student whom he had earlier selected to be a companion to his own son Stephan. Touchette was about twenty, with the clean-cut looks of an athletic fraternity boy. Jones told the young man that he had been watched closely and others had vouched for his trustworthiness. Jones said he was pleased with Touchette's church work and wanted him in p.c.

Mike had progressed a long way since a first visit from Indiana. His entire family—a half dozen of them—had made the big move to California in two stages in 1970 and 1971 after several years of anguished indecision. The years transformed Mike's life. He had first discovered the humanity of black people—as people—during that earlier stay in Ukiah in the summer of 1966. One image had stuck with him: Jimmy Jones, Jr., plopping himself on a towel near the Golden Rule pool and saying, "I wanna work on my tan." Now Mike was married to a pretty young black woman, Archie Ijames's daughter Debbie. He had performed commendably as Stephan's companion, as a driver and personal aide to Jones and as a security guard at general meetings. And he had sacrificed football and track for the cause. A year earlier, Jones had privately talked with him and found him receptive and knowledgeable about the prison movement, George Jackson, the Vietnam war and other topics. He also explored Touchette's attitudes about homosexuality, perhaps to test his tolerance and humility.

Now, Jones flattered him with an invitation to join p.c. It appealed to Touchette because he believed, as Jones said, that p.c. planned the strategy and direction of the Temple. Besides, it would be another shared experience with his friends on the commission, Wayne Pietila and John Biddulph.

Touchette joined as others had joined, feeling honored and rewarded. Once inside, he saw contradictions that he either repressed or could not act upon, out of fear or faith in Jones. The minister would recline on a couch with blankets and pillows, stretched out comfortably while dozens of others packed into a tiny room, most sitting on the floor. Next to "Father" stood a table with juices and other drinks, and a platter with cheese, turkey, chicken breasts, sliced beef or the like. Jones usually munched on peanuts to replenish his "burned-off" protein, and constantly "flushed" his kidneys with fluids because of a urinary tract problem. Jones would order the platter passed around, yet everyone politely declined. Father, because he took everyone's problems upon himself and drove himself around the clock, needed the fuel more than anyone else, as he also needed the pills always at hand.

Usually, catharsis ate up the meeting time. Hardly anybody except those in the inner circle seemed to be immune, and Jones would even talk about them behind their backs. Marceline attended the meetings infrequently, and when she did, Jones would build her up one minute and tear her down the next. Archie Ijames was humiliated at least once, and the old Becky Beikman adoption matter reappeared with new wrinkles. But often Archie, the diplomat, would get away with going against the grain. Though potbellied Jack Beam oftentimes would lead the lambasting with his usual bombast, he was not spared from attacks either. Tim Stoen, excused to work at his office, would show up very late or not at all.

Almost everyone was poised, dreading an attack. Many got their lashing. Jones made it clear that defending anyone else, especially a friend or a loved one, was forbidden. It would undermine the whole concept of catharsis, allow the person to avoid "confronting himself." This purging of ego was supposed to make one a better socialist, but members could not escape the pain of being cursed and criticized by brothers and sisters in the cause. Often the sting did not stop when the session ended.

A person never could be 100 percent certain about his tormentors again. Friends, spouses and lovers were divided by degrees.

It became all too apparent after a while that Jim Jones, though he sat back as others brought up people for criticism, was choreographing the encounters. Sometimes he would pass a note or would be so indiscreet as to point at someone. Instantly, his closest aides were interrogating, humiliating, ridiculing the target.

Some people were on the receiving end more often than others. Once Jones approached Touchette and asked him to "bring up" Grace Stoen for failing to raise John properly. Touchette felt sympathy for Grace, yet a request from Jones was a command. Touchette thought Grace had been verbally abused too often already, badgered to tears over her son John: people even criticized her for failing to hold up her little son at meetings, to point out Jim Jones and say; "That's your father"—an ambiguous lesson, since Jones was known as "Father" to all his followers. During one session, Jones seemed to have a heart attack as Grace was ostracized. That made others even more angry with her.

In a number of such attacks, Jones would fall back, clutching his chest. He was cut to the heart, he moaned; he had wanted Grace to get an abortion but she had refused. His attendants would quickly give him oxygen or nitroglycerin pills. As much as anything, these so-called heart attacks seemed to be brought on by his own manipulative bent. Once in a while, the nurses supposedly would draw a pint of his blood to stimulate him and thin his blood. Jones would lift up the blood for all to behold: "This blood is so good that if they could put it into sick people, they would be healed."

Sometimes Tim Stoen was present when Jones claimed John was his own flesh and blood. Tim would say nothing to contradict his pastor. The young prosecutor's behavior convinced some people that John was indeed Jones's biological, not just spiritual, offspring. Within the decade, many would put their lives behind that very claim.

EIGHTEEN

Lourdes on Wheels

For some time, Jones had been recruiting in California's metropolitan areas. Weekend bus trips established strong constituencies in San Francisco and Los Angeles as well as satellite congregations in almost a dozen lesser cities. By 1972, the Temple was calling Redwood Valley the "mother church" of a statewide religious movement. Moving the seat of power into an urban area seemed a strategic necessity. The Ukiah area afforded no room for expansion, and bus trips did not build loyal congregations.

On September 3 and 4, 1972, the Los Angeles temple was blessed and dedicated as thousands witnessed scores of revelations and healings. The imposing brick Moorish-style complex that had once housed the First Church of Christ, Scientist was located at the corner of Alvarado and Hoover in the heart of Los Angeles, within easy driving range of Temple believers in the far-flung metropolitan area and largely black suburbs. The dedication provided a spectacular kickoff.

"During the Sunday meeting, one elderly brother was felled by a stroke," according to a Temple announcement. "While the Pastor was ministering to others, registered nurses . . . rushed to give aid and comfort, but could detect no signs of life! Pastor Jim Jones then came . . . and reached down and said, 'This is our new church in Los Angeles. This cannot happen here! I am the Temple of the Holy Ghost. I command you to arise!' . . . The man bolted back into consciousness, . . . becoming the 40th person to return from the dead in public meetings this year. Praise God!"

From the start, the Los Angeles temple was set up chiefly as a way station and recruitment center. Los Angeles was much bigger than San Francisco and included large black communities in the center city, Watts, Compton and elsewhere. Jones set up a permanent staff there and showed up with his busloads of northern California members every other weekend. Vast collections helped keep the Temple growing, and the number of attendees figured heavily in Temple's false claims of twenty thousand members statewide.[30] But the real commitment came when Los Angeles–area blacks began moving to the north. Four hundred miles up the jagged California coast, a mere two-hour drive from Ukiah, lay Jim Jones's city of conquest.

The Temple descended on the hilly city with the missionary zeal of the Franciscan padres and the naked ambition of the Forty-niners. To get people to the church, healings were promoted in the most sensationalistic way. But that put the Temple into a sort of Catch-22. Healings tended to draw right-wingers and religious nuts—the very sorts of people to keep out of a closet socialist group. People who presented themselves as radical, particularly the whites, were screened closely too. The ever-present specter of infiltration became an obsession; Temple members believed that someday the government, through the FBI, CIA or another agency, would try to destroy "the most promising hope for world socialism."

When an interested person came to the heavy front doors of the San Francisco temple, he or she would not simply pass unmolested into the inner areas of the building. All newcomers were met at the door by a mostly white greeting party assigned to chat with them and size them up. In the lounge, various counselors further screened potential members, as subtly as possible. Based on written thumbnail evaluations, people were shunted to the counselor best equipped to handle their type.

The interrogators asked in a friendly and conversational manner about the newcomer's background. Those flagged as troublemakers were allowed to stay to chat in the lounge, but they were told it was a closed meeting. "We'll call you for the next meeting," they would be told, then never phoned.

As a rule, moderates could attend the first meeting unless they had terrible personality problems. A victim of circumstance, such as a black drunk or drug addict, most likely would be admitted. In fact, few blacks were barred, except rigidly religious people who might rebel upon hearing Jones's blasphemy and profanity.

Attendees each were assigned an interpreter of sorts to sit with them. The escorts explained the rationale behind Jim Jones's cussing, or his dancing on the Holy Book, and they also observed the neophyte's reaction to such things and to the political and social content. Plenty of religious people, especially older blacks, stomped out. Jones's aides tried to intercept them so they would not leave angry. Once, a woman was furious about Jones's praise of Marx. Cartmell assuaged her by saying, "Jim didn't say 'Marx.' It was 'Mark' as in Matthew, Mark, Luke and John."

After the first meeting, people desiring to join were asked to come back. They were expected to attend five consecutive Sunday meetings before acceptance. By the second meeting in the upstairs, high-ceilinged auditorium with the elevated podium, each person would be adopted by a sort of guardian angel. The newcomer could select a seat by himself, but someone would watch discreetly from a distance; any comments were added to a three-by-five-inch evaluation card. The newcomer would be allowed to stay for the Sunday potluck dinner in the downstairs dining hall, which gave people a chance to evaluate one another and get acquainted.

Between the third and fifth week, the newcomer was checked out as thoroughly as possible. He could expect to lose some of his garbage to Temple trash sifters, or be called for a phone poll or some other ruse designed to weed out agents and conservatives. Temple ferrets looked for negative or incompatible reading habits, attitudes and lifestyles. By the fifth week, the recruit received a membership card to be shown at the door before services. Later he would be directed into a church program, or job.

In its own ghostly blue light, the convoy ate up miles and miles of blacktop. Eleven big Greyhound-type cruisers, with destination windows reading "Temple," ran California freeways every weekend and the nation's interstates quarterly. In the space of several years, the church had advanced from charter buses to a few used clunkers to a trim fleet of large passenger buses housed in a well-equipped garage that looked like a small airplane hangar. These mobile and highly visible signs of rising fortunes were themselves one of the most important recruiting and fund-raising tools.

From the outside, nothing differentiated Bus No. 7 from the rest of the diesel-powered fleet. But the flagship cruiser was Jim Jones's personal bus, outfitted with armed guards and special creature comforts. Having seen Jones trying to nap on the back row of the bus in his rumpled clothes, some of his aides closed off the last few rows of seats with a partition. So that Jones could shave and freshen up before his next sermon, they put in a tiny sink. They installed a small bed with protective metal plates at the head and hung curtains on the windows. The furnishings were then rounded out by a clothes closet, an ice chest and a short-wave radio. When Jones found out about his relatively posh accommodations, he acted furious at this affront to his egalitarian principles. He accepted them nonetheless.

Getting close to Father was as desirable on the road as it was at home. Those assigned to Bus No. 7 were privileged. Naturally, the inner circle was allowed to share the bus with Jones, as was the Jones family. For Jones's fellow passengers, the monotony of the trip was broken when he emerged from his compartment to joke and visit. The sound of Jim's laughter—as high-pitched and as cackly as a midwestern granny's—pushed their own laughter to deafening extremes. Fat Patty Cartmell would team up with Jack Beam for some slapstick, being loud, witty and nearly lewd. Tickled, Jim Jones would lead the applause as they played off each other, encouraged by their captive audience. Jack would ham it up as Geraldine, the Flip Wilson character; Patty often poked fun at her own obesity.

When Jones retired to his compartment to rest, the others quieted down as well, though now and then a woman would slip into Jones's private boudoir. But little John Stoen, just a few years old, was precocious. Late one night, as the buses carried slumbering members between San Francisco and Los Angeles, John sat in deep thought for several miles, apparently not happy to be the only one awake. He marched up to the front of the bus and picked up the driver's intercom CB. "Come in. Come in!" he called. "All Peoples Temple, attention please!" The drivers on all the other buses responded quickly, assuming some emergency was at hand.

"Drivers, awaken your people," John commanded. "Tell them Father loves them every one and no harm will come to them. Ever. Then tell them to go back to sleep again." The drivers followed the orders; everyone's spirits lifted.[31]

On bus trips, Sandy Bradshaw and other staff maintained positions outside Jones's parlor. Their leader often required secretarial services and other assistance. Jones would pop out of his compartment unannounced at all hours to ask them to take dictation or write down notes for tasks that had to be performed as soon as the buses stopped. There was time to do recommended reading, such as "Introduction to Socialism," but generally the exhausted staff women catnapped when they could.

Jones's clock-be-damned style of administration dazzled his aides. From a dead sleep, he could get up and rattle off a letter of several pages, or distill a convoluted problem into a precise solution. His thoughts cascaded; his decisions and commands made sense. But his demands placed his secretaries under great stress as they struggled to keep up. In turn, Jones tried to show his appreciation. Except when exhausted or ill, he always was patient and took care to thank them.

Jim Jones bragged that the Temple never would embark on a cross-country trip that did not net $100,000 to $200,000, and he told Richard Cordell, one of his early adherents, that a million dollars a year was a realistic goal. Still, even with the tremendous loyalty of Temple members, it was a chore to gather seven hundred people to fill eleven buses; and sometimes Jones would have to settle for trips with three or four buses.

In the early 1970s, Temple buses traversed the nation a few times a year, making one- and two-night stands in the largest cities. During a stopover in Washington, D.C., the Temple called on California congressmen and a lengthy and laudatory description of the Temple was placed into the *Congressional Record* in June 1973 by Democratic Representative George Brown. The praise came after the church donated several thousand dollars to California newspapers "in defense of press freedom." During the stopover, the *Washington Post,* in an editorial page item on August 18, 1973, provided still further kudos for the Temple's public relations folder: "The hands-down winners of anybody's tourist-of-the-year award have got to be the 660 wonderful members of the Peoples Temple . . . this spirited group of travelers fanned out from their 13 buses and spent about an hour cleaning up the [Capitol] grounds. . . ."

Inconveniences and sacrifices notwithstanding, Temple travelers derived benefit from their trips. Whatever Jones's ulterior motives, many of his people were being afforded their first opportunity to see the United States, to visit the nation's capital and meet their Congressmen in person. They felt pride in being part of a recognized group. For many, the collective identity helped erase lifelong feelings of powerlessness.

Travel conditions, however, bordered upon the inhumane. At rest stops, Temple members were reduced to bathing in sinks. They gobbled their food in transit, sandwiches of cheese and peanut butter on day-old bread, cold cans of chili or ravioli. A hot meal was as rare as a warm bed. Some people actually sought out sleeping space in the unventilated luggage compartments under the buses because that was one place for sleep uninterrupted by the frequent offering calls that Jones made over the CB radios.

Two, three and even five collections were taken each day as they traveled between cities. Telling them "The ends justify the means," Jones asked his collectors on each bus to use various ruses to keep the travelers reaching into their purses and wallets. Sometimes, the buses would stop and passengers would be told that they needed an inflated amount of money to get across a toll bridge or to make repairs on a bus. The buses would sit until the collections satisfied Jones.

Not even the poverty-stricken were excluded from these desperate pleas for money. Some members actually competed to see who could donate the most. Even people working menial jobs or on government assistance were pleased to part with their money. Some bragged. They were supporting an institution that belonged to them. They sought the approval of their leader, and their comrades. No one wanted to feel or appear greedy or selfish. And no one who sacrificed a great deal wanted to look across the aisle at a tightwad or a holdout.

The pressure did not cease when the bus engines cooled off. Advance teams had set up services and leafletted in cities all along the way. Ads were placed in local newspapers and on local religious radio stations. In the lobbies or outside auditoriums, the Temple set up tables to peddle pictures of Jim Jones, holy oil blessed by him and other religious artifacts. And people who did not know Karl Marx from Harpo Marx came to see what the leaflets promised:

COME AND SEE THE MOST MIRACULOUS SPIRITUAL HEALING MINISTRY IN THE LAND TODAY! ALL NINE GIFTS OF THE SPIRIT MANIFESTED IN REV. JIM JONES' PEOPLES TEMPLE MINISTRY (OF THE NEARLY 2 MILLION MEMBER DISCIPLES OF CHRIST DENOMINATION) REV. JONES OFTEN CALLS SCORES OF PEOPLE FROM THE AUDIENCE WHO ARE HEALED OF ALL MANNER OF DIS-EASES! THE BLIND SEE! THE DEAF HEAR! CRIPPLES WALK! SEE A MODERN DAY APOSTLE . . . HEAR HIS URGENT MESSAGE FOR THESE TROUBLED TIMES.

Jones's bus caravans were billed as a traveling Lourdes. Lest the skeptical stay away, the leaflets quoted without permission from letters and comments by prominent people—a physician who said he believed the healings were genuine, Disciples of Christ officials who praised the humanitarian works of the Temple.

Jones's healing techniques had been polished over time, but they received a great assist from the climate created by his travelers. The several hundred California members often were presented as local people, so attendees in places such as Detroit, Cleveland and Houston did not always realize that the newcomers were a distinct minority at a staged event. Jones's huge entourage imported enthusiasm, and some members functioned as shills during offerings. Witnessing miracles and revelations —and donations of hundreds of dollars—made the uninitiated even more inclined to donate generously. The needy and not-so-needy—wage earners, unemployed, runaways, winos and others—were collected along the way.

While the numbers who headed west stayed limited, the names of those who did not were nearly as valuable. Church mailing lists ranked among the most precious Temple possessions. By the early 1970s, the Temple had set up Truth Enterprises, a direct mail branch sending out

30,000 to 50,000 mailers each month to people who had attended Temple services, written in response to Temple radio shows or otherwise come in contact with the church. Money poured into the Temple from all over the continental United States, Hawaii, South America and Europe. In peak periods, mailers grossed $300 to $400 a day.

The tone of the mailers was an amalgam of Rev. Ike, Father Divine and brassy old Christian hokum, appealing to people's desire for financial deliverance, spiritual guidance and physical health. Thanks to the law of averages and the innate gullibility of people, the church received many reports of the bounty of blessings from Jim Jones—and used those in future mailers. People attested to the power of pieces of his robes, healing oil or pictures of him in frames, rings, key chains or lockets. People sent offerings in thanks and anticipation of benefits. Even Jim Jones was surprised by their number.

An early mailer bore a photo of Jones in his robes, yet without sunglasses. His arm was outstretched toward an empty retangular space where the believer was to glue either a photograph or a piece of a garment as a gesture of faith. Space was provided for the recipient to write an "urgent need" and to designate a "love offering" of $5 to $50, or "other." The message was clear: "As you send your letter, if you are able to send a Gift of Love to help the work financially, God will honor your faith." However, on the same page in very fine print was a more temporal disclaimer: "Peoples Temple assumes no legal responsibility for the truth of any testimonies. . . ."

Jones's old friend Jack Beam was the star of one mailer with a photograph of a horribly twisted and overturned Temple truck and caption: "Saved from Certain Death." Wearing a tractor cap and his broadest country smile, Jack stood before the wreckage flashing the peace sign. "When the truck overturned, my head was thrown through the windshield," said a testimony befitting one of Jones's loyalist functionaries. He said that he had been decapitated, but that a dashboard photo of Rev. Jones had made him whole again.

By the Temple's own count, it received more than one thousand similar testimonies to the power of Jones's anointed and blessed photographs sold through the mails and at services. It was $5 for the deluxe model with plastic frame. Stationery depicting various scenes of Temple life, including Pastor and Mrs. Jones, sold for $1.50 a packet. Lots of money was made, but Jones used to fret, "They're gonna get me for mail fraud someday."

The pictures were the brainchild of an enterprising couple, Deanna and Elmer Mertle, who after defecting would call themselves Jeannie and Al Mills. Earlier, Jones had asked everyone to destroy photos of him because he did not wish people to worship him like Catholics kneeling before plaster statues. With this new idea, however, he allowed his pictures to be promoted as protection from various evils—one picture was designed to safeguard the owner from fire, another assault, a third from cancer, and so on. Some pictures were to be worn over the heart, others framed for the home.

On the mainstay weekend bus trips to San Francisco and Los Angeles, it was not uncommon to sell a few thousand dollars' worth of photos of Jones, holy oil that was nothing but vials of olive oil, and anointed prayer cloths that originally were pieces of Jones's discarded robes but later merely remnants from fabric shops. The oil went for $5, the cloths for $2.

Offerings at healing services in the two large California cities dwarfed those sales. The weekly take in Los Angeles often ranged from $15,000 to $25,000 or more, and in San Francisco from $8,000 to $12,000. There also were smaller Redwood Valley collections. The counters, gathered in a back room, started piling and tabulating bills before the services ended. Jones at times would demand a total before they were finished. When an aide relayed the incomplete count, the preacher sometimes would deflate even that figure. Then he would deride the paltry total, and the bucket would be passed some more. To stimulate generosity, Jones would promote future projects, some of which never materialized. In addition to asking for support of the church's social service programs and college dorms, Jones took up collections to purchase airplanes and boats and bulletproof cars. He began talking about setting up a mission in South America. And, he said, several members would be sent to flight school.

During one of the Temple vacation trips in 1976, Jones directed the caravan toward his hometown; the side trip would provide a triumphal return, allowing his followers to see his birthplace firsthand.

Jones evidently was bringing up the rear when the first buses rolled into Lynn at about seven one weekday morning. One of the drivers motioned a passing motorist to the side of the road to ask for assistance. It turned out that the driver was Jones's boyhood friend, Don Foreman, who had stopped in Lynn for breakfast on the way to his engineering job in Dayton.

"Can you help me?" said a black man who approached.

"I'm not sure. Can you tell me what you need?"

"I'm from California with a church group, and we're looking for the birthplace of God."

"The birthplace of God?" Foreman was bemused.

"Yes."

"I can't help you until you tell me who God is."

"Jim Jones."

"In that case, I can help you," said Foreman. "Jim Jones lived over there in a house that was behind that grocery store."

While Foreman went on to work chuckling to himself, eleven buses lined up on Grant Street by the site of the Jones home. Jones himself arrived on Bus No. 7 with his entourage. He introduced his family and followers to his former baby-sitter, Myrtle Kennedy, the sweet Nazarene lady. He spent two hours talking to the aged woman whom he called his spiritual mother. And after he hugged and kissed her good-bye, he did not forget her. He remembered her birthday and made sure she received a shower of birthday cards from his followers as well. He called her occasionally on the telephone and had his secretary write her letters when he could not.

N I N E T E E N

Sex in the Temple

One night, after a long meeting in Redwood Valley, Jones toppled over in one of his apparent coronaries. The congregation was sent home quickly while Dale Parks, a young inhalation therapist, administered oxygen. A few aides—Jack Beam, Archie Ijames and Larry Layton—anxiously hovered over their stricken leader. Supine on the blue-carpeted pulpit platform, the pallid-looking preacher took a draft of oxygen, looked up at Larry Layton and declared: "Larry, I'm in love with your wife." It was probably the first public declaration of the Jones-Layton liaison, and it left no room for misunderstanding: Jones went on to relate that he and Layton's wife had each come to climax no fewer than sixteen or seventeen times in their first illicit encounter. With his aides looking on, Jones talked Layton into divorcing his wife.

Other twists soon followed. When Layton went to Nevada to finalize the divorce, Jones dispatched Karen Tow, one of the Temple's most beautiful women, to keep him happy.

Like Layton, Tow came from relative affluence and was politically reborn in the 1960s. Temple opinion about her was divided: some thought she was a sweet, sensitive young woman; others saw her as a vain flirt who needed humbling. In any case, she and Larry Layton made a handsome couple—and eventually married. Karen characterized her tie to Larry as a friendship, perhaps warm and sexual, but her devotion belonged to the Temple, and her real sex life revolved around Jim Jones.

In fact, Jones usurped both of Larry Layton's wives. However, this sexual double duty taxed even the master juggler. Carolyn, he swore publicly and privately, was his first true love; Karen became expendable. Claiming he was irritated by her demands, he asked Archie Ijames and Jack Beam to extricate him from the relationship. Karen, rebuked by these Temple old-timers, became indignant and refused. They in turn threatened to expose her to the general membership as a selfish woman sapping Father's energy. "If you don't back off, he'll tell it all in public."

"He wouldn't do that," she snapped.

"The hell he wouldn't."

The bluff worked, and Karen Tow Layton acquiesced. Jones, however, was not through with her newfound husband. Having stolen sexual favors from both his wives, Jones now proceeded to humiliate Larry Layton by portraying him as a homosexual in front of the planning commission. The effect of Jones's triple blow to Layton was to turn a deeply feeling, onetime activist with a drug problem into a puppyish functionary. Demeaned, Layton was dismissed by other Temple members as "spacey," while the church newspaper proclaimed him as a drug reform success story.

Though Jones stopped short of exposing lurid details of his trysts from the pulpit, he was not so discreet in other forums. Word of his affairs traveled through the church. Jones bragged about his conquests to his longtime buddies like Beam and Ijames, belying his strident public calls for women's liberation. Like one of the boys in a beer bar, he boasted of his triumphs in raw language. Nothing was too crude or intimate to relate. He loved to talk about venereal warts, the smell of genitals or hygiene in the anal canal, and always in the most graphic and clever terms. He would talk about rooting around in the grass with some young girl and how, once she stood up, her behind was plastered with stickers. Finally, Ijames, using diplomatic double talk, took a gentle jab at his pastor: "Brother Jones. I think you trust people too much. They don't deserve the trust you give them."

The Temple's sexual politics meshed with the changing sexual mores of society, but most of all with Jones's own changing attitudes and habits—and his organizational needs. Jones had become a student of sex. He recognized it as a primal force closely tied to the will to survive. Sex, like hunger or the need to sleep, could be channeled and controlled. A charismatic leader like Jones could literally conjure up the sexual energy of his congregants and turn it toward the needs of the organization. Since ultimately Temple goals were synonymous with his goals, he inevitably abused the energy, fulfilling his personal sexual and psychological fantasies.

Jones also used sex to tie people to the group. Like a matinee idol or some politicians, he promoted himself as the ultimate sex object, dispensing favors to an adoring following, drinking up their adulation. He used his body to discipline, elevate and reward, as well as to assert his own superiority and to humiliate. In his own insecurity, he became an addict who needed the sexual fix. And he also had discovered the reputation-destroying power of sexual rumors and innuendo.

Jones tailored his sexual theories and rulemaking to a functional opportunism. For instance, in a time of free love and women's liberation, he preached the sharing of love, encouraging his members to share sexual favors freely. Conventional sexual mores and jealousies he denounced as egotistical and hypocritical. He criticized narcissistic sexual game playing that made the less-favored and shy feel inferior.

Such policies, in practice, served to bind people to Jones and the church. By violating old taboos, people morally compromised themselves. Jones had disoriented them, like the devout Christians whom he taught to cuss. And he had seized control of a powerful force in their lives.

Still, Jones's sexual standards changed like the wind, and were rife with special privileges. The dogma seesawed between sexual awareness and total celibacy. Did not sex squander energy that could be better applied to building socialism? Was it not elitist to continue marital relations when so many Temple members had no partner at all, selfish to make babies when so many were starving? Good socialists ignored the sex drive.

To convince people to abstain—and perhaps for his own psychological needs—Jones bullied them by attacking their sexuality on many fronts at once. One device was his absurd thesis that he alone, among Temple men and women, was the only true heterosexual. All the rest were hiding their homosexuality, he declared; having heterosexual relations was simply a masquerade. Perhaps out of shame for homosexual tendencies within himself, Jones made his members publicly admit homosexual feelings or acts, past and present, latent or overt. Planning commission members were forced to list all the sexual partners in their lives, male and female, as well as type of sex. He had wives stand up and complain about their husbands' lovemaking. He had male children fill out questionnaires that asked, among more doctrinaire matters, about their sexual feelings for Father. And he personally had sex with some men in his church, ostensibly to prove to them their own homosexuality.

Using all this ammunition, Jones created a sexually eclectic climate of intolerance disguised as tolerance, of guilt, repression and division. Some, particularly the elderly and very young, stayed celibate with no great sacrifice. Some members found it a great strain; some had sex on the sly and felt guilt; some had sanctioned sex in arranged relationships. Some had sex with Jones, others resented it. The labels "homosexual," "queer," "lesbian," "male chauvinistic pig," "sexist" and "narcissist" were flung about. Members censured one another in meetings at home: any behavior perceived as selfish or elitist or snooty warranted attack. Any behavior seen as homosexual, even a friendly kiss or an embrace between two members of the same sex, was criticized, and sometimes punished. Conversely, those who showed an interest in the opposite sex —and were therefore "compensating" for their homosexuality—were humiliated, or sometimes sodomized by Jones to prove their homosexuality.

Partly as a bonding ritual, partly as an escape valve, the church did sanction some marriages and arranged others. Usually people without real romantic feelings for each other were asked to form a marriage of commitment to the cause. Some lovers, especially interracial couples, were asked to marry for the sake of appearance.

Jones promoted interracial marriage, despite his general condemnation of all one-on-one relationships as counterrevolutionary. Such marriages advanced the interracial lifestyle and also served to tie the couples more closely to the Temple, which remained a rare, racially hospitable environment.

Marriage was one thing, but childbirth another, especially in the Ukiah days. There are too many unwanted and neglected little ones in the world, Jones would cry, perhaps lamenting his own childhood. Bearing children instead of adopting was construed as greedy. Some women in their childbearing years were clearly frustrated by this policy; others who went ahead anyway, like Grace Stoen, were showered with abuse.

"Elitist bitch," some called Grace Stoen behind her back. Childbirth seemed to be just one more special privilege for the church attorney and his wife. Yet soon after the birth of John Victor Stoen, Jones took extraordinary steps to bind the couple to the church. First, he had Stoen sign the paternity statement. Then, almost immediately, he elevated Grace to the planning commission. By Jones's own admission, Grace was mistrusted, a waverer; the appointment was an incentive and reward but also an obligation, as was the house down payment Jones gave the couple.

For a while, he allowed them to live as a nuclear family with their beautiful, bright little boy. But Jones then turned the screws. Grace was pushed into quitting junior college and getting a job: she worked the night shift at a convalescent hospital so that she could spend days with her son. And when John was only two years old, Tim announced it was time to move the boy out of their home and into the larger Temple community, to be raised communally. Grace was upset and angry, but she yielded, and John was moved out.

The church gradually took the energies she once had devoted to her child. Grace found satisfaction working with the elderly. But in August 1974, that too was pried away from her when she was asked to work full time in the church's newly opened Redwood Valley commercial complex. Grace objected, and even broke down in tears. "I love the patients," she pleaded with Jones. "It's the first job I've ever enjoyed in my life."

"Grace," Jones told her. "These people were racists when they were younger. . . ."

Out of guilt and a need to please her fellow Temple members, Grace gave up the job. She poured her energy into her Temple duties, answering church phones for Jones, paying bills, immersing herself in the organization. She even put in extra hours beyond the sixteen expected of all members, hoping the criticisms of her in planning commission would stop. Slowly, things got better. People came to her with problems. Counselors took note of her dedication. Jones promoted her to the church council and eventually to head counselor. For the first time, she had attained a coveted position of responsibility—and she was deeply gratified. A disinterested appendage had been converted into a key member.

As Grace's status in the church improved, her relationship with Tim deteriorated. She had grown tired of asking Stoen for time and attention, of hearing him say she was a shabby socialist or too possessive. Once in Los Angeles, when she asked for a few minutes together, he brushed her off. It did not matter that Jones had put him up to such behavior with the rationale that it would harden Grace, make her a better socialist. Chasing her own husband humiliated her, and Grace gave up on him. They stopped living together.

Tim Stoen's mere presence raised those old inferiority feelings in Jones. He was many things Jones was not. But he also was naïve and prone to zealotry and idealism, and Jones exploited that. Having elevated Stoen to the highest standings, Jones made his fall all the more calculating and cruel.

Jones went after Stoen's sexual identity. As if getting his signature on the paternity document were not enough, Jones tried to get Stoen to admit homosexuality publicly, as had other church members, under bullying and false logic. At one point, he tricked Stoen into going out and buying some women's undergarments, while at the same time letting the word slip to Grace that Tim had transvestite tendencies. The trap worked: when she saw the clothes, Grace reported Tim in writing.

In 1975, Jones also wanted Stoen to proclaim his "homosexuality" at a church meeting. To Stoen, it would have meant, at the very least humiliation, at most the kiss of death for any future political aspiration. Once Jones was able to lead him through a logical sequence, to make Stoen acknowledge that there were male and female traits in everyone and a certain latent homosexuality in all, but the lawyer always balked at the final step. Stoen was the sort who could not even have a fleeting homosexual experience without being consumed by guilt. Jones had pushed his lawyer's pride too far. Though Stoen would not act on the incident for two years, it planted a seed of disillusionment.

Talk of sex was not confined to the planning commission or the council; Jones made policy from the pulpit, with a graphic and witty style. He gave earthy commentaries that made the audience howl. With a clever sense of humor, he tossed off all pretensions of piety, adopting the language, intonations and vocabulary of his inner-city people and mixing it with a vocabulary nearly as florid as his mother's writing. The brew was spellbinding. No subject grabbed his congregation like sex.

Whereas an ordinary preacher might have been uncomfortable with the subject, Jones spoke with candor, giving off the sexual magnetism of a crooner. Women of all ages adored the good-looking preacher in dark glasses and satiny red or blue religious robes from New York religious suppliers, and the men admired and envied his macho, straight-talking manner. The bawdy words and gestures provided vicarious thrills.

Whatever Jones's demands for celibacy, rank-and-file members might transgress in the privacy of their own bedroom. To prevent this, Jones relied on guilt, public cross-examinations, on his own reputation as a clairvoyant, and informants. Some confessed their weaknesses. Some spouses turned in each other for "having sex," but others formed pacts to continue their relations in secrecy. Some, especially those who lived in Temple communes and had ample opportunity for sleeping around, simply yielded to their desires haphazardly. Couples formed and dissolved, people gossiped. Jones could not program his people like robots, but he did limit and direct them.

Those who ascended to the planning commission and of course to Jones's staff had an inside view of the Temple's sexual dynamics. As Jones's roster of lovers lengthened, he tended to dote over sexual conduct.

The p.c. often met in the attic of the Redwood Valley commercial complex owned by the Temple. In this adult Loft, Jones played games with people's lives. The planning commission members were often sexual partners. Continually he tested their allegiance, playing men against women, polarizing. The men were charged with "male chauvinism" or homosexuality; in turn the men thought the women were "bitchy" man-hating feminists. In one of his more mind-boggling statements, Jones claimed that all good socialists had to know themselves in all ways, including sexually—which meant all good socialists must be sodomized.

Jones's sexual contact with men generated tremendous conflicts within some of them. He made his lessons in buggery all the more humiliating by always assuming the dominant position. As he conquered his partners, he told them again and again that it was for their own good. He derived no pleasure at all from the act, he told them, but made sure they did, arousing them with practiced physical manipulation, stimulating their prostate glands so as to bring them to climax. He left his victims both guilt-ridden and humiliated.

Jones went out of his way to find male partners who showed not the slightest homosexual inclinations. Backstage at a Los Angeles service, he looked at a newcomer named Tim Carter in a fatherly fashion and patted him on the back of the head. "Son, if you want me to fuck you in the ass, I will," he offered. When the shocked Vietnam veteran replied in the negative, Jones left the door open, saying, "Just so you know I'm here if you want me."

He particularly liked awakening macho types, respected church members or "studs" to their "homosexuality," though he rarely took on black males. As he said later on tape, he delighted to hear brawny men squealing with pleasure as he mastered them. Yet Jones also engaged himself with more effeminate men, some of whom were already practicing homosexuals or bisexuals.

Although Carter was not humiliated or punished for his strict heterosexuality, Mike Prokes was. Prokes—a former Modesto, California, high school football player—had bragged to friends in the Temple about a time he and a high school buddy took turns in a darkened motel room with a girl who believed she was with only one lover. In the church, he was accused of making plays for teen-age girls and was called up in front of the church leaders, who concluded that Prokes did not feel comfortable with women his own age and needed to face up to his homosexuality. Jones was there, ready to help.

Jones helped others too, humbling and compromising them in a number of ways. Later, their confessions reinforced Jones's image as a selfless heterosexual superlover. One particular man committed his feelings to paper as part of his postsex therapy:

"I felt that when you related to me, you were doing so to serve me without being condescending at all. Your choice of words, your warmth and tenderness made me feel that you deeply loved me.

"Your fucking me in the ass was, as I see it now, necessary to get me to deal with my deep-seated repression against my homosexuality. I have at times felt resentment at being fucked even though I knew your motives were utterly pure. . . . It was also due in part to the humiliation of being discovered by [my wife] and Karen.

"I did find being fucked in the ass pleasurable, but I felt so 'unnatural' about it that the fear outweighed it. . . . I know beyond doubt you are the very best sexual partner in the world and I don't think I've ever thought I could really compete with you."

Jones's relations with women were characterized by his own insatiable ego, garnished with elements of therapy, the reward system, the "groupie" phenomenon and the old minister–troubled parishioner gambit. Despite his selfless posturing, Jones reveled in his exploits, demanding that his partners publicly praise his prowess and telling his congregation, "I've been reported to be a good lover. . . ." Some women sought out Jones for sex because he was, by his own definition, the only sex symbol available, the "only heterosexual" male, the ultimate lover, selfless and sensitive and all-powerful. Other women naturally turned to him for their sexual needs just as they turned to him for other types of sustenance and guidance. And they surrendered to him if he approached them.

The stories—or myths—of Jones's sexual "generosity" were aired openly in p.c. Once, Jim and Marceline were called to a house where a young Temple girl threatened suicide with a butcher knife. According to the story, Marceline suggested that Jones make love to the girl. In another story, "a traitorous bitch" was rendered malleable—and loyal to the cause—by Jones's "selfless" gift of himself. Some subjects of such stories, despite their alleged instability, won places on Jones's staff. For example, there was Annie Moore, Carolyn Layton's younger sister. Artistic, whimsical, witty, she had a knack for making others laugh and feel good about themselves. Like Carolyn, who was nine years older, Annie was a dedicated worker—her profession was nursing—and she was also sensitive to the disadvantaged. But, although she sympathized particularly strongly with black people and studied Yazoo Delta blues music, she disdained Peoples Temple at first for isolating her sister from the family. The week after she graduated from high school, Annie visited Carolyn in Ukiah and toured the Temple care homes. She came away moved by the experience and, like her sister, could not pass up Peoples Temple.

This same young woman, according to Temple lore, soon needed Jones's loving sexual therapy because she was suicidal. Supposedly, her own sister summoned Jones to make love to her, thus "saving" her. As a Temple member, Annie Moore went on to nursing school, where she once again became her old self with an outrageous sense of humor.

Jones did admit to a strong sex drive, though he never acknowledged any selfish pleasure seeking. In private, he told the women he was "helping" that he "needed it." Sometimes he forced himself on them; later, he would explain to his confidantes that he had asked the women for sex only so they would not feel guilty about pressuring him into it.

Jones's affairs created jealousies within the church. When others realized that he was engaged in special relationships, some envious women criticized his partners for being selfish or petitioned him for similar favors. Childishly, they squabbled for Jones's attention. Finally Jones, tired of all the demands, announced one day: "Okay, who wants it?" By his count, Jones satisfied that day sixteen men and women. Later, he represented it as a leveling experience, meant to wipe out petty competition and jealousy.

The wisdom among those who had enjoyed Father's special attention was that sex with Jim Jones was incomparable. Jones convinced his partners that his own needs were secondary, his lovemaking an alternative to the abusive, inconsiderate sex of male chauvinists. Jones seduced with his mind as much as his body. But this student of people's needs did not neglect the physical. He jogged to keep his oversized calf muscles in tone; he claimed a larger-than-average organ and experimented with drugs to prolong his erections.

Though some were unsatisfied or found him clumsy and rough, many a woman came away in a blush, feeling she was his favorite. But those who nursed such delusions for long found themselves called elitists. The competition and rivalry was particularly bitter within Jones's own staff; some who had regular or multiple sexual contacts with Jones became possessive. Some fell in love with him and went through all the stages of a love affair, from infatuation to seduction to letdown, to the realization that Jones was community property and that they better accept the bittersweet role of sometimes lover. In a much shorter time span, they repeated Marceline's experiences. And like Marceline, most remained loyal church members.

In the topsy-turvy world of Peoples Temple, those who felt worthless could be elevated and energized by a brief session with Father. Intimacy with the Temple's man-god fountain of principle raised self-esteem. Jones motivated some of his followers this way, making them feel special, vowing his love and showing it physically. Always behind the lovemaking was an implicit form of blackmail: the compromising sexual encounter might later serve to silence the person or keep him or her in the cause.

When his partners were called upon to sing of their lover's talents, some embellished or fabricated. Sometimes Jones, in turn, complained about them. Twice he stood on the stage during a planning commission meeting, ranting about insatiable sexual demands being placed on him. On one occasion he invited all his partners to stand to describe the exquisite sessions with him. Of a hundred people, about thirty took to their feet. His sexual practices caused some dissension, however. He seemed to always sleep with whites—in fact, the p.c. was only about a quarter black, and few if any of them had had sex with him. In his defense, Jones noted that black people had been sexually humiliated over the centuries by whites, so he did not want to impose on them at all.

Though deeply wounded by her husband's extramarital sex, Marceline tried to repress any overt signs of jealousy or disapproval. Nonetheless, Jones's references to his philandering, indirect and otherwise, drove her out of meetings in tears. Some members felt sorry for her; others thought her selfish or overly emotional.

Marceline's pain made Jones feel guilty, though not guilty enough to stop his affairs. In a way, Jones still loved her—and they did have a semblance of a man-wife relationship. But from an organizational standpoint, he had to placate her because the potential for an internal Temple split lived within her broken heart. The image of the "rainbow family" remained a valuable one to him, and Marceline was a popular church figure, revered as "Mother" for her demonstrated sensitivity and kindness. Jones extended token privileges to her, some of which caused resentment among other members. She was permitted to keep her wedding rings and jewelry when others surrendered theirs to the cause. She drove a better car than most. And she and the children dressed better than most members, in partial compensation for the other sacrifices associated with being kin to Jim. Marceline apparently accepted the pain as a natural consequence of being wife of a movement leader. Yet every day, she came closer to realizing that her presence in the Temple could no longer be based upon her love of Jim Jones.

Like a teen-age girl in a small town, Carolyn Layton retreated from Redwood Valley before her pregnancy became obvious. The Temple taboo against bringing more children into the world applied to Jones's favorite mistress as well as to other members. But she, unlike a number of other women the dashing minister impregnated, did not abort the baby. Instead, she spent her pregnancy in Berkeley with her parents, Rev. and Mrs. John Moore, while Jones concocted a story that she was on a mission in Mexico.

The Moores, though happy to see their daughter again, were less than pleased about her relationship with a married minister. Repeatedly they suggested she somehow clear up the sordid entanglement. Barbara Moore wanted Jones to divorce Marceline in order to marry her daughter, but that was a mother's wishful thinking.

During Carolyn's pregnancy, Jones often visited the Moores' home. Around her parents, he acted attentive and concerned for Carolyn's well-being, and everyone survived the ambiguity and tension of the visits. Once they even dined out at a restaurant together. Carolyn, not at all depressed at the prospect of giving birth, anticipated the event as might any expectant mother. She seemed to enjoy the time with her parents, who bent over backwards not to appear judgmental.

In January 1975, Carolyn gave birth to a dark-haired boy who was named Jim Jon but called Kimo. So the child would be legitimate, Mike Prokes, at the request of Jones, went through the formality of marrying Carolyn and giving the child his surname. Yet on the paternal side of the family tree listed in Kimo's baby book, Carolyn made only two entries—Lynetta Jones as grandmother, "Carolyn" as father.

In the church, it became common knowledge that Jones was Kimo Prokes's father. In fact, in order to explain his contradictory action of allowing a pregnancy, Jones claimed that it happened accidentally while he was teaching Carolyn how to use her body if she got in a jam on a secret mission. Kimo—and John Stoen—became extensions of the Jones family.

TWENTY

Training Young Minds

At 7:30 A.M. sharp, Esther would stand at the door to the boys' room, crowing, "Time to get up!" With varying degrees of reluctance, Stephan, Jimmy, Jr., and Lew would pry themselves out of bed in the dormitorylike quarters. Breakfast was mandatory. When their bellies were full, they walked out to the road to await the school bus.

Although he had many reasons to enjoy school, Stephan Jones also dreaded it. He may have been the toughest kid in his age group, the guy the girls chased, a fine athlete and a good student, but he wondered whether he was normal. No one ever invited Stephan Jones home after school, nor did he invite them. He did not feel free to make friends with nonchurch members. Like other Temple children, he was conditioned to think that nonmembers disliked black people.

In his early school years, his brothers were among the few non-white students. Although he and Jimmy fought like banshees at home and once in the school cafeteria, Stephan defended his brother when outsiders were involved. In the third grade, he did nothing more than shake in anger when a girl sang a ditty with the stanza, "Ran like a nigger through the woods." But by the eighth grade, he was taking physical action. He shut a boy's head in a drawer for calling Jimmy a "nigger," and he was pelted with rocks and chased home once for sticking up for his brother. And in high school, he and other Temple members would fight back when redneck boys hassled the Temple's black students.

Throughout school, there was extra pressure on Temple children not only to get good grades but to behave, to properly represent an integrated organization. They were to keep the church secrets and do nothing to call attention to themselves. Despite the guidelines, they managed to lead fairly normal school lives. And even Stephan Jones, with additional pressures and image responsibilities, met the triple standards of school achievement—academics, athletics and leadership.

Temple children, like others, fell in love with athletics, and no amount of sermonizing against the evils of competition could spoil it. Though Jones himself usually stayed away from the school games, Marceline came out to root for her boys as they ran track and played football, baseball and basketball. She was proud and happy for them. The family kept clippings about the athletic achievements of the Jones boys, including those of Tim Tupper, a school chum of Stephan's adopted by the Jones family and treated as a son.

For the sports-minded, weekends were a washout. The grinding thousand-mile bus trips to Los Angeles left no time or energy for sports. But shorter San Francisco trips and longer trips with layovers sometimes provided opportunity for basketball—and to Stephan and his friends, that was a gift from heaven.

Temple buses returning from these weekend trips would rumble into Redwood Valley early Monday morning. Stephan would drag himself into the house, curl up with a blanket or a sleeping bag in front of the heater in the kitchen and snooze until roused for school. . . .

Teachers in Redwood Valley, Potter Valley and Ukiah were seeing fatigued children arrive for classes without breakfast, baths, or sleep, Monday after Monday. Some youngsters dropped their heads to their desks as soon as they warmed up. Many teachers let them rest, covering them with coats, and one teacher let them snuggle up in a cloakroom.

In Potter Valley, school officials sent representatives to the homes of Temple children and found them living communally with more than a dozen people. But nothing could be done. Resources of little country schools already were strained by Temple children. Youngsters imported from the big cities showed up with hard-core behavior problems; kids turned on to shivs and sex were introduced to schools with budgets for a staff psychologist only half a day a week. Teachers accustomed to respectful country kids had to regularly handle bitter rebellion. They were told to "fuck off," or called "goddamn bitches" by some problem kids. Some of these rough Temple kids were veteran San Francisco Bay Area juvenile delinquents, and they intimidated their classmates. In fact, a group of parents became so upset with the changing character of their schools that they wanted to bar Temple members from the PTA.

But the vast majority of Temple children were hard-working, more socially aware than the locals. They dressed at least as well and, in the case of the urban imports, often with a good deal of flair. They tended to hang around in their own cliques in the yard. Many were enlisted in the poverty lunch program.

Often a teacher named Ruby Bogner was assigned children with behavior problems, so she had many from the Temple. An independent sort who wàs rearing two children of her own, she used unconventional teaching methods and would not permit herself to be pushed around. Bogner had had an unpleasant introduction to the Temple and its pastor in her first teaching stint at Calpella Elementary School. One of her second graders was Jimmy Jones, Jr. Mrs. Bogner found Jimmy militantly uncooperative, seemingly hyperactive—and he tested out as a genius. She called on the parents for help. But the Joneses took Jimmy's side, using lifelong conflicts with racism to explain his behavior.

A couple of years later, as the fall term began, Ruby Bogner was given a note by one of her fifth graders, a tall, toothy boy with straight dark hair. "You won't like me because of my brother," it said. "But I will try to be good in your class." The unsolicited promise came from Stephan Jones. He made good on his word and emerged as a leader in the fifth grade class of 1970.

Mrs. Bogner encouraged her pupils to express themselves and to make themselves at home in her classroom. Her students could sit anywhere they wished, and they worked around long utility tables rather than at desks. They had so much fun together that some children spent recesses and lunch periods with her. Sometimes she bought a box of apples, and they lounged around, munching and talking. A few Temple kids came to her house to help with her yard work.

Although Stephan kept his distance and believed Mrs. Bogner disliked him, he became her favorite. His natural leadership qualities were combined with a form of fifth grade "macho." He viewed himself as an instrument of righteousness in a poem that said, in part, "Among the blooming flowers I walk, and I am the Fist." His teacher was impressed with his sensitivity, honesty and decency.

Mrs. Bogner relied on him in small ways and was never disappointed. If she was umpiring a class baseball game and missed a call, she would holler, "Stephan, was he safe or out?" Stephan always made fair calls, and the children accepted his verdicts. Sometimes Mrs. Bogner would let her students play teacher. Stephan, an excellent student, usually chose to teach geography and social studies. Like his father, he took charge in a classroom, covered the material with apparent ease and kept everyone on their toes. Still, he had a tendency to be condescending toward slow students, and he was inclined to get overbearing. To Mrs. Bogner's dismay, he started giving orders to Temple kids.

Mrs. Bogner made no connection between Stephan's sometimes domineering behavior and his father. But she noticed that he never spoke of Jim Jones in the same affectionate or admiring way that other children did of their fathers. In fact, he called his father *"him"*—never "father" or "dad." It became just as obvious that he loved his mother. Whenever a problem arose, Stephan always entreated Mrs. Bogner to contact his mother, not his father. "My father doesn't have time," he said.

It was from other Temple children that Mrs. Bogner began to get hints of murky Temple activities that contrasted with admiring local newspaper stories. Bogner did not like what she saw in her microscopic view of the church's future leaders.

Small things came to her attention at first. Temple children did not participate in giving Christmas gifts at school; they told her they got only three dollars each in gifts from their parents and the rest went to the church. Then some Cordell children abruptly stopped coming by her home to use her plastic swimming pool; they begged her never to tell anyone they had visited her. One of the Temple's exceptional students, Julie Cordell, wanted a *B* in English changed to an *A*, explaining, "I don't want to be whipped in front of the church."

Bogner took the plea in earnest and made a special point of generally awarding Temple kids at least *B*s. It was not difficult to believe there was corporal punishment. She had seen them exhausted after weekend bus trips; they told her they were stowed in luggage racks and in compartments beneath the overcrowded buses. (Jones denied it, of course, and the sheriff's office told her they checked and found the allegation untrue.)

The teacher protected the identities of her informants. Every so often Temple kids huddled with Mrs. Bogner to ask her to clarify various mysteries of Temple life.

"Mrs. Bogner, do you believe people could be raised from the dead?" Mark Cordell asked. Another time, one asked whether it was possible to heal cancer. A third time: "Mrs. Bogner, can you change water to wine?" They were hungry for explanations for "miracles" they could not fathom, whether or not their parents and grandparents seemed to believe in them.

Once the Temple kids came to school with their hands all scratched up. One was also bruised. When Mrs. Bogner asked what happened, they said, "We were wrestling in a berry patch." At lunchtime, she pulled one child aside and was told the truth: during a "survival drill," they had been dumped at 11:00 P.M. at the summit of the Tomki Road area and instructed to find their way home, a few miles away. They had to descend a deep ravine to the river, then follow it back to Redwood Valley in the dark.

Though furious, Mrs. Bogner did not want to betray her source.

She waited a number of months before cornering Jim Jones at a school open house. He tried to change the subject, yet she would not allow him to slip away. "Those kids were scarred and scratched, and I know what happened," she said.

"They were wrestling in the berry patch," he insisted.

"Knock it off."

"They were just playing."

"They were in a canyon! And the way they were bruised and scratched, it looks it."

Without admitting anything, Jones said, "It'll never happen again." He added the teacher to his mental list of enemies.

Had Mrs. Bogner been aware of some other Temple practices, she might have been even more shocked. To harden them, Temple children were taught to swim long distances underwater, under the covered Temple pool. And Jones required them to fill out questionnaires with a number of strange personal and religious questions.

Eddie Mertle, the twelve-year-old son of Elmer and Deanna Mertle (later known as Jeannie and Al Mills), was one of those who answered a sheet of thirty questions. Number 12 was, "Who is Father; do you see him as Savior, Creator, or both?" Question 13 for a child was, "What are your sexual feelings and attractions to the pastor?" Eddie answered, "None." Questions 16 and 29 were identical, "What are your hostilities to the pastor?" Question 4 was foreboding: "When and why have you thought about suicide?" The boy replied, "I don't think I ever have."

The Temple's college dormitories were born simply and innocently enough at the end of the 1960s, as communal-style housing for a few Temple youths. Ideally these rented duplexes were to provide a home environment for serious students attending Santa Rosa Junior College, allowing young Temple members to gain a higher education without falling victim to outside influences. The structure did not permit outside political activities, let alone romance and recreation outside the communal context. The dormitories amounted to an extension of Jones's control.

The student housing project evolved from just a few men and women into a church institution with thirty to forty students. Most took up residence brimming with idealism and talked of devoting their lives to helping other people, as their leader had. They targeted socially useful careers and occupations. Like many other college-age people, they sought a resolution between political ideals and their own ambitions and interests.

In discussing ways to contribute to this miserable world's betterment, Jim Cobb and other dorm students came up with an ambitious idea: "We could build a hospital." The very words sent ripples of idealism through these would-be doctors, dentists, nurses, therapists. Their hospital, they decided, would never reduce a human being to a mere gallstone or root canal fee. More practically, such skills would provide the Temple with a full range of social and health services.

Temple college students lived in a middle-income Santa Rosa neighborhood. About a dozen young men roomed in a half duplex, and about two dozen young women occupied a full duplex across the street. Accommodations were makeshift and crowded—but no more austere than those for students in many college towns. The students cooked their own meals, ate communal-style, rotated the chores. They were provided with transportation to and from school in a car pool arrangement, using their own cars and Temple gas money. They tried to take the same classes so they could tutor one another and study together. In most respects, it was like other college dorms, with the tedious routines broken by cookouts, some socializing, dancing and sports, even wrestling and waterfights. Personalities ran the range from extremely serious students to cutups, from popular students to outcasts. The dorms were governed not only by peer pressure but also by an external bureaucracy. Their often-restated fealty to the Temple, however, was a source of pride as well as control. At least the Temple young people had an outlet for their activist energies, more meaningful and more enduring than many of the issue-oriented outbursts of the sixties.

All in all, the dormitory arrangement was not a bad tradeoff for those committed to the Temple. But not all students came because they were enamored of college credentials or with the concept of achieving their highest human potential for the cause. Mike Touchette, who had been perfectly happy with a post-high school job as a forklift operator, was pressured into it. Jack Beam called him one day to ask his future plans, then told him: "Well, you have a choice. Go to school or go to Vietnam. Jim had a prophecy you would be drafted."

Although cliquishness was frowned upon, Touchette formed his closest friendships with other amiable young men who came to the dorms without real personality or drug problems. Among his best friends were Jim Cobb, who shared Mike's interest in sports, and Wayne Pietila, a Ukiah local who knew what it was like to play a trout or to bring down a deer. Touchette himself was both athlete and outdoorsman. He was easygoing enough to roll with the dorm regimentation, and the cooperative spirit appealed to him.

Dale Parks, a dark-haired serious young man, was the dorm administrator. Cobb, bursting with ideas, idealism and talent, was a sort of leader by acclamation and conducted many of the meetings. Pietila was the treasurer, hard-working, tough and forceful enough to become leader a year later. Among the women were Jones's adopted Korean-American daughter Suzanne, Jim Cobb's sister Terri, Mike Touchette's sister Mickey and Archie Ijames's daughter Anita.

A lot of the students did their best to get a college education, to remain faithful to their social and political ideals and to enjoy life. But some fanatics lived as though Jim Jones *was* omnipresent, and they set themselves up as guardians of absolutism.

David W., who trained for Temple life on Hare Krishna mantras, could not cope very well with levity. Often his disapproval was nonverbal, but it was always felt. One night when the natives were bombarding each other with tennis balls in the dark, David went outside in a huff and bedded down in the backyard. To teach him a lesson, the revelers hosed him with water.

Another fellow who liked his solitude was Larry Schacht, one of the Temple's most heralded reformed drug abusers. Although the former Texas art student had short-circuited his brain with psychedelics, Jones had decided that he would make a good Temple physician. The pastor pulled enough strings and provided enough encouragement to motivate Schacht and point him toward medical school in Mexico. During his premed studies at Santa Rosa, Schacht still would have drug flashbacks. And if people around him became too loud, he would start screaming wildly.

Eventually Schacht lost his zombielike intensity and buckled down to work, alone with his mission, his thoughts and his guitar. "What we are learning, we are learning for the love of Jim Jones," he used to say. His odd combination of total devotion and terrible temper translated into slavish study habits.

For Jeanette Kerns, the first six months of the 1971–72 school year almost met her expectations. After moving out of the Stoen household, she enjoyed herself rollerskating and signing up for classes. At first, the Santa Rosa duplexes seemed very much like the church-operated dormitories she envisioned when she came from Florida. But she stood out among the Temple students—a blond ex-surfer with a bank account, jewelry and fashionable clothes—and the others resented her. One night in the dorm living room when the students were analyzing the problems of another Temple woman and Kerns volunteered to help her with studies, the tables turned suddenly. "Let's talk about *you,*" someone said.

A mild catharsis became an unfettered purge of pet peeves. Kerns was informed that her classical and surfing music, her dressing habits and bleached light-brown hair offended the others. From accusations of vanity, they leaped to racism. "I like my hair and I like the way I am," she cried, fighting back. "If I was a racist, why would I live with you?"

Confused and intimidated, she unintentionally revealed her disenchantment on a holiday trip to Seattle and Vancouver. Jones turned to her at lunch one day: "You've been thinking about leaving, haven't you?" He probably read it on her face or had heard about the conflicts.

Trapped between her own condescending attitudes and the dorm students' hypersensitivity, she admitted, "Yeah, I have." She considered the Temple people the rejects of society, and could not understand why she should take abuse from them.

"You can leave," Jones said kindly. "But you won't be able to finish college. Give it another try. It will be better when you get back to the dorms. You can grow from this experience. You're a humanist." At that time, she was flattered by Jones's sensitivity. His encouragement worked. She resolved to try again.

At the dormitory, her popularity declined nonetheless. The students had vowed to stamp out every remnant of middle-class consciousness. Once a catharsis session developed because Jeanette was wearing her glasses too far down her nose, a sure sign of snobbishness. People began to call her names. One white woman who was accepted by the blacks because of her Jewish heritage leaped to her feet, slapped Kerns across the face, knocking off her glasses, then shoved her into a corner. Others jumped after her before it was stopped. Sobbing, Kerns ran out and packed her clothes. The others blocked the doors and would not allow her outside until she calmed down.

Leaving was more difficult than it had been on the bus trip. She was more securely locked into the church because, in seeking acceptance and peace, she had donated most of her savings. The Temple was her ticket through school, her only foreseeable means to the education she had worked for years to finance. Besides, staying was the only way to really keep in contact with her mother and brother, who were church members. Locking her jaw and sweating out nightmares that caused her to jump in her sleep, she decided to get a good education in spite of her tormentors.

In addition to long church meetings, the dorm students were following another agenda. Kerns, basically conservative but against the war, found herself living among young people who talked of someday being urban guerrillas or dying for socialism. Like communards in Berkeley, Ann Arbor and elsewhere, the dorm students had study groups in Marxism and socialism. Certain leftist books were required reading. Jones had condoned and fed a more-radical-than-thou attitude among his young followers. He converted the dorms gradually into a training center for his future professionals, his socialist vanguard.

Jeanette Kerns hated the socialism classes, which Jones asked Jim Cobb to teach. Mike Touchette enjoyed them, especially discussing such issues as Vietnam and South Africa. The students also researched corporations supporting or benefiting from the war, and they studied the effects of nuclear fallout.

The church monitored the progress and content of the classes. Jones would check with Cobb for an assessment, sometimes taking him aside at weekend services. The pastor seemed pleased usually, but on several occasions he ordered actions that seemed contrary to education about socialism.

At Redwood Valley and in the college dorms, there were purges of socialist books and books that the U.S. government might perceive as subversive. In the valley, men in pickup trucks, led by Jack Beam, made sweeps of Temple residences collecting books for burning or burying. The college students were trusted to purge their own bookshelves. Although some students began to wonder why the raids never materialized and why Jones kept such a tight rein on their political education, their critical attention was not directed at Jones or his policies—not yet.

TWENTY-ONE

Her Father's Daughter

Whenever her father worked bare-chested on their little farm in Redwood Valley, Maria Katsaris could see the sun glint off the cross that hung from a chain around his neck. Each morning of Maria's nineteen years, Steven Katsaris had brought that familiar cross to his lips, like a priest vesting himself. In fact, Steven Katsaris had been an active Greek Orthodox priest most of his life—until recently. Maria remembered that the cross had always been one of her father's dearest possessions, when she was a toddler in Pittsburgh, a buck-toothed six-year-old taking ballet lessons in Salt Lake City, a gawky teen-ager on the San Francisco Peninsula. Beautiful in its simplicity and message, the cross carried the early Christian symbols of Fos, for light, and Zoe, for life. Maria told her father that she wanted to wear it after he died.

When her parents were divorced, Maria lived with her mother a brief time in a San Francisco suburb. But after her graduation from high school in 1970, she and her brother Anthony joined their father in the Ukiah area. Though an authority figure, Katsaris seemed to be on the same side of the generation gap as his children. He criticized outmoded practices in the Greek Orthodox church, and he made a conscious decision to help troubled children rather than build big churches for his denomination.

At first, Maria and Anthony found jobs at a Ukiah kennel. But Maria wanted the challenge and satisfaction of working with children. She applied for a job at Trinity School for mentally disabled students, and she was hired as a teacher's aide through normal channels, though certainly her chances were not harmed by her relationship to the schoolmaster, her father.

Although she was a principled teen-ager and could toss cuss words when appropriate, Maria was reticent and prone to defer to her father in public. She impressed some people as a wallflower. She seemed to lack confidence, and was unsure of her life's direction, though she vaguely wanted to enter nursing school.

At Trinity, she embraced the students as she did her pets. She worked hard to understand and help youngsters suffering from parental abuse, hyperactivity and other emotional disturbances. She loved the job. Each night on the way home to Redwood Valley, she told her father about the day's events—and sought his advice as a psychologist. They laughed, shared their ideas and discussed the state of the world.

At home, they worked together on their several acres. Maria loved animals, so they kept dogs and cats, and maintained a pet cemetery. They constructed a fence around their vegetable garden rather than corral their horse. Together, the father and his children put down new roofing and flooring on the house.

At home and at work, bearded Steve Katsaris remained the patriarch he had been when Maria sat in the front church pews watching him say mass, when they went fishing and horseback riding, and marched against the war. That summer, neither Maria nor Anthony had time for social contacts, and anyway Maria had always led a parochial life.

She had never dated. As a teen-ager she had worn braces to straighten her teeth, and she still thought of herself as a tall, bony ugly duckling. But her face was drawn in long, thin lines that suited her frame. Unpretentious, she wore her dark hair in pigtails and chose jeans over dresses.

Maria made her outside friends among the staff at Trinity, and one of her favorites became thirty-four-year-old Liz Foreman. Maria revealed something of herself to Foreman—the stabbing pain of her parents' divorce during her high school years; her present feelings of isolation in a sheltered lifestyle that seemed to preclude the social life she never had.

As their friendship developed, Maria discovered that Foreman was a member of the kooky church called Peoples Temple and, oddly enough, kept a picture of Jones in her home and a blessed prayer cloth near her heart. Maria's view of the Temple began to change when she saw that it attracted a respected friend who was fifteen years her senior and much more worldly.

Maria's initial negativity toward the Temple may have come from her father. His intelligence had been insulted by the Temple's fawning welcoming efforts when he arrived in Ukiah. Still, the Temple intrigued the humanistic former priest because he was familiar with socialistic and communistic religious groups and had attended numerous tent meetings in the Ohio Bible Belt. Furthermore, he believed in the phenomenon of healing through faith, whether at the Roman Catholic Lourdes in France or various Greek shrines. He had become more curious when he too discovered that Liz Foreman was a member. One day, while having lunch with Foreman in the school cafeteria, he inquired about meeting this purportedly clairvoyant minister named Jones.

In one sense, it probably seemed prudent to welcome a humanitarian like Katsaris. He had a slightly "hip" appearance, had recently divorced, and was drifting away from the rigidity of the Greek Orthodox church. But great risks would be inherent in opening the doors to the former priest. First, he had influence in the religious community. Second, he had theological training and experience. Third, as head of the school and as a fair-sized employer, he came in contact with influential people. Fourth, he was a psychologist who was likely to see through Jones's tricks, and perhaps to spot his mental disorders. At this time, Jones had already run afoul of the psychology community in Indiana. Katsaris could harm—or help the Temple cause on several fronts.

In the end, Jones directed Liz Foreman to extend an invitation, and one Sunday, Katsaris, Maria, her brother Anthony and a Trinity School psychologist who was curious, strolled into the Redwood Valley church.

The obligatory hour of hymns and testimonials was unremarkable. Then, just as they were expecting Jones's act, a church member, Bob E., tapped their shoulders. "Rev. Katsaris, this is a closed meeting." He was polite yet firm.

"You're mistaken," Katsaris said. "I got invited by Liz Foreman." Maria was miffed too. "We're not gonna stay if we're not wanted."

The following morning, Rev. Jones called to apologize. "Rev. Katsaris. I didn't know you were there. It was in fact a closed meeting. I'm sorry. If I had known you were there. . . ."

"Thanks for calling," said Katsaris.

Now even more anxious to see Jones in action, Katsaris soon attended a public Peoples Temple "tent meeting" in a big hall at the county fairgrounds. Anthony and Maria tagged along again. Again, when Jones's appearance neared, Katsaris was tapped on the shoulder. A Temple lawyer, Eugene Chaikin, escorted him deep into the parking lot, some distance from the hall.

"Pastor Jones," the attorney said, "asked me to ask you if there's anything he can do for Trinity School."

Peeved that he had been lured outside, Katsaris said abruptly, "Thank you. If there is anything that comes to mind, I'll let you know." He was eager to return for the finale.

As he started back toward the hall, however, the mellow-sounding attorney clamped a hand on his arm. "Is there any painting you need done?"

"I'll have to talk to the maintenance department." There was a loud outburst inside the auditorium. Katsaris impatiently brushed aside Chaikin and hurried back inside in time to see that a nurse showing a joyous audience something in a handkerchief.

Maria and Anthony wanted out. "Let's go, Pop," she said, disgusted. "Yeah, it's really creepy," added Anthony. As they hurried away, they quickly told their father about the discharged "cancer." "Was it phony?" they wanted to know.

"You'd have to see it first," Katsaris answered. Their hasty exit was cut off by a concerned-looking law student named Harriet Tropp. "Why are you leaving? Did you see something you didn't like?"

Katsaris was angry at being stalled. Later he wryly told Liz Foreman, "If it was a miracle, I missed it."

The phone rang at Katsaris's home late one night following the tent service. An apologetic Jim Jones invited Katsaris and his family to a service that very night, August 1, 1972. Katsaris graciously accepted, unaware of the extraordinary groundwork being laid for his supposedly informal visit.

At the church, with the full congregation before him, Jones criticized his people for allowing Katsaris to go away upset from the church and fairgrounds. "Name-takers," Jones addressed those who screened visitors at the door. "The minute you hear a 'reverend,' say, 'Oh, we're so glad you came. We're sorry. But we're having a confession. Our people feel more at ease when they confess their faults to one another.' Don't say, 'Members only.' That sounds too uppity, too proud. Handle it discreetly. What we'll do if enough people want [to visit] is to call a special Saturday night service and be the straightest bunch of people you've ever seen. We'll have a devotional service and have Purity sing and Joy read from the Bible and we'll not cuss that night." His congregation burst into laughter at that—Purity and Joy were old followers of Father Divine who had never brought themselves to use foul language like the rest.

Next, Jones wanted to know what "feedback" had followed the Katsaris family's rude treatment at the tent service. Taking the microphone, Liz Foreman recounted how she had acted "naïve," as instructed, when Katsaris asked her about it. But, she reported, Katsaris was suspicious of the Temple's motives and he thought the treatment might have been deliberate because the Temple detected the family's negative feelings about the church. He went so far as to ask Foreman to find out why Chaikin "really" wanted him in the parking lot during the healing.

"Well," said Jones. "We didn't handle it right from the start, so I have to meet them [now]. I'm not threatened by those blowhards. . . . What kind of political stand do they take openly?" He was thinking aloud, trying to shape his strategy.

Liz Foreman, his expert on the Katsaris family, could not place the priest politically. "He's never said what his politics are. He's never committed himself. . . . He feels he just wants to observe."

Jones was suspicious. Undeterred by that rather neutral evaluation, he blustered, "I'll probably threaten him so badly [that] when I'm through he'll want to fight me that much more, because the truth usually threatens hypocrites. . . .

"He's up to something," Jones declared. "He's got ahold of a wind he thinks he can agitate a little."

Foreman then portrayed herself as an infiltrator in Katsaris's school and family. "The daughter says she's thinking about becoming a member and wants to talk to you personally. I said it's a very difficult thing to talk to our pastor."

Mocking the sincerity and naïveté of the girl he never had met, he said to laughter, "Oh, dear God. Tell her to come too."

Quickly the plan was fixed. "We'll throw them some loops tonight," he confided. "We'll have no healing here tonight, you hear? Only what I do under the table." They laughed. "We'll talk about humanism and service work to our fellowman and God," he explained like a coach chalking up plays. "If I say you're an atheist tonight or a fundamentalist, you be that tonight. Right?"

"Right," they shouted.

"We have some really bad enemies up to no good and we have to give them the wrong scent. . . ." Jones was sharing secrets, and his people were delighted at being in on the game. He assigned specific roles to some, such as Chaikin, who was told to attest to a healing.

"Don't call me 'Father' or 'Savior' tonight," Jones cautioned. "We don't want anything controversial. I'm ordering you to say, 'Jim' tonight, no exceptions. . . . You won't be taking respect away by calling me 'Jim.' "

Soon the Katsaris family—Steve and his second wife Ann, plus Anthony and Maria—entered and introduced themselves at the microphone, to a tumultuous prearranged welcome. Jones ventured the first move: "I understand there was a communications breakdown between you and the group, and I thought the best way was for you to come and get to know us. . . ."

In shorthand fashion, he then described the Temple: "We have liberal and orthodox here, agnostics and fundamentalists. Some see me as a spiritual being, but most just think of me as Jim Jones." He asked if Katsaris had any questions. Katsaris said he was happy to be there, pleased to meet Jones and did not feel any enmity. In fact, he said, he knew little of the Temple.

After an exhaustive recitation of Temple achievements, Jones confided some of his plans for expansion in the San Francisco Bay Area, and noted, "We've run into a problem [here] based on the liberalism of my theology." Jones had pegged Katsaris as a liberal—and as someone concerned about his daughter. To counter any fears Katsaris might have of the church courting Maria, Jones announced that the Temple was deemphasizing local recruiting.

Though reserving some skepticism, Katsaris formed a favorable opinion of Jones. Rather than hurl stormy oratory, Jones caressed his people with talk of social justice, functioning more as a moderator or provoker of ideas than an omniscient voice. He seemed to be addressing important social issues in a practical, Christian way. And the meeting ended with no act of clairvoyance, no "cancer miracle." The only unusual things Katsaris noticed were a pair of signs. One said, "Take as much food as you want, but only as much as you can eat," and the other explained that Pastor Jones wore secondhand clothes and had only one suit to his name. The apologia rang a little phony, but overall the experience was a warm and positive one.

At the invitation of Tim Stoen, Steve and Maria Katsaris walked to the Jones home for a nightcap of coffee, tea or milk. About ten members were sitting around talking, among them Marceline and Grace and Tim Stoen. Jim Jones, wearing dark glasses, strode into the room a half hour later. Though Jones was outgoing and friendly, Katsaris distrusted the dark-glasses routine and was disturbed by the adulation waved around like great fans to Jones's ego. "Our pastor is very kind to animals," an apparently mature adult would pipe up, while someone else would chime in: "Our pastor says we should be good to children and to our seniors."

Maria sat quietly through the session. She had already contacted the church, unbeknownst to her father. Jones would take a strong interest in her, and would tell Liz Foreman, "Maria is a highly evolved person, and we have to attract her and keep her." It would not take much work to make her a loyal and dedicated member, thanks in part to the humanitarianism and sensitivity instilled by her family.

But other factors made the winning of Maria Katsaris more desirable, and easier. If Jones could steal her love from her father, she might eventually become as dedicated to his Temple "Family" as she had been to her own. The conquest would be all the more gratifying because Maria was another cleric's daughter—in that respect another Carolyn Layton or Annie Moore. Jones's disdain for Katsaris—a hypocrite he called him—was raw, and he relished duping him, outwitting him, making him the fool. His tactic was this: he would attempt to convince part of Maria that she was achieving independence from a powerful father figure while actually she was becoming totally dependent upon another.

By small increments, Maria became involved in the Temple. Under Jones's instructions, Foreman brought her to services and sat with her. Jones sold Maria through his message and his manner, as well as through the Temple people and good works. One day she told her father, "I'm going on a bus trip to San Francisco and won't be back until Sunday. I'm going to help some people in the ghetto."

Katsaris was proud of her; but he soon became increasingly uneasy with her detachment. Their communications stiffened, and she spent more time with Liz Foreman than with her own family. It became difficult to talk, especially about the church. In response to questions, she would offer only terse answers such as, "I worked in the day care center."

"What do you do there?"

"We take care of kids."

She would not lie, but spoke only in generalities. Maria's secrecy soon made Katsaris desperate, and he turned to his own staff. "What's going on with Maria?" he asked her contemporaries and friends. Various theories were offered—delayed teen-age reactions, rebellion or overreaching for independence.

Whatever it was, Katsaris hoped that she would outgrow it. But their relationship became more strained. Maria never would talk freely about the church except to make pat defenses when her father challenged her beliefs. She steadfastly refused to fill in her cliché-ridden sketch of a do-gooder organization.

This was the same pattern experienced by the Houstons, the Moores, the Laytons and others. Families were torn by two conflicting forces—appreciation and pride over the humanitarian work, unhappiness and suspicions about the isolation and subtle alienation manifested in flat communications and unwillingness to discuss the Temple in detail. The secrecy drove a wedge between members and their families; on one side, it created family resentment toward the church; on the other, it made continued family communications awkward for the member.

In the case of Katsaris, the pain of separation from his daughter was prolonged over a period of years. His daughter's love would not be quickly obliterated or transferred to someone else. Also, Katsaris, like Rev. Moore and his wife, was relatively invulnerable to divide-and-conquer tactics commonly used against other families. For instance, Jones could not score points with Maria by labeling her father a racist or a fascist. Furthermore, Katsaris was astute and understanding enough to avoid serious direct confrontations with his daughter over the church. He realized that Maria's feelings had become so hardened that he would risk losing his child altogether with ill-considered words and actions. His basic tactic, his natural tendency, was to keep extending love to Maria.

For all his restraint, occasionally concern overwhelmed him. One night, for instance, he drove Maria to a meeting at the Temple and came upon formations of men wearing uniforms and berets. Their arms were folded like lightweight imitations of the Black Panthers in the 1960s. To Katsaris, it looked like a parade of paramilitary punks, and he told Maria so. "Maria, that is uncalled for," he said. "If you don't want the local population to be concerned, you shouldn't do that."

"But, Pop," she pointed out, "people threatened Jim Jones. They honk their horns during church services, and they call us 'nigger lovers.' "

Something serious was happening to Maria, but her father felt helpless to draw her out of her isolation. Since joining the church in 1973, she always had found excuses to avoid her father's home. When invited to dinner, she would accept then cancel at the last moment. During her only weekend home, she looked haggard and worn and slept until noon the next day. Her father was tempted to look through her purse for drugs but was afraid to violate her privacy or push for answers.

Maria showed the classic signs of a dedicated Temple member. The cause consumed her life, and she thought that outsiders, including family members, were frittering away theirs. She was living in Temple dormitories, going to school, working on church finances and attending services. Another job, another fragment of routine, always awaited her. She had not yet discovered the difficult realities beneath that catchphrase of other children of the 1960s: "Revolution in our lifetime."

Jones had touched her and claimed her by meeting her needs.

Recognizing her inferiority feelings and insecurity, he elevated Maria on his organizational chart. Taking an average student who had shown little leadership aptitude, he built her confidence and gave meaning to her life by giving her an expanding role in the church.

In the Temple climate of radical feminism, her father was a convenient target—the domineering male ready to be blamed for Maria's insecurity. That became the conventional Temple wisdom, along with the myth that Maria hated her father. Though Jones could demand pounds of effort from her, he could not decimate her love for her father. He had, however, created a tremendous conflict in her. She felt guilty about going home and was discouraged from doing so, but in her conversations with her friend in the dorms, Jeanette Kerns, she exuded respect and love for her father. No doubt Maria dreaded the day of decision, but with each passing year it became more inevitable. She would have to choose between her own father and "Father."

Since he could make no headway with his own daughter, Katsaris chose another course, one that carried him into Jones's lair. Knowing the Temple was inclined to isolate its enemies, Katsaris went to county counsel Tim Stoen's office to plead his case. He told Stoen, whom he knew through official county business, that he was disturbed that Maria felt she could not maintain a close rapport with her family. To put the church at ease, Katsaris reminded Stoen that he had donated money to support the church's good works.

"Let me talk to Jim," Stoen said. Two days later, he reported back to Katsaris, "Jim is concerned. . . . And he wants Maria to maintain the highest possible contacts with her family." Actually, Jones had told Maria to do everything possible to soothe her father's concerns, meaning she should call, write or visit often enough to keep him at bay.

Maria's contacts with her father, like the contacts of other members with their families, fell generally into three categories: the guarded conversations when she was at the Temple; more open conversations when she called from pay phones; and contacts she made for the express purpose of extracting favors that related to the church.

Maria had no trouble obtaining money and donations from her father, even if it meant lying to him. Once, when the church fined her and another woman four hundred dollars for improperly dispensing toilet articles, she told him she was seriously ill and needed that much money for a hospital stay. She got it. Then, around Christmas 1974, she called to ask for a favor that would prove fateful.

The Temple had chartered a plane to carry Jones, some top aides and a few settlers to Georgetown, Guyana, to inspect the overseas mission that would become Jonestown. Maria had apparently been invited along at the last minute. But she needed a passport, quickly. "Pop, I have a chance to go to a jungle mission in South America," she announced enthusiastically. "Some people dropped out, so there's room for me. I can go but I need a passport right away, and I need a birth certificate to get it."

Katsaris had no objection to the trip; after all Maria was in nursing school at the time, and it made sense to visit a "medical mission," as the newly founded settlement was described. He made a few phone calls and, as a result, Maria's passport was processed in time. When Maria returned, she would tell him virtually nothing—though the voyage had changed her, permanently.

On the flight to Guyana, Maria had barely settled in before Jones sauntered over to her and took the seat beside her. He said something to her; she shook her head as he walked away. Patty Cartmell, who was laughingly known to aides as Jones's "fucking secretary" because she wrote the names of his sexual partners in a slender notebook, took his place beside Maria.

The next time Jones returned to Maria's side, he stayed for several hours. It was evident to all around that Father was about to take the next step in "building her self-esteem." The other passengers watched him work on her. Some approved the display, others envied it, still others ignored it. But no one would have dreamed of interfering even had they known she was a virgin.

Instead they gazed on voyeuristically as Jones, at forty-four old enough to be her father, casually draped his hand around the back of her seat and showered her with his silvery voice, his engaging manner, his complete attention. Summoning every bit of his charm, he went through his well polished routine. Yet Maria responded without warmth or animation; she seemed more intent on finishing the book on her lap. Jones finally fell asleep, his hand gently resting on her shoulder.

But something happened during the next few days in the tropics. Maria was observed repeatedly at Jim's elbow. On one occasion, she became excessively protective of him, almost possessive. While a Temple photographer was snapping pictures of Jones, she suddenly snapped at him: "Can't you see Father isn't feeling well? You shouldn't be taking his picture now." She was having trouble coping with what must have been a multitude of feelings, anxieties, uncertainties. She would start sobbing for no apparent reason. Jones would comfort her. After a few days, she looked awful, with her eyes red and puffy, marks all over her neck.

Only after the contingent came home to the States did word filter down that Jones had accepted a new mistress on the trip. The story current among Jones's staff was that Maria, devastated by jealousy when she learned Jones had made love to another woman, demanded he sleep immediately with her, even though it meant giving up her virginity. Staff members were not surprised that Maria had "sought" Jones's love, since they thought the young woman had a low self-image and a history of domineering men. It never seemed to occur to them that Jones's lovemaking could be less than selfless.

By 1975, Maria had been fully established as one of Jones's principal mistresses. She had quit school and moved into the San Francisco temple as a full-time worker. Those who had known her prior to her rise were dismayed by the changes in her. Her self-effacing humor evaporated —she became an ultraloyalist. As was expected of her, she reported people for minor infractions such as smoking and once turned in another member for an imagined homosexual overture. Occasionally, and with a few select people, her plucky sense of fun returned. But sleeping with Jones was a punishing experience—it thrust a companionable young woman into an arena of rivalries, hostilities and jealousies for which she was ill prepared.

Once word got around that a particular woman had been intimate with Father, she was competing directly with other mistresses, and the unchosen would turn on her. Once she had been a wonderful person, they would carp—now she was just another bitch. The hypercritical posturing and snappishness of a Carolyn Layton or Maria Katsaris may well have been a defense to such resentment. They knew they could expect nothing better: the reward was the curse.

Steven Katsaris was surprised to learn that Maria was taking flying lessons with Debbie Touchette at an Oakland flight training school. Maria had shown almost an aversion to flying since childhood days in Utah where Katsaris, an experienced pilot, had used a plane often for both priestly duties and pleasure. Frequent airsickness had caused the kids to vow to stay earthbound. Now, Maria maintained to her father, she hoped to become a commercial pilot—she did not mention the planned church migration to South America, and the possible need for pilots there.

This newfound common interest in aviation became a tenuous link in the father-daughter relationship. Seeking his advice as an experienced pilot provided Maria with a safe rationale for maintaining contact and flying provided her with relative freedom of movement.

Fatherly concern took over at the outset. At one point, Katsaris and a friend who was an airline pilot checked out Maria's technique. Although it was a gusty spring day with difficult flying conditions, Katsaris was comforted to see Maria's light touch on the controls, her calm professional manner. The lessons had not been wasted. "How am I doin', Pop?" she asked, still seeking approval. Proud, he complimented and encouraged her, and offered her use of his airplane. She thanked him, but never took the offer.

Katsaris called Maria once or twice a week at the San Francisco temple. He noticed the long delays before she took the line and the strained conversations, and wondered whether the calls were being monitored. Sometimes he offered Maria use of the plane. Sometimes he invited her to dinner. There always was an excuse, distance politely interposed. His feelings were hurt, but he took comfort in the fact that Maria's calls from pay phones, presumably unmonitored, brought out more warmth.

One morning in 1976, while Katsaris worked on the roof of his house, a small plane circled overhead, knifed between two pine trees and buzzed him. It was a neat pass. A short while later, Maria called from Red Bluff to tell him she was on another cross-country flight. But that swoop of her plane had said it all: she was still her father's daughter.

TWENTY-TWO

The Arms of God

Steve Katsaris had been correct in his reading of the local people. They viewed the Temple's strange behavior and security precautions with alarm. Certainly there were some rednecks who talked about driving the church out of town, but generally area residents were more than happy to keep their distance from the large, increasingly militant group. Yet they were curious about the many people who seemed to come and go in secrecy. And they wondered what kept lights burning and traffic flowing until early morning.

The crew at the volunteer fire department often watched the bustle of the Temple office-apartment complex next door. They could not tell which children belonged to which adults, or who was married to whom. For inexplicable reasons, most Temple members acted distant or unfriendly, though Grace Stoen always made it a point to exchange cheery hellos. The church members who came to shop at the local market were polite, but they never bought cigarettes or liquor. Sometimes they brought along a baby chimpanzee named Mr. Muggs.

At first all this merely baffled the locals. Then things became disconcerting.

First, Temple members started taking down the license number of every vehicle parked near their complex or in front of their laundromat, which was open to the public. They even jotted down the numbers of cars pulling up to the adjacent volunteer fire department during a fire emergency. Then, using an old black and white police car outfitted with a CB radio, church security members started tailing people who drove past the church late at night. A woman walking home passed the Temple one night and suddenly was bathed in an eerie gray: the church grounds had lit up like a prison courtyard.

Gradually the church had taken on the appearance of an armed compound. Chain-link fencing topped by barbed wire circled the place. Floodlights attached to telephone poles were spaced around the perimeter, facing outward, apparently to illuminate or blind intruders. A guard shack was built atop a tall cage for the chimpanzee; now and then a local would spot a Temple patroller with a gun.

Locals wondered if they had a paramilitary army on their hands. One hot summer day, dozens of Temple security guards with black uniforms and berets stood at attention in 100-degree heat across the front of the property. The reason: the Hell's Angels had been observed in bars in the area en route to a Lake Mendocino outing. Ostensibly, the Temple wanted to be ready for any attack. It was a long wait.

Local people did not doubt that some individuals with bellies full of beer might have shouted racial slurs at the church, or honked pickup truck horns or tossed a rock or beer can while driving past the church grounds. But they had not heard or read about any incidents warranting extreme measures.

About the only mention of harassment came in the early 1970s in a Kathy Hunter article headlined: LOCAL GROUP SUFFERS TERROR IN THE NIGHT. The few incidents it detailed were reminiscent of those in Indiana —a breather making phone calls in the middle of the night; an anonymous caller threatening, "Get out of town"; references to right-wing retaliation, and the random comment of some dim-witted gas station attendant: "We ought to rock 'em out of town."

Church members saw the menace of the surrounding population in much more vivid and violent terms than the alleged incidents committed to print and police blotters. Every minor incident inflamed the growing security panic which sprang from organizational needs and personality changes in Jones.

Despite his "big scare" rhetoric in the 1960s, Jones had maintained an appearance of Gandhian or Kinglike nonviolence, the Christian posture of turning the other cheek. Still, it was no great task for Jones to inure his pacifistic flock to violence. He had long since perfected the trick of keeping the audience's attention on one hand while the other did the magic. Though he condemned the outbreak of leftist and antiwar violence, he began to drift, almost imperceptibly at first, toward the acceptance of force. Through fear, violent rhetoric and fakery, he conditioned his people gradually to accept defensive violence, and he enlarged the definition of self-defense until it became: attack at my command and in defense of principle—socialism—and of me.

At the end of the 1960s, as the Temple began to expand into larger cities, Jones engaged himself in greater conflict. Now he was competing directly with urban ministers and to some extent with militant groups such as the Black Panthers or Black Muslims. He sought and took on the trappings of a movement leader.

Jones protested on many occasions that he did not fear losing his own life for the cause. Martyrdom—in the style of other great leaders of the 1960s such as Martin Luther King, Jr., the Kennedy brothers and Malcolm X—was a sort of inspirational vision to him. He foresaw himself at a podium going down in a spray of hot lead: Malcolm X in New York in 1965. He promoted this image through the most underhanded means, manipulating the love of his people, filling them with his own fears of hostile or threatening outsiders. He even convinced them that never-definable enemies had been making attempts on his life.

Jones fantasized attacks on the church and magnified some real hostility from the outside community, blowing it all into a siege mentality that would remain to the end. He conditioned his people to self-defense and armed an elite and put them in uniform. He involved both men and women in unarmed security duties around the church and in taking karate lessons. Having stripped his men of false macho attitudes, he exploited those same tendencies by urging them to heroic and protective feats. He encouraged the natural tendency toward radicalism in Temple students, prodding them in the direction of urban guerrilla game playing, even arranging weapons training for some.

By the mid-1970s, all the military elements were in place. The church had stockpiled almost two hundred guns; a security squad of a few dozen people had been trained; Jones traveled everywhere with body-guards; there were procedures for searching all who entered Temple services, and Temple buses had armed escorts. Paranoia, an inflated view of his own importance and the need for an atmosphere of apprehension kept security as a primary concern. But Jones could not rely on drunken rednecks or an occasional epithet to keep his people in a besieged state of mind. Thus he found it necessary to whip them up with sermons and absurd, orchestrated attacks. Feigning violence was but a short step beyond phony healings. All Jones required were some gunshots fired from a mysterious source; then he would take over with a routine that combined both the heart attack and stigmata acts. At first, the culprits were as-sumed to be local rednecks. Later, the villains—none were ever ap-prehended—took on other identities.

The collision course had been set, because Jones could not elude his own sickness. Lynetta Jones, lamenting the unsolved killings of two Tem-ple dogs, provided a wrenching portent of things to come:

". . . These animals, instinctively seeking help, dragged themselves home to die. To die in the excruciating pain of one spasm closely followed by another. The rigidity of jaw, the foam-flecked mouth, the glazed eyes, mute testimony to the present day savage who kills for the joy of killing. Grim handywork of the cowardly poisoner who would prolong the agony of death to sate the devil within himself."

In addition to threatening phone calls and verbal assaults, various other incidents of harassment were reported to church members. Some were relayed to the sheriff; many were not. Garbage was dumped on the Temple grounds. Someone threw crayfish on the driveway and crushed them with a car. Someone hung a Temple dog with a spike through its neck. As in Indiana, dead animals were hurled at the church. A burned-out firebomb was found at the building (in Indiana it had been a stick of dynamite on the coalpile). And someone apparently tried to run down some black children walking to school.

It was a fairly convincing array of attacks. Yet most members still did not conclude that they were engaged in a life-death struggle. No one had been seriously injured, let alone killed. The closest brushes with death were near-accidents from faulty car components—dangers predicted by Jones. Members would find that a tire was about to fall off or their steering mountings were completely loosened, or a vehicle would almost run them off the road at a place described by Jones.

Their only constant reminder that Jones would die in defense of his principles was his permanently bent pinky. This was the result, he told his followers, of his intervening on the side of a black man against a white knife-wielding attacker in Indiana. According to the story, Jones, though suffering a severed tendon, had managed to bludgeon the assailant with a brick, probably killing him. The message was inspiring enough that some children—and a few adults—started holding their pinky the same way.

Finally on a pleasant Redwood Valley afternoon in the summer of 1972, the church's paranoia exploded into genuine fear. The congregation had gathered, a few hundred strong, in the parking lot between the parsonage and the Temple. While food and plates were arranged on long rows of utility tables, the church band performed. Teen-agers were shooting a few baskets. Some older folks took to the shade.

Then a boom froze the scene. Stephan Jones, thirteen, thought that a musician had stomped hard on a bass drum. Then he turned and saw his father hit the ground with a thud. Dozens of terrified faces turned on their leader. The shot had originated among the tall, dense grapevines, to one side of the lot. Stephan's big mongrel Husky bolted in that direction, barking and ready to do battle. The people started to take off that way too, but Jones, clutching his hands to his bloody chest, stopped them. "No. No," he choked. "That way." He pointed weakly in almost the opposite direction, ordering everyone toward the rear of the house.

In the pandemonium, the pack obeyed Jones. One older man almost had a heart attack; still he managed to pick up a shovel and join the pursuit, ready to brain someone. Old ladies trembled, and one woman screamed hysterically, thinking Jones had been assassinated, just like the other great leaders of recent years. Stephan stood by as people fussed over his father; something did not seem quite right. Why did his father direct the pursuers away from the vineyard?

With Marci and the nurses swarming around him, Jones struggled bravely to his feet, and was helped toward his house. Jack Beam suddenly appeared and took one arm. The people feared they had lost their God.

A half hour later, Jim Jones walked out of the house under his own power. The crowd gasped in relief and praised the heavens. Jones turned

to his nurses: "Tell them. Tell them about the hole I had in me." While
Jack Beam held up the bloody shirt with a hole, one Temple nurse testified,
"I could stick my fingers in the wound." Lack of a hole in Jim's chest was
proof of the miracle. He had healed himself, he said. And to underscore
his capacity for forgiveness and mercy, he confessed that he had sent his
people away from the shooter, so the would-be assassin could make a
clean getaway and not be harmed. An emotional, uproarious meeting of
thanksgiving followed.

To remind his followers of his miracle, Jones commissioned Archie
Ijames to build a wooden case with a glass front to display the bloody
shirt. The relic was shown for only one meeting, however. The sheriff's
office heard about the shooting incident somehow and made an inquiry to
Jones. That scared him more than the shooting. With miraculous speed,
the display case went into storage.

Those who were familiar with the mechanics of his healings were
unbothered by the shooting incident. The manipulation was valid because
the outcome was positive: the shooting unified people and made them
realize that they had enemies, real enemies who would stop at nothing to
destroy them.

Meanwhile, Jones encouraged the dorm students to take more direct and militaristic action than socialism classes. Suddenly, without a
graceful transition, Jim Jones, the man who named his firstborn after
Gandhi, had begun quoting Che Guevara's pat phrase: "The bullet or the
ballot." His vanguard of young people was told they might have to protect
the Temple family against attack. Shoot straight and survive, they were
advised.

The dorm students supplemented their political theory readings
with study of military strategy, wilderness survival techniques, explosives and weaponry. Members were given military problems related to
safeguarding Temple buses traveling to and from their cave shelter during nuclear warfare.

The cadre took to the woods regularly, too, for maneuvers in steep
and densely forested terrain. For some it was torture, but for many it
blew away the tensions of the classroom as they raced up and down hills,
fantasizing revolution and timing each other. They rappelled down cliffs
with ropes or learned to hide in the bush, to travel silently, to use binoculars and compasses, to find the enemy, to ambush.

At the urging of Jones, some dorm students went out and bought
a few M-1 carbines. Target practice was great fun, but deep down they
knew that they were not Che Guevaras, and no revolution had arrived.
Yet, in the summer of 1972, Jim Cobb and four other Temple members
would be admitted to a special three-month course in weapons and legal
training conducted by the San Francisco Police Department. Jones finally
had sneaked some of his best people inside the belly of the beast. At the

conclusion, the students were entitled as reserve or special police officers to carry a gun and do private security work.

Self-protection became a preoccupation with Jones, almost as though he believed in the incidents he himself faked. In the space of a few years, security went from a one-man operation to a Secret Service-type blanket force. Armed protection was inaugurated in about 1969. At first, Marvin Swinney, a husky five-foot-eleven, 190-pounder whose family had been following Jones for years, worked alone, legally armed with a gun permit. Then he was augmented by Jones's trusted aides, Jack Beam and Archie Ijames. In August 1972, Jones told the whole congregation, "I'd like to see you get your minds and spirits so you could hold . . . guns and not feel any hypocrisy." By late 1972, ten or eleven Temple members were attending special meetings for holders of gun permits, and Jones's coterie of guards at services numbered at least thirty men and women, about five of them armed.

As the church flourished, more security personnel were needed to pat-search all men who entered services and sift through the purses of women. Very few guns were confiscated, but knives piled up. At each meeting, security officers also checked around the podium and elsewhere for bombs and listening devices. Jones dreaded the thought that a tape of one of his socialistic Bible stomps might fall into the hands of an enemy.

"Security" trained with weapons at a private gun club off Highway 101, or simply went into the woods. Jones chose the group from staff, planning commission, and the rank and file. Some members were brought to security mainly because of physical stature, others because they knew how to handle firearms. The same team did not serve at every event. Sometimes, if Jones wished to impress people with muscle, he brought out the meanest, most hulking crew he could assemble. If he wanted a lower profile, he used women and less intimidating men.

When they put their bodies around Jones, it was as though they were shielding a world leader. All orders had to come from Jones himself. They were his personal police force.

Despite the formalized training and snappy uniforms—usually leisure suits of various colors, shirts, ties and berets—it was on the whole a ragtag group of amateurs. No doubt that was why Jones imposed strict regulations on firearms use, especially in crowds. No one was supposed to show a gun except on the command of Jones, yet some guards flaunted them. A couple of times Jones even ordered security to display their weapons in meetings, a show of force like a scene from a bad gangster movie.

Teddy Ballard, at seventeen hardly a professional teacher, conducted karate classes for about fifty people twice a week. Claiming martial arts expertise, Jones would come watch the lessons. But he phased them out after a month because the students shouted too loudly during practice. He was afraid the locals would feel threatened.

To maintain the same high level of vigilance on the road and to protect the offerings money, Bus No. 7 was heavily armed, usually with a shotgun, a rifle and at least one pistol. The bus escorts, converted black and white Highway Patrol cars, were equipped with CB radios so they could communicate among themselves on trips. Security squad cars often met returning buses several miles outside of Ukiah and escorted them home in event of some threat or crisis.

Despite their ultraloyalist demeanors, security people came to recognize that Jones was afraid for his life. Some were disguised to look like Jones so that they would take any bullets meant for him. One of these "doubles," Wayne Pietila, wondered why the self-sacrificing Jones was unwilling to take bullets when he supposedly could cure himself anyway. Security guards also were among the first to doubt the authenticity of attacks on Jones.

Most curious was the phantomlike ability of would-be assassins to vanish, of alleged bullets to penetrate a plywood antiassassin screen without making holes, of Jones to know almost as though on cue exactly when the shots would ring out. Once as the congregation went into hysterics, Jones clutched his head and shouted, "Calm down. I've been shot in the head, but I'm all right." His explanation? "I dematerialized the bullets."

In close quarters, the guards got intimate glimpses at Jones's healings too. Jim Cobb was assigned to guard the "cancers" as they were paraded around the church after healings. If it looked as though someone might get their hands on one of the putrid things, he was supposed to destroy the evidence by eating it first.

Accidents happened too. One day, a telephone man was making some repairs at the Jones house, and he found a small overnight case. The first urgent phone call went to Marvin Swinney, since he was head of security. Swinney, thinking the case might contain a bomb, hustled over. He opened it gingerly, first the clasp, then the lid, ever so slowly. A terrible smell invaded his nostrils. In a plastic bag was a blob of chicken guts fermenting. When Swinney brought the find to Jones's attention, the minister erupted: "It's somebody trying to plant something to make me look bad. I'll take care of these."

At one point, the gun situation started to slip out of control. It was a wonder that no one was shot when crises developed. Some guards were wearing guns on their hips Western-style, bragging about pistols in front of kids and showing off. A number did not understand the first thing about gun safety. Swinney was not particularly comforted when he saw Jones himself carrying a little .25-caliber automatic pistol—which he claimed the sheriff suggested he carry.

Finally, Jones too decided that his people were using their guns as phallic symbols and that an excessive number owned weapons. Out of concern that someone—even he—might be shot, he ordered everyone to turn in their firearms. Members surrendered more than 170 of them— everything from expensive deer rifles with scopes to Saturday Night Specials to shotguns. The guns were stored at the Stoen house. Then one day, a church member transported them to a secure place in San Francisco. Some later would be sold or junked and others would be secreted in crates bound for South America, where they would be turned on outsiders for the first time.

PART FOUR

A DELICATE BALANCE

Wherever you have lied,
permanently or to stop awhile,
you will make your little lies come forth,
little thin wisps of lies at first,
then larger windblown ones,
complete with all the anger
that seethes within yourself. . . .

LYNETTA JONES
"Ode to Liars"

TWENTY-THREE

First Cracks

During the California period, Jones had kept a nominal outpost in Indiana, mainly so he could recruit there on the Temple's periodic cross-country bus excursions. It made sense to keep a foot in the fertile midwestern recruiting territory. In fact, a small group of loyalists left behind in Indianapolis had been managing the nursing homes, the former church and other Temple income properties. And Jones probably envisioned a permanent base in the Bible Belt. But his return to Indianapolis in 1971 brought on trouble with dire implications for the future.

On this stopover, the former Indianapolis human rights director downplayed socialism in his services, as he usually did on the road. But he made the mistake of failing to temper his healings, which caused the vigilant local press to jump on his grandiose claim to be a Prophet of God, with power to raise people from the dead. Suddenly newspapers which had ignored or missed Jones's healing ministry in the past were exposing him. The story was a bizarre one: the city's first paid human rights director had returned as a healing huckster.

CHURCH FILLED TO SEE "CURES" BY SELF-PROCLAIMED "PROPHET OF GOD," read the headline of a skeptical first-person account in the *Indianapolis Star* October 14, 1971. Though the reporter did not accuse Jones directly of fakery, he did comment: "The people who were called upon in the evening [service] had a striking resemblance to some who were called upon earlier in the day." The news coverage set the Indiana State Psychology Board to investigating Jones's claims of curing "psychosomatic diseases" through "parapsychology."

Stung by the story and afraid of the investigations, Jones moderated his pitch when he returned to Indiana two months later. On this December 1971 visit, he downplayed the miracle-working, emphasizing instead the Temple's social work in California. He also launched a diatribe against faith healers who spent their money on Lincoln Continentals and opulent houses of worship. Jones did manage a little healing—he had a woman pass a cancer and then ordered it paraded around like a saint's relic—but he also made a disclaimer: "Don't give up on the medical profession or on parapsychology."

The press and the local establishment were not appeased by such peace offerings. A doctor joined the opposition, expressing public concern that genuinely sick people might defer crucial medical treatment because of Jones's quackery. When the doctor and others challenged Jones to submit the "cancers" to laboratory analysis, Jones said that he would welcome such tests, but that his publicity-shy church leaders would not allow it. Besides, he went on, someone might switch the bona fide cancers with a phony substance. His "enemies" would do anything to discredit his powers. In fact, he noted, there had been no fewer than twenty-three threats on his life since the *Indianapolis Star* story two months earlier.

Seeing he would be hounded and investigated in his home state, the Prophet retreated. At the tail end of his healing campaign, he indicated he would permanently discontinue his Indiana ministry because, he said, of the great distance from his main church in California. After that graceful exit, the Temple did sell the nursing homes, the church and other properties. Two corporations chartered in Indiana were so inactive that they had their charters revoked. And Tim Stoen flew to the state to convince the psychology board to drop its inquiry. Everything was cleaned up, except the press. The newspaper was not finished with him yet.

A few months after Jones's departure, *Indianapolis Star* reporter Carolyn Pickering wrote the *San Francisco Examiner* inquiring after the transplanted church. The inquiry was passed along to the *Examiner*'s religion editor, Lester Kinsolving, who had already learned of the Temple from one of his newspaper column readers, and was curious. After some delay, he went after the story.

Kinsolving and *Examiner* photographer Fran Ortiz drove to the Temple one morning in the summer of 1972, parked their car and approached the Redwood Valley church as people arrived for a service. The two journalists were soon intercepted by four or five clean-cut young men wearing white shirts, neckties and slacks. These Temple security guards first told the newsmen they could not enter, then, after checking with Jones inside, said that both could come in, but without cameras. Kinsolving plunged ahead, but Ortiz refused to leave his cameras unattended. While the service went on, he took exterior shots, with the security guards tailing him. He noticed that three wore sidearms and one was cradling a shotgun. When Ortiz asked why they carried guns, his escorts said that someone had tried to assassinate Jones by firing through a window.

After Ortiz's photos documented the allegation that Peoples Temple had become an armed compound, Kinsolving continued his research. He found that church members often were afraid to talk. But in a few weeks, he began to penetrate the organization's wall of secrecy and developed some confidential sources.

The "investigation" threw the Temple into a frenzy of defensive actions. The first major crisis was breaking out. Lester Kinsolving was no small-town reporter, but a nationally syndicated columnist and well-known "ecclesiastical curmudgeon," as *Time* magazine called him in a full-page 1971 profile. At news conferences, he shot questions like a prosecuting attorney. During Watergate he had asked Nixon whether he had stopped going to church. A fourth-generation Episcopal priest who had abandoned a career in advertising and public relations, Kinsolving had a nationwide reputation in religious circles. He reached many readers in the Temple's prime recruiting areas. And he was sharing information with the *Indianapolis Star*, Jones's nemesis.

Believing that the best defense was a good offense, Jones had church members send some fifty-four letters to the *Examiner* praising himself. When it became clear that Kinsolving's story would not be killed, Jones pretended to cooperate with the reporter, selecting Tim Stoen as intermediary to answer questions raised by Kinsolving's interviews with former Temple members and other detractors. But Stoen, apparently overzealous, stumbled into a public relations blunder with his September 12, 1972, letter answering Kinsolving's inquiries. After providing church statistics and extolling Jones's humanitarian virtues, Stoen confirmed one of the most serious allegations against the church:

"Jim has been the means by which more than forty persons have literally been brought back from the dead this year. . . . I have seen Jim revive people stiff as a board, tongues hanging out, eyes set, skin greying, and all vital signs absent. . . ."

The logic in Stoen's closing appeal was as well knotted as a ribbon. "In case you wonder why I am so deeply interested in the matter of publicity of Jim Jones, it is this: it hurts him, even good publicity. He is antitotalitarian whether communist or fascist, and therefore we have extremists who recurringly try to do him in. . . . Whenever there is publicity, the extremists seem to show themselves."

Kinsolving was unmoved by the appeal from a man who would become his number two target. Less than a week after Stoen's letter, Jones was put in a cross fire of accusation, from Kinsolving at the *San Francisco Examiner* and Carolyn Pickering at the *Indianapolis Star*. Their first installments hit newsstands with large headlines and prominent photo displays, actualizing the Temple's worst fears in black and white.

Stoen's letter had accomplished nothing except to provide Kinsolving with a sensational lead for his inaugural story on September 17, 1972:

"Redwood Valley—A man they call the Prophet is attracting ex-

traordinary crowds from extraordinary distances in his Peoples Temple.
. . . His followers say he can raise the dead."

Kinsolving's exposé quoted from Stoen's letter and church newsletters and implied that the Temple had free rein in Ukiah.

The next day, in part two, Kinsolving led off quoting a true believer:
" 'I know that Pastor Jim Jones is God Almighty himself,' cried one of the more than 1,000 people who overflowed the auditorium of Benjamin Franklin Junior High on Geary Boulevard. . . .'' There followed a skeptical eyewitness account of two resuscitations and of testimonies to healing powers and revelations.

Stoen himself absorbed Kinsolving's third blast, on September 19: "Mendocino County's assistant district attorney—who has written that his pastor, the Rev. Jim Jones, has raised forty people from the dead—has confirmed that he himself has solemnized the marriage of a girl who joined his church." The story contended that Stoen had no legal authority to officiate at a wedding, an allegation he denied, saying, "I meet all the requirements of the State Civil Code." Kinsolving implied that the Temple was arranging marriages of its young people, getting them to sign on welfare rolls, then obliging them to turn over their welfare checks to the church.

In an attempt to muffle the bad publicity, Jones already had sent out Temple members with fists full of change to buy every copy of the *Examiner* in the Ukiah area. Now this third installment, actually hinting at violations of the law, provoked Jones into action. He mobilized his troops to march against the *Examiner*.

A Ukiah member showed up at the Santa Rosa dormitories with the announcement: "There's gonna be a bus here in ten minutes." About three dozen students put aside books and classes and boarded the bus. They disembarked near the corner of Fifth and Mission streets in downtown San Francisco, where they joined contingents of members from the city and from Ukiah.

About 150 Temple members picketed outside the modern three-story *Examiner* building, waving signs that said: THIS PAPER HAS LIED; THEY SAW HEALING UNDENIABLE. AND WOULD NOT PRINT.

Kinsolving, apparently not content to let matters be, appeared personally out front, holding an *Examiner* security guard's cap and mocking: "Brothers and sisters, nice to have you here. Alms for the poor." While he tried to pass the hat, television cameras whirred. Tim Stoen was delighted with the foolery; it strengthened the Temple's legal hand.

Kinsolving's fourth story appeared on schedule, despite the pickets. It disclosed that the state attorney general's office had been asked to investigate the Temple by Rev. Richard Taylor, former pastor of Ukiah's First Baptist Church. "What is of utmost concern," wrote Rev. Taylor, "is the atmosphere of terror created in the community by so large and aggressive a group." The story noted that Temple security men were openly carrying weapons.

The Temple pickets returned in force. Perhaps as many as two hundred marched in a block-long loop outside the *Examiner*. Many had not read the stories they were protesting. Jones walked among them, scowling, determined. When acting city editor John Todd came out to speak with him, Jones demanded that the series be halted. Todd replied that he would give Jones a chance to tell his side of the story, in the interest of fairness. Jones called off his picketers.

The next day, Jones called the *Examiner* city room and told Todd he wanted to talk about interview ground rules. Todd invited him to the office. Jones would not come in to the *Examiner*. Instead he said he would send someone to pick up Todd.

Soon the newspaper security guard phoned upstairs to tell Todd he had a guest from the Temple waiting at the front entrance. Downstairs, Todd met a hulking black man named Chris Lewis—a community activist and thug who had choked a public official at a meeting a year earlier and who would shoot a man to death at another public meeting a year later. Of this, Todd was blissfully unaware. A block away, at the corner of Fifth and Howard streets, Lewis opened the back door of a limousine. Jones, sitting on the far side, motioned Todd in. Todd went ahead, and Lewis piled in after him.

The car pulled away from the curb. Crushed between Lewis and Jones in the back seat, Todd became extremely uneasy. Behind the wheel was an unidentified black man. Riding shotgun was Tim Stoen, who did not identify himself. It was not a friendly get-acquainted session. Stoen and Jones ganged up on him verbally, haranguing the editor ceaselessly as the driver cruised aimlessly past the rotting old docks of the Embarcadero and through industrial sectors near the bay.

Jones kept pounding him with the question: "Why do you want to attack me?"

And Stoen said: "You're destroying a good man. It's morally reprehensible and legally libelous."

They argued about the handling of the Kinsolving stories, which Todd had had no part in editing, since Kinsolving worked under the executive editor. Jones maintained that Kinsolving's attack was part of a personal grievance. In some ways, he was right. Once the Temple marched against him, exposing Jim Jones had become a sort of crusade to the opinionated columnist. Moreover, Kinsolving's taunts on the picket line had pegged him as a hostile investigator. In that light, Jones was successful in demanding his exclusion from the agreed-upon interview. But he failed to persuade Todd, despite his strong-arm tactics, to agree that the word "Prophet" would not appear in any printed rebuttal.

Jones was trying to recover lost ground. He was not ready to go public with the title "Prophet Jones," because it broke down the dual identity he had tried to maintain. Inside the church, or on fund-raising tours, he could bill himself that way for purposes of control and stature to attract crowds and money. But to the Establishment in Ukiah, and even more so in the big city of San Francisco, where he was cutting a toehold, he needed to uphold a purely humanitarian image.

While John Todd had been getting an hour's worth of Jones's bully tactics, *Examiner* management, in consultation with the newspaper's lawyers, had decided to hold off on the remaining stories in the Kinsolving series. The series had run for four days, with three stories to go. The picketing, and phone calls from Temple friends to publisher Charles Gould, were not in themselves enough to do the trick. But by now the Temple had threatened to sue and had brandished its attorneys. Furthermore, the remaining installments were not well substantiated, and they went beyond Kinsolving's expertise in religious matters into areas of possible criminal wrongdoing. Kinsolving too, by antagonizing the pickets, had helped spike his own stories. Continuing the series seemed a risky proposition, at least without more work from an investigative reporter.

Kinsolving's unpublished articles delved into Temple internal affairs in a way that no other stories would until 1977. But though he had collected pieces of the mosaic, he had failed to form a coherent picture. He had put his finger on Jones's claims to be the reincarnation of Christ, on his predictions of nuclear doom and the secret cave, his visit to Father Divine, on Temple tithing, catharsis, socialist readings, survival training for children, on Temple political power in Ukiah and more.

The *Examiner* did not intend to drop coverage of the Temple altogether. But the remaining stories required substantiation. It was hoped that the upcoming question-and-answer session might provide material to beef up Kinsolving's canceled stories. But Jones was too clever for that.

Jones's first on-the-record confrontation with the press was waged in the conference room of the *Examiner* on September 20, 1972. The interview was conducted by *Examiner* reporter John Burks, with Todd looking on. Jones brought his two Temple attorneys, Tim Stoen and Eugene Chaikin, to advise him during the two-and-a-half-hour tape-recorded session.

When Jones confirmed the claim of raising forty-three people from the dead, with no failures, Burks voiced skepticism. "In sports terminology, that's like pitching a no-hitter. The implication is that you and your people can somehow live forever. . . ."

Replied Jones: "We haven't evolved that far. . . . If there's some dimension that the mind can conquer, I'm all for pursuing it."

Burks pointed out to Jones one of his own contradictions. "On the one hand, you are preaching nonviolence, brotherhood of man, racial harmony, all that sort of thing," he said. "On the other hand, you seem to feel a necessity to have armed guards at worship services. Isn't this a contradiction?"

"I don't think it necessary [to have armed guards]." Jones explained at length that the guards were posted because the church board of directors had overruled him.

As Todd listened, he was impressed with Jones's abilities as a con man. Jones could fend off any questions convincingly, slide out of a tight spot, tell a boyhood story, then return to the subject from his own point of view. The harder he was pressed, the cooler he got. He could look Burks in the eye and lie through a smile. Rev. Jones was one of the smoothest salesmen these newsmen had ever seen.

On Friday, September 22, Todd reviewed the question and answer story with Jones and assured the pastor that it would not be doctored, though there would be an introduction to provide the context of the interview. Jones objected heatedly to use of background material and objected specifically, again, to any reference to "Prophet Jones."

Saturday's preview edition read: "Jones doesn't exactly like being called a Prophet, not that he denies he's got some powers along those lines. It's just that to him the title seems sort of unseemly."

On Saturday afternoon, the *Examiner* newsroom began getting irate calls from the Temple. The desk man, who was unfamiliar with the story, suggested that they call Todd at home and unwisely gave out his home phone number. Soon the phone sounded in Todd's Marin County home. Todd recognized the caller by voice as Tim Stoen; speaking as a lawyer, the man demanded that the story be pulled from the remaining editions and alleged that it was defamatory and libelous to Jones. Todd refused.

A half hour later the phone rang again, in the bedroom. Another anonymous voice: "Is this John Todd?"

"Yes."

"You're presenting a story about our Rev. Jim Jones, and what you're doing is hateful. May the devil never forgive you."

The caller clicked off. Barely five seconds later the phone rang again. Same damning message. After fielding a half dozen calls, Todd walked to the kitchen to fix himself a drink. He hoped the calls would stop. But the phone started ringing in the kitchen too.

Three hours after the first phone call, Todd and his wife and children—who had been planning a quiet weekend—were moving into a motel. When Todd went home to check Sunday, the phone still was sounding off like clockwork. On Monday night, after forty-eight hours away from home, Todd's family moved back to their house. The calls had relented.

When upper-level *Examiner* management heard about Todd's travails, they remained cautious and did not run the rest of Kinsolving's series. Again, the risks seemed to outweigh the benefits.[32]

And so the *Examiner* quit the story. A nobody named Jim Jones had worn down a big San Francisco daily. It would be almost five years before the *Examiner* embarked on a major effort to untangle the Peoples

Temple story. By then, the stakes would be much higher and the target more elusive.

Virtually nothing came of Kinsolving's stories. The state attorney general's office concluded they had no jurisdiction. The Mendocino County sheriff's office concluded there was nothing illegal about members carrying guns on Temple property. Mendocino County District Attorney Duncan James privately told Stoen that he was concerned about Stoen's professional reputation being tarnished, but Stoen and others stated their defense in the *Ukiah Daily Journal.* In fact, several months after the series, Stoen was keynote speaker at a Boy Scouts meeting in Santa Rosa.

Meanwhile, the Temple debated continuing the offensive, though church attorneys decided that a lawsuit might expose the Temple's peculiar practices, jeopardizing both its tax-exempt status and its standing with Disciples of Christ.

Already the Temple had stepped up donations to the Disciples in response to the crisis. The church sent $2,000 within a month of the Kinsolving series, then $2,000 more in January 1973. This apparent strategy paid off. When inquiries from member churches and others inundated the Disciples national headquarters in Indianapolis, national president A. Dale Fiers wrote a form letter dated February 8, 1973: "The article is inaccurate, prejudicial and misleading. For one thing, the main charge that the Rev. Jones claims to be the reincarnation of Jesus Christ has been categorically denied by Jones himself. . . ." About two weeks after the letter was drafted, the Temple sent $2,000 more to the church.

To try to neutralize the press, the Temple simultaneously went after Kinsolving and promoted its own image as an advocate of press freedom. In the months after the exposé, it donated several thousand dollars to various newspapers in support of freedom of the press. To its credit, the *Examiner* returned a $500 donation. But the *San Francisco Chronicle,* which did not print any allegations against the Temple, passed its $500 donation to the journalism society Sigma Delta Chi. It was during this well publicized "free press" campaign that Representative George Brown placed flattering stories about the Temple into the *Congressional Record.*

Meanwhile, the Temple set sights on Kinsolving as a declared enemy. At one strategy session, an overzealous church leader suggested that he be kidnapped, stuffed in a bag, then beaten or "eliminated." Instead they launched a full-scale effort to destroy their tormentor's reputation and effectiveness. A week after the series ran, Kinsolving's home was burglarized by unknown persons who took nothing but duplicates of his newspaper articles and his checkbook stubs. They kept his Berkeley home under surveillance and sent negative letters to newspapers that carried his syndicated column—most of which would later cancel him. In looking for dirt on the reporter, they used phone books from all parts of the country to locate relatives. The Temple had started a dossier on Kinsolving. They clipped virtually every word written by him or about him. Over the years, the file would swell to half a foot in thickness.

By early 1973, no law enforcement agencies and no newspapers were investigating the Temple. The only people doing anything about the Temple were members of an informal Christian prayer group in Ukiah, a group run, appropriately enough, by Ross Case, Jones's onetime associate in Indiana.

Case, though he had bid adieu to Jones some eight years earlier, had not been forgotten by his former pastor. To Jones, Case may well have been living too nearby for comfort. The previous year, someone threatened Case by phone. Though Case strongly suspected the Temple and urged a police investigator to look into dangerous trends in the church, he did nothing on his own. But this time he started his own investigation.

The situation arose by accident when Case, visiting a neighbor in Ukiah, met Birdie Marable, a Temple dropout who was operating a care home for several elderly women. Case offered to drive the ladies to church sometime. A short time later, when he paid a visit to Marable's house, he found several elderly black ladies waiting for him on the porch. Immediately they began complaining to Case about Jones's sacrileges—the spitting and stomping on the Bible, his swearing like a drunken sailor.

Seeing Case was all ears, Marable spurred on one of her charges: "Mother Brown, why don't you tell Brother Case about the miracle?"

Obligingly, Janey Brown told how she had been lured out of a service in San Francisco, deliberately jostled by some Temple girls, then rushed to a hospital by Temple nurses. Without being examined by a physician, her arm was diagnosed as broken and put in a cast. Before the plaster had fully hardened, she was back in the church service. The moment she reentered the building, Jones cried from the pulpit, "Uh-uh. Ain't nobody comin' in here like that. Take that cast off, and that arm will be healed." Poor Janey Brown did not know what to do except hold still as Marceline Jones cut off the cast with surgical scissors. The suspense mounted. Finally, Father handed Mother Brown a ball and instructed her to toss it with her "broken" arm. As the ball went sailing into the air, Jones danced back and forth on the stage, delighted: "That arm ain't broken now, is it, Mother Brown?"

Brown's was only one of many anecdotes collected by Case as he conducted Bible study classes for the five women. He passed on information to the sheriff's office. Again he was told there was not adequate evidence to prosecute Jones. But this time Jones found out: two of the ladies in Case's class had returned to the Temple and informed on him.

On August 24, 1973, less than a month after he had started his informal investigation, Case was attending a religious conference near Disneyland when he got a call there from Leo W., a black acquaintance from the Temple's Indiana days. Case had opened Leo's first checking account and, when Leo wanted to marry a white woman, had gone out of state to perform the ceremony.

On this day Leo's conversation was, as usual, nearly incoherent. But what had started out as an oddly casual long-distance call suddenly turned desperate.

"I've been thinking about you," Leo said in an overly friendly tone. "Want to know how you been getting along. Like a brother, long time ago, thinking about coming up to see you." Then he began to lay the snare. "Get kinda hot. Get kinda hot. You and I had a pretty good time together . . . in the parking lot."

An uneasiness crawled over Case. His mind raced. He asked Leo whether he loved the Lord Jesus, and said curtly, his voice tense, "I don't understand the word 'hot.' "

Leo, unwilling to elaborate, pushed for a meeting, despite Case's protestations that he was too busy. "I got to see you. You know how we got together before. . . . How you talked about love and how you loved. . . . We can get along, love each other, pet one another. . . ."

When there was no mistaking Leo's intentions any longer, Case said abruptly, "I can't help you, Leo. See if you can find someone else to find that affection."

"No one else, no one else," he entreated clumsily. ". . . Hey, listen . . . I like to feel your lips."

Confused and indignant, Case finally hung up the phone.

Case concluded after some reflection that Jones was trying to alienate him from Leo, so that Leo could not feed Case any information if he left the Temple. But Case had underestimated Jones's deviousness.

The genesis of the allegation was this: in discussing ways to destroy Case, Jones remembered that Penny Kerns had once stumbled upon Leo W. having sex with an unidentified man. So Jones coached Leo about ways to draw Case inadvertently into a compromising taped conversation, and made Penny Kerns agree to swear falsely that Case had been Leo's partner.

On August 28, a Jones aide phoned Case asking him to come to the church. Supposedly, a young man there was highly agitated about his relationship with Case. Knowing Jones's kangaroo court tactics, Case passed up the invitation. However, a few days later, on September 4, while Case was readying his classroom for the fall term, he was summoned to the school superintendent's office. Case arrived to find Leo, Penny Kerns, Temple attorney Gene Chaikin and an unidentified woman making accusations. While Kerns provided corroboration, Leo said that he and Case had engaged in sex the previous October. Therefore, Leo claimed, Case was unfit to teach children.

After the Temple contingent departed, Case explained the peculiar background to the accusations—and saved his job. The superintendent even seemed ready to testify if Case wanted to sue for slander.

A little while later, Jones called Case—twice in one night—to apologize, to deny any part in the allegation and to promise to kick Leo out of the Temple. Case responded to Jones with icy skepticism, but that did not prevent Jones from chirping: "Why don't you and Luella, and Marceline and I get together?"

Nonetheless, Case reported the harassment to the police and sheriff's office. Once again, there was no basis for prosecution.

TWENTY-FOUR

The Eight Revolutionaries

"Hey, big brother," Jim Cobb's sisters and brothers would call when he came home from college. He loved to take them out for an ice cream. Not an alienated college kid, but a hard worker proud to be paying his own way, he enjoyed coming home to bathe in the respect of his younger siblings and the love of his parents. They had a close family, so Jim Jones went to work on them.

Jim Cobb's father, who had opposed the move from Indiana, resisted joining the Temple himself, though he allowed his family to be active and he lent a hand around the church. But Jones still viewed Cobb, Sr., as a crack in his fortress. Waging psychological warfare on the churchgoing part of the family, Jones criticized this good provider for smoking, for drinking beer, for eating chicken while the Temple dabbled in vegetarianism. "He's out to destroy your mother," Jones told Jim Cobb. Given church peer pressure, young Cobb could not help but feel guilty for liking his father so much.

Then Jones moved in boldly. A contingent of Temple men, black and white, arrived at the family home in Ukiah and told Jim's father: "You got no home, no children, no wife, no family. Get your black ass out of here." They grabbed him by his ankles and threw him out of his own house.

When Jim Cobb arrived home from school that Friday night, the gang of Temple members was still there. Jim's father had been drinking heavily, they said. He supposedly had threatened to kill Jim's mother and kidnap the children.

"What? He's gonna do what?" Jim Cobb shook his head, incredulous. But there was no way to escape the Temple verdict. His family, his world, was rent. Baffled and shaken, Jim Cobb was sent to meet with Jim Jones and various church leaders.

"Are you willing to kill your father?" Jones asked him.

"I won't kill my old man, but I'll see that he won't hurt anybody," Cobb responded quickly.

It would be years before Cobb would hear the true story, from his father. In the meantime, as groundwork was prepared for his parents' divorce, young Cobb wallowed in confusion. What Jones and the others said made no sense. His father had been a devoted husband, had never missed a day's work, had always treated him with respect. He had not spanked his son since grade school, and he was not a violent man. At most, Jim thought, his parents might have clashed over the church—but he could not imagine his father threatening to kill his mother. "How could my father come out here and just change like this?" he asked himself.

While Jim Cobb lived with his doubts, he gradually fixed his rancor on the real culprit behind the white domination, the double standards, hypocrisy and divisiveness within Peoples Temple. He no longer believed that white zealot staff was the major problem; it was Jones himself.

In fall of 1972, as the Kinsolving series was running, as Jim Cobb prepared to move to San Francisco to start dental school there, he decided it was time to make his break. When classes began, he quit going to services and stayed away from Ukiah altogether. Leaving his mother, brothers and sisters was the hardest part of quitting. There was no middle ground after his defection. He had turned traitor. Still, the family tie remained.

One day during final examinations, his mother located him at the U.C. library, and they had an emotional reunion in the hallway. Mrs. Cobb wanted to see what had become of her oldest son in the months since he had deserted the cause. She inspected him, critically, frowning at his stubbly face—the church prohibited beards. "What's my son coming to?" she reproved him.

Mrs. Cobb had come on a mission—to get back her son. She pleaded with him to return to the fold. She and Jim's brothers and sisters were living in San Francisco now; the church was not so far away.

When pressed, Jim, at long last, bared his feelings. "Mama, I don't want to pop no bubbles. I love my family and I love my friends, and there are good people in the church. But I've looked at it, and ya know what? Jones is the one."

Mrs. Cobb disagreed strongly. Of course there were failings, she conceded, but they had to be blamed on Jones's staff, not on the great humanitarian. "No, he isn't the one," she said. "He has people who tell him things. He's like the President. He has advisers. And he listens to them."

"No." Jim knew better. "I've seen things you haven't. I was there at his door, standing guard, and overhearing things. . . . He's behind it all; it's him. It's hard for me to realize how someone could put together a movement with so many good people and all these different colors of people—attorneys, people with lots of money, and poor ones—yet could be so rotten. Yet it's true."

His mother was unswayed. "If you can't come back for anything else, come back for the family," she said. "The kids need you. Your father's not there, and you were sort of that image. They're asking where you are and what you're doin'. It's in a state of turmoil at home."

Jim digested the conversation over the next few weeks, then took a step back. He began to drive his mother to San Francisco temple services. He never went inside, just parked outside or dropped her off and departed. But more and more the church intruded on his thoughts. Like so many others who left later, Jim Cobb missed the Temple atmosphere and the constant message of cooperation and caring for people.

One day in late spring of 1973, while he was driving his mother to church, the spirit of penitence pulled him through the Temple doors. Though still not convinced he was wrong about Jones, he tearfully stood in front of the congregation and delivered a standard prodigal-son spiel, believing it at that moment. "I've been out in the world and there's nothing out there," he said. "There are a lot of bad things and bad people out there, and there are a lot of loving people and good things going on here."

As a onetime defector, Cobb's role had changed. Jones pampered him by honoring his request to be a church photographer. But Cobb felt the disdain of others, particularly white women staffers, who viewed him as an ingrate and snubbed him.

Staff members had reason to be suspicious of Cobb. He had been openly critical of the holier-than-thou loyalty of the white leadership. Worse, upon his return Cobb became a confidant to many members, particularly young blacks with complaints about the white staff.

Despite his temporary reconversion, Cobb soon realized the situation was hopeless. In September 1973, just a few months after rejoining, Jim Cobb decided to drop out again. He did not tell anyone, not even family and close friends, for fear they would inform as they were obligated to do. Cobb did not ask his wife Sharon to defect, at least not directly. They had a typically loose Temple-style marriage, and, as a nurse, she had been helping with the healings and was very loyal.

Cobb figured it would take about a week to get his car ready and to square away his personal affairs in secret. During that time, his dorm friend Wayne Pietila dropped by Cobb's commune in San Francisco, behaving mysteriously, asking him to come for a ride without telling anyone else.

Cobb guessed Pietila had come either as a Jones agent or to announce his own plans to leave. Neither young man revealed anything of his intentions over lunch. Finally, while driving back to the commune, Cobb rallied the gumption to say, "I want to tell you I'm leaving the church next week. I wasn't gonna say that, but I don't give a shit. If you're here to spy on me, that's okay. Whatever, man. But I can't take it anymore."

Wayne exhaled through his teeth in a whistle. "Man, we're goin' too!"

Disillusionment had come gradually for Wayne Pietila but accelerated as he became privy to Temple secrets and more philosophically committed to socialism. Pietila, a Ukiah local, had joined the Temple as a withdrawn thirteen-year-old when his mother, Wanda Kice, and his stepfather, Tom Kice, cast their lot with Jones. Like Jim Cobb, he spent his adolescent years soaking up Temple guilt, feeling horrible when he indulged in a movie or junk food. Then, when he was elevated to the planning commission and became the college dormitory leader, he was exposed to the church scandals.

The first discovery occurred just after Pietila finished high school, when Jones took him for a walk. The minister disclosed that he was having sex with various women—"to keep them loyal"—and that John Stoen was his son. At the time Jones was telling the church body to abstain from sex altogether.

On p.c., Pietila was exposed not only to Jones's excesses but to a disgraceful double standard. Those in the church inner circle—mostly white—went to restaurants and movies routinely and took special privileges, while the rank and file—mostly poor and black—did without. And, though socialism was being preached, Jones's staff kept coming by to gather up political theory books. Pietila had to bury about three dozen of his books so they would survive the purges. It seemed that as soon as the college dorm residents started to strengthen their group with study of political theory and self-criticism, the larger church cracked down on them.

Discouraged, Pietila stopped studying and started breaking church rules. He missed regular meetings and went deer hunting with another member, John Biddulph. When Pietila flunked all his classes and dropped out of school in spring of 1973, Jones knew something was wrong. The pastor tried to appease him by making him a key bodyguard, but that just exposed him to more shenanigans.

Finally, Pietila was called onto the floor in a p.c. meeting. He was accused, falsely, of having sexual intercourse with a fourteen-year-old girl. Even his friends took turns lambasting him. Belittled, he looked over in the corner and spotted Biddulph laughing and pointing at him, out of Jones's line of vision. The message was clear: "Don't worry, friend, I'm on your wavelength; this catharsis business is a bunch of bullshit." For an hour Pietila stood there like a forgotten child while Jones went on to another subject. Then Jones turned his attention back to sex. He implied that Pietila was compensating for homosexuality: "Son, I can understand your problem. In a way, it's my fault because I didn't spend enough time with you. I need to spend more personal time with you. It's something only a true father can cure."

Nothing could have scared Pietila more. A private encounter with

Jones could mean only one thing. "Oh, no," thought Mike Touchette, who was living in the same commune with Pietila and Biddulph. "Wayne, what did you get yourself into now?" And Biddulph, who could not keep a straight face, began mockingly making lewd gestures from the corner as Wayne squirmed.

"Jim, we don't need that kind of a relationship," Pietila said, still frightened that the group might pressure him into sex with Jones. Other p.c. members shot him dirty looks, but he escaped.

After the meeting, Biddulph came up to him. "Father's gonna fuck you."

"No, he isn't," Pietila said.

The two started to talk about leaving the church. They visited the secret cave off Highway 101 where Jones maintained the congregation could hide from nuclear fallout—all they found was a bottomless pit with a rattlesnake in residence. The two began looking for allies. With numbers, they could defend themselves better against search parties sent out by Jones. Their core group numbered four—Biddulph and his wife Vera, Pietila and his wife, Terri Cobb, who was Jim's sister. The four lived together in a commune with Mike and Debbie Touchette, but after much agonizing, they decided it was too risky to invite the third couple. The Touchettes were too close to their loyal parents.

The first real recruits were Wayne's dorm friend Tom Podgorski and his girl friend, Lena Flowers, a black woman whose family came from Indiana in about 1970; the original four had known the outspoken Podgorski felt negative about the church. They then added Jim Cobb and college student Mickey Touchette, Mike's sister. Cobb had left once already, and Mickey's attitude indicated that she was fed up. Also, she and Jim Cobb had been interested in each other for years, though Jones discouraged the match.

These eight agreed to leave. They were four interracial couples—all college students or ex-college students. Because the group had formed quickly and without a concrete plan, they needed time to prepare. Yet delay made them anxious.

People in planning commission began asking Pietila why Cobb was spending so much time visiting his house on Tomki Road. Then Pietila was brought up for missing some work at Masonite. The eight feared they were on the verge of being discovered. They decided the time for action was upon them.

One of the last things Jim Cobb did was confide in his younger brother Johnny. "I'm leaving," he told him. "Sometimes people have to work away from the people they love and go on missions." In the language of the Temple, a "mission" was an assignment for the cause. Cobb did not want his brother to believe that he was a traitor. "I love you and I love the whole family regardless of what happens and who says what."

At the selected hour, the eight converged on Pietila's place on Tomki Road and packed everything that would fit into an old Dodge, a

Ford and a Chevy truck. They stowed a few firearms as well. Defecting was no lark: too many sinister statements and threats had been leveled against those who might desert the cause. And the talk of killing for the cause was not entirely rhetoric.

The eight correctly suspected that Jones would at least send out a search party or notify the Highway Patrol. So instead of taking nearby Highway 101, they traveled east, then north toward Sacramento. With adrenalin gushing, the "Gang of Eight" headed north toward green and wild Canada, refuge for draft evaders, religious communards, cultists and genuine fugitives. As the miles lengthened into hours and days, and the tires drummed monotonously, the implications behind their flight dulled their euphoria. It hurt to be leaving behind friends and loved ones, and it hurt to think of the pain they would endure when the eight were denounced. For Cobb, it was especially difficult because he knew that this time he could never go back to the church and his family.

The group decided against crossing the border into Canada because they were worried about being caught with their weapons. In their fear, they presumed that Jones would have alerted the border authorities to watch for three carloads of "violent revolutionaries." They wound up staying in the wilds of Montana and having a great time. Smoking cigars, they drove from place to place and exchanged talk about their Temple experiences. They camped at lakes where they fished, swam, partied and got drunk, indulging in all the forbidden pleasures, as Temple defectors often did.

Within a week, most of the eight knew where the others stood on the Temple and Jones. They had analyzed the church endlessly and shared great volumes of information. As their gripes were aired and argued openly, they began to realize that no one had the total picture, that they could not all agree on something so elementary as an opinion of Jim Jones. Jim Cobb and some others thought him "an asshole"—that for all his gentle protestation, he was the source of all the game playing and double standards, the evil. But Wayne Pietila and others believed that Jones was a positive influence, that staff was to blame for everything. They still could not see the puppeteer for all the puppets.

After several weeks, when funds ran out, the eight headed for Washington to look for work. When they landed in Spokane, Mickey Touchette and John Biddulph posed as a white nuclear family and rented a house. The other six moved in and lived out of an ice chest until they could find jobs.

During their travels over about two and a half months, they found it necessary to communicate with Jim Jones. All of them had lived within Jones's "family" for at least a couple of years, and they were not sure which parts of their experience to discard. Like other important defectors later, they believed it critical that Jones understand their thinking. Furthermore, they needed to know he would not harm them or poison their reputations and relationships with people inside the church, family members included.

The manifesto the eight drafted while drifting through the Pacific Northwest was a compromise. Rather than placing blame directly on Jones, it instead faulted staff for everything because that was the only blame all eight could agree on. Unanimity was important, they felt; they did not want Jones, back in Ukiah, to be able to point to any division in their ranks. Besides, a moderate position might keep Jones uncertain as to whether he might command a modicum of loyalty from the eight. That way he would be less likely to do them—or their families—any harm.

Sex was the first topic on the list of grievances. "A revolutionary, as you and staff would say, does NOT engage in sex. . . . However, who takes the privileged liberty to abuse such a decision? STAFF." They illustrated their point with specifics, naming various high-ranking members, male and female, who had been penetrated by Jones.

The letter said that members who made lots of money for the church got away with being racist, were elevated to staff and special projects, and became untouchables, outside the egalitarian standards of the Temple.

"You said that the revolutionary focal point at present is in the black people. Yet, where is the black leadership? . . . Black people are being tapped for money, practically nothing else. . . ."

The eight characterized staff as a nitpicking bunch of women "hungrily taking advantage of a chance to castrate black men" and freely tossing around "male chauvinism" charges. They said the meetings of the central church body were laughable. "All planning commission does is call each other homosexual, asking if each other suck cock, planning to plant dope on people. What a contribution to socialism! . . ." Why was anyone who wanted to become an active socialist put down as a homosexual and belittled as "a big revolutionary"? the eight asked. "How does one half of Peoples Temple manage to know zero about socialism?"

The defection of the so-called Eight Revolutionaries immediately set off Jones's defensive reactions. Although other individuals and groups would leave the church, no other defectors would put Jones into such a tizzy until the late 1970s. And perhaps no single act of defection touched as many members in a personal way as that escape by eight young people with families and numerous friends. In that one night, Jones lost bodyguards and p.c. members; and the church lost a large segment of its would-be professionals, essential contributors to a would-be self-sufficient countersociety.

Already the strategist had dispatched his search parties. He had Norman Ijames rent an airplane to scan the highways for the wayward members. While the search was on and eyewitnesses were being interviewed, Jones wrestled with his own feelings of rejection. Over the years, each defection would strike him as if he had been physically wounded. He would fly into terrifying rages at the slightest provocation, the slightest sign of wavering loyalty. Teeth gnashing, facial muscles ready to snap, he would unleash the most abusive, almost maniacal language against potential traitors. He would menace the potentially unfaithful; he would wave a pistol inside p.c., telling his followers not to dare leave him, not even to doze while he was talking. Losing even one person from the inner circle infuriated him. It was a failing, a punch to the groin.

When he had learned enough facts, Jones called an emergency meeting in Redwood Valley, even summoning members from San Francisco. The minister branded the eight as Trotskyite adventurists, provocateurs crazed enough to take his teachings literally and plot something like the demolition of dams or the bombing of the Masonite corporation. He ridiculed them as "Coca-Cola Revolutionaries"—as pleasure seekers playing at revolution, as phonies and lightweights who wanted the easy romance of instant results rather than prolonged struggle through socialism. In one breath he called them terrorists; in the next, he painted them as cowards. He tried to make it sound as though the eight were running from trouble. "Their theory is this: 'Father's gonna be killed. We're all gonna end up in concentration camps.'" He paused to let that sink in. "Well, even if it were true, does it justify what's being done?"

Angry vitriolic shouts of "No. No."

"I promised that if you kept my teachings and followed me, you couldn't go to concentration camps," said Jones, knocking down his own straw man. "I made that an unconditional promise. And I never have made an unconditional promise I haven't kept." Cheers and admiring applause, though restrained.

Jones began working over his audience with guilt, to turn their love for him into hatred for the eight. He shared his feelings of betrayal, casting the eight as ingrates, as foolish to leave him: "If I had a leader —oh, how I would love to have a leader. . . . If I had a God—and oh, how I wish I had a God like you [do] . . . because I'm the only one there is as far as I could see. And I have searched all over heaven and earth and I certainly looked through the belly of hell."

Talking almost in riddles, he pleaded with his people to be selfless. The eight, he concluded, had gone for selfish reasons—sex among them —and would be miserable. The message: don't chase mirages, or you will be unhappy too. "Don't love your life." He paused for effect. "Move on like I have until you hate your life. Move on till you lose it, then you [really] find it. When people try to hold onto it through sex . . ." He turned again to the eight, portraying them as casualties of their own rebellion. "They all teamed up in little couples [thinking] that they are gonna have romance now. Their romance has turned to bitter, bitter agony already. They've got a black and white suicide squad. . . . An accident looking for a place to happen." He even pointed out a disturbing irony: that this rebellious group was better integrated than the Temple leadership. "How tragic it is for us to see black and white go fifty-fifty."

Hatred for the eight was promoted with a vengeance in meetings and in sermons. Fellow students and their relatives were enlisted in the purging as Jones made the Eight Revolutionaries a useful target for unfocused feelings of discontent. Jones used the affidavits of various members, accusing the eight of idolizing Che Guevara, displaying anti-white racism, conducting cruel catharsis sessions, discussing political terrorism, engaging in sexual misconduct and so on. As usual, the alleged crimes of defectors carried, at most, kernels of truth, or were activities encouraged by Jones himself.

Defections of important members threatened the Temple walls from both sides. Inside, defections harmed morale and created danger of a domino effect. But the major concern was that defectors might go to the press or the police. Each prominent defector was a torpedo loaded with explosive secrets. Jones had to either get it back or disarm it somehow.

Jones followed the same general strategy with most defections. First, he and his aides investigated the circumstances of the defection, looking for a way to level an allegation of theft or misconduct of any sort. Second, Jones decided whether to report the defection to other members or to keep it secret and try to get back the defectors. Third, he cast the defectors in villainous roles; he fed the membership's genuine feelings of betrayal and loss by belaboring his own. In that climate, he was able to convince friends and relatives of the defectors to sign affidavits attesting to their dastardly past acts.

Finally, Jones limited the damage. He partly closed off one avenue to the press and the law by documenting allegations and damaging the credibility of defectors. At the same time, he tried to reestablish contact with the defectors to induce them to come back or, failing that, never to harm the church. Sometimes he sent heavyweights to intimidate them or tried to blackmail them with their own false written confessions.

But the Eight Revolutionaries were not intimidated or neutralized as easily as past or future defectors, as Jones discovered just a few months after launching his propaganda attack on them.

The eight had learned, through phone calls to relatives and others, that Jones had been ridiculing them and telling lies about them. One day after three or four pitchers of dark beer at the pizza parlor where Lena worked, Pietila and Biddulph became infuriated with Jones's lies. They went to the rest of the eight and developed a plan to set things straight with Jones.

In secrecy, Pietila and John and Vera Biddulph made their way back to Ukiah. From town, they placed a phone call to Pietila's mother, Wanda Kice. Wayne said he was calling long distance. He asked her to call Jones and tell him to be at her house at 5:00 P.M. to take an important call from the eight. No one else was to be alerted, and no one else was to come.

At about 4:30 P.M., the three defectors pulled up to the Kice house. While Vera stayed in the car as a lookout, the two men went around the back of the house, where they found Wayne's mother washing dishes. She almost fell over with surprise and joy. Her son hugged and kissed her.

The trap had been set, and for once Jim Jones was the prey. As they waited for the pastor, the two defectors were keyed up, ready to defend themselves if necessary with the pistols in the back of their waistbands.

About ten minutes later, Jones drove up to the house with Carolyn Layton. Excited and for some reason disguised in a big trench coat and businessman's hat, he almost trotted up to the house. Then, looking like Sam Spade, he pushed open the door and stepped into the lair. He found himself face-to-face with Pietila and Biddulph. He blanched then caught himself quickly. He spread a grin across his face. "I'm glad to see you, my sons."

But when he reached out to hug them, Jones felt a gun. His expression changed ever so slightly, as Pietila pushed him back an arm's length and gave him a good handshake. "Good to see you, Jim."

The two traitors took command of the situation. They ordered Carolyn Layton out and told her under no circumstances to call anyone, especially not security or p.c. Jones, clearly concerned about the guns, told her, "Do everything they say." He looked intently at the men and added, "They will not harm you."

Jones tried to assert his authority. It was not proper for Wanda Kice, who was not on p.c., to overhear serious discussions about secret church business, he said. But the two traitors insisted she stay as a witness; they did not want Jones to be free to distort what they said.

Having won that point, Pietila and Biddulph pulled out the letter from the eight and read it to Jones line by line. The grievances were so sweeping and struck so close to the heart that Jones could not restrain himself. He tried to answer it item by item, disputing all but the part blaming his own staff. "You understand," he said, "that in an organization like this, I can't have complete control. People do things that I don't agree with."

They were getting nowhere. Jones kept on arguing. Biddulph gathered himself and got serious, acting as if he were about to issue the ultimate verdict. Pointing his finger at Jones, he snarled, "And here's another goddamn thing. . . . We hear you're calling us the *Coca-Cola* Revolutionaries. And, dammit, we want you to know we're the *Pepsi Cola* Revolutionaries!" The humor went past Jones. He stared straight ahead, frightened.

Pietila deliberately turned so that Jones could see the gun tucked in his belt in the rear. Then they made their final point, which was really a message from all eight: we're minding our own business in another state. We don't want you to hurt us or our families who are still in the church, and we won't hurt you. We have an intelligence network of our own and we will hear any lies you tell about us. We want the lies stopped.

Jones tried to placate them with double talk. He admitted some past lies and tried to rationalize it all in terms of socialist ideology. "You understand that 'the dictatorship of the proletariat' means I have to go to these extremes. The end justifies the means. But I will not bother you, just so long as you don't undermine the good name of Peoples Temple."

But the eight had vowed when they defected that Jim Jones never would forget them. They were right. Some would come back to torment him years later.

TWENTY-FIVE

Playing with Fire

Within a year of the Kinsolving series, the Temple was taking serious steps to build stronger inner-city bases of political and economic power. By shouldering into these dangerous and crowded arenas almost immediately after his near-catastrophe, Jones put all his urban aspirations into jeopardy. By seeking a forum of high visibility, he seemed to deliberately risk embroiling his organization and himself in conflicts that would show others that he indeed was under attack.

By moving his focus to San Francisco and Los Angeles, Jones was transplanting the Temple into the political volatility of the early 1970s. This period saw remnants of the New Left rechanneled into everything from electoral politics to the prisoner rights struggle to terrorism.

While the Black Panthers made forays into the political arena, a host of revolutionary cadres operated in the San Francisco Bay Area in 1973–74. The mysterious New World Liberation Front bombed banks and public utilities with a Robin Hood fervor. The Black Liberation Army, believed to be behind the political murders of police, infiltrated and took over at least one black community group. The Maoist group Venceremos carried out some sensational prison escapes. And a prison-spawned group called the Symbionese Liberation Army went on an outlaw odyssey with its November 1973 assassination of black Oakland school superintendent Marcus Foster and the February 1974 kidnapping of Patricia Hearst.

Since Jones empathized with the inner-city frustrations that nourished these guerrilla vanguards, he began condoning the violence he had once condemned. In church, he even took responsibility, for example, for the unsolved explosion of a Vietnam-bound munitions train in Roseville. He began to cast off his Mendocino County Republican image, but only up to a point. He still husbanded a liberal humanitarian image while playing dangerous games on the side.

Two Los Angeles incidents in 1973 serve to indicate Jones's recklessness. In one, the Temple was nearly exposed as a violence-prone militant organization. In the other, Jim Jones nearly was unmasked as a sexual exhibitionist.

The first incident took place on January 7, 1973, outside the Moorish-looking brick temple building. An ambulance had been summoned to take away an elderly black woman who had fainted and was still feeling ill.

When the ambulance arrived, a crowd of Temple members gathered to watch their "sister" being loaded by the attendants. The procedure was supervised by Temple security, all wearing policelike uniforms. Some, like Johnny Brown Jones, a San Francisco youth worker adopted by Jones, were wearing sidearms. All went routinely until the white attendants had the black woman sit on a bench inside the ambulance. "Let her lie down," Johnny Jones demanded, protectively. Heedless of the demand, the attendants shut the ambulance doors. Young Jones opened the door and persisted. The ambulance crew shut the door again. Once again Jones pulled it open.

Tempers sparked. Others joined in the argument. Temple members accused the ambulance attendants of treating the woman badly, of making racist remarks. The disagreement escalated. The attendants radioed for assistance. Quickly Johnny Jones and Cleveland Jackson jumped the attendants. The melee that followed continued as police squad cars roared up with flashing lights. Flailing clubs, officers waded into the nasty brawl. Temple members grappled with police and screamed as bodies tumbled and heads were bashed. Then, as a police helicopter circled overhead, Jim Jones defused the near-riot by ordering his members to drop to their knees.

The police took three Temple members—public relations man Mike Prokes, Johnny Jones and C. J. Jackson—into custody. At nearby Ramparts Station, Jim and Marceline Jones attempted to intercede. Grabbing the arm of an officer, Jones proclaimed: "If you're going to arrest anyone, arrest me." He was detained briefly and cited, but the case was too weak for prosecution. However, Johnny Jones and Jackson were convicted of disturbing the peace.

To outsiders, this incident came as the first and only clash between the Temple and law enforcement. To the Temple, it was yet another example of racism and police oppression.

The Temple responded by inviting officials to make a presentation of their neighborhood anticrime programs. Prior to his speech, Captain Joe Marchesano met alone with Jones, who explained that the Temple was not militant or antipolice. During Marchesano's address, the congregation roared approval at his every utterance, particularly his anticrime references. But Marchesano was disturbed by this experience and by the bodyguards stationed at various doors. As a result, he turned down a $250 Temple donation to the police youth program which was brought to him a week or two later.

Despite his friendship gestures, Jones wound up seeing the police again before the year was out—to be exact, on December 13, 1973. That afternoon the Westlake Theater, a movie house across from MacArthur Park and about a mile and a half from the Los Angeles Temple, was playing the Clint Eastwood movie *Dirty Harry*. MacArthur Park was reputed to be a meeting place for homosexuals, and patrons of the Westlake had been complaining about homosexual solicitations there. In response, Ramparts Station had assigned two vice squad officers, Arthur Kagele and Lloyd Frost, to work the place in plainclothes.

In the nearly empty balcony, a dark-haired man in a green coat motioned Kagele to join him in the rear seating section. Kagele had seen the same man in the restroom earlier. But he ignored the overture and went back to the restroom to check for activity.

Within a minute, he heard the restroom door open, and the black-haired man strode back to the same toilet stall. The man's right arm began moving, and he turned toward Kagele. He was holding his penis erect in his hand. Masturbating provocatively, the man approached the officer. By the time he reached the middle of the room, he had crossed the boundary of lewd conduct. Stepping outside the restroom, Kagele signaled his partner, and they made the arrest.

At 4:00 P.M., while handcuffs were closed on the man's thick wrists and his Miranda rights were read, the incident still seemed to be a routine bust. Things changed a little later when, driving along in an unmarked police car toward Ramparts Station, the remorseful arrestee said that he was a minister of a local church. But that did not matter; the case seemed airtight to Kagele.

James Warren Jones, forty-two, was booked for investigation of lewd conduct and held on $500 bail. On his arrest sheet, he listed his employer as Disciples of Christ, his occupation as pastor. Significantly, the only physical malady he reported was "possible hemorrhoids." Jones was bailed out promptly, and his followers went immediately to work.

Within twenty-four hours, they had an outside attorney on the line and a medical defense in the mails. The Temple promptly retained Los Angeles lawyer David Kwan, who was known for his ability to get things done. On December 14, 1973, a San Francisco urologist wrote to Kwan: "Reverend James Jones has been under my urological care since October 1970. He has obstruction of the outlet of the urinary bladder due to strategic enlargement of the prostate gland. . . . Moreover, there is chronic inflammation of the prostate. These conditions cause urinary frequency. Even prior to seeing me, Reverend Jones had learned that jogging or jumping in place afforded improved initiation of urination. I encouraged his continuing that technique. . . ."

The Temple prepared a press release to be used if the matter ever leaked to the public. It hardly tallied with Jones's medical defense—the release maintained that the arrest had been prearranged as retaliation for the near-riot. "When Rev. Jones turned and told the officer, in startling plain English, to get lost, he was arrested."

With his groundwork readied, Jones asked to meet with his acquaintance Captain Marchesano to discuss the charge. The captain first checked with the arresting officer, Kagele, who insisted that Jones's behavior could not have been health-related. Then Marchesano met with Jones at the Temple but refused to intervene.

Jones and two or three aides also paid a visit to Ramparts Station where, according to Vice Squad Lieutenant Bob MacIntosh, they offered $5,000 to Marchesano and him for the stationhouse fund. The veiled bribe offer was phrased so as to be unprosecutable. Marchesano refused the donation.[33]

When the case arrived in court on December 20, 1973, Municipal Court Judge Clarence "Red" Stromwall, a former police officer, dismissed the charges at the request of the city attorney's office. The city attorney's file listing the detailed reason for the dismissal motion vanished, and none of the prosecutors later recalled having made such a decision.

Jones was not yet in the clear, however. As part of the dismissal, he had signed a "stipulation as to probable cause," a document admitting that the officer had had reason to arrest him. This protected the police against a false arrest suit but also reflected negatively on Jones. He and Tim Stoen worked to keep the records from prying eyes. In January 1974, Jones visited the Los Angeles police records division, then Stoen followed up with two phone calls. He was told that only minors qualified to have their records sealed. Stoen, then Mendocino County assistant district attorney, made similar calls to state agencies—always careful to say he was operating in a private capacity. All his requests were turned down.

Yet on February 7, 1974, in chambers, without notifying the prosecutor or arresting officer and without a court reporter present, Judge Stromwall ordered all the case records sealed and destroyed. He also instructed various law agencies to destroy their files on Jones's arrest, an action rare if not unprecedented in Los Angeles sex cases.[34]

To make sure the order was executed, Stoen went to the state attorney general's office and asked that Jones's record be pulled and destroyed. Stoen said he was afraid that undefined malevolent people might use the records to "get Jones." His argument struck the state records expert, Deputy Attorney General Mike Franchetti, as downright bizarre. Franchetti refused Stoen's request.

The seal-and-destroy order rankled Officer Kagele so much that he filed an internal protest in the police department, actually taking his complaints all the way to then-Police Chief Ed Davis, who referred him to future Chief Daryl Gates. Gates said nothing could be done about the court's order. But others besides Kagele, mainly city police records personnel, were concerned, because they feared the minister might have access to children. Eventually, the State Department of Justice special services division asked Stromwall in writing to vacate his "invalid" sealing order but he refused. That put in motion some slow legal machinery. Jones would not learn that records of his lewd conduct case had survived after all until the fall of 1977. By that time, he had moved abroad permanently—and had too many problems already.

In the cities, Jones wanted his organization to be rooted in the streets of the black community. But as a practical matter, he did not have the energy or inclination to do more than send representatives to community meetings and to recruit a few of the young black community activists. As a white preacher from the Midwest, he was at a decided disadvantage in rough neighborhoods and housing projects where traditions of hard survival and violence ran deep, where turf battles were fought over dope, prostitution, federal dollars and jobs.

Jones only dabbled in this bare-knuckles world, and usually with stand-ins. Chris Lewis was Jones's most notorious second in the ghetto— the perfect Temple antihero, a black Robin Hood with the physical equipment of Sonny Liston. He was a likable freewheeling street person when he was in good humor; but he was as unpredictable as a bleeding bull. The six-foot-two, 220-pounder had earned his street scars, smarts and rapsheet on the heroin-fencing-burglary circuit.

When Lewis was introduced to Jim Jones through a relative in 1969, he was a heroin addict and community activist in the Western Addition. He joined the Temple and went to Redwood Valley for detoxification—one of the few true needle users to come to the Temple's antidrug program.

For about a week in 1969, Chris Lewis went cold turkey. Sweating and shaking, his withdrawal took place under the supervision of other Temple members, Jim Cobb among them. They talked to him, played chess with him and took turns being supportive. Toward the end, they brought him outside to chop wood to take his mind off the pain.

After Lewis beat the habit, he wore many hats for Jones—bodyguard, chief enforcer and reformed junkie. During the Temple's urban expansion campaigns, the ex-con probably was Jones's most prized recruit. Lewis effectively lectured troubled teen-agers about the ugly realities of prison: "It's blood on your knife, or shit on your dick." He bolstered Jones's security forces directly as a guntoter and indirectly as a threatening presence to discourage traitors. Chris Lewis was a special case; Jones liked and admired "Teddy," as he fondly called him. While he built up Lewis's image as an enforcer and a virile stud, Jones also realized that he never could break Lewis's independent spirit. Lewis did pretty much what he pleased. He walked out of meetings without being challenged. He broke church dietary rules himself and took kids out to hamburger joints for junk food.

The other members respected Lewis. But they feared the wide mood swings that had enabled him to survive in community politics that were as rough as street fights.

Lewis was very much involved in internal politics and power games of the Western Addition Project Area Committee (WAPAC), a community group that provided a check on the San Francisco Redevelopment Agency and its urban renewal projects. At a Redevelopment Agency meeting in July 1971, Lewis got in an argument and tried to choke redevelopment Executive Director Justin Herman with his own necktie. Two years later, Lewis carved an even deeper notch in his reputation:

In November 1973, at a meeting attended by about a hundred people, an altercation developed between WAPAC factions. On one side was Lewis, an affirmative action officer for WAPAC. On the other was twenty-two-year-old Rory Hithe, the WAPAC director and a secret Black Liberation Army member, who had pleaded guilty two years earlier to conspiracy in the 1969 torture slaying of Black Panther Alex Rackley in New Haven, Connecticut.

With the crowd looking on, a fight started between two women— Hithe's sister, Michelle, and Lewis's wife, Mae, who was a Temple member. Chairs were thrown and people tumbled to the floor as Lewis and Hithe became involved in the scuffle. Lewis pulled his .38-caliber revolver, then three shots rang out. People screamed. Lewis had killed Rory Hithe with a bullet to the head and wounded Michelle Hithe in the thigh.

With Lewis booked on murder and assault charges, Jim Jones came to his aid, footing the bill for the famed defense lawyer James Martin MacInnis and putting up Lewis's $100,000 bail.

Just prior to the trial, newspaper accounts alleged that the BLA had infiltrated WAPAC, and several top WAPAC officials resigned amid accusations of death threats and stolen payroll checks related to BLA activity. The disclosures meshed nicely with Lewis's defense. His attorney contended that Lewis had fired in self-defense, though his victims were unarmed. Portraying his client as a political moderate, MacInnis said that Lewis was attacked for his opposition to radical political corruption.

Although the prosecution pointed out that Lewis had come to the meeting armed and although two ministers testified that Lewis did the shooting, it took the jury only seven hours to acquit him.

Jones claimed at a Temple meeting that the shooting sprang from Lewis's failure to follow his instructions that night. "I have to bleed my people for you," he told Lewis, noting that he had spent $36,000 in Temple money on legal fees and other expenses.

Although Jones later would say that helping Lewis was the biggest mistake of his life, some benefits accompanied the expenditure. First, Jones proved to his people that he would stick up for them all, no matter what the cost. Second, he put Chris Lewis deeply in his debt. The events also bespoke both Lewis's willingness to kill and Jones's power to play the justice system like a cello. And Lewis's reputation on the streets was not damaged either; black politicians and community leaders knew that Jones had a strong henchman as a bulwark in his security squad.

Knowing he had been saved from prison, Lewis promised contritely to pay back every penny. Faithful to his word, he hand-delivered $500 and $1,000 cash payments. To raise the money, Lewis returned to his days of fencing, selling "hot" car radios, dresses and other wares in quasi-government agencies or on ghetto street corners.

It was almost inevitable that the Temple would be caught up one way or another in the Symbionese Liberation Army's kidnapping of Patricia Hearst. This kidnapping-brainwashing by a ragtag group of eight revolutionaries became the center of news media attention in the mid-1970s and thrust one of the world's most powerful publishing families into contact with the radical community in the San Francisco Bay Area. The primary mechanism for this intercourse was a multimillion-dollar food giveaway program demanded as a ransom by the newspaper heiress's captors. The SLA simultaneously named a watchdog coalition of community groups to oversee food distribution to the poor in the Bay Area, and asked WAPAC to chair the coalition.

Jones's statements inside the church, and to sympathetic radicals outside it, probably best indicated his true feelings about the SLA. His rhetoric was unrestrained. He as much as said that terrorism was understandable, that the kidnapping of Patricia Hearst was an important lesson to the ruling class. Expressing admiration for the SLA, he had the Symbionese Declaration distributed among his members. Later, he even allowed circulation of a rumor that Chris Lewis helped put up the SLA during its underground sojourn.

At the same time, Jones followed a circuitous strategy designed to convince his primary enemies—law enforcement and the press—that the Temple deplored the SLA and terrorist violence.

On February 13, 1974—just nine days after the kidnapping—members hand-carried a $2,000 check to the Hearst family mansion in Hillsborough, a suburb of oak-shaded dales and winding streets. While reporters from every imaginable news agency camped along the street outside the Temple members presented their contribution to the $2 million People-in-Need food program. The Temple's $2,000 was meant as a good-will gesture toward Patty Hearst's family, especially her father, Randolph Hearst, president of the Temple's nemesis, the *San Francisco Examiner*. Thanks to an introduction by Bob Houston's father, AP photographer Sammy Houston, news of this "antiterrorist" largess went across the nation on the AP wire.

Yet two weeks afterward, the San Francisco police intelligence unit opened a file on Rev. Jim Jones which it shared with the department's antiterrorist unit. Based on an intelligence inspector's interview with a Temple member described only as a black woman housekeeper in her mid-fifties, the report said, "Jones advocated to the congregation the overthrow of this established government by means of force and violence . . . and it was discussed approximately one year ago that Hearst would be a target as he represented the Capitalistic Society."

The report went on to say that, based on newspaper photos, the informant recognized Hearst's boy friend, Steven Weed, and SLA members Donald DeFreeze and Nancy Ling Perry at various meetings. The informant also said she saw armed guards in cars outside Temple meetings in Ukiah.

The rather sensational and disjointed information was thought unreliable and was not publicly disseminated. Nevertheless, the intelligence division received two letters from Tim Stoen within the next month, both of which took pains to explain the Temple's antiterrorist convictions and to dissociate the church from Chris Lewis.

In his April 8 letter, Stoen said he was writing at the suggestion of two patrolmen who had investigated a kidnapping and assault reported by Temple members. "The circumstances suggest that a 'militant' group may have been involved. . . . As an assistant district attorney, I can attest that Rev. Jones consistently . . . attacks scathingly the B.L.A., the S.L.A. and other groups. . . . Moreover he and the rest of us are most grateful for the excellent response of the SFPD . . . when the bomb was planted last month under his bus."

Police records showed no evidence of a bomb being reported. And the alleged kidnapping incident did not check out at all.

A week later Stoen again wrote the intelligence division, reporting inexplicably that Chris Lewis—"recently acquitted of second degree murder against a B.L.A."—had no connection with the Temple, except that his wife had attended services and that members had been trying unsuccessfully to get him into drug rehabilitation work.

"Since the trial, however, Lewis seems to have finally realized how much grief he's caused. . . . As a result he has agreed to leave the community. . . . If Chris Lewis ever returns to San Francisco and gets involved with any issue with the police, we will not only ask our members to wash their hands of him but to completely oppose him."

The letter did not mention that Lewis had been dispatched to the Temple's new mission in South America. . . .

Between 1971 and 1974, Jim Jones had suddenly found himself challenged by three serious enemies—the press, Temple defectors and the Establishment, including law enforcement agencies. Traitors had breached security from the inside, and outsiders were threatening to reach behind closed walls. The cracks could grow and merge and ultimately bring the walls crumbling down, and Jones knew it.

With a combination of offense, defense and limited retreat, he mini-mized his losses and in some ways turned liabilities into assets. But like an injured daredevil, he kept repeating his dangerous stunts, always putting himself in conflict with the larger world, always showing his allies that enemies really *were* out to get him.

At every turn he made new enemies and increased the likelihood of the old ones forming alliances. When he applied his absolute and amoral pragmatism in defense of the church, the remedies tended to come full circle and do additional damage. When he intensified church discipline to prevent defections and disloyalty, Jones utilized harsh practices that actu-ally caused defections. When he tried to build a political power base for ego needs and as a defensive tactic, that would backfire too. Though he might win powerful friends and make the church less vulnerable to at-tack, he would increase the church's visibility and subject it to new scru-tiny containing the seeds of destruction.

Still, Jones did not lose sight of reality entirely. He knew only so many lies, deceptions and cruelties would go unnoticed. In an effort to stay one step ahead of his enemies, Jones advanced a new vision of a faraway sanctuary. In fall of 1973—shortly after the desertion of the eight and about a year after the Kinsolving series—he and Tim Stoen prepared "immediate action" contingency plans for responding to a crack-down by the press or police. In a handwritten outline, Stoen listed means of fleeing the country—a flight to Canada on twenty-four hours notice; a flight to Canada and then to "a Caribbean missionary post" on three weeks notice; and a mass exodus to the Caribbean on six months notice. The "Suggested Long Range Plans" were: "1. Stay here in California until first sounds of outright persecution from press or government. 2. Have already developed a mission station and Christian retreat in the Caribbean, e.g., Barbados, Trinidad. . . ." The plan also called for flying all members to the settlement at the first signs of persecution.

As the plan was refined and fleshed out, the Temple zeroed in on Guyana, a small underdeveloped country on the northeastern shoulder of South America. As an early step, Temple researchers studied the coun-try's economy and extradition treaties between the United States and Guyana.

Why Guyana? For one, Jones had been favorably impressed back in 1961 during his stopover in what was then British Guiana. Its politics were socialistic and moving further left. It was the only English-speaking country in all South America and, perhaps more important, was governed by blacks. Besides, it was small enough and poor enough that Jones could easily obtain influence and official protection there.

On October 8, 1973, in Redwood Valley, the issue was put squarely on the table, as Resolution 73-5. Should the board of directors of Peoples Temple vote to authorize establishment of a branch church and agricultural mission in Guyana? Jim and Marceline Jones, Tim Stoen, Carolyn Layton, Archie Ijames, Sharon (Linda) Amos and Mike Cartmell made it official with a unanimous vote.

T W E N T Y - S I X

Escape Valve

As the tropical sun beat down, Emerson Mitchell interrupted his pacing for a moment to wipe perspiration from his brow. He was waiting for an airplane to touch down on the narrow patch of dirt that was the airstrip for Matthews Ridge, a tiny jungle community about 130 miles from the Guyanese capital of Georgetown. As he waited, Mitchell could not help but fret about his recent track record. He had a mission that was not being accomplished. He had been sent by his government to somehow convert remote jungle terrain into habitable productive farmland. After two years of false starts and disappointments, he was frustrated. But perhaps this new group of Americans that Georgetown was sending him would prove helpful. It was late December 1973.

This region was commonly called the Matarkai area—acronym for Matthews Ridge, Arakaka and Port Kaituma, an even tinier outpost some thirty-five miles northeast of the Ridge via a bumpy dirt road or by railroad.

With the aim of settling people there, Mitchell had come to the area under the orders of Dr. Ptolemy Reid, Guyana's deputy prime minister and also minister of agriculture and of economic development. As the government representative, Mitchell was to get houses built, help clear the land of the thick jungle and virgin timber, and provide food and farm implements until the settlers could fend for themselves. In 1972 the first government project brought about fifty national youth corps settlers to the interior. As they cleared the jungle and built more roads and houses around Port Kaituma, Mitchell was encouraged. But later the youths found the local Amerindian girls more attractive than the farming. Within two years, the youth corps was gone.

Also in 1972, a group of about eighteen jazz musicians came down to Guyana from New York for a Caribbean festival of the arts. They soon learned that the government was encouraging settlement in the interior and decided to take up the offer. As time went on, Mitchell discovered that the musicians were most interested in playing music, lying around and drinking. And their only successful crop turned out to be marijuana. Within two years of their arrival, they were kicked out of the country. Another failure for Mitchell.

As these thoughts and bitter memories floated through Emerson Mitchell's head, the plane he had been awaiting finally arrived. Out stepped Jim and Marceline Jones, their sons and a dozen trusted aides. Mitchell knew immediately this group was different. They were serious. They seemed well educated, they had money, and they struck him as enthusiastic about developing the land and making a life in the jungle.

Mitchell was a sophisticated man, but he had more than met his match in Jim Jones. When Jones showed him the photo albums and press clippings that legitimized his movement, Mitchell could not take his eyes off the pictures of costly Temple buses. As he studied photographs of senior citizens whom the Temple had transported across the country for vacations, he remembered *Time* magazine exposés about America's neglected old people. He saw what Jim Jones wanted him to see, and he liked it.

In any case, he was predisposed to like Peoples Temple. Unlike the previous attempts at settlement, this would not cost Guyana a penny. Jones said that he had $5 million Guyanese, the equivalent of $2 million U.S., to spend at the start.

Furthermore, Mitchell had received instructions from Georgetown to make these people comfortable and welcome. For centuries a border dispute had been simmering between Guyana and Venezuela over the western two-thirds of the country, mostly unsettled jungle. A town of a thousand or so Americans less than thirty miles from the Venezuelan border would help Guyana maintain its tenuous foothold and would lessen the possibility of a Venezuelan invasion or seizure. They would hardly want to provoke an international incident with the American government. There were other benefits as well for Guyana Prime Minister Forbes Burnham, who viewed himself as an important Third World leader. His status would be enhanced by the very fact that a predominantly black, socialist group of Americans voluntarily had chosen to emigrate to his country. Furthermore, the Temple's wealth would help ease Guyana's critical balance of payments problems. But most of all, Peoples Temple would develop resource-rich but untapped hinterlands, as the Guyanese government had been desperately and unsuccessfully trying to do for years.

There was something else Emerson Mitchell liked about Jim Jones: he was a midwestern minister talking and living integration. Mitchell had lived in Chicago from 1944 to 1949; he knew the storefront churches of black Chicago and the Father Divine types. So, when a man from Indiana appeared to be motivated to help black people and establish a multiracial settlement, Emerson Mitchell was ready to believe him.

As if he needed any more convincing, the two days the Jones entourage spent in Matthews Ridge confirmed Mitchell's impressions.

White people there, Mitchell knew, never fraternized with the natives. But Temple people not only fraternized, they treated them as equals. They won the hearts of the village people. Mitchell could not help but feel elation, amazement at the minister's ease in dealing with people. He wondered whether Jones did not "have a touch of the tar brush in him," and at one point he put the question that way to Archie Ijames. Ijames tried to disabuse him of that notion but with only partial success.

A member of Mitchell's staff saw so many adoring women with Jones that he could not figure out if they were all "his." In Jones's presence, the man commented: "I don't think he's capable of handling all those women. We must give him some capadula to drink." Capadula, made from the bark of a local tree, was looked on by the natives as an aphrodisiac. Jones did not hesitate. "Yes," he said, "I would like some."

Next morning they served it with breakfast and Jones drank it with relish. This, too, was well received. Instead of bringing in his special foods from America, he would eat the eddoes, cassava, plantain and morocot, a local fish caught in the Barima River and preserved in salt.

After breakfast, Mitchell took Jones around to the proposed development sites. Traveling to Port Kaituma by train, he showed Jones the land cleared by the American settlers and the youth corps. And it was soon decided that Port Kaituma was the general region where the Temple wanted to plant its roots. It was a little hilly, but otherwise acceptable. The "agricultural mission" would be called Jonestown. (Jones later would tell his people that the name had been suggested by Emerson Mitchell, but Mitchell knew otherwise.)

After the two-day tour of the Matarkai region, Mitchell sent Jones and his entourage back to Georgetown to nail down the land lease terms with Deputy Prime Minister Reid. Jones was visibly excited. There was so much to do that he wanted somebody to stay behind and get to work immediately. No one had come prepared for more than a three-week visit, yet Jones was talking about many months. They had lease details to be worked out, land to be surveyed, supplies to be ordered. First Jones turned to his old loyalist, Patty Cartmell, but she said it was impossible for her to stay.

Next Jones appealed to Archie Ijames, who had the construction skills and administrative experience that Cartmell lacked—and was black. Ijames, however, did not feel his wife Rosie could get by without him back in Redwood Valley. Besides, he had property in the valley, dentures to pick up, a myriad of things awaiting his return. Jones and his aides assured him they could handle all the little details. When it seemed everyone wanted Ijames to stay, he began to think he had been set up. But he remained adamant.

Then, suddenly, Jim Jones grabbed his chest and collapsed. But before lapsing into unconsciousness, he turned to Ijames and said, "See? If you don't do what I want, you're going to lose your leader." Ijames had witnessed similar collapses caused by other people, and vigilant nurses always had responded swiftly with oxygen. Nevertheless, Ijames was scared to risk his leader's life this time. When Jones came around, Ijames agreed to stay behind, to lay groundwork, to safeguard the $100,000 initial investment in the Promised Land. Shortly thereafter Jones dispatched attorney Gene Chaikin and Paula Adams to help Ijames.

It was a typically humid day in February 1974 when Ijames and Chaikin walked into the government office in Georgetown to submit their lease application. An afternoon cloudburst had cleansed the air. A young black clerk took their document, read it and asked in the lilting rhythm of the Caribbean, "Who is going to be listed as project director?" Chaikin replied without hesitation, "Archie Ijames." Archie duly signed.

But as they turned to leave, Ijames turned to Chaikin and said, "Back in the States I've signed papers and that sort of thing for window dressing, and I understand that. We're here in a black country now with a black prime minister, and you want more window dressing. But if I put my name down on this piece of paper as project director, I intend to be just that."

Ijames had swallowed his pride for years, but now he was extra sensitive: he had just learned that a white man—Charlie Touchette, his daughter's father-in-law—would be arriving that summer to take command.

Back in a Redwood Valley meeting some time later, Jones, uncharacteristically, began talking disparagingly about Archie Ijames. As a preliminary slap to his rebellious associate, Jones had decided to dredge up a long-forgotten controversy: the Becky Beikman affair. Jones said he had copies of a letter from Ijames to the young Indiana woman Archie had tried to adopt many years before. The envelope, Jones told the planning commission, contained contraceptives. Then, baring his real concern, he asserted that Ijames was building an alliance for himself in Guyana, asking the church to send down only people he could easily manipulate and control. Jones was not about to let that happen. "We'll fix Archie's ass," he sputtered. "We'll send him down a bunch of people he won't get along with."

Jones wanted six people to leave for Guyana the next morning. He tapped Mike Touchette, his uncle Tim Swinney and Phil Blakey, all of whom would obey Jones's orders to the letter and would take on Archie if need be. The other three had been delinquent kids in the valley; Jones figured it was a good opportunity to shuttle them out of the States.

Touchette had only six hours notice. He was sad to be leaving behind his wife Debbie, Archie Ijames's daughter, but was assured that she would follow shortly. Still he was eager to get away from the California Temple and to learn new skills, such as operating a Caterpillar bulldozer. Like the Eight Revolutionaries, he detested staff's holier-than-thou attitude and their special privileges, and he would not miss them or the all-night p.c. meetings.

When the group arrived in Georgetown in mid-March, Mike Touchette instantly found himself in an awkward situation. He was very fond of his father-in-law but not so much so that he still could not spy on Archie for Jones. Moreover, his own father, Charlie Touchette, would be arriving within a couple of months to displace Ijames as project leader.

Within a week, the group chartered a plane into Port Kaituma, where they would base their early operations. From the airplane there was nothing to see but jungle, mile after mile of dense green bush, broken only by the silty brown rivers that cut loops through the trees or an occasional sandy beach with a cluster of small thatched huts.

At an inlet of the Kaituma River lay Port Kaituma with its tiny graveled airstrip, a couple of rum shops and roughly fifty simple houses built on stilts. Several hundred people lived here, most of them Amerindian farmers, government workers or railroad hands. They were dirt poor.

Most of all, the village was remote, thirty-five miles by rough road or rail to Matthews Ridge. There was no direct road anywhere else. The only regularly scheduled flights were between Port Kaituma and the Ridge; direct flights to Georgetown had to be chartered.

The first boatload of Temple settlers was expected in August. The Temple had purchased a seventy-two-foot trawler, the *Cudjo*, to carry people and supplies from Florida and Georgetown to the interior. Jones had told prospective settlers it was a phenomenal boat. But the boat actually was too small, too crowded. And it leaked too badly to do any serious fishing or to bring fresh fish into the region, as Jones had promised Guyana officials.

Matarkai was not the tropical paradise Jones had promised either, yet from his first day in Port Kaituma, Mike Touchette was happy. He liked the Amerindian children running around naked and free. He felt the thrill of pioneering as he watched a man surveying the Temple's leased land. All that existed was a footpath into the jungle three and one-half miles long. But soon that would be a road, cut twenty-five feet across.

Over the next few months the group set to work, cleaning and painting the buildings left by the earlier settlers, cutting the grass and planting a small vegetable garden. When they were ready to bring over more settlers, Touchette and the others left Guyana aboard the *Cudjo* on June 11, 1974. Seven days later they sailed into Key West to pick up Archie Ijames and the supplies he had purchased there. The next day, they sailed into Miami to meet a Peoples Temple bus with the first sixteen settlers bound for the Promised Land.

During his stay in Florida, Archie Ijames went through a crisis. He found that Jones had turned his own family against him for his insubordinate remarks. With Archie thousands of miles away and unable to counter Jones's allegations, Rosie had been swept along by the stories of her husband's alleged infidelities with Becky Beikman. Jones then hit Rosie with an old letter in which Archie vowed that his allegiance to Jones outweighed his personal commitment to his wife. Ijames tried in vain to write or phone his wife to patch up things. Then, when he finally reached her through a third party, Rosie felt obligated to report it to Jones.

Meanwhile, Jones had sent a church member to Florida on a special mission to persuade Ijames to deed his Redwood Valley house to the Temple. But Ijames refused to sign, knowing it would provoke Jones's fury. When Jones heard about Ijames's obstinacy, he instructed Rosie to call long distance and chew him out. It was the couple's first conversation in months. So Archie initially thought the woman had gone out of her mind. But when Jones took the phone from her, Ijames saw through it all. "I see now that you got done what you were trying to do, so I'm through," he declared.

"You're through?" Jones exploded. "What do you mean, you're through?"

"That's it!"

"Who the hell's gonna run things down there?" Jones demanded.

"You should have thought of that," replied Ijames. "I've been trying to tell you that all along, but you wouldn't hear me. So get yourself another man."

However, Ijames's burst of independence was short-lived. Jones calmed him down. He persuaded him to stay on and meet the bus soon arriving from California.

Among the bus passengers were most of Mike Touchette's family: his parents Charlie and Joyce, his brother Albert and his sister Michelle, and Mike's wife Debbie. The reason for the en masse emigration of the Touchettes was simple: daughter Mickey had defected with the Eight Revolutionaries the year before, and Jones wanted her family out of the country. Besides, the Touchettes, especially Joyce, were loyal and had no compunction about giving Ijames a bad time. Neither did anyone else on the bus, including Archie's own daughter, Debbie. Had not Archie disobeyed the Father to them all?

The harassment began before the bus engine cooled off, and it continued daily. When Ijames brought supplies back to the boat, Joyce Touchette would scream at him for spending too much or buying the wrong things and sometimes would order them returned.

When his wife arrived from California, Ijames failed to break through her wall of defenses. And that night, he slept in the car, rather than in the boat with everyone else. Things seemed hopeless.

Next morning, however, Rosie and Archie went for a walk that saved forty years of marriage. She told him she had been hurt by the Becky Beikman revelations and by his letter of allegiance to Jones. Then he told her the truth, without the intrusion of Jim Jones. They realized that their years together did mean more to them than Jim Jones did.

This did not instantly transform Archie into a rebel, however. Now reconciled with his wife, Ijames signed over the deed to his property. He still desperately wanted to belong and believe in Peoples Temple.

But the rest of the entourage continued to make life miserable for him. On a rough twelve-day journey aboard the less than seaworthy *Cudjo*, Archie's movements were restricted to the cabin and the deck; he was the only passenger not allowed to take the wheel. High seas buffeted the boat, designed for six and carrying sixteen. The psychological punishment battered Ijames: isolation, humiliation, needless verbal abuse. At times, Rosie Ijames objected. But his tormentors would reply, "Well, Father told us to give him hell."

What had started out as unpleasant was approaching the unendurable for Ijames, a sensitive man, acutely conscious of race. His family and in-laws had been treating him shamefully; the man to whom he had pledged everything had betrayed him. He thought that he had no reason to live.

On one rare day of calm seas, he walked to the stern of the boat. The water looked inviting. It would be an escape from the pain. At sixty-one, he had been in Peoples Temple for seventeen years. "After all these years," he thought to himself, "all I put into this movement, it's come to this. We thought we got away from racism in America, but white people are pushing us around this way."

Archie Ijames contemplated jumping overboard, but did not want to hurt his wife.

Soon Archie found himself an ally aboard the *Cudjo*. Ironically, Chris Lewis, Jim Jones's chief enforcer, took the Ijameses into his protection. No one wanted to tangle with Lewis, so the couple enjoyed a little reprieve for the rest of the trip.

When the *Cudjo* finally eased into its berth at Georgetown Harbor, the Temple public relations crew welcomed the new arrivals—but for Ijames, it meant more trouble.

Paula Adams immediately pulled Ijames aside and asked what had happened to $45,000 entrusted to him. He told her what he had already told Jones by phone from Florida: "I don't have it. Ask Gene." Before Ijames had left for Florida, he and Gene Chaikin had crawled under a Port Kaituma house, buried the money and marked the spot with a large rock. Chaikin had gone back looking for the money but could not find it.

A few nights later, the Ijameses were lounging quietly in a Temple house in Port Kaituma when Rosie began telling her husband about a p.c. meeting in Redwood Valley. She said Jim Jones had asked for volunteers to kill Archie. Several who had raised their hands that night had abused the Ijameses on the boat trip from Florida—and now they were living right next door. "Honey," Ijames softly exclaimed. "Why didn't you tell me this before?"

"I was afraid to," she said. "Jim got me to believe that you weren't trusted and that if I told you, I'd be in trouble myself."

"Don't worry," Ijames assured her. "I'm not afraid to die, but I'm not going to stay here like a sitting duck waiting for it to happen, either.

I'm getting out of here, and I'm taking the money. I'm getting it to pay for our house. Let them try to put me in jail."

The morning that Ijames and Chaikin were to make another search for the money, Ijames got up ahead of time, crawled under the house in darkness and hit the packet of money with a screwdriver with his first stab. He laughed to himself: How could Chaikin have been so blind as to miss it? He dug up the treasure, took it into the house, unwrapped it and counted out $45,000 in $100 bills. Ijames then walked across a bend in the road and hid the money in a bush.

Later that day, after he made his excuses to Chaikin, Ijames retrieved the money, rewrapped it and addressed it to himself in care of Georgetown General Delivery. Then he tucked the package under his arm and walked down the road to the tiny Port Kaituma post office. He had the clerk register and insure the package for the maximum. He had been in Guyana long enough to know that nothing was reliable.

When Archie Ijames dug up the money from under the house, he felt he had taken an irreversible step. Within a few days someone would notice the money was gone. He decided to act first by calling a meeting with Charlie and Joyce Touchette, Chaikin and a few others.

"This is not what we've given our lives for, the way we've been treated here," he told them, speaking for Rosie, too. "We're leaving." He already had guaranteed a police escort to Georgetown by going to the constable in Port Kaituma, saying their lives might be in danger.

The loyalists tried unsuccessfully to persuade the Ijameses to stay, though they did convince Archie to cancel his police escort. The couple flew back to Georgetown, where their daughter Debbie met them at the airport and took them to a hotel in town near the Central Market on Water Street. As soon as she left, they checked into another hotel a few blocks away, under another name. But when they returned there after dinner, they discovered that someone from the Temple had traced them there already. They moved again, this time to a private home, where Guyanese acquaintances harbored them. They bought airline tickets home with money Rosie Ijames had saved from her rest home, but could not get a flight out for a week.

A few nights later a knock sounded at 2:00 A.M. Jim Jones and a church member had found them. Ijames was embarrassed but not surprised.

During that meeting, Ijames broke into tears: "I've lived in a racist society," he said. "I've looked long and hard to find a group of people with whom I could live without having to deal with racist attitudes. The church is supposed to be integrated, and yet *it* has racist attitudes. I felt you were the last hope. And the way I see it, that's not real either."

"I'm sorry if you feel that way," said Jones. "I'm sorry if you think I'm a racist."

"I don't know how else you can interpret it," Ijames replied.

There was nothing left to say. There was no longer any point in even talking. Saddened, the Ijameses finally boarded a Pan American jet and returned home. Jones flew into Port Kaituma to check the progress of the settlers, then he too returned to California.

The first thing Ijames did in Ukiah was to put the $45,000 in a safe deposit box. Despite the Temple's wealth, Ijames's bundle was no pittance to Jim Jones; it equaled the take from a good weekend of preaching all over California. Jones was determined to get back that money and shrewd enough to realize that Ijames really did not want to leave. He decided to give Archie what he wanted: a public apology at a general meeting.

Within a few days of the apology, Archie resolved to return the money. "Now if we're really going to work with these people," he said to his wife, "then we've got to trust them." When Ijames brought back the money, Jones turned to him and sneered, "You should have died in Guyana."

Despite his humiliations, Archie Ijames could not bring himself to fully leave Peoples Temple. Making a clean break would force him to admit to himself that he had been deceived all those years. He felt he was too old to start over. The Temple was his life and identity.

At last, after over a decade of dreaming about it, Jim Jones's Latin American haven was established, in the middle of tropical rain forest, miles from the nearest outpost. But Jim Jones exaggerated what was in reality a notable achievement. He could have told his Redwood Valley congregation that the Temple settlers were doing backbreaking work, clearing the bush and trying to grow food in the middle of a jungle. Instead, Jones had to claim that Jonestown was a Caribbean paradise with ripe fruit bursting from every tree, that food was so plentiful you could just sit back and let it fall in your lap.

During the summer months of 1974, Peoples Temple Agricultural Mission became more than just a nice phrase on a piece of paper. The new settlers built a trailer to haul supplies, made arrangements to install a generator in Jonestown and built an open-faced banana shed there, the first structure. The pioneers commuted to the site at first from Port Kaituma, close to seven miles by road. Assisted by Amerindians paid six and eight dollars a day, they cleared land and erected the first buildings out of jungle hardwoods—the kitchen, a cage for Mr. Muggs the chimp, and a recreation room for the seniors next to the kitchen. They gathered huge mounds of vegetation into piles and torched them—the "heap and burn" method. And they planted the first corn.

Jonestown was designed to be the place where Jones would make a fresh start, abandon the mistakes and deceptions of the past and be free to live openly the true socialist principles of the church. But people close to Jones soon realized that this was false billing, too. Within six months of the groundbreaking, Jones staged a faith healing service in Georgetown that left heads shaking. . . .

On a sticky August day in the capital, Paula Adams and five other Temple members had rung the bell at Brickdam Rectory. They asked to see Father Andrew Morrison, a Jesuit born in Guyana of English parents. A thin, hollow-faced man in his mid-fifties with eyes that lit up in excitement, Morrison served as church rector and as editor of the *Catholic Standard*, a small, mimeographed weekly started as a parish newspaper. The *Standard* had become the most reliable source of political news, an alternative to government-owned dailies that were propaganda sheets for Burnham's regime. Morrison had remained in Guyana despite the turbulence, poverty and government efforts to suppress him.

On this particular day, Paula Adams asked Father Morrison if Peoples Temple could use Sacred Heart Church for a service. Adams had done her homework. She knew that both Morrison and his parish council were strong believers in ecumenicism. For his part, Morrison found these Temple members to be emotional Christian idealists who believed strongly in integration and in helping to develop Guyana. He told the group he would need to speak to the parish council.

Months slipped by. Then one day in November, the group suddenly reappeared at a 5:00 P.M. mass, demanding an answer. Then, at Father Morrison's invitation, the Temple representatives made their presentation, to the council. They said there would be a prayer service and a little healing, which Father Morrison thought normal for an evangelical group. No one on the parish council voiced any objection. And the Temple picked a date and left.

In late December 1974, a large chartered plane carried Jim Jones, his top p.c. aides, female staffers and a new contingent of settlers to Georgetown. Archie Ijames swallowed his pride and came along for the ride. After touchdown at Timehri International Airport, Jones exited smiling and holding Mr. Muggs on a long chain. As the others followed happily, Mike Prokes filmed the arrival.

The group then took several small planes into Port Kaituma. During a week's stay, they took daily trips to Jonestown. Little John Victor Stoen, a dark-haired toddler nearing his third birthday, played on a small red tractor while his mother Grace posed for the camera and ate a grapefruit. This was for home consumption, as was a brief shot of Jones, with a hint of a smile on his lips as he fed a bird from his hand, then freed it.

For further promotional shots, Jones drew on his stagecraft. Unfazed by the fact that Jonestown had grown no fruit, he spread the store-bought fruit on the ground before him as the camera whirred away.

The settlers had been ordered in advance by radio to avoid saying anything negative about jungle life. Everything was to appear perfect. Jones had already told his fellow visitors that the trees grew fruit the flavor of ice cream. To cover for him, Mike Touchette was supposed to say that these trees had been ordered, but had not yet arrived. Likewise, he was instructed to say that the settlers had not yet planted crops or built houses in Jonestown because of difficulties getting equipment. One visitor who took Jones at his word expected to find lush tropical fruit growing wild everywhere and more nuts than he could eat. When he got to Port Kaituma, he asked Charlie Touchette where the bounty was. "There ain't any," came the reply. "You could go into the jungle and starve."

For a whole week, work came to a stop. Several tractor-trailer loads of settlers and visitors bumped along the road to Jonestown, marveling at the cleared land and the few primitive structures. People walked into the bush and swung on the jungle vines. Everyone laughed at the antics of Mr. Muggs as he was introduced to the cage built for him.

Meetings every night lasted until three or four in the morning. The first was devoted exclusively to catharsis, with emphasis on the settlers —Jones was afraid they had grown lax in his absence. In subsequent meetings, Jones mostly expounded on the state of the world or his plans to develop Jonestown. Jones and his top aides told the settlers they should feel privileged to be allowed to work in paradise, while the rest slaved away back home, "in the belly of the beast."

Overall, the visit was a happy get-together, though the early settlers were irritated that many new arrivals were troublemakers. Mike and Charlie Touchette had been begging for workers, not juvenile delinquents. Still, progress was good, and the reunion gave everyone a chance to get caught up on gossip from back home. It also allowed Jones to bring a respectable-sized contingent to nationwide celebrations for the tenth anniversary of Prime Minister Burnham's election. The Temple sent a delegation to the festivities at Matthews Ridge, and some church members met Burnham personally.

Back in Georgetown, Father Andrew Morrison was very worried. With the December 30 church service fast approaching, he noticed half-page advertisements in the *Guyana Chronicle* attesting to Jim Jones's supernatural healing powers. THE BLIND SEE! THE DEAF HEAR! THE CRIPPLED WALK! screamed the box in the center of the ad.

About a week before the service, Morrison told a contingent of Temple aides that he felt deceived: they had asked to use the church mainly to describe their agricultural mission—not to demonstrate healing powers of Jim Jones.

The Temple group pleaded innocence: "Our advertising department must have slipped up, Father. We'll fix it."

But on the following morning, the *Chronicle* carried an even larger ad for the healing service. It pushed Morrison and the parish council into a dilemma: should they cancel a publicly promoted event, or be used by this newcomer Jones? In the end, they decided that they would get more criticism if they stopped the service.

Long before the 11:00 A.M. service, the people began streaming past the large white sign for "Sacred Heart National Shrine" and the three windswept palm trees in the front courtyard. Soon the spindly whitewashed wooden church was packed from the main floor to the organ loft. Most were black Catholics; some were simply curious, drawn by the advertisements.

Wearing a white suit, a black shirt with white tie and his ever-present dark glasses, Jones opened the service slowly. He sang American hymns and talked briefly about the agricultural mission. Then he began the healings, with Marceline assisting at the altar. "Someone in the middle of the church has trouble with his legs." Jones scanned the audience. "Yes, it's the knees. Put your hand up."

When a tall black man raised his hand, Jones walked down the aisle, flanked by assistants. "You are going to be healed. Bend your knees and squat," the preacher ordered. The man squatted and came up again.

"Do you feel any pain?" Jones asked. The man shook his head. "No." As the man did deep knee bends, Temple assistants led the crowd in applauding Jones's miraculous powers.

Jones did several more healings, one involving a young white woman with breast cancer. At the conclusion of the spectacle, Jones softly called people to the front. In a single file line, they passed along the communion rail, murmuring thanks as Jones touched their shoulders.

Father Morrison watched the service with mounting horror. At first he thought to himself, "Either this man has enormous healing powers or this is an enormous hoax." As the service wore on, his uncertainty fell away. The slick well-dressed American was not talking about Jesus Christ, but about himself—how he devoted his life to helping others and wore secondhand clothes. The performance left Father Morrison red-faced.

Two days later, Father Morrison was able to confirm that those "healed" were members of Jones's congregation. But when he went to confront Temple leaders at their residence, he was told everyone had gone to Jonestown. The priest complained about the fraud to Christopher "Kit" Nasciemento, a high-ranking government official in Burnham's cabinet. Nasciemento sympathized, but said he was helpless. So Father Morrison decided to keep his own file on Jim Jones and Peoples Temple. It would grow substantially over the years.

Many inside the Temple were likewise disappointed by the healing service. Though tame by stateside standards, it proved that Jones was importing the same cheap, theatrical deceptions used in American ghettos. His settlers had hoped he would leave home the religion and concentrate on the church's social and political goals. Several aides had advised him against the healing service—and they were right. It became a public relations disaster. A January 10, 1975, article in Father Morrison's *Catholic Standard* emphatically disassociated Sacred Heart Church from "the alleged healing service" and asked embarrassing questions about Jones's orchestration.

Jones responded by organizing his public relations aides into two-person teams and sent them to patch things up with officials, priests and ministers all over town. The teams succeeded to some extent in down-playing the healing service, but the incident shook Jones.

In a moment of candor, he took Tim Stoen aside and confessed that he had horribly misjudged the public reaction. He wondered aloud whether he had lost touch with the masses, whether his years living in Redwood Valley and making whirlwind healing tours had not eroded his ability to read people. Jones told Stoen that he had decided to regain his feel for the people by shifting the Temple's U.S. emphasis almost entirely to the big cities.

PART FIVE

PARADISE, GAINED AND LOST

*It's two steps forward,
one step back. . . .
Sometimes you can't win
for losing.*

JIM JONES

TWENTY-SEVEN

Communalists

During December of 1973, Joyce Shaw languished on the upper bunk of her Redwood Valley commune. She was sick with the flu and so depressed that she wondered whether she would die. She had endured enough of provincial Ukiah.

For a year, she had worked full time in the church publications office. This was considered a privilege, but Joyce was getting tired of getting only two or three hours of sleep a night and competing with others who bragged: "Oh, I only got one hour last night." Once, to get out an issue of the church paper, she and Bob Houston went for four or five days at a stretch without sleep. Worse yet, it was becoming obvious to Joyce that some tasks were contrived by Jones.

Living conditions began to seem oppressive, too. Joyce had forfeited her own rented house in 1973 when she accepted the position as full-time publications worker. Like other full-time workers, she went "communal." At first, she slept in a bed in the hallway of a little house on Road K. Later, she camped in the publications offices in her sleeping bag, and borrowed showers elsewhere. When she finally complained, the church council let her and other workers occupy a member's vacant house. Archie Ijames installed triple-decker bunks, improved the garden and erected a pen for some dogs. The commune was called West House; another one was known as East House.

Joyce still was unhappy with her lot. Ill in her upper bunk, she wrote Jones a letter saying she did not believe that full-time church work was the optimum utilization of her talents. She requested and was granted permission to find an outside job.

Soon, she and Bob were summoned to a meeting of the full planning commission. They were asked to get married, for missionary duty in some vague African project. These lovers were hesitant. Their relationship had bounced over rough shoals. Joyce was not anxious for a permanent tie; at the time, their relationship mainly revolved around church duties. And Bob resisted the idea of divorcing his wife Phyllis, largely because of their two children.

With church permission, Joyce and Bob spent some time off by themselves discussing their orders. It was unusual for Jones to allow a marriage of two white middle-class, college-educated lovers. So Joyce and Bob assumed that Jones mistakenly thought there was no romantic love between them. After some deliberations, they decided they would wed on the basis of intellectual and ideological compatibility, and warm feelings for each other.

Actually, the determining factor behind Jones's order may have been his fear that Shaw would leave. He apparently acknowledged the stress she was under by telling the couple to move to San Francisco. "Hallelujah!" Joyce thought. She was overjoyed to escape the rural Ukiah area that reminded her so much of her Ohio homeland.

Within a day, she had packed and was on her way to San Francisco. Wearing a borrowed suede coat, tottering on high heels unworn for many months, thrilled but lost in the big city, she went job hunting.

Bob welcomed the change of scenery too. In October 1973, he either had quit or been fired as a sales representative for Xerox in Mendocino and Lake counties. Driving a beat-up old Pontiac, wearing bags under his eyes and his only suit, he had tried to be a salesman, but he could not succeed in that competitive sales world without the trappings and energy denied him by the church lifestyle. After leaving Xerox for a milling factory where he lost about thirty pounds, San Francisco sounded like paradise.

While waiting for Bob's divorce, Bob and Joyce took up residence in a studio apartment located at Fillmore and Haight streets, an area known as "Needle Alley" among narcotics cops. As the only whites in the area, they were conspicuous as they marched out each morning, neatly dressed for work. Joyce had found a job as a psychological tester at the University of California Medical Center, and Bob, after a stint as a substitute music teacher, worked as a Youth Guidance Center counselor and for the railroad. They sacrificed their own comfort and risked their safety so they could accumulate as much money as possible for the church. Adhering to the principle of giving according to ability and taking according to need, they turned over at least $10,000 to the Temple that year. They even swept wine bottles and heroin debris out of the apartment building hallway each day to defray half the rent.

As soon as the divorce came through in September 1974, Bob and Joyce hand-carried their marriage papers to Redwood Valley. It was October 2, 1974. While Temple members milled about, folding chairs after a meeting, the couple presented the papers to their pastor. There was no ceremony, no elation, no rice and no cake. Jones signed the legal documents and, as the newlyweds walked away, he called after them irreverently, "What God hath joined together let no man put asunder."

Like good socialists, Bob and Joyce abstained from the frivolity of a honeymoon. Their wedding night was spent in their $80-a-month apartment. But soon the close quarters were not theirs alone anymore.

About six weeks after the marriage, church head counselor Grace Stoen asked them to take in a teen-age boy having difficulty adapting in Ukiah. They did so. Less than a month later, the church decreed that Bob's daughters would move in too. Phyllis, it turned out, was dating another member who had once left the church and was viewed as potentially disloyal; giving the children to Bob and Joyce might bind the mother to the church.

To accommodate their expanding family, Joyce and Bob went house-hunting on Potrero Hill, a racially mixed poor and working-class neighborhood with some housing projects. The hill, where football star O. J. Simpson was reared, overlooked downtown San Francisco from one slope and the industrialized bay shoreline from another. After only three hours of looking, Joyce and Bob rented a spacious three-story frame house on Vermont Street with a playhouse and a garden in the backyard. Soon, this commune was bulging with people too. The Houstons had started out with seven children—including Bob's daughters. Throughout 1975, additional children and several adults moved in as Jones encouraged people to go "communal" and shifted the church emphasis wholeheartedly into the big cities.

Communalism was no revelation to Jim Jones. The revival of communalism in the 1960s simply put that living style back in public consciousness. Using biblical justifications, Jones had practiced it to a very limited extent in Indiana with his extended family of about a dozen. But in California, the organization was sufficiently large to reintroduce it. Philosophically, Jones favored the communal life because it was a leveling and unifying influence. In a commune, all theoretically would have the same housing, use of communal transportation, equal sharing of food and even clothing. No one would own anything. No one would feel inferior. No one would lack parents, or children. Everyone would live under Temple rules.

People were encouraged—and at times pressured—to "go communal." Anyone privileged enough to be elevated to the p.c. or important church positions was expected to adopt a communal lifestyle. But it was more than a badge of commitment. The money saved through a collectivistic lifestyle, along with the possessions of the communards, could be donated to the church. Their children would be raised communally too, often in other Temple communes and even under guardianships.

The communal system was almost self-generating. The church converted houses and property donated by communards into new communal living units. Over thirty pieces of property were signed over to the church in Mendocino County alone. At least several dozen additional properties, including a rest home, were donated in San Francisco, mostly by black people who had worked all their lives to buy a home or build a business.

In the mid-1970s, as the Temple shifted to the cities, communes became important as a means of tightening controls and of improving church finances. Rather than use wholesale recruiting and risk another Kinsolving series, Jones concentrated on deepening the loyalties of existing members and making revenue through them. Their possessions were sold through two Temple antique stores and through weekend flea markets. People signed over pay checks and disability, welfare and social security checks, receiving in return room, board, medical care and other benefits. Contrary to the stereotype promoted by the Temple and embraced by the news media and others, the masses of Temple members had not been ne'er-do-wells on welfare. They were hard-working black people who had been productive all their lives and who often had maintained strong Christian church ties. When they retired, they collected their social security with pride. They had toiled hard for it.

The attractions for people on fixed incomes was obvious. A social security check did not go far toward paying for necessities. But pooling resources meant all could live better communally, with companionship and brotherhood and people to care for them in their final years. Likewise, single parents were attracted to a lifestyle with religion, political activism, companionship and child care. For all, the standard of living, while perhaps not comparable to white middle-class neighborhoods, was far superior to that of many urban ghettos. The diet was healthy, the shelter safe and adequate, the supervision of students and children good. And the environment was interracial.

During the urban transplanting process, some Temple good works were negated. There would not be room in San Francisco communes for the animals sheltered by the church in rural Mendocino County. Reluctantly, the Temple had to dispose of animals that could not be placed in homes. Three pits were dug on one member's property, and security chief Jim McElvane, a towering black activist and vegetarian, supervised the extermination. Dozens of dogs were shot, their bodies thrown into the mass graves.

For their commune, Bob Houston and Joyce Shaw tried to pick bright rebel children with church or school adjustment difficulties. The total population fluctuated, reaching twenty-four at one point, including several adults. It was so overcrowded that some children had to be hidden when social workers came to the house. But with as little money as they allowed themselves for support, the communards performed admirably. Bob adopted the role of handyman and father figure. Joyce, the mother figure, mended old clothes and prowled secondhand stores so the children could be dressed in presentable fashion. The commune spent $400 a month or an average of 60 cents a day per person on food, with an emphasis on fresh fruit and vegetables. Yet five adults netting $45,000 one year still were able to turn over $19,000 to the church. The commune became known as the Temple's most successful one.

As a treat, all children with a birthday in a given month were allowed to select an activity or outing—a parallel to the monthly birthday parties held by the larger church body. Playing parents, Joyce and Bob would shepherd the children to places they never had seen before—the beach and Chinatown, ice skating. For all intents and purposes, the houseful of children belonged to Joyce and Bob, whether foundlings and orphans, kids on loan or permanently adrift, black or white. Six were under guardianships to the couple. If any had troubles at the nearby grammar schools or junior high, Bob Houston went as a parent to talk to teachers and administrators. He and Joyce provided individual tutoring at home to help some children keep up with classes. They supplied instruments to four children taking music lessons at school, and Bob supplemented that with lessons at home.

The harmony thrilled Joyce; her dream of a family was fulfilled. Her first husband never had wanted to have children, but her second took in children and treated them as his own. Though not particularly demonstrative, erect and dedicated Bob Houston saw to their needs. Bob was careful never to show favoritism to his own flesh and blood—that was the Temple way. In fact, he had been reprimanded for allowing his daughters to sit on his lap at a church meeting. After that, he followed the rules so strictly that Joyce finally encouraged him to reserve an extra bit of love for Judy and Patty.

Temple children at Potrero Hill Junior High dressed on a par with other students. Though exceptionally meek and retiring, they blended well in a school that was nearly a third black, though school staff did notice that they shared a group identity. They would not play kickball or participate in yard activities. They always ate lunch together—as part of the free lunch program. Whether black or white, they called each other "brother" and "sister." And after school, they met on the front steps to go home together.

Eventually, Principal Thomas J. Sammon asked Bob Houston's cooperation in dissolving the clique. The children then did start developing some outside friends at school. But when they brought them home after school, one church member objected that having a nonmember, even a child, inside a Temple commune was a breach of security.

After school, commune children, like children in nuclear families, had an afternoon snack, then free play time. When Joyce came home from work at dinnertime, there were often up to ten people lined up, waiting to hash out their problems. She did not mind being mother and counselor. But she wanted a measure of authority if she was going to shoulder the lion's share of responsibility.

Soon a conflict arose. Bob believed in total democracy and extreme egalitarianism, with children having an equal voice. Joyce, as a p.c. member, was more in tune, at this time, with Jones's drift toward an authoritarian structure. She contended that crowded conditions necessitated more rigidity.

The issue resurfaced whenever the house became dirty or in disarray. Joyce's patience ran out when she found herself alone on one weekend, faced with a huge cleanup job. She drafted a schedule designed to guide everyone in the commune from 7:00 A.M. wakeup until 10:00 P.M. quiet time. When Bob and the others returned to the house from a bus trip at 5:00 A.M. Monday, Joyce had planted herself at the front door. She handed out copies of her typed schedule. Bob did not like this reception one bit; he thought Joyce was usurping his role as commune leader. They quarreled.

When other adults in the house supported his wife, Bob became defensive and uncooperative. Frustrated, Joyce took the drastic step of writing up her husband in a report to the church council. The matter came to the floor during a church meeting. In compliance with Jones's wishes, the counselors officially designated Joyce as sole commune leader. The decision emasculated and demoralized Bob, but he abided by it, playing in the band, holding his mouth shut, avoiding conflicts. He did not question Jones's healings, and he did not challenge the most intellectually troubling practice, the deification of Jones. Bob Houston so strongly believed in the value of the Temple's social service that he accepted the guideline: the ends justify the means.

Still, Bob Houston was operating on more precarious ground than most. The combination of his stubborn personality, vocabulary, education and perhaps his father's occupation as a newsman made him a suspect member, a frequent target of Jones's tirades against elitists. It did not matter that he worked two paying jobs, that he served as a church bus driver on weekend trips to Los Angeles, that he kept himself running on coffee, or that he knew his Marx. He had the disturbing habit of taking Jones seriously when Father invited questions. Bob asked them—sometimes the tough or esoteric ones about socialist theory. What to Bob was simply exercise of intellectual curiosity seemed to others a pretentious flaunting of multisyllabic words and complicated concepts. Worse, he was clearly better educated than Jones.

At meetings, Jones handed carte blanche to anyone who wanted to antagonize or harass Bob Houston. By ridiculing Houston as an "insensitive intellectual," by poking fun at him for priggishness (Houston seldom swore), Jones indirectly intimidated anyone who might think of exercising his or her intelligence independently. The articulate potential challengers to Temple practices were silenced. Like the college dorm students, like Tim Stoen, Houston needed subduing and humbling.

Tearing Bob Houston apart became a sadistic sport condoned by Jones. He was mocked, even by children, even at home. His stubborn, honest defenses only encouraged more of it; he was derided even for dozing off at meetings. Jones labeled him a "narcoleptic," victim of a disease marked by sudden and deep sleep. Then he attacked him as a traitor and class enemy. Though some members were disturbed, none came to Bob's defense. No one wished to share the animosity. Besides, it seemed sometimes that Houston brought it upon himself, stubbornly doing the same things over and over. Stoically he tolerated the punishments that grew more extreme with each month in 1975.

Like so much with the church, the physical discipline began in a small way and only gradually reached extremes. It had started with a few light spankings for children. Then a paddlelike one-by-four-inch "Board of Education" was introduced. The paddlings became more severe and were often administered by a rotund black woman named Ruby Carroll, who was chosen for her physical strength, not a mean disposition. Like a master of ceremonies, Jones supervised, but the audience participated, particularly when the disciplined person was deserving or disliked. The swats varied in number and intensity. Some were spanked almost half-heartedly, or in fairly good humor. Other spankings qualified as beatings. In one of the most extreme, teen-age Linda Mertle (later known as Mills) was hit seventy-five times for becoming too affectionate with an alleged lesbian.

The normal practice was for church notary publics to obtain signed permissions from parents and guardians before the public floggings. Then, once he had guided the jury to the proper verdict and sentence, Jones, for the most part, sat back and watched silently. At times, he seemed pained; at times, he laughed at some humorous aspect of the punishment, a joke that the spectators either shared or were expected to share. Other times, he would command the hitter to use more force or to increase the number of strokes. He might show compassion, calling off a particularly painful beating, or reducing the number of hits.

Boxing matches were soon inaugurated for the children—almost as entertainment. Laughter and lightheartedness predominated as an errant child was pitted against a stronger opponent who was supposed to win. Some were as young as five. If the wrong child won, tougher opponents would be called into the arena until the child was taught a lesson.

The next step was introducing adults to the matches. The brutality became severe as full-grown people donned gloves and began throwing punches seriously. Sometimes they knocked each other silly or bloodied each other. A person stupid enough to fight too hard would go toe to toe with bigger and better opponents until vanquished. But if he did not fight at all, he was ridiculed and hit anyway. Every punch carried the message: one cannot fight the "collective will." The will of Father.

The battling conditioned people to believe that they would win if they fought for the church and would lose if they fought against it. Jones justified his psychodrama by saying that society was full of rough conditions, that people needed to be rugged and capable of self-defense. Yet it really was an extension of the catharsis sessions, with physical pain added to the psychological. Through corporal punishment, Jones could simultaneously strengthen internal order, mete out justice and indoctrinate.

No one, not even Jim Jones and the white elite, was exempted, technically speaking, from the punishments. In 1975, Joyce Shaw volunteered for five swats with the "Board of Education" for shoving her stepdaughter, Judy Houston. Jones, who claimed that his own father had spanked him as a child, took some swats too, to demonstrate that his followers had caused him pain by their rules violations. Stephen Jones was paddled once. Even little John V. Stoen took a spanking in front of the group, stood with tears in his eyes, raised a clenched fist and said bravely, "Thank you, Father."

Punishment was applied not just for deviation from policy but for serious cases of delinquency. In some instances the Temple was substituting its own punishment for an act that might well have led to a jail term on the outside: for example, there was the man whose penis was beaten with a hose after he was caught molesting a child. Another in this category was a fourteen-year-old boy who had karate-kicked his sister in the back, putting her in traction.

Jones confronted the boy, whom we will call Mason, at a Redwood Valley meeting. "What the hell you doin'? With all our enemies, you put a hand to one of our sisters?"

Jones asked the congregation to prescribe a punishment, but suggested himself the severity and rationale: "How many should he get, Church? Ten? [Remember] he's been kicked out of school. He kicked his sister after doing karate. You who don't want to do it or who want to do it mild are the worst enemies they've got, because when he winds up in jail, you won't be there to get him out.

"If anybody does, it'll have to be me, and I'm overworked."

After asking for a show of hands on various punishments, he announced that the majority had voted for twenty whacks. Mason's mother seconded the penalty. The crowd applauded her.

"Which black brother will take this on?" Jones called. A volunteer came forward.

As the sound of swats echoed throughout the church, he explained, "Part of this is humiliation more than physical pain, so all you standing up, get out of the way [so the others can see]." Jones counted the licks out loud. "Eighteen . . . nineteen . . . twenty. . . . Now what do you have to say, son?"

"I'm sorry," Mason said. "I won't do this anymore."

Softening, Jones explained that the discipline was designed to kill rebelliousness that might land the boy in prison. "Don't fight the world," he advised. "If it hadn't been a sister, you'd be in jail. . . . You'd be up the river, like George Jackson, who was just about your age. We're trying to help you. We're not trying to be mean."

Bob Houston was sent into at least two gladiatorial events. In one boxing match, he suffered a bloody nose and a shiner and was greatly embarrassed in front of his family. He tried to fight back, with little luck. As he was pummeled, Jones sat behind the podium on his stool and chortled.

Another time, after troubles in the commune became public, Bob's punishment was to sit in the front row at services—like a troublesome child—and to show unqualified enthusiasm for Jones by waving his arms in the air, swaying and shouting praise like the Pentecostal blacks. But the discipline that hurt Bob most resulted from Joyce's March 1975 memo complaining about his obstructionism in the commune.

On one recent night, the Temple had been gutted by fire under mysterious circumstances. Jones had kept his congregation an extra long time in Redwood Valley services, delaying departure to San Francisco time and time again, telling his people he had a premonition of danger. When the buses rolled up to the San Francisco temple, fire trucks still were parked outside the smoldering building. While church members praised Jones's prescience for saving them from certain death, arson investigators concluded that the stairway had been doused with flammable liquid. By whom, it was never known.

The restoration provided a ready project to occupy Temple kids, unemployed members—and Bob Houston. At a Sunday night meeting in the partially restored church, Jones decreed that Houston should start work immediately, without even going home to change out of his business suit. Houston, though taken aback, agreed to Jones's Maoist-like "reeducation."

For over three months, Bob was absent from the commune and saw little of his wife and daughters. The punishment was expedient: at the time there was a railroad layoff, and Houston would not have a good-paying job anyway. This way he could collect unemployment benefits and do church work. For his part, Houston tried to make the best of a painful situation by learning about building trades.

In July, when the railroad began rehiring laid-off workers, Bob wanted to return to work and also move home. "What do you think about my coming back?" he asked Joyce. She replied, eagerly: "I'd love it." Though she had been responsible for his being disciplined, she regretted it. She needed and missed him. With Jones's permission, Houston rejoined his family.

Running the commune on her own had taxed Joyce's energies beyond capacity. In addition to commune duties and her regular job, she coordinated medical care for Temple members in San Francisco. As in

Ukiah, the church provided the best available. Despite Jones's so-called miracle healings, he encouraged his people to see doctors.

When people needed medical attention, they came to Joyce with their symptoms. Every few weeks, she took her list of people and ailments to Dr. A. for a consultation. The doctor, who also happened to be one of Jones's personal physicians, would take an hour and a half of his time at no charge, then make referrals to some of the best doctors in town.

To his own doctors, Jones was an enigma. The "great healer" spent long hours visiting various physicians. He always arrived with bodyguards, tough-looking but deliberately low-key, who would hang around the waiting room door. Jones spoke openly about his biggest fear—that the government and others were out to get him—and expressed concern about the rise of fascism in the United States. Although his only physical ailment was a chronic, nonserious urinary tract problem, he also exhibited signs of stress and hypochondria. He complained of chest pains and talked incessantly about his sacrifices; he even spoke of his sexual services as part of his duty. The doctors presumed he was sleeping little, eating improperly and irregularly and carrying too large a burden.

At one point, a doctor suggested that he enter a hospital for complete rest and an examination. Jones consented to a psychiatric examination. The diagnosis: "paranoid with delusions of grandeur." Once out of the hospital, Jones boasted of having undergone the examination, as if to show his people there was no onus attached to it. Jones, who had once bragged that he could beat any lie detector, said that the psychiatrist had found his mind "in perfect working order."

TWENTY-EIGHT

San Francisco in Thrall

By the late 1960s, the city with the magical fog and hilly white look of a Mediterranean seaport had been energized by its second "Gold Rush"— tourism. But though downtown San Francisco had been transformed into a West Coast Manhattan of glass and concrete towers full of white-collar commuters, important political developments were afoot in the neighborhoods.

From the sunny "Mission" to the often foggy Sunset District near the beach, San Francisco had been a proud, mainly white, working-class town. For many years, labor and "Downtown" had controlled the balance of political power. But in the 1960s the rules of the game changed. Asians, either recent immigrants or descendants of the Gold Rush's cheap labor force, had moved into white enclaves in western San Francisco and enlarged their numbers. At the same time, more Latinos had arrived, the population of blacks in San Francisco had almost tripled—and a new power equation emerged in local politics.

There was a shift from citywide elections of county supervisors to district elections, which many felt would give black, yellow and brown people a better shot at representation.[35] Campaign spending limits and reporting requirements were introduced in the early 1970s. And together these factors bestowed unprecedented power on neighborhood associations, ethnic groups, interest groups and others who could be pulled together into coalitions. The days of calamari clubs and fat cat contributors seemed at a close; the days of Peoples Temple and community alliances were dawning.

It was only a matter of time before Jim Jones, operating in the black community, would meet Dr. Carlton B. Goodlett. A physician in the San Francisco black community since 1945, Goodlett was a curious mixture of civil rights fighter, black businessman and political kingmaker known by some as the godfather of the city's black politics. Since 1948, he had published the weekly black newspaper, the *Sun Reporter*. In the 1966 gubernatorial race he had placed third, and by the early 1970s Goodlett was president of the black National Newspaper Publishers Association and served on just about every board of distinction in the local black community. Reportedly a millionaire through his three-pronged business ventures—medicine, publishing and urban developing—Goodlett put money behind his politics. And although some viewed him as abrasive, abrupt and cantankerous, he was an important and consistent voice for minority rights.

Goodlett first encountered Jones in the course of his medical work —and at political rallies. Jones patronized Goodlett's medical offices himself and sent some members of his own family, including his mother. Contacts with the Joneses—plus hundreds of other Temple patients— acquainted Goodlett with the church's human services ministry. These visits made it easier for Goodlett to buy Jones's explanation that his controversial healings were really the elimination of psychosomatic ailments.

Goodlett was most impressed that people he had known for years seemed to be leading happy and functional lives. The Temple, like the Black Muslims, showed a capacity for turning wayward youths into dedicated social activists. Temple bus trips took the elderly poor and ghetto children, some of whom had never left San Francisco, across the country. Goodlett respected Jones's demonstrated longtime commitment to equal rights, enough to present him with the *Sun Reporter* Special Merit Award in April, 1972. Somehow, a warm rapport had developed between the white minister who wished he could be black and the fast-talking black physician who could well have been a preacher.

Sun Reporter editor Tom Fleming, as burly as Goodlett was wiry, also developed a rapport with Jones. Fleming had defended the Ukiah church in print against the 1972 *Examiner* stories, believing that Kinsolving was motivated by racial prejudices. A year or so later when he was invited to the Geary Boulevard Temple, Fleming at first declined because visitors were pat-searched at the door. When that humiliation was waived, he did visit—and liked what he saw: a nursery school, a printing plant, a free physical therapy clinic and more. Fleming concluded that Jones was using religion to recruit blacks and was an uncompromising integrationist.

Though anything but religious himself, the journalist fell into an informal relationship with the Temple. He went there to chicken dinners a few times, and out to a coffee shop for lunches with church people, usually public relations man Mike Prokes. Fleming, old enough to be his father, told Prokes about being black in the pre–civil rights days, while the white former television newsman launched into accounts of what he said was FBI and CIA harassment.

There was no more devout advocate than Prokes, and few more sincere members. He had arrived some years earlier as an unexpected windfall from the Kinsolving series. A TV newsman in Modesto at the time, he had come to the Temple to do an exposé on Jones in October 1972, but liked the people and respected Jones's forthright critique of the American system. When he joined, Prokes provided exactly what Jones needed to combat a prying press: an imagemaker and media adviser.

Increasing paranoia soon marked Temple contacts with Tom Fleming. The *Sun Reporter* was called with reports of the arson fire at the Temple. Then calls reporting unprovable threats against Jones started coming once and even twice a week. Finally Fleming told the minister, "Jim, you got to learn to live with it."

Meanwhile Goodlett was receiving visits from alarmed citizens. A delegation of black ministers complained that Jones was stealing their members, breaking up families and collecting property. "Listen," Goodlett told them, "this man looks to me like he's pretty successful in interpreting the functional gospel. I don't know what brand of whiskey he drinks, but if he drinks a special brand of whiskey, you better drink it yourself."

Despite these and later complaints to be laid on his doorstep, Goodlett would steadfastly maintain the value of Temple work. Though head of a sometimes crusading newspaper, he never attempted to delve into allegations that continued to surface. (Later he would maintain that church controversies were sticky business for a community newspaper and that he did not have the staff to investigate properly.)

But the publisher also had a personal, political and business association with Jones. Goodlett had permitted the church to use his medical license to open the physical therapy clinic at the church and had used his influence to help Temple member Larry Schacht get into medical school. He allowed the Temple to print its newspaper, *Peoples Forum*, on his presses, with payment only for printer's time. In 1976, Goodlett and Jones became involved with others in an import-export company. Later, Goodlett and the Temple each invested $35,000 to help save the failing Norfolk, Virginia, *Journal and Guide*, the third oldest black newspaper in the nation.

The Goodlett–Jones relationship was of mutual benefit. When the Temple first went to Guyana, Goodlett wrote a letter of recommendation to the editors of the *Guyana Chronicle*. And while the *Sun Reporter* bestowed its blessings on Jones, the Temple newspaper returned the compliment by praising Goodlett and by encouraging all Temple members to subscribe to his publication.

Goodlett teased Jones sometimes about his dark glasses, and Jones fondly called Goodlett a "Cadillac Communist" behind his back. But they enjoyed their shoot-from-the-hip conversations, which sometimes slipped into theology. Jones would argue that Christ's church had been in effect a communal organization and cult. Goodlett told him he thought the Temple was a cult too, and the two talked about various cult leaders such as Father Divine and Daddy Grace. Goodlett was too admittedly egotistical to be threatened by Jones's presence, and was little impressed by Jones's so-called charisma.

The charisma of Jones did not awe Rev. Cecil Williams either. And like Goodlett, he felt a kinship with the new maverick minister and his progressive church.

Among black ministers, Williams had long been an exception. His services at Glide Memorial Methodist Church, the same church once pastored by Carolyn Layton's father, had been likened to nightclub performances. Williams, hirsute and wont to wear dashikis, orchestrated "celebrations of humanity" conducted in a singalong atmosphere complete with guitars and drums. The message not only lured blacks and whites, poor and not so poor, into the Tenderloin area church but also reached across the nation via the mass media.

At rallies for progressive causes, Williams was frankly surprised to see large numbers of blacks enthusiastically cheering on a white preacher named Jones. He was given a taste of Temple methods on the tenth anniversary of his San Francisco ministry, in November 1975. The event, a testimonial service at Glide followed by a jazz-soul music concert at the Cow Palace auditorium, was marred before it could begin. There was an anonymous threat on Williams's life. Then, when the Temple contingent descended on Glide, Jones announced that his security team wanted to frisk everyone entering. Williams refused politely.

Thousands of Williams's friends and supporters thronged to services highlighted by tributes from influential liberal and leftist leaders.

Among them were future Temple friends and allies: Goodlett, black communist Angela Davis, State Assemblyman Willie Brown and future mayor George Moscone. In that perfect setting, Jones could hardly conceal his rivalry.

Resplendent in a suit, Jim Jones was dramatically escorted to the stage by bodyguards. With his thousand faithful casting adoring shouts and applauding, Jones spoke, alluding to threats on his own life, praising Williams's work, attacking the "terrorism" of U.S. government agencies at home and abroad. When he finished his speech with a ringing oath of solidarity—"[If] you come for one of us, you damn well better come for all of us"—his members burst into a tumultuous forty-five seconds of applause.

Williams received only a smattering by comparison. Then the insult was compounded at that night's Cow Palace concert when Jones's one thousand members, occupying a bloc of seats that had cost the Temple $5,000, stood up in the middle of the show and walked out en masse.

Two days later, Jones called Williams and explained that a church emergency had necessitated the rude early departure. Not wanting to hear the lie, Williams retorted: "Jim, I don't need an explanation."

Soon Williams was getting 2:00 A.M. and 3:00 A.M. phone calls from the solicitous Jones. Seeming paranoid, the white minister expressed fears for his life. In particular, he wanted to discuss the problems he was having with black ministers, whose members were flocking to the Temple.

One of the major contradictions for black leaders exposed to the Temple was the gap between Jones's antiracist rhetoric and Temple practices. Though Jones affected black speech patterns in addressing them and used to say, "I would give anything to be black," he could hardly disguise the racism in his own organization. Goodlett, Williams and Assemblyman Willie Brown could not help commenting on the fact that few blacks were around Jones making decisions.

It was not Williams, but Assemblyman Willie Brown, who provided the bridge to the Establishment power structure. Shortly before the Cecil Williams testimonial, Brown and other prominent San Francisco Democrats were discussing the 1975 mayoral candidacy of State Senator George Moscone. The conversation had turned to recruitment of volunteer workers—an especially important consideration due to new campaign spending limits.

Since Moscone's opponent, conservative realtor John Barbagelata, had great strength in the populous white western sectors, it was incumbent on Moscone backers to get out the vote in traditionally liberal areas, particularly black areas. During the discussion, someone suggested that Brown line up Peoples Temple volunteers. Soon the Temple was being bandied about as one of the community groups needed to pull together a winning liberal coalition—and install the city's first liberal administration. Some felt that using the Temple amounted to hiring mercenaries with loyalty only to Jones and his church. In the end, though, the response was:

"They can get hundreds of people, they are disciplined, and they'll take [the work] we have to give them."

The Temple leaped at the chance to help. Before the election, they turned out about two hundred volunteers who saturated black neighborhoods for two days. They efficiently distributed slate cards bearing the names Moscone for mayor, Joseph Freitas for district attorney and Richard Hongisto for sheriff—all white liberals, though not formally allied. In the November local election and December mayoral runoff, the Temple did get-out-the-vote work and also dispatched several hundred members to help at Moscone's campaign headquarters downtown. By all indications, they had done a good job: Moscone won, though by only four thousand votes. Freitas and Hongisto won more easily.

In the postelection euphoria over the victory, various organizations claimed credit, the Temple included. Jones made sure that Moscone felt indebted not only for volunteer assistance but for votes: he boasted that the Temple had eight thousand San Francisco members among twenty thousand statewide. Ukiah Democrats had already relayed the observation that Jones's people voted as a bloc. So it left the impression, logically, that the Moscone margin might well have been provided by the Temple.

That is exactly what Jones wanted the politicians to think. In truth, Temple membership figures were greatly exaggerated. At best three thousand to five thousand persons belonged to the Temple and few—not even Jones—were registered to vote in San Francisco. (In fact, voter rolls showed later that only several dozen of the 913 persons who died at Jonestown had been eligible to vote in the 1975 San Francisco election.) That fall, Temple members probably provided no more than a few hundred votes.

Politicians had wrongly assumed that any group which could turn out several hundred volunteers was huge; they failed to see how the Temple's communal and authoritarian structure meant Jones could produce a high percentage of his members at will.[36]

Through illusion, public relations, misrepresentations and exploitation of political greed, Jones expanded his influence. He invited politicians to the Temple and fed them punch and cookies, or a chicken dinner. He showed them partially staged services and "free" food and medical programs which actually were closed to outsiders. Most politicians came away with positive impressions. As honored guests, they were invited to address the congregation, unaware that Jones ridiculed them later or even literally behind their backs. For instance, Jones once flicked his middle finger behind Assemblyman Brown, whose personal style—Wilkes Bashford suits and Porsches—offended him.

Jones asked favors of his political "friends" with characteristic aggression. For instance, a few months after the 1975 election, Jones and Willie Brown met face to face for the first time, over lunch at Bardelli's near Union Square. Jones, sitting erectly in dark glasses and a leisure suit, talked politics with a socialist flavor. After lunch, Jones's ever-present companion, Mike Prokes, stopped by Brown's law office and asked Brown to come to the Temple to be interviewed for a "documentary" about the church's good works. When on the assigned day Brown was brought to the interview area, he was joined by newly elected District Attorney Joseph Freitas and Sheriff Richard Hongisto. Prokes amateurishly directed the camera crew while Jones asked leading questions designed to elicit praise. After each politician made a statement, they left, unaware that that film of their statements would be spliced into the middle of a film of Jones's "miracles," leaving the false impression that distinguished public figures, even law enforcement officials, condoned his healing.

On the color footage, hundreds of members clap and sway to spirited music, caught in the euphoria of a Los Angeles temple service. In rapid sequence, Jones cures a woman who ostensibly cannot see without her glasses, as well as a woman complaining of a chest pain. As the rejoicing breaks off, a narrator introduces the politicians and the film cuts to the interview setting in the San Francisco temple—and the politicians praise the church's social work.

In fact a number of politicians and some journalists and radical figures did witness either healings or testimonies to healings. Rather than hide his hokum, Jones both compromised his visitors and delighted his followers with his shenanigans. His guests rationalized them as mind over matter, psychosomatic healings or as a mere aberration in an otherwise good organization, no more improper than what evangelists do on television.

Within days of the 1975 election, Mike Prokes was named to the forty-eight-member committee Moscone would use to screen names for one hundred commission appointments. Peoples Temple was hardly a household word, yet Prokes's presence on that panel of community, labor and minority leaders affirmed the Temple's political emergence. Still, it became clear, when the committee began selecting candidates, that the Temple would not be a mainstay in Moscone's early administration. Not a single Temple member was recommended for an appointment, though Prokes persistently put forward lists of candidates for each post.

Jones could not accept defeat. With the patience of a water torturer, he kept dropping his people on officials. About a year after the 1975 election, Prokes and others complained that the Temple's support had not been properly rewarded. The squeeze was put on a Moscone aide over lunch at the Copper Penny, and the Temple netted a handful of jobs.

Meanwhile, they pressured Moscone to come up with a suitable appointment for Jones himself. Seeing that the minister's pride had been hurt, Moscone appointed him in March 1976 to the Human Rights Commission, an appropriate place for a liberal preacher. But to Jones, it was a lateral appointment—the same post he had held fifteen years earlier in Indianapolis. At least sixty members sent letters to Moscone telling him off, saying Jones's talents were underutilized. The letter campaign was all the more outrageous since Moscone had stuck out his neck to appoint Jones in the first place. Moscone knew that Jones resided outside San Francisco, and thus was ineligible for appointment under the city charter.

On the official day, just minutes before Jones was to be sworn in as a human rights commissioner, he slipped into the mayor's inner office through a side door. With Mike Prokes standing by for moral support, Jones announced, with great tension in his voice, that he would not accept the post after all. As the ticklish matter was discussed, Jones remained unsmiling. Moscone, always the gentleman, was solicitous. After some fifteen minutes, Jones came up with an explanation for the press waiting outside. Then the two reached an understanding that Jones would be appointed to something else, and parted on friendly terms.

Moscone kept his word. In a press release on October 18, 1976, his office announced that Jones had been named to the San Francisco Housing Authority, the agency which oversees operation of public housing. The appointment surprised Jones's friends and supporters, partially because the minister always denied having political ambitions. Jones's advisers, such as Tim Stoen, were concerned that a public appointment would expose him to scrutiny and attacks. "You're treading on very dangerous ground," Goodlett warned, "because you're gonna have a lot of people who are enemies, and the few friends that you've helped will be friends during fair weather times." The warnings proved all too correct.

Before Jones's arrival, Housing Authority meetings had been dull, poorly attended affairs. After Jones, the meetings became spirited public rallies. Jones bused in his own cheering section. They applauded him wildly, no matter what he said, whether it was a call to end corruption, a promise to improve the living conditions of the inner city poor, a vow to tighten the expense accounts of agency staff. The meetings became so jammed by Jones's entourage that the sessions were moved across town to larger quarters. Though the agency had its own police, Temple guards patrolled, watching doorways, roving through meetings. They even barred anyone from using the bathroom while Jones occupied it.

Commissioner Jones worked with the same dedication he displayed in Temple endeavors and soon became chairman of the body, thanks to lobbying by Moscone's office. He came to his first meeting as chairman equipped with a parliamentary procedure reference book; the agenda and his own remarks were outlined with the meticulousness of a Tim Stoen. Jones became a public voice for the rights of minorities and the poor. He also built political and personal alliances, from the highest levels of administration to a tenants organization. A few hard-working Temple members were employed there too, one of them Carolyn Layton.

Though pleasant, Jones was wary of reporters. He knew he was being watched: the local press routinely covered Housing Authority meetings and always kept an eye open for a good story. Among the journalists was an *Examiner* newsman who remembered quite well the Kinsolving series and Jones's response. Another was a young *Chronicle* reporter named Marshall Kilduff.

Jim Jones realized that he was flirting with the law—and could be stung at almost any time. So he consciously set out to establish good rapport with the chief law officers of San Francisco County, just as he had done in Mendocino County. Here he did not need to falsely present himself as a law-and-order Republican, because the liberal San Francisco trio shared the Temple's progressive social views.

Although the Temple delivered slate cards endorsing Joseph Freitas for district attorney in 1975, Freitas first heard about the group from Willie Brown after the election. Then Tim Stoen came down from Ukiah looking for a job in Freitas's administration. After interviewing him, Freitas wanted to place Stoen in his consumer fraud division, but the only available job was being held open for a minority appointee. Later, when newspapers pointed up a lack of progress in the office's politically sensitive voter fraud investigation, the head of consumer fraud reminded Freitas about Stoen. The Temple attorney—who came highly recommended by an assortment of Mendocino officials and by Jim Jones—got the job. Stoen was being hired as chief prosecutor in an investigation into allegations that large numbers of nonresidents had voted illegally in the 1975 election. Stoen would end up using volunteer clerical workers from the Temple in this sensitive investigation. Later, similar voter fraud allegations would be leveled against the Temple itself, though not proved.

The strategic importance of having a Temple member in the prosecutor's office did not elude Carlton Goodlett. "You always got a man pretty close to a law enforcement agency in a town, don't you?" he once remarked.

"You're very perceptive," Jones laughed.

As in Ukiah, Jones tried to get gun permits from law officials. Sheriff Richard Hongisto, nationally known for his antiwar views and jail reform views, was courted after receiving Temple assistance. During the 1975 election, Prokes, Chaikin and other church members had started to drop by the sheriff's office offering favors, talking nebulously about providing refuge for jailed prostitutes and drug addicts, seeking advice about petty ordinances.

Then Jones called, alarmed over his personal safety. He asked for gun permits so that his people could defend themselves against harassment. When Hongisto checked into the alleged incidents, he became convinced that Jones had fabricated the story.[37] Diplomatically, Hongisto suggested the Temple hire private security guards, or else contact Police Chief Charles Gain. But Gain, another controversial progressive, turned down the Temple requests for gun permits too. The setback, however, did not prevent Temple guards from illegally carrying guns or, reportedly, from getting permits by working with an existing security guard company.

Public concern over terrorism provided a marvelous opportunity for the Temple to ingratiate itself to others outside the church's normal sphere, even to ideological enemies. In late 1975 and in 1976, while the New World Liberation Front waged a terrorist campaign against county supervisors over demands for upgrading county jail health care, conservative supervisors John Barbagelata and Quentin Kopp were mailed bombs disguised as candy boxes. They escaped unharmed because the boxes were not opened. After the incidents, Jones phoned Kopp at City Hall and offered Temple members as guards for him, Barbagelata or any other supervisors. Kopp declined the offer saying he and other officials already were given police protection.

Late in 1976, an attempted bombing at the home of supervisor and future mayor Dianne Feinstein caused Prokes to write a December 17, 1976, letter offering Temple protection. To imply that they faced common enemies, Prokes attached a two-page Nazi hate letter which he said was received by the *Peoples Forum* newspaper. Nonetheless, the offer of Temple protection was declined.

The Temple's relations with the black establishment were mixed too. By the end of 1976, the Temple had purchased hundreds of memberships in the local NAACP branch, and Jim Jones, Johnny Brown Jones and another Temple member were elected to the board of directors. But some NAACP members felt that the Temple, with control of about a tenth of the board and with several hundred votes out of two thousand members, had grabbed the reins of the civil rights group. When the Temple tried to sign up thirty members, including Jones, at the Black Leadership Forum, a warning bell went off. Some feared that Jones was attempting another takeover, and they argued that as a white he had no right to belong to a black political endorsement group. Rather than barring someone on the basis of color, the membership voted to set up a membership screening committee. Jones did not fit through the mesh. The defeat upset him a great deal.

For Jones and the Temple, the fibers of his political network were unraveling almost as fast as they were woven. But progress was still made because, as Jones would say near the end, the church took "two steps forward, one step back." Jones had created a moving target which with each stride added political armor. The vigorous activity in the 1975 election established the church as a factor in local politics, as a force within the black community and as a potential ally for those with compatible political goals or the pragmatism not to care. With that momentum, Jones transformed potential enemies into a second line of defense—his image of respectability and power.

Even those politicians disturbed by Jones's personality problems, militarism or manipulation did nothing. First, who would want to risk opposing a church doing such worthwhile work in the community? Second, who would want to offend a machinelike political organization with friends in high places? Third, how could anyone speak against such a secretive organization with any certainty? Uncertainty—the psychological factor that kept some Temple members from defecting—inhibited political figures too. Those with misgivings about the church kept them to themselves. Looking around, they saw only forces of the Right speaking against the newfound political power of community groups such as Peoples Temple. With his constant chatter about the government, rightists, Nazis and others being after him, Jones implied that anyone who challenged him would be in bad company.

Most bases in San Francisco were covered neatly by 1976—Jones's self-proclaimed Year of Ascendancy. A favorable rapport was established with virtually all important public figures. Where could opponents, skeptics or victims turn if Jones had friends or admirers in the state legislature and the U.S. Congress, the offices of the governor, the mayor, the police chief, the sheriff, and district attorney, as well as on the leading black newspaper and the largest daily newspapers?

TWENTY-NINE

Backwater

Guyana—in the native tongue "land of many waters"—had been blessed with neither the sandy white beaches of its northern neighbors, such as Barbados and Jamaica, nor the vast oil reserves and natural resources of its western and southern neighbors. Its economy had never quite recovered from slavery and sugar plantations under the Dutch in the sixteenth, seventeenth and eighteenth centuries nor from British colonial rule and the system of indentured servitude in the nineteenth and twentieth centuries. The country seemed doomed to remain a British vassal state, until the early 1950s.

It was then that British Guiana saw the first stirrings for independence. A Marxist dentist, Dr. Cheddi Jagan, an East Indian educated in America, founded the People's Progressive party, which quickly assumed power under colonial rule. Jagan was assisted in the drive by a brilliant British-educated Afro-Guyanese barrister named Linden Forbes Burnham. Within several years, however, Burnham broke with Jagan to form his own party, the People's National Congress.

With the Cold War and the Cuban revolution to the north, the

United States was absolutely determined not to let another "domino" fall in the Caribbean. So it entered the power struggle in obscure Guiana. Burnham had a more opportunistic side than the more doctrinaire Jagan, whose pro-Soviet sympathies were no secret. When the Central Intelligence Agency injected $1 million into labor unions to finance street disturbances, enough internal instability was created that Forbes Burnham toppled Jagan in 1964.

Two years later, Burnham announced independence, and two years after that, in 1968, his party swept the elections. Burnham became prime minister. On February 23, 1970, the country became known as the Cooperative Republic of Guyana. To the surprise of the CIA, Burnham moved his country on a socialist path, flirting with Castro, the Soviets, East Germans and North Koreans, and nationalizing most of the country's resources, including sugar, rice and bauxite, of which it is the world's fourth largest producer. In any case, the economy worsened. There were chronic shortages of just about everything, particularly imported goods.

Burnham was essentially presiding over a minority-run government. He could not hold honest elections, since the East Indians, who outnumbered blacks 55 percent to 35 percent, voted for Jagan. Burnham won in 1968 because of a new provision that allowed Guyanese overseas to vote in national elections; the "proxy" votes went right to his party. He got the same help in 1973, when the army counted the ballots. A 1978 referendum on whether to keep him in power until a new constitution could be written was so patently rigged that Jagan told his people not to even show up at the polls.[38]

To keep his support, Burnham set up an elaborate system of patronage. For this reason, close to 90 percent of the army and police were black, as were most government ministers and high-level bureaucrats. Ensuring absolute loyalty became a tricky feat, however, as the economy worsened, and as churches and other institutions became alarmed over the erosion of civil liberties formerly enjoyed under British rule. As people began to chafe under Burnham's regime, he cast about for allies.

One was Rabbi Edward Washington, an ex-convict from Cleveland, Ohio, who managed to persuade several hundred Afro-Guyanese that blacks were the original Jews. His House of Israel became a political enforcement arm of the Burnham regime. The organization broadcast a weekly radio show on the government-owned radio station in Georgetown, a sure sign of official favor. Another group that would get a weekly radio show was Peoples Temple.

Temple publicist Paula Adams was learning to find her way around Georgetown, the capital and major port at the mouth of the Demerara River. The city, protected by seventeenth-century Dutch dikes, had a certain backwater charm, though it housed the national offices for Guyana's various ministries, nationalized industries and other government bureaucracies. Georgetown's principal boulevard, Main Street, began near the muddy Atlantic Coast beaches, at the Hotel Pegasus, Guyana's most modern hotel. Alive with cabs and donkey carts and parasol-carrying Afro-Guyanese women, the avenue stretched about a half mile to the center of town, to a thin marble shaft known as the Cenotaph, a memorial to Guyanese soldiers who died in World Wars I and II.

Main Street's tree-lined esplanade, with its small cement canals for rain water and raw sewage, split the avenue in two. Government buildings, foreign embassies, airline offices and banks from all over the world were interspersed with the unlikeliest of neighbors, some with a touch of the slums.

At the American Embassy, hundreds of Guyanese began waiting in line by 7:00 A.M. to explore ways of emigrating to the United States. Down the street stood the British High Commission, and across the esplanade rose the splendid white Sacred Heart Church, where Jim Jones held his healing service. Next to that, the Presidential Palace was graced with lush gardens. It was along this boulevard that Paula Adams would do most of her work, currying favor with officials and influential private citizens.

Adams had joined the Temple several years before. An attractive young white woman with delicate features and a pleasing personality, she was utterly devoted to Jim Jones. In a testimonial written for Jones, she confessed that when she first came to Peoples Temple she was a mixed-up woman of twenty-two with no hope beyond the drinking, doping life of a manic-depressive. She had been a student in the Santa Rosa dormitories, but was not doing well academically, and Jones decided she could better serve the cause in Georgetown.

It was a shrewd choice. Attractive white women were not only rare, but real objects of desire in Guyana's machismo-steeped culture. Adams's soft good looks and relaxed style won the Temple many friends there, not least among them Laurence "Bonny" Mann, Guyana's ambassador to Washington. Mann would squire her around town to social and diplomatic functions during the next few years when he was on home leave.

By having Adams, along with Debbie Touchette, establish the Temple's full-time public relations team in the capital, Jones set out to wire an entire nation. This was not an overwhelming task in a small, impoverished Third World country with potentially corruptible officials and a monolithic government. In Guyana, the "media" consisted of employees of the Ministry of Information. If Jones could lead San Francisco politicians around by the nose, the Guyanese should fall into step as readily.

The fledgling Temple crew moved into a rented house at 121 Third Street in Albertown, a district of Georgetown. It was a fairly new, spacious home, with three bedrooms, a large living room, dining room and kitchen, and was built in the traditional fashion, on stilts. The church public relations staff worked and entertained there while getting to know and influence figures in the Guyana power structure, writing upbeat notes to government officials describing Temple accomplishments in the interior and arranging passports and visa matters with the Ministry of Home Affairs. There were some notable successes:

In late 1974, government officials gave the Temple permission to import "duty free" certain items of household and personal effects, as well as construction and agricultural equipment. And on February 26, 1975, less than two months after the healing service at Sacred Heart, the National Assembly, Guyana's Parliament, passed the Peoples Temple of the Disciples of Christ Church Act, which incorporated the church in Guyana.

Father Andrew Morrison, still smarting over the phony faith healing, did not see or hear of the Temple for several months. Then, to his amazement, two members approached him and asked to be admitted to the Guyana Council of Churches. When the Council discussed the application, Father Morrison strongly expressed his own reservations, and the Council delayed.

As the Temple mobilized an intensive lobbying campaign, the Council did further checking. One member, Rev. Paul Tidemann, an American-born Lutheran minister, made an inquiry to a friend in the United States. He wrote on February 18, 1975, to Rev. Dr. Carl Segerhammer, at the Pacific Southwest Synod in Los Angeles:

"Needless to say, I am more than a little skeptical about this group. . . . Guyana, as with many Third World countries, is deluged with crazy religious outfits and personality cults. We are struggling with this Korean fellow, Moon, and his Unification Church. We don't need another cult here, if that is what Peoples Temple is."

Segerhammer passed the letter on to the Northern California Ecumenical Council, among whose members was Karl Irvin, president of Northern California Disciples of Christ and a friend of the Temple. The Ecumenical Council group wrote back to Rev. Tidemann, giving the Temple a clean bill of health. With the reluctant assent of Father Morrison, the Council of Churches admitted the Temple. Over the next few years, membership would give the Temple continued visibility and prominence in Georgetown affairs, despite its basically passive role.

As time went by, the Temple public relations machine kicked into high gear—with results. In January 1976, Ambassador Mann—Paula Adams's friend—wrote to a Temple secretary in Redwood Valley, saying he had heard many fine things about "Bishop Jones" from Adams and from Mike and Debbie Touchette.

The following month, two years after the Temple had applied for the Jonestown lease, the government finally granted it. The Temple originally sought 25,000 acres, but after a survey, it was cut down to 3,000 acres. Under the lease, the rent would be 25 cents an acre for the first five years, then would be revised at five-year intervals. The original application called for a minimum investment of $1 million Guyanese (about $400,000 U.S.) during the first two years. As part of a requirement to cultivate and occupy at least half the land within five years, the Temple had to submit progress reports.

The jungle pioneers had moved permanently from Port Kaituma into Jonestown in 1975. They slept in the large building next to the banana shed. Mike Touchette's parents ran the place, Charlie as chief planner and administrator, Joyce as head of the kitchen. Charlie, in his early forties, was independent-minded, resourceful and well organized. Once a success-ful salesman in the Midwest, he now produced in the jungle too, getting the most out of his workers, winning their respect, pitching in to help.

Touchette's wife, thoroughly and unquestioningly committed to Jim Jones, was the mother figure for all the children. She lent a sympa-thetic shoulder to older men who were homesick or missed their wives. Joyce even took on the role of daughter to Mom and Pop Jackson, an elderly black couple who flew to Guyana when the first settlers arrived by boat. (Jones had always bragged that Pop Jackson was one hundred and eight and his wife one hundred four, but Mike Touchette once peeked at their passports and discovered they were only eighty-nine and seventy respectively.)

In Jonestown, Mike Touchette's lifelong wish to live like a lumber-jack in the wilderness was fulfilled. After the Guyanese workers cleared jungle, young Touchette would let the trees sit for ninety days, then burn the debris. At that point, he would scrape the field smooth with his Cater-pillar tractor, forming nutrient-rich piles of brush and vegetation. It was a delicate task for heavy machinery. He had to push the debris into windrows without disturbing the thin and precious topsoil. But Touchette became known as the best bulldozer operator in the area.

Sometimes workers would cut loose from their jobs. They threw fifty-five-gallon diesel drums on the windrows, lit them, and watched the explosions blow huge logs into the air. The young men hiked the jungle trails and tasted the thrill of exploration, the pride of owning a vast tract of land.

But from the start, Mike Touchette doubted the project would ever become self-sufficient. The soil was too poor. The high temperature in the jungle oxidized the organic matter, leaving the ground hard as concrete. In the ongoing quest for the right soil nutrients, the group bought hun-dreds of tons of commercial fertilizer and crushed sea shells to spread over one hundred acres of land. But each application of fertilizer lasted for one crop only, and was effective only if the weather was decent and heavy rains did not wash away the thin topsoil. Jim Jones told the settlers to keep experimenting. But it was costing a fortune.

In December 1974, the Jonestown settlers requested some essen-tial machinery: a four-wheel-drive vehicle, a ten-ton truck and a four-wheel-drive tractor with a winch—as well as all sorts of small tools and farm implements. Archie Ijames and J. R. Purifoy, back in the States, sent word they had located Army surplus trucks, off-road models that could negotiate even Jonestown's mud. They also made a bargain deal on a ten-ton dump truck and mobile crane that could lift twenty tons once they were rebuilt. And they promised to send down a warehouse full of parts and a generator.

The equipment finally arrived at the Kaituma River dock on September 29, 1975, nearly ten months after the requests for it. During unloading from the boat, the crane, its tires completely bald, slipped on the wet and steep dock, so the Jonestown crew had to borrow a government Caterpillar to pull it off. The Temple's newly rebuilt truck lost its brakes on a dockside incline just as the hydraulic hose on the rebuilt crane broke. The crate of parts fell open as it was unloaded. Inside was rusted, no-good junk. Only a windshield wiper motor worked. The Temple had also shipped three generators—one would not start, the others blew up within three weeks.

The settlers were angry. They were sweating in the heat and mud clearing the jungle, building paradise for Peoples Temple, and their reward was equipment that qualified as scrap metal. They blamed the money-saving mentality of the folks back home. Disgusted and rebellious, Mike and Charlie Touchette went into Georgetown and, without authorization, bought new generators. Later, they would find out that Temple mechanics in Redwood Valley had just begun to rebuild the equipment when Jim Jones ordered them to ship it off immediately.

The settlers were further handicapped by a scarcity of funds in Jonestown, even to buy lumber. Little construction was going on, though nationals were paid to erect structures from Jonestown's own harvested timber. The large wall-less pavilion was the most prominent of these.

In the early years, the settlers held meetings there on Sundays, with Joyce and Charlie Touchette presiding. When problems arose, the group dealt with them in a civil manner. They had decided never to have heavy catharsis sessions like those in the States; games and browbeating would only hurt the project. The meetings would, however, open with the "Three Miracles," a ritual instituted in the California church. Everyone would be called upon to attest to the miraculous protection accorded by Jones that week. In the States, Mike often had to make up at least a couple of his three miracles, things such as "Father's love saved me from certain death on the freeway Tuesday. . . ." In Jonestown it was easier, because the work was physical and hazardous. "Thank you, Father, for saving me from an accident where the machine threw a rock up and almost hit my head," was one Mike Touchette recited often, whether he believed it or not.

The meetings would last anywhere from thirty minutes to six hours, with much time devoted to planning. They discussed building a large number of cottages, each to house two or three couples or eight singles and kids. And there were the nuts-and-bolts matters—generator repair, ordering materials from the States and Georgetown, construction of septic tanks or showers or toilets, and agricultural concerns.

Just when the settlers got too complacent, just when they were beginning to forget their holy mission, hour-long tapes of Jim Jones's sermons and teachings would arrive from California. Listening to each tape eight or ten times would jar them into remembering how bad things really were back home. Then their productivity would improve noticeably.

Jim Jones did not visit again until November 1975, when he, Mike Prokes and Stephan Jones came to check the settlement's progress. Mike Touchette was glad to see them, if only for a few days, especially because his wife accompanied them out from Georgetown. Mike and Debbie had been going as many as six months without seeing each other, even though they were only 150 miles of jungle apart.

Charlie Touchette was looking forward to Jones's stay for another reason: he had been entreating Jones for more money to keep the place running. At times, shortages of funds and fuel almost dragged work to a standstill. A number of times, they had to shut down the Caterpillar—once for two weeks—until they could get more diesel fuel. But when Mike's father Charlie made a plea for more money, Jones threw him a withering look: "I'm bleeding for money," Jones told him. "I'm dying for you and you're just bitching about money, just throwing it around."

Instead of money, Jones brought his catharsis sessions with him. He thrived on the emotional upheavals the settlers had hoped to avoid. Just before the Sunday meeting, he went up to Mike Touchette. "I want you to jump Tim Swinney's ass for being a bully. He's treating people bad. And I want *you* to do it so people don't think there's an alliance between you two."

Jones knew that Mike and Swinney, his uncle, were inseparable. Swinney did have a tough exterior that put off some people. But when Touchette confronted him, as instructed, he felt very uncomfortable. It reminded him of the day Jones told him to confront Grace Stoen in p.c. He got a glimmer that Father might be trying to keep people apart, rather than mend their problems. After the confrontation, Touchette and Swinney stayed friends.

In 1976, Jones visited his settlers only twice. While he was away, they lived almost autonomously, and more happily. Though there were still fewer than fifty settlers, many more organized activities were available. Rented 16-millimeter movies from Georgetown—everything from *Hello, Dolly!* and Bruce Lee's *Enter the Dragon*—were screened in the jungle. A print of *Z*, the Costa-Gavras film about corruption and fascism in Greece, was run a dozen times a month for a year. Settlers memorized the screenplays so well that they walked around during the day spouting lines from the movies or singing songs from the musicals.

On a typical day, people were awake at sunup and at work by seven. They broke for lunch, often a hearty vegetable stew. Quitting time was about five thirty, then people scrubbed up for dinner. Having no cold storage facilities, the settlers ate meat only when fresh-killed—usually two or three times a week. The Amerindian hunters sold them deer, "bush cows," wild boar, two types of South American rodents and a variety of small jungle animals.

Except for Sunday nights, people had the evenings free. They could read, catch up on their sleep, play cards and dominoes or watch movies. For Mike Touchette, it was a great life. He loved hanging out on the porch outside the kitchen with Swinney, Jim Bogue, Phil Blakey and others. They would turn off the generator and talk quietly in the dark, or listen to the sounds of the jungle, the baboons howling in the wind, the crickets, frogs, night birds and vampire bats.

THIRTY

Radicals

Like all con men, Jones had learned the value of keeping his followers and pursuers off balance. He even managed to obscure the nature of the Temple—perhaps the biggest juggling act for such a highly visible personality.

In Indiana, the Temple was more of a church than a social movement or cult; in California, it was more of a social movement and cult than a utopian community; in Guyana, it would become a utopian community and in some ways the ultimate cult.

The most respectable and accurate label in the Temple's early years, even in California, was "church." To most people, the California Temple remained a humanitarian, activist Christian church. The Pentecostal style of the services and the conventional religious trappings kept religious people in a familiar theological sphere while moving them in other directions. However, in terms of the intimacy among members, the Temple most closely resembled a utopian community. Like dozens of communal groups in the nineteenth and twentieth centuries, the Temple came to the West Coast to escape some perceived outside threat and persecution and harbored a self-righteous group mentality that raised natural barriers to outsiders.[39]

While he never publicly called his organization a cult, Jones, with his paranoid idiosyncratic personality, ventured toward the extremes of cultism—toward the pinnacle of human control. His extremist internal methods demanded secrecy and caution in recruiting, which doomed him to mediocrity in the numbers category. Yet in some sense, the personality cult surrounding Jones was similar to those around Dr. Martin Luther King, Malcolm X, Elvis Presley or John F. Kennedy. There was a sort of rock-star sex-object mentality, along with hero worship and a respect for his personal sacrifices as the ultimate socialist. In another sense, Jones's exploitation of power carried the same scars as Hitler's and Charles Manson's—though on a much smaller scale than Hitler's, on a different and less maniacal scale than Manson's.[40]

In the end, Jones's people were subjected unwittingly and gradually to sophisticated mind control and behavior-modification techniques borrowed from postrevolutionary China, North Korea and perhaps from other cults. Though he had always been domineering, it is unlikely that Jones, a reader of books on psychology and mind control, would have arrived independently at common cult techniques, such as isolation of the recruit and renunciation of self, family and previously held values. Like the Temple, most cults set out unattainable goals such as heaven on earth, because attainment would leave the organization without a justification for its own existence. The cult really strives to preserve a state of mind with defendable borders. As in the Temple, most significant violations of the cult borders are defections by "traitors" and investigations by the outside "enemy." And this alarmist view is promoted by the charismatic leader who constantly asks his followers to push a juggernaut of paranoia. There are no checks on him, for he defines reality and makes all rules. His power is so institutionalized that organizational contradictions go unchallenged. In the Temple, for instance, Jones promoted his infallibility while convincing his people that they could voice dissent. Each unchallenged contradiction in turn nourished the leader's delusions of grandeur. Charismatic personalities such as Jones start viewing themselves as divine or as representatives of the divine, with the power to punish, instruct, command, reveal. Some seize power over life and death. In the Temple, Jones not only took divine powers but also allowed himself earthly privileges: typically, sexual gratification and, to a lesser extent, material things.

The Temple distinguished itself from most cults with its overtly political message. The church involved itself in political processes and formed political alliances, not just for the sake of expediency but also out of some real political sympathies. In the final analysis, the Temple did act most often—in the outside world—as a social movement, with a dual purpose of improving this world and aggrandizing the group. As the social direction of the Temple became more openly socialistic and communistic, it depended more upon the political world, in particular on the Left, for its identity and its protection.

Winning the good will of elected officials like George Moscone was just the means to an end for Peoples Temple, a safeguard against attack. Their first sympathies went out not to conventional politicians, but to those who shared the revolutionary vision. These they cultivated with flattery, political support and often a great deal of money.

The endorsement of the Temple by political radicals was a two-way bonding process. Figures such as the communist Angela Davis and Laura Allende, sister of the late Chilean leader, validated the Temple as a social movement to those on the Left, while their presence and support validated the Temple to its own members. Besides Davis, the church proudly numbered among its friends actress Jane Fonda, Black Panther Huey Newton, American Indian Movement leader Dennis Banks and others whose radicalism was to Jones's liking. Jones desperately wanted their recognition, for he considered himself a lifelong revolutionary and communist.

Angela Davis had been quick to emerge as one of the Temple's darlings—militant, bright, black and a woman. The Temple participated in rallies on her behalf, and she made visits where she chatted privately with Jones and top aides in his apartment in the San Francisco temple. Angela Davis was both a "sister" and a celebrity of the Left who could strengthen Jones's radical credentials. But other radicals, chief among them Dennis Banks, were considered more reliable friends.

In early 1976, the Native American activist received what was probably the largest Temple donation—$19,500. The church previously had bestowed large sums, mostly for humanitarian and public relations reasons, on a variety of charities and causes—for instance, $6,000 to save a senior citizens escort program, $500 each to Cesar Chavez's United Farmworkers Union and the San Francisco Police Fishing Program, and $1,000 to a Marin County drug treatment program. But the huge contribution to Banks gave the church predominance in the effort by progressives to block the Indian's extradition to South Dakota for trial on weapons charges indirectly related to the 1973 Wounded Knee uprising.

The Temple stepped in, as the *Peoples Forum* reported in April 1976, with nearly $20,000 bail to free Banks's wife Ka-mook and their newborn daughter from an Oregon jail. "A week ago, my wife was behind an iron door, my children were in Oklahoma. You, in your love, have moved the iron door," Banks told 2,500 persons at the San Francisco temple.

AIM was only one of several groups Jones was cultivating. Though philosophically Jones considered his Western Addition neighbors, the Black Muslims, to be sexist and racist, he respected their discipline and effectiveness in youth work and business enterprises. At one time, Jones feared that friction, born largely out of close proximity, might precipitate violence. He contributed to the superheated climate by speculating without cause that the Muslims were responsible for the Temple's arson fire. Once after Temple photographer Al Mills allegedly was hassled by Muslims for taking photos of them, Jones became furious and sent a few of his biggest young black men, including Chris Lewis, to the nearby mosque to issue a warning. The Temple wanted no trouble, but would take no abuse.

Gradually, however, relations with the Black Muslims improved. The Temple bought fish from Muslim fish stores. They even exchanged visitors at some services, which must have been particularly gratifying to Jones in light of the Muslims' rebuff of him in Chicago years earlier. And, in 1976, the two organizations planned a historic event for the Los Angeles Convention Center. For their joint "Spiritual Jubilee" on May 23, 1976, the Muslims and the Temple invited political figures to their gigantic "demonstration of brotherhood." Among those converging on the convention center were some of the Temple's most treasured friends and political contacts—Dr. Goodlett, Angela Davis, San Francisco District Attorney Joe Freitas, Lieutenant Governor Mervyn Dymally, not to mention Los Angeles Mayor Tom Bradley, whom the Temple had wooed with little success.

A half moon of at least fifteen to twenty Temple and Muslim guards sat, shoulder to shoulder, below the stage. The Temple had selected its beefiest men for the security ring out front and instructed them to look as mean as possible. Backstage several other bodyguards were posted, all packing pistols and instructed to protect their leader from the Muslims if necessary.

In the audience, Temple members in red and black intermingled with Muslims in white, creating a spectacle of contrasting color. In those thousands upon thousands, Muslims far outnumbered Temple members, despite Temple claims to be the largest Protestant church in California. Jones felt compelled to make excuses: some Temple buses from northern California, he said, had broken down on the so-called Grapevine grade on their way south. The Temple compensated for the empty seats by putting on a very professional musical revue.

With magnificent presence, Jones planted himself behind the microphone. "Peace, peace," he uttered, motioning for silence. "We are grateful of this symbolic merging of our two movements. . . . If the Peoples Temple and the Nation of Islam can get together, anyone can. . . . A few years ago, we couldn't walk down the streets because of tensions, and one might have thought we could fight."

In his strong staccato voice, Jones blazed an impressionistic trail of rhetoric, leaping abruptly from "unity" to Christianity to the need for a free press to Watergate to—totally out of context—a reference to himself as an object of sexual desire. Finally, Jones pledged support to the Muslims, declaring that he wished Wallace Muhammad were running for President of the United States.

Despite such fleeting moments of grandeur, most of Jones's pronouncements centered on local housing politics, not national politics. As a housing commissioner, Jones consistently took the side of tenants. So when, in late 1976 and early 1977, the Four Seas Investment Corporation tried to evict the mostly poor and elderly tenants of the International Hotel, he was quick to seize on the incident. Four Seas wanted to raze the decrepit residence hotel not far from the North Beach "topless" nightclub area for more profitable purposes. Jones saw a classic confrontation in the making—a greedy corporate giant versus the poor and helpless. Joining other community groups, Jones threw the weight of his office and the Temple against the planned eviction.

With Jones as chairman, the Housing Authority voted to acquire the hotel, using $1.3 million in federal community development funds; they would then turn it over to a nonprofit tenants group. The Authority's proposal, however, ran into unbridgeable obstacles in the courts. The evictions were ordered.

The issue was heating up. Crowds of five thousand ringed the hotel. Sheriff Hongisto, a Jones political ally, said he lacked the manpower to carry out safely the evictions and was found in contempt. Meanwhile, picketers rallied around the clock, forming a human buffer zone to keep out the sheriff's office. Protestors inside laid plans to barricade the doors at the first sign of an eviction squad.

During a mid-January 1977 demonstration, the Temple supplied two thousand of the five thousand persons chanting, "No, no, no evictions!" The explosiveness of the situation was growing by the hour; police received reliable eyewitness reports that a gunman had been stationed on the hotel roof with a rifle and that Molotov cocktails were being poured by tenants' supporters. On the streets, Jones's people barely avoided a spontaneous violent incident involving an outsider. In this climate, Jones and Stoen had conferences with go-betweens for Sheriff Hongisto, who was in a tough spot, since his ideological sympathies probably were pro-tenant. Jones, wearing sunglasses although it was midnight, stood outside a car several blocks from the hotel surrounded by bodyguards; he looked like a Mafia don. His lawyer, Stoen, climbed into the car and did most of the talking, though at one point Jones interjected: "I'm concerned about the possibility of violence."

Though Jones contended there were no guns in the hotel, the situation had become so unstable that Superior Court Judge Ira Brown, Jr., stayed his eviction order. But, by June 1977, after Hongisto had served a five-day contempt sentence in his own county jail, the courts ruled that the Housing Authority could not acquire the hotel through eminent domain. The battle was lost.

The International Hotel incident was not a total loss for the Temple, however. It incidentally introduced the Temple to many progressives and leftists, as well as labor and community leaders. More important, it reestablished the Temple as an organization which could turn out more "troops" on short notice than any other in San Francisco.

To heighten his membership's understanding and empathy for progressive and socialist struggles around the world, Jones provided political education in his sermons, in the church newspaper and in guest speaker programs. Most important, he imbued his people with fear so that they —no matter what their backgrounds—might feel oppression. The spec-

ters of Klan lynchings, a revival of Nazism, earthquake, nuclear holo-
caust and global famine exploded from the pages of *Peoples Forum*.
Then Jones was handed evidence of what he had always suspected—that
Big Brother was watching.

One Sunday in November 1976, Unita Blackwell Wright, a Mississippi mayor and longtime civil rights activist, was delivering a speech to
the San Francisco temple about her trip to China with actress Shirley
MacLaine in 1973. Two men caught eavesdropping at the front door suddenly took off by car.

Temple sleuths eventually traced the rental car to a government
electronics expert, Thomas Dawsey of Biloxi, Mississippi. In response to
inquiries from Representative Phil Burton, Democrat from California, the
Air Force wrote on January 26, 1977, that Dawsey, a civilian electrical
engineer, had been working temporarily at California air bases but was
off duty on the day of the Temple speech.[41]

In two other letters, the Air Force said that Dawsey was assigned
to a Keesler AFB, Mississippi, group that installed and maintained electronics and communications equipment. But it insisted that the group
would not and did not spy on the Temple or Wright. The curious episode
was added to the list of conspiratorial actions against the church.

Jones's inflated claims of power in the United States and in the
international community of the Left, including Guyana, evidently did not
excite Cuban Premier Fidel Castro. On January 24, 1977, Tim Stoen wrote
Castro: "I have just learned that Rev. James W. Jones, the founder and
leader of Peoples Temple Church (with more than 250,000 active members, considered the nation's largest single church) will soon be visiting
Cuba with Dr. Carlton Goodlett. . . . I would respectfully recommend that
you consider making this occasion a Visit of State. . . ."

As it happened, Jones returned to Cuba with no more fanfare than
on his first visit in the 1960s. In any case the real reason for the trip,
arranged by Goodlett, was old-fashioned *business*. Goodlett and Jones
wanted to establish an import-export trading relation with Cuba for a San
Francisco Bay Area company that he, Jones and other unnamed persons
had founded.[42]

In Cuba, while visiting Goodlett's business contacts and touring
schools and other facilities, Jones was annoyed that Castro had not consented to see him. Ruefully he remarked that Castro must be living better
than the people.

The highlight of the trip was a visit to fugitive Huey Newton's
residence. Goodlett had provided the entrée to the Black Panther leader,
Newton—who had run from California charges of murder and assault and
who, incidentally, had never met Castro during his two years in Cuba—
was teaching at the University of Havana and living in a modest apartment complex. During their hour visit, Jones and Newton talked about the
Panther's family members who had attended the Temple—his parents and

a cousin. They also discussed Newton's desire to return to the United States struggle—a notion that Jones ridiculed privately, saying that Newton missed his luxurious apartment and his favorite bars in Oakland.

The March 1977 *Peoples Forum* played up the trip in a big way. Jones offered basically a positive appraisal of Cuba, with exceptions:

"With as much dissent as he saw, Rev. Jones felt free to suggest that it might be a good idea to allow someone with a different perspective to run against Castro. There have been elections for all the lower level offices, and Dr. Castro himself was reelected, but he ran unopposed. . . ."

In the meantime, Jones's efforts in another leftist Caribbean state met with a series of successes. They had led off with an overblown pretentious letter similar to the one to Castro. In October 1976, Temple spokesman Mike Prokes requested that Guyana Prime Minister Forbes Burnham receive Jones as a dignitary during a visit later that year with some "high ranking U.S. officials."

To impress the Guyanese, Jones landed in Guyana on December 27 accompanied by California Lieutenant Governor Mervyn Dymally. By Temple arrangement, Dymally was accorded VIP treatment: Jones and Dymally had a private meeting with Burnham and Foreign Affairs Minister Fred Wills. In the session, both Burnham and Wills said Guyana wanted to keep the door open to cooperation between the two countries, and Dymally agreed to convey the message to the U.S. State Department.

In a letter to Burnham, Dymally would call Jim Jones "one of the finest human beings" and later would say he was "tremendously impressed" by his visit to Jonestown.

THIRTY-ONE

Flight of the Princess

Behind Jones's international diplomacy and the Temple's barrage of public relations, problems were popping up faster than they could be resolved. Jim Jones feared Treasury Department scrutiny for political activity and tax improprieties. He feared the FBI, although the agency had shown no interest in him. He feared the news media, although he had cultivated *San Francisco Chronicle* city editor Steve Gavin, its popular columnist Herb Caen and several local reporters on daily newspapers and in television. With one hand he raised a clenched fist to figures on the Left, while with the other he shook the hands of politicians. All the time he kept a sturdy hold on his organization. But behind the walls of Temple image, political alliances and hocus-pocus lurked the truest threat—disloyalty from the ranks.

Some defectors knew so much that Jones must have considered them high-grade explosives waiting to be detonated. In the past, Jones had covered himself fairly well. Linda Dunn, who once had dug through garbage as a Jones staffer, had been tailed by a private investigator, then intimidated by Chris Lewis, who spat at her feet. Marvin Swinney, the first head of security, had moved across the country after Jones bought his silence and tried to threaten him. Deanna and Elmer Mertle, who defected in the mid-1970s to become Jeannie and Al Mills, received vaguely threatening letters that implied trouble if they broke silence. And the Eight Revolutionaries mostly had been placated. The net effect was that those who could have hurt Jones most had refrained from doing so. Until Grace Stoen turned against him.

In July 1976, Grace Stoen vanished from the San Francisco temple without a word. Shortly thereafter she showed up in Redwood Valley to collect belongings. "Can we help you?" some people asked. "No, thanks," she replied, "it's just garbage." She threw boxes of possessions into the car and sped away from the valley where she had spent six difficult years.

No single deception or episode had driven her away. It was, rather, an unending accumulation of demands, contradictions, emotional traumas and disappointments. As her negativity deepened, she had confided in her friend Jack Arnold Beam, the Temple bandleader and son of Jack Beam, Sr. They commiserated. When young Beam defected, he invited her to come along, but she was not yet ready. Before leaving, he advised her to seek out Walter Jones, his co-worker in the bus garage. Jones—a sandy-haired master mechanic known as Smitty—had stayed behind when his wife Carol and her family, the Purifoys, had moved back to the Central Valley, but now he too was wavering. In him, Grace found a new ally. They became friends. They spent more and more time together. Word around the church was that Jones had assigned Grace to Smitty in the hopes her "special attention" would keep him from following the path of his in-laws. If so, the plan backfired. Grace did not keep Walt Jones in the church but in fact led him away.

Grace Stoen had seen her marriage dismantled, her child given up to be raised communally. She had been berated in p.c. meetings for not publicly proclaiming Jones to be father of the child. She had watched her little boy paddled in front of the church. She had seen Jones portray her husband as a homosexual. She had sat in p.c. while Jones waved a gun and threatened to shoot her if she fell asleep. She had seen poor people treated like cattle on bus trips and fed poorly at home, while Jones ate good meat. She had seen the fleecing and the fraud. As head counselor, and part of the Temple justice system, she had been compromised. As one of the notary publics, she handled guardianships and property transfers that tightened the church's grip on other members. As a p.c. member, she had witnessed atrocious statements and actions.

In the summer of 1976—after witnessing dozens of spankings and boxing matches—Grace Stoen finally drew the line. A forty-year-old woman was being pummeled by some dozen members for saying that Jones had turned them all into robots. The animal rage of the attack, the violent squelching of dissent, was too much. She told Walt Jones afterward, "Walt, I'm leaving. This is too heavy duty."

"Can I leave with you?" he asked.

On the Fourth of July weekend, the head counselor of Peoples Temple—the woman Jones had asked to administer the San Francisco temple, the wife of the assistant district attorney in San Francisco—made her dash for the outside world. To avoid hampering church operations, she left behind her church-related keys and instructions about unfinished business. She also left a note expressing her pain at leaving so many people she loved, one of them her son. Grace would say later that she did not want to put his life in danger. She was all too aware of Jones's claims on the child, his attempts to track down traitors, his threats to kill them.

As Grace and Smitty struck out on their own for Lake Tahoe, on the California-Nevada border, the double betrayal put a damper on the Temple's Independence Day picnic. While the general congregation sat attending a service inside the Redwood Valley church, Jones conducted an emergency p.c. meeting under the evergreens outside. His inner circle before him, he swore and ranted like a wounded animal. "How could she do this to me?" he screamed. "How could she do this to me after all I have done for her?"

Jones scorned her selfishness. Many nodded agreement: they had resented the special privileges extended Grace Stoen—the house, the nice possessions and, most of all, the privilege to carry a child to full term. Those special privileges made the betrayal all the more infuriating. In his tirade, Jones led step by step to the one link Grace Stoen could never deny: her child.

"Father" proclaimed his own version of history: he had an affair with Grace, but only to counteract her disloyalty. A few years earlier he had learned she had been smoking cigarettes—a sure sign of imminent defection. Then, on one of the bus trips, she had looked at him in that special way. He had known then there was only one cure. "That's what she needed, and that got her into the proper perspective."

Despite this gift, Grace had been an abusive and neglectful mother to his son, Jones railed. And now, after deserting the cause, she had already called him and wanted their son back. He vowed that she never would get the boy.

Jones was not bluffing. The child, whatever his parentage, was revered and loved in the Temple. Though raised by his legal parents the first two years, he was soon being given a mix of communal living and special upbringing as part of the Jones family. Stephan Jones considered him a half-brother, along with Kimo Prokes, Carolyn Layton's son sired by Jones but given legitimacy by Mike Prokes. John Victor's situation became particularly complicated when Maria Katsaris, who resembled Grace in some ways, was installed as his surrogate mother.

John Victor was systematically trained in the image of Jones, so even adult Temple members were reluctant to reprimand him. He was encouraged to swear, as Jones had as a child. His black hair was groomed like Jones's. With the assistance of Tim Stoen and others, this budding little antihero developed a socialistic rhetoric and an accompanying hatred for capitalists by the time he was three and a half. As cute as he was, this precocious child dominated his playmates. He could shift from charmer to a little terror with a flash of his dark eyes and a mischievous grin. As with Jones—and with other lads his age—the temper tantrum was a part of his repertoire. Once he stood up among the adults in the press room when they would not allow him to do a job he wanted and then plopped himself down in the middle of the floor: "Forget it! I ain't working here no more."

To some, John Stoen was a ruined, spoiled, confused little boy, weaned early from his mother and passed around an extended family without ever deriving a clear concept of parentage. To most, however, he was a living tribute to progressive, interracial child rearing. Among p.c. members, John V. Stoen was almost a reincarnation of Father as a child and was to be loved in the same way.[43]

Even Lynetta Jones, whom John called grandma, saw great profundity in the child's actions and reveled in his spunkiness, a quality she had nurtured in Jim. Around this time, she wrote:

"John Stoen, 3½ years of age, is a sage in his own right. He is . . . habitually too involved with the world's problems and the complexities of human kind for one of his tender years. . . . His solutions are as direct as the flight of a well-aimed bullet. He recognizes no monitor without reservation, except the Rev. Father Jim and his father, Tim, a very able attorney. When he doesn't like what he is called and reasoning fails to impress the tormentor, John resorts to quotes from Father Jim's teaching. Failing this, and having figuratively exposed both cheeks, he promptly utilizes fisticuffs to level off the zeal of the aggressor. . . ."

Like others, Grace Stoen had been unable to make a clean break. She still loved people in the church and, for complex reasons, still sought the approval, or understanding, of the very man she had fled. Worst of all was the guilt over her child.

Only a day after leaving, Grace Stoen called Jones from Nevada. She wanted understanding for what she had done; instead Jones twisted the knife of guilt, trying to get her back. In the low, pained tones of intimate friends, they spoke of their feelings. There was no rancor and no threatening. While she confessed the pain of leaving, he talked about the pain of abandonment.

"My heart inside me wrenched," he said. "I didn't expect this from you."

"I feel bad about a lot of people," she confided. "A lot of people, I respect; a lot of people, I like a lot. It really tore me up [to leave]. . . . But I couldn't keep on going on. . . . I couldn't stand being yelled at by you or anybody."

"But there was no idea of yelling at you," Jones replied. "I don't know where you got the idea anybody was ever yelling at you."

The two then talked about the child. Grace felt inadequate as a mother, and regretted the mother-child distancing demanded by a Temple lifestyle. Jones argued that the child still needed the Temple, and that she in turn was needed by the child; thus she must come back. Jim Jones wanted them both.

"I wouldn't any more let this baby down. . . . You got greatness in your child," Jones advised her after telling an anecdote illustrating John Victor's egalitarian tendencies.

"I know, but I just feel so inadequate with him," she replied.

"Well, who doesn't? How inadequate do you think I feel with you gone, my head counselor? . . . It's hard when I've got a few of you I put so much faith in, to have it jolted."

Whenever Grace began talking about her problems, he retorted with flagrant self-pity. He accused her of thinking too much about herself. And he emphasized that John Victor was dedicated to the Temple. "He knows the truth. You were sensible enough not to destroy him [by taking him with you]. I think that's a great measure of devotion. I'll always respect you for that."

Perhaps the communal environment was good for little John. But Grace wanted to clarify that she had not abandoned him out of lack of love: "Of course, I always wanted to take him . . . I knew it was selfish. I know it would be more for me than John."

"Yeah, it would have been," Jones agreed. "No individual can give what a group can. . . . He could have been destroyed. He'd have a personality problem. You'd probably have a mental case on your hands. . . ."

When Grace then talked about the emotional tug-of-war involving little John as some sort of unresolved sticking point, as something that "hangs me up," she tipped off Jones that she did indeed want her son.

Finally, Jones asked her to promise she would not tape-record him; all the while, of course, he was recording her. He tried to trip her into revealing her present location. Had she gone to Colorado, as she once planned? No, Grace said, not volunteering her whereabouts. A little huffy, Jones said: "I'm not going to trace you down. I just wanted to know where in hell. . . . I'm worried about you," and the conversation petered out.

Despite Jones's disavowal, the Temple, using phone records, was able to trace Grace's general location. They telephoned dozens of Nevada businesses where she might conceivably be doing clerical work. But they could not pinpoint her. Grace and Walt had driven to Carson City where they would live and work for six months.

In the two weeks that elapsed before the next recorded conversation—on July 15, 1976—Jones had discovered that before their flight, Walt Jones had encouraged Grace to take John with her. This time Jones bared his bitterness on the phone. As Grace defended Walt, it stirred up her own conflicting emotions about John Victor.

"He's not trying to hurt you," she explained. "Honest. I don't think he understands. . . . He thought that I couldn't handle being without John. . . . I don't think he would understand how involved John is. . . . I could never do that to you.

"I'm the one who left, not you. John is so involved with that. . . . To take him out . . ."

"Would have destroyed him," Jones finished the thought. Was Grace merely playing along, knowing she was being tested, recorded? Jones suspected Grace wanted the child, although so far she had not stated it explicitly.

When she insisted on talking to her son, Jones agreed to the request, but set the guidelines in such a way that notice was served: I control your son and your access to him. Grace tiptoed, acting agreeable, not doing anything that would cause Jones to change his mind.

"Just tell him you love him," he instructed. "Don't show any emotions. You can never tell a child too much about love, but [show] no emotional reaction if you can avoid it."

"I hope I can," she murmured.

At that, Jones threatened to cancel the call. "Please now, if you can't [restrain yourself], better not do it. . . ."

John Stoen came on the line, sounding a little uncertain: "Hello."

GRACE: "Hello, John? How are ya doing, hon'?"

JOHN: "Fine."

GRACE: "That's good. You sound great. I miss you."

JOHN: "No."

GRACE: "No?"

JOHN: "Yes."

GRACE: "You busy?"

JOHN: "No."

GRACE, talking with animation, tried to stir more of a reaction out of the black-haired boy: "You're not? Don't you help them with the dishes and stuff, and get the glasses?"

JOHN: "No."

After more of the same, Grace, evidently trying to find out why she was getting one-word answers: "Were you asleep?"

JOHN: "No. They just put me in bed."

GRACE: "Well. . . . You know, Jim loves you very much."

JOHN: "Yes."

Wisely Grace had said nothing to undermine Jones's position with the child, but the answers from a bright, talkative little boy who had not seen his mother for at least a couple of weeks rang false. Apparently hoping to draw him out of his reticence, Grace asked about John's friends, his surrogate mother Maria Katsaris, his new shoes, his trip to the park, about Kimo Prokes and Stephan Jones—his brothers for all intents and purposes.

"Well," Grace finally said, hiding her worry. "I don't want to keep you up anymore."

"Bye," John said.

In a moment, Jones grabbed the line again. "It's amazing how children know when we are testing them."

"It didn't even sound like him," Grace said, distressed. "He just sounds so different." Why had John showed no emotion whatsoever? Had he been instructed to hide his feelings, as she had been told to hide hers?

An unspoken deal was struck during a conversation between Grace and Jones on July 29, 1976. Each wanted something from the other. A month had elapsed since Grace's defection, and Jones needed a solid cover story for her absence. Grace wanted to see her boy.

They talked as they had in their other long-distance calls, Jones adopting the paternalistic, long-suffering tone of a martyr, Grace sounding weary and worn, admitting to some classic withdrawal symptoms—depression, insomnia, dreams about the church and her son.

"I miss him terribly," said Grace.

"I'm sure you do," said Jones. "I know it being a natural factor, but you preferred evidently . . . leaving him. You knew when you left and went to Smitty that that was more important to you than your child. . . . If you had taken him from his daddy, you'd have a very, very sick child. If you'd taken him, he'd have been destroyed. And, leaving, naturally you're not going to see him as much. . . . Did you think of that when you took off?"

"Sure I thought of it," she said.

Then, reminding her who regulated contact with her son, Jim Jones asked her to make a taped statement that would permit him to hide the couple's defection for another month or so—something he could play for other members to convince them that Grace and Walt were away on church work.

Puffing up like a talk show host—and giving away what Grace must already have known, that she was being recorded—Jones began to interview her about her church missions. Then he stopped the charade abruptly. "It doesn't sound real, Grace. I'd come on more like your buoyant self and give love to various people and say the date."

"Oh, God," she sighed, hopelessly. Then, after more instruction from Jones, she adopted her false broadcast voice. "Okay," she said. "I have the privilege of speaking to our friend Jim, and I'm calling from the mission. And I just wanted you to know I miss you very much, although it's much more pleasant over here in the Promised Land. A lot of things are being accomplished, although I'd rather be with my family, the greater mass of family. I'm here trying to help all of us. I miss everybody. I miss John and . . ."

As the names trailed off, Jones broke in, "Good enough."

Later in the conversation, Grace asked for something in return. "I'd like to see John if I could. I could come there."

Jones was reluctant to set up a meeting. "It's gonna be hard, because he's happy now and content. . . . How are we gonna tell him you come, and then you go? . . . You're playing with a little child's life, playing with his mental health."

She assured him, "I wouldn't do anything to upset him." They eventually reached agreement.

One Sunday in September 1976, Grace Stoen made her way from Carson City to Los Angeles. She was full of apprehension as she entered the Temple there for the first time as an outsider, a "traitor." "John's mother is here," other children cried when they saw her. John appeared; he was excited to see his mother. They hugged, and they talked. Grace marveled at how much he had grown in two months. He was only four.

After the brief reunion, Grace met with her husband and Jones together. Tim was hostile, and Jones did most of the talking. He told her he wanted her back in the church, apparently under any terms—including giving her John. Grace replied that she did not want to rejoin; she merely wanted her son. Her estranged husband and pastor insisted she could not have him. However, they said, she could visit the boy when he got to South America, and they handed her a round-trip ticket to Guyana. By taking it, she was playing into Jones's hands, allowing them to say she, in effect, accepted the arrangement.

For the most part, Grace Stoen had fenced beautifully with Jones. But as she later continued her informal efforts to retrieve John, she tipped her hand. Out of exasperation, she told Tim Stoen: "There are other ways to deal with you." Interpreting that as a threat to take legal action, Jim Jones and Tim Stoen decided to insulate themselves from a possible court order for the return of the child. John Victor would be sent to Guyana, beyond the jurisdiction of California courts. To protect himself legally, Jones asked Tim, John's legal father, for permission.

"Yes," said Timothy Oliver Stoen. With that one word, the little boy's fate was sealed.[44]

In an early November 1976 phone conversation with Tim, Grace learned that her son was in the Promised Land. He had been spirited off in October. Grace was numb with shock, stricken. Her voice became nearly inaudible. It made her sick, she said; she thought she would die.

Stoen reassured her that she could use her plane ticket to see her son in Guyana. And he promised, in a sort of unilateral child custody settlement, that the Temple would pay her expenses for twice-yearly visits.

Then, using the child for leverage, he returned to the theme of Jones's earlier conversations. "Have you thought about coming back?"

"It doesn't matter," she said, still reeling.

"There's a welcome here," he went on. "Our friend [Jones] really does have respect for you. . . . There's a lot of excitement there [in Jonestown]. . . . Eight new buildings. In one week, they cleared seventy acres. The prime minister himself came with the foreign minister. . . ." Getting no response, he added, "Our friend keeps telling him [John] that you love him and care for him. . . ."

Again, no response from Grace. Then Stoen asked: "Do you have any regrets about letting John go over there?"

To answer at all would be self-defeating, and Grace knew it. Any response would be used against her, would blow up in her face some-day. The heavy breathing was audible over the wire, but that was the only sign of the churning inside her. Not a word escaped Grace Stoen's lips.

"Our friend knows you are doing the highest thing a mother can do," Stoen continued. Then he made his final plea in a scattergun ap-proach: "I hope you'll be coming back, okay? . . . I know what a fucking lousy husband I've been, but I'm willing to learn so we can help people together. Please know you've been built up in little John's eyes, and he has a lot of good feelings about you. . . ."

THIRTY-TWO

One Gallant, Glorious End?

I don't mind losing my life. What about you? I don't mind losing my reputation. What about you? I don't mind being tortured. What about you? . . . I'm no longer afraid. I've lost interest in this whole world of capitalist sin . . . I'd just as soon bring it to a gallant, glorious scream-ing end, a screeching stop in one glorious moment of triumph.

JIM JONES

Since about 1973, Jones had been discussing openly what he certainly had pondered privately for years—the destruction of a Temple he was still building. It had become apparent that sooner or later someone—defectors, press, police—would topple his walls, exposing the intolerable state of internal affairs. When that happened, Jim Jones's reputation and life's work would be crushed. He had fashioned an organization that could not survive his death or imprisonment. He had never decentralized authority, never set up a truly socialist organization. He had conditioned his people to believe they could not live without him.

Slowly, insidiously, Jones let his people in on the secret plan for coping with his downfall. They would leave an indelible mark on history. It was the cleverest twist of all; in death, they could achieve new life. A bunch of common people and a preacher named Jones could take their place alongside the great nations of history, the heroes of the Russian and Chinese revolutions, the martyrs of the American civil rights movement, the Jews at Masada.

By choosing the time, place and manner of the death of his movement, Jones could deprive his enemies of the chance to bring him down; he would avert defeat. And this escape would not be forgotten—it would have meaning. Their statement: that members of Peoples Temple could no longer tolerate the cruelties of this world. That statement would define Jones's place in history: from the filthy depths of defeat, "one gallant, glorious screaming end."

In 1973, several months after the Kinsolving series, Jones first broached the subject of mass suicide. At the time he also made clear his own intention to remain behind to explain the self-destruction. Jack Beam protested that Jones ought to perish with the rest, but that was the only major note of dissent.

By 1975–76, with more serious trouble brewing, Jones actively began promoting his plan again. He started by testing his inner circle of one hundred. Jones hoped to gauge people's willingness to throw aside their will to survive and to make the "ultimate sacrifice." The first experiment occurred during an unusually festive planning commission meeting at the San Francisco temple, in the very room where the church entertained some of the most important politicians in California. On this particular night Jones suspended a Temple prohibition. He announced that some very good wine had been made from grapes grown on the church's Redwood Valley properties. And he ordered wine poured and passed around for a rare celebration. Some p.c. members hesitated—it was against all practice, after all—but finally they tried the wine. Sipping and socializing, the group began to feel loose, even relaxed. This certainly beat catharsis or a business meeting.

Jones went around making sure everyone had tasted at least some wine. Then, suddenly, he called for everyone's attention in a foreboding voice. The party mood snapped. The wine contained a potent poison, he informed them. They would all die within forty-five minutes. Jones proceeded to explain the rationale for his unilateral decision: by killing themselves, they would be protesting the inhumanity of the world.

To show he was serious, Jones sent cups of wine upstairs to his own living quarters, ostensibly for his sons. Soon various people around the room slithered out of their chairs like dead fish. Jones warned: Anyone who tries to escape will be shot by Mike Prokes or other armed security watching the exits.

No one rose to question the judgment of Jim Jones. No one rebelled, no one challenged his insane logic, no one called for an antidote. No one questioned the right of Jim Jones to make the decision for them to die. In fact, some even voiced concern that children and others not attending the p.c. meeting would be left behind to suffer in the cruel world. Could they not be brought in to take the potion as well? It was not necessary, Jones assured them: he would soon detonate a nuclear bomb that was sitting nearby in a van, thus mercifully destroying San Francisco and all the children with it.

As some members keeled over, apparently dead or dying, other p.c. members held their seats. Some, like Joyce Shaw, believed they were dying but did not react; death sounded like a long vacation from an exhausting and unsatisfying life, and they were consoled by thoughts of reincarnation. Some shared Jones's vision of a glorious final statement. Some, no doubt, were in a state of shock, afraid of the oncoming death from poison or afraid of the bullets from Mike Prokes's gun, afraid of being seen as cowardly or disloyal. These people froze, blank, uncertain. Many were skeptical, thinking the ritual surely could not be real. Most could not be sure, and others, like Sandy Bradshaw, did not care one way or the other.

Only a few, the actors, knew for sure. Even Patty Cartmell, Jones's longtime stagehand, may have been left out of this secret—at least Jones wanted the others to think that. At one point she made a wild, screaming dash for the door: she was going to "kill enemies," she shouted. Prokes intercepted her and a shot rang out. The explosion, almost point-blank, knocked her to the floor. It was only a blank, but the percussion had torn her clothing and she had seemed to pass out. Momentarily, she recovered, dazed and sputtering angrily. One of Jones's lieutenants had failed the loyalty test and the others were amused.

Soon the slapstick was over. There was no poison after all, Jones announced.

But there had been a test, and Jones wanted to evaluate the success of his experiment. He ordered two Temple women, one of them Joyce Shaw, to ask p.c. members on tape whether the charade had fooled them. The interview result: about half had believed, and half were skeptical. The nonbelievers did not so much doubt that Jones would do such a thing; rather it was the poor acting, the amateurish "dying" of the "victims," that had tipped them off.

A 50 percent credibility rating on the suicide rehearsal was no mean feat. Only one person had tried to escape—and perhaps had been acting. Most of all the little exercise had been unifying. The thought of dying had raised expressions of loyalty, and sacrifice, even of the lives of their children. For some, incredibly, it was a beautiful sight to behold.

The mechanism was tested and in place.

Although Jones often denigrated Bob Houston, he wanted to keep him in the fold. He was a devoted member. This could not have been more dramatically demonstrated than when he returned to his commune after doing time on the Temple work crew repairing damage from the fire.

Instead of diminishing his commitment, Bob Houston rededicated himself. Wholeheartedly he threw himself into a positive-minded critique of the Temple's communal structure, which involved over 400 people and a few dozen communes in San Francisco. He systematically assessed its strengths and weaknesses, and suggested solutions. His thoughtful and detailed written evaluation noted that some 50 key people were bearing the load for the entire system and that the talents of the 350 others were being wasted, at the expense of their sense of belonging and personal commitment.

"Members are becoming increasingly resentful and disgruntled that the promises of 'all your needs being met' are not being fulfilled, and the buck keeps being passed around and around," he declared.

Little was forthcoming in the way of improvements. If anything, the communal amenities became more meager, the overall strategy more desperate and the structure more centralized. In 1976, despite the Temple's newly acquired political might and upgraded public image, the deterioration became pronounced. High visibility had heightened Jones's fears of government crackdowns and renewed media inquiries. In April 1976—through numerous phone calls and letters, and by badgering newspaper personnel—Jones was able to defuse a *San Francisco Chronicle* story by reporter Julie Smith. Nevertheless, such scares made the building of a sanctuary seem more urgent.

Inside the church, Jones told his followers to tighten their belts to save money for the exodus to Guyana. They all might be forced to flee sooner than expected, he said: civil war might break out if Jimmy Carter, a southerner, was elected in November. As an added inducement to sacrifice, Jones showed his people a silent film of the December 1974 visit to Jonestown, complete with store-bought fruit.

As a first step in consolidation, the church initiated a rule in January 1976 that all members must eat meals at the Temple dining hall on Geary Boulevard. That economy move represented great hardship for the Houstons. The church was a ten-minute drive across town from Potrero Hill, and there was only one commune car to bring twenty-four hungry mouths back and forth. Practically the entire evening was spent shuttling people to dinner.

The new mealtime arrangement was accompanied by a new bookkeeping policy too: all communal money would be handled through central bookkeeping. The Temple would monitor and maintain control of every dime, paying rent, phone bills, and other allowable expenses. Wage earners signed over their checks; in turn, they were allotted a certain amount of money for their needs and had to submit requisition slips for the rest, even personal articles such as toothpaste, shampoo and sanitary napkins.

The meals policy, coupled with the intrusion of some problem adults on Potrero Hill, caused Joyce and Bob to request new quarters. In April 1976, the commune moved into a more convenient Victorian house on Sutter Street, within easy walking distance of the Temple. The house was stuffed with people, nearly twenty living at least three per room in six rooms, including the living and dining rooms. Joyce roomed with two girls, and Bob with two boys. There was no space for socializing or conducting communal activities. In this flophouse, sleeping was the primary activity. As far as Temple leadership went, that was just fine: it mitigated against any independent communal identity.

The Sutter Street commune's refrigerator was barren; without mealtime gatherings, there was no forum for discussing problems and solving them, or for sharing interests. Instead they marched to the church, where they endured food lines and often were unable to sit together. Every night was a cafeteria meal. Discipline in the house deteriorated; the children sassed adults and showed no respect. Joyce and Bob soon became miserable.

The ironies did not escape Joyce. The very day she handed the church an $800 paycheck, she had to submit a request for $10 for the children's monthly birthday outing. The bureaucratic requirements were stifling and nonsensical, and the poor diet drove her to complain repeatedly. "This is a rich organization," she told Jones in planning commission meetings. "So why don't our children have [even] the standard of living of kids in the slums?" Jones reiterated his statements about the need for money to flee the country, and Joyce was ridiculed by others as a selfish white middle-class intellectual.

The verbal punishment persisted at meetings in spring and early summer of 1976. She and Bob were ostracized for taking a "white" attitude, ignoring the fact that children were starving all over the world. Maintaining a white middle-class dietary standard was expensive and unnecessary, they were told. Besides, Joyce and Bob were becoming territorial about their little group. A self-centered communal identity undermined the larger community, Peoples Temple.

Righteous doubts as troubling as a suicide rehearsal had flooded Joyce Shaw's consciousness. To her, there seemed to be no free exchange of ideas, no effort to encourage criticism, no attempt to adopt the sorts of positive changes Bob had suggested. The lifestyle was growing more spare, the organization more autocratic and authoritarian. Her respect for Jones was fractured.

In June 1976, as her discontent deepened, Jones elevated Bob to the planning commission. Joyce interpreted the move, correctly, as an attempt to placate him and control her. Although Bob did not join in the criticism of Joyce at the next p.c. meeting—much to Jones's chagrin—the appointment nevertheless added an element of mistrust to their marriage. Joyce did not share with Bob the details of her growing disaffection.

Meanwhile, she had started having late-night conversations with a couple of women members who had secret doubts about the church. The three of them broke a taboo one night by smoking cigarettes and drinking wine in a bedroom. As they savored each puff and sip, breaking the rules together, they established a bond of trust. They talked rebelliously, but were still too scared to act on it.

At about this time, happenstance provided a climate for Joyce to make a decision. Because her parents were coming to visit from Ohio and because she made good wages as a legal secretary, she was allowed to remain in San Francisco during the church's annual cross-country bus trip.

With the children away from the commune, she slept longer, and fell into a more conventional routine. As the effects of sleep deprivation wore off, her misgivings about the church came into focus. Her willpower strengthened. She assured herself that she possessed the skills to earn her way in the world and that her family would shelter her if necessary. In that regard, she differed from many Temple members without the youth, education, background and outside resources to make a clean split.

On the night of July 15, 1976, Bob drove her to work. She was a little early, so the two sat talking in an old Pontiac on California Street. There were warm feelings between them, despite a certain wariness. Bob suspected she was anxious to leave but did not suspect her defection was just hours away. "If you leave, it will hurt a lot of people," he said. Her responses were awkward and restrained, revealing nothing. It was too late. She had already put aside a couple of paychecks, stowed belongings bit by bit with an outside friend and purchased a bus ticket.

That night after work, with a little Buddha statue and few other belongings in a bag, she stepped onto the street in her high heels and hailed a cab. She was leaving behind her husband, six children under her guardianship, and several years of her life. At the Greyhound bus station in downtown San Francisco, she boarded the 1:15 A.M. bus to Santa Rosa, where an old friend had offered her a place to stay.

Less than twenty-four hours after defecting, Joyce called Bob at the San Francisco Youth Guidance Center, presuming that phone would not be bugged. Predictably, Bob pleaded with her to return. He reminded her of the Temple's good deeds and told her he felt doubly hurt because they had been planning to move back into the same room together in the commune.

Joyce tried to explain herself, but shied away from criticizing Jones or contradictions in the church. Bob would not even acknowledge that their own relationship had been victimized by Jones. The conversation got nowhere. She knew the prestige of a p.c. seat still meant a great deal to him, and it would take time for the luster to wear off.

For three weeks, Joyce lived on the midway at the Sonoma County fairgrounds and other fairs, selling T-shirts at her friend's concession stand and learning to slow down. Still, she kept reaching back. She called Bob two or three times and also placed a call to Jones. As did many defectors, she nearly apologized to him. She was trying to find herself, she said. "And I don't believe the revolution is coming," she added. Instead of abusing her, Jones salved her with understanding, encouraged her to go ahead with her search. And he extended her an open invitation to return.

Amiable as the forty-five-minute conversation was, Joyce did not trust Jones. She wrote her first husband, the Hungarian, in Vienna, briefing him on her defection and warning him that if any harm befell her, the church was responsible. The letter alarmed him so much that he sent a copy to Joyce's mother. The family tried unsuccessfully to contact Joyce through the Temple and were given phony excuses for her absence. They became frantic. Finally, as her mother and brother made plans to fly to California to search for her, Joyce telephoned home to ask for asylum. She had remembered Jones's admonition to defectors: If you go five hundred miles away, no one will harm you.

Still nearly in shock, she flew home to Ohio. The Temple dominated her dreams; she flashed back in time. She slept and slept, sat around idle, incapacitated, asking herself what had happened to her. It was therapeutic, she discovered, to tell her parents about her experiences. But she knew that her next step must take her outside her own closed cosmos; she needed to occupy herself and regenerate. One day in the shower, she decided the best option was to return to school. Within two months of leaving, she enrolled for the fall term at Wright State University.

Though more convinced than ever of Jones's deceit, she could not forget Bob. She called him on their second anniversary, October 2, 1976. It seemed apparent that Bob wanted her back as much as she wanted him. But his words offered little hope that he soon would quit the church. He said he was looking forward to a vacation in Guyana. Secretly, he was recording the phone call.

"Bob, I don't believe the ends justify the means," Joyce said, refusing to return.

"I *do* believe that," he said. "I do believe that."

"I can't make your decision to leave," she said. "But I want you to know where I can be reached. If you want to leave, we can get together and I will do anything to help the girls."

The invitation to reunite hung there, openly. Was some part of him listening?

At the end of their conversation, Joyce had asked Bob to send some clothes she had left behind. The clothing was mailed to Joyce's parents' house the morning of October 4, 1976, before Bob went to work at Juvenile Hall. After his first eight-hour job, he went to work at the railroad.

In the small hours of October 5, 1976, the general yardmaster of the Southern Pacific railroad yards, Ben Rhoten, drove south from San Francisco to San Bruno. He parked and walked up to the door of the single-story house where Bob Houston's parents lived. Rhoten was a golf partner of Sam Houston's, and he had visited the house previously. This time he was dreading it.

Nadyne Houston answered the door in her nightgown. She went immediately to get her husband out of bed. When Sam Houston walked to the front of the house, his friend Ben greeted him with a taut expression. "Sam, I've got something to tell you." His face said it all.

"Is it Bobby, Jr? Is he dead?"

About a hundred people, including a contingent of at least fifty Temple members, gathered at the San Bruno Funeral Home for Bob's services. The turnout provided some consolation to the grieving parents; it indicated that Bob had been a popular Temple member. But these were not Bob's friends. Most of his friends had left the church, and none of the friendly senior citizens Bob used to shuttle around had been selected for the Temple contingent.

The family abided by Bob's wish—and Temple practice—that he be cremated. His remains would be put to rest at Skylawn Cemetery, where he had played taps years earlier as a Boy Scout. The Temple would contribute $200 to the burial cost.

At the mortuary, Joyce Shaw sat with the Houstons; Phyllis refused, both for herself and for her daughters. The relationship between Mrs. Houston and Phyllis had never been particularly warm, but it meant a great deal to Bob's parents to have their granddaughters beside them. Instead, the girls sat tearless among the Temple contingent, showing no emotion.

Nadyne Houston's minister presided over the services. Bob's former bandleader said a few kind words, and some ex-Temple members delivered short but complimentary eulogies. Jim Jones did not attend, but his son-in-law and onetime designated successor, Mike Cartmell, stood to say that Bob had been working too hard recently and that Rev. Jones had encouraged him to trim back his schedule. Joyce Shaw was disgusted at the self-serving eulogy: now no one could say the Temple, by overworking him, had indirectly contributed to his death.

After the services, the Houstons opened their home. Mourners from the Temple showed up with a half-dozen coffee cakes. Lines of tension immediately crackled between current and former members. Carolyn Layton and others stood around with folded arms and stern expressions. Many of the young blacks, obviously assigned to attend the funeral, fidgeted nervously.

Even the Houstons noticed the charged atmosphere. They thought it odd that Joyce never put down her purse, as though someone might lift it. In fact, she held it purposely so that Temple members would think it concealed a tape recorder and would not bother her. Nonetheless, Phyllis Houston privately tried to show her a letter in which Bob had supposedly tendered his resignation the day before he died. Joyce assumed the contents had been added later above Bob's signature on a blank sheet of paper. "Bob never typed anything," she noted. But the so-called resignation letter told her what the church line was: Bob had been a traitor who had suffered the consequences.[45]

In that climate of barely submerged hostility, Joyce Shaw attempted to speak with Judy and Patricia Houston. She believed that the girls were not being permitted to grieve openly for their father because his memory was being destroyed inside the church. Judy looked as though her stomach ached, from suppressing her feelings for her beloved father. On the way to the bathroom, Joyce managed to get a moment alone with Patricia, enough only to say, "You know, I love your father," before the conversation was clipped short by a church member.

At the end of the reception, Joyce stood on the front walkway as Temple members piled into cars and drove away. As a car swung away from the curb with Phyllis and the girls, Patricia turned in her seat, smiled at Joyce and raised a clenched fist. To Joyce, it meant: we're still together, you mean something to me.

The following day, Joyce and the Houstons drove to Bob's Sutter Street quarters to pick up his personal effects. While Sam straightened out some matters with Phyllis, Carolyn Layton called Joyce into a bedroom. Tim Stoen and Harriet Tropp were already there waiting for the confrontation. The three wanted her to read some papers behind clear plastic in a black notebook. She refused, demanding that they state any message aloud. Apparently afraid she was taping them, they merely stared at her threateningly. She turned heel and walked out.

Moments later, in the kitchen, Carolyn Layton warned: "If you ever decide to start talking, there are certain things that you and Bob did to the children. . . ."

"You let us have the children live with us. So if those things are true, why did you give us the children?" Shaw knew Layton was threatening to use the phony confessions she and Bob had signed, admitting physical or sexual abuse of the girls.

"We'll let people know that you beat those children," Layton shot back. "You admitted it in writing." The threat was not complete without a seething oath of total commitment: "The Temple is my only reason for living. I'll do anything to save it, if anyone tries to harm it."

Not knowing what the Temple might do, Joyce wrote her cautionary letter to the Houstons, preparing them for possible allegations. This was the letter that first carried details of the Temple's insidious blackmail-like practices to Sam Houston and, in turn, to me, an Associated Press reporter at the time.

The warning arrived fortuitously just after the *Fresno Bee* requested that our San Francisco AP bureau provide a profile of the Temple. In late August–early September, Jones's group had picketed for days on behalf of the Fresno Four, four *Bee* newsmen and editors jailed for failure to divulge sources of published information about secret grand jury proceedings. The four, all white, had been heartened to look out the Fresno courthouse windows upon Jim Jones and strings of mostly black pickets supporting them. No other group had come over two hundred miles to defend freedom of the press—and no one else attracted national news media coverage, including space in the *New York Times*. It was natural enough that the *Bee* would like to run a feature on the Temple.

But after the bureau management talked to photographer Sam Houston, the routine story request had turned sticky. AP management could neither ignore the *Bee*'s request nor an employee's negative experience with the church. A full-scale investigation at the time was ruled out, since other stories were already taxing bureau manpower. Instead it was decided that a bare-bones story, based on another reporter's interview with Jones, would be written for the *Bee*. The resulting story, though it reflected caution, pleased the Temple a great deal. It provided the implicit imprimatur of the world's biggest news agency, with no hint of scandal.

Meanwhile, *Bee* religion writer Ray Steele had been assigned to look more closely into the nasty rumors about the Temple. His investigations revealed allegations similar to those that had appeared a few years earlier in the *San Francisco Examiner*. The *Bee* did not publish them. Not only were they thought to be unprovable, they had been leveled at a preacher perceived widely as an advocate of press freedom.

THIRTY-THREE

Presidential Embrace

In the fall of 1976, as Walter Mondale's private jet touched down at San Francisco International Airport, a party of Democratic dignitaries gathered on the runway to greet the vice-presidential candidate. Climbing the steps with Mayor Moscone for a private visit with Mondale was a man in a white leisure suit, black shirt and sunglasses. Looking more like a country-and-western singer than a minister, Jim Jones viewed his fleeting session with Mondale as a valuable steppingstone. No sooner had the vapor trail from Mondale's jet faded again than the contact was being bandied about to increase Temple standing with the Guyanese government. The Temple told Guyanese officials that Jones had engaged Mondale in private talks about outside attempts to destabilize Guyana and other Caribbean nations.

But for Jones the political event of the fall session had come in an earlier visit from Rosalynn Carter. The San Francisco Democratic Central Committee had mailed out about a thousand invitations for the dedication of the local Carter-Mondale campaign headquarters. But even with Mrs. Carter as an attraction, officials still doubted that they could fill the new headquarters downtown on Market Street. At the suggestion of someone who recalled the Temple's work in the previous mayoral campaign, Peoples Temple was called to the rescue. In return, the Temple asked that Jones be seated on the speakers' platform with Mrs. Carter. The organizers agreed, since Jones was, after all, a bona fide civic figure on the Housing Commission.

Several hours before the rally, the Temple upped its demands: now it wanted four assistant ministers on stage, and Jones himself seated near Mrs. Carter—whom he claimed to have met previously. The head of the Democratic Central Committee agreed to rearrange the seating, to put Jones on one side of Mrs. Carter and Cecil Williams on the other side, a sort of ministerial buffer.

As rally time neared, Secret Service agents combed the building looking for bombs and checking exits, no doubt mindful of the attempt on President Gerald Ford's life in San Francisco a year earlier. Curiously, a group of Temple security people soon arrived and followed many of the same procedures as the Secret Service. Then, as busloads of Temple members filed into the headquarters, an agent and a committee official both spotted an exposed pistol on one of the Temple assistant ministers. When the agent caught up with the Temple official at the corner, some questions were asked. There was no disarming, no hostility, no trouble. "It's okay," the agent said, returning to his post at the door.

The hall was jammed and stifling as the rally got under way. So many Temple members had piled into the building that some party regulars could not squeeze inside. As usual, remarks by Jones triggered waves of applause punctuated by whoops and foot stomping. The reception for Mrs. Carter was polite and restrained by comparison. During the rally, while sitting with Mrs. Carter, Jones consulted with his security chief Jim McElvane, who leaned over his shoulder. Scanning the audience for signs of danger, they spotted a suspicious-looking black man standing on something to elevate himself above the throng. They pointed at him, and the alarm went out. A moment later a Secret Service agent whispered to the head organizer: "Don't worry, but one of the Temple guards says he thinks this guy has a gun. We'll check."

Two agents closed in on the mysterious man who was wearing a sports coat and tie and writing on a note pad. The man smirked when agents said they wanted to frisk him. They found nothing. The mystery man turned out to be Lon Daniels, a reporter for the *San Francisco Examiner.*

For most luminaries, the rally was the end of the Rosalynn Carter visit, but for Jim Jones the finale came later. Jones requested a chance to chat privately with Mrs. Carter. Her advance team had heard that Jones's grass-roots political organization had made the difference in Mayor Moscone's victory, so they decided Jones would be worth ten minutes of Mrs. Carter's time.

That evening the Jones motorcade crawled up Nob Hill and swung into the courtyard of the posh Stanford Court Hotel. In white suit and sunglasses, Jones stepped out of an older Cadillac limousine and, with a coterie of about fifteen bodyguards, swept into the lobby. When a member of Mrs. Carter's advance team asked why so many guards were needed, he received the standard reply: "There was a threat on Rev. Jones's life today." The entire squad intended to accompany Jones downstairs to a restaurant for the meeting, but the advance men talked them out of it, averting the spectacle of twenty-five Temple guards and Secret Service agents hovering over Jones and Rosalynn Carter as they sipped coffee. The tête-à-tête lasted only about fifteen minutes, yet the *Peoples Forum* staff soon would ready photos of Jones and Mrs. Carter with the caption, "Rev. Jim Jones, by invitation, dines with Mrs. Jimmy Carter."

A short time after her visit, Mrs. Carter phoned the minister as a sort of follow-through courtesy call. After all, San Francisco was a key area in the nation's most populous state. While Jones fell all over himself in his attempts to charm Mrs. Carter, she was cordial and noncommittal, though she evidently did not know he was taping the conversation.

Jones expressed admiration for Mrs. Carter's "Christian ethics" and "broad liberality," then stumbled. "Is there anything in particular we can do for you?" he asked.

"No," said Mrs. Carter. ". . . I just wanted to call because Jimmy had gotten this letter from [unintelligible]. He said you've been saying some nice things . . . and told me to call you."

"I don't know whether you received my letter of encouragement," Jones continued; ". . . not that you need it. We're going to win! We're going to win!"

"I appreciate that," Mrs. Carter replied, explaining that Jones's letter might have been lost in the stacks of mail piling up.

"Well, you call us [if you need anything]," Jones reiterated. "We have many, many thousands of members. And I have considerable influence in the Disciples of Christ denomination of which I am an official. . . ."

Keeping the subject on religion, Mrs. Carter asked Jones whether he knew her sister-in-law, Ruth Carter Stapleton, an evangelist.

"I have heard . . . uh . . . read of her, with a great deal of admiration . . ." Jones replied sweetly. Then he went after this plum with the enthusiasm of the boyish Indiana preacher who had once lined up the great William Branham. "I . . . we would be more than honored to help her," Jones said. "And if she's having a meeting [we would be willing] to sponsor it or to advertise it. We have quite a number of radio broadcast outlets and television outlets. We also have the *Peoples Forum* that has six hundred thousand circulation in the Bay Area. So anything you'd like us to print, don't hesitate to send us. . . ."

That gross exaggeration of the Temple newspaper's circulation was too much for the future First Lady to pass up. She asked Jones to repeat the address of *Peoples Forum*. Jones left her with: "Your slightest wish is our command. God's blessing be with you."

Despite such vows of loyalty, the Temple was covering its bets. Jones ordered an aide to offer financial contributions to the campaign of President Gerald Ford, in case Carter lost. Still, Jones was elated when Mrs. Carter took up residence in the White House. He cultivated the contact as well as he could, writing her a March 17, 1977 letter, which began:

"I regret I was out of town and missed meeting your sister-in-law Ruth Carter Stapleton when she was in San Francisco recently." Evidently, the President's sister could not reach Jones by phone. To avoid future communications problems Jones gave Mrs. Carter his private number.

Jones then wrote the First Lady suggesting that he and a group of prominent doctors and businessmen could arrange for Cuba to receive much-needed medical supplies and equipment. Such humanitarian aid, he declared, might well win that country away from the Soviet orbit!

In response, Jim Jones received one of the Temple's most highly prized letters. It was on White House stationery, written in pen:

> *Dear Jim,*
> *Thank you for your letter. I enjoyed being with you during the campaign and do hope you can meet Ruth soon.*
> *Your comments about Cuba are helpful. I hope your suggestion can be acted on in the near future.*
>
> *Sincerely,*
> *Rosalynn Carter*

The successes of 1976 and 1977 did not quench Jones's often-denied ambitions for political recognition and power. It was not even enough that Governor Brown appointed church attorney Tim Stoen in April 1976 to serve on the California Advisory Council to the Legal Services Corporation—the body that handles federal legal aid programs. Jones wanted titles and authority beyond the chairmanship of the San Francisco Housing Commission. He wanted more than to host the January 15, 1977, citywide celebration in honor of Martin Luther King, Jr., more than to share the podium that day with Governor Brown and the head of President Carter's transition team. Jones exposed his ambitions by denying in

Peoples Forum "rumors" that he was planning to run for mayor. He had talked with aides about running for the state legislature or Congress. With a former Brown cabinet member, he discussed his chances for appointment to the University of California Board of Regents, the state's most prestigious nonsalaried appointment. And he made a bid for an appointment to the prison-related state Community Release Board. Yet the pinnacle of his Year of Ascendancy was undoubtedly the September 1976 testimonial dinner.

The printed invitations read like something prepared for an official visit of a head of state. Yet Jones knew he had to retain his "humble" image, so the Temple sent a silly follow-up letter to the invitations: "Dear Friends, Upon being informed that a testimonial dinner was planned in his honor, Rev. Jim Jones insisted that the occasion be changed to a benefit for various humanitarian causes. . . ."

The several hundred people who pulled their cars into the Temple's "patrolled" parking lot on the night of Saturday, September 25, 1976, had no illusions. They were paying tribute to Jim Jones. The Temple on Geary Boulevard had been rearranged into a formal dining room with linen tablecloths, proper place settings and an ample number of ferns. Well dressed Temple members ushered the guests to their places. The head table was filled with familiar faces—Lieutenant Governor and Mrs. Dymally, Assemblyman Willie Brown, Mayor George Moscone, District Attorney Joe Freitas and others. In fact, the guests were led to believe that it was an honor to be seated inside the main building at all, that the bulk of the "8,000" attendees were dining at various other auditoriums around the city and had to watch the festivities on closed-circuit television.

The guest list read like a register of the city's luminaries—Democrats, Republicans and radicals, including Angela Davis. Also present were *Chronicle* city editor Steve Gavin, leftist lawyers Charles Garry and Vincent Hallinan, and Mendocino County Republican head Marge Boynton. Ukiah Bircher Walter Heady and his wife, startled to find Jones so immersed in the liberal-progressive San Francisco Establishment, survived meeting former Black Panther and Born Again clothing designer Eldridge Cleaver.

As Temple members waited on tables and the band provided music, the guest of honor, dressed in white, assumed his position at the head table. He was flanked by his wife Marceline, elegant with her golden hair heaped in curls and her satiny gown hanging like a choir robe. They looked for all the world like the ideal husband-wife team, aglow with the adulation coming their way.

Some Temple leaders were delighted to see so many opponents of socialism assembled to clap for Jim Jones. Other members took tremendous pride in the event: the Temple *was* getting somewhere. Jim Jones *was* a great man—or so many bigwigs would not have coughed up $20 and their time to make homage.

All went smoothly. The dinner was edible, and Temple entertainers charmed their audience. At one point, a little black singer named Shaun Baker weaved through the audience like a polished nightclub star. "I'm just a soldier in the army of lu-uh-uv," he sang. "Now hate is my enemy, I got to fight it day and night." Although stage fright sometimes cracked his clear voice, he bravely marched through the song. The boy would be a few inches taller and his voice a little deeper and surer two years later when he performed for Jones's last "testimonial" in the jungle of South America.

Witty and wordy Willie Brown served as master of ceremonies. He introduced his fellow politicians so that they could present their gifts: Republican State Senator Milton Marks handed Jones a plaque bearing a resolution passed by the entire State Senate: "This is an outstanding institution which has shown that hope and love still reside in this city." Marks's Democratic opponent in the race for his seat, San Francisco Supervisor Robert Mendelsohn, presented a certificate of honor on behalf of the Board of Supervisors.

Among church leaders present, the Reverend Cecil Williams gave Jones a plaque on behalf of Glide Memorial Church. And Gerald McHarg of the Disciples of Christ Southern California region said, "I am honored to be part of a denomination that includes Peoples Temple and its minister."

Claude Worrell, deputy Guyanese ambassador to the United States, commended Peoples Temple for not "intruding" in the internal affairs of Guyana. "The Peoples Temple has identified with and become a great part of [the Guyanese government's] direction."

And Lieutenant Governor Dymally, a Trinidad native who had first introduced the Temple to Worrell, offered what *Ukiah Daily Journal* reporter Kathy Hunter termed "perhaps the most poignant accolade." He said that Jones was bringing together all ages and races: "I am grateful he is showing an example not only in the U.S. but also in my former home territory, the Caribbean."

The Fresno Four were introduced with a partial reading of their letter of thanks to the Temple: "There is no doubt that what you, Rev. Jones, and your flock did in Fresno . . . is the most eloquent testimony possible to the brotherhood of man." Thus Jones, the man who had used everything in his arsenal to suppress the Kinsolving series, was saluted as a champion of press freedom.

Praise echoed throughout the auditorium like reverent chanting. The speakers had been asked not to mention the name of the humble host being honored. That was being saved for Temple public relations man Mike Prokes. "Here's a man who says as long as I have a home, you have a home," cried Prokes. "Here's a man with only one pair of shoes and no car, one suit of clothing—I think the suit he's got on tonight was borrowed. Here's a man who works over twenty hours a day. Here's JIM

JONES!" As the applause rose like a fountain, Prokes shouted an apology for mentioning, in his enthusiasm, the name Jim Jones: "I'm sorry Jim. I just had to say it."

Still Jones did not rise: one adoring introduction was not enough. Willie Brown took the rostrum again: "Let me present to you what you should see every day when you look into the mirror in the early morning hours. . . ." he declared. "Let me present to you a combination of Martin King, Angela Davis, Albert Einstein . . . Chairman Mao. . . ."

Then, to the tumultuous applause, Jones stood with his chest thrown forward. . . .

THIRTY-FOUR

The Writing on the Wall

Stephan Jones came down from Ukiah to the big city in 1975, with sports still on his mind and with the burdens that once had driven him to attempt suicide. In his sophomore year at Ukiah High School, he had played on the basketball team with his brothers and other Temple members. His father had tried to cool the teen-ager's basketball mania, saying, "How would it look if people don't see you at services? You should be setting an example." But Stephan overcame his guilt and had a ready answer: athletes were important in the Soviet Union. His father granted grudging permission.

Stephan looked forward to playing in San Francisco, too. But he and other Temple high school kids were sent to Drew School, a college preparatory hardly known for athletic predominance. Not surprisingly, Stephan found the atmosphere snotty at Drew, just a few blocks from ritzy Pacific Heights. After a short spell, he and the rest of the Temple kids moved to Washington High, a larger, inner-city, public high school. Stephan Jones let his B average take care of itself, but he worked hard on the basketball court. He was excited about making the team—then abruptly his father pulled Temple students out of Washington.

Jim Jones enrolled them at Opportunity II High School, for troubled students, dropouts, unwed mothers and others who did not or could not make it in regular schools. Jones had made the move because the potential existed for turning a public alternative school almost into a Temple school. Also, he respected the political activism of the school's coordinator, Yvonne Golden. The black educator raised issues and raised hell at school board meetings. At school, she energized naturally rebellious youth; she invited guest speakers such as Angela Davis, Dennis Banks and Rev. Jim Jones.

During the school year 1976–77, one year after Stephan Jones moved to San Francisco, Peoples Temple students filled one-third to one-half of the several hundred desks at Opportunity High. No one at school seemed particularly concerned about the disproportionate numbers, nor did it bother them when some students were absent for weeks at a time on bus trips or gave names and addresses of guardians that did not quite fit.

Generally, the students impressed many of Opportunity's teachers as respectful, well motivated and eager to improve. Temple students made their mark in athletics, too. The Temple dominated the lineup of the 1977 baseball team, Opportunity's first one. Though it did not win a game against the other full-size city high schools, it was undefeated in preseason play.

During a student-teacher night, the Temple band provided entertainment, and Jim Jones presented the school with a $200 check for its athletic department. Some non-Temple parents were left scratching their heads, wondering who Jim Jones was. "For those of you who don't know him," Golden told the gathering, "he's the best thing that ever happened to San Francisco. . . ."

Yet Temple ties at Opportunity would start to unravel as the church experienced larger problems. Some faculty would begin questioning the relationship between Jones and Golden, who attended some Temple meetings but denied membership. School district officials would wonder whether the Temple had deliberately filled the school with students not eligible for enrollment there. A schools attorney would write an assistant superintendent:

"How did one-third to one-half of the student body of Opportunity II come to be Peoples Temple members within a short time? . . . how is it that all or most of the adolescent members of Peoples Temple met [admission] criteria, while only 300 of all adolescent students in all of San Francisco qualify? The case of Rev. Jones' sons, who are apparently academically successful, athletic, 'all-American' boys, seems particularly incongruous with the purpose of a continuation school."

During this time, Stephan Jones's relationship with Michelle Touchette flowered. Happy to be together, they would throw a football around, take walks in Golden Gate Park, and sometimes go to the movies. Since most members were living on two-dollar weekly allowances, Stephan had to filch money for his dates. He would sneak into his father's room in the San Francisco temple and rifle the pockets for loose change or a couple of bills. Jim Jones never locked his doors, and sometimes Stephan had the misfortune to barge in when his father was entwined with a lover. Most of the time he could steal away undetected. Despite his relationship with Michelle, Stephan Jones began feeling overwhelmed by conflicting emotions, the instability of his family life, the uprooting and transplanting, the rivalries with his siblings. He stayed behind one weekend in the San Francisco temple while the others made the long trek to Los Angeles. When he thought all the buses had pulled out, he took an overdose of Quaaludes. It was his second suicide attempt. But he was mistaken: not everyone had left. Jim Jones walked back into the Temple and found his unconscious son. Frantic, Jones called for help. Jim McElvane slapped Stephan conscious. They wrestled him to his feet, walked him downstairs and pumped his stomach. They forced coffee into him and gradually he came out of his stupor.

A short time later, Stephan was sent to a psychiatrist. His father insisted that no one, including the psychiatrist, was to know that Jim Jones was his father. Sharon Amos posed as his "mother" for these sessions. As a disguise, Stephan wore dark glasses and piled his hair under his hat. He felt he could talk about everything except what really bothered him—his father. After a few sessions, the psychiatrist told Stephan he need not come anymore because he seemed to have analyzed and worked out his problem.

The episode had one important consequence: it gave Marceline Jones an excuse to spend more time with her son and to move to San Francisco. She transferred to the nearby Berkeley office of the State Department of Health. And in early December 1976 the Temple fixed up a San Francisco apartment for her with an extra room for her family to stay overnight.

Marceline Jones knew about Stephan's hostility toward his father, but they talked about it only with restraint. Although she sometimes shared her problems with her son, more often she gave him motherly support. When Stephan showed an interest in acting, Marceline accompanied him to the American Conservatory Theater, San Francisco's principal repertory company, to investigate acting classes there. When Stephan wanted a place of his own, he and his mother found a second-story $250-a-month studio apartment. She even paid the first and last month's rent from her own salary and bought him a bed and television set.

Stephan's father had opposed the idea as elitist and only relented on the condition that Stephan not tell anyone about it. But living alone was an odd feeling for the lifetime communalist so Stephan soon had friends coming over at every chance. To pay expenses, he parked cars in a Chinatown garage. At last he was asserting his independence.

Christmas of 1976 was Marceline Jones's happiest holiday in years. With Stephan nearby, and Jimmy and Lew living with her, she felt like a new person; to make the holiday complete, she called her parents. She also invited them to visit.

The Baldwins arrived in San Francisco on February 5, 1977. The reunion was a joyous occasion. Then one week later the phone rang. It was Jones. When Marceline got off the phone, she was distressed: Jones wanted to take Stephan to Guyana the next morning. She had pleaded and argued against it, knowing Jones might well keep him there.

Marceline did not want her son six thousand miles away, especially at an age when he was ready to think about college and career. Yet she could see why Jones wanted Stephan in Jonestown. After all, their only natural son had already tried to commit suicide and now had his own apartment. How would it look if Jones's own son defected?

At first Stephan refused to go, then Jones gave assurances that he would be home within a week. When Marceline finally told him, "I want you to go," Stephan agreed to leave. Sadly, Marceline and her parents saw off the group the next morning.

Almost immediately upon arrival, Stephan was asked to remain in Jonestown permanently. He refused. Though he enjoyed the physical work and renewing his friendship with Mike and Al Touchette, Stephan longed for the San Francisco life—his new apartment, his newfound independence, acting lessons.

But two days later, as the entire group sat around the kitchen porch after work, Jones steered the conversation to the sacrifices people should be willing to make for the cause. Stephan became even more uneasy when Paula Adams—who disliked Jonestown's administrators—volunteered to quit Georgetown and settle for good in the jungle. Under pressure, Stephan, too, offered to stay. It was not so much that he was still intimidated by his father. He did not want to appear selfish, to feel like an outcast in the church, the only life he had known.

After returning to San Francisco without Stephan, Jones laid plans to ship down another of his sons. Despite the fact that Lew Jones and his wife Terri Carter were expecting their first child and were in the midst of Lamaze classes, Jones packed them off to Jonestown. The pretense was that Lew's work was lagging, and he had been picking up evil ways from an "outsider" who drank.

For the second time in a month, Marceline's family was wrenched apart. The departure crushed Mrs. Baldwin, who had loved Lew since the day he had arrived as a malnourished Korean orphan. But it soon was followed by the departure of another adopted son, Tim Jones, and his new wife, Sandy Cobb. Jimmy, Jr., was to be next. Once Jones had all the children in Jonestown, there was no chance that Marceline would renew her threat to leave him and take the children.

By late 1976, the Jonestown settlers had voted to step up their work. Instead of taking the evening off, they toiled until 11:00 P.M. They had built a large dormitory to house workers, but they badly needed more people to fill it—and to beef up the work crews.

By early 1977, Jonestown still had fewer than fifty settlers. The only buildings had been constructed of poles and canvas roofing, with crude floors. While awaiting a large load of lumber for building permanent structures, they cultivated several hundred acres of land. Sawmill construction was getting under way. The piggery and chickery were already built; the mill was grinding flour from cassava root. The *Cudjo* chugged regularly to Georgetown for supplies.

Despite his sacrifices, Stephan Jones came to love Jonestown. With his own work crew and responsibilities, Jim Jones's tall, skinny kid matured quickly. The troubled boy who had retreated within himself, sometimes to the point of aloofness or surliness, loved attacking the hardwood timber. As they cleared land with chain saws, axes and wedges, his muscles soon matched his newly found enthusiasm. His shoulders and chest thickened, and as he approached his eighteenth birthday, he acquired a powerful athlete's body—six feet five, broad shoulders tapering to a narrow waist. His legs were strong like his father's. He pulled his long black hair behind his neck and secured it with a colorful bandanna, accentuating his high cheekbones. He wore khaki fatigues tucked inside high-topped boots that protected him from snakes. At last, he looked like the tall Indian warrior his mother had envisioned at his birth.

Young Jones's arrival coincided with the first real construction spurt. He worked with Albert Touchette at manual labor, building bunk beds and toilets, digging wells and the like. On a typical day, Charlie Touchette made first calls at 5:00 A.M. If they overslept, they could always count on rambunctious Vincent Lopez to awaken the whole dorm when he jumped crashing out of bed. They ate a hearty breakfast of eggs, pancakes, chipped beef and toast, and by 6:30 were on the porch getting the day's assignments from the elder Touchette.

Once a couple of dormitories had been framed, Stephan and Albert laid flooring, learning as they went. During breaks the guys would line up and do calisthenics, jumping jacks, sit-ups, push-ups and some clowning around. Stephan liked to tackle Albert when his back was turned and have a good wrestle.

The settlers toiled till about six each day, with a lunch break and a midafternoon slowdown because of the hot sun. After an hour's break for dinners of barbecued chicken, macaroni and cheese, or pizza, Stephan and his crew returned to the sawmill until about ten, where they cut and finished wood for the next day's building. Charlie Touchette stood by with his sheet listing sizes and dimensions for the lumber cutting. A team of six men would pick up each huge slab of board and run it through the blade.

The next day, one crew would lay the posts, another the floors. A third would prefabricate the walls, and a fourth crew, Stephan's, would carry the frames out and set them up. Later they would install the doors and add roofing. Most of Jonestown was built that way, in little more than six months, thanks to sweat and long hours under the debilitating sun. Altogether, the crews built about sixty cottages.

The young men slept little more than about five hours a night, because they worked hard and played late. On nights when they did not work until ten, they would watch a movie and later fool around, running through the half-built dorms or playing cards, dominoes or chess in the recreation room. With so few women in Jonestown, some of the younger men caroused with the local girls in Port Kaituma.

Charlie Touchette's authority was undisputed. He kept track of the work and made assignments. The construction side ran beautifully, but the agricultural problems remained, largely because of the poor soil. To make matters worse, the settlers sometimes improperly rotated crops. And most suggestions for improvements were turned down by Jones because they cost money. It was particularly frustrating for attorney Gene Chaikin, who threw himself into the study of crops, plants and agriculture, and wrote memo after memo to Jones.

Perhaps the hardest worker was Tom Kice, the stepfather of Wayne Pietila, one of the Eight Revolutionaries. Kice, once a deer-hunting, dope-smoking millworker, could not shake some hostile feelings for Jim Jones, but was grateful for the church's positive influence on his trouble-prone son, Tommy, who learned to work on Jonestown crews. Tom, Sr., used to vow that he would kill a redneck some day. Kill he would —but it would be no redneck.

For Stephan, San Francisco seemed a distant memory. He missed his mother terribly, but still he was happier than he had ever been. He had become a big brother to John Victor Stoen, and he loved his tiny nephew, Chioke, newborn son of Lew and Terri. (Chioke had been Lew's Korean name before the Jones family adopted him.)

There was no paycheck at the end of the week—only the pride that came from building. Sometimes Stephan's crew worked into the small hours of the morning just to put up one more cottage than they had the day before. Stephan would stroll through the three hundred acres of cleared land and aluminum-roofed buildings and tell himself, "I put every nail in that cottage. I knocked down the trees to cut the wood to build that house." Others felt that pride too, and the enthusiasm was contagious.

One day late in 1976, Marshall Kilduff of the *San Francisco Chronicle* got to talking about Jones with some fellow observers of the Housing Authority scene. He, an *Examiner* reporter and an Authority executive customarily killed time before meetings, chatting over coffee in the executive's office; on this day, the office door was ajar and some of Jones's bodyguards loitered in the hall. Kilduff had never put much stock in the Kinsolving series in 1972 because he did not think much of Kinsolving's work, but he had observed the Temple's treatment of *Chronicle* reporter Julie Smith when she attempted a story in spring of 1976. He recalled aloud how Jones had tried blatant flattery on Smith and had somehow learned the exact contents of the story draft in her desk.

Jones's spies were working on this particular day as well. After the commission meeting, the minister approached Kilduff. "I hear you think I'm eccentric, and try to butter up the press." Kilduff replied: "I don't know how you would know that, but I would not say those things in public."

"I get the feeling you don't trust me," Jones said.

Rather than intimidating Kilduff, the exchange provided a catalyst. In the back of his mind, the intrigued reporter formulated an idea for a story—not a hard-hitting exposé, but the profile of a colorful local figure with a Pentecostal flair.

One Sunday at 11:00 A.M. in January of 1977, Marshall Kilduff walked into the labyrinth. By prearrangement, he passed through the iron-grille front gate and heavy wooden door to meet Dick Tropp—the Temple's resident professor—and a black woman from the Housing Authority who took him and about ten other visitors on a standard Temple tour. After a while, Kilduff became aware that the other visitors, who kept asking benignly leading questions about the church's good works, were Temple shills. Also, he noticed that, while the tour dragged on, about two thousand people were sitting in silence in the main auditorium, evidently waiting. Surely, he thought, they could not be holding up services for his sake. But they were.

On being escorted to a seat near the front of the auditorium, Kilduff discovered his own boss, *Chronicle* city editor Steve Gavin, and *Chronicle* reporter Katy Butler among the congregation. As they exchanged greetings awkwardly, he felt intimidated. He was unaware that his own co-workers would be attending the Temple services. Actually, it was Gavin's first visit, Butler's second. Kilduff, now decidedly uncomfortable, witnessed a service complete with testimonies, entertainment and a question-and-answer period in which Jones spoke against investments in South Africa.

The next day at the *Chronicle* Kilduff remarked to Gavin, "Quite a show. Don't you think we should do a story about this guy? I hear he's powerful politically."

"We've already done it," the city editor said, mentioning the Julie Smith article.

"That's right," Kilduff agreed, concluding that the *Chronicle* would not accept another story unless he could find something entirely new. But rather than dropping it, he decided to consider doing the piece free-lance, for a magazine. In digging deeper, he found strong opinions —opposition from some black ministers, approval from some community organizations that received Temple donations. One Communist party member said she and Angela Davis had misgivings about Jones's total discipline approach. Some applauded the Temple's radical Christianity; others voiced suspicions or talked of the humiliation of being pat-searched upon entering the Temple. Oddly enough, most did not want to be quoted.

In the meantime, Kilduff continued to gather personal impressions at the twice-monthly Housing Authority meetings. Jones stationed his aides near Kilduff and other newspaper reporters. The spies were so obvious about eavesdropping and peeking at their notes that the reporters were amused.

The Temple, worried about Kilduff's story, checked with friends and contacts at the *Chronicle* for an assessment of the reporter and his work. Eventually, they went through his garbage at home, looking for clues, and followed him around town, even to bars. They concluded that Kilduff, a San Francisco native and a Stanford University graduate, intended to vilify them because he was politically more conservative than the Temple and had never warmed to Jones.

The January issue of *Peoples Forum* alluded to Kilduff's research as an upcoming "attempt to 'smear' our human service work." And in March 1977 the Temple spread an editorial across the second page explaining their rationale for barring reporters from the Temple, refusing to grant interviews with Jones and opposing any article on the church. "The number of interested reporters is becoming overwhelming and . . . is disrupting our work," the editorial claimed.

What reporters might see at the Temple was of less consequence than what they might hear from defectors. And the worst potential defector from Jones's standpoint was Grace Stoen. Though drifting toward open opposition, she did not yet know that Kilduff was looking for people like her to interview.

In a sense, Grace Stoen already had declared war. On February 1, 1977, in a phone conversation with her estranged husband, she cast off past caution, graphically detailing her reasons for leaving and vowing her determination to wrest her son John away from the Temple. She wanted John Victor to live in San Francisco so she could at least have visitation rights. Instead Tim Stoen suggested she visit her son in South America. She commented sarcastically, "We don't have millions of dollars like some people." Then she complained, "He's not with his mother or father. . . . Why won't you let me see my little boy?"

In defending himself, Stoen parroted Jones's excuses. He said John was destined for a leadership role not just in the church but in the world. It was as though the five-year-old were heir to a throne.

Grace insisted that John be brought to San Francisco, where he could make a free choice between the Temple or her. Stoen in turn reminded her that she had once—while still in the Temple—granted permission for John to go to Guyana.

In a subsequent conversation with Jones, she asked whether John would be coming back to the States. Jones postured helplessness and answered as though the decision rested in the child's hands: "You never know what a little guy will want to do." He then made it sound as though Grace had endorsed the move to Guyana: "I think it was wise on everybody's part—yours, too—to allow it to take place."

Given his other documentation, Jones hoped to build a case that both legal parents had granted permission to have the child transported to Jonestown, thus insulating himself against charges of child stealing. In one undated document, Grace had written: "I gave my full permission to have my son, John Victor Stoen, go to the Promised Land for any reason." There were similar 1976 documents bearing her and/or Tim's signatures. In the most recent, dated September 30, 1976, during Grace's efforts to get John, Tim had named Jim Jones, Joyce Touchette and five other Temple members as his attorneys: "I specifically authorize . . . them to apply for passports or other travel documents on said minor's behalf; arrange for said minor to travel . . . out of the country. . . ."

At first, Grace Stoen had hesitated to seek a court order for John's return because she feared the Temple would hide the boy in Guyana, then claim no knowledge of his whereabouts. But now it looked as if all hope of reaching an out-of-court settlement had been destroyed. In February 1977, she threatened to file for divorce, and then did it.

The battle had escalated. Jones realized that Grace, as mother, would likely win any custody dispute in court, and that Stoen would be held in contempt if he failed to surrender the child. A contempt citation in the San Francisco district attorney's office would expose the paternity dispute to the public and fire up press interest. So Jones ordered Stoen to take a leave of absence from his job and hide out in Guyana.

After the voter fraud prosecutions, Stoen had moved over to the district attorney's special prosecutions unit. Now, in the middle of his first case, he called in two investigators: "Hate to do this to you," he apologized, then explained that his international law practice demanded that he take a leave of absence for business in London and South America. The investigators, who were not particularly happy to see their prosecutor leaving, were then asked a final favor: could they please take some of Stoen's packed belongings to his friend Billy Hunter's office for safekeeping? Stoen entrusted a trunk and a couple of boxes of personal things and papers to William Hunter, a black prosecutor who was about to be appointed U.S. Attorney in San Francisco. Stoen planned to send for the belongings when he needed them.

In mid-February 1977, just a few months after escorting Lieutenant Governor Mervyn Dymally to Jonestown, Stoen boarded a plane for his new home. Unlike other settlers, however, he kept himself means of escape. Before leaving San Francisco, he obtained a new passport and had his father begin to set up private bank accounts for him in Colorado.

Did he want the passport as a backup in case the Temple confiscated his old one? Was he simply trying to preserve his personal options, his freedom of movement? Was he guilt-ridden over his complicity in the exile of John and actually trying to rescue the boy, as he later would claim? Or was he simply preparing a quick escape route for himself in case the Kilduff investigation proved particularly damaging?

These very questions quickly came to preoccupy Jones. Just after Stoen left San Francisco, Jones intercepted a letter from Tim's father along with checks from his new Colorado bank account. "Dear Tim, We followed your instructions. . . . Your savings book came today. You did not say when you were leaving so hope this reaches you in time. Were photos all right? . . . Love, Dad." The letter was dated February 16—the very day Stoen had left for Guyana. To Jones, these unauthorized bank accounts spelled disloyalty at the least and possibly desertion. In a frenzy, he immediately arranged to fly to Guyana with several aides.

Stoen, working in the sawmill at the time, had caught sight of Jones's chartered plane as it passed over the settlement. A short time later, he found himself being taken to a cabin for interrogation. Jones did not seem at all worried about Stoen skipping out with millions of dollars from the Temple accounts he had set up. He accused Stoen of plotting to kidnap John Victor. Stoen denied it. The personal bank accounts were aberrations, remnants of his irrepressible materialism, the lawyer said. Eventually Jones appeared to accept this story, though in private he told Mike Touchette to make sure that Stoen did not take the boy out of the camp. He then left.

Touchette would not have allowed Stoen to snatch John Victor anyway. As John's "big brother" in Jonestown, he felt the last thing the boy needed was another emotional wrenching. From Touchette's perspective, the boy had been kicked around all his life, from Grace to Maria and now to Mike's own mother, Joyce. Like Jim Jones as a child, John Victor craved attention and affection. His dark eyes glimmered every time someone showed him love. He had been confused and used, turned gradually against his traitor mother, told that she was a "capitalistic whore bitch." Tim, on the other hand, despite the paternity question, was held high in the boy's esteem—as his "second dad," behind Father Jim. Perhaps it was less a biological than an organizational distinction.

Thinking he had outsmarted Jones, Stoen worked nearly fourteen hours a day in the Jonestown sawmill so that no one could accuse him of being an elitist. He knew his fellow settlers were scrutinizing his own conduct and were guarding John. They found Stoen's nice-guy demeanor suspect, and did not appreciate his complaints about back pains or his tortured faces. Some were relieved when his output tapered off and he was assigned to do paperwork.

Despite Jones's concerns that Stoen might nab John, some settlers felt Stoen neglected the boy, and that John's feelings were hurt. In his delicate position, Stoen really could not win. He did set aside time each day to be with John, to help him with studies. He sat with him during meetings or entertainment, though he was circumspect about showing his feelings in public. In the bunkhouse one day, however, he told John that he was so proud of him that he had written someone a letter praising him. John leaned back in his bunk, hands behind his head, and said like a true egalitarian, "Ya know, you shouldn't brag about your kid."

After almost a month in the jungle, Stoen had written a postcard to attorney Gene Chaikin, who was then in the States: "I am really enjoying Guyana. People are so considerate and helpful. . . . My son, John

Victor, is with me and doing great. He can read, has developed motor coordination and . . . is happy as a lark."

When Stoen mailed the postcard about March 18, he had already moved to Georgetown to do legal work. He set up meetings with the deputy prime minister and the ministry of home affairs, did legal research at Georgetown libraries and wrote the University of West Indies in Trinidad, asking how to obtain a law license for the Caribbean. But, at the same time, he drew up another agenda. He felt a growing need to get away. He needed to think about the future, and perhaps return to California to see his latest love, a nonmember.

On March 13, he drafted a tentative travel schedule and the message he apparently wanted to be left behind him: "I have gone to States [with my] own money. Am planning to return to teach at Univ. [of Guyana] end of Sept. Am in love with a black woman—must *see* her and handle on own. Will call before entering Calif."

Stoen's escape took a different form than originally planned. On Sunday, March 20, the Temple issued him $147 Guyanese for travel to explore admission to the Caribbean bar and to tend to other legal business. According to entries in his trip log, he stopped in Barbados Monday, Trinidad Tuesday and Wednesday. On Wednesday, still in Port of Spain, he took a taxi to the law school to see about being admitted to practice. The last entry: a milkshake at the Port of Spain Holiday Inn. Tim Stoen then vanished.

Two days later, a telegram arrived at the Peoples Temple house in Georgetown: "Must stay nine more days. Due Timehri [Georgetown airport] 2 April 1905 British Airways . . . Timothy."

The telegram panicked the Georgetown Temple staff. Immediately they began calling hotels and guest houses in Port of Spain. Finding no trace of Stoen, they transmitted the news to San Francisco. Word reached Jones. At the conclusion of a Housing Authority meeting that day, with his guards huddled around him and in full view of reporters, Jones suddenly crumpled to the floor.[46] As aides helped him to his feet and a commission member checked his pulse, an *Examiner* reporter asked guard Chris Lewis: "What happened?"

"He works day and night," Lewis said. "He attends conferences and counsels drug addicts."

As an aside Marshall Kilduff commented: "He pulls it all the time."

In fact, this collapse might well have been planned, even though loss of Stoen—even temporarily—would traumatize Jones. Real or not, the public fainting spell created an excuse for Jones's own absence from upcoming Housing Authority meetings. It allowed Jones to slip out of town unnoticed the next day.

While their pastor flew to Guyana, Temple members were assigned to find Stoen. Two of them went to the district attorney's office and learned that Stoen, without letting on that he was secretly fleeing the church, had recently sent word to prosecutor Billy Hunter, asking that his baggage be sent on to London. Thinking fast, they volunteered to take care of shipping the belongings themselves. Hunter accepted the offer.

Sandy Bradshaw and Mike Prokes loaded the baggage aboard an eastbound jet and boarded the same flight. At the end, they deduced, they would find Stoen. In London, however, they waited hours and hours in the baggage claim area. No sign of Stoen. After a long flight and a sleepless night, they were exhausted. Had their quarry avoided the trap?

Several days earlier, Stoen had checked into the London Musical Club, a sedate place where he could listen to classical music, relax and sort out his life. Like other vacillators, he felt he needed pampering and peace from the years of crisis. He bought tickets to plays, planned to set up jazz piano lessons, took long therapeutic walks and neatly jotted it all in his diary. He felt free at last on the streets of London.

Then, on Monday, March 29, after doing his laundry, he called the airport and found that his baggage had arrived. The next day, he went to pick it up.

In the airport cargo area, he was startled by Prokes and Bradshaw; he had not expected to be tracked down in London. His decidedly unfriendly pursuers made it clear that Jones believed Stoen was defecting; their orders were to bring him back. When Stoen balked, Bradshaw and Prokes told him, falsely, that Chris Lewis was waiting outside. Stoen finally agreed to call Jones, who was in Guyana.

On the phone, Jones's approach was to bribe Stoen into staying. "What do you want to convince you to stay with us?"

"I want women and jazz," Stoen replied.

"We'll buy the Holiday Inn in Grenada, and you can run it as a socialist convention center," said Jones. He always had said that everyone had his price.

Hotel or no hotel, Stoen finally agreed to return to Guyana to assist Jones in legal matters. But first he wanted to stay in London for a few days to see a Shakespeare play.

"Do you realize Shakespeare was a homosexual?" Jones retorted.

"I don't want to talk about it," Stoen snapped.

While Prokes returned to the United States, Sandy Bradshaw stayed behind to make sure Stoen boarded a plane for Guyana soon. Though Bradshaw despised Stoen, they made the best of their time together. They dined out and saw *Julius Caesar*, which Stoen followed in a book. On April 3, they went to Heathrow Airport together. But Bradshaw stopped outside the British Airways passenger gate as Stoen boarded the plane for Guyana. He looked back, surprise on his face. She had led him to believe that she would be going to Georgetown with him. Instead, she took a flight back to the United States, her mission nicely accomplished.

When Stoen landed, Jones and his aides exerted unrelenting pressure on him. They desperately wanted him to stay, though they would never completely trust him again; he knew too much to be let go. To reinforce his pleas, Jones suffered a "heart attack" or collapse almost every evening. Teri Buford and Carolyn Layton kept pleading with Stoen: "Jim will die unless you commit your life to the cause." But it was Jones himself who finally brought his majordomo into line one day as they strolled nearby along Third Street, airing their feelings. Stoen said he believed in Temple teachings but found the authoritarianism hard on him. The warm, loving environment with talent shows and camping trips had dissolved, he said, and now a life-or-death seriousness tinged everything about the church. As they walked, Jones stopped to gesture at some fruit trees in a yard. "Tim," he said with utter sincerity, "I don't think anyone in the world has a right to enjoy that fruit until everyone has." That appeal to his socialistic instincts touched a chord in Stoen's heart. He agreed to rededicate himself to the cause.

Stoen bore close watching, but he was too valuable now to be put on a Jonestown sawmill crew. The focal point of Temple activity was finally shifting to Guyana after two years of preparation. As Jones and his chief lieutenants converged on the country, the Jonestown administrators were called into the Guyanese capital for meetings at 41 Lamaha Gardens, a spacious house recently purchased in an attractive section of town.

In recent weeks, Jones had decided to move the church yet again. The pressure in the United States was too much for him—or rather the prospect of what might be revealed was. One day about this time, he paced the house, obsessed with the Kilduff article, certain that it would be negative and destructive. Suddenly, he stopped his railing and turned to Mike Touchette: "What do you think about moving a lot of people down here quickly?"

"It's impossible," replied Touchette. "We don't have the wood for housing."

Pacing again, obviously irritated, Jones persisted: "How many people could we accommodate now?"

"About 150 to 200 people at the maximum." Touchette explained that the Jonestown crews had been hampered by the financial bureaucracy and by the rainy season. Although to date only one permanent structure had been built—a dormitory—Jones pressed ahead with his plans to bring a thousand Americans to the jungle. From April 27 through May 1, 1977, Jones and his top aides—Stoen, Gene Chaikin, Hastings law student Harriet Tropp, Teri Buford, Carolyn Layton and, occasionally, Marceline Jones—met for sixteen to twenty hours a day in the master bedroom of the Lamaha Gardens headquarters.

The other church leaders echoed the worries of their leader. They had agonized over their problems so much that they were becoming self-fulfilling prophecies. The only handwriting on the wall, in May 1977, was their own. Marshall Kilduff had yet to locate a single damaging informant and had not even found a publication to print his story. That did not matter to Jones. He was a prophet, and he had foreseen it all. Of course, no one suspected that the apparent machinations of the church's enemies really were plotted—at least invited—by Jones. In fact, the exodus to Guyana would follow in almost every detail the organizational blueprint drawn up four years earlier, prior even to acquisition of the Caribbean sanctuary. Jones's contagious paranoia—not enemies—was driving them out of the United States.

The threats could have been survived, but through tactical blunders and overkill, Temple leadership would aggravate their existing problems and create new ones. Though they fretted about government investigations, government agencies in reality were uninterested in them. The FBI, still smarting over disclosures of its antileftist campaigns in the 1960s, was not involved and would not be until it was too late. The Federal Communications Commission was monitoring Temple amateur radio transmission but only for minor infractions of amateur radio rules that could easily have been stopped. Some defectors were talking to the Treasury Department, but efforts to intercept smuggled weapons would be feeble and ineffective. The IRS was only questioning whether the Temple's political activity exceeded standards for tax-exempt organizations—and only after the church wrote repeatedly asking whether it was under investigation.

Fear of the unknown played upon Jones's fixations. He returned to San Francisco in a morose mood. The future looked grim. Of course no one on the outside knew of the plans for an exodus. But, by coincidence, the Temple was asked a short time later to participate in a Golden Gate Bridge demonstration opposing suicide. The organizers called the rally to dramatize their objective: the installation of suicide barriers along the span to prevent people from climbing the low railing and jumping off.

On Memorial Day, 1977, Jones and some six hundred of his followers showed up at the Golden Gate, each wearing an armband bearing the name of one of the bridge's victims. With local news media and wire services looking on, Jones delivered a generalized appeal of concern for suicide victims. Then abruptly his tenor changed: suddenly *he* was the one being driven to the brink: "Suicide is a symptom of an uncaring society," he said. "The suicide is the victim of conditions which *we* cannot tolerate, and, and. . . ." He paused, realizing he had misspoken. "I guess that was Freudian because I meant to say, 'which *he* cannot tolerate,' which overwhelm him, for which there is no recourse."

Jones then became even more direct: "I have been in a suicidal mood myself today for perhaps the first time in my life, so I have personal empathy for what we are doing here today." Then he ended with an abrupt "Thank you."

While Tim Stoen and others took notes, the Georgetown group considered various plans for the evacuation. About 450 people could be transported in each of two large trips, with the remainder trickling down; or 100 a month could be brought down, fully populating Jonestown by

February 1978; or 250 a month could be transported for a completion date of August 15, 1977.

A rapid exodus entailed certain disadvantages. It would take time to prepare members so they would not rebel or tattle to reporters or the government. Also, the plan required that the church sell off its stateside properties; if the process were rushed, prices would be lower. Finally, by moving everyone to Guyana too quickly, the church would lose job income and some government payments, not to mention offerings at services.

Workers and people on fixed incomes would come first, it was decided. Maria Katsaris would be sent early because the Temple believed her father might try to get conservatorship over her, a tactic used by parents of Moonies. But generally key people would stay behind in the United States to hold together the organization and present a front of business-as-usual. Jim McElvane, whose sister owned a Los Angeles real estate office, would sell off stateside properties—including the Los Angeles and San Francisco temples—producing an estimated $1.2 million.

For hours, the hierarchy debated whether Jim Jones should return to the United States or hide in Guyana. By staying, he would confuse defectors and news media. But staying also would create a higher risk of violence—either *to* Jones or *from* him. Furthermore, in Guyana Jones could avoid the threat of arrest over the John Stoen custody matter. Jones decided to go back to San Francisco, but only temporarily.

The arrival of the immigrants was planned: everyone, no matter what his status, first must work two weeks in the Jonestown fields to become conditioned to the regimen of jungle life, to give leaders time to assign jobs, and to save money by allowing the layoff of local Guyanese field workers.

The housing plans did not jibe with the earlier visions of Charlie Touchette—of nice cottages housing two couples each, or three in a pinch. The church leadership now wanted cabins that would hold twelve people; they wanted five dormitories to hold forty-two people each, and a mess hall. Sitting in that spacious Georgetown house, the leaders allocated jobs to people by name and set their daily schedules. Work would begin at 6:30 A.M. and continue until 6:00 P.M. seven days a week, with an hour for lunch —"but try to limit to one half [hour]," added Stoen's note. The nights were filled too: on Sunday a meeting, Monday a movie, Tuesday free time or a meeting, Wednesday a meeting and socialist classes, Thursday free time, Friday children's night with wieners, Saturday farm night.

Though Stoen helped plan the mass migration, other members viewed him with mounting suspicion. Jones did not trust him; he felt nagging concerns about Stoen's short-lived defection and wanted to know step by step what he had done in his travels. He soon found the answer. One day while the lawyer was out on business, Jones and his aides stood staring at the small leather briefcase Stoen had left behind. "I wish there was a way to open that," Jones said. It took a member ninety minutes to pick the combination lock. Two staff women took a quick inventory, then relocked and replaced the briefcase before Stoen returned. Stoen was none the wiser.

The conclusion drawn from their examination, as expressed in a memo to Jones from "T.B.": "I am convinced that Stoen is so absolutely dual that it is not funny." The inventory took note, facetiously, of a love letter to a woman named Beverly; more important, it noted that Stoen was carrying a picture of him with Grace, and many pictures of him with John. A few other items were bound to exacerbate Jones's paranoia, too. One was a newspaper clipping about Stoen's arrest in East Germany, and his strange anticommunist diary from that period—these alone would be enough to allow Jones to say that his attorney was a government infiltrator. The second item was the diary Stoen kept during his brief defection —in that, Jones discovered indications that Stoen held various private bank accounts. The kicker was Stoen's new, secretly obtained passport, dated February 9.

With the rifling of Stoen's briefcase, Jones had come to believe that his chief attorney might well be a government agent and potential thief. Stoen was certainly a potential enemy. And his later explanation—that the East Berlin affair had happened years ago and he merely had neglected to mention it—did not ease Jones's fears. Nevertheless, Stoen kept on working for the church. He and other top aides joined Jim and Marceline Jones and their four sons on a May 7, 1977, flight to Grenada, a newly independent Caribbean nation with a fragile economy which desperately needed investment dollars. The Temple contingent met with Prime Minister Eric M. Gairy to discuss Temple plans to put one million dollars in banks there. The group, in turn, received government assurance that land could be made available for establishment of a mission. Before leaving, the Temple leadership explored the purchase of the Grenada Holiday Inn.[47]

Back in Georgetown, under the watchful eyes of other members, Stoen continued helping with preparations for the influx of new settlers. It became clear that continued Temple membership held hazards for the attorney. In fact, he composed for himself a memo outlining "factors" in his future. Under "PT/JJ," he noted: "Publication negative article, removal tax exempt status, prosecution of individual members. . . ." Under "Personal Factors" he wrote, "Indictment, divorce, new job, remarriage, protecting John, helping Jim."

Such prospects weighed on Stoen, and it began to show. One of his compatriots at Lamaha Gardens reported his disenchantment in a memo to "Mr. Hill" (code for Jones). "Mary Ruth" said that "George" (Stoen) had hinted at unhappiness, had said he would be useless to the church if Guyana authorities did not allow him to practice law or teach at the university. "He is completely detached from everything going on here," Mary Ruth went on. "He leads our organization meetings but . . . he is detached, and before a point is settled, he wants to go on to the next item.

"I think George is making groundwork to split," she concluded.

"He has his passport, he has money, and he has enough freedom of movement. . . ."

On June 12, Paula Adams reported to "Mr. Hill": "George left in the van at approximately four-thirty this morning without letting anyone know where he was going."

The Lamaha Gardens staff checked all flights and found no reservations for Stoen to New York. Stoen did return, briefly, only to vanish again later that very day. Two days later, Debbie Touchette was able to confirm that he had slipped out of Georgetown, most likely aboard a Pan Am flight for New York, with his friend Mike V. The last Guyana sighting of Stoen was Sunday at the Tower Hotel, where he had mentioned to a clerk that he was in a rush to catch a plane.

By way of New York, Stoen returned to the San Francisco Bay Area to see the love he had left behind. He was stunned to find her engaged to someone else. Shaken, he retreated home to Colorado for a while, then made another trip to Europe to straighten out his thoughts and make decisions. He did not want to turn against Jim Jones publicly, but he did want to help Grace retrieve John from the jungle. In July, with Kilduff's Temple exposé about to appear in *New West* magazine, Stoen met with his estranged wife in Colorado and discussed strategy for getting John back. They disagreed. She wanted to use the courts; he wanted to negotiate. He still identified with the Temple.

Stoen later would say that his departure had been triggered by the noblest of motives. Citing the guards around John, he would deny abandoning the boy. In fact, he would say that his flight from Guyana had been designed to bring the boy ultimately home to his mother: he could serve as an agent of reconciliation between Jones and his enemies back in the United States—and in return for his loyalty, he could demand the child. But Stoen would be in no position to act as intermediary. He too would become a primary target of press and government attacks.

THIRTY-FIVE

Scandal

While the Temple leadership, afraid of Marshall Kilduff's story, secretly drew up their evacuation plans, they anxiously watched each frustrating step that the reporter took in search of a publisher. In about March 1977, *New West* magazine finally gave Kilduff the go-ahead for his story. When he requested an interview with Jim Jones, however, a Temple spokesman wanted a pre-interview interview to size up the reporter. Several church members, including Mike Prokes, tried to put him on the defensive, pressuring to make him to write either a favorable story or no story at all. "We hear you are very conservative. . . ."

Kilduff assured them he would be objective, but they argued that even positive coverage hurts church work and invites racist attacks. The Temple promised to call Kilduff soon with a verdict on his interview request. Instead, a delegation visited Kevin Starr, then editor of *New West*, and convinced him that a story would harm their humanitarian work.

Again without a publisher, Kilduff went to *San Francisco* magazine. They became interested, so Kilduff began writing and further researching the story. The Temple watched his moves and reported everything to Kilduff's boss at the *Chronicle*.

Soon Gavin called in Kilduff, told him the church was very upset with his story and admonished him not to identify himself as a *Chronicle* reporter or to do the article on company time.

Kilduff's finished story for *San Francisco* fell miles short of Jim Jones's fears. It did not even include the allegations from the days of Kinsolving. Not a single defector was quoted. It was an admittedly muddy story about a peculiar public official. *San Francisco*'s editors rejected the piece because Kilduff had neither proved his suspicions nor drawn a concise portrait of Jones.

The news was disheartening. Kilduff felt beaten. Almost as if to flaunt its victory, the Temple carried the following item in the April issue of *Peoples Forum*, without naming Kilduff: "To date he has not been able to get any periodical to ally with him. However, he continues to make the rounds, trying to convince different periodicals that a 'smear' of a liberal church that champions minorities and the poor would make 'good copy.' "

Within a few months of *New West*'s refusal Kilduff went back to the magazine. In the interim, Rosalie Wright had replaced Kevin Starr as editor, and on the second go-around, *New West* agreed to publish a revised story with new material. Furthermore, it also assigned one of its own reporters—Phil Tracy, who had become interested in the church while living with the brother of Temple member Carolyn Looman. This time the writers concentrated on the political rise of Jones. The new story raised questions about Temple guards, hostility, paranoia, secrecy. It asked: Why is it that a politically important group is unwilling to talk about its inner workings?

In fact, there was little explosive material even in this revision, and the story would have inflicted minimal damage, if any, were it not for the Temple's overreaction. As the church called in debts and pushed its friends forward, *New West* began receiving dozens of letters and phone calls from prominent citizens. Politicians contacted the owner, Australian publishing magnate Rupert Murdoch, on Jones's behalf. Dozens of the magazine's advertisers were encouraged by callers to drop ads in protest. At the height of the campaign, the magazine's editorial offices received as many as fifty phone calls and seventy letters a day.

The letter-and-phone campaign proved to be a godsend to Tracy and Kilduff. *San Francisco Examiner* political columnist Bill Barnes had heard about it, and decided to write up "the story behind the story," inevitably raising the question: What exactly did Jim Jones have to hide? As advance interest was building, defectors in the Bay Area were alerted that someone was willing to listen to their stories.

The holes in the Kilduff-Tracy piece were soon filled in by defectors who started to call *New West* two days later, some anonymously. Their allegations, though not dissimilar to those in the Kinsolving stories almost five years earlier, went far beyond that article's charges of eccentricity. They included beatings, mysterious deaths and sexual deviations. Suddenly the story had spread into something much broader than the profile of a politically well-connected church.

But the reporters needed sources to make public their allegations. So one night in the home of Jeannie and Al Mills, Tracy and Kilduff met with a group of a dozen or so defectors—Grace Stoen, Walt Jones, Jim Cobb, Wayne Pietila among them. The reporters convinced them that their safety could best be ensured by going on the record with photographs; if any harm then came to them, the Temple would be blamed.

Meanwhile, the Barnes article had struck a personal chord in me. Since my conversations with Sammy Houston in the fall of 1976 and the first few months of 1977, I had moved from the Associated Press to the *Examiner*. A short time later, by coincidence, my AP news editor Jim Willse joined the *Examiner* as city editor. We both remembered Sam's story and thought the *Examiner* should take a look at the church. Willse pulled me in from the East Bay bureau to San Francisco to work full time with veteran reporter Nancy Dooley. Now the church faced two major news investigations.

Before either the *Examiner* or *New West* could publish a word about internal church activities, the Temple received another blast of adverse publicity: on July 17, *New West* reported a break-in at its San Francisco offices. It took four days for the police to issue a report finding no evidence of a burglary after all. The Temple labeled the episode a publicity-generating ruse, and Temple friends took solace, convinced that the story was going to be an irresponsible broadside.

While the Temple pushed its prominent supporters to commit themselves publicly and battered *New West* with harassing calls and letters, Jones made flight plans. One day in July 1977, Cecil Williams took a phone call during a counseling session. It was Jones, sounding far away. "I'm at the international airport in Los Angeles. I'm getting ready to leave the country for Guyana. I wanted to talk to you first. Should I go or shouldn't I . . .?" Jones explained that the news media were destroying him with false accusations, and that he expected the government to gang up on him too. "The motherfuckers don't have the power, and I'll show them."

"You don't have the power if they can make you run," Williams said. "They have the power."

"You don't understand."

Williams advised him to stay and take on the accusations, whatever they might be. It was still several weeks before *New West* and the *Examiner* published. But Williams would never again hear from Jones directly. The pastor of Peoples Temple had run, ignoring friends and allies who had admonished that it would be perceived as an admission of guilt.

Finally, in late July, the long-awaited August issue of *New West* appeared. Entitled "Inside Peoples Temple," the article told the stories of ten defectors and displayed in counterpoint Jones's political trophies and connections. It documented the "crimes"; yet it did not—and could not —provide a cogent explanation. Despite the sensational new disclosures, the nature of the organization remained murky: ". . . life inside Peoples Temple was a mixture of spartan regimentation, fear and self-imposed humiliation." The article went so far as to add a section: "Why Jim Jones Should Be Investigated." It cited areas of possible wrongdoing and danger—operation of care homes, property donations, treatment of young charges and signs of an exodus. "The story of Jim Jones and his Peoples [Temple]," the article concluded, "has only begun to be told. . . ."

Locally, the article created a stir; it was picked up by wire services and described briefly in newspaper articles. Tracy appeared on local talk shows and started preparing a second article, about suspicious deaths in the Temple. Kilduff went back to the *Chronicle*. His rather contrite city editor Steve Gavin came to him and gave him free rein to cover new developments.

Many Temple friends in the liberal and progressive communities dismissed the story as bad-mouthing by disgruntled former members or as part of a rightist campaign. Some viewed the story as the second volley of an attack that had started with an uncomplimentary *New West* story about Mayor Moscone. The article, though hard-hitting, did not in any sense deal a lethal blow to the organization; much of the damage could have been repaired, some of the allegations blunted, the ugly picture tinted if only Jones had dug in for a fight.

Lavish expressions of solidarity marked a July 31 rally designed to unify Temple members and their supporters. Some public figures stood before the Geary Boulevard congregation to impugn the motives of the attackers; others simply, and safely, reiterated their endorsement of the church's good works. Public officials across the spectrum leaped to Jim Jones's empty pulpit to defend him without ascertaining the truth of the *New West* allegations. Some of the Temple's siege mentality had actually rubbed off.

State Assemblyman Willie Brown: "When somebody like Jim Jones comes on the scene, that absolutely scares the hell out of most everybody occupying positions of power in the system."

Yvonne Golden, principal of Opportunity High School: "We who support Rev. Jim Jones will continue to stand behind him. We find solace in the eloquence of Thomas Paine: 'Tyranny like hell is not easily conquered. . . .'"

The climax of the rally was Jones's long-distance speech, transmitted by radio from Guyana. His voice a combination of Billy Graham-on-amphetamines and petulant, foul-mouthed child, he delivered a long scatalogical diatribe, calling his enemies "bitches" and "bastards," vowing that the press never would get him. "I know some of you are wanting to fight," Jones shouted over the loudspeakers. "But that's exactly what the system wants. They want to use us as sacrificial lambs, as a scapegoat. Don't fall into this trap by yielding to violence, no matter what kind of lies are told on us or how many. . . ." The crowd sprung to their feet time and time again, jutting their fists into the air. Their sustained screaming bordered on hysteria.

When Jones finished, State Assemblyman Art Agnos, who was visiting for the first time, turned to county supervisor candidate Harvey Milk. "Harvey, that guy is really wild."

Milk smiled. "Yeah. He's different all right."

Particularly ardent support came from the black community's watchdog and guardian—the *Sun Reporter*. Without investigating, Dr. Goodlett wrote a lengthy front-page editorial dismissing the article, upbraiding the authors and questioning the sources.

In the meantime, Nancy Dooley and I had found many of the people interviewed by *New West*. Other defectors came forward, given courage by signs of media interest. When word spread that the *Examiner* was pursuing the story too, I was invited to meet with a group of former members at Mickey Touchette's apartment.

Her Cole Street apartment was located several blocks from Haight Street in an area crammed with cars, stucco duplexes and a good number of Victorians, all gently rising toward Twin Peaks. I was the first arrival. As she set out nibbling food, I found myself wondering how she had got mixed up in all this: it was difficult to imagine Mickey Touchette as anyone other than a San Francisco office worker in her mid-twenties. I had no idea that her parents were the "administrators" of Johnstown.

She spoke with the pleasantly softened twang of a midwesterner. "My grandparents heard about Jones in Indianapolis in the early 1960s, and my family came in 1966 and spent the summer in Ukiah." She explained how the ties gradually became closer, through Jones's "healing" of her grandfather's heart attack and through Jones's predictions of nuclear holocaust in Indiana. "We thought we were part of the chosen people."

As this young woman who had attended Indiana University and

California colleges talked about Jones's paranormal powers and healings, she smirked with disgust, "The power of positive thinking can do a lot for you." Yet not a word about socialism or the political content of Jones's earthy sermons slipped into her account; it was as though she was afraid the outside world would discount her story as political differences with Jones. Although I did not know it then, Jones would claim exactly that, calling Mickey Touchette and other members of the so-called Eight Revolutionaries "violent terrorists."

The rest—including most of the Eight—arrived in bunches, some carrying potato chips, six-packs of beer or jugs of wine. They embraced one another like long-lost relatives or friends. Most were young whites in their twenties.

Soon Tracy and Kilduff wandered in. They greeted their sources and welcomed me to this incredible story. They appeared a little weary, almost jaded about the material, though they seemed to inspire the respect and confidence of the eighteen defectors there, some from as far away as Ukiah and Los Angeles.

As the afternoon sun poured into the room, we settled into seats and drinks were poured. While others shared experiences or became reacquainted, I had my first opportunity to sit down with a large sampling of former members. It was no easy job to size up or define Peoples Temple. No label seemed to fit. At the time I looked upon the Temple as a church with a survivalist outlook, a charismatic leader, a dose of political-social activism and a Mafia-like code of silence.

That last characteristic—of secrecy enforced through intimidation—fascinated me. It was—and would remain—the biggest obstacle to me as a reporter. After the frustration of trying to find willing talkers, this gathering was almost an informational overload. One person after another stated fears about "going public," as they called it. "It's hard to believe that a few months ago, all of us were in fear, of each other and of Jones," said Elmer Mertle, who explained that he had changed his name to Al Mills in order to hide from his past and any pursuers.

The ex-members recited other incidents, some of which were revolting, cruel, almost incomprehensible to me. As they did so, it became apparent to me that Jones was a very clever man who protected himself legally; terrible as they were, the incidents hardly seemed provable or prosecutable.

—Anthony Rubin was drugged so Jones could raise him from the dead.

—As punishment, Danny Pietila was drugged with a piece of cake, then raised by Jones.

—A boy was forced to eat his own vomit.

—Someone named Marvin Wideman was beaten.

—A woman was stripped and ridiculed after expressing sexual desire for Jones.

—Twelve-year-old Curtis Buckley died, possibly of a drug overdose, because church members tried to treat him by putting a picture of
Jones over his heart.

The ultimate cruelty recounted by these defectors was the story of
the poisoned wine. They described it as a test of loyalty. "Jones suggested
that we commit mass suicide to leave our mark on the world," said Walter
Jones. "He tested us every minute one way or another. Daily, you could
see him getting crazier."

The group session provided an abundance of new leads and new
contacts. Nancy Dooley and I expanded our list of sources among former
Temple members to more than two dozen, and confronted the politicians
and other Temple supporters.

Given the remarkable contrast between the Temple's public image
and the internal practices, we had to apply a high degree of caution in
weighing our information. Generally, we used a two-source rule to determine whether to use a given story, but often we had a half-dozen backup
sources supporting particularly serious allegations. Even then, some
statements from the defectors seemed too wild or explosive to use; for
example, it seemed irresponsible to use the faked poisoning incident because it appeared a test of loyalty rather than a plan for mass suicide. It
had been presented to us as theatrics, a cruel mind game mixed with
gallows humor.

The credibility of our sources was another important consideration,
no matter how many confirmed the allegations. Numerous times we asked
ourselves, "How could intelligent, seemingly well adjusted people join and
put up with that abuse? How reliable is information from people who
would follow such a man?" The answers were never 100 percent conclusive. Yet members who went public seemed to have nothing to gain by
doing so; many apparently dreaded it. Their stories jibed well with documentation the *Examiner* obtained; their stories appeared consistent with
a pattern of Jones's past troubles and disregard for legal formalities. And
most important, the accounts of various members—whether interviewed
personally in the Bay Area or by phone all over California—meshed and
matched to a reassuring degree.

After a few weeks of investigation, Nancy Dooley and I wrote what
would be the first of two lengthy front-page packages for the Sunday
Examiner. Probably more than a million people saw the headline story
on August 7, 1977. "Rev. Jones: The Power Broker; Political Maneuver-
ings of a Preacher Man." An opus by newspaper standards, the story filled
dozens of column inches and featured sidebars, including a history going
back to Jones's monkey-selling days in Indiana.

The Temple responded, predictably, with a gush of mail. They had,
however, learned a lesson from the Bill Barnes exposé—and refrained
from calling out their political friends.

The next story appeared on August 14, 1977. "The Temple, a Nightmare World," went beyond the *New West* article in describing a dehuman-

izing lifestyle—of children being assigned to beg in the streets, of two-dollar weekly allowances for adults who turned over everything, "catharsis" sessions, faked healings and resurrections, boxings and beatings. We also had been told about, but did not print, stories of children being punished with an electric shock device called the "blue monster" while their screams were amplified for the rest to hear. Though I had been told people would kill for Jones, it was not printed. There was no evidence, and I did not fully believe the accusation.[48]

Jones's departure made it easier for some people to abandon the Temple; but most of those in liberal and progressive circles adopted a wait-and-see posture without drawing definite conclusions. The church's most important supporters—namely Willie Brown, George Moscone and Carlton Goodlett—stood behind the Temple publicly.

Moscone was deeply disturbed by the *New West* article. His closest aides had the impression he felt duped. Nevertheless the mayor believed that until someone proved the allegations, his only tenable public position was support for his Housing Commission chairman. Moscone refused a political rival's demand that he launch his own inquiry into the Temple. But the mayor privately made it clear to Temple representatives in San Francisco that he did not want an absentee commissioner: he demanded to know how long Jones would be in Guyana. Housing officials, after checking with the Temple, assured him that Jones would be coming back soon. But a short time later, August 2, 1977, Jones dictated his resignation over the radio-telephone.[49]

THIRTY-SIX

Exodus

One afternoon in August 1977, a frantic man called the *Examiner*. He was desperate to speak to someone about his "common-law wife" of several years, Le Flora Townes. The call was transferred to me, and after a brief conversation I agreed to meet with him.

His upstairs Potrero District flat looked out over a block where Latino children played tag around cars left disabled on the sidewalks. After almost a minute of rapping, the door swung inward and there stood Harold Turley. His ebony skin glistened, and a few beads of water trickled down his neck to his clean white T-shirt. He smelled as though he had stepped out of a bath; his boxer shorts hung almost to his knees, nearly meeting his gartered black socks. We scaled the steep stairs.

In a back room, he cleared some clothing off the only chair, for me, then hunkered on a mattress; behind him the pastel-painted rooms were as naked as his knees. "She gave the furniture away," he explained. "She wants that new stove and icebox to go to the Temple."

It pained him obviously to talk to a stranger about his personal life, yet he had no hope of winning her back. "I wouldn't want her back because I'd be afraid of her," he snapped. "But somebody has to know the truth." Compulsively he told me his story:

Le Flora had followed Jones for almost seven years. A short time after her conversion, she and Harold began living together. They had never married because Jones opposed marriage. She badgered Harold to join her church, but he was turned off by the fifteen or twenty members he met over time; they always talked against the American system.

Their routine had been common enough. Le Flora had worked for a decade as a maid at a downtown hotel, while Turley did odd jobs and sometimes collected welfare or attended City College. Then Jones came between them.

"She's fifty-five and ignorant," he said. "She always tried to get me to go to the church. She'd talk all night long about Jim Jones. She used to brag about what she gave the church. She went four or five nights a week and gave well over a thousand dollars a year. She bought a brand-new washer and dryer and gave it to them too."

He held open a tiny notebook in the palm of his hand—a record of donations, in Le Flora's own shaky hand. Under the initials "P.T." ran columns of dates and amounts ranging from $5 to $100, some on back-to-back days. During three months she had donated a total of $572. She also contributed to the church by moonlighting at a Potrero Hill convalescent hospital donated to the Temple by her friends, James and Irene Edwards.

She began behaving strangely, Turley said. Before the Temple, her life had revolved around Christianity and church bingo games. But when she came home after Temple activities, including exercise and karate classes, she threw karate chops and kicks at dumbfounded Harold. She was full of vinegar. "She said they had her on guard duty at various times around the church and there were guard dogs too. This was after the arson fire at the church. She told me, 'We got girls who can whip yer ass.'"

All this confused and aggravated Harold Turley, especially when Le Flora visited the Temple every day for a solid week and would not tell him a single word about it afterward. It also miffed him when she paid $150 and took off from work to join a Temple trip to New York. He had his own Svengali theory to make sense of it:

"Jones had intercourse with every one of them. He had control of them sexually. When she tells me she'd sell her pussy for the church, what does that tell you?"

In disgust, he pushed to his feet and paced. Turning to face me, he went on, "She can barely read. She's ignorant, I tell you. And Jim Jones is a master of speaking. He's crude and clever. That's how he did it."

"But what was he after?" I asked.

"Her money," he said, explaining that she had accumulated some $98,482 in social security in forty years of working. "I saw the slip myself," he said. "Almost $100,000! And she can collect her social security payments in the other country. That's what they want."

For some time, Le Flora had talked about the Temple's Garden of Eden. "Jim's telling us to get our passports because something bad's gonna happen here," she told Harold. She had seen some films of the mission, and it did look like paradise, just like Jones said. Apparently jungle life agreed with her friends James and Irene Edwards; Edwards, a six-footer well over 200 pounds, had trimmed down to a fit 160 pounds in the tropics, she told Harold.

Then the phone calls from the Temple increased in frequency and urgency. One Wednesday, a caller told her, "You better get your passport quick." The next day she was gone. She took one suitcase, all that the immigrants were allowed to bring. She left behind a closet full of clothes, kitchen implements and appliances.

On the way out, she grinned and called to Harold: "I'm leavin'. I'm not supposed to say where I'm goin', but I'll write." She was tickled to be resettling in the Promised Land.

"When people get old, what will he do with them then?" Harold shouted back at her. "And suppose you don't like the place and want to come back? He's not going to permit that."

But Le Flora did not want to hear it. At midnight, five buses pulled away from the front of Peoples Temple: in one of them sat Le Flora Townes.

For many months, workers at the Immigration and Naturalization Service in San Francisco's Federal Building had observed a strange phenomenon. Hundreds—perhaps as many as five or six hundred by July 1977 —had come through the lines requesting passports for the obscure country of Guyana. They came in little groups. Most were either very young or very old people, and there was always a supervisor. Each was already prepared with the necessary shots, passport photos, passport fee and proof of citizenship. Nothing about the preparations was illegal. There was nothing to report to any authorities.

Earlier the Temple had required everyone to obtain a passport so that they could leave on short notice. If they did not have the money, the Temple paid. If they did not have birth certificates, the Temple wrote away for them. In some cases this was very difficult, since some older black people from the rural South had been born at home and their births were never recorded—but the church managed.

The Temple treated each of its immigrants as an important element in the new settlement. They were not simply herded aboard buses to airports. Extensive efforts to make the migration orderly required incredible paperwork for each individual. A check list for each traveler called for a submission of address change forms to the post office, disposing of pets, transfer of car title to the church, giving home keys to spouses staying behind, notification of relatives, payment of outstanding bills, discontinuation of some government payments, rerouting of others. The church collected brief medical histories on each settler. People signed medical releases and gave the church power of attorney over their children. Social security and bank account arrangements were made so the church would not lose those sources of income. In essence, the church took responsibility for putting in order the personal affairs of each future Jonestown resident.

In like manner the church straightened out its own business affairs. Before Maria Katsaris joined the exodus, she and other financial officers went around San Francisco closing many Temple bank accounts—one with at least $1 million—so the money could be moved overseas. The aides wired money to Guyana, sometimes as much as $500,000 per transaction, through local Canadian bank branches and New York. On a smaller scale, the Temple sent down $5,000 with each trusted immigrant. Some cash was carried by hand and declared; other large sums were hidden in baggage or on people's bodies. Much of this money was deposited in banks; some went into Jonestown, where hundreds of thousands of dollars were kept readily available. In the future, Jones's penchant for moving funds outside the United States would cause the Temple to wire excess money overseas whenever local bank accounts reached $300,000 to $500,000. To finance what became a $5 million capital investment in Jonestown, the Temple also would be selling off its California properties.[50]

Money was a serious business to Jones. Tim Stoen's betrayal had left him feeling financially vulnerable, and for good reason. Stoen—who once wrote "transfer all substantial monies to International Banks" as part of the Temple escape plan—had set up the theory behind the Temple's investment and monetary practices. His mandate came directly from Jones, who feared the U.S. government someday might freeze or seize Temple assets, which had grown to $10 million by 1975 and kept growing.[51]

Despite such wealth, amateurism and incompetence marked Temple finances. Stoen had been no financial wizard, and Jones had placed serious limitations on investments. Always wary, Jones wanted to keep his assets liquid for any sudden emergency. That prevented the church from making any semi-long-term investments that might bear excellent returns. Instead, the church mainly confined itself to thirty-day to ninety-day time deposits.

Secrecy had dominated the handling of Temple funds. Jones not only feared the government and private lawsuits, he also wanted to preserve the image of a poor, hand-to-mouth organization that poured all income into humanitarian endeavors. The deprived and frequently dunned church members would have been shocked to learn the extent of Temple holdings.[52] But the financial practices reflected Jones's frugality, in part inherited from his mother, and his lifelong dread of debt. Fat bank accounts lent a measure of power and security to a man with great and costly ambitions, and potentially expensive problems. He even kept an account for legal defense. And although Jones did not divert millions of Temple dollars to his own luxury, he did take steps through the so-called Valley Trusts to ensure that the Temple would meet his and his family's financial needs in the long run.

As the Jonestown development accelerated, the Temple had acquired foreign bank accounts so it could conduct its business throughout the world, including in Guyana. For its banking center the Temple had selected Panama because of that country's proximity and unrestrictive banking laws. Stoen had contacted a pair of Panamanian lawyers who set up two secret corporations. Once those corporations were functioning, control of banking and finances fell mainly on Carolyn Layton, because Stoen was occupied with other duties. Another staff member, Teri Buford, who knew mathematics but not finances, assisted her. And in late 1976 to early 1977, Jones added two other women to the financial circle—Maria Katsaris and Debbie Layton Blakey, sister of Larry Layton and wife of Temple member Phil Blakey. Without any explanation, both were ordered to Jones's apartment in the San Francisco temple one day.

Jones questioned Blakey closely, looking for signs of hesitation. "Debbie, will you ever leave the church?"

"No," she said quickly. Maria then passed the same test.

Satisfied, Jones told them weightily, without divulging specifics: "I'm going to send you on a very important mission."

A few weeks later, Jones sent the two neophytes and Carolyn Layton to Panama City, where they were greeted by Teri Buford and attorney Gene Chaikin. Katsaris and Blakey were instructed to make themselves look "mature." When Debbie Blakey, then twenty-three, finally glanced at herself and her bulbous "natural" hairdo in the mirror, she thought she looked about fifty.

The group went to several Panama City banks. In each, they signed papers and left in short order. Since no one besides Chaikin spoke Spanish —and his was shabby—everything remained misty to Debbie and Maria as they tagged along. The trip was so steeped in intrigue that Debbie, thinking her discretion was being tested, was afraid to tell one bank official one of the few things she did find out—the name of one Temple corporation.[53]

That first trip had been merely a preliminary. When Stoen defected in June 1977, a new flurry of financial transactions became imperative. Debbie Blakey, by then Maria Katsaris's assistant financial secretary, was told: "We're leaving tonight. Pack for both hot and cold weather. Bring enough clothing for a month." Maria Katsaris gave her a money belt with $5,000, the legal maximum exempted from declaration. They were to pay cash for everything.

At about 6:00 A.M., Debbie and her senior traveling companion, Teri Buford, made final preparations for their mission. Buford impressed Blakey with the urgency of the assignment by giving her a piece of paper with three phone numbers to call in case of emergency. According to instructions, Blakey memorized the numbers, then ate the paper. At the airport, Buford expressed fear that someone either was watching them or would be during the flight. She told Blakey to pretend they did not know each other, and warned her that agents or enemies might try to pose as friendly men. But the flight was uneventful.

After a couple of days of running financial errands in Panama City, during which Buford kept all specifics from her companion, the two headed for the airport again. "Where are we going now?" Blakey asked. "London," Buford replied succinctly.

In London, they spent their days at a local library, poring over books about socialist and communist countries, trying to identify which ones offered the most advantageous banking systems and laws. Although she had been told the experience would be educational, Blakey felt like a flunky. She read little, because she was too busy running for change to Xerox two inches of pages on banking systems while Buford did research.

Next stop was Paris, where Buford informed her on arrival: "We'll be flying to Zurich. We'll do it late tonight so that nothing will be shown on our passports." Proceeding according to plan, the two soon found themselves carrying their suitcases over a river bridge in Zurich that night. They hiked up a long series of steps to a building, formerly a convent, and they spent the night.

The next morning, Blakey took a curling iron and straightened her "natural" hairdo. Looking more presentable as a young businesswoman, she accompanied Buford to a Swiss bank. They were ushered from one plush sitting room to another. A bank official checked their identification so there would be no mistakes. Treating the transaction soberly and seriously, he pulled out some papers that had been prepared in advance.

Teri seemed anxious to reveal as little as possible to Debbie. "We don't need to discuss anything," she insisted to the bank official. "Let's sign the papers." But he plowed ahead, mentioning something about the Temple having $2 million in the main account. That amount jolted Blakey. Then he read the account number out loud, revealing to Blakey yet another "secret" bit of information.

After completing the transaction, Buford and Blakey retreated to the convent. Since the mission was accomplished, Teri took Debbie to the bus and train depot and sent her to France with a final instruction: "Don't fall asleep on the flight back home." Apparently she had seen too many spy movies in which people divulged valuable secrets in their sleep.

Much of the trip, with all its silly cloak-and-dagger games, had left a fuzzy impression on Debbie Blakey; but its purpose was clear and significant. Jones hoped to put money into an Eastern European socialist country, most likely Rumania. He desired to win the good will of the Soviet Union, so it would welcome a Temple migration. Already Jones was looking beyond the Caribbean for a backup sanctuary.

The exodus from San Francisco had begun in May, shortly after the legal conference at Lamaha Gardens. It intensified in June, July and August as the lid came off Temple horror stories. The plan had originally involved transporting 380 people on April 3 aboard charter planes, but the Guyanese had asked for a postponement of several days. They needed time to review the surge of immigration applications; after all, Guyana was a country most people wanted to *leave.* After Jones described the immigrants as "skilled and progressive" and "most vulnerable to the state repression" in the United States, and after he showed off an envelope he claimed contained $500,000 to be deposited in the Bank of Guyana, Guyanese officials granted permission. Jones had promised to transfer all or most of the church's assets to Guyana—a promise not kept.

Several weeks after the Guyanese government approved the plan, nearly 400 members arrived in groups of 40 and 50 in Guyana via commercial flights. By the end of July 1977, approximately 850 members had resettled in Jonestown, and by September, nearly 1,000 had immigrated.

The San Francisco temple teemed with activity in the summer months of 1977. The radio room hummed with messages from Jonestown, calls for supplies, instructions about the exodus, reports on progress in Jonestown, reports about press coverage. Outside in the church parking lot, supplies were crated and stacked. Buses were serviced for the cross-country trip. Plane reservations were arranged by phone.

Secrecy covered all departure details because the church feared that someone might attempt either to stop the exodus altogether or else to stop certain people—particularly children. The magnitude of the flight was effectively hidden from news media and others until mid-August. In order to disguise the shrinking congregation, Jones instructed his people to be boisterous at the regular services conducted by Marceline and others in San Francisco.

Meanwhile, small caravans of fifty-passenger buses pulled away from the Temple in the dead of night, loaded with optimistic people, heading to the East Coast—for plane flights south. On Jones's instructions, they had covered their tracks. In some cases, they told relatives that they were going on vacation or on another routine summer bus trip east. They resigned from their jobs suddenly; some merely stopped showing up for work. A number of them left relatives and friends without even a parting phone call; they were afraid someone might try to stop them.

In their wake, they left pained and confused loved ones. Butcher Freddy Lewis came home from the meat market one day to discover his wife and seven children gone, along with most of their possessions.

The shock for Sam Houston was delayed. One day in August, Phyllis Houston brought Sam's teen-age granddaughters to see him and

Nadyne. He gave the girls $20 each, and they all went on a shopping excursion. The girls, he noticed, were buying warm-weather clothes: straw hats and other light things. Having heard speculation about a Temple exodus, Sam feared the worst. The next day, the girls boarded a Temple bus for what was supposed to have been a "vacation" to New York. A short time later, the Houstons received a letter from Guyana: "Dear Grandma and Grandpa, Real soon, I'll be going to an agricultural mission and I'm very happy. When I get there, I will write. . . . Lots of Love. . . ." It was signed by Judy. A letter from Patricia arrived the next month from Jonestown.

The Temple scandal had pushed District Attorney Joseph Freitas into a no-win situation. As chief law enforcement official of San Francisco County, he could not ignore allegations of criminal wrongdoing without being accused of cronyism and coverup. If he investigated and came up with nothing, it would appear that he had gone easy on Jones. If his investigation did turn up something, he and his friends would appear to have been duped in the past. In fact, the first word of Freitas's investigation did upset some Temple supporters, who believed he had bailed out too quickly.

The six-week inquiry, carried out by the unit Stoen had once headed, was initiated on July 18, 1977, and involved all five Special Prosecutions investigators. They conducted more than seventy interviews. Mostly they heard the same stories that had been given to reporters.

The investigators were hampered by dated information and by lack of a single inside source among current members. As they made the rounds to Temple communes, they found many deserted and others geared up for a quick departure. Whenever they attempted to talk to anyone, they were given the silent treatment; members had been advised against talking by attorney Charles Garry, hired on the eve of the *New West* story. In one case, the investigators visited a commune with a large number of suitcases stacked downstairs. When they started to talk to the residents, a Jones secretary referred them to Garry. When they returned to the commune the next day, the suitcases were gone, the building empty.

The Temple's conduct appeared highly suspicious, but there was no lawful basis on which to stop the exodus, and investigators could not penetrate the remaining communes, which were locked down tightly. At one commune on Scott Street, the investigators spotted people peeking out the windows, but no one would admit them or identify themselves. One woman finally exchanged a few words through the door with one investigator, but as someone else approached, she broke off mid-sentence and pretended she had not been speaking.

Although defectors had meanwhile provided hundreds of leads, none firmed up as a prosecutable case. The investigators were running in circles. When they confessed their frustration, Freitas—who was later accused of foot-dragging—pushed them to keep probing. In fact, Freitas's former assistant, Tim Stoen, soon became one of the best prospects for prosecution.

The investigators turned to other agencies, to see whether they might be of assistance. They found that the FBI was conducting no investigation, although some defectors and relatives claimed they had gone to the agency with their complaints. The lone investigator at the California Secretary of State's office was looking into illegal use of notaries public. U.S. customs was investigating possible weapons smuggling to Guyana. State welfare officials were checking into possible fraud.

After six weeks, having referred some matters to the Los Angeles and Mendocino County authorities, the San Francisco district attorney's office gave up. It did not bring the matter before the grand jury, although it had employed the jury in other difficult cases. It quit before Tim Stoen —the single most important potential source—could be interviewed. Impeded by the exodus, outdated information, jurisdictional limitations and the unwillingness of some key defectors to cooperate, Freitas's office went on to other matters. The special prosecution unit chief wrote to Freitas: "No evidence has been developed that would warrant consideration of criminal prosecution. . . ." The report added at the end, "Obviously nothing in this memorandum should be read as approving of the practices of Peoples Temple, many of which are at least unsavory and raise substantial moral and non-criminal legal questions." And of Stoen—the original draftsman of the exodus plan which had effectively killed the investigation—the report said, "There are a lot of stories flying around [but] so far, no evidence has surfaced that would link Stoen with any criminal activity in San Francisco. . . . We have found no evidence to date of misconduct by Stoen as a deputy district attorney in San Francisco." The report was not made public until a year later, when events in Guyana made it imperative to do so. Failure to do so in August 1977 left a festering climate of severe charges and countercharges.[54]

Already questions were being raised about living conditions in Jonestown. Phoning Mike Prokes at the San Francisco temple, I asked why Jones would not answer the press allegations. "He'll be back, but nobody knows when . . ." Prokes replied. When the public relations man mentioned that he was leaving for Jonestown that night, I asked to visit the paradise he had described. It was the first of my four attempts to see Jonestown. "We'll have to discuss it," Prokes replied.

The morale of the original Jonestown settlers had shot up as new arrivals poured into the compound. Years of work suddenly took on new meaning, and the dream of a functioning agricultural encampment seemed only short steps away. But construction could not keep apace of the influx, and soon the available housing overflowed. When mission administrators complained to Jones, he said, "Make room." They stepped up their work, but were always one step behind the population growth.

The crowded conditions irritated and inconvenienced everyone. Because the kitchen was designed for the small pioneer crews, the new settlers had to endure long food lines like those at the San Francisco temple. They ate in three shifts. Living in exceedingly close quarters in jungle cabins and dorms produced friction, too. Some people arrived with unsuitable clothes for the tropics, others with only the clothes on their backs.

The productivity of the newcomers often fell far short of the "skills" they had listed on forms prior to departure. And some could not work at all. So much energy had to be devoted immediately to training them.

A larger problem remained unspoken: that Jonestown was not the Promised Land depicted in promotional films and brochures. The soil described as rich was poor, even by Guyanese standards. The trees did not even produce mature fruit, let alone a fruit that tasted like ice cream sherbet. The people could not fish and swim; the nearest body of water was almost seven miles away on muddy roads. Jonestown required sweat and strain for survival itself.

The grim transition sapped the pioneer spirit and enthusiasm of many. Nevertheless, Jones continued the same old propaganda on the shortwave radio, trying to convince his people in San Francisco and perhaps himself that Jonestown was indeed the fulfillment of their dreams.

Using Albert Touchette's license, he spoke oftentimes over the international radio network, as if he were a head of state. He assumed, correctly, that people eavesdropped on Temple communications. In fact, those radio relays probably entertained hundreds of amateur radio operators around the world. They also provided the best source of intelligence information for defectors, such as Elmer and Deanna Mertle (Al and Jeannie Mills). Even the *Examiner* enlisted a ham radio operator to monitor the transmissions in hopes of finding out something about Jonestown.

The *Examiner*'s radio operator was listening at 6:00 A.M. on August 23, 1977, while Jones spoke from the settlement to the San Francisco temple. Sounding tormented, Jones pleaded unjust persecution by the news media. "I have always heard that it was the government that represented corporate elite interests, and that it was the press that exposed things like Watergate. What in the world is going on?"

On the radio, his loyalists in the Bay Area relayed the day's press treatment. He sighed relief each day nothing was reported. He would not face the press in a news conference or interviews, but spoke to the world at large about these allegations, proclaiming his innocence like a man already convicted.

"People are saying it's all work down here, no time to play," Jones said over the radio. "They haven't seen the community center, the TVs, the videotape. We have comedies, documentaries on social conditions. We had a dance tonight. We will go for a hike this weekend. It's really fantastic."

Speaking of the 130 young people the Temple claimed to be rehabilitating from lives of crime, he sounded like an American patriot: "We're serving our country in two ways, taking a burden off the taxpayers, reducing crime, astronomically, and then helping good relations by building agriculture in a country that is trying to feed, clothe and house their people."

In times of crisis, the Jones family, like any family, drew closer. The spate of negative publicity united them on the airwaves this day. Marceline Jones put her mother, Charlotte Baldwin, on the radio, and she asked Jim how he was feeling.

"I'm a little concerned, you Republican lady. . . . It's wonderful being out here in a part of the jungle where you don't get any news. . . . We've got some marvelous laying hens and some broilers and fryers. You got plants of every variety, and tea . . . the papaya aren't really ripe yet. . . . Here comes your grandson, who looks healthier than I've ever seen him in my life. . . . He's learned every kind of skill available. Here's Steve."

After Stephan chatted briefly with his grandmother, Marceline then came on to talk to her son: "How are you, sweetheart?"

"I'm fine because, thanks to Dad, I've got a job I'm happy with. I'm happy where I can pretty much work by myself. I'm really enjoying it here."

"That's beautiful. I'm so glad. I know that Dad recognizes your leadership abilities. I know that you're a great help to him. I'm so proud. Did you get my note?"

"Yeah, I did."

"Well, I meant every word of it. I'm telling you what I'm seeing happening here [with the press] makes me so glad that all of you are there."

There was a long pause, then Stephen said: "Mom, I love you and miss you."

"I love you too and miss you, but we'll be together before you know it."

After having a similar conversation with Jimmy, Marceline concluded the transmission: "I feel so optimistic about everything. I think everything is going to work out just fine."

PART SIX

THE EMPEROR JONES

"I can do anything I want because I've sacrificed to give everybody the good life."

> JIM JONES
> *September 1977*
> *ham radio broadcast from Jonestown*

THIRTY-SEVEN

Heaven on Earth?

Despite the litany of allegations back home, no outsider visiting Jonestown for the first time could fail to be impressed by the physical site itself. The people, through sheer hard work and perseverance, had converted three hundred acres of dense jungle into a neatly laid out, administered and maintained town of nearly a thousand people. One needed only to walk the boardwalks to see the pride that had gone into constructing the colony—the row upon row of weeded crops on either side of the long road into Jonestown and around the cottages and dormitories, the vegetable beds and citrus groves planted in and around the settlement.

     Visitors coming from Port Kaituma passed under a large sign hanging over the road: GREETINGS, PEOPLES TEMPLE AGRICULTURAL PROJECT. Behind the sign was a guarded gate—nothing more than a chain across the road—and a small security shack equipped with radio and tall antenna; routinely the guards advised Jonestown of approaching visitors. Along the roadsides, plantain groves and acres of cassava flourished. A final turn into the compound revealed the banana shed, kitchen and eating area on the right. Surrounding buildings included showers and toilets, sheds to dry and store food, an outdoor laundry area and even an herb center. On the other side of the road rose the dominant structure—the Jonestown pavilion—an open-air structure with a peaked aluminum roof. Here Jim Jones held his meetings and here the band played. Immediately adjacent to the pavilion stood two long school rooms with green canvas roofing. Beyond the pavilion, five large sexually segregated dormitories had been built for single women, problem children and the elderly. Beyond those lay a cluster of small wooden cottages. Other buildings were interspersed throughout the compound: the nursery, preschool center, the radio room and an outdoor play area. On opposite ends of Jonestown stood East House—accommodations for overnight visitors—and West House, home to Jim Jones; these cabins were named after early communes in Redwood Valley.

With the logistical problems of the initial influx behind them, the Jonestown administrators could practically watch the place run itself. The organizational plan, with modifications owing to the poor soil, was essentially working. Joyce Touchette ran the kitchen, central supply and laundry. Charlie Touchette oversaw construction, mechanics, the wood and machine shops, transportation and power generation. Marceline Jones, who commuted between Jonestown and San Francisco, ran the medical department when she was around. Tom Grubbs ran the school. Johnny Brown Jones, Carolyn Layton and Harriet Tropp served as Jim Jones's chief administrative officers: "the triumvirate." Stephan Jones sat on the steering committee, which planned for the farm's future, basing its decisions on reports from heads of various departments—banking, sewage, sanitation and engineering, roads, public relations, movies, video and guests, livestock and agriculture.

Jonestown's workforce was comprised of about 950 Peoples Temple members, two-thirds female. Nearly 70 percent were black, 25 percent were white, and the rest a smattering of mulatto, Hispanic, American Indian and Asian. Nearly three hundred were under eighteen years old.

An extensive report to the Guyanese government in the summer of 1977 detailed the progress of these pioneers. A preliminary draft was sent to the San Francisco temple with a note from Harriet Tropp: "[It] does show that the project is indeed something other than a 'penal colony.' "

The section on cassava production illustrated the care taken to use every bit of the precious resources available: the cassava mill could grate one hundred pounds of cassava root in three minutes. The gratings then were pressed; when the starch settled in the resulting liquid, the remainder was boiled, strained, then cooked down to a heavy syrup called cassareep. This was used to flavor foods and to make fudge. The starch was used for cooking and in the laundry center. The leftover cassava pressings were made into flour that was mixed in pig feed or turned into bread.

Eddoes, a root similar to sweet potatoes, were planted in 900-foot beds. The orchard, upward of a thousand immature trees, yielded only small fruit. But the agriculture section expected a crop of 1,000 pineapples and harvested 2,000 pounds of bananas a month. As the settlers invented a mechanical planter and their farming methods improved, they experimented with a wide variety of crops: onions, mung and cutlass beans, even coffee.

The pig population had grown from one young boar and five small pigs in 1975 to 130 animals. Pork, though served only when outsiders visited, was plentiful—and regularly sold downriver to earn income for the farm. The chicken population of several hundred soon multiplied to a thousand.

The Jonestown kitchen, though spartan by American standards, nevertheless was efficient and came equipped with large commercial refrigerators and icemakers, two gas and kerosene stoves and large aluminum sinks. It stayed open around the clock, as teams of workers took turns preparing the meals. At first the diet was varied: fresh fruit and vegetables, rice, chicken, cheeses and bread, among other things. A hand-dug well provided excellent water for cooking, drinking, cleaning, laundry and bathing.

The medical unit was well staffed and supplied. A large room served as an infirmary and drug dispensary. Detailed medical records, even a gynecological history on each woman, were kept.

Don Fields, who held a doctorate in pharmacology, manned the dispensary. The medical personnel included Dr. Larry Schacht, who had interrupted his internship to come to Jonestown, plus a pediatrics practitioner and a respiratory therapist. A registered nurse was on duty twenty-four hours a day.

The hard-working staff soon learned to cope with health hazards of a jungle life. They had workers kill off mosquito larvae to prevent outbreaks of malaria. The herb staff experimented with various teas to treat serious cases of constipation, a common consequence of the increasingly starchy diet. The seriously ill were taken to Matthews Ridge or, if necessary, to Georgetown.

The preschool nursery was a wood frame cottage with a corrugated metal roof. A rising sun had been painted on its wall, in back of the sandbox. Toys, crayons, children's books and dolls were arranged on ledges. A clipboard held "preschool stool reports." The day's lesson plan was chalked on a blackboard: "1) Perceptual motor skills; 2) water colors; 3) play dough; 4) paper cutting; and 4) sandbox, manipulative toys."

Elementary school classes were organized according to ability. The learning pace was individualized. In addition to the three R's, the students were taught physical and earth sciences, social science "with emphasis on Guyanese history and culture," socialism, arts, crafts and music. The high school provided vocational and technical education, stressing agricultural skills.

For many of the several hundred senior citizens, Jonestown might well have seemed better than life in America, especially for southern blacks who came via the ghettos. Nearly two hundred seniors turned over monthly social security checks to the church, but in return they enjoyed a measure of security. All their needs were met, and they no longer had to fear urban crime. By and large, seniors could relax. Those not desiring to work on communal projects could tend small gardens. All could visit the library for books or watch videotapes. Sometimes they took short nature hikes on carefully marked trails. It was difficult for some, but they adjusted out of necessity to crowding, strange food and weather, and other negative conditions. Still, they shared a sense of community in Jonestown—and some believed that Jones was God. None was in a position to pack up and leave.

Not all was work, hardship and structured activities. Occasionally, Stephan Jones would face his stereo speakers toward the cottages and turn up the volume. People would gather spontaneously to sing and dance. Visitors provided relief from the routines, too. When outsiders came to Jonestown, Jim Jones would pull out the stops; the settlers could count on pork or chicken for dinner, with several kinds of vegetables and sometimes a piece of pie. The Jonestown Express and the Soul Steppers would provide the musical entertainment while comedians did their slapstick routine. When the band got cooking—soul, gospel, rhythm and blues, disco—everyone would join in.

Above all, the pioneer spirit kept Jonestown alive. Despite the hardship, this group of city people had carved a new life in the rain forests of South America. Most new arrivals felt a special sense of adventure. They also felt their experiment was significant: that they were building a model for socialism.

Nevertheless, factionalism developed with the sudden arrival of so many people. Stephan Jones and some other early settlers resented the well educated new arrivals, who second-guessed their work. When one so-called expert suggested "a better method" for milling lumber, they invited him to try. Then they gloated after he managed less than 10 percent of the regular crew's production and gave up.

It did not take long for one woman to realize that Jonestown was not for her. During her May 1977 visit to the Promised Land, "Mrs. B." became convinced that people were losing weight rapidly on a high-carbohydrate diet. As a city person, she was put off by jungle sanitation; she did not like using a cold water shower and an outhouse, or wiping with a newspaper. The flies pestered her so much that she had to eat with one hand and shoo them off with the other. It rained nearly every day, leaving the ground constantly muddy. Mildew crawled everywhere.

Mrs. B. got the impression that Temple leaders did not want her to speak with her friends from San Francisco—James and Irene Edwards and Emmett Griffith, Sr., and his wife Mary—who had arrived earlier. Yet the two couples privately told Mrs. B. that they were not getting enough to eat. Edwards, a powerful man well over six feet, looked as though he had lost fifty pounds. Both couples wanted to go home. (Earlier, of course, I had heard what another friend, Le Flora Townes, believed about Edwards's weight loss—that he was not emaciated but fit, and happy, in Jonestown.)

Such revelations had made Mrs. B. afraid to speak to anyone else about leaving; she feared being reported. She believed others were unhappy, too, but were stranded without money or passports. Someone advised her to pin any cash she had to her underwear, so it would not be taken away or stolen.

Though she was squired around hospitably, some hardship and brutality could not be hidden from her. People worked from sunup to sundown, performing the most grueling physical work in the broiling sun. The children were pushed to the point of unquestioning obedience. In one case, a child who defecated in his pants was forced to wear the soiled garments on his head and to go without food while watching others eat. An eleven-year-old boy who said he was tired of hearing about Father's sacrifices was knocked down by one man, and Charlie Touchette had to throw his body over the boy to prevent him from being hurt further. As punishment, some were made to eat hot peppers. Edwards told her of one offender who had a pepper jammed up his rectum. Other guilty parties had their heads shaved. Mrs. B. also heard Marceline Jones and Maria Katsaris lecture a women's meeting, saying sex was banned, because there was time only for labor.

To complain was to be punished. So Mrs. B. used ruse to return to the United States. The others—the unhappy and the true believers alike —were doomed to stay behind.

On a daily basis, Jones had to deal with the dashed expectations of the many settlers who recognized that Jonestown, their tropical paradise, really resembled a primitive jungle workcamp. Jones had to crush any thought of leaving or escape, but that was no more difficult than disabusing them of their fantasies. At last, he had people where he wanted them —on another continent, in a jungle with no law except his own. Their isolation was complete. Events in the world—and reality itself—would be filtered exclusively through him. His lust for control could be almost sated.

During a May meeting taped by the Temple, Jones was in a lighthearted mood as he played with his power. He would interrupt the meeting with hideous laughs, prolonged, high-pitched whinnies that were both eerie and sadistic. Perched in his light-green wooden chair at the front of the pavilion, he singled out an eighteen-year-old black youth named Jerry.

"Tell me why you want to go back to America?" Jones began almost playfully, "so we can reeducate you."

Jerry thought for a moment, then repeated what Jones had said for years: "It will be destroyed by nuclear war. . . . I just want to go back, when probably it'll be taken over by socialists."

An opening had been provided. "When nuclear war comes," said Jones laughing, "and they blast everything to dust and you can't drink the water and you can't breathe the air and your apartment is blown to hell, there'll be damned little left."

"It was always my impression that some of us would go back and take over the States," Jerry said.

"All the black folk'll be blown up because they don't give us no caves, no bomb shelters, so I'd be going back to help white folks," Jones said, shooting down that argument. "You want to make another case for me to go back there?"

"We can just wait a while till the radiation cools," Jerry offered, hopefully.

"I'll tell you, son," Jones said, after one of his long squeals. "Your balls will have done shrunk up by the time that happens. Till it's safe to wander around, it'll be fifty years." Everyone was laughing now.

"I figure," said Jerry, undaunted, but a trifle more tentative, "if we go back and probably kill off white folks, I mean . . ."

Laughter.

"You're my best argument against going back," said Jones. "Keep on, Jer."

"I figure it this way. It wouldn't make no sense to let that land go to waste."

Another opening. "You lazy ass fuckers," Jones bellowed. "We got twenty-seven thousand acres here. Why don't you want to develop this land . . . ? "

Jones continued ridiculing Jerry for suggesting the very things he himself had promised. Jerry kept suggesting they go back and "run things" after the nuclear war Jones had prophesied. And Jones kept mocking him, to roars of laughter:

"[All you'll find] is just toothless slobs with long stringy hair down the side of their faces and balls all radiated away and sunk up inside 'em. . . . all you'll have is dirt and cockroaches, big as a bulldog. You gonna take them over, Jer?"

Sobered, Jerry confessed, "At first I wanted to go back, but I don't want to go back now."

Jones had just gotten what he wanted: a public acknowledgment that Jonestown was infinitely preferable to going back to the United States.

THIRTY-EIGHT

Close Encounters

Joe Mazor had come upon the scene like a hired gun. At one point in the summer of 1977, access to ex-members who had "gone public" was unrestrained; the next, reporters and law enforcement investigators found themselves contacting a hard-boiled private detective whose name sounded like some sharpie's pseudonym and whose voice dragged through a leathery throat full of cigarette smoke. The arrangement was all the more curious, given Mazor's background as a onetime convict who served a sentence for passing bad checks and who in newspaper file photos wore a patch over one eye.

Among Mazor's first Temple clients were Jeannie and Al Mills—prime sources of the *New West* and *Examiner* articles. Soon his covey of clients numbered over a dozen, and he was serving as both conduit to the press and a shield from us. Meanwhile, he was reportedly trying to spring his clients' children loose from the Temple.

"Private" investigator was hardly an apt title for Mazor, given his inordinate appetite for publicity. One day in August 1977, Mazor phoned me. One of his clients possessed documentation that would hang Tim Stoen, he said. This was particularly tantalizing because it was not publicly known that Stoen—who appeared to be the Temple's number two man—had defected.

"What kind of documentation?" I asked.

As usual, Mazor had a knack for avoiding the direct answers. "Come to my place this afternoon. Bob Graham of the district attorney's office will be here to pick it up."

Nancy Dooley and I drove to 1800 Pacific, an elegant high-rise apartment building in the heart of Pacific Heights.

In a moment, a blond woman was showing us to Mazor's conspicuously posh living room, accented by a fireplace and large windows framing a panorama of the bay. As we sank into a velvety sofa and waited for Mazor, we were left in the company of Mr. S., a gnomish man in a drab brown suit who crouched at the edge of the fireplace. Though introduced as Mazor's legal counsel, Mr. S. volunteered not a syllable. When we asked the name of his Temple client, he muttered, "I don't know." Soon another member of Mazor's team walked in—Bob K., a public relations expert from a well-known San Francisco public relations firm. This all seemed a bit excessive. Joe Mazor was either doing a wonderful business or gambling on instant fame that would bring wealthy clients to his door.

Finally Mazor himself entered, playing the gracious host. In place of the eye patch was an eye that seemed to swivel independently of its owner. In sleek suit slacks and a dress shirt, powerful but paunchy, he looked more like a successful attorney than did his retiring Mr. S. In the course of our conversation Mazor dribbled out information designed to make his business seem flourishing and exciting.

Then Mazor, in effect, promised to give us the first concrete evidence of criminal wrongdoing by a top Jones aide, Tim Stoen. The private eye contended that the Temple illegally took the property of one of his clients—former Temple security chief Marvin Swinney—then paid him off for his silence. The proof? A tape recording of a conversation between Swinney and Tim Stoen, plus the photostat of a grant deed from Mendocino County.

The grant deed to Swinney's house in Redwood Valley indicated the "gift" was made in June of 1973, yet the ownership transfer was not recorded until September 22, 1975, shortly after Swinney and his wife Mary defected. Though the deed was notarized by Tim Stoen, Swinney and his wife had given sworn affidavits that they had never signed it.

Producing the documents with a flourish, Mazor pronounced the whole property transfer a phony. "Tish Leroy [a Temple member in Jonestown] told three other members who are clients of mine now that she did it—using liquid paper and Temple membership card signatures."

In the spirit of good showmanship, Mazor waited for the arrival of DA's investigators Bob Graham and Dave Reuben before playing the tape. It contained two conversations recorded on Swinney's answering service recorder in December 1975; in each, Swinney had reached Stoen in the Mendocino County district attorney's office.

"My only involvement is to get [you to sign] the paper thing," Stoen was saying on the recording; he wanted Swinney to sign a new document stating that the church had purchased the property and authorizing it to assume Swinney's loans. There was also money changing hands. Under an agreement negotiated with Jones, the Swinneys had been slated to receive $10,000 upon leaving Ukiah, with a promise of $3,000 later. Jones had not wanted to pay out until the Swinneys were packed and ready to leave.

In the second conversation, Stoen got down to business. "This [document] will acknowledge that the property was purchased in full, that it authorizes us to pay it off, to deal with the bribe problem."

"To deal with the what problem?" Swinney replied.

"The bribe problem," repeated the attorney. "Somebody can say you were bribed. . . . This is a goddamn legitimate transaction."

Later that day, I phoned the Swinneys in the Carolinas and found they had been threatened by Chris Lewis and had never received the balance of $3,000. Meanwhile, the district attorney's office listened to the tape. Since it had been made while Stoen worked in Mendocino County, they had to pass the buck. The recording was kicked among several law enforcement agencies, none eager to accept jurisdiction. Eventually, the secretary of state's office took up the matter but would drop it because documents experts could not prove forgery: Mazor had produced only a photostat, and the original deed was still missing.

Since the story was shifting from the United States to South America, the *Examiner* wanted to send me to Guyana with or without permission to enter Jonestown. Already conflicting reports had surfaced about the quality of life, with Temple supporters describing Jonestown as a utopian community and with defectors—such as Mrs. B., whom I interviewed around this time—calling it a concentration camp. At this point Joe Mazor surfaced again.

Mazor had a plan, an ambitious plan for an expedition to Guyana. Once there, he hoped to use U.S. court documents to wrest some eight children from the Temple on behalf of their parents or guardians. He was inviting the *Examiner* to cover the trip.

Despite Mazor's obvious ulterior motives—publicity, for one—it seemed worthwhile to see whether his trip did shape up: covering efforts to bring out several children would more likely produce a story than wandering around Guyana without an entrée to Jonestown. With each phone call, Mazor kept me posted. Chances for the trip looked better and better.

The day-to-day delays stretched into weeks. Mazor then explained that in order to save money, he was trying to persuade Ed Daly, the colorful president of World Airways, to donate a charter to undertake a mercy mission like controversial Operation Babylift during the fall of Saigon. But postponements continued. Daly himself probably would not go after all, Mazor said; he was ill. (The airline later denied that Daly had ever negotiated for a plane with Mazor.[55]) Eventually the timeliness for the trip had been lost.

By late September, after the initial surge of Temple stories, I had returned to my East Bay beat. Now and again Mazor would call, preoccupied with his plans to rescue children, and with the idea of bringing Tim Stoen to justice. The ex-convict seemed to have a visceral hatred for the ex-prosecutor.

That fall, in the course of one conversation, Mazor coyly talked of going into Jonestown with some "backup," using an amphibious approach through the Venezuelan jungle. He seemed to be inviting me to cover an armed assault on Jonestown—first there would be a rocket launcher attack on the radio transmitter and tower to create confusion, then a quick commando raid to nab children. Though he spoke hypothetically, hearing this made me extremely uncomfortable.

"Look, Joe," I said, "there's no way we would be part of anything done by force." It was hard to tell whether he was joking or just spreading his macho thick. I seriously doubted this paunchy private detective could ever pull off such a caper. I wondered whether he was trying to bait me into saying something supportive.

Meanwhile, Mazor pursued his other agenda. It did not matter to him that Tim Stoen had left the Temple. He wanted to see Stoen penalized—and perhaps to get some decent commissions out of the business as well. But Mazor's efforts collapsed. The detective complained to me one day that some former clients—Jeannie and Al Mills and the Swinneys—had dropped complaints against Stoen after Mazor arranged to have the lawyer's notary revoked on their behalf. Mazor was particularly offended that the Millses had put up Stoen at their Berkeley home, like a long-lost brother. "With or without them, I'm going to keep after Stoen," he vowed.

While Mazor's and other probes were stymied, another futile investigation wound down. Since February 1977, the U.S. customs service had been looking into Temple gun smuggling. Over a dozen former Temple members had alleged that 170 weapons—most collected in earlier gun turn-ins—had been shipped secretly in the false bottoms of crates of machinery bound for Jonestown. Within three months, the Temple had learned about the investigation and taken evasive action. David Conn, a longtime friend of Al Mills, had inadvertently tipped off Jones by mentioning the investigation in a talk with radical Indian leader Dennis Banks—and Banks had informed Jones.[56]

Although the Temple continued to buy and send guns and ammunition to Guyana during the investigation, they exercised more caution. Jones used code when ordering weapons over the radio. In one conversation in August 1977, Jones spoke to security chief Jim McElvane in San Francisco:

"I want you to go to the Bible Exchange at Second and Mission," Jones began. "They have a flashlight, the kind with black metal and it's twenty-four inches long. Do you copy?" The only "exchange" on Second Street was the San Francisco Gun Exchange—"Bible" was the church code for "gun."

In this particular case, Jones might well have been ordering flashlights. But several days later, the orders were more direct: "For God's sake," Jones demanded at one point, "send me ten copies of the book and I'll review it."

Clever as the Temple's smuggling techniques were, there still were several close calls both in Guyana and in the United States. When a customs inspector at the Georgetown airport questioned one Temple woman who was carrying six guns in her crate, she became flustered and sputtered: "All I have . . . is arms and other things." Sharon Amos covered for the terrible slip, and the officials permitted her to pass unsearched.[57]

The Temple took pains to avoid a repeat of that experience. Amos found that inspectors tended to check crates more diligently than duffel bags, so the church started using those. And there were other diversionary tactics as well: using people in wheelchairs to arouse sympathy; using women to flirt with some inspectors and handsome men to flirt with the gay ones; putting Kotex on top of sensitive cargo to embarrass the inspectors and hurry the procedure; arranging for inspection at night, when it was easier to turn the head of a customs agent with a few well-placed bottles of liquor.

In August, U.S. customs watched ports in Houston, New Orleans and Miami for Temple cargo—a fact the Temple soon learned from Guyanese Police Commissioner C. A. "Skip" Roberts, who received a copy of an August 26, 1977, U.S. customs report through Interpol. Meanwhile, on August 29, customs agents made a spot check in Miami of the shipment bound for Jonestown. The weapons search was pure hit-or-miss—in fact the agents apparently checked only one crate out of ninety located. Nothing was found, and the shipment went through.[58] By early September, customs had discontinued its investigation altogether.

During the customs investigation, the Temple purchased at least three guns in the San Francisco and Ukiah areas which eventually found their way into Jonestown. An undetermined number of other guns were smuggled into the settlement from the States. On October 31, 1977, about two months after customs halted its investigation, Jack Beam, Sr., walked into what the Temple called "The San Francisco Bible Exchange" and purchased a Remington Model 700 .308-caliber bolt action rifle that, one year later, someone else would use to kill Representative Leo Ryan.

Although my Guyana trip had been postponed indefinitely, I kept monitoring the conflicting reports about conditions in Jonestown and listening to tapes of intercepted radio traffic. One day I received a call from Mrs. B. about a mystery escapee. "Come to my house tomorrow if you want to meet a man who escaped from Jonestown," she said.

It was my day off, but I agreed. My hopes for a useful encounter, however, were low. There always seemed to be a problem with accounts about Jonestown. Mrs. B. had already told me her story of degradation, yet admitted she had been well fed and not beaten or abused; also, she was unwilling to be quoted by name.

Among some San Francisco row homes, I located Mrs. B.'s house. Mrs. B. welcomed me warmly, then introduced me to a black, bearish man in a heavy woolen overcoat. The coat clearly served as shelter night and day; it marked him as a derelict.

Shyly, Leon Broussard shook my hand and smiled. His face was roundish, his eyes sad to the point of liquefying. His silvery hair appeared thick and healthy, but the yellowness around his eyes and the dry pink tongue made him appear ill. His speech was a smooth blend of inflections right out of Cajun country. He talked quickly about the tribulations of his nearly fifty years—birth in New Orleans, a career as a merchant seaman and cook, more recently his life on the skids. At one point, he slid a merchant seaman card from a battered wallet as proof of his story, and showed me a passport paid for by the Temple and dated April 14, 1977— early in the exodus period. Unfortunately it did not even show whether he had, in fact, traveled to Guyana. The used pages had been torn out; the blank ones now served him as an address book.

Dates seemed to slip his mind. While on the skids in San Francisco, he had wandered into the Temple somehow. He slept there several weeks. Then they invited him to the tropics where, they said, Leon could munch popcorn all day and listen to exotic birds and watch children play. "They told me I was going to the Promised Land, and they paid my way."

Shaking his head forlornly, he insisted, "I don't hate Jim Jones or those people, but the way they treated me, I couldn't do a dog like that."

Though he did not know exactly where he was, at least he was warmly greeted in Jonestown. Jim Jones personally wrung his hand and said, "Nice to see you." But he soon realized those were the only kind words he would hear. That very night at the welcoming dinner, Jones had said, "I know you all came here to work. But I'm afraid you'll have to wait until tomorrow to start."

To Broussard, Jonestown was like a work camp in the southern swamps. They issued him clothing, rubber boots to keep his feet free of swamp rot, and a toothbrush. They assigned him sleeping quarters in a canvas-roofed barracks.

The former cook found the food so unpalatable, with rice in everything and everything on rice, that he sneaked into nearby Port Kaituma without authorization and feasted on chicken, papaya and watermelon. For his binge, the Temple confiscated some pocket money he had been given en route to Jonestown.

Though it was little incentive, Broussard knew the rule: no work, no food. He cut grass at first. Next, he toted lumber from the sawmill back to the camp. But the wood was heavy, the haul long for a man whose toughest recent labor had been panhandling.

Under the watchful eye of club-wielding Johnny Brown Jones, Broussard labored until the lumber rubbed a raw spot on his shoulder. Then the pain and disillusionment came pouring out of him. He pleaded: "I'd appreciate it if you would let me rest for fifteen minutes." But the young foreman made him work until he broke down crying. "I'd appreciate it if you'd just kill me and get it over with," he said at one point.

Finally, Broussard had the temerity to take his grievances to Jones. It was only about a week after he had arrived. "I want to go home," he told Jones, in front of others.

"You'll have to pay your own way home, Leon," Jones replied. "I brought you to this wonderful place, so you'll have to get back on your own."

While Broussard protested that he had no funds, James Edwards hit him and others yelled, "Don't fight back. Don't fight back, Leon. If you do, we'll make you wish you'd never been born." A crashing blow to the chest forced the wind out of him and knocked him to his knees.

Edwards—who had confided misgivings about Jonestown to Mrs. B. months earlier—stood over Leon screaming, "The next time, you watch your mouth and what you say to Father." Leon regained his feet slowly.

Then other men and women shouted, "Get on your knees, Leon. Get on your knees. You crawl to Jim and beg forgiveness." When Leon reached the polished black shoes and khaki pant cuffs of Jim Jones, he cried, "I'm sorry, Jim."

Looking down at the top of Broussard's graying head, Jones said,

"You're not so good that I can't put a bridle on your mouth and blinders on your eyes, and put you in that hole."

There was a trench, roughly nine feet deep by nine feet square, where the slackers were dumped, Broussard knew. A few children who maintained they were sick and unable to work were lowered into that excavation and made to dig in the mud, first light till last light.

Leon could see the penalty was worse than the work, even though the crater in his shoulder was the size of a half dollar. When Leon went back to work that day, Johnny Brown paid him special attention, brandishing a club and telling him, "I might wanna use this if you get out of line." Leon's only reply was to retch his last meal all over the ground.

Even more dreaded were the meetings when Jones presided from a chair on the stage at one end of the pavilion. "Get up there, Leon," they would shout. "Run, Leon. Double time."

Broussard would lumber up as fast as his fat legs would carry him. Jim Jones, his face white, black hair glistening under the generator-powered lights, prodded him with snide condescension, designed to stimulate venom in the others. "I heard you didn't want to work," he would say.

"I was sick," Leon said.

"You're not a sick man," Jones said. "Get back to work. There's important work to be done here."

Feeling the hostility and the ponderousness of his own tongue, Broussard could not summon the courage to argue. But he resolved that he had been abused long enough. They were discriminating against him: no one else was beaten up. He suspected his food might have been drugged. He longed for that muddy red clay road to Port Kaituma.

One morning about two weeks after his arrival, he woke up in darkness shortly before 5:00 A.M. He heard not a noise other than the whirring of jungle insects and the restful breathing of his roommates. He pulled on his rubber boots and khaki pants.

Tiptoeing out, he slipped past the pavilion, past the lodgepole cage where Muggs the chimpanzee lived, past the playground. Then he ran in the deep jungle, parallel to the road so he would not become lost. He did not care anymore whether the monkeys, snakes and tigers grabbed him in the darkness. He was beyond that sort of fear.

As day broke at about six o'clock, he encountered an Indian near Port Kaituma. "Hello," Leon called weakly. "I need help."

"What kind of help you need?" the Indian inquired.

"I need help to get back to the United States." There he was, in a clearing in the middle of the South American rain forest talking to a man who probably made less than $500 a year. "I'm from Peoples Temple."

The man took Leon to his home in the town. It was a simple place for the man, his wife and their two baby children. One room was for sleeping, one for sitting and eating, and one for a pig. Hospitably, they put the pig out of its room and put down a mattress there for Leon. Though exhausted, he told them that the Temple would not allow him to leave and would not give him money for travel. "I was sick, but they forced me to work," he said, telling them about the hole.

Later, a tall, brown-skinned policeman came to the house. He carried a pistol and a long-barreled gun as well. When Leon said he wanted to go home to the United States, the policeman asked him why.

"Because I didn't like Jonestown," Leon replied. "They are cruel to me." Leon showed the hole in his shoulder, told about the beating and mentioned the pit in the ground. He looked a mess after his marathon run through the thick jungle.

Later that day, three policemen transported Leon by jeep to a hospital thirty miles away, presumably Matthews Ridge. Leon did not know where he was. A woman came to his room and treated his wounds.

Then a white man came with a little boy. The white man wore a khaki shirt jacket which was the national men's attire. With him was Johnny Brown Jones, without his club. Leon became frightened.

The white man asked Leon whether he would prefer to go back to Jonestown or to the United States. Leon said he wanted to fly back to America. But he was too upset by Johnny Brown's presence to get to the part about the hole in the ground.

The white man assured Leon, "I'll get in touch with Jim Jones and come back tomorrow."

The next day, Johnny Brown Jones brought Leon's plane ticket and his passport. He told Leon to keep his mouth shut and never to talk about the Temple. He assured Leon that Temple people would meet him at the airport in Miami and give him $200 to $300 cash and some food so he could get back to the San Francisco area.

After Leon flew back to the United States, he waited and waited in Miami, but no one came to meet him with food or money. After hours of begging and hanging around the airport, an airline, seemingly out of pity, gave him a ticket to San Francisco. Actually, the Temple had paid for it.

The departure of Leon Broussard, the only person ever to escape Jonestown successfully before the final day, had touched off an extraordinary sequence of events:

The unidentified white man in the Leon Broussard story was U.S. Consul Richard McCoy, the boy his son. The forty-three-year-old consular officer provided services to Americans in Guyana—registering births, marriages, deaths, offering help with passport difficulties and the like.

It was an accident of timing that McCoy had stumbled onto the Leon Broussard escape. En route to Jonestown for his first visit, McCoy was met at Matthews Ridge by a district official who told him a Jonestown escapee had been hospitalized at the Ridge. The official said Broussard was telling disturbing stories about mistreatment. The official was vague about what offenses might have been committed there.

McCoy went to the dispensary—without Johnny Brown Jones, according to McCoy's version—and questioned the bedridden escapee for about a half hour. Identifying himself, he asked, "What's happening? . . . I understand that you made a complaint you were mistreated."

Broussard denied the mistreatment and said simply that he could not adjust to Jonestown life. When McCoy asked him about ugly-looking cuts on his shoulder, Broussard said he incurred them carrying rough-hewn lumber. Finally, after trying to assure Broussard that he could speak freely about any abuse, McCoy promised to make sure the Temple sent him home if he wanted.

Although Broussard had told the two Port Kaituma constables about forced labor and other mistreatment in Jonestown, McCoy felt he could act only on the basis of what Broussard told him personally, not on hearsay. Besides, McCoy prided himself as a smart questioner with the ability to speak the language of urban blacks, and this caused him to think he had probably coaxed Broussard into leveling with him.

Later, when McCoy went into Jonestown, he confronted Jim Jones about the escape. "A member of your organization is in Matthews Ridge. His name is Leon Broussard."

"Oh, that's where he is," an aide replied. (Stephan Jones and Albert Touchette already had gone into the bush looking for Leon.) Aides then began to impugn Broussard's character, calling him a drug addict. That did not sit well with McCoy, though he already had pegged Broussard as an uneducated derelict.

"I don't care what he is," the U.S. official replied. "As consul, I serve all Americans in this country. You brought him here and you are responsible for getting him back."

McCoy wanted to establish the precedent that the Temple, not the U.S. Embassy, would pay for repatriating unhappy communards. Seeming embarrassed by the whole affair, Jones agreed to pay for Broussard's return and sent Johnny Brown Jones to get his passport and personal effects. Jones also seemed apprehensive about what Broussard might be saying. But because Broussard had not made any accusations of mistreatment to him directly, McCoy felt he could not broach that with Jones. He knew, too, that Broussard could be easily discredited.

Even if he had the inclination, Broussard had little opportunity to expand on his story to McCoy. The presence of Johnny Brown Jones next to him on the plane flight to Georgetown must have been inhibiting. When the consul asked Broussard if he had any objection to returning to the Temple house in Lamaha Gardens with Johnny Brown Jones, Broussard said no. Then, less than twenty-four hours later, Broussard left for Miami —and McCoy confirmed his departure with a friend in the immigration office. Jim Jones had passed the test: he had let Leon Broussard leave, and paid his fare.

McCoy's original mission had been to establish ground rules for consulate–Temple contacts during the quarterly visits he planned to make, and to see Carolyn Looman. Her parents feared that Carolyn—

whose brother had roomed with *New West* reporter Phil Tracy—was being held against her will. They based that upon a phone call she had made from Georgetown before being taken into Jonestown; they said she did not want to go.

In Jonestown, McCoy wanted to check into the concerns of parents in the United States and to bring out anyone desiring to leave. After dealing with the Broussard business, McCoy established ground rules for consular visits and "welfare and whereabouts" inquiries such as the Looman case. People must have their passports with them so that he could be sure of their identity, he said. They would talk alone in an open area, where they could not be intimidated or overheard. McCoy would conduct interviews near the pavilion, so that if people wanted to leave, they could cut diagonally across a nearby field to a waiting vehicle, before anyone could interfere.

McCoy told Looman that she was free to leave immediately with him, that Jonestown was under Guyanese law and that a Guyanese official was waiting with a vehicle and driver. Moreover, he said, he had an airplane ticket for her from her parents.

McCoy, of course, could not know how thoroughly all Jonestown residents had been conditioned by fear. He could not know that the Temple was aware of Looman's failed escape plan, that she was under suspicion, that Jones, with advance notice of the visit, had had plenty of opportunity to work on Looman's attitude.

Carolyn Looman told McCoy she was fulfilled teaching seventh and eighth grades—and wanted to remain in Jonestown. What her parents told McCoy had been wrong, she said. The consul felt her answers were unrehearsed. He had no choice but to report the bad news to Looman's parents. But no one would ever know whether Looman was telling the truth or not.

THIRTY-NINE

Siege

The Broussard escape, the Looman inquiry and the Embassy visit had frightened Jonestown. The Temple leadership was worried further when a Ministry of Home Affairs official came to investigate Leon Broussard's accusations about forced labor in the "hole." But nothing would shake the fragile community like the custody battle for John Victor Stoen.

The Stoen case was heating up. Grace Stoen's attorney, Jeff Haas, was currently in Georgetown to convince a Guyanese magistrate that Guyana should honor a California order for the return of the boy. And Jones closely watched every move Haas made. On September 3, Harriet Tropp and Paula Adams, posing as American tourists, had befriended the young lawyer in his Georgetown hotel. They reported to Jones that Haas expected to have the case wrapped up by the end of September. A court date was set for September 6 in Georgetown.

Meanwhile Jones learned that the Temple's three best friends in the Guyanese government—Deputy Prime Minister Ptolemy Reid, Foreign Minister Fred Wills and Home Affairs Minister Vibert Mingo—were all traveling outside the country the week of the hearing. Could that be mere coincidence? What about the prying visits earlier in the week by the Guyanese official and the U.S. consul? Would there be a CIA-inspired coup to topple the anti-American government and get Peoples Temple at the same time? To a paranoid personality, the possibilities were endless.

The night before the September 6 court date, Stephan Jones, Johnny Brown and several others were with Jim Jones when he pulled out a .357 magnum revolver and ripped off a few shots at a banana leaf. This was the first time that seventeen-year-old Stephan realized there were guns in Jonestown. After they left Jones's hut and were walking back toward the center of the camp, Stephan and Brown heard a gunshot. Racing back to Jones's hut, they found him face down on the floor, apparently in shock. Jones told them that he had been standing by the window when he had a premonition. Luckily he had bent down, just as a shot whizzed through the window, narrowly missing his head. Enemies were sniping at him, Jones cried.

Taking a shotgun from the hut, Stephan took off into the bush. He fired two rounds in the general direction of the first shot, then came back. His father, surrounded by aides, placed him in charge of security. Immediately, Stephan stationed himself and another man at Jones's hut, and others around the compound's perimeter. The alert was on.

Stephan knew that his father was not above staging such episodes. Still, he felt this attack had been real, though he had detected no trace of bullets or shells. After all, he had spotted a suspicious-looking broken limb on a tree not far from the Jones hut. His father did have enemies. And in the volatility of the past months, it seemed anything could happen. But there were no further disturbances that night.

Early the next morning, attorney Jeff Haas walked into the Georgetown courtroom of Justice Aubrey Bishop with his local counsel, Clarence Hughes. After a brief hearing, with no Temple representation, Justice Bishop ordered Jim Jones to produce John Victor Stoen two days hence and to show cause why a final order should not be issued giving the boy to his mother.

Armed with an interim writ of habeas corpus, Haas accepted the offer of a Guyanese Defense Force airplane and flew into Port Kaituma to serve Jones with the documents. As Haas and Guyana Supreme Court Marshal Billy Blackman waited near the Kaituma airstrip for a four-wheel-drive vehicle, the attorney noticed the Temple's shrimp boat moored at the port inlet. Locals told him that its radio posted Jones on any arriving planes or boats.

After riding over the bumpy red clay road, Haas arrived at the settlement. Two hundred inhabitants watched his approach, most of them very old or very young. There were more white people than Haas had expected, maybe up to a third. When the jeep stopped, Maria Katsaris demanded to know their business. Marshal Blackman stepped forward and asked to see Jim Jones on official Supreme Court business. Katsaris replied that Jones was "on the river somewhere" and had not been seen for two days.

The Haas party had no choice but to return to Port Kaituma. Once there, they ran into two immigration officers who said they had seen and spoken to Jim Jones in Jonestown that very day. Jones's deception merely renewed Haas's determination. He pleaded with the two officials to return to Jonestown with him to confront the Temple. But they refused, instead promising to report the episode.

Back in Jonestown, a panic was building. The government had let Haas get this far and, indeed, had supplied a plane and a marshal. What other tricks would Haas pull to bull his way in, to "kidnap" John?

By September 7, two days after the "sniper attack," Jones had blown up the custody business into a full-scale crisis. "Alert, alert, alert," Jones screamed on the public address system, while sirens summoned the community to the pavilion. It was bedlam. Guards with guns ran through the camp, ordering frightened people to assemble. Juanita Bogue, a nine-teen-year-old field worker, was terrified when the Temple dump truck appeared in the field to round up farm workers. "We're all going to die," the guards cried as they loaded workers into the truck. Back in camp, the workers were forced to stand with their hands up while guards frisked them. Then they were handed "cutlasses" (machetes), knives, crossbows, hoes and pitchforks and told to encircle the settlement, facing out toward the jungle.

Once they were assembled, Jones addressed his shaky troops, telling them they were about to be attacked by mercenaries backed by Tim Stoen. The Guyanese army would be invading as well, probably by air. Already the enemy had fired at him from the bush, he said. At any minute, they would storm the settlement to take away all their children. Jones swore that he would not let them take John or any of the other little ones. If they come for one, they come for all, he warned.

The whole camp must fight to the death for socialism, he yelled urgently. Smear your faces with mud, he cried; form your line around the perimeter and show them we mean business. Jones told his army they should wave their weapons while scanning the bush for enemies. They would eat and sleep on the line. Deserters fleeing the battle must be killed.

Jones, who always had admired the Russian stand against Hitler's troops, now was defending his own Leningrad. The siege was on.

Jones ordered his son Stephan and Tim Swinney to the front gate to halt every incoming vehicle and conduct a thorough search. A number of Temple immigrants were welcomed to Jonestown for the first time this way.

As the two waited behind a barricade of rubber tires, the full impact of Jones's words washed over them. Stephan wondered why invaders would come boldly down the road when they could approach Jonestown through the jungle. And he wondered how Jonestown could defend itself with an arsenal consisting of Jones's .357 and a few other pistols, an old M-1 carbine, a couple of rifles and a temperamental sawed-off shotgun with "Boss" painted on it. "We don't stand a fucking chance," he commented to Swinney.

On the face of it, the crisis made no sense. There was no sign of enemy aggression. But people conditioned to believe Jim Jones did not doubt his call for the final showdown on the basis of one mysterious gunshot. "We built this place, and we're gonna defend it," was the prevailing attitude.

As Jones evoked images of bloodthirsty invaders and the sounds of gunfire, he urgently, even hysterically, deployed his foot soldiers. People brought sleeping bags to the defense lines and ate pathetic rations of rice at their posts. They stood guard for hours, grabbed sleep between verbal sieges. Then the silence would be punctuated once again by the shrill voice of Jim Jones: "Alert, alert, alert!"

Meanwhile, top aides closeted themselves with Jones in the radio room, where they maintained constant communication with Georgetown and, to a lesser extent, with San Francisco. From the radio room, Jones could talk simultaneously to settlers over the public address system and to San Francisco by radio. A tape recorder was running:

"I'm hit. I'm hit. I'm hit. I'm hit. I'm hit," screamed Jones into the microphone. "Keep calm. Whatever you do, don't take offensive action. Be sure you don't take offensive action. We only want peace. We want asylum somewhere. They're now trying to negotiate, trying to contact a socialist we trust, so don't do anything rash, I beg you. Out of seven hundred people, it's easy for someone to make a mistake. . . . Don't put that spotlight to my right on anybody's head. We do not know how many people are on our left." He shouted at the top of his voice to "enemies" in the jungle: "WE HAVE FIRED NO WEAPONS!! WE HAVE FIRED NO WEAPONS!!" Then more softly to his people: "So keep calm and keep down. Do you copy? Let me hear you."

There were loud noises and yells of support from the crowd.

"Please do not move from the ranks," Jones screeched, his voice raw from overuse. "We still do not know if you are friend or foe, and it could cause someone to act rashly. If you need to go to the bathroom, ask one of the stewards or stewardesses to assist you. If you need medical help, you know the procedure to follow. Do not take moves that aren't planned. Because, if you're wandering about, something could happen that would be just chaos. We must behave as pacifists. This may be an attempt to get us to make an offensive move that would destroy the years of pacifism that we have built for. Do you understand me?"

Loud cheers.

"I cannot hear the left field." Cheers. "Center field!" Cheers. "To the back." Cheers.

"The people have formed a perfect circle," a woman told Jones.

The siege continued. Time became a blur. Caught in a furious rush of events, few slept. Fear and confusion outweighed their exhaustion. At one point, Jones trucked about fifty people into Port Kaituma and began loading them into the boat for Cuba. As people rushed to clamber aboard, one woman fell off the side and broke her hip. People began crowding around Jones, including one who had faithfully thought to bring along a tape recorder.

"My God," Jones said. "If they won't let us all go, none of us go. . . . I won't go without you."

"Thank you, Father," came the response from a dozen voices.

Jones continued: "They'll let me and my family in and a few leaders, but no one else. The rivers are blocked to the rest of us. I say the hell with it. I wouldn't be a leader worth a tinker's shit if I just went. Those miserable sons of bitches [in Cuba] are afraid to stand up to the United States."

"Thank you, Father," they cried.

"If I'm the only socialist alive, then I'll die a socialist." Cheers.

This "escape" was little more than a stunt. But in the emotional frenzy, no one thought to ask Jones why he went so far as to load the boat just to proclaim his political purity and his loyalty to his people.

By September 8, the fourth day since shots were fired, Stephan Jones was wondering about the validity of the crisis. Things did not add up. During the day, his father would send some people back to work, then suddenly call another alert so that people would have to run back to the defense line. They were no longer grabbing their cutlasses and pitchforks with the same urgency. And Stephan, equally jaded, was making a game out of surprising people on the Temple trucks.

It seemed that every time he stepped into the shower, his father's voice would burst forth from the loudspeakers again. Once, his friend Mark Cordell came running in. "They're trying to get Father," he cried. "I saw it." Cordell was hysterical, and Stephan slapped him. With the shampoo still on his scalp, Stephan had Cordell show him where the bullets hit. From the trajectory, it appeared that someone had fired from the nearby bushes. Jones told Stephan to charge into the jungle and start shooting.

Taking off with an M-1 carbine, he ran barefoot through the windrows, braving snakes and spiders. Cordell followed with a shotgun. Once in the bush, Stephan fired off a few rounds at the invisible attackers then returned.

He was confused. He looked again at the ground to the point of impact and figured a rough trajectory. It did not make sense. If the bullets had been fired from long range, they would not have entered at that angle. The gunman had stood very nearby—not in the jungle.

Back in Georgetown, oblivious to the impact of his visit, Jeff Haas awaited Jones's next move. The unserved writ had ordered Jones to bring John Victor Stoen to Justice Bishop's court on September 8. Not surprisingly, neither showed up. As his next step, Justice Bishop decreed that the writ could be served simply by posting it in three Jonestown locations or by handing a fourth copy to a Jones assistant. Haas made plans to fly out the next day to post the writ.

When Jones learned from his Georgetown aides that Haas was coming, he made preparations. On the morning of September 9, he asked his son Stephan to clear a concealed place in the bush. Taking John and an umbrella to shield them from the sun, Jones went into hiding. Several security guards followed with his wooden chair and a metal strongbox, which Stephan Jones assumed contained gold and the Temple's vital banking information.

The whole community heard the noise and looked up. An old twin-engine, ten-passenger GDF airplane made a pass, dropping some papers. When Christine Lucientes bent for one, people screamed, "Don't pick them up!" Someone might be taking pictures from the plane—and picking them up might constitute "service."

Haas brought along extra backup. This time, Marshal Blackman was joined by Tony London, Guyana's superintendent of police, and a Port Kaituma constable. At the gate, they noticed that the security shack, with its radio antenna, had been camouflaged with branches and leaves. London pocketed a pistol.

As they approached Jonestown, hostility charged the air. This time, Haas saw no children or old people milling around. About thirty pairs of eyes peered from the community center. Young toughs glared from the steps. One big guy in jungle fatigues walked by and grunted at him. Haas was glad to have the police with him.

After a few taut minutes, Joyce Touchette and Harriet Tropp came running up. Haas recognized Tropp as the American "tourist" who had befriended him back in Georgetown. She and Touchette screamed at the Guyanese officials that "two whites" had shot at Jones last Tuesday. They all but accused Haas himself, yet policeman London was unimpressed. When Tropp demanded to know their business, Marshal Blackman stepped forward again, as he had three days earlier. He identified himself and said he had come to serve legal papers. He wanted the person in charge.

"I'm in charge," said Joyce Touchette. "My husband is in the fields." Blackman asked to see Jones. Tropp interrupted: "On the advice of our attorney, we are not authorized to accept service."

Blackman drew himself up to his full height and read the judicial order aloud. As he tried to hand it to Tropp, she withdrew, letting it fall to the ground. He laid it at her feet. But she angrily kicked it away.

"Okay," said Blackman, "if that's the way you want to have it. . . ." He proceeded to nail the order on the freshly painted buildings. A young man in jungle fatigues—Stephan Jones—got up menacingly and ripped them down. "You have no right to deface our property."

"Shut up," Tropp snapped at Jones. The last thing she wanted was to provoke a weapons search or arrest. Mr. Muggs could not be so easily disciplined; he tried to urinate on Blackman while the marshal nailed up the order. But Haas and his escorts got their job done, turned and left.

Shortly thereafter, Jim Jones emerged from his hiding place, leading little John Victor Stoen by the hand. When Touchette and Tropp told him what had happened, he was pleased that his son had yelled at the invaders. Then he and the others laughed as the confrontation was recounted—how everyone had postured in high school-style, how Tropp had kicked the papers and so on. The immediate danger had passed, but the laughter died quickly. The siege was not yet over.

The action once again shifted to the courtroom. On September 10, 1977, the day after the marshal and Haas visited Jonestown, Justice Bishop issued his third, and most serious, order:

". . . IT IS ORDERED that a Bench Warrant be issued for the arrest of the infant JOHN VICTOR STOEN now in custody of the Respondent, and that the said child be made a ward of the court and that leave is hereby granted for contempt of Court on JIM JONES. . . ."

Georgetown aides immediately relayed the news to Jim Jones in Jonestown. No longer was it simply a matter of the child. Now the GDF could march in and arrest Jim Jones—legally. And his friends in the government—Ministers Reid, Mingo and Wills—were still out of the country. The radio traffic between Guyana and San Francisco crackled. The tone was desperate. It was the sixth day of "the siege," and this day Jones's mood darkened. No longer would Jones's people make a stand in defense of their land, children and principles. Now, unless they were given asylum one way or another, they would all die by suicide. The concept of "revolutionary suicide" had been enlarged since 1975, when the wine had been poured for his trusted circle. Now he extended self-destruction to the entire Jonestown congregation. Jones was throwing the ultimate tantrum, because *he* had no other place to go, no other option. His enemies were cornering him. . . .

Marceline Jones awoke September 10 in her small apartment at the San Francisco temple, where she was trying to keep the U.S. movement together in Jones's absence. She headed almost at once for the radio room. The radio connection was poor, with static drowning out words and bending voices, making them sound eerie and disembodied.

"As you know," her husband informed her, "there's been an order for my arrest. . . . People are conspiring. We are going to have to make a stand. We are prepared to die. Do you copy?"

"Roger, roger."

"The last few days has been nothing but harassment. People shooting at us."

"Roger, roger. But can I say just one thing? Give us time to let us work something out. Please do it."

"We will give people as much time as we can afford. We've been lied to and deceived. The foreign minister of this country promised us we'd have complete sanctuary. We've also gotten the promise of Dr. Reid. I can't imagine them going back on their word. . . . I can be arrested at any moment."

"Roger, roger. But surely they can stop that from happening. Please, please give it some time." Her voice cracked and she broke down into uncontrollable sobbing.

Jones reproved her: "If you don't get control of your emotions, you can destroy the greatest decision in history. We will not allow any of us to be taken. We will die unless we are given freedom from harassment and asylum somewhere—Tanzania, Libya, even Uganda—that chap [Amin] seems to be able to stand up for what he believes."

The death threat had been issued. Marceline knew her husband was desperate enough to carry it out. Somehow she had to calm him, restrain him, salve his paranoia. It would not be easy. To Jones, the threat was immediate and palpable. He had been living with it, most likely without sleep and with the assistance of drugs, for days, perhaps for a week or two.

Jones came on the radio again. Matters had become critical. He no longer would remain silent, as his attorney Charles Garry had advised him. With the audacity of a monarch, he ordered a doomsday press conference to be held in San Francisco, with invitations issued only to sympathetic reporters.

Jones then put Jimmy and Stephan on the line. Neither son would buck his father.

"Hello, Ma, this is Jimmy. I want to die. . . ."

"Jimmy, it was not too bad a few days ago. If you and your dad could kind of hang on there. The other's so final, Jimmy." Marceline started crying again.

Stephan then came on: "Mom, don't get too emotional. Dad loves all of you there. We're the ones standing here, and he's holding up. He's trying as hard as possible, and you don't have to worry about me, because as I've told you before . . . all I've ever done in my eighteen years is to anticipate what would happen . . . and I know this is the way I want it."

"Okay, I sure love you. Let me talk to the other boys, but let me tell Jimmy I love him too . . . I'm sorry for being so emotional, but it's hard not to be."

Sandy Bradshaw sat along with Marceline in the tiny radio room, waiting breathlessly for the words coming from the small ham radio set. Also present were Teri Buford and Mike Carter, the radio operator. It was the first time that Carter, a gawky nineteen-year-old with glasses, had heard anything about guns or threats of suicide. He was shocked and utterly helpless to save his wife and baby in Jonestown.

The other three knew more. Buford seemed genuinely scared. Marceline Jones was hysterical. Bradshaw did not know whether Jim Jones was bluffing or not, but she thought it a forceful strategy to get the Guyanese government to withdraw its arrest warrant and contempt charge. And if the group did die for its beliefs, would not that at least show the world how seriously the church took socialism?

The four of them took shifts to hold the radio connection twenty-four hours a day. They also tried to keep a lid on the crisis, but word leaked out. Soon the fifty people living in the San Francisco temple were aware of it. Their whispering and somber faces heightened the already tense atmosphere.

Jim Jones was growing more insistent. Not only did he want a press conference, he also wanted his leftist friends to address his troops via radio. San Francisco members searched frantically for Carlton Goodlett, Dennis Banks, Yvonne Golden, Angela Davis and Huey Newton that Saturday afternoon. "We might not be alive much longer," Jones instructed in his sternest voice. "Perhaps that might make them come over a little more quickly than they would have ordinarily. Make this very clear."

Marceline Jones, desperate to save the movement, redoubled her efforts to resolve the crisis. More than fifty phone calls had gone from San Francisco to the Midwest in an effort to reach visiting Guyanese Deputy Prime Minister Ptolemy Reid and get his assurance that the government would not arrest Jim Jones or take away the child.

Jones was on the radio with Marceline again: "Well, we're gonna die if anyone comes to arrest anyone. That's a vote of the people. We'll die because we've done no crime. I offered to go, to make that painful sacrifice, Marceline, but the people said no The morale would not stand it. I don't mind chains. But it's an illegal arrest order based on an illegal proceeding.... Our people, as you can tell, have surrounded the perimeter of our property.... They have cutlasses and are ready to defend themselves." He turned his attention to those hearing his voice over the pavilion sound system. "You are the most beautiful people in the world."

Then he thundered: "TURN THAT LIGHT OFF!! KEEP DOWN!! KEEP DOWN!! I have said you would hear everything that's going on. I've told you everything about my life. I've told you everything about my beliefs. You've known that I've been a Marxist from the beginning, have you not?"

"YES," the crowd cried. And they cheered and cheered as he asked the question again and again.

Perhaps the sound of the cheering crowd made Marceline Jones realize the desperation of her own pleas for Jonestown's survival; not only her own sons but also the populace were ready to carry out Jones's instructions. She never had been able to successfully stand up to Jones —not even in person—so it was now impossible to do so, by radio, six thousand miles away. If she started to protest, he could simply switch off her voice. There was really no choice but to be with him, or to be silent. She would not desert him now, in perhaps his final moment. She would play the good wife, the public wife.

"I want to say a few words," she told him, her voice breaking.

"Yes, my good wife."

"I just want to say that I am your wife. I've been your wife for twenty-eight years. And I know the pain and suffering you've gone through for socialism, for complete economic and racial equality. . . ."

Marceline had collapsed into weeping, but Jones wanted her to repeat her message. "I missed your copy, darling. . . . I want to tell you that I've been glad being married to you. You've been a very faithful wife, but most important, you've been a true humanitarian. . . . I love you very much."

Marceline repeated her previous statement, and then went on: "And as far as my children are concerned, I guess I love children about as much as anybody could love children. . . ." Again, her voice halted while she wept. "I do love children. As much as it's hard for me to be away from everybody there, I wouldn't have them back here. I want them to be with you. . . ."

After hours of delicate negotiations and complicated logistics, the stage was set for radio phone patches that would cheer the seven hundred front-line warriors. First the voice of the Temple's favorite black communist was carried from the United States to Jonestown and broadcast over the loudspeakers.

"This is Angela Davis. I'd like to say to the Rev. Jim Jones and to all my sisters and brothers from Peoples Temple to know that there are people here . . . across the country who are supporting you. I know that you're in a very difficult situation right now and there is a conspiracy. A very profound conspiracy designed to destroy the contributions which you have made to the struggle. And this is why I must tell you that we feel that we are under attack as well. . . . We will do everything in our power to *ensure* your safety. . . ."

Jim Jones asked his people to respond. The crowd's roar, audible even through the radio to San Francisco, lasted twelve seconds. "I guess you can hear the ovation of the people, Angela," Jones broke in, "all races, all backgrounds, that appreciated this more than words could possibly [express]."

The next phone patch was with Huey Newton, the Black Panther leader whom Jones had visited in Cuba. Newton's cousin Stanley Clayton was among the Jonestown residents listening as Newton delivered a pep talk through heavy interference:

"I want the Guyanese government to know that you're not to be messed around with. Keep strong and we're pulling for you."

The third and final phone patch was with Dr. Carlton Goodlett, who was reached in New York. He gave Jones some advice: "You knew there was going to be pressure from the U.S., and if the Guyana government is that weak-kneed, you aren't running anywhere. . . . You ought to demand that the government protect you as an American citizen and preserve your rights, and forget the matter of friendship—it is more a matter of international law."

"As always, my good doctor, you are very wise," Jones responded. "I offered to be arrested; it doesn't matter anything to me. . . . it is much easier to die for [your people] than to live for them."

Though the crisis was in its sixth day, Pat Richartz, aide to Charles Garry, had been notified of the Guyana developments only that morning when she was awakened at 4:30 A.M. by a weeping Teri Buford.

At 10:30 A.M., Richartz had called the FBI office in Chicago in her search to locate Ptolemy Reid, the Guyanese official and friend of the Temple who was visiting the mayor of Gary, Indiana. Reid was at that moment in a police-escorted motorcade on the way from Midway Airport on the south side of Chicago to Gary, less than a half hour away. Richartz told the FBI and Chicago police that it was an emergency: Jonestown could be invaded within the hour and only Dr. Reid could stop it. Both agencies turned down her requests to contact the motorcade, she would later say.

As a last resort, Marceline Jones and two Temple aides flew to Chicago to try to find Reid. At O'Hare Airport, they rendezvoused with Charles Garry, who had been in Detroit. Driving to the house in Gary where Reid was staying, they could find only his wife. But Mrs. Reid assured Marceline that Guyanese Defense Forces would not invade Jonestown and that Jim Jones would not be arrested.

Marceline immediately communicated the news to San Francisco staffers, for relay to Georgetown, then she headed for Guyana. When word reached Jim Jones, he called off the alert. The six-day siege had drawn to a close. His exhausted people had proved their readiness to die. Less than one month after his move to Jonestown, his power was total. Should members start to doubt that enemies lurked, that the settlement's very existence was threatened, they had only to think back to those days on the line, their faces streaked with mud, their arms aching from brandishing pitiful weapons.

The week following the six-day siege, Ptolemy Reid returned to Georgetown, and attorney Haas immediately sensed that the government had jammed the legal machinery. Haas's Guyanese cocounsel, Clarence Hughes, also began noticing strange things. The legal file on the Stoen case vanished from the Registry for days, then the judge locked it up. On September 16, Haas and Hughes filed another motion for the jailing of

Jones for contempt of court. Nothing happened. However, unbeknownst to them, two letters were written that day:

One from Guyana's Washington ambassador, Laurence "Bonny" Mann, to Foreign Minister Fred Wills noted that the U.S. State Department had alerted him that Guyana might receive "widespread and unfavorable media coverage of what is now becoming known as 'L'Affaire Jones.' " Though acknowledging Jones's noncooperation with the Guyana courts, Mann said his government told inquiring reporters that the Temple had not violated any Guyanese laws. But, he added, "the Temple would be injudicious to allow emotional affections for a child to embarrass the relationship with the Guyana government. . . . We ought to be concerned [about future] media or Congressional accusations that the Guyana Government is harbouring a fugitive, or blocking the execution of a court order."

The second letter to the Guyanese Foreign Minister alleged precisely that. U.S. Consul Richard McCoy wrote: "It is our understanding that the Government has issued instructions that the Court Order [in the Stoen case] not be implemented. For instance, the warrant for the arrest of the child remains unsigned. . . . The Embassy is concerned over the apparent intervention on the part of the Government. . . . On the surface, it appears that Jim Jones is impeding the resolution of a case involving the well-being of a young child."

The letter pointed out that the Embassy was concerned about precedent, because similar cases involving a number of American children in Jonestown could arise in the future.

The Temple was also concerned about precedent. "Pragmatically, the issue of John Stoen is not an isolated custody case to us," wrote Carolyn Layton in a Temple chronology. "From the political perspective we know that if we do not get backing on this issue, how could we ever have confidence in the government backing us on far more controversial issues? We also know that if John Stoen were taken from the collective, it would be number one in a series of similar attempts."

Believing he no longer could trust Guyana, Jones ordered a search for other havens. On September 30, the Temple sent letters to the Washington embassies of more than a dozen countries, many in the Third World, asking their policies on immigration and cultivation of farmlands. The church got initial replies from the Ivory Coast, Brazil, Greece, Tunisia, Bangladesh, Malawi, Canada and others. The Temple also wrote the U.S. State Department asking about several countries including North Korea and the Stalinist state of Albania.

At the same time that the Temple was making these rather peculiar inquiries, the Federal Communications Commission was monitoring the church's radio broadcasts in response to complaints from amateur ham radio operators. In fact, the FCC overheard strange discussions on September 12, only two days after the siege.

"Tonight," one official cabled to another, "I heard a 'Mr. Hill,' one of the leaders, talking about an arrest warrant and something illegal that they had done, also talk of extradition. It appeared that Mr. Hill had been shot at and harassed."

A week later, on September 19, the FCC actually taped two Temple members discussing the events of the six-day siege. One said, "It was an ordeal I wouldn't want to repeat, but you would have been proud of your friends, the seven hundred-plus; you would have been proud of them as they were prepared to lay their lives down for what they believed."

Again Jones's madness had come dangerously close to discovery by outsiders. But inside his walls all was strangely serene. When San Francisco radio operator Mike Carter arrived in Jonestown at the end of September, he expected to find a camp of solemn people, shaken by their brush with death. Instead, people were looking healthier and happier than he had ever seen them.

Several months later, Stephan Jones was standing by the kitchen in Jonestown when sixteen-year-old Vincent Lopez approached him. "You know, I saw something," Vincent began, "and I'm just gonna tell you. (You know) that time Dad got shot at from the bush? I saw K. run into the bush, turn around and shoot."

Stephan looked at him for a moment, then turned away.

FORTY

On the Defensive

With the *New West* story on press, with Tim Stoen gone, and with worries mounting about government inquiries, Peoples Temple had turned to Charles R. Garry. In the eyes of many, the selection of Garry—a nationally renowned lawyer of the Left and chief counsel to the Black Panther party since 1968—conferred additional credibility upon the Temple as a political organization. With so many seemingly nonpolitical accusations flying about, the choice of Garry helped the church present itself as a victim of political conspiracy. In practical terms, the Temple was retaining not only a fine trial attorney but also a master at handling news media.

Garry, while not the most eloquent of barristers, was the tough, blunt advocate Jones needed during stormy times, a sort of folk hero with a personal history that meshed with the openly leftist image Jones wanted. Born the son of Armenian immigrant parents who had escaped the Turkish massacre, Garry had been reared in a farm town in California's Central Valley, where as a youth he taught Sunday school and felt poverty and prejudice. As an avowed Marxist lawyer, Garry had the reputation of a fighter on behalf of the underdog. He prided himself on his street fighter's image and his trademarks—his flashy clothes and cars, his creatively direct language. Now, silver-haired and balding, nearly seventy years old but hardly mellowed, Charles Garry made perhaps the worst mistake of his career by accepting the Temple case. Garry, like so many others, was about to become a victim of Jim Jones. Because of Jones's deceptions and because Garry sincerely believed in the Temple's espoused political aims, because of Garry's own style and his willingness to forgive eccentricities and excesses in political cases, the lawyer was drawn into the accelerating current.

On his desk Garry kept a sign that read: "The only clients of mine who go to San Quentin are the ones who lie to me." He always insisted on hearing the truth, and he made no exception in the case of the Temple. In fact, Gene Chaikin and other Temple representatives at least went through the motions of confessing all. They admitted that some *New West* allegations were true technically—there were beatings, for instance. But the alleged offenses, they said, were placed in improper context, exaggerated or instigated by the very people now making the charges. They provided Garry with seemingly strong documentation showing the corrupt nature of their detractors.

Garry accepted the Temple's general thesis—that practices such as beatings had been discontinued long ago and certainly did not exist in Guyana—and set about defending the church to the best of his ability. He treated it as a political case. His office became intimately involved with church members.[59]

Over the next year and a half, Garry served as adviser to the Temple and as insulation between Jones and his enemies. Temple representatives visited or called almost daily to discuss mounting problems. While relatives and others attempted to retrieve children from Jonestown, Garry blocked their efforts at each juncture. He believed, based on affidavits which he took personally in many cases, that the Jonestown residents wanted to remain there. He supported his client against press inquiries too, making information available when it tended to help the Temple's case, holding it back when it did not. He insisted on controlling the Temple's public stance.

Garry and his office helped the church file hundreds of Freedom of Information Act requests of various government agencies to determine whether the Temple was being investigated. And when the Temple went public with Dennis Banks's disclosures about the Treasury Department gun-smuggling probe, Garry told a September 8, 1977, press conference: "We've come to the conclusion that there is a conspiracy by government agencies to destroy the Peoples Temple as a viable community organization." The results of FOIA requests, however, caused Garry eventually

to change his assessment, to conclude there was little government interest in the Temple, let alone a conspiracy. But, as the Temple's advocate,
he did not make those findings public.

Garry found himself defending a church under siege in a constantly
fluctuating situation. The initial problems posed by the *New West* article
expanded quickly: a paternity suit and litigation on two continents; lawsuits filed by Tim Stoen and concerned relatives; a countersuit against Tim
Stoen; new press disclosures; accusations of libel.

At the same time as these pressures built, Garry was confronted
by discoveries of his own. His client was exhibiting dangerous behavior;
his people showed a complete lack of independent thinking. Garry could
not overlook the problem, though he kept his criticisms within the lawyer-
client relationship.

About a month after the six-day alert, the spirit of that crisis was
resurrected in a letter Teri Buford left Garry aide Pat Richartz before
going to Jonestown. The disturbingly fatalistic missive, dated October 9,
1977, befuddled and concerned Richartz. She asked some San Francisco
members to interpret the letter for her, but they merely shrugged and
acted mystified.

Buford wrote: "Should anything happen that would kill Jim or
bring about a last stand . . . in Guyana—please try to put both his life and
death in perspective to the people.

"I am sure that many will say it was perhaps a 'crazy or hysterical act' [but] we maintain the right to choose the circumstances of our
deaths. . . ."

In response to September's terrifying events and to Buford's letter, Richartz typed a very forthright six-page answer, criticizing the Temple. Expressing uncertainty about the Temple's retreat itself, she said, "I
am not convinced that . . . revolutionaries have the right to leave the 'belly
of the beast' free of the conflicts and contradictions. . . ." Like others on
the Left, Richartz could not comprehend how an organization could fight
for socialism in a jungle six thousand miles away. And she sincerely
doubted that the Temple functioned socialistically, particularly in reaching decisions. "You feel," she wrote, addressing Jones, "that the answer
lies in establishing a socialist colony—a model. But the model isn't really
visible to us [in San Francisco], and the model panics when you panic or
are disturbed. . . . All roads lead to you—there doesn't seem to be any
independent thinking or . . . collective element in the decision making
. . . we should be thinking in terms of what happens when you are gone
—sick—not available? And perhaps I don't really know all there is to
know. . . ."

Richartz did not understand that Jones had no intention of allowing
his people to survive him. In the closing pages, her letter quoted Black
Panther Huey P. Newton's writings on a concept that Jim Jones had bent
to his own ends: "revolutionary suicide." Jones had redefined the term as
self-destruction in the face of the enemy. This twist allowed Jones to

transform a cowardly defeatist act of final protest into a dignified revolutionary "conquest." The concept described by Huey Newton, however, was something else entirely. Newton had called for incessant struggle against oppression no matter the odds (*that* was the suicide part of it). There was no room in Newton's view for surrender to the oppressor, nor to conditions created by the oppressor—poverty, drugs, street crime etc. He used the word "suicide" not literally, but to mean a fight to the death against overwhelming adversity. The defeatism and petulance implicit in Buford's letter and Jones's actions could not have been more contrary to the spirit of Newton's term. As the Panther expressed it: "You do not beg because your enemy comes with a butcher knife in one hand and the hatchet in the other."

That month, October 1977, Charles Garry hand-carried the written critique to Jonestown, along with some of his own misgivings. The events of September had troubled him. The willingness to sacrifice everything for one person—John Victor Stoen—conflicted with his collectivist principles. Also, he wanted to meet privately with his client and see for himself whether Jones actually was mad or merely prone to overdramatize, or whether he had actually manipulated Garry and his friends on the Left.

It was a pity Garry could not have seen the antics that preceded his visit, for they might well have provided the definitive answer. Jones had wanted his son Stephan, while walking down to the plane to greet Garry, to suddenly act as if he had been shot, with fake blood and the works—all to convince Garry there was really a conspiracy. Stephan discouraged the idea, and Jones finally agreed it would be counterproductive.

As it turned out, Charles Garry was impressed with Jonestown. It seemed a clean, efficiently operated socialist utopia, exactly as the church had billed it in its brochures. The people—some of whom he interviewed at length for various court cases—appeared healthy and happy. Garry soaked in the atmosphere, taking in details that would help him later describe Jonestown's virtues to the San Francisco press.

At one point, Garry had a private talk with Gene Chaikin, the seemingly sincere lawyer who had told him by phone during the siege that Jones was a madman. For several hours, they inspected the settlement together. This time Chaikin was singing a different tune. He talked of his blossoming love of agriculture and allayed Garry's worries. He conceded Jones had become overly emotional during the six days in September, but insisted that Jones now was on an even keel. As for the threats to commit "revolutionary suicide," Chaikin said they were merely means of coercing Guyanese authorities to back off. In other words, Garry and his friends had been duped so that Jones could get what he wanted—John Stoen.

Garry fumed at the thought of being used, and under the corrugated metal roof of the open-air pavilion, he cross-examined Jones. "I want to clarify some doubts in my mind," he said sharply. "I have problems with an organization which professes to be Marxist yet is willing to sacrifice the whole for one person."

Instead of arguing, Jones put on his soapiest preacherly manner, common as an old shoe. While his aides flitted around him like children, he tried to soothe the lawyer. "We overreacted," he explained. "We got panicky. It was a mistake. No one ever intended to die."

"Well, it was a stupid fucking thing to do," exploded Garry.

Jones claimed that it was his "emotional" followers who had pushed him into the whole business. Then Jones said that he personally agreed with the criticisms contained in Richartz's letter but that everyone else disagreed.

One evening after entertainment in the pavilion, Jones drifted into a discourse about sex in the church. While Marceline, Maria Katsaris, Teri Buford and others listened, Jones said, with self-sacrifice dripping from his voice, that he gave his body to church members to keep them happy and to preserve his little socialist society. And he boasted of having sex with sixteen in a single day. He then turned to his wife: "You know, I gave you the same opportunity, to have sex with anyone you wanted."

"I never did," said Marceline.

"You could have," he repeated.

The discussion over sex gave Garry pause—but not enough to negate his positive feelings about the mission and its people. Garry went back to the States and defended his client, overlooking Jones's eccentricities and forgiving his past excesses. "I have seen paradise," he told me and other inquiring reporters.

Soon new problems reached toward "paradise," reminding Jones of his vulnerability. On October 31, 1977, Jones's attorney in the lewd conduct case in Los Angeles, David Kwan, wrote him: "It is most urgent that you contact me as soon as possible." Eventually the matter was referred to Garry. The problem: On October 17, the state attorney general's office moved to overthrow the judge's order to seal and destroy Jones's lewd conduct case records. Hundreds of pages of legal documents would be filed during the next year's legal fight. Though the state lost two key decisions, it kept pushing to preserve records that would rend Jim Jones's reputation beyond repair, appealing higher and higher. The exile's problems would simply not go away.

One afternoon around the beginning of November 1977, Sam Houston phoned me. His voice sounded raspy, as though he had a bad cold. "I'm ready to tell my story, Tim," he said. "My doctor says I've got throat cancer. I might lose my voice and everything else—so I've gotta say it now. . . . Maybe if I tell my story, it will get . . . someone to find out about this church."

In the Houston family living room, Sam and Nadyne placed photo albums before me as I sat on the sofa. Sam, his voice already partially throttled, sat beside me. Nadyne took a chair by the fireplace across the room, her beauty-shop curls framing a soft face. The heavy albums introduced the family in an intimate, slightly awkward way. As we turned the pages of the album together, the life of a model child materialized in photographs taken by his proud father, in mementos and newspaper clippings of his achievements. Bob Houston had done all the right things—from grade school through the University of California—he had studied hard, attended church faithfully, excelled in the Scouts, took music lessons, played in the school band, won awards for scholastic and artistic achievements. With each page, the terrible tragedy of his death became clearer.

Now, more than a year after Bob was found on the railroad tracks, his parents were fighting back. In the past, they had tiptoed around the Temple, afraid to offend, hoping the postfuneral visits from their granddaughters would continue. Since the girls had been spirited away to South America without their mother, the grandparents were desperate. They feared the worst about Jonestown. "If my grandchildren are happy and it's real—they can stay," Sam said. But he added, "It would be a great memorial to my son if we eventually proved a salvation to the people who got into this."

Before printing Sammy Houston's story, I researched his son's death and interviewed Bob Houston's ex-wife and his widow. The conversation resolved nothing about conditions in Jonestown nor about the mysterious death. "I last heard from [my daughters] about a week ago and they said they really like it there," said Phyllis Houston. "There also is a condition that if they don't like it there, they can come back."

"I figure many of the adults down in Guyana made their choice," Joyce Shaw had told me. "But children don't have the same choice."

Our conversation gravitated toward the question of Bob Houston's death. Was it accident, suicide or murder? If it was an accident, why were his brakeman's glove and lantern neatly left on the train which sliced through him? If it was suicide, why did he leave no note and choose such a painful way? If it was murder, why was his wallet untouched and why were there no signs of struggle? None of the possible explanations could either be proven or excluded—the suspicions of foul play would not go away.

Joyce Shaw, probably the person who knew Bob best, could not provide any more conclusions than the district attorney's office, coroner's office or police reports. No, she said, Bob never had been suicidal, though he spoke in terms of life being grim with little reward. As for an accident, she said, Bob was known to be careful. On the question of murder, there were also counterbalancing factors. The death followed the defections of some others from the p.c., and the church did put out the story that Houston had written a resignation letter the day before he died. But there was no way to know whether Houston had, in fact, turned traitor, thus subjecting himself to retaliation—or whether the resignation letter was a phony to allow Jones to explain Houston's death as a bolt of God's lightning.

"There will always be lingering doubt in my mind," Joyce Shaw concluded. "Always."

The front-page Sunday article on the Houston family brought about 150 Temple protestors to the *Examiner*, waving signs, shouting and chanting to the beat of drums. But more significantly, it produced results for Sam Houston: his old friend, Congressman Leo Ryan, had promised to do what he could to help Sam's granddaughters.

FORTY-ONE

Sins of the Father

On November 18, 1977, one year to the day before the end, Grace Stoen, Marshall Kilduff and I found each other outside a courtroom in the San Francisco City Hall. We were joined soon by Grace's attorney, Jeff Haas, and by an owlish-looking man in his late thirties, who pecked Grace on the cheek and shook hands all around. Tim Stoen was as I had imagined him: handsome in a square-jawed way. His physical resemblance to Jim Jones was remarkable—black hair, the same compact body type minus a couple of inches. He could have passed for Jones's studious little brother from Stanford Law School.

For unstated reasons, this onetime Temple official now was joining his estranged wife to wrest away a child of disputed paternity from their former pastor. It was a strange turn in the story. My own deepest misgivings related to his status vis-à-vis the Temple: had he really turned against Jones? Or was he going to stand up before the judge and lambast Grace as an uncaring mother who abandoned her child? Would he claim Jones was the father?

Inside the tall court chambers with high windows along the left wall, Grace ventured a thin smile. She sat near Stoen, her legal adversary in these custody proceedings related to her divorce suit. A glance around the court revealed no one from the Temple, not even an attorney for Jones. Actually, the church lacked legal grounds for fighting the custody award. Under California law, a child born in wedlock is presumed legitimate—the offspring of the married couple—regardless of true paternity.

When their case was called, Tim and Grace approached the bench.

The judge asked them questions about the child's whereabouts, then asked Stoen, "What is your opinion of Grace Stoen's fitness as a mother?"

"She is a very fit and proper mother," he said—though previously he had tried to keep the boy from her. "An excellent mother. . . ." He then stipulated, as the legal father, that Grace could have John as long as he had visitation rights. With that, the judge awarded the mother physical custody and the estranged couple joint legal custody. The quick simplistic solution did not touch upon the more complicated issues—and did not even allow for the possibility that Jones might be the father. Without fanfare, the judge ordered Jones, wherever he might be, to hand over the child to Grace Stoen.

Their legal standing affirmed, the Stoens strolled out of the courtroom. They were no closer to regaining the child, but they had closed one more avenue for Jones; now, if he returned to California yet failed to turn over John, he could be cited and jailed for contempt. Further, having exhausted all legal remedies in the United States, they could use that fact in making their plea to authorities in Guyana, where a California court order was not binding.

Stoen was still trying persuasion on Jones. That day he showed me a letter asking Jones to cooperate in delivering the boy to Grace and him by November 25, 1977. The faintly threatening tone offered little to Jones. The minister's paternity claim had been leaked to *Chronicle* columnist Herb Caen—so he was effectively on record. Acceding to Stoen's request could spare Jones a court fight in Guyana and a public relations fight in the States—but those were hardly trump cards against a man who already had run from U.S. publicity and stalled the Guyana court system. The only concessions were Stoen's assurances that the child would be reared in an "interracial, sharing environment consistent with the highest teachings." The way Stoen couched his own faded commitment and spoke about the treatment of John must have galled Jones to no end:

"I have received reliable information to the effect that Grace is being seriously discredited in John's eyes," the letter said. "Not only is this deeply offensive to me, but it could easily cause irreparable emotional harm to John. I ask you to immediately reverse the hate campaign and to advise John repeatedly what you and I both know to be true: that Grace loved him deeply and has never abandoned him. . . . May the goals we shared be realized at Jonestown."

By joining Grace, Stoen was at last exerting his independence. His unwillingness to give up the child, whatever the reasons, had multiplied the stakes profoundly. Stoen knew the battle involved more than ego, even more than the life of John Victor. And he must have realized that Jones would not back down after this opening skirmish.

Outside the courtroom after the custody hearing, Stoen told me that he had promised himself that unless John Victor was back with Grace by January 1, 1978, he would personally go down and get him. But such fighting words and the letter to Jones produced nothing but enmity.

Thanksgiving, Christmas and New Year's passed without positive results. In early January 1978, the Stoens were forced to venture into Jones's territory, Guyana, again with negative results.

In February 1978, for the first time, Stoen turned to the press. He called me and said he was ready for the open-ended interview I had requested.

High in a monolith along Montgomery Street, Tim Stoen looked up from his desk. The lawyer had finally arrived at the polished world of Mont Blanc pens and appointment secretaries. Almost at the outset, Stoen acknowledged that he had signed the most important single document in Jones's paper-intensive church:

"I, Timothy Oliver Stoen, hereby acknowledge that in April 1971, I entreated my beloved pastor, James W. Jones, to sire a child by my wife. . . ."

By leaking it to the press, the Temple had provided a rationale for Jones's self-imposed exile and, no doubt, embarrassed Stoen. Why would the lawyer ever have committed his name to such a document?

Stoen maintained that Jones had wanted it to ensure John would be raised communally in the Temple if anything ever happened to Tim and Grace. Stoen said he had signed the document, expecting Jim Jones to place it in a safe somewhere. Trusting Jones with the life of John, he said, was the most regrettable thing he ever had done.[60]

While conceding that Jones had genuine affection for the boy, Stoen declared: "I am the legal, biological father and because John identifies with me far more than Jim, I am his spiritual father. He's holding my son because he needs an excuse not to come back to America."

The phone rang around 7:30 A.M. on February 17, 1978. "It's Jean Brown of Peoples Temple," my wife whispered urgently. The Temple was the last organization I would entrust with my unlisted phone number, so I made a mental note to find out how they got it and to change it that same day.

Leaping out of bed, I grabbed the phone with an abrupt "Hello." A woman blurted, "Mr. Reiterman, the Rev. Jim Jones is on the radio-telephone line from Guyana, ready to take your questions."

My head whirled. Sitting there in my shorts, fuzzy-headed, blurry-eyed, without a pen or paper, let alone a tape recorder or a list of questions, the Temple was offering me an unrequested and completely unexpected interview with the most elusive character I had ever experienced. If Jones had wanted to catch me off guard, he certainly had succeeded.

I had been seeking out the Temple's side for an article about the custody fight. At the suggestion of Charles Garry, I had left a message at the Temple for Marceline Jones, who recently had been interviewed by the *New York Times*. Two days had elapsed without a word. Now, suddenly, I was being given the first—and only—such interview with Jones after his flight to Guyana.

"I don't have the written questions we submitted to the Rev. Jones," I told Brown as my wife brought me a legal pad and pen.

"The Rev. Jones will only answer questions about John Stoen at this time," she said curtly.

She explained the procedure. My questions would be relayed through her to a radio transmitter at the San Francisco temple for radio routing to Jones. The answers could come in reverse order through a process that precluded rapid follow-up questions. The Temple would be controlling all circumstances of the interview.

"My first question. . . . Who is the father of John Victor Stoen? And how can the claim be supported?"

Over radio interference, my question was relayed to Jones. "Do you copy? Do you copy," Brown asked.

"Roger, roger. Roger," said a fainter voice in Guyana. Then Jones's voice cracked through the radio speaker so loudly and clearly that I could hear it before the words were repeated for me. "I am the father!!" he said in a chilling staccato. "I have taken statements from both parents —one sworn under penalty of perjury. I have sworn statements from hundreds of people. I challenge him [Tim Stoen] to take all the blood tests and challenge him to take polygraph tests under objective circumstances or truth serum.

"Why," he asked rhetorically, "would I risk my reputation for a child they have abandoned unless it was mine? I have spent thousands of dollars for legal defense in the custody [matter]."

Jones quickly proved his reputation as a compulsive talker. His thoughts tumbled out in a strident voice, with the abandon of a man accustomed to captive audiences. His answers strayed almost immediately from the questions.

"Would you be willing to come back to the United States or some neutral turf and take the same tests?" I asked.

"It can be done here," said Jones stiffly. "We can do it in the capital, with advertisement [in the Pegasus Hotel] if necessary." Then he became snide about being asked to leave Guyana for scientific tests. ". . . They would not be calling this country biased or backwards, would they?" And after only two questions, he rambled into a speech, frustrating his own relay people as they tried to keep up.

"This is ceasing to be an interview," I interjected angrily to Brown. "I've got other questions to ask. Please stop him."

When Jones became calmer, I asked about the biggest subject of speculation: "Are you willing to come back to the United States?"

"Absolutely," he said. "If they want to put the child through it, I will comply. I do not want to put my child through this publicity, but I will naturally defend my right of parentage and use every legal means possible not to let my child be used as a pawn by them. . . ."

"Why haven't you claimed in a court of law that you are the father of the child?" I inquired.

"My lawyer is there doing so now, if he hasn't already," Jones replied, an apparent misunderstanding or lie. "I would have done so earlier but would not want to cause embarrassment for a little child."

"Why have you not returned to the United States to answer allegations?" I continued.

"Certainly not because of lying allegations," he said defensively, "but because this is the way I have been advised to protect my child, and furthermore I am doing valuable humanitarian work. . . ."

"Why were you not present at the birth, why is your name not on the birth certificate and why did you not rear the child after the child came home from the hospital?" I asked.

"I was present at the birth, at the hospital, Santa Rosa Memorial Hospital, and she introduced me as the father in front of people and took me around to see the child in the nursery," Jones said. "She made out the birth certificate and did not consult me. Naturally, I did not want the child stigmatized. . . ."

I knew almost certainly that Jones was lying because I had already talked to the attending physician, who recalled Stoen, not Jones.

Jones, the Guyana radio operator, San Francisco radio operator Tom Adams and Brown all seemed to be shouting, so my voice kept climbing too. "How did you come to sire the child? Or why were you having relations with Mrs. Stoen, if that's the case?"

The minister shot back. "See Stoen's sworn affidavit. It was printed by Herb Caen." A smart answer—Stoen was to bear the embarrassment.

"Why, as an advocate of adoption, did you feel it was necessary to sire a son for one of your church members?"

After a long pause, Jones evaded the question. "I would rather not embarrass the relatives of Mr. and Mrs. Stoen, because it has to do with Mr. and Mrs. Stoen's very personal lives, and I am sure they do not want it aired."

That nettlesome question had caused the most severe crackling and popping on the radio—interference and fading signals that I later would learn were manufactured by the Temple. Aides and advisers in the radio room with Jones had become concerned that he was fumbling, and that he had told at least one lie that could be exposed as such.

As the transmission faded, I requested that Jones call me again so we could discuss some written questions submitted by the *Examiner*. His answer was pieced together between garbles: "I am working on them very thoroughly now. Your fairness with the information you got today . . . will determine whether I . . . give interviews here to your paper. . . ."

The same day, Temple attorney Gene Chaikin sent a similar warning to *Examiner* publisher Reg Murphy, dangling as bait the Jonestown interview with Jim Jones that I wanted. The heavy-handed approach continued the next day when Jean Brown called with another teaser. If the *Examiner* article was fair and if the *Examiner* also "exposed" Joe Mazor, she said, I would be provided with an opportunity to get "fantastic insights" into Jonestown and the life of Jim Jones.

Later the Temple agreed, at my request, to supply a tape of my interview with Jones for the sake of accuracy and completeness. However, a transcript—not a tape—was delivered to me. Oddly, the transcript carried less, not more, information than my notes. Some key passages—such as Jones's claim that he was present at the birth and was introduced as the father of the child at the nursery—did not appear. The transcript had been censored. My efforts that day to hear the Temple tape itself were unsuccessful—and finally a church spokesman confessed angrily, "It's been erased. It had no importance after the transcript was checked against it."

On Saturday, the day preview editions of the Sunday paper appeared, the Temple hand-delivered an undated letter from Temple attorney Chaikin. "This is the straw that broke the camel's back," the letter said. "Tim Reiterman has now shown the most outrageous bias by refusing to accept the answers . . . because undoubtedly they were not to his liking. . . . We . . . will litigate."

Contrary to the threats, no lawsuit came. The bannered story was balanced and did not identify either Stoen or Jones as the father, but it did signal a new escalation in the war of words between Jones and the defectors. Stoen, knowing the harm the paternity debate would do to his reputation, nonetheless had gone after Jones with the same zealotry he had poured into the Temple. He told me frankly that he was now trying to tear down what he had spent eight years building. Once part of the problem, he now felt responsible for providing a solution.

The exchange of claims in the *Examiner* tore Jones's credibility beyond mending. Jones himself anticipated negative fallout from the article. Though he had initiated the interview, he did not want Temple friends and supporters to learn of the paternity tangle in the newspapers. On his orders, the San Francisco staff scrambled to contact them all to prepare them for the latest publicity blast.

For some, it was one blast too many. The repercussions of the article, picked up by wire services and others, were devastating. Once again the peculiar self-exiled preacher became a topic of conversation and gossip in the liberal-progressive political community. Former supporters found it increasingly difficult to dismiss the long-standing allegations against the Temple as a rightist vendetta. Even Temple friends had to ask themselves what kind of a man would agree to sire a child for a church member, then keep that child from his natural mother. Were they to believe that Jones's stand with the boy in the jungle was only coincidentally related to published allegations against the Temple? Were they to believe that a man involved in such a bizarre carnal transaction was above beatings, forced property donations and manipulations of all sorts?

Even before Jones went public with his paternity claim, Steven Katsaris was becoming increasingly anxious about his daughter Maria's well-being. Like others with family in the church, the former Greek Orthodox priest had learned too much through newspaper and magazine articles and his own exposure to trust Jim Jones—or anything his daughter told him while under the Temple sway. Bureaucracy, distance and expense kept many relatives from visiting their loved ones, but not Katsaris.

When the *New West* article appeared in midsummer, 1977, Katsaris had been heartbroken, though Maria had forewarned him and even persuaded him to send a telegram to the magazine's owner. The serious allegations—some made by Maria's former friend Grace Stoen—frightened him, and he felt betrayed. When Maria called from Georgetown a week after the article appeared, he gave vent to his disappointment.

"It's all lies," Maria replied. "Jim will be coming back to refute them."

There were more calls. In one, Katsaris believed that his daughter, by seeking his permission to stay in Guyana, was actually signaling him that she wanted to come home—that she wanted him to order her back to the United States. Otherwise the call made no sense; his children normally did not ask permission, and Maria was over twenty-one. It was a tipoff, he thought, that something was wrong. Sick with worry, he let ten days pass. He became convinced that Maria finally had realized she was in a crazy group, but was too deeply involved to walk away.

Resolving to get her out, Katsaris called the San Francisco temple's radio operator to relay a message to Maria: he would be in Guyana on September 26, 1977, and Maria should prepare a list of things she wanted him to bring.

When a week went by with no response, Katsaris got panicky. Had he overstepped the line? He called the radio operator again, and was told Jonestown had been out of radio contact. Katsaris tactfully informed him that he was familiar with ham radio communications and suggested atmospheric conditions would improve.

A few days later, he was jarred out of bed at 4:00 A.M. by a phone call. Adrenalin surged through his body. He had visions of something terrible happening. The woman on the line was calm and friendly. "Mr. Katsaris, I am part of the group that left Peoples Temple. We hear you're going to see your daughter. We don't think it would be a good idea." She hung up. The next morning, a call came at 3:00 A.M. "If you are thinking of going to see Maria, you shouldn't," the woman said. "It's a very strange group." Two nights later came the third call. This time it was a man, and he sounded nasty. "We know you live on a ranch by yourself," the man said. "If you go, you'll get burned out."

By the following night, Katsaris was ready for anything. He had not reported the calls to the local authorities because he had no faith in them when Temple matters were involved. But this time the call came from the church radio operator. He was connecting Maria Katsaris. "Those bastards," thought Katsaris. "They tell me four nights ago that they can't reach her, and then after repeated threats, they put her on."

Loud screeches of interference interrupted their initial attempts to say hello. Katsaris thought the people at the Lamaha Gardens house were deliberately jamming the station. As chance would have it, the Federal Communications Commission was monitoring the call on September 15, 1977, less than a week after the end of the six-day siege. The FCC investigators could not hear Maria, only what was relayed to her father as her words.

"Maria, I'm going to be in Washington next Thursday," Steve Katsaris was saying: "I'm going to ask the [Guyana] government if it's okay for me to come down. . . . I would like to have you come in to Georgetown to see me. You are my daughter and we are family, and I would like to talk to you."

Relay: "She says she will not be here that particular day you are coming. Why that particular day, she wants to know?"

"Because the following week when I come back, Maria, I'm going to go to the hospital for extensive surgery, over."

Relay: "What's wrong with him?"

"She knows what's wrong with me and I don't want her playing this cat-and-mouse game. She has known about it before."

Relay: "She says she isn't playing any cat-and-mouse game. She says what you need to know, she's already told you on the telephone."

"I can't understand why she won't meet me in Georgetown."

Relay: "She's going with her boy friend to Venezuela. . . ."

"Do you copy, Maria? I'll meet you in Venezuela. . . . I'd like to meet him, too. I won't take too much of your time.

"I don't need to see the project. I need to see my child. . . . I'm beginning to get extremely anxious as to why my daughter doesn't want to see me. . . . The only thing that comes to my mind is that she would not be permitted by someone within the church to come and meet with her father, in which case I'm now desperate and I'll take whatever legal means there are to be able to come down and see if my child is all right. Over."

At that point, the Jonestown radio signal faded.

More determined than ever, Katsaris sent Jim Jones a telegram through the U.S. Embassy, summarizing the phone call, communicating his anxiety and puzzlement at his daughter's refusal to see him and reiterating his intention to arrive in Guyana on September 26. There was no reply. Katsaris had sent the cable because he wanted to proceed openly, not in a threatening manner. To Jim Jones, there was no such thing as a nonthreatening approach.

When Katsaris landed in Georgetown, Maria was nowhere to be

found. After a few days, he boarded a homeward-bound flight, dejected, but not defeated. He already was planning his next trip.

In the interim, Maria Katsaris sent her father two letters. The first was very conciliatory. She explained that she had declined to meet him on his September 26 visit, because she had wanted to be alone in Venezuela with her "fiancé," Dr. Larry Schacht, but had been too embarrassed to go into details over the radio. She then expressed concern over rumors that her father had seen several congressmen about her situation and may even have contacted "that guy Mazor, a man who is part of the conspiracy against the church." She concluded that she could understand his concern, but she insisted she was fine. She signed the letter, "Love, Maria."

Maria's next letter, dated October 28, 1977, hit Katsaris with a one-two combination of hostility and the threat of total cutoff:

"The board said it was ok for you to go ahead and come on your own. . . . However, there is something I want to know first. I have heard from rather high sources in the States that you have been cooperating with the worst kind of people, stirring up trouble. You did not tell me the truth [when you denied] that you had contacted that bunch of criminals and others. . . . I know you are up to trouble. If you want my love and respect for you ruined totally—you are succeeding. If you do not come straight, and you do not stop this immediately, that's it. I will never see you anymore."

That was only the prelude to the bombshell, dropped during a tape played for Georgetown consul Dick McCoy by Paula Adams. On it Maria Katsaris accused her father of sexually molesting her as a child. The same allegation went out in a Temple press statement.

For a former Greek Orthodox priest who now directed a school for emotionally disturbed children, this was a lunge for the jugular. Maria's accusation inflicted a deep wound, yet Katsaris fought back. He prepared to sue Peoples Temple for defamation, a tactic that would drive his daughter further away. And he flew to Washington again.

This time he met with Guyanese Ambassador "Bonny" Mann and persuaded him to intervene. Later, however, in Guyana, oddities and hitches surfaced, though Jones had assured Mann that Katsaris could see Maria. First, it was discomfiting to discover that "Bonny" Mann was playing house with a Temple woman at the residence of Arthur Chung, the President of Guyana. Worse, that woman was Paula Adams, who had run the "child molester" tape for Dick McCoy. In fact, when Mann invited Katsaris over for drinks, Adams fixed them. The depth of Temple-government rapport became even more evident when Mann took Katsaris by the Lamaha Gardens house, and the people there greeted Mann like a long-absent friend.

Katsaris spent the next three days in limbo, trapped between contradictory signals from the church. Yes, he could see Maria. No, her flight had not come in yet from Matthews Ridge as expected. Yes, she was in Georgetown, but she had gone out to dinner. And so on.

On the fourth morning, Paula Adams called. It was seven fifteen. She said Katsaris could see his daughter in forty-five minutes at President Chung's residence. "Bonny" Mann would be there, as would consul McCoy, if Katsaris wished.

The air was sultry as Katsaris arrived at the large white house with the beautifully landscaped gardens. They retired to the terrace off the living room, so they could catch the Caribbean breezes. A circle of wrought-iron chairs had been arranged. Maria walked in with Carolyn Layton and two large men; one man kept his coat on, which prompted Katsaris to wonder if he had a gun. Her father was shocked by Maria's condition. He knew she would be pale and too thin. But her complexion was terribly sallow, and there were bags and dark marks under her eyes.

When he embraced her, she remained stiff, with her hands at her sides. She turned her cheek away. He wanted to sit opposite her in the circle so he could observe her closely, but he was partially deaf in one ear, so he sat beside her instead, with his good ear toward her. She was cold and distant and wasted no time in launching an attack on her father.

Katsaris had left the priesthood, but his spiritual life was still very important to him. When he mentioned God, she stood up abruptly. "We don't believe in God," she burst out. It was an awkward overreaction, almost a conditioned reflex. Carolyn Layton tried to temper that peculiar admission by a "Christian" church member. "It's true we don't believe in God," Layton said soothingly, "but we believe in good things." But the outburst confirmed Katsaris's fears that Maria had been rehearsed, maybe even worked over during the four-day delay.

Jim Jones knew how potentially dangerous this encounter was. Steve Katsaris, a respected, trustworthy man in Ukiah, possessed the professional and financial resources to mount an attack, publicly or legally. To Jones, losing Maria would be more than simply losing a mistress or a capable financial secretary. Out of Jonestown and the church, Maria could lend new ammunition to attacks upon the church; John Stoen's surrogate mother could join his natural mother.

But Katsaris's hopes were melting away. Maria kept up her hostile barbs. She accused him of hiring a criminal—Joe Mazor—and of getting Guyana blackballed from some international human rights organization. McCoy and Mann corrected her on both counts.

Katsaris was outraged at the transformation of his daughter; still he kept a grip on himself. One false move, and he might never see her again. He looked around for ways to hustle her out of the room, but one man stood directly behind Layton, and the other blocked the path to the door.

If she showed any sign of wanting out, Katsaris planned to ask for asylum in the American Embassy and somehow get her there. But Maria never vacillated, never deviated from her cold exterior. Steve Katsaris thought she might have been deprived of sleep.

"Maria, I just want you to listen," he said. "You know I was here last month." He was not even sure she had been told.

"Yes." The answer was too abrupt. Then, when he tried to raise the child molesting accusation, Maria said, "That is a subject we shall not discuss."

"You have to discuss it," McCoy broke in. "He came six thousand miles to discuss it."

Mann could not restrain himself either. "I have children, too," he said, "and if they refused to discuss it, I would be pained to the point of death."

"That is a subject we shall not discuss." Her words seemed wooden, hard, inappropriate, coming from one so frail.

"Maria, I'm worried about you," her father pleaded. "I've been told you signed an undated suicide note and that they would kill you if you showed signs of wanting to defect."

"What is the source of your information?" she said sharply and much too fast.

"That's not important," Katsaris replied. "If you're afraid they'll kill you, tell me, and I'll get you out. If you didn't sign the note, tell me and I'll stop worrying."

"If you will not reveal your source of information," she repeated, "that is a subject we shall not discuss."

Katsaris was on the spot. His source was Temple defector Liz Foreman, his former employee and Maria's former friend. She had been present when Maria had signed the suicide note, but was now a Temple enemy. Katsaris had not spent a fortune, traveled this far and ignored threats back home in order to betray a Temple defector.

The father wanted his daughter at least to reassure him about her own safety. And yet she would not answer. He suspected the worst of the Temple. He could not help noticing that Maria's brown woven purse was roomy enough to hold a small tape recorder. And when Carolyn Layton hiked up her rather revealing sleeveless dress, Katsaris recognized it as a deliberate distraction.

"Maybe you want to give Maria time," Layton offered, playing the conciliator. "She'll be all right after a while."

As a last resort, Katsaris tried to appeal to his daughter's sense of family, to her love for her Papou, her Greek grandfather, who helped raise the kids.

"Maria, I tried to think what Papou would do in my position," he said. "I know he'd do what I have done. I love you, Maria. I came all this way to see you, yet there are all these people and lawyers."

"There are certain things called guardianships," Maria replied tersely.

Finally, it was clear what Jones's worst fear had been and why he had wanted the Temple's local legal counsel present for the meeting. They had suspected that Katsaris might serve conservatorship papers on her, as parents of "Moonie" children were doing in the States.

It was futile to discuss anything. So Katsaris turned to McCoy. "Thanks for the meeting. I'm convinced she wants to stay here. I'll be leaving on the afternoon flight."

To Maria, he added, "There will be a ticket home at the Embassy if you want it. If you want to cash it in, you can do that, too." He embraced her again, but she was cold. The only option that remained, he felt, was abduction. But, true to his word, he made plans to leave that afternoon. As he got to the Pan Am ticket counter, he saw a message to phone Dick McCoy. He dialed in a trembling hand. Had Maria defected? No.

"Both Ambassador Mann and I think that something was strange there this morning," McCoy said. "I stayed behind to talk to him. We want you to know that because you are very upset, I'm writing a full report to State, and you will get a copy."

Katsaris never did get a copy, but he felt relieved to know that at least one State Department official now believed something peculiar was going on.

Less than a month after Katsaris's visit, some other anguished parents, Howard and Beverly Oliver, came to Guyana to retrieve their sons, Billy, seventeen, and Bruce, nineteen. The black couple had given them permission for a brief Jonestown vacation. However, the passage of weeks and reports of the Temple exodus had convinced them that their sons were gone for good.

When the Olivers first demanded that their sons return, they had received gushing letters about life in Jonestown. But the letters did not wash with Mrs. Oliver, a former Temple member.

Next, the Olivers obtained a court order in San Francisco for the return of Billy, still a minor. But Billy would be eighteen soon, and Jones could stall until then. Furthermore, the boys had told visiting attorney Charles Garry that they were happy in Jonestown. In fact, Bruce had said he would rather "run into the jungle" than return to the United States.

On December 19, 1977, Howard and Beverly Oliver arrived in Georgetown with their attorney. It was a heavy financial burden for Oliver, a security guard. For eight maddening days they tried to see their boys. At one point, Howard Oliver thought he would get an audience with the prime minister, but that turned into another runaround. The U.S. Embassy tried to arrange for the boys to come into Georgetown to see their parents, but the Temple kept postponing. Finally, the Olivers were told that the church council decided it was best that the couple not see their sons. Frustrated, they left. They would be back to try again, even though they had to borrow travel money.

FORTY-TWO

White Nights

When Mike Touchette returned to Jonestown in December 1977, from a four-month stint in Georgetown, he was dismayed by the living conditions there. Instead of eight to ten people crowded into each cottage, there were fourteen. Instead of free time after work, there were catharsis sessions and long rambling discourses by Jim Jones three or four nights a week. Instead of the entertaining movies rented from Georgetown, they saw propaganda shorts on Soviet life supplied by the Soviet Embassy and video-cassette documentaries about the abuse of old people in U.S. convalescent homes or problems of returning Vietnam war veterans. Attendance was mandatory, and everyone was tested on the programs afterward.

The worst aspect of the deterioration was the permanence of the sort of "siege and suicide" routine first used by Jones in September. By now this routine had even acquired its own name, White Night.

Initially, Jones had called the ordeals *Omegas,* but then had said, "It's not the end, it's the beginning," and changed the name to *Alphas.* That did not stick either. He tried the term *Black Night,* but was concerned about the racial connotation. He settled on the term *White Night,* and soon these rituals were being held with astonishing regularity—about every two weeks.

During the first few White Nights he witnessed, Touchette still believed, more or less, in the correctness of Jim Jones's concept. The place Father had built was worth protecting from invading enemies, fighting to the death if necessary.

"Alert, alert, alert," Jones screamed over the loudspeaker, summoning everyone to the pavilion for a White Night. Jones would wait in the radio room until all were assembled. His security guards would surround the pavilion with guns and crossbows. Usually, the crisis began during the day and lasted far into the night.

Touchette served on security. But he had learned from his friend Stephan Jones that these drills were tools of manipulation and that Jones had orchestrated the gunfire during the six-day siege. Once Touchette realized that Jones had no intention of carrying them through to death, he sometimes returned to his room to read or sleep. During a two-day

White Night, Jones said he wanted an escape route to the Venezuelan border or a camp built deep in the bush and stocked with food. Touchette jumped on his Caterpillar immediately and began clearing jungle. It was an easy way to escape the unpleasantness of the pavilion.

For nearly everyone else in Jonestown, White Nights were terrifyingly real. Jones would play their emotions like a symphony conductor, making his moods their moods, making them do and say what he wished. "I want to know how you feel," he would say. People would stand up and spout: "I think it's a good thing to die for what we believe in." Even the malcontents knew that unless they demonstrated the appropriate responses, unless they clapped loudly enough for lurking "mercenaries" to hear them, they would be punished.

During a White Night in the spring of 1978, Jones's rhetoric shifted suddenly from self-defense to self-destruction: "We're going to drink poison and kill ourselves." A large batch of fruit punch was brought forth, and people lined up. Martin Amos, Sharon's little boy, pleaded with Jim Jones. But Jones insisted that Martin trust him—just as many years earlier Jones had insisted that Ronnie Baldwin stand in the rushing waters above Niagara Falls. And Martin drank, too.

A few people plopped over and were carried out, but the shoddy acting caused Tommy Bogue to snicker. Stephan Jones sat on the edge of the stage hating his father and grinding his teeth until he finally stood up, went over to his father, and whispered, "You're putting people through unnecessary pain." Jones stopped the ritual soon, saying it had been a loyalty test.

Sometimes new arrivals or a young macho guy would stand up during a White Night and oppose suicide, saying, "I think we should fight." Jones would reply, "We're going to kill you." Despite such threats, the dissenters at least gave Jones a public reason for backing off.

When the White Nights ended, Jones gave everybody the next day off to sleep and recover, to let the tension run from their bodies. It was like hearing that your relatives' plane had crashed, killing everyone, then learning they had missed the flight. People in Jonestown were not allowed to take living for granted.

Jonestown had degenerated physically as well as emotionally. Sloppiness was rampant. Buildings needed paint and fields were overgrown by weeds. Bureaucratic requirements became counterproductive, and needless paperwork consumed far too many hours. Too little time remained for the labor itself. Life became increasingly difficult for everyone.

Before Jones moved permanently to Jonestown, people had been able to take days off occasionally, even relax a bit or stroll to the "waterfall," a shallow creek with rapids about a quarter-mile from the settlement. Now that too had changed. Sundays were free, but people had to catch up on their laundry or sewing, or study for the quizzes on the news Jones read day and night over the public address system. And if people wanted to visit the waterfall or the bush, they had to coax a security guard to go along, ostensibly to keep them on the trails and protect them from snakes, tigers or mercenaries.

Jonestown institutions also broke down under the strains of overcrowding and an increasingly irrational leader. Even the Jonestown school suffered—as the notebook of fourteen-year-old DeeDee Lawrence reveals. The workbook provides a glimpse of the instructional topics—the preceding night's news and Jim Jones's paranoid visions of apocalypse, revolution, traitors and enemies. Her spelling lesson was especially revealing:

1. Tim Stoen has hire *mercenaires* to come over here and destroy us.
2. Guyana has an *alience* with the Soviet Union.
3. Yemen has offered *sancturary* to the Red Brigade.
4. Albania is a *non-aliegn* country.
5. Dad wants us to use *stradgy* when we are in a crises.
6. We are jungle *Guerillas.*

In another section of the workbook, DeeDee offered her own fantasies of how she would like the news of the day to develop:

The Red Brigade has kidnaped Carter, the Rockefellers and Moboto. They said if they don't let some political prisoners go that they would exsicute them.

China droped a bomb in the middle of the USA.

Jonestown has the most gold, copper and silver in the world. Ever goes to them for money.

The highly touted medical program did not instill confidence in everyone. If it were a choice between doing without treatment or seeing Dr. Larry Schacht, Mike Touchette would do without. He once had the misfortune of seeing Schacht trying to suture a friend's smashed finger; the doctor's hand was shaking so much he looked as if he had Parkinson's disease. Even Schacht's two nurses, Joyce Parks and Judy Ijames, complained. They said he would throw fits, ranting about inconsequential things. In retaliation, Schacht brought them up during a catharsis session for not cooperating.

Schacht could be reasonable at times, but the former drug abuser lived on a hair trigger, under great stress. Jones sexually compromised him, calling for him whenever he desired a male lover. His work allowed him little sleep. Any time Jones had an "attack," day or night, Schacht was summoned immediately. His loyalty to Jones came before his medical ethics.

Although Schacht's medical textbook knowledge was adequate, his clinical experience could not match that of some of his technical assistants. One of these was Dale Parks, the inhalation therapist.

In 1976, Jim Jones shaking hands with San Francisco mayor George Moscone. Moscone would be assassinated by a political enemy eight days after Moscone's friend, San Mateo congressman Leo Ryan, was murdered by Temple gunmen near Jonestown. RICHARD BARNES. REPRINTED FROM *New West* MAGAZINE.

The Rainbow Family in San Francisco. Jim and Marceline Jones, and from top left, Stephan, Jimmy, Jr., Lew and adopted son Tim Tupper Jones. COURTESY STEPHAN JONES.

Jonestown from the air. In the middle of the photo is the pavilion and directly be-
hind it are two long narrow structures that housed the Jonestown school. To the left
of the school are the five dormitories for seniors and behind them the cottages that
housed up to fourteen people each. To the right in a cluster of three buildings is Jim
Jones's house. LEE ROMERO, *San Francisco Examiner.*

The Peoples Temple boat Cudjo, *around 1976–77, docked on the Kaituma River. The seventy-two-foot trawler sailed between Georgetown and Port Kaituma bringing settlers and supplies.* PEOPLES TEMPLE FILES.

The original settlers in Jonestown, around 1974. Jones is third from the left in the top row. At far left is Mike Touchette. Below Jones is Temple attorney Gene Chaikin and to the right of Chaikin are Michelle Touchette, Paula Adams, Debbie Touchette, Al Touchette, Charlie Touchette and Chris Lewis, who was known as Jones's enforcer. PEOPLES TEMPLE FILES.

Mr. Muggs, the Temple's chimp, in his cage in Jonestown with Joyce Touchette.
PEOPLES TEMPLE FILES.

Jim Jones showing fruit during a Christmastime visit to Guyana. The fruit was storebought (Jones has neglected to remove the bag it was carried in), yet it was filmed and presented as produce raised by Temple pioneers. STILL SHOT MADE BY THE *San Francisco Examiner* FROM TEMPLE FILM.

Peoples Temple's Georgetown headquarters in Lamaha Gardens. The radio room was the bottom room on the left. GREG ROBINSON, *San Francisco Examiner.*

Main Street, Georgetown, November 1978. At left is Examiner *photographer Greg Robinson photographing NBC cameraman Bob Brown playing with Guyanese children, as NBC sound technician Steve Sung looks on.* RON JAVERS, *San Francisco Chronicle.*

Lobby of Hotel Pegasus in Georgetown during negotiations over whether Ryan party will be admitted to Jonestown. From left to right: Temple attorneys Charles Garry and Mark Lane, Temple aide Sharon Amos, Ryan staffer Jackie Speier and unidentified Guyanese. GREG ROBINSON.

Members of Concerned Relatives huddling in Georgetown. From left to right: Steve Katsaris, Beverly Oliver, Mickey Touchette, Anthony Katsaris and, at bottom right, Grace Stoen. GREG ROBINSON.

Journalists covering the Ryan trip at Port Kaituma. From left to right: Tim Reiterman, Don Harris, Gordon Lindsay, Bob Brown, Steve Sung, Bob Flick, Ron Javers and Greg Robinson. GREG ROBINSON.

Congressman Ryan in Jonestown with the Houston family. Clockwise from Ryan: Judy Houston, Carol Houston Boyd, Patricia Houston and Phyllis Houston, the girls' mother. TIM REITERMAN.

Jim Cobb in Jonestown with his family. GREG ROBINSON.

Leo Ryan in Jonestown pavilion during Friday night entertainment. Saxophonist second from left is Brian Bouquet, whose mother was awaiting his return in Georgetown.

Jonestown residents explode in applause when Ryan says that for some Jonestown was the best thing that ever happened to them. Cobb family is in foreground. GREG ROBINSON.

Jim Jones showing off six-year-old John Victor Stoen to the press, claiming that similarities in teeth and bone structure proved the boy was his son. GREG ROBINSON.

Jim Jones being interviewed by press Friday night. From left to right: security chief Jim McElvane, Jim Beam, Tim Carter, Johnny Brown Jones, Jim Jones, Charles Krause, Dick Tropp (background), Charles Garry, Ron Javers, Tim Reiterman and Bob Flick. Reiterman is asking Jones for permission to remain overnight, but is refused. GREG ROBINSON.

Marceline Jones in front of the Cuffy Memorial Baby Nursery, during aborted Jonestown Saturday morning tour. TIM REITERMAN.

Anthony Katsaris and his sister Maria standing together during Jonestown tour. The previous night Anthony tried in vain to persuade his sister to leave Jonestown with him. GREG ROBINSON.

Jim Jones in pavilion area Saturday afternoon, after getting word that some of his people wanted to leave Jonestown. From left to right: Mark Lane, Leo Ryan, Jones's aide Harriet Tropp, Jones, Charles Garry and U.S. Deputy Mission Chief Richard Dwyer. GREG ROBINSON.

Jim Jones confronting potential defectors Edith Bogue and Harold Cordell as security chief Jim McElvane looks on. GREG ROBINSON.

A defeated-looking Jim Jones waiting to face reporters. Already he knew that over a dozen of his people would leave with the Ryan party. White woman on right is long-time Temple loyalist Patty Cartmell. TIM REITERMAN.

Jones (back to camera) at his last press conference in Jonestown. GREG ROBINSON.

Jones (center of playground) as truck is about to leave for Port Kaituma. He is surrounded by his top aides, and nervous Temple members look on. Minutes later, Jones stood by impassively as one of his members attempted to slit Congressman Ryan's throat. GREG ROBINSON.

Truck leaving Jonestown for the last time. Chris O'Neil in foreground. Edith Parks in plastic raincoat and baseball cap. Tim Reiterman looking on from back of truck, with Bob Flick (wearing white cap) to his left and Dale Parks on his right. Anthony Katsaris wearing sunglasses on far right. GREG ROBINSON.

Congressman Ryan in shack at Port Kaituma as he describes the knifing attack on him in Jonestown. The blood of his assailant, Don Sly, is visible on his shirt. GREG ROBINSON.

Defectors waiting to board the small Cessna as Tim Reiterman, Jackie Speier and Charles Krause look on. A tractor and trailer full of Temple loyalists has approached in the background. Waiting on the steps behind Teena Bogue are Patricia Parks and Tommy Bogue. GREG ROBINSON.

The aftermath of the Port Kaituma massacre. Tim Reiterman used Greg Robinson's camera to photograph the destruction the following morning. The five dead are, clockwise, Congressman Ryan, NBC reporter Don Harris, cameraman Bob Brown, Temple defector Patricia Parks (on right near baggage) and Examiner *photographer Greg Robinson (near the left plane wheel).*

Temple loyalist Larry Layton being brought to courthouse in Georgetown for preliminary hearing on the murders at Port Kaituma airstrip. ERIC MESKAUSKAS, San Francisco Examiner.

The Real Thing

If the potion we drink had been the real thing, then it would have been the end of Dad's pain. He would not have to suffer for us anymore. Just like last night the more he talked, the more pain in his tongue. The rest of the people would be in peace with our loving leader if it was the real thing there would be no more pain and no more suffering we would be in peace today. That would have have been the best way to die. Everyone wouldn't have to go to the pavilion there would be no more toots of the horn or talking about strategy. If it was real, ofcourse we would have been free. We would have died the best way. Any other way we wouldn't be sure if it would work or not and we would have suffered. I know that Dad wouldn't let us suffer like that. Thank-you Dad for the test and not letting us suffer.

Thank-you Dad

Copy of a "Dear Dad" letter recovered from Jonestown by the San Francisco Examiner.

Jim Jones's house in Jonestown. LEE ROMERO, *San Francisco Examiner.*

Nine of the more than 900 bodies recovered from Jonestown by the U.S. Army. The aluminum casket on the middle right of the pallet is identified as "Rev. Jimmie Jones." ERIC MESKAUSKAS, *San Francisco Examiner.*

Parks's family had followed Jones since the mid-fifties in Indiana, when his grandmother Edith Parks, the spiritualist, joined. Dale had become disenchanted with Jones in California; however, Marceline Jones pleaded with him to give Jonestown a chance—and said he could leave whenever he wanted. His family—parents, grandmother, sisters, and a sister's boy friend—soon discovered Jonestown was not the Promised Land. But it was too late. Like everyone else, they had been stripped of their valuables, passports and other identification. They made the best of a bad situation. While avoiding overt signs of disloyalty, they waited for an opportunity to leave.

Although few other families made escape plans, many people chafed under the restrictive rules and practices. Sex guidelines were a major irritant. As in the States, Jones gave contradictory sexual instructions. There was no sexual freedom. The true homosexuals were not allowed to practice it, without fear of being ridiculed or confronted on the floor. Unmarried or unsanctioned couples slept together at their peril, and married couples never could be intimate with any degree of privacy in their crowded cottages.

In the case of one couple reported for having sex, the woman was married to someone else and had three children. "If you're so hot," Jones leered, to laughter from the crowd, "let's *all* see how good it is." He brought the couple to the front and told them to disrobe. Someone ran to get a red light and a mattress. The couple stripped to their underwear but were too embarrassed to do anything. Jones was in a good mood and laughingly let them off the hook.

A Relationships Committee was established to set ground rules for sex and marriage. If a couple wanted a union, they needed committee approval. During a three-month trial period no physical contact—not even kissing—was permitted. Next, they were allowed a physical relationship for a six-month trial period. If the relationship survived, they were considered married. Pregnancy automatically meant a permanent relationship. People came to the committee for contraceptives, dispensed according to established rules. But, as expected in any large community, people had affairs on the sly.

Some Jonestown residents resented the constant presence of security guards who reported all signs of lackluster attitudes. Day and night, sentries with binoculars manned a searchlight tower. Other security guards roved the settlement looking for cutups, loafers and slackers. Anyone loitering could be issued a warning. Anyone not smiling or clapping enthusiastically during a meeting could be warned. Three warnings a month meant work on the Public Service Unit (PSU) or the "Learning Crew," which did nasty jobs such as cutting grass by hand, or cleaning the outhouses or ditch digging in the mud.

For younger children, punishment could be especially terrifying. At first Jones would threaten to turn disobedient children loose in the bush to see how long they could survive there by themselves. Those who continued to act up were blindfolded then lowered by rope into a well. Adults, on Jones's orders, would hide in nearby bushes or even in the bottom of the well, making noises and pretending to be monsters.

In evening meetings, Jones would read a list of the people given warnings that day. They could contest the issue—but not very effectively, because their accusers never were identified. Then Jones would decide the appropriate punishment or would have a catharsis session to "correct" the counterrevolutionary attitude or behavior.

"I have people out there among you," Jones would warn from his thronelike chair. "Nobody knows who they are, but they are my spies." Stephan Jones knew there were no secret superspies, but he also knew his father's bluff was effective. It guaranteed that people would be afraid to talk to one another. Jones tried to divide even his own sons, from the community and each other.

Tim, Jimmy and Stephan Jones and Johnny Cobb were seen by most people as heads of security, as bodyguards stationed around Jones's house. Stephan carried a gun during the six-day siege, and during subsequent White Nights. He kept a gun at his bunk and used it for target practice or when his father sent him off into the bush looking for enemies. Jones said publicly that his son could plug a quarter at two thousand yards with a rifle, which was absurd, yet good for Stephan's ego. But soon Jones was not merely deploying his bodyguards and security guards against imaginary outside enemies—he began to use them as intimidators.

Once when Tommy Bogue and another boy ran off, a Temple search squad caught them near the railroad tracks to Matthews Ridge, then put the boys in leg irons. Back in Jonestown, their heads were shaved and they were forced under armed guard to cut logs into small pieces until Stephan Jones got his mother to intervene.

The most extreme punishment, the sensory isolation box, was the idea of chief schoolteacher Tom Grubbs. The four-foot-tall plywood shipping crate, measuring about six by ten, was first placed on top of a nearby hill, but the prisoner could hear sounds from the settlement. Then the box was placed in a ditch.

The first victim was Jeff Carey, twenty-seven, an early Jonestown settler from Flint, Michigan. Jones did not trust Carey, an inveterate note-passer who kept trying to make himself look good. Carey once came back from Georgetown and said Lew Jones was borrowing lots of money to take out white women—an untrue accusation against Jones's own son. To "cure" him, Jones ordered Carey into the box. It was not total sensory deprivation: Carey could hear the news over the loudspeaker, could see enough light to know whether it was day or night. But he could not stand, and was brought only water and mashed-up, unappetizing food. After a week, he was released. He unlimbered his stiff, cramped body, and then told Grubbs during a public meeting that the box was "great," that he had been transformed by the experience. It was exactly what he was expected to say.

Other victims included Michaeline Brady, a thirty-five-year-old white woman from Long Beach who was having severe emotional problems and would walk around the camp staring straight ahead. Barbara Walker, a twenty-five-year-old black woman who would sometimes lash out unexpectedly at people, was drugged, then put in the box.

On one of her trips down to Jonestown, Marceline Jones discovered the existence of the box and insisted that people placed inside have their vital signs checked by nurses every couple of hours. That was as far as she went—or felt she could go—toward opposing it.

December 1977 was not a good month for Jim Jones. His first trauma was the loss of his mother, Lynetta Jones, who had arrived in Jonestown before the six-day siege.

Knowing her love of nature and wild animals, Jones had arranged for her to take the boat voyage and river trip from Georgetown. But the Caribbean waters were rough, and she was up all night vomiting. The trip seemingly had weakened her beyond recovery.

Lynetta Jones never had the strength to venture out of her Jonestown cabin. It frustrated her in particular to be so close to wild animals yet unable to walk into the bush to see them. Still, she remained her lucid and plucky self. Once, when Stephan carried her to the porch for fresh air, she overheard Jones say he had shot a bush turkey nearby with a pistol, at two hundred yards. Laughing, she called over her daughter-in-law. "That man didn't shoot any turkey," she told Marceline. "I didn't see anything flying out there. . . . Anyone knows you can't shoot anything with a pistol from two hundred yards. That boy!"

But fifty years of cigarette smoking had taken its toll, and Lynetta Jones's emphysema worsened. Finally she had a stroke. She could not talk or move her eyes or get enough air, and several days later she died. Her death devastated Jones. He loved his mother. She always had stood by him. When she left him, he lost one of the few small constraints on his power and sickness.

To a lesser extent, Jones was upset by news from San Francisco that Chris Lewis had been murdered in the Bayview-Hunters Point district of San Francisco. The local papers ran stories, quoting police as speculating that the killing may have been drug-related, or revenge from one of Lewis's many enemies. The trail of blood to his body indicated that two gunmen had chased him on foot, then executed him, without bothering to take the $1,000 in his pocket. The church was worried it would be blamed for the shooting because Lewis had been persona non grata since leaving Guyana. As usual, Jones took the offensive, claiming that Lewis had been murdered by anti-Temple conspirators.

Jones was in a foul mood already the December night he was passed a note about a suicide attempt by Tom Partak. The thirty-two-year-old Vietnam veteran was one of a handful of Jonestown residents who had been asking to go home. In meetings, he always took the bait when Jones asked in his sympathetic voice whether anyone was homesick. Partak missed his mother terribly. After several months of being reprimanded regularly for wanting to leave, he had become suicidal. And now he had tried to kill himself with a cutlass.

On this night, Jones was in no mood for fun and games. The tape recorder was running.

"You should have been black," Jones told Partak, his voice oozing contempt. "You wouldn't worry about suicide if you were a nigger like us. Where you come off with all this whiteness? You like pain?"

"No, Dad."

"Don't you think the cutlass causes pain?"

Partak hesitated. His voice was halting and his tone uncertain, fearful, on edge. "I thought, sort of, the mental pain I go through every day."

"You think you'll stop pain by one act of killing yourself?"

"I just wanted to get out of, uh, the particular situation," Partak replied, hesitantly.

"You think the situation's that bad, huh? How many places in the world are worse than this? I could show you places in Chicago where boys are castrated every day. Nobody's bothering you, molesting you, castrating you. You have food, shelter, you're not cold. You people amaze me with your total inability to think. You've been conditioned to go back, programmed like a robot. Ever consider the blessings of this place, you idiots?"

The words came so fast that few could catch them, let alone an inarticulate fellow who was already terrified. As usual, Jones identified a real problem—the robot conditioning—but deflected the blame from its real source, himself. Frighteningly, this refractive logic worked.

"I'm, uh, grateful," Partak stammered, "for people finding happiness and contentment here, Dad. I'm happy that's the case. I'm sorry it hasn't worked for me."

That last line sent Jones into an uncontrollable rage.

"Do you know why, sir, it doesn't work for you?" He was screaming now, mixing unadulterated fury with the old cadence of the Pentecostal preacher. "You're an elitist! You're a fucking miserable capitalist. You should be shot. I suggest that. SHOT! Through the hips, so you can lay. LAY! AND SUFFER! You're a bigot. A spoiled child of the middle class. A petit bourgeoisie. Yet I love you enough to live for you." There was applause.

"What you said is true, Dad."

"Through the hips," Jones continued, now menacing again, "so you can lay. So you can feel pain. You don't give a goddamn about anybody."

He paused for a moment before shouting at the top of his voice: "It's a good thing I'm a loving savior."

More applause.

"You better respond. We'll get you out of your goddamn fucking shell and your bourgeois attitudes and your emotional insanity. We're not privileged. We're niggers. We don't have the privilege to go insane and be on expensive tranquilizers and have some stupid shrink stand over us and tell us why we want to fuck our mothers. You thought you had an easy out. You thought you wouldn't have to suffer. You been playing with our mercy. TALK!!!"

Partak was terrified by the torrent of verbal abuse. He could barely get an answer out, but when he did, it came from the gut. "I, uh, don't like the structure."

"I don't give a fuck what you don't like," Jones cried, defying Partak to desert them all. "Want to go now? Just say so. We got a path. We'll send you. YOU WANT TO LEAVE TONIGHT?"

"No, Father."

"You miserable goddamn person. If you don't have any compassion on me . . . I've lost my mother. You miserable, goddamn, self-centered son of a bitch." Jones began striking him and sobbing at the same time. Then his sobs turned again to shrieks. "I'm gonna give you more and more. You're gonna stay awake twenty-four hours. You're gonna be crazy. Goddamn you."

There were cheers all around.

"One of my black sons [Chris Lewis] just died, was shot for the likes of you. I've dealt with your insanity for the last time. I don't give a shit what you do. You can commit suicide and come back a goddamn fishworm. Let the fish eat you. See if I give a damn."

The session continued, with the crowd joining in the catharsis. People walked to the microphone to accuse Tom Partak of being a capitalist agent because he had been a private security guard, an exploiter of Third World people because he was white. One critic started thumping poor Partak, and Jones joined in.

"You heap more pain on us," Jones cried. "Is it not enough I lost my mother, a heroine of the faith, and a black son? How do you think I would have felt if I'd gone out there and found *you* wounded or dead?" Jones neatly turned the guilt around.

"Sorry, Jim," Partak said. "It was just completely selfish of me. I'll make it up to you. I'll work as hard as I can."

"It's a rage of love that causes all this," said Jones, excusing his own loss of temper. "Otherwise, every indulgent act would be endorsed. You understand that?"

"Yeah," Partak said, gratefully.

"Son," said Father. "Life is not going to appeal to you. But there are several hundred of us, and we can make one hell of a noise for socialism. It's not gonna last forever. . . . We gotta teach that this kind of behavior can't be tolerated. We don't hate you. We love you. Dismissed."

Jones's criticism of suicidal church members was but one example of the double standards of Jonestown. Another was the leader's lifestyle itself. It had become relatively lavish since the old p.c. days when Jones would curl up on pillows and eat from a plate of meats, nuts and fresh fruits. Now, aides in San Francisco sent him crates with Courvoisier cognac, chocolate bars and assorted treats that went directly into the small refrigerator in his house.

Jones lived in West House, the best and roomiest structure in Jonestown. The two-bedroom house with a screened porch was shared with his two closest aides and mistresses, Carolyn Layton and Maria Katsaris, the stand-in mother of John Stoen. Jones slept in the largest bedroom, alone when he wished, while Katsaris, John Stoen, Layton and sometimes her sister Annie Moore slept in the other. The bedrooms were separated by a tiny room with an army-type field telephone to reach the radio room and public address system. Jones could literally spend days in his house, reading the news by phone into the loudspeaker or holding the nightly meetings by hook-up to the pavilion.

His bedroom was dominated by a large four-poster wooden bed, with clothes drawers underneath. Wooden trunks held his personal items: hypodermic needles, alcohol swabs, liquid Valium, morphine, many other kinds of drugs, sugar substitute, laxatives, Maalox, cocoa, Allercreme, hair spray, and Miss Clairol hair coloring, used to keep his graying hair jet black. Next to the bed an oxygen machine and several large canisters were ready to revive him from his attacks. Across the room, next to the small refrigerator, his file cabinets held farm reports, memos from his Georgetown staff, reports on discipline problems and digests of the day's news, taken from radio broadcasts.

Carolyn Layton still ranked as Jones's top assistant, yet Maria Katsaris had come far in her few years in the church. In Jonestown, she acted as a kind of palace guard, shielding Jones from people he did not want to see. Sometimes, she hardly ventured from West House for days. Though some resented her, Stephan Jones liked Maria and joked around with her. He appreciated her often biting wit, and her protectiveness of John.

Once when Jones asked his son to stage a kidnapping of John, Stephan found an ally in Maria. Jones had ordered Stephan to scoop up John, throw him in a bag, fake a fight with himself, disguising his voice, then save John from the would-be kidnapper. Stephan thought it was crazy and would do psychological harm to John. On the way to Jones's house, he encountered Katsaris and confided in her. She said, "You've got to talk him out of it." Stephan did so, impressed that Katsaris would take his side.

By the end of 1977, Jones's madness filled the air almost incessantly. He harangued over the loudspeaker for hours on end. The news with his paranoid, doomsaying interpretations became sickening to his own son. One day, at the sound of his father's voice, Stephan snapped, "Oh, fuck. That lying son of a bitch. Who wants to hear that shit?" Mike Touchette was startled to hear such irreverence, and to hear Stephan refer to Carolyn Layton as "that bitch." Such pronouncements and private conversations with Stephan reinforced Touchette's doubts about Jim Jones, but not enough to prevent him from reporting his friend.

Jones already had taken steps to neutralize Stephan and Marceline —in case they tried to stop his final march. Earlier, he had told Touchette that Stephan was unstable and had tried to kill himself. "Be a friend, a brother, to Stephan," Jones said. "And if he says anything strange, let me know so I can put a stop to anything serious that might happen." After overhearing a conversation between Stephan and Marceline, Touchette reported that they commiserated, about Jones.

The great majority of Jonestown residents were not privy to enough information to be skeptical of Jones or of the White Nights. And while some labored under discontent and a few, like Dale Parks, bided their time and fantasized about killing Jones, they still took Jim Jones at his word. Unlike Stephan, they did not have a front-row view of Jones's games and manipulations and were kept submissive. Those who showed their unhappiness were humiliated in front of their entire world—one thousand people. Those intellectually and verbally capable of taking on Jones publicly were smart enough to stay in line. And most probably did not want to leave anyway. In their faith, they believed Father when he said conditions would improve. And if Jones acted irrationally, they could forgive him: Father was always under such pressure. People directed their resentments not at him, but at themselves, at each other or at the enemy.

Meanwhile, Jones's paranoia had brought about the very IRS investigation he had dreaded for so long. On February 21, 1978, the IRS notified the Temple of its examination of the church's political activity. For years, the church had escaped such scrutiny, even after the damaging *New West* article seven months earlier. But an ongoing series of letters in 1976 and 1977 to the IRS—asking what level of church political activity was acceptable and including a list of political supporters—probably had aroused the agency's curiosity. Further, the Temple had filed one Freedom of Information Act request after another to see whether the IRS was investigating, despite continued IRS assurances that it was not.

Although the 1978 IRS probe soon tapered into nothing, it further legitimized Jones's image as a persecuted rebel. He was more convinced than ever that the government was after him. When Jones felt pressed, his people suffered. . . .

By early 1978, Jonestown's inhabitants accepted White Nights as part of their routine. They dutifully trooped to the pavilion as often as twice a month, not knowing what to expect. During the White Night of April 12 and 13, 1978, for instance,[61] Jones dwelt as much on sex as on death. One man was raked over the coals for having sex with an off-limits woman. After ridiculing some people for sexual inadequacies, Jones bragged of his own powers: "You people who believe in love are stupid," he announced. "You can't fuck for seven hours, like I did. I only saw one [woman] who could do it and she's a stupid masochist. . . . I'm not fucking her now. She's in Georgetown, and I never seen nobody fuck through a jungle. My dick's supposed to be fair-sized, but it don't reach that far. . . .

"Shift, please!" That instruction, issued at various times during the meetings, was an order for people to stand and stretch, so they would not fall asleep.

"Don't wave, honey," he continued, as the kitchen crew brought food to the assembly. "They'll get the food to you. You'll eat before you die. If it's the last meal, we'll kill the chickens and have fried chicken."

An old black woman stepped to the microphone: "I been in this movement since 1971," she said. "And when they hurt you, they hurt me. You [are] the only father I have. I love you, Father. I have no family but you."

As the White Night wore on, someone brought Jones a drink. After a while, he began to slur his words.

"Whew, that's strong brandy. You should'a told me it was brandy before I drank one-fourth of the glass. Shit." Jones laughed. "I'm drunk. You fuckers did that on purpose. But don't start no shit. I may stagger, but I can still get you. Laugh, Jeff, or your ass'll still be on the learning crew. You all right, my son? Stone-face Steve, they call him. You want some brandy? . . ." Jones laughed again. "What is it, dear, wanna fuck? I just feel relaxed enough to fuck." He then whispered to an aide. ". . . I know how serious a White Night is, drunk or sober. But things are getting calmer. Smile, bitch, or I'll pour it up your vagina." More laughs. "It don't make me happy, but it makes me not feel my headache."

Though she was one of the few restraining influences on Jones, Marceline was often traveling or in San Francisco. When she was in Jonestown, it was a more harmonious place. When she took part in the catharsis sessions, her criticisms had more impact than her husband's almost indiscriminate attacks. Though she cut with a sharp tongue, she had the respect of her audience because she tried to be constructive. She was the mother figure.

Near the center of the compound, Marceline lived in her own simply furnished green cottage with a small sitting porch enclosed by mosquito netting. All her children dropped by to see her. Marceline took special delight in Chioke, her new grandson and Lew's firstborn. As often as he could get away, Stephan would visit, and they would talk for hours. He shared her meals, delivered by a kitchen aide. Often, he would catch a few hours sleep there.

Marceline, while going through a difficult menopause and marital problems, continued to confide in her only natural son. Her husband's philandering still bothered her, Stephan knew, but what really set her boiling were Jones's insinuations in public meetings that they were still sleeping together or that she still desired him. She would smile agreeably and hold her tongue, but when she got back to her cottage, she would let loose. "I can't believe what the son of a bitch said."

Sometimes Jones would make loving gestures toward her. But they were gratuitous and insulting and angered Marceline even more. She told Stephan she still loved his father, though more as a sick child than as a husband. She knew he was addicted to drugs, and once she told Stephan: "We've got to isolate him. We've got to get him off these drugs." And Stephan replied, "Mom, you keep forgetting. There's no way he's . . . even gonna admit he has a drug problem."

In late 1977, on one of her periodic trips to the States, Marceline felt exhaustion overtake her. She had been pushing herself at an almost superhuman pace since the exodus. Now she had developed a chronic cough. On the way back to Jonestown, she decided to stop in Indiana to see her parents. When she got off the plane, her mother immediately recognized the toll of strain: Marceline appeared drawn, sickly and older.

The family doctor hospitalized her for a checkup and to diagnose her cough. After a week, cancer cells were detected in her sputum. Her week-long stay stretched into a month of tests. As she lay there, her husband heaped pressure on her by always calling from Jonestown with urgent orders. In a quandary, Marceline was almost ready to check herself out of the hospital. But her sister Sharon called Jones and talked him into giving Marceline's health precedence.

Later tests showed no cancer cells in the sputum, and Marceline was discharged. She wanted to go home to Guyana, but Jones instead sent her to San Francisco to field problems with the Stoen custody case. Then he dispatched her to Washington to persuade congressmen to ignore Tim Stoen's appeals for help.

When Marceline finally did make it to Jonestown, she wanted to convey her happiness to her parents. She wrote them several letters over the next few months extolling the joys of working in the medical facilities and the nursery, of being with her children and grandchildren.

"We have such darling children here," she said in one letter. "I can sit on my porch and watch the toddlers walk the path to their school. You know I would enjoy that more than the greatest stage production in the world." And in another she said of Stephan: "[He] is a great comfort to me. At times I feel I depend upon him too much. He is so very wise."

Stephan Jones was spending many of his days alone in the bush, far from his father's madness and the sycophantic palace guard. The bush was a special place, dangerous to a newcomer but comforting and serene to those learning its mysteries. It became Stephan's private world, his refuge. Instead of enduring the drone of Jones's amplified voice, he could listen to black ants buzzing from their nests or the jungle birds announcing his arrival.

The day finally came when Stephan Jones shared his world with his mother. They took a long-promised walk to the hilltop where they could overlook the entire settlement. Marceline's back still bothered her, so they moved slowly. At the summit, she broke into a wide smile.

"When you were first sent down here, I really just fell apart," she said. "I thought, 'He's going to destroy you. You'll never have a chance to create.' But now, when I see all that you've built, I'm so grateful you were able to be here. I'm so glad all these people could come here and see something other than the United States. But none of them are as lucky as you, who were able to build it and see it when it was nothing."

Stephan took her in the opposite direction, about a mile, a long walk for her. He had cut a special place in the jungle. It was his alone and very beautiful. A small waterfall plunged into a gentle pool. He was showing his mother his university. Seeing it, Marceline too marveled at the beauty. She sat down to rest and breathe in the tranquil surroundings. It was a day she always would treasure.

By her very role as a peacemaker and mother figure in Jonestown, Marceline Jones, despite her private reservations, helped legitimize her husband's power and dulled people into living amid impossible circumstances, rather than revolting against Jones. Because she loved Jones and also believed so strongly in the positive aspects of Jonestown and the settlement's founding principles, she tried hard to dismiss the negatives. She knew her husband was dangerously out of control at times, but she was terrified of him. She also knew that she was watched closely.

Marceline's only real ally was her son. Stephan told his mother to pick her fights carefully. He also felt that a rebellion was not likely to succeed. Since these two—the key to any revolution in Jonestown—had resolved to wait until Jones was out of the way, there was no prospect for an overthrow.

In the first half of 1978, the U.S. Embassy made two visits to Jonestown to check on relatives and perform the normal consular activities. On February 2, Frank Tumminia, Guyana desk officer visiting from the State Department in Washington, flew out with John Blacken, the deputy chief of mission or number two man to the ambassador.

Tumminia spent three hours in conversation with Jones. The minister appeared completely rational, but dominated the conversation and talked of persecution by right-wing forces in America. Though impressed by the physical site, the desk officer felt some people responded to him like robots. He did not know, however, that Jim Jones prepared his people for outside visitors.

On May 10, 1978, Blacken's replacement, Richard Dwyer, made his first visit to Jonestown, accompanied by Consul McCoy. Dwyer, an Indiana native and graduate of Dartmouth College, was a robust gray-haired man in his forties. Dwyer already had logged twenty years in the Foreign Service, including time in Chad, where he survived a grenade attack.

An associate had told him Jonestown looked like a summer camp, but Dwyer found it to be an impressive development—run by calculating people. During lunch, Jones suddenly was called away from the table, leaving Dwyer alone with Marceline Jones. The diplomat was surprised to hear Mrs. Jones bring up the Stoen custody case. "That was probably the worst mistake Jim Jones ever made, to father that child," Marceline said. "But I want you to know it was done with my complete support and concurrence, and as far as I'm concerned, Jim Jones is among the greatest men alive."

McCoy, meanwhile, spent his time attending to consular duties, interviewing church members on behalf of relatives in the States. He told everyone he ran across that the consulate would provide a new passport if they needed one for any reason.

Somehow, the same message reached Deborah Layton Blakey in Georgetown.

FORTY-THREE

Secessions and Skirmishes

As assistant financial secretary, Debbie Blakey knew the overseas banking system when she traveled from San Francisco to Guyana in December 1977. She was trusted and seemed to be tightly bound to the church. She had family in Jonestown—her mother Lisa Layton and her husband Phil Blakey, who worked on the boat and the bulldozers. Her brother, Larry Layton, was still in the States.

Even though Debbie Blakey ordinarily worked in Georgetown, she saw enough of Jonestown to know it was not paradise, not with such long hours, poor food, armed guards, White Nights. By May, she was having trouble keeping her hostile feelings private. On May 12, her sister-in-law, Karen Layton, wrote Jones from Georgetown:

"Debbie is very difficult to deal with. . . . Sometimes she is so kind and thoughtful and other times she's short-tempered and pissy. I have not found her helpful in organizing here."

The next day, Debbie Blakey disappeared, leaving the public relations staff very worried about her intentions. They confirmed the worst when Debbie Touchette spotted her at the post office with an Embassy political officer.

"What's wrong, Debbie?" asked Touchette.

"I'm leaving," Blakey replied. "I'm sorry. I know this comes as a shock to you, but I just can't take any more of this."

Touchette pleaded with Blakey to reconsider, or at least to call Jones and explain personally why she was leaving. Blakey finally agreed to dictate a note through Touchette, saying she wanted to leave and settle down:

"I have nothing vindictive against the church," Blakey said. "I'm just tired. I thought it was unfair to have a crisis when there wasn't one. People can't live on a string. A lot of times [Jim] says [for] people to give opinions, [but] they are put on a list to be watched . . . I always had the fear I wouldn't explain myself well, and it would be the learning crew [for me]."

As a member of the financial team and an experienced radio operator, Blakey had made herself almost indispensable. She had persuaded Jones to let her work in Georgetown, so that she could plot her defection. She had called her sister collect in the United States to say she wanted to leave. Then her sister had sent her a return ticket, and McCoy had provided her an emergency passport.

The Temple tried again to stop Blakey. Terri Carter Jones of the Georgetown staff tailed her to the airport, then concealed herself among the passengers for the Pan American flight to New York. As Blakey walked through the electronic security gate with Consul McCoy, Terri Jones popped out to confront her.

"It would ease the mind of the one who loves you most if you would just keep in touch," said Jones. Blakey nodded slightly.

Terri Jones started to cry. "Why are you doing this to Jim?"

"I'm not doing anything."

"Can you imagine how he feels right now? He's so sick, Debbie."

Unmoved, Blakey boarded a United States–bound jet with McCoy, who was returning to Washington for scheduled consultations. The consul was delighted to have a defector on his hands. He had been frustrated in Guyana, deluged by both angry relatives and the Temple. He thought a defector, especially such an articulate one, might clarify matters. But, as she talked, it seemed that she was exaggerating.

Back in Jonestown, the effect of the Blakey defection was predictable and instantaneous. "Alert, alert, alert," Jim Jones shrieked over the loudspeaker. It was his forty-seventh birthday, but there was no celebration. Everyone streamed to the pavilion. Another White Night was about to begin.

The alert sent Stephan Jones running to the radio room, picking up bits of information on the way. His father, talking to Georgetown, was learning details of Blakey's desertion. In the radio room, a crowd had gathered: Carolyn Layton, Harriet Tropp, Larry Schacht, Marceline Jones and the Jones boys. Jones asked the doctor how everyone could commit suicide.

"Well," Schacht replied, "we could sedate everybody and give them an injection into the heart."

"We could shoot everyone, too," Jones added.

Stephan and Marceline Jones felt Schacht was just telling Jones what he wanted to hear. As usual, Marceline opposed such talk, and Layton and Tropp began arguing heatedly with her.

"Do you really think you can take the lives of a thousand people?" asked Stephan. "It's not that easy." His mother was vigorously nodding her head.

Jones shut them off. "How many bullets do we have? Count the bullets. I'll do it myself. I'll walk around and put a bullet in everyone's head."

Young Jones thought his father was posturing, but he continued to argue. "Do you know what a bullet does when it hits a human body?" Stephan asked. He thought his father was basing his idiocy on TV and movie violence.

Yet Jones was certain that Debbie Blakey could open up the camp to its enemies. "It's better for us all to die together, proud, than have them discredit us and take us apart and make us look like a bunch of crazy people," he said.

"What do you think everybody committing suicide will look like?" Stephan wanted to know.

"Well, at first, maybe they'll think we're crazy," Jones said. "But it's going to go down in history as a great act."

By then, all of Jonestown had been assembled and waiting at least an hour. The people in the radio room were poised. Jones stopped before a mirror in an adjoining room, combed his hair, painted on his sideburns and adjusted his black Mao hat. Then he strode into the pavilion with his pistol. Stephan Jones thought to himself, "There goes the warrior, this little fat man, with his .357, which he thinks is a .45."

The Emperor Jones took his throne, the green chair, and sat back against the pillow. His arms folded, his gun holstered, he scanned nearly a thousand human beings and listened as Harriet Tropp explained the dire situation.

The people were not told who defected—only that the traitor was involved in finances. Speculation centered on Tim Carter, whose brother Mike was on stage with Jones, handling the sound equipment. This death rehearsal began in the afternoon, and by 3:00 A.M., young Carter would be sick of it—and ready to die.

"Yes, let's do it now and end the constant pressure," would say many who approached the microphone. A small minority would say, "No, why now? We still have the children to live for." And they usually would be called "chickenshit" and shouted down.

Jones, meanwhile, tested and pushed people to their limits. How much did the cause mean to them? How far were they willing to go? Would they defend Jonestown to the death? Would they kill themselves to make a revolutionary statement for socialism?

Several people consistently argued against death or suicide. One was Kay Rosas, a woman with emotional problems whose opinion carried no weight. Another was Christine Miller, a black woman in her early sixties from Los Angeles, who used to wear furs in the States with the special permission of Jones. She would argue that there was still too much to live for. But she betrayed her "materialist tendencies" when she argued, for example, "I sold my car and my forty-thousand-dollar house to come down here. I could be living comfortably. I didn't come down here to die." Miller's arguments were counterproductive.

No one challenged Jones on the basic issue: that self-destruction was insane, meaningless and sure to be interpreted differently than intended. Enormous peer pressure kept them from saying so. Mike Carter, for one, was afraid to tell anyone his feelings, for fear of being reported. When Jones asked how many would be willing to die, Carter was careful to show uninhibited support along with the rest. It was impossible to tell how many were swept along, screaming for death just to protect themselves.

Dinner was served in the pavilion as the White Night continued. At 4:00 A.M., nearly everyone had dozed off. Looking around, Jones said, "Fuck it, let's all take a nap," and people stayed asleep on the wooden benches. When they awoke, Jones dismissed them. As Carter yawned, he saw the sun come up. But by noon, the meeting had started anew, with the same wearisome discussion of the same issues. Jones delivered progress reports on the anonymous defector, even changing the gender.

"He's in Venezuela now," Jones said. "He might be coming back. . . . We're not calling him a traitor yet."

Finally, Jones terminated the White Night. "It isn't our time to go yet. We have too much to live for. . . ."

Jones's first corrective action had been sending Maria Katsaris and Teri Buford out of the country to change all the bank accounts and rearrange the Temple's finances in case Blakey tried to raid church funds. He also ordered Larry Layton immediately to Guyana. He did not want the defector preaching anti-Jones doctrine to her brother. When the church reached Larry, he was in his father's swimming pool in the Berkeley Hills. He obeyed orders and was barely dry before he was at the airport boarding a plane.

Without doubt, the Blakey escape represented a real crisis. But perhaps, with some fast letter-writing, Jones could neutralize the press in San Francisco, and defuse Blakey altogether. . . .

Several weeks after Debbie Blakey left Guyana, accusatory letters came to me at the *Examiner*. Since there was no way of knowing that she had defected and was agonizing over whether to go to the press, the nine letters were particularly baffling. They ranged from mild to vehement, all with the same innuendo: Tim Stoen and other unnamed persons were plotting a mercenary attack on Jonestown, and Tim Reiterman had been identified either by Stoen or by "reliable sources" as a supporter of violence against the church. Only later did I see that the Temple might have wanted me on the defensive in case Debbie Blakey suddenly appeared and began talking, which is exactly what happened. It was June 15 when the phone call came inviting me to a semiprivate news conference, with just Marshall Kilduff and me representing the San Francisco news media. It was held at the offices of attorney Jeff Haas in a renovated brick structure across the street, coincidentally, from the Housing Authority.

Debbie Blakey arrived without fanfare, looking every bit as icy as I had imagined upper-echelon Temple women to be. It appeared that she had joined forces to help the Stoens; Haas was their attorney, too. Blakey appeared childlike, little more than a teen-age refugee from Berkeley's Telegraph Avenue. She seemed reserved, and dressed tastefully. She was pretty. Ever-protective Haas explained how reluctant she had been to speak out and how difficult it was. Only a month had elapsed since her escape. But why was "escape" necessary?

"They have armed guards, about fifty, and they encircle the camp to make sure everyone is working," she said. "They have weapons— handguns and rifles, not machine guns. They have twenty-five guards in the daytime and twenty-five at night. There's one at Jim's house around the clock.

"It's really depressing there," she added. Blakey sounded somehow unconvinced, as if her heart were not in it. Her speech seemed hollow, her allegations sensational. "In San Francisco, it was beatings, but down there, it was literally torture.

"There was a guy, Don Sly, [who] put his knuckles in your temple and pressed. There were free-for-alls. Faces were bashed in. People tried to not show their expression when the torture was going on. They looked at Jim. The tortured were indoctrinated and tested . . . in front of 1,100 people."

Blakey portrayed Jones as a fat, pistol-toting tyrant at the command of a group that sounded more militant and better armed than the California church had been. "They've got guns and enough poison and liquor to put people asleep," Blakey said, when asked about her reference to "mass suicide" plans. Yet she also conceded that guns never had been used on members, just for target practice. And she admitted some had been purchased in Guyana under legal permits for security and hunting.

"But there's no meat and no hunting," she said. "When there's a crisis, two hundred to three hundred rifles and about twenty-five handguns come out. There's lots of ammunition, and some people are working on a bazooka. I never saw the bazooka."

After the interview, I felt anguished. I wanted badly to write a story from the Blakey material and realized its importance—as an inside view of Jonestown—but my gut feelings were negative. Though she may have shown real courage in escaping and speaking out, her story conflicted with Broussard's and Mrs. B.'s in some ways, and more than that, it presented the familiar problem: How could I write an extremely damaging, uncorroborated account about an agricultural mission six thousand miles away? Was it not possible Blakey was a plant, sent to seed the news media with false accounts? Given the Temple's past strategies, the chances of a Temple agent provocateur did not seem remote—and an irresponsible story, even a hoax, could discredit everything the media had printed about Jim Jones.

Although the *Chronicle* did run the story, the *Examiner* decided to hold off on the Blakey allegations; one story would not resolve conclusively our questions about Jonestown, and probably would put me further away from a visit there. With positive appraisals being offered by Charles Garry and others, things had become too muddied for me to settle for anything less than a personal visit.

Meanwhile, in a hospital in Georgetown, Debbie Blakey's mother, Lisa Layton, was dying of cancer. Everyone had taken pains to keep the news from the fading woman, but Jones got her to sign an affidavit criticizing her daughter's character and motives.

"Her attitude is positive," said Karen Layton in a daily reports to Jones about her mother-in-law. "She has said many things against Debbie, including that she thinks Debbie has a criminal mind. . . . Of course, I gear a lot of the conversation, but she adds a lot, too." Soon thereafter, Lisa Layton went home to Jonestown to die.

In about October of 1977—between his two futile trips to Guyana —Steve Katsaris had systematically contacted all the ex-members mentioned in the original *New West* story. He first gathered with them at the Berkeley home of Jeannie and Al Mills, defectors who were starting a Human Freedom Center to shelter and counsel refugees from cults. After Katsaris's November 1977 trip to Guyana, the group met again and expanded sufficiently—to a dozen or so—that they planned a public protest at the San Francisco Federal Building. Sherwin Harris—the ex-husband of Temple public relations woman Sharon Amos and father of her oldest daughter—had written a flyer for the protest, dubbing the group the "Concerned Relatives." The name stuck.

Tim Stoen had begun to participate in the meetings, although he had been reluctant to switch sides entirely. The group met at night and talked into the small hours of the morning; sometimes the meetings were staked out by Temple surveillance teams which checked out the license numbers of the parked cars to determine their enemies. While defectors gave the relatives an education in Temple history and practices, the group talked strategy and studied transcripts of the Temple's coded radio transmissions, intercepted by the Millses and others. And they shared details of their frustrating individual experiences.

A common sense of impotence and frustration now allied some defectors and relatives. Media disclosures heightened their concerns each passing month. Letters from Jonestown appeared almost childishly contrived; phone patches arranged through the Temple also sounded artificial. Many concluded that something was terribly wrong—yet could not reach Jonestown. And on March 14, 1978, the Temple raised another red flag. In a letter addressed to members of both houses of Congress, Temple member Pamela Moton complained of alleged harassment and threatened: "I can say without hesitation that we are devoted to a decision that it is better even to die than to be constantly harassed from one continent to the next."

By the spring of 1978, anxious relatives and the beleaguered church had fallen unwittingly into a peculiar symbiotic relationship. Each action fed a reaction by the other side, and each exchange made a collision course that much more certain.

The Concerned Relatives made their strongest and best-organized public plea on April 11, 1978, when a contingent of about fifty persons led by Steve Katsaris and Howard Oliver assembled outside the San Francisco temple. Though stopped by the chain-link fence surrounding the Temple, the group delivered a petition along with a list of "accusations of human rights violations."

At the head of the list of grievances, the relatives excerpted the "decision to die" statement sent to Congress by the Temple. "We frankly do not know," the relatives said, "if you have become so corrupted by power that you would actually allow a collective 'decision' to die or whether your letter is simply a bluff designed to deter investigations. . . ."

The Concerned Relatives protest touched off public relations skirmishes and an exchange of lawsuits. Taking the offensive, the Temple arranged during the next week for various Guyana residents to contact their relatives. With reporters listening, the Jonestown residents insisted they wanted to remain in Guyana and criticized relatives for attacking the church. Their voices could be heard over radio-telephone hookup in the law offices of Charles Garry, accusing the Concerned Relatives, in their presence, of being perverts, drug addicts, heavy drinkers and so forth.

One of the organized relatives, bearish and bearded Sherwin Harris, received a 10:30 P.M. call on April 13. After fourteen months, the Temple finally had put his daughter Liane in touch with him—but the hardness in her voice shocked him and convinced him she had been coached. Harris wrote himself the following note about the call: "I had only a few minutes . . . to talk to her. 'Liane, I love you, I miss you. I want you to come home for a visit.' She answers me, 'Dad, are you a robot or a machine? Is that all you can say?' It is not my daughter. . . .''

In May of 1978, a Burlingame schoolteacher and divorcee named Clare Bouquet experienced a similar feeling of futility. Since the initial exposés in 1977, she had felt deep concern over her grown-up son Brian's membership in the Temple. When she read my story about the Stoen-Jones paternity suit, she clipped the article, wrote on it—"Whoever is telling the truth, how can you respect these people? They've got to be a bunch of kooks"—and sent it to Brian's Los Angeles address along with a five-dollar check for Easter. Because the check went uncashed, she wrote her son a follow-up letter. Finally, in May, still with no reply, she telephoned the San Francisco temple and was informed that Brian had been living in Guyana for months. Hanging up the phone, she cried in despair.

Brian Bouquet had been brought to Peoples Temple in 1975 by Tim Carter, another white Catholic Burlingame boy. Of the four Bouquet children, Brian seemed the least likely to submit to an authoritarian organization. The thin, brown-haired, brown-eyed boy was open-minded by nature, appreciative of good music and good writing, but also inclined to challenge authority. As he grew older, Brian became a conscientious objector and let his hair grow longer.

When he met Tim Carter, Brian was working in a local food market, sharing a place with other young men, mastering the saxophone, partying, and visiting his strong-willed Irish Catholic mother several times a month. When he came face to face with Jones, something clicked. The minister detected a certain receptiveness in him. "*You* know what I'm talking about," Jones said after his humanitarian spiel. He wanted Brian, and Brian was flattered. Instead of starting the fall 1975 term at San Francisco State University, Brian moved to Redwood Valley, became a true believer, cut his hair short and found a job at a Ukiah Safeway.

Clare Bouquet had trouble staying in touch with her son. He would drop by her place unannounced every three or four months, but he told her the only way to contact him was by mail. A rebellious son had been transformed into a zealot who kept a picture of Jim Jones over his heart to protect himself from auto accidents, who collected all his possessions of value, including an heirloom diamond ring. His mother hoped he would pass through the phase. But the brief visits grew less frequent.

Along the way, Brian had met a pretty young woman named Claudia Dillard. Her mother, Esther Dillard, the daughter of a Baptist preacher, had drifted to Catholicism and spiritualism before joining the Temple several years earlier. The large family was musically inclined, and Claudia sang beautifully. When the singer met this saxophone player, the two fell in love. Brian wrote his mother, breaking the news, describing his girl friend as very pretty, "the kindest person I have ever known," and black. For a couple of years, Clare Bouquet urged her son to bring his girl friend home with him for Christmas Eve with the family, but Brian always had an excuse. Then, on January 20, 1978, Brian showed up unannounced at his mother's apartment and introduced Claudia. "This is my wife," he said. "We were married last Tuesday at the courthouse in Los Angeles." Clare Bouquet hugged Claudia and welcomed her to the family.

The newlyweds brought belated Christmas presents—a flower vase from Claudia, an antique spyglass from Brian. But when Clare mentioned getting them a wedding present, Brian discouraged it, saying the present probably would be sold when they left the country. A happy occasion suddenly turned frightening as he said, "We might be going to the mission for a while. We have a beautiful experiment down there." His mother begged, "Don't go down there, Brian," and she elicited a promise that he would come to see her and discuss it before going.

In May, when Clare Bouquet discovered Brian already was gone, the San Francisco temple arranged for her to talk to him by radio-telephone. "Brian, why did you leave like that without even saying good-bye?" she said.

"Well, we didn't know what you were up to," he said, implying she might have tried to stop him. "We think you're in cahoots with Tim Stoen."

Clare Bouquet had never met Tim Stoen. But this phone conversation prompted her to contact Stoen and the other Concerned Relatives. Meanwhile, she continued doing what every American supposedly should do to resolve a grievance. For the entire summer of 1978 she tried to enlist the help of government officials in the United States and in Guyana, and of law officials and even the Catholic Church. She received only the most callous sorts of bureaucratic responses. Clare Bouquet wrote Prime Minister Burnham with copies to President Carter, Secretary of State Cyrus Vance and Guyana's U.S. Ambassador Laurence Mann. She wrote to her congressmen, one of whom was Representative Leo Ryan. "I am desperately worried about the safety and well being of my son, Brian Bouquet, and his wife Claudia. . . . The very lives of those 1,100 Americans may be in jeopardy."

A short time after sending the letter, she received a radio-telephone call from Brian. "Why did you send those lies to . . . Washington?" he asked. Though he did not tell her, Brian had been ordered to write a letter to some California congressmen saying his mother was upset merely because he had married a black woman.

With only a thin partition for privacy, Brian and Claudia lived in the loft of a cottage shared with about a dozen other people. They did love each other and their music. They went before the Jonestown relationships committee to ask for permission to have a child. As a test, they were first required to go through a trial parenthood, taking care of some children.

Brian's few letters to his mother, with sweetened accounts of Jonestown life, did not console her much. He described the trade winds, a pet parrot and his performances with the Temple band in Georgetown, where he said he made much money. He sent a picture of himself and Claudia smiling in front of their "very own cottage," but Mrs. Bouquet became alarmed when she learned from Debbie Blakey that it actually belonged to Marceline Jones.

Tortured with worry, Clare Bouquet wanted to know about her son's true living conditions and well-being, but the State Department handled her inquiry sloppily. Consulate officials promised to visit Brian in August 1978 and to report back. But no one from the Embassy would set foot inside Jonestown until November, less than a week before Mrs. Bouquet arrived in Guyana with her congressman.

FORTY-FOUR

41 Lamaha Gardens

News of the fuss in California had reached Guyanese newspaper publisher Brindley Benn. Once the deputy prime minister under Cheddi Jagan and later founder of the pro-Chinese Working People's Vanguard party, Benn was more than willing to reprint allegations of Temple misconduct in one of his several antigovernment newspapers to embarrass his political foes. On Christmas Day 1977, his paper *The Beacon* carried a small inside story repeating accusations made by ex-Temple members in the United States.

That Sunday, Sharon Amos and Paula Adams of the Lamaha Gardens public relations team dropped by Benn's home to demand a retraction. They said they were surprised by an attack coming from a comrade in socialism. But Benn thought his visitors did not know the first thing about socialism. And when they suggested his story was an indirect jab at Burnham, he replied, "When I want to attack the PNC, I will [do it directly]."

The Temple group left him with a batch of documents and articles bearing on the alleged conspiracy against the Temple. Benn became so intrigued by their contents that he went to see Guyana's commissioner of police and related accusations about guns, people held against their will in Jonestown, snipers shooting at Jones from the bush and other troubling reports. The commissioner listened politely but did not appear interested.

The January 22, 1978, edition of Benn's *The Hammer*, a four-page mimeographed sheet, devoted the third page to Jonestown. Its headline: [Police Commissioner] BARKER MUST PROBE PEOPLES TEMPLE.

"Vanguard Publications believes," wrote Benn, "that all is not above board with the Peoples Temple, although Rev. Jones appeared photographed with the Prime Minister. Vanguard is determined to secure every [bit of] information, local and foreign, on the sect." For the educated classes of Georgetown, who cherished every scrap of news from nongovernment sources, the stories rivaled the *New West* exposé; they were a potential embarrassment to the Burnham regime.

The Temple considered suing Benn to clear its name, even though he had no money and sold bakery goods to survive. Amos and Adams went to see their old friend Fred Wills. Though fired as foreign minister, Wills still met periodically with the Temple and imparted valuable information about government matters. Wills told the Temple it would be foolish to sue Benn. "You'd be a laughingstock," he said. "It would be like suing Bobo the Clown."

The house at 41 Lamaha Gardens could not have been in a more desirable location. Bought April 17, 1977, for 33,000 U.S. dollars to accommodate the Temple's burgeoning public relations staff in the capital, the spacious, two-story yellow stucco building stood on stilts in one of the quieter sections of town. One could gaze out the large picture window and see cows or goats grazing in green fields.

Inside, the house was well appointed because the residents regularly entertained prominent Guyanese government figures. The wood-paneled living room was tastefully simple, with hardwood floors, throw rugs, a couch, several comfortable blue and red chairs. With the stereo tape deck went a good selection of jazz and popular music from the States. The walls were decorated with Jones's political trophies, most prominently the California State Senate commendation.

The downstairs served as nerve center, housing the radio room and office with a Xerox machine, three phones, typewriters and taping equipment. Upstairs and down were rooms, some with cement floors that were perpetually jammed with bunks, mattresses and sleeping bags; these primarily were accommodations for visitors from Jonestown or the States and new settlers on their stopover.

By late 1977, the mainstays of the public relations team, Paula Adams and Debbie Touchette, had been joined by Mike Prokes and Tim Carter. But internal problems already had beset the Georgetown operation, too. Jones correctly suspected that Paula Adams had been pulling punches in her reports to him. For instance, he would get on the radio at 3:00 A.M. and tell her to call the home affairs minister about some immediate problem. Knowing that calling at that hour would be counterproductive, Adams would sit tight, then tell Jones the minister's schedule was full.

When Sharon Amos was sent into Georgetown in early 1978, her mission was to keep Paula Adams honest. Humorless and absolutely obedient, Amos took Jones's every word literally. It did not take her long to discover that Paula Adams held back information from Jones, a fact Amos immediately passed on to her master.

In January 1978 the Stoen case was again reactivated, after a long period of dormancy. That month, Tim and Grace Stoen slipped into Georgetown for another go-round in the protracted legal proceedings. From the moment their plane arrived, Stoen felt their movements were being observed closely. Most officials seemed suspicious and unfriendly. Nevertheless Stoen was encouraged by remarks from the high court bench and believed the matter would be resolved in a few days. While they waited, Stoen wanted to charter a plane to Jonestown to see John. But his lawyers said he should not risk arrest or force the issue until the judge's decision. That was prudent advice, because the U.S. Embassy seemed hesitant to get deeply involved.

At 4:00 P.M. in his hotel one day, Stoen was approached by an immigration officer and officially ordered out of Guyana by the following evening, one week before his visa expiration.

Stoen saw the influential hand of Jim Jones at work. He told the Embassy he would stay and resist, but would send Grace to neighboring Trinidad. While at the ticket counter the next day, they were approached by a second immigration officer who informed them the order had been rescinded. Consul Dick McCoy had intervened on the Stoens' behalf. Stoen decided to send Grace to Trinidad anyway.

Before leaving the airport, the American lawyer found himself surrounded by three Temple members who threatened his life unless he dropped his lawsuit. Stoen reported the incident to Skip Roberts, Guyana's assistant commissioner of police, who later warned the Temple against taking the law into their own hands.

Meanwhile, Sharon Amos visited McCoy to protest Embassy involvement in the Stoen case. When her pleas seemed to get nowhere, she said, "We're all going to sit down and die if they take John from us."

"Quit talking nonsense," McCoy snapped.

Though Amos began to cry, McCoy did not take her threat seriously. This was before the Blakey defection, and he could not believe that a group with so much of an investment in Jonestown would take such drastic action over one child.

The consul was getting heat from both sides, fending off the Temple public relations aides, yet trying to placate frustrated and hostile relatives who did not comprehend that the Foreign Service was not an investigative agency. He was using chits with the Guyanese government to help the Stoens; already the Embassy had devoted more time to the case than any in his experience with the Foreign Service. And although he secretly admired the tenacity of the Stoens' attorney, Jeff Haas, McCoy finally lost his temper when Haas accused him of being chummy with the Temple.

"You come to us accusing us of doing nothing," McCoy shouted. "Well, tell me. . . . Who left that child and who are the parents? So don't say it's my fault. . . . I'm a father, too, and I wouldn't leave my kids." That outburst only tended to confirm the Embassy's alleged unresponsive attitude toward the Stoens.

After days and days of waiting, the Stoens heard that Justice Bishop had taken the matter under submission. The Temple began lobbying in earnest, besieging all its lawyers and government friends daily about the case's status.[62] The Temple's Georgetown barrister, Sir Lionel Luckhoo, finally became sick of Amos and ushered her out of his office, telling her not to come without an appointment.

Technically, Jones stood in contempt of court for refusing to surrender John. However, in a March 22, 1978, meeting, Home Affairs Minister Mingo told Amos that the commissioner of police would not arrest Jones unless the court ordered him to do so.

Somehow, the case bogged down even longer. In May, Justice Bishop called a meeting of attorneys for both sides and told them he had received hostile phone threats from people with American accents. On August 3, 1978, nearly a year after the Jones arrest order, Justice Bishop disqualified himself from the case. "In this matter," the judge told the court, "there have been persistent and continuing efforts of an extra-legal or opprobious nature . . . intended to influence the outcome of the proceedings. . . . I consider those acts mean and despicable."

Chief Justice Harold Bollers suddenly found himself with a difficult case to reassign. Everything was back at square one.

The Temple's lobbying efforts may have been effective as far as the Guyanese government was concerned, but they were more clumsy and harmful when directed at the U.S. Embassy. Dick McCoy was exasperated by their repetitive visits. He did not appreciate Sharon Amos's rabid approach to public relations. When he joked or teased, they took him seriously. Once when they accused him of being the CIA chief in Guyana, he grinned and said, "What if I am?" They looked at him as if he had just sprouted horns.

A key dispute was whether McCoy would give the Temple in advance the names of everyone to be interviewed on his trips to Jonestown, including those whose relatives had inquired about their well-being. The Temple said it needed the list so McCoy would not arrive to find them "on the river" or "in town," or otherwise unavailable. McCoy agreed but kept a few names secret until his arrival. That way, he thought, Jones and his aides would not be able to coach them. He was wrong, though. Jones coached everyone.

When McCoy's successor, Douglas Ellice, arrived in Georgetown as the new consul, the Temple tried to play him off against McCoy. They told Ellice that McCoy always had provided a list of every person he wanted to see. Jones gave his Georgetown crew specific instructions to tell Ellice they would be neither intimidated nor interrogated. If he wanted to ask questions, he could do so in front of a thousand people.

Ellice, however, stood his ground and refused to give the Temple a complete list of names.

Outside Georgetown political and legal circles, Peoples Temple was not a familiar name. Occasionally, a resident might run into somebody who had attended the 1975 healing service or who had donated to a government-licensed Temple solicitor. Or a resident might accidentally tune to the Temple radio show, though its propaganda would not hold many listeners.

On one show, Sharon Amos interviewed Dr. Jose Louis DeSilva, a Georgetown optometrist who spent three days in Jonestown giving eye exams and taking orders for glasses from 187 people. Amos served as cheerleader, while DeSilva raved about his royal tour as Jonestown's official optometrist.

"And the food," he said, "you should cut down on the food you serve—two eggs, bacon, three kinds of jam. It's just too much to eat."

Said Amos: "Well, that's what we all eat. . . ."

In late October, Dr. DeSilva would ship more than a hundred pairs of glasses to Jonestown. He would never receive payment; by that time, it would be too late.

The Temple generally enjoyed favored status with the Burnham regime. The editor of the government-owned *Guyana Chronicle* told Sharon Amos that he would never reprint any of the accusations, because, "We need your agricultural techniques. You can show us what a little hard work can do."

The friendship ran deeper than that. The thirty-member National Relief Committee for aid to victims of fire and disaster had three Temple public relations members on it. Additionally, Tim Carter, Mike Prokes, Debbie Touchette, Sharon Amos and Paula Adams took active roles in the Guyana-Korea Friendship Society, which sponsored two seminars on revolutionary concepts of North Korean leader Kim Il Sung. And the Ministry of National Economic Development (headed by Ptolemy Reid) put Touchette and Amos on a committee to mobilize worker support for a May Day celebration.

The Temple's biggest contribution to the Burnham government was voting in the June 1978 "Referendum." Burnham's term was up, but as usual he was afraid to call for an unrigged general election. To avoid that, he suggested adoption of a new constitution, and if a referendum on that passed, his party, the PNC, would stay in power to write it.

Again, according to Amos the Temple contact points were Wills and Mingo. In a March 9, 1978, note regarding Mingo, Amos said: "He seemed to appreciate the donations we were making and also the donations to the PNC." Touchette also reported on an April meeting with Mingo: "He said in confidence Dr. Reid wanted to make it possible for us to participate in the voting (he let us know it wasn't really legal, though). Sharon agreed we would like to do that."

Most of the electorate, particularly the Indians, boycotted the election, and the referendum measure passed overwhelmingly, with help from the Temple. Jones had picked the winning side once again.

Aside from the Stoen case, there were two primary areas of conflict with the government. One was the Jonestown school, the other a medical internship for Temple doctor Larry Schacht.

Because Guyanese law prohibited private schools, the Education Ministry wanted Jonestown to integrate its school with Guyanese children and Guyanese teachers. For obvious reasons, Jim Jones could not bow to that. So the church claimed additional children could not be accommodated.

The issue came to a head in early 1978. A team of four education officials inspected the Jonestown school, and Education Minister Vincent Teekah made a personal visit, before which Fred Wills had advised the church to make Teekah feel "as if he runs education in Jonestown."

The strategy paid off. On March 8, Wills had good news—the "merger" of Jonestown's school system with Guyana's would be only a technical one, with no intrusion by Guyanese students or teachers.

Dr. Schacht's medical certification presented a stickier issue. Guyana's chief medical officer, Dr. George Baird, wanted to stop Schacht, who had served only a few months of a prestigious internship program at San Francisco General Hospital, from practicing without clinical experience. Baird showed some flexibility and even suggested that the Matthews Ridge doctor could treat Jonestown patients while Schacht was doing a Georgetown internship. But Jones again refused to buckle. And Baird never forced the issue.

The Temple's standard public relations gimmicks worked even better in Georgetown than they had in the United States. In this impoverished nation, many people were delighted with the cakes on their doorsteps and other gratuities. Sharon Amos mentioned in a note "the monthly booze to Barker," a reference to Police Commissioner Lloyd Barker, never known to be sympathetic.[63]

Another recipient of Temple kindness was Eileen Bollers, a short, rotund woman of East Indian ancestry, who just happened to be married to Sir Harold Bollers, Guyana's chief justice of the Supreme Court, the man reassigning the Stoen custody case. Sharon Amos and other Temple public relations people took a sudden liking to her.

The Bollerses first met the Temple contingent at a Lamaha Gardens open house. Along with other prominent Guyanese guests, they saw a film of Jonestown and heard Marceline Jones's narration. Mrs. Bollers was surprised to learn such a group was trying to settle the interior. How could these friendly Americans, she asked herself, give up so much—chocolate, television, other luxuries—to develop land spurned by even the most hardy Guyanese? Soon after that, Mrs. Bollers took a

Barbados vacation and contracted an illness the Georgetown doctors could not diagnose. While visiting her, Sharon Amos suggested she go to Port Kaituma to see Larry Schacht, but Mrs. Bollers was too weak to travel.

One day Amos appeared at her house, a beautiful home opposite the prime minister's residence. She brought along Jonestown nurse Joyce Parks, who accurately diagnosed Mrs. Bollers's problem as viral pneumonia and prescribed the correct medicine. During Mrs. Bollers's long recuperation, Amos would drop by twice a week, bringing her books and providing company. Sometimes, Amos brought over her children—Martin and Christa—to play with Mrs. Bollers's son. Several times the Bollerses were invited to visit Jonestown, but Sir Harold, who also became friendly with Amos, was always busy.

There were also hints and rumors floating about the capital that the Georgetown Temple women were using their bodies to win friends and influence people. It was true that for two years Paula Adams had been carrying on a rather public affair with "Bonny" Mann, Guyana's ambassador to Washington—and Jones did brag about his public relations women in Georgetown giving all for the cause. But Stephan Jones, for one, felt his father exaggerated: Jones wanted his women to flirt but not deliver.

Aside from official and unofficial public relations, the Georgetown staff had plenty of other duties. They had put behind them the enormous job of clearing everyone through customs during the 1977 mass exodus. But now, in 1978, the task of keeping Jonestown supplied became monumental. They shipped everything from diesel fuel to underwear to the free Gideon Bibles that Jones ordered for toilet paper. And some staff also handled the logistics for smuggling contraband—guns, drugs and American currency—into Guyana.

Although payoffs to customs officials helped safeguard firearms and plentiful drugs that came in as medical supplies, the most valuable import, American cash, usually entered Guyana quite legally. Everyone was allowed to bring up to 5,000 American dollars. On the black market, an American dollar could bring between five and seven Guyanese dollars —two to three times the official exchange rate of about 2.5 to 1. And Guyanese officials preferred their payoffs in hard American dollars.

Keeping the project well stocked with essentials was a herculean task for the Georgetown crew. All goods ordered by radio from San Francisco were shipped through the capital. There was, for example, a $2,938 order of truck and tractor tires. There was a $5,690 order for 67,000 pounds of wheat. And the Jonestown Express band, which was gaining popularity and making money, needed an emergency $835 order for uniforms and instruments.

Keeping more than nine hundred people in clothes and toiletry articles was a huge job. And contrary to the image of bare survival, the

Temple purchased "frivolous" items, such as art materials for adult drawing classes. One order included $150 worth of bobby pins, $500 of Toni
Perm Wave, $1,500 of Afro straight combs with handles, and $110 for a
hundred boxes of Clairol Black, presumably not all for Jim Jones. Hundreds of pairs of briefs were ordered at a time, as well as jeans, T-shirts,
rain gear, thongs, work shoes and rubber boots, and the amounts went
into the tens of thousands of dollars per monthly order list. And, despite
the claims of some defectors, special individual needs were sometimes
filled, such as the "RIGHT AWAY! RUSH!" order of six 42 DD bras for Patty
Cartmell.

Some commodities were ordered for the store operated upriver by
Patty Cartmell and Rheaviana Beam. One order noted that $2.50 (U.S.)
bedsheets could be sold for $50 (Guyanese) each. Because the Guyanese
were so starved for imports, they would also pay, in their own currency,
$50 for dolls, $20 for T-shirts, $150 for used watches and $50 for jeans.
The Temple bought these items at United States prices, sent them down,
then turned a tidy profit of several thousand dollars a week.

As the summer of 1978 wore on, the public-relations crew in
Georgetown, like the rank and file in Jonestown and the faithful in San
Francisco, succumbed to exhaustion. The Concerned Relatives' relentless
pressure meant more strategy sessions, and longer hours on the radio
transmitting messages. Without adequate sleep or relief from the constant crisis mentality, morale declined. Moreover, the staff rebelled
against public relations chief Sharon Amos's strong-arm tactics. At one
point she wrote Jones: "My type of p.r. seems to raise a storm with almost
every person who comes in new to it or who works with me. . . . Paula
thinks we should use techniques for crisis only in a crisis. I think that
when anyone says anything that is hostile . . . we have to let them know
we don't sit by and take it."

In July, depressed and upset, Amos took to the typewriter to complain about the condition of the house and the two vans. "People are
abusive and treat things like shit," she reported to Jones. Things were
falling apart.

In passing through, Marceline Jones realized the problem was in
large part due to unnecessary pressures Jones was placing on the Georgetown staff. His "strategic messages" over the radio sometimes kept the
staff awake until 4:00 A.M. He insisted that his every word—and sometimes repetitive or contradictory orders—be transmitted. If carried out,
some of his craziest orders would totally backfire. "Communication is a
very difficult thing," she wrote her husband, "especially if under pressure
. . . I have told those here to not carry out an instruction unless it makes
sense to them. Questioning it does not mean they are questioning your
wisdom. . . ."

FORTY-FIVE

No News Is Good News

From late 1977 on, a number of very determined relatives and journalists had tried to answer the serious questions about Jonestown. The U.S. government was not much help. Even after the defection of Debbie Blakey in May 1978, Washington essentially adopted a waiting attitude. While the U.S. Embassy kept finding excuses not to visit Jonestown, two U.S. reporters landed in Guyana in May and June, hoping to see the settlement and find out about the lives of a thousand Americans. Both failed because of Temple resistance.

For one of these, Kathy Hunter, the trip was pathetic from the start. The former *Ukiah Daily Journal* reporter landed in poor shape, hobbling and in pain from a recent hip operation. Her mission was to chase down the story that had eluded reporters on larger papers—the real Jonestown. She tried to get backing from a number of publications, including the *San Francisco Examiner*, before leaving California. But she and her husband George, editor of the *Journal*, ended up financing the trip.

Having written so favorably about the Temple in the past, Hunter believed she had the perfect entrée to Jonestown. The church previously had told her it would welcome a visit. Moreover, she embarked after getting a phone call from Prime Minister Burnham, whom she had interviewed years before in California. But Hunter learned upon arrival in Georgetown that the call had been a hoax and that the Temple had withdrawn the welcome mat, angered by her sympathetic recent stories about Tim Stoen and Steve Katsaris.

By her third day, May 19, 1978, three anonymous bomb threats had been called into her hotel, the Pegasus. Temple members had followed her everywhere. She had chatted with Tim Carter, Mike Prokes, Debbie Touchette and others, who demanded to know why she had not contacted the church in advance. After more bomb threats and delaying tactics, Hunter told the Temple crew she had come with an open mind, but that they were rapidly closing it. Her May 20 journal entry began:

"The plot sickens. What a script for a 'B' movie. Seems as if a lot of people, including the hotel management, believe I'm the target [of the bomb threats]. I'm being moved from room to room and under security guard with strong 'suggestions' that I not leave the hotel if I don't want to risk a permanent 'disappearance.' "

After several minor fires at the hotel, Hunter found herself whisked into an immigration office and informed that her visa was canceled and that she would be leaving on the Wednesday plane. "Do you understand?" the official said. "You *will* be on the plane." Upon discovering there was no Wednesday plane, Hunter became so paralyzed by fear that she began vomiting uncontrollably in her room. A doctor came and gave her shots.

Meanwhile, four Temple members, staking out the Pegasus lobby twenty-four hours a day, were picked up for questioning by police. One had been discovered wandering near Hunter's room upstairs. The four were interrogated at police headquarters from about midnight to 6:00 A.M. and some were reportedly slammed against the wall. None confessed, and they were released without being charged.

The day after the detainment, Temple members complained to Skip Roberts. "What gives you the right to do private surveillance?" he demanded. They replied, "She's an evil woman."

Dick McCoy of the U.S. Embassy helped Hunter obtain a visa extension, and ten days later, she limped aboard a plane, sick and defeated. The Temple had repelled the threat, but it paid the price in bad publicity—California newspapers published accounts of Hunter's frightening experiences.[64]

U.S. Consul Dick McCoy's last consular visit to Jonestown had been in May, only a few days before Debbie Blakey defected and signed an affidavit alleging mass suicide rehearsals. This affidavit was now gathering dust in the Embassy safe, although McCoy repeated his conversations with Blakey to Ambassador John Burke. This information would not be forwarded to the State Department in Washington until early November. And McCoy, though armed with all of Blakey's information, never managed to make it back to Jonestown to even inquire into her horrifying allegations. In fact, no one from the Embassy would enter the camp for six months, even though they had set up a quarterly visiting schedule. There were always excuses to defer the trip, the usual one being the unavailability of aircraft.[65]

Communications among State Department personnel and divisions were handled ineptly and carelessly. No one, neither from the Embassy, the consulate, the Guyana desk of the State Department in Washington, nor the consular section there, ever had all the information at his fingertips at one time. In fact, neither the Georgetown Embassy nor Washington ever was certain what the other knew about the Temple. Embassy officials assumed that Jones was using the threat of apocalypse only to maintain control—which is serious enough in itself.

They knew as much about the true conditions in Jonestown as any outsiders did. They had heard the allegations from ex-members, two escapees, relatives and the news media. They had placed the *New West* article and other negative California newspaper articles in the Embassy files. But they were getting contradictory information from the Temple, as well as bully tactics designed to keep them on the defensive. Embassy officials, acutely aware of Temple mail campaigns to Congress, the State Department and elsewhere, had severe constraints of their own. For one, they could not exercise any authority over a group of Americans in a foreign country.

Another constraint handcuffed them: their limited understanding and sometimes misunderstanding of the Freedom of Information and the Privacy acts, two recently enacted laws. It was enough to know that between October and December 1977, the Temple filed multiple FOIA applications, requesting all information the State Department (and other government agencies as well) had gathered about the church. The inhibiting effect of the FOIA requests, intended or not, was dramatic. Burke and others feared that any written reports about the Temple might later be read by church members. As a result of their caution, Embassy reports of Temple activities lacked analysis, conjecture, texture and—as others later would report—a healthy dose of skepticism. Washington never fully understood the implications of them.

The misinterpretations, communication breakdowns and excessive caution probably did their most severe damage when Burke sent a cable to Washington on June 14, 1978, nearly a month after the Blakey defection. The ambassador tried, under his perceived limitations, to convey his concerns to Washington superiors. His precisely drafted cable noted the isolation of Jonestown, the press inquiries and congressional interest, as well as accusations against the group. He said, "the settlement's autonomy seems virtually total," and that the "rather primitive administrative machinery" of Guyana was already overstrained without having to police the community.

"What we have, therefore," the cable stated, "is a community of American citizens existing as a self-contained unit in a foreign land."

Burke was asking for guidance. He wanted to know if his Embassy was doing the right thing in treading middle ground, in never identifying the Temple as the problem. Did the Embassy, given the widespread revelations, have any authority at all to probe? And could he ask the Guyanese to see that their laws were being enforced and to tell Jonestown residents they were free to leave the settlement?

Burke was sure that State would give him a go-ahead to approach the Guyanese. Yet because the cable was so carefully drafted—without even bare mention of the Blakey defection—it never set off alarm signals. Those who received the cable at the Special Consular Service Office (SCS) were annoyed by it and assumed that Burke, like a good bureaucrat, was papering his files to protect himself. A junior officer drafted the reply, essentially telling Burke to do nothing. To Burke's consternation, the cable concluded that any approach by the Embassy could be viewed as American interference in Guyana's internal affairs.

Washington's Guyana Desk Officer Frank Tumminia—who was familiar with the Temple problems and had personally visited Jonestown —was perturbed by the reply, but he took no exception to it. Neither did Burke. Within two weeks, he returned to Washington for consultation and, significantly, never brought up the matter.

The Temple was convinced that CIA agents not only worked in the U.S. Embassy but also had infiltrated Jonestown. Jones's fears were not entirely fantasy. The CIA's presence in socialist Guyana—a major producer of bauxite, an ingredient of aluminum—could be assumed. Although the CIA had been legally proscribed from spying on American citizens overseas since 1976, the Agency almost certainly was monitoring the Soviet Embassy—and would have noticed weekly visits by Temple aides. It is also likely that the CIA came in contact with Temple members at the U.S. Embassy, where at least some intelligence operatives would be based.

Beginning in early 1978, Sharon Amos, Debbie Touchette, and other public relations people met with Soviet official Feodor Timofeyev to discuss sending an exploratory delegation to Russia, and later possibly relocating the entire Temple colony there. Amos and Touchette kept Jones informed via lengthy memos which made clear that Timofeyev heard more than he wanted to know about Jones's health problems, the "conspiracy" and past Temple troubles. The prospect of allowing a thousand dissident Americans into USSR began to appear unattractive.

Though Timofeyev would open the sessions by turning on the radio in his office to counter any bugging equipment, news of their meetings circulated all over town. The gossip even reached the U.S. Embassy. In late May, U.S. Consul McCoy told Amos he knew about these meetings. If the church was so peaceful and only wanted to be left alone, why, he asked, was it seeing the Soviet, Cuban, Yugoslav and even North Korean missions?

Another time he actually ribbed the Soviet consul at a cocktail party. "I understand you're letting Peoples Temple go to the Soviet Union," he teased. "How could you . . . ?"

"We're not going to," the Russian grumbled. McCoy got the feeling the Russians were wary, but also appreciated the eventual propaganda value of such a move.

But whatever the Russians thought, they did not want their contacts with the Temple spread around. During a September 22, 1978, meeting, the Russian diplomat lost his temper. He told Amos and Touchette that Dwyer had approached him at a cocktail party at the Yugoslav Embassy and had jokingly asked about Soviet-Temple contacts. Timofeyev said the entire Soviet Embassy was extremely upset about Dwyer's chance remark, and he warned Temple people to practice absolute secrecy. He said they divulged too much over the phone when they called the Soviet Embassy, and said he would have to report the carelessness to Moscow.

Others would charge, much later, that the CIA had not only infiltrated Jonestown, but also that Jones and his top assistants were CIA tools using the settlement as an experimental base for the CIA's MK-ULTRA program involving mind control drugs. (That program, begun in the late forties, employed a multitude of experimental drugs and coercive techniques designed to gain information from enemy agents.) It is extremely unlikely that Jones was in any shape to administer such a program, even if he had suddenly turned sympathetic to the CIA. Moreover, the CIA would have wanted a controlled situation to monitor test results, not the chaos and uncertainty of Jonestown.[66]

While the Debbie Blakey defection did not aruse much excitement at the State Department, news articles about her allegations did prompt worry at the Social Security Administration. On October 13, 1978, SSA official Ted Girdner, director of the Division of International Operations, requested that the State Department determine whether social security recipients had full control of their checks or were not coerced into signing them over to the Temple. The State Department, which had conducted about a dozen such interviews earlier in the year, agreed to conduct new interviews in January 1979. But January would be too late for approximately two hundred social security recipients who were receiving about $40,000 a month in government checks in Jonestown.[67]

FORTY-SIX

The Downward Spiral

One late night in spring or summer of 1978, while Stephan Jones was lying in bed, he heard the shots. When he charged barefoot down to his father's house, he was greeted by the business end of a shotgun. Joe Wilson, a young black security guard, had not recognized him at first.

Al Simon was already there too. "I was on security," said Simon, "and I heard these shots. From the sound of them, I'd say they were from a .22."

"It doesn't seem strange to you they'd be using a .22?" Stephan asked.

"Naw," said Simon. "It happens all the time."

Stephan thought Simon was a know-it-all, and he did not like the fact that Joe Wilson had moved into the hierarchy to a top security guard post. He thought Wilson was unbalanced and did not know how to use firearms properly.

Stephan turned to his father as they headed toward the pavilion. "Do you think," he said, "that if anyone was going to attack you, he'd run up on a whole group of you with a .22?"

Ignoring his son, Jones scanned the bush beyond the dorms and pavilion. "We need to give the people some inspiration. They feel we're losing because our enemies have the upper hand. We need somebody to go out there and act like they've had a fight, and have killed [the enemy] and come back and say, 'I got 'em.'" Then he offered the bait: "I'll get Joe Wilson."

Stephan's pride was too great; he volunteered to help pull off the hoax.

"I don't know. . . ." His father was hesitant.

"Look," said Stephan, "Joe Wilson doesn't know anything about the bush. He'll get himself killed. I can do it better."

The plan was for Jones to point out in the field, to call over Larry Schacht and say, "Hey, do you see that?" Schacht was to acknowledge an imaginary mercenary. Then Stephan was to run into the fields and eliminate him.

All went according to plan. Stephan took off, barefoot and armed with a hunting knife, through one windrow, past a field and past another windrow. He stayed out for a while, then cut his own chest slightly. When he walked back into the radio room, he felt like a fool.

With Dr. Schacht working on Stephan, Jones announced over the loudspeaker, "Well, we got one of them. It was a mercenary." Everybody cheered. Schacht continued the fiction by pretending to go out into the bush to bury the mercenary. But later, when someone asked what happened to the body, Jones replied, "Oh, we put him in the soup. You ate him last night." Some people believed him and became ill.

Despite his youth, Stephan Jones at eighteen had enough insight to realize he could not challenge his father very often. Yet Stephan did stand up publicly to Jones on occasion. Once it happened during a White Night. Jones sat erectly in his wooden armchair facing the congregation assembled on benches in the pavilion. Behind Jones, Stephan leaned on a small wooden table awaiting results of a test of his own:

Jim Jones sometimes counted on the combined opposition of Stephan and Marceline to prevent White Nights from going too far. This time Stephan wanted to see when his father would stop it on his own. So he had urged his mother earlier in the evening to go along with anything that Jones was saying.

But suddenly the plan backfired. Carolyn Layton gave a long speech exhorting everyone to die, leaving little room for squirming out.

Poison was the next step. As she wound up her harangue, Stephan muttered, "Oh, fuck." Jones lunged for the opening: he wheeled around to face his son. "Obviously, *you're* afraid to die," Jones said, in a loud voice.

"No, I'm not," Stephan said. "You know better than that. Come on. I've proven I'm not afraid to die."

"I say you are afraid to die."

"Bullshit."

The reaction was immediate. People stood up and yelled, "You can't talk to Father like that." Jones signaled to Marceline to control her son.

"Stephan . . ." she reproved.

"Fuck you, too," he said, knowing he should show no less public disrespect for his mother.

This time the crowd began to heap abuse on him. Eventually, the White Night was called off.

It was difficult for Stephan to feign respect for a man he saw at his most childish, petulant, eccentric and perhaps delusional. Once he was summoned urgently to Jones's house. At the house, he felt a heavy weight against the door. It was Jones, pretending he was a Russian Bolshevik during the days of the 1917 October Revolution. On this day, his enemies happened to be Carolyn Layton and Maria Katsaris, and evidently he had been scuffling with them for a while before they called for reinforcements. Jones was babbling in an awful Russian accent. Carolyn was visibly angry, Maria confused. Stephan grabbed the revolutionary around the waist, just as he raised his feet in the air. It felt to him as if his father weighed 230 pounds. Stephan could not hold him for long. He dropped his load and kicked him away, sending him sprawling onto the floor.

When Jones scrambled to his feet, he went after the two women again, spouting pseudo-Russian. Stephan threw him on the bed and dove on top of him. "You're very strong," Jones told his son. "Don't waste your time on this. It's not what you think."

As Stephan relaxed his grip, Jones kicked him clear across the bed and rose to his knees. Now angry, Stephan came after him, hitting Jones full force with a shoulder tackle, sprawling him again. The young man pinned him, and this time Jones could not move at all.

"Let me go," Jones babbled. "I don't want to use what I know on you. You're too young. I don't want to hurt you." Finally, the revolutionary bumped his head on the back of the bed and came to his senses.

Not only was Jones under emotional stress, he was also experiencing physical problems, and taking drugs, alcohol or both. He could not urinate at times; as edema swelled his body, his mind seemingly showed the ill effects and his behavior became more erratic. Even so, Stephan was convinced that, since he pulled such stunts only in private, most of it was theatrics. Within a few days of the Russian Revolution, Jones, dressed only in pajamas and a silly-looking hat, dashed into the bush with his .357 magnum. It was his reincarnation act again. This time he was being held prisoner. But as he trudged over a rotten bridge, it collapsed, and he wound up stuck in a tangled heap of termite-and-scorpion-infested logs. Stephan, thinking his father would be bitten, rescued him.

"Where am I?" Jones asked.

"You're in the bush," Stephan replied.

"How'd I get here?"

When Stephan told him, Jones made unconvincing sounds, as though he were coming out of a trance. Jones explained his miraculous recovery by saying that he must have sweated out all the accumulated body wastes and poisons on his jungle jaunt.

Feigned or not, Jones's illnesses made him a recluse in West House, where his tyranny, not only unchecked, would also be unobserved. He no longer performed even symbolic physical labor, such as hauling a little wood. He spent his days at home or in the radio room, often not emerging until nightfall. In a halting, increasingly slurred voice, he would use his house phone to relay information to the radio operators or to announce the world's news to the community. He told his people he was too sick to preside over the meetings, which by midsummer of 1978 had become nightly and often lasted until early morning.

The meetings were lengthened in part by a new addition—Russian language classes. Feodor Timofeyev of the Soviet Embassy in Georgetown would be paying a visit soon, and Jones wanted to impress him with the group's knowledge of Russian. But no one learned more than a few conversational Russian phrases, and those only because of constant repetition.

Because of his poor health, Jones also announced that Johnny Brown Jones would conduct the nightly meetings from the stage, while Father addressed the congregation from his house. Johnny always would try to dispense with the catharsis sessions first. But sometimes Jones would come to the pavilion during the middle of a meeting and repeat the criticism session, rehashing it, dragging it out, churning people's hostilities toward each other.

After spending May and June in Georgetown, Mike Carter took the *Albatross*—a second Temple boat, purchased to make money carrying freight in the Caribbean—to Port Kaituma, then traveled overland to Jonestown. To his dismay, Jonestown had come to a standstill. There were no signs of growth or progress; people were demoralized. Bureaucracy had completely taken over, and Jones was too irrational to make intelligent decisions about day-to-day life. Time and effort went to waste everywhere.

Carter's department was electronics, and he was luckier than most. He managed six to seven hours sleep. After breakfast, he made tapes of news broadcasts from Radio Moscow, Radio Sweden, and, when he could get them, Voice of America and BBC. He relied on Radio Sweden, because he considered the others biased. Carolyn Layton or Maria Katsaris culled the hard news and transcribed it. Jones made news broadcasts based on these transcripts and his own opinions. He went on the air at 6:15 A.M., so people could listen during breakfast.

About three in the afternoon, Carter would fire up the radio for about ten straight hours of transmission to the States and Georgetown. As in the past, top aides such as Harriet Tropp and Karen Layton sent most of the messages. But now ordering supplies and discussing strategy took twice as long, because radio operators had switched to Morse code to deter eavesdropping. A typical message to the States, with reply, would consume forty-five to ninety minutes.

Whenever the Concerned Relatives did something noteworthy or newsworthy, Jones reacted with a strategy session and a counterattack. On one occasion, he assembled people in the Jonestown radio room and, with considerable prompting, had them make almost laughable statements, branding their relatives in the Concerned Relatives as addicts and pushers, violence-freaks, terrorists and sex perverts. And these were sent to the news media gathered in lawyer Charles Garry's San Francisco offices.

On another tape, at the urging of Jones, people described imaginative plans for torturing or killing their relatives, while in the background he injected his high-pitched chortles. Like the testimonies in the States, their statements were designed to please Father—and were not necessarily true feelings. One girl, for example, said, "I'd like to string my father up by his nuts and stick a hot poker up his ass and make him realize what he's doing." Added Jones, after a good laugh, "I'm sure he *will* realize. . . ." Joyce Touchette said this about her daughter who had fled with the Eight Revolutionaries: "I gave Mickey up as a daughter years ago. I'd be willing to go back and shoot her. I talked to her on the radio, and she sounded like a robot." Finally, John Stoen came on the tape with all the enthusiasm of a six-year-old child pleasing the adults who had trained him:

"I'd like to kill Grace Stoen and Tim Stoen. I'll go back and do it right now." Maria Katsaris was with him. She elaborated: "He says he wants to tie a rope around Grace's titty and hang her down in the water until she drowns. He's six years old and [is] this imaginative." Jones cackled: "She wouldn't like that."

One day in July, Dick Tropp sat down to write a letter to Jim Jones. It was not a casual note, but an intensive critique of himself, in keeping, almost, with a Maoist concept of revolutionary self-criticism. A New Yorker of Eastern European Jewish heritage, a former instructor of English at Santa Rosa Junior College, Tropp was Jones's chief propagandist and author of press releases. In fact, the professor currently was gathering material for an authorized biography of Jim Jones.

Jones considered this self-critical letter from one of the Temple's resident intellectuals to be brilliant. He praised Tropp lavishly. Over the loudspeaker, Jones announced that he wanted self-criticisms from everyone within the week. For Jones, here was another chance to evaluate and increase his control. By ordering people to bare their souls to him in print, he could identify potential troublemakers and measure the effectiveness of his conditioning. He wanted certain topics addressed: the eight-hour day, elitism, anarchy, nostalgia for the United States and thoughts of returning home—also, feelings about Dad, defending Jonestown, past waste of money or personal problems and failings.

The results were mixed, in some cases pathetic. Many letters were barely literate, grim recitations of people's dreary lives before they met Jim Jones. Many simply told him what they thought he wanted to hear. They confessed sinning back in the States by spending money on Big Macs and other junk food, money that then went to corporations that killed babies and murdered Allende in Chile and Lamumba in Africa. They often repeated exactly what he had drilled into them, day after day, in his reading and analysis of the news: the world according to Jones.

People confessed to homosexuality, even though some said they had abstained from sex for years. Children who could not spell the word "elitist" admitted their elitism. Many thanked Dad for rescuing them from fascist America. Some agreed with Dick Tropp's assertion, appropriately tinged with self-loathing, that all intellectuals should be shot once the revolution came.

In the most honest attempts at self-evaluation, thoughtful people revealed their agonizing unhappiness with Jonestown life. Yet Jones's conditioning was working on them too. Rather than blaming him for the hardships and the frustrating emotional climate, they blamed themselves for not living up to his ideals and his example.

Jane Mutschman was one of the rank and file, a thirty-one-year-old white woman, pudgy at five-feet six and 155 pounds. She had been a Temple secretary in San Francisco, answering phones and writing letters. In Jonestown, she helped care for seniors and did guard duty at the front gate. Her letter mirrored the agony of life in Jonestown and her regret for having once left the Temple:

"My main thought since returning to PT has been to get life over as quickly as possible without committing suicide," she began. "That basic notion running through my brain has made me feel like a burned out cinder. I have no right to communicate this to Dad, who obviously feels like he wants to die and has every right to. . . . I think constantly about why Debbie [Blakey] and others left, why I left and came back, and on and on. I'm sick of analyzing. I don't even want to think. I know I have the same elitist pattern Dick [Tropp] does. . . ."

This was the crux of it. Jones had so twisted people with guilt that to think at all was to be elitist. To perceive that not all was right in Jonestown was to be anarchistic. Even without Jones's constant reminders of Jonestown's beauty, these people had conditioned themselves to shut out the bad. They had given up so much to come to Jonestown that to even contemplate trouble in paradise would be incapacitating. It was far easier to blame themselves for failing to be contented amid impossible surroundings. And yet, when things did not improve, when decisions were announced that seemed crazy or arbitrary, when more and more people were crammed into tiny living spaces and the food deteriorated, these doubts were impossible to dismiss. Some, like Jane Mutschman, hoped that by their giving voice to the doubts, Jim Jones could reassure them that their tremendous sacrifices were not empty gestures.

"Where is my goddam energy," Mutschman's letter continued. "Does the term battle fatigue accurately describe my non-actions? . . . but how can I write a note to Jim Jones and say, 'I'll go through the motions,' when he deserves so much more? So I renew my commitment here and now. This movement doesn't need another lazy ass-hole. If I have to, I'll put the 'barrel of the gun' up my butt and start a self revolution."

Tish Leroy, a middle-aged woman, had been a temple accountant and notary public for years. Her job in Redwood Valley and San Francisco, among other things, had been to affix her seal to documents she knew to be false, forged or made under duress. Her letter captured precisely the dilemma of perceptive people in Jonestown:

"I observe a lot in silence, and though I can always justify the lies that get told, I deeply resent being told them—I understand the ends justify the means. The undersurface of me resents terribly being stifled and stopped in expressing—we are not allowed to give honest opinions, for these are dictated as policy and it is treasonous to have differing thoughts. Yet, I can also give you a whole list of 'wrong' thoughts I did express, to the tune of being blasted and humiliated for it and told how wrong I was—only to watch events prove me right. . . .

"If we must 'conform' our thoughts, I'll never make it. I must say yes with my mouth if it's good for the collective, but my mind will scream 'no' till my dying breath. I feel at times like a misfit, but I know I'll never leave. I love what we have too much. It's far more important than me or mine."

As with Mutschman and Tish LeRoy, Larry Layton repeated the general pattern—honestly stated criticisms and/or expressions of self-hate and a death wish, followed by a renewed dedication.

"I trust Jim Jones as the most sensitive of all leaders and would follow him to the end of the world, but would hope that we need not live that long. I as a person don't like people very much and thus could be termed an elitist if not a reformed hermit. I am grateful for the kindness you have shown to all of us although you are in great pain constantly. I was especially touched by the care you gave to [my mother] Lisa and myself. I will rededicate myself to bring about success of our revolution."

Another letter was scrawled anonymously in a childish hand on a wrinkled piece of yellow paper, then turned over and copied more neatly on the other side. The tone was naive and trusting, the import clear: Jim Jones would never let down his people. Even unto death he would guide them peacefully, painlessly:

"If the potion we drank had been the real thing, then it would have been the end of Dad's pain. He would not have to suffer for us anymore. Just like last night, the more he talked the more pain in his tongue. The rest of the people would be in peace with our loving leader. . . .

"Everyone wouldn't have to go to the pavilion. There would be no more toots of the horn or talking about strategy. If it was real, of course, we would have been free. We would have died the best way. Any other way we wouldn't be sure if it would work or not and we would have suffered. I know that Dad wouldn't let us suffer like that. . . . Thank you Dad."

These letters also revealed inequities in the camp, and some people "confessed" to having privileges. For example, anyone with friends on the kitchen or bakery crews could get treats. Joyce Touchette slipped her son Mike and his friends iced tea, pies, bread, chicken, hamburger, even popcorn, and they had little parties in their living quarters.

But such practices rankled other people. Dale Parks was furious one day when he saw Mike Prokes get an extra bit of food from the kitchen. Moments before, Parks had seen his own mother, who had lost thirty pounds in Jonestown, refused food at the same window.

Those who scored an "excellent" on the latest weekly news quiz made their request for special treats in their letters. One man said he would like a cup of coffee and another a piece of pie on Sunday. And one poor woman whose grandson likely was working in isolation on the Public Service Unit wrote: "What I want for my excellent plus is for Wayne, my grandson, to hurry and learn principle so I can talk to him again."

In his letter, Tom Grubbs, creator of the sensory deprivation cage, confessed that a "schizophrenic" split between his emotions and his intellect made him a potential deserter.

"I am isolated, insulated, alienated and at times show elitism though usually I feel too insecure and inadequate [around adults] to feel elite . . ." he wrote.

"I am [also] having a difficult time with all the news. I cannot quit work to listen . . . but I cannot shut it out either, so it just plain interferes with my work and frustrates me. Sometimes I get a panic feeling, then frustration, then fearless hostility, then rebellion. . . ."

Despite his complaint, nothing was done. The "news" problem obsessed Grubbs almost to the point of violence. As hard as the thirty-seven-year-old teacher worked, he could not spare the time to study for mandatory news quizzes or to retake the test if he failed. The test insulted his intelligence and made him so negative about Jonestown that his wife reported him.

Jones ordered Grubbs to the radio room for a lecture, but Grubbs ended up raging at Jones. When Stephan Jones happened by, the big, athletic-looking teacher seemed to be scaring Jones. A lot of people crowded around, as Jones was telling Grubbs, "I can't believe you're saying this. I heard what you've been saying through my electronic equipment."

"I'm no fool," spat Grubbs. "I know there's no electronic equipment. My wife keeps turning me in. She's the only person who could have. I know that."

Jones denied it again, and they argued some more. Finally, Grubbs said, "Look, let me go. I'll take my chances in the bush. I don't want to go back to the States. I hate what it's all about, but I see the same thing happening here."

Jones looked around for someone big enough to take care of Grubbs. His gaze landed on his son. "Stephan, come here. Arrest this man."

"What?" Stephan said, incredulously.

"Take him away."

"Where am I supposed to take him? I don't know where to take people."

At that point, Grubbs interjected. "You better arrest me," he told Jones, "because I don't know what I'm going to do in the next couple of hours. Right now, I'm very hostile to you. I have the potential to kill you right now. . . ."

This was a rare burst of outrage, and to Stephan's great surprise, Jones backed down and excused Grubbs from the tests. He wanted Grubbs, a community asset and hard worker, to stay relatively happy.

The agonizingly long meetings and catharsis sessions continued, as did the Russian language drills. News reports were broken by Jones's petty announcements from his house, such as "Attention, attention, attention. My fever is down, slightly, to 104." The food worsened. On many nights, the rank and file saw little other than rice and gravy. Whereas bananas had once been plentiful and freely available, people now were disciplined for swiping them from the banana shed.

In August, anticipating a series of visitors from the United States, Jones added a new routine to the meetings. Playing interrogator or reporter, he would fire hostile questions at his people, then give critiques of their taped replies. He wanted to make sure that no one, wittingly or unwittingly, would ever confirm any of the accusations against Jonestown.

One night he ordered Carl Hall, a seventy-four-year-old black man from Los Angeles, to approach the microphone:

"Tell me, sir, what do you like about Jonestown?" inquired Jones, adopting a broadcaster's tone.

"We're all treated the same, on an equal basis," stammered Hall. "And the great work you're doing."

"Don't talk to *me*," Jones corrected. "Talk to me like you're talking to a *reporter*. . . . How's the food here?"

"The food is excellent," Hall said quickly.

"What kind of food do you eat?" Jones pressed.

"We eat three meals a day and they're all good."

"What kind of food," Jones insisted. "Tell me about your diet!"

"Well, in the morning, I have one to two eggs and toast." At that, people broke up with laughter. Eggs for breakfast were as rare as a U.S. Embassy visit.

"You're sharp, brother," Jones said, approvingly.

"And at lunch we have bread and soup, and the soup is very delicious," Hall added, warming to the exercise.

"Bread and soup, hmmm," said Jones, thinking out loud. "Mention fruit and salad. What's that soup the Russians eat, and they're the healthiest people in the world? Borscht. But you know Americans. They gotta have a bunch of shit that gives them cancer. . . . How many people live with you?"

"Fourteen." At that, everyone groaned and laughed.

"That's what I was afraid of," Jones said sharply. "Don't ever say that. Say four or five. Say 'two couples. My wife and I are retired.' Don't talk about fourteen 'cause the average American wouldn't understand it."

This exchange, like those in other nightly sessions with other participants, continued for more than an hour. Jones patiently coached Hall on how to answer such questions as why he decided to come to Jonestown and why he did not want to return to the United States. When Jones ran out of questions, he asked for help from the audience. A little kid named Jim came up with some winners, such as "Do you have any weapons here?"

"No, we don't," Hall said.

That was not good enough for Jones. " 'We are peaceful people,' " he coached, " 'nonviolent.' I'd look shocked. 'Weapons? What are you talking about?' That's a very good question. 'Do you beat people here?' "

"No, they don't," said Hall.

" 'Do you sock people, hit people, any kind of brutality?' " pressed Jones. " 'No, of course not,' " he said, answering his own question. "Look shocked. Even though some people in the past have grown up because of strong measures. But reporters don't give a good goddamn. They just want copy."

The little boy asked Hall, "Do you put people in boxes?"

"Yeah," echoed Jones. "Do we ever put people in boxes?"

"No, they don't," was all Hall could manage to reply.

"I'd say, 'That's ridiculous. That's a stupid question, sir. I don't mean to be offensive, but that's ridiculous. We don't use any form of brutality. We reason things out.' "

The little boy piped up again. "What's the tower back there?"

"That was a bright question," Jones said. "Give him a treat. Call it the pagoda. 'You mean the pagoda?' Act like it's a pagoda. 'They're making slides for children to play from there, and if we have dry spells, they can spot fires.' That makes sense, you hear? Don't initiate anything with people if they're trying to harm you."

Jones's "pagoda" was indeed the security tower, manned twenty-four hours a day by guards, scanning the camp for malingerers and potential deserters.

FORTY-SEVEN

Con Games and Hijinks

Had Karl Marx lived in the late twentieth century, he might have been tempted to reverse the order of his famous observation about all events in history happening twice, first as a tragedy, then as farce. In the case of Peoples Temple, the farce came first, in the St. Francis Hotel in downtown San Francisco one day in fall of 1978.

All Jones had intended initially was a sympathetic book telling the Temple story from a left-wing perspective. The Temple had been approaching reporters and other authors with leftist credentials for some time. Finally, at the suggestion of Charles Garry, they turned to Don Freed, a writer perhaps best known for his joint efforts with conspiracy gadfly Mark Lane. Freed had coauthored with Lane a 1973 novelization of the John Kennedy assassination called *Executive Action*.

Most recently, Lane and Freed had reopened their "Citizens Commission of Inquiry" into the 1968 assassination of Dr. Martin Luther King, Jr., hoping to prove that King had been assassinated not by James Earl Ray but through a government conspiracy. It was the King assassination, and not Peoples Temple, that claimed the major attention of Don Freed and Mark Lane in the fall of 1978; but the pursuit of that case required money. That was where Jones came in.

Freed had first met Jones during a two-day Jonestown visit in mid-August. His trip coincided with a long-requested jungle "house call" by Dr. Carlton Goodlett, who tentatively diagnosed a lung fungus and wanted Jones hospitalized.[68]

However reluctant a patient, Jones did not hesitate to use medicine on others, especially his other visitor, Don Freed. Freed had come to confer about the book or other favorable publicity for Jonestown. As a "courtesy," the Temple offered him a physical examination which supposedly pointed up venereal disease of the sort contracted only through homosexual activity, something Freed had not engaged in. Nevertheless the unsuspecting author accepted both the diagnosis and the treatment —all of it tape recorded. And during optical tests, he accepted extra-strength doses of eye medicine, which blurred his vision for nearly ten hours. Whatever the cause, Freed slept through much of his visit and suffered from diarrhea during the rest.

Jones had struck Freed as a minister in the Elmer Gantry tradition —neither evil nor pure, lucid, with an earthy sense of humor. The minister had confessed that the machinations of Tim Stoen had stretched him to his wit's end. After dismissing a book project as too time-consuming and articles for sociological journals as too academic, Freed and Jones had finally agreed that a film—or at least the lure of a potentially big film deal —would best serve their purposes of cracking "the conspiracy." To Freed, it had seemed that the weakest link among these "conspirators" was the man in it for the money—private investigator Joe Mazor. For $1,000 or so, he could rent a hotel room in San Francisco and offer Mazor consultant's fees for the film about the Temple.

Jones himself had provided the first prop for the pitch to Mazor. In an August 22, 1978, letter authorizing noted filmmaker Paul Jarrico to make the Temple film, Jones wrote: "Based on your magnificent film, 'Salt of the Earth,' Peoples Temple has decided to cooperate with you in making a feature length theatrical film [about] . . . the Jonestown community. . . . We understand that you will author and co-produce the film . . . and . . . are currently negotiating with a major star to play the role of myself."

In truth, Jarrico, who had weathered the McCarthy era red-baiting in Hollywood, had never even heard of the church. According to Jarrico, Freed had first proposed such a film to him in late August or early September, but the filmmaker had dismissed Jones as a phony religious huckster. As an alternative, Freed then had asked Jarrico to meet with Joe Mazor in San Francisco, and to *pretend* to be producing the film. The aim of the charade, Freed told him, was to induce Mazor to switch allegiances. Jarrico would say later that he had refused categorically to take part.

But Freed, undeterred, went ahead without Jarrico. On Monday, September 4, 1978, he and Mark Lane checked into single rooms at the St. Francis Hotel on Union Square in San Francisco. The next day, Freed moved to a $150 day-room suite, a more impressive place for what he called "the presentation." The Temple had agreed to pick up the tab.

Freed acted as moderator, with backup from Lane. When "both sides" had arrived—Charles Garry's office representing the Temple, Mazor representing Temple detractors—lunch was ordered from room service. With the consent of all present, a tape recorder rolled. Freed handed Mazor and Garry aide Pat Richartz two sheets of paper—the Jones letter to Jarrico and a letter of intent:

"The film group . . . intends to make a theatrical motion picture, tentatively entitled JONESTOWN.

"In exchange for their cooperation and information, the producers intend to employ Mr. Joseph A. Mazor and his offices and Mr. Charles R. Garry and his offices. . . . The producers offer to pay a good faith advance . . . as soon as the funding for the film has been secured. The amount to be paid to both Mr. Garry's and Mr. Mazor's firm is $25,000 each. . . ."

Even Richartz, who was aware that Freed hoped to lure Mazor over to the Temple's side, was convinced that a movie was in the offing. But Lane and Freed were really after information from Mazor.

With the inducement of a $25,000 movie consultancy, Mazor was more than willing to entertain them with the same rambling, sometimes inaccurate grab bag of fact, half-baked information, rumor and fantasies he had opened to reporters. He even apparently convinced the two late-comers that they had cracked open the "conspiracy" against Peoples Temple.

When Mazor quickly made clear his availability for hiring, Freed, seeming surprised, said with chumminess, "Joseph, let me say this. . . . It seems to me that this gives us maneuverability I did not know we had. . . ."

The movie plot discussed by Freed implied that an intelligence agency manipulated defectors and other Temple opponents. "This sort of war breaks out between this very large group on one hand, Jonestown, and a very small group on the other hand. But the small group is getting help. Now somewhere along the line comes a sort of independent investigator, like yourself, and who may be an ambiguous figure and either becomes a hero or what have you."

Freed kept coming back to Tim Stoen as a central figure in the movie. "We are interested in Stoen," he said, his voice damning with innuendo. "Here is a man who travels to countries all over the world. A man who is spending a lot of money flying around to meetings and organizing people."

Without blinking, Mazor growled, "Well, I'll tell you this. He got a lot of dough out of Venezuela. . . . from a very nice right-wing group. . . ."

Lane took over the questioning. "Let me ask you, Joseph. Do you think that is possibly an organization which fronts for an American intelligence operation?"

"Like the CIA?" Richartz added.

Then Mazor dropped two bombshells.

One came after Freed shifted discussion to the John Stoen case. "The child belongs to Jim Jones," Mazor said flatly.

"Absolutely," Freed agreed but was clearly taken aback.

"It was conceived in the back of a bus. . . ." There were wows around the room. "That came from Grace. Okay?"

"She told you that?" Lane asked.

"Yes. I had her in my office one day and she laid it out. . . ."

Had Mazor, the onetime investigator on behalf of the defectors, betrayed the intimate confidences of a former client, or had he lied? Grace

Stoen and Walt Jones would say later that they had never even discussed the paternity of John Stoen during their one session with Mazor.

Mazor had just awarded Lane and company a major coup, but was not finished.

In the course of their conversation, Lane and Freed introduced a spurious connection between Tim Stoen and the minerals exploration firm that employed his brother. "We know he is working with them, and we know they do high-resolution photography and they do overflight," Freed revealed. "We know there have been overflights down there [in Guyana]."

"Overflights is nothing," said Mazor. "I did an overflight."

"You did an overflight over Jonestown?" asked Lane.

"Yeah, sure. Back last year with a Cessna."

"But you didn't send the mercenaries in, I take it," Freed suggested, taking the bait.

"No comment," Mazor said, tantalizing them.

"Or did Stoen?" Freed laughed, cleverly.

Lane asked, ". . . If you have got this guy going behind the Berlin wall in the fifties, and then the idea's later on to destroy the Temple, is it possible he is in deep cover, setting up a whole series [of problems] which even the Temple didn't know about at the time?"

"Very possible," said Mazor.

"You say it's possible that he was doing this as an . . .?" Lane wanted him to repeat, to elaborate.

"Well," said the detective, "I look at Stoen in one of two ways. Either Stoen set the Temple up or Stoen is a second Lee Harvey Oswald."

"He's the one we're looking for!" declared Lane.

During a discussion about the movie plot, Mazor returned to his "overflight" disclosure, which would become a vital element in the Temple's conspiracy scenario. "My problem is very simply this. I cannot have a full agreement on [how to portray] Jones because the last time I was in South America, I was there," he said mysteriously. "And I didn't really get a chance to view the scenery. I had to leave very quickly. The Kaituma River is very swift. But, ah, the river raft was very rough going across."

Lane and Freed did not rise to Mazor's loud cue, but Richartz, who remembered vividly the six-day siege, picked up what had slipped by the rest. "When were you last in that area [of Guyana]?" she asked Mazor.

"Last year."

"And you were on a raft?"

"Well, Charlie made the news announcement." Mazor dropped the hint obliquely.

"About the raft?"

"Didn't Charlie make a nice news announcement?" Mazor said. "[Didn't he say,] 'Somebody tried to kill my client yesterday'?"

"That's true!" Richartz then remembered that Garry, during his September 1977 news conference with Dennis Banks, had mentioned the shot reportedly fired at Jones. "He did make an announcement like that. There was a shot fired."

"I know," Mazor said. "I was flying back at the time it happened."

Lane, apparently thinking he could put Mazor in bed with Stoen, said, "Did you have the feeling Stoen was trying to use you in any way?"

"No," said the detective. "I have never talked to Tim Stoen . . . because as far as I was concerned, Tim Stoen was always as dirty as Jones was."

"Let me tell you this," Freed told Mazor. "I think that the Jarrico office is going to be probably swayed by your assessment."

That exchange and Mazor's earlier "no comment" to questions about mercenaries left the impression that the detective had led an expeditionary force to Jonestown and might well have been responsible for the shot fired at Jones. He seemed to be on the verge of confessing to an attack staged by Jim Jones himself.

After Lane left for a Los Angeles television appearance, Freed told Mazor, "I think we've broken the case, Joe. I really do. . . . Suppose I submit a request that you would at least talk on the telephone with a Peoples Temple agent to negotiate the ground rules for your own investigation [in Jonestown]?"

A short time after Mazor departed, the Temple's tired and shell-shocked San Francisco staff descended upon the hotel suite with party food. Freed put them in a euphoric mood by telling them that Mazor's information would expose Stoen and the rest of the Temple enemies as conspirators in a plot to destroy the church.

Already Freed had started work on a memo that aroused great hopes. "Bring Mazor to Jonestown at once," the writer recommended. "He is ready to turn around. . . ."

Charles Garry had been planning a trip to Jonestown to prepare legal documents in the tangle of Temple suits and countersuits. The church asked Garry to invite Mazor along, which he did. After some negotiations with Mazor, and balking by Jones, the Temple agreed to pay Mazor his trip expenses and $2,500. According to the plan, Garry would fly down first, and Mazor would follow.

En route to Guyana, Garry and a Temple staffer listened to tapes of the St. Francis Hotel meeting. The lawyer reached a speedy conclusion: "This is all bullshit." He was particularly annoyed that Lane and Freed were promoting a useless movie at a time when serious lawsuits already burdened the church.

In Jonestown that September day, Garry discovered Jones in ill health, incoherent, complaining that he had not urinated in four days. With Garry looking on, Jones was catheterized. The minister and everyone else were in a tizzy over Mazor's approaching visit. They feared Mazor would smuggle in guns and cameras, and talked of canceling the visit. A short time later, when Mazor arrived on a Temple truck, Garry informed him, "Mazor, you've got to be searched."

When the two men finally met, they hit it off straight away, though Mazor had no stomach for Jones's politics. "You're a socialist, and I'm a capitalist and want to live on the hill," he said. Nevertheless, the two con men spoke the same language, which became clear in the ensuing conversations.

With Garry and Temple aides looking on, Mazor told Jim Jones that he had the goods on Tim Stoen, that he possessed a tape of Grace Stoen admitting that Jones sired her child and that he had led mercenaries through the Venezuelan jungle to Jonestown in September 1977.[69] Mouths agape, Jones and his aides nearly drooled over their good fortune. The glib private eye did everything but say outright that he had fired the shot at Jones which set off the six-day siege. Mazor confessed to a plan to blow up the Temple communications tower and, in the confusion, to rush into the settlement and grab about a dozen children for his clients. He mentioned a plan to use an airplane supplied by World Airways President Ed Daly—the aborted plan he had mentioned to me a year earlier (see note 55). Mazor even explained why the alleged mercenaries had left without fully executing their plan: from the jungle perimeter it appeared that the defectors had lied about the settlement—there seemed to be no guards, barbed wire or unhappy people.

As he sat back and let Mazor describe his phony siege for the benefit of others, Jones almost glowed. He was vindicated. A man once in the employ of Jones's most ardent enemies had confirmed the only "attack" on Jonestown.

The Temple believed, rightly so, that it had purchased an important functionary. Jones wanted to put Mazor on the payroll, but the detective wanted to work independently, free to take information to police or the press if warranted. The private eye may have accepted money from Jones —about $2,400 on top of the initial $2,500—but he never lost sight of his other agenda.

As a postscript to the visit, Garry said in a taped message sent to Jones, "I think we are very fortunate to have Mazor." But his optimism was unwarranted. Mazor could not come up with the promised tape of Grace Stoen, though he would sign an affidavit repeating his contention. For its money, the Temple received precious little. Mazor did, however, go to the press.

His phone call amazed me. Without explaining his elaborate arrangement with Jones, Mazor told me that he had traveled to Guyana alone, had been admitted to Jonestown and had spoken with Jim Jones at length. He offered me and a television reporter his story, exclusively.

Mazor had given me the impression that he would project a somewhat positive appraisal, which made me wonder what turned him around. The *Examiner* decided that Mazor's story, whatever it was, would not carry much weight. We would not write about Jonestown conditions until we could visit.

Meanwhile another writer was already in Jonestown on the heels of the detective. Mark Lane's visit just days after the Garry-Mazor stay excited Jones's sense of persecution. Jones had grown impatient with Garry and his lie-low strategy. He ached for the resolution of all his problems. He was flushed now with the achievement of having obtained an internationally known conspiracy theorist such as Lane. Perhaps Lane's headline-grabbing, pugnacious counteroffensive would finally free Jones from his tormentors. There would be no more punching it out in the courtroom over individual cases. They would go for broke with the contention of massive conspiracy.

At his father's request, Stephan Jones had greeted Lane with these words: "You've given us new hope." That is exactly what Lane's visit did. The prospect of blowing away the defectors, the government, and the press with one grand conspiracy case had caused Jones to start thinking even of escaping his self-made jungle prison. Living in the bush, isolated, without a telephone to call important people, without a real pulpit, the bus trips, the high energy of rallies or the ecstasy of healing services, Jones felt lifeless, a shut-in surrounded mostly by children and the elderly. His only entertainment was playing with the lives of his people, indulging in drugs and sex.

He told Lane in the pavilion area that he would like to pull an "Eldridge Cleaver," referring to the fugitive Black Panther who had returned to the United States as a Born Again Christian patriot. With his son looking on, Jones claimed that he was drafting a letter to the CIA and other government agencies, promising that, if they left him alone, he would repatriate and cause no trouble for the government. While playing the penitent religious man, he actually planned to come back in Elmer Gantry style, with a healing tour. And to show Lane he could pull it off, he ordered his aides to run a Temple promotional healing film. When Stephan Jones and some of his friends saw footage of Teri Buford, enthralled, nearly swooning over the miracles, they snickered.

Jones would not let Mark Lane slip out of Jonestown without sharing the good news with the inhabitants. In a speech about the King assassination, Lane drew parallels between the fate of one of the greatest civil rights leaders of our time and of Jim Jones.

After Lane left, Jones nearly burst with excitement. He ticked off items in the conspiracy case to be exposed. "Lane told me . . . Lane told me. . . ." Stephan Jones and some others were not as impressed. One quipped, "This guy makes a conspiracy out of everything."

On September 20, 1978, on his way through Georgetown, Lane stopped and called a news conference. He announced in grand fashion that he and Freed, through their Citizens Commission of Inquiry, had "investigated" conditions in Jonestown and interviewed various people in California. "We are able to state conclusively . . . at this time that none of the charges . . . made against the Peoples Temple are accurate or true," Lane declared. ". . . there has been a massive conspiracy to destroy Peoples Temple and . . . Jim Jones . . . initiated by the intelligence organizations of the United States." To support this contention, Lane alluded to Mazor

without naming him: "We have uncovered in recent days . . . a key witness
. . . who has now made in essence a full confession to us . . ."

Though actually on Jones's payroll, Lane presented himself to the
public as a disinterested seeker of justice and truth. Also, the California
interviews he mentioned—with Steve Katsaris, George Hunter, some ex-
members and Joe Mazor—had not produced the clear-cut picture he drew.

After trying to discredit the Temple's detractors in Guyana, Lane
swung through San Francisco to do the same thing. In a speech at the San
Francisco temple at the beginning of October, he scoffed at the Concerned
Relatives' accusations and told church members that the settlement was
"the closest thing on earth like paradise that I have ever seen." (Later,
he would deride Charles Garry for having said essentially the same thing.)

A couple of days later, at an October 3 news conference covered
by San Francisco newspapers and broadcast stations, Lane formally announced the conclusion of his independent investigation and declared once
again that there was no substance to charges against the Temple and that
the government was conspiring to destroy the church.

These news conferences were the opening volleys in a public relations and legal counteroffensive which Lane and Jones had agreed to
without Garry's knowledge. According to Temple notes, Lane, at $6,000
per month for three months, had promised to work full time filing Freedom of Information Act requests and preparing a federal court suit
against Tim Stoen, federal agencies, news media, some John Does and
"probably Joe Mazor."

In an enthusiastic return letter, Temple attorney Gene Chaikin sent
a list of investigation targets—a dozen law enforcement agencies and
court officials, two dozen publications. He suggested doing "backgrounds"
on nine reporters. Heading the list: Marshall Kilduff and Tim Reiterman.

Lane's first assignment was to counteract an impending article by
free-lance Gordon Lindsay for the huge weekly tabloid *National Enquirer*. In a rambling October 2 monologue, Jones told his people: "Dr.
Mark Lane . . . got that article killed because he paid to get somebody that
lied on us, and he went into the *National Enquirer* and said, 'Here's one
liar and I got his affidavit. You print this and we'll sue you for seventy
million dollars' . . ."

A few days later, on October 5, Lane took Mazor to lunch in San
Francisco with two newsmen—Hal Jacques of the *National Enquirer*
and Bob Levering of the *San Francisco Bay Guardian*. The purpose of
the meeting was in essence to have the private eye confess to being a
former conspirator; later, there was some dispute about whether the
Enquirer article was discussed at all.[70]

In any case, on November 8, the Temple's Jean Brown delivered
$7,500 to Lane at Los Angeles International Airport and he in turn pro-
duced a draft of the *Enquirer* article. The story never appeared in print.
Mark Lane later would contend he had played no part in killing it, but had
accepted the Temple money merely to counter the damaging article.

PART SEVEN

NIGHTMARE

They whip dreams of madness out of their own nightmares.

JIM JONES
October 1978

FORTY-EIGHT

In the Hands of a Madman

If there were any lingering doubts that Jim Jones had lost touch with reality, his September 25, 1978, letter to President Jimmy Carter should have silenced them. The minister, who had chatted on the phone with the First Lady two years earlier, now felt compelled to tell the President of the United States his rationale for siring John Stoen. The five-page, single-spaced letter was marked URGENT URGENT URGENT, with copies to Secretary of State Cyrus Vance and the State Department's Guyana Desk.

The tone was frantic: Jim Jones and the Peoples Temple were being destroyed by enemies, including rumormongers at the U.S. Embassy, and by defectors who stole thousands of dollars and "planned to blow up bridges . . ." and "poison the water supply of Washington, D.C." For one not intimate with Temple developments, the letter must have read like the incoherent ramblings of a lunatic. What Jones wrote about the Stoen child was particularly telling:

"The schemes against us include some of the most devious stratagems imaginable. One of the principles told me several years ago, in tears: 'I have to quit my job . . . I have to leave the church. My wife is going to leave me. But she is attracted to you. Will you please have sex with her?' . . . Well, I checked with my wife and the church board, and they thought it would be alright if I went ahead to satisfy this desperate man's plea—they reasoned that this woman was distraught or confused enough to tell all kinds of lies about the church. . . . I went into the relationship, and although I used preventatives, she got pregnant.

"And now, six years later, a big issue is being made over the child.

... these people are attempting to use a child as a pawn to discredit and ruin my work."[71]

Jones had begun to see himself as a ruler of a sovereign city-state: writing letters to the President of the United States, receiving visiting foreign dignitaries. His letter to Jimmy Carter was tame compared to his daily broadcasting over Jonestown loudspeakers.

Life there was growing more surreal by the week. The drugs—injectable Valium, Quaaludes, uppers, barbiturates, whatever he wanted—had taken hold of him. His voice, once so riveting, now sounded pathetic, raspy, as if he were very drunk or his tongue coated with peanut butter. Words collided with each other in slow motion. He would read from typed notes, but often not finish sentences. Sometimes, as he sat in West House, barely gripping the army field phone that connected him to the radio room, he could not read at all. In that case, Larry Schacht or Mike Prokes might prompt him by reading the sentence first and urging him to repeat it or, if Jones was really in bad shape, they would read it themselves after making excuses. Once, Schacht announced that Jones was in the next room combing his hair in anticipation of a visit from King Hussein of Jordan.

Somehow Jones got himself in shape on October 2 for the long-awaited visit from Soviet Consul Feodor Timofeyev. Timofeyev's colleague from Tass had visited in April and sent a glowing report back to the Soviet Union. But Timofeyev was the man who really mattered, the man on whom the Temple pegged its naïve notion that nine hundred expatriate Americans would be welcome in Russia. They spent countless hours practicing phrases in Russian to impress the Russian diplomat.

The program for Timofeyev got under way with Temple singer Deanne Wilkinson delivering a political protest song in a rich and hauntingly beautiful voice, with organ accompaniment. Then Jim Jones stepped to the microphone.

"For many years," Jones said, "we have made our sympathies publicly known. The United States is not our mother. The USSR is our spiritual motherland." A tremendous ovation greeted his words. "Ambassador Timofeyev, we are not mistaken in allying our purpose and our destiny with the destiny of the Soviet Union."

The Russian consul stepped forward, greeting the eager crowd in Russian. "On behalf of the USSR," he said, switching to a halting English, "our deepest and most sincere greetings to the people of the first socialistic and communistic community from the United States of America in Guyana and in the world."

He continued with lavish praise, pausing to explain at length the history of the Soviet Union since 1917 and to defend its policies. Wishing the collective continued great success, he concluded: "It is a great pleasure to see how happy you are being in a free society."

After the speech, Jones led everyone in a hand-clapping, gospel-style rendition of various socialist songs, including one that was repeated again and again:

> "We are communists today and we're communists all the way.
> Oh, we're communists today and we're glad."

Whatever personal strength and discipline Jones had marshaled for the Timofeyev visit was exhausted the next day. When he returned to the loudspeaker for news, announcements and lectures on fascism, he sounded drugged again. But he poured out his words faster than he could enunciate them, as if he were on stimulants. At one point, he threatened Public Service for anyone who said Christ's birth was more important than the Russian Revolution. Then he leaped to the subject of Charles Garry, whom he first described as a nice, even admirable, man, then mocked as a cowardly old fool. "Every time I wanted to sue, he'd say, 'no, no, no, no. They don't bother you.' The hell they don't! Those lies hurt you. I'd take an entirely different course of action now. We were stuck with him . . . when you deal with an attorney, you have to tell him everything. He knows certain facts about our organization, and when he goes against you, you have difficulties."

On another tape, Jones was considerably more charitable toward Garry's rival, Mark Lane. He told the people that Lane had called him a saint. Jones would talk rapid-fire, run out of words briefly, then fire another burst. He would drop subjects, then resurrect them. It was clear Father was not feeling well:

"Dr. Lang [sic], Dr. Mark Lang said he would make every person who entered this community go naked, and he would look in their vagina and in their penis and in their mouth. You know damn well [that] private messages are not supposed to go out. They're supposed to be read by censors. . . . They know how little words can be taken wrong and used by the CIA."

Jones was ensuring that his closed universe stay closed by controlling all access to the outside world, by body searches and censorship. It was not enough that he regulated letters and phone calls home, availability of newspapers or periodicals or anything else that would contradict his own insane vision. He lambasted his people for writing home at all: "Some of you break my heart. Here I sit with a 105 temperature, and some of you won't do so much as to try to save a stamp on an envelope by writing some suckle" —he stumbles over the words—"son, hump, damn! I haven't got the words for it, I haven't got the damn words. It's just low down and unthankful. . . ."

Then his gratitude for his conspiracy theorists gushed out: "The next children born here should be named after Mark Lane and Don Freed. That is the good diplomatic sense. Whoever happens to have the next child, if it's a boy—or you can fix up a girl version—name it after Mark Lane and Don Freed."

As in the past, the emperor realized that his subjects, given time to think, would compare notes and catch him in his lies. So he riveted their attention on his version of reality, on his amplified voice:

"All departments should be talking about the news. I don't want to hear chit-chat. And you should be practicing Russian together. We should be above our brainwashing. . . ."

And then, more craziness was spewed:

"Nursing staff, you should be kind to our seniors. You must smile. You must be warm when you pick their body up. It is a fearful thing to be sick. Let me tell you, I'm sick much of the time, but I'm not in the nursery. I have work to do. My temperature is now over 105. I'll be all right whenever I take whatever they put up [pause] this depository. . . ."

Any escape from this madness, from that voice was welcomed. And not surprisingly, the Jones boys and their friends found more diversion than most inhabitants, one that would save their lives. Basketball came to Jonestown one day when it occurred to some of the young workers, including Stephan Jones, that the hardwood floor of an unfinished building would make a good half court. A stout pole was sunk into the ground, a standard erected and a floodlight trained on the court for night play. Jones was receptive to the idea once it became clear he could use a Jonestown basketball team for propaganda purposes, as he did with the band or the karate and drill teams. He even let team members leave work a half hour early for practice.

Stephan Jones and Lee Ingram, who became the coach, picked the team with help from Tim Jones and Johnny Cobb. Emmett Griffith, a big, fast hustling player, bulwarked the defense. Jimmy Jones, Jr., at six feet four an inch shorter than Stephan, played center, while Stephan played power forward. Johnny Cobb and Tim Jones started at guard. Mike Touchette, a former high school athlete, became trainer. About sixteen young men tried out, and eleven made the team.

When the broadcaster for the Guyanese National Cricket team came to Jonestown, the basketball team put on a show—warm-up drills where they dunked the ball, and a scrimmage with flashy passing. It was the creative basketball style found on U.S. ghetto playgrounds, but not on Guyanese courts. It so impressed the announcer that he decided to arrange a tournament between the Jonestown and Guyana national teams. People would pay to watch the American wizardry, he said.

For a group of young hoopsters who wanted to have some fun and escape the endless community meetings, this indeed was welcome news. The prospect of a tournament in Georgetown gave them incentive to polish their skills. And now if anyone questioned their "frivolous" pastime, they could justify it more easily. Friends and family respected the boys. Other residents, however, noticing that three of Jim Jones's four sons were starters, considered the team another example of special privileges for the elite. And many feared them. After all, the same young men buttressed Temple security.

Although he recognized the propaganda value of the basketball tournament, Jones was unsettled by the team's sudden plans to play in Georgetown, away from his reach. But Marceline, realizing how important the sport was to her sons and their friends, smoothed the way. When Jones wavered, she promoted the tourney behind the scenes. And to avoid jeopardizing it, she insulated her husband from any rules infractions committed by team members.

For many years, Jim Jones had advertised his movement as an alternative to the fascism he predicted for the capitalist United States. He defined fascism as "when capitalism gets mean." He even posted the words—more or less—of American philosopher George Santayana, "Those who cannot remember the past, are condemned to repeat it." Santayana's words stand as a terrible reminder in the Dachau memorial outside Munich. Yet Jones had crafted a concentration camp of his own, complete with armed guards, an elaborate system of informants, and special places where people were disciplined or fed powerful drugs to subdue them. Punishments seldom fit the crime. For example, Mike Lund's write-up of Vincent Lopez: "Last Monday night about ten, Vincent went into the banana shed and stole three bananas in front of my and Wesley Breidenbach's eyes. He obviously didn't think we'd report him." Lopez was sent to Public Service Unit (PSU) then—and later for stealing a boy's flashlight.

Alleane Tucker was reported because she refused to authorize sale of her 102 acres of U.S. land without first talking to her brother. Barbara Simon was put on PSU for two days, her second time, because she took ice from Jones's water pitcher after a meeting.

In a sort of "brownie point" system, two "praises" canceled out one warning. Three warnings a month resulted in PSU punishment—which Jones found inadequate for some cases. By late summer, he had established an ECU or "Extended Care Unit," for unmanageable people such as captured escapees. Their keepers sedated and drugged them under twenty-four-hour observation.

Jones, concerned that investigators somehow could confirm Debbie Blakey's stories of Jonestown corporal punishment, had turned to the ECU as a replacement. Overseers at the eight-bed ECU had access to enough behavior-controlling drugs to equip the city of Georgetown. Among the drugs later recovered from Jonestown were: 10,000 injectable doses and 1,000 tablets of Thorazine, an antipsychotic; 20,000 doses of the pain-killer Demerol; 3,000 liquid doses and 2,000 tablets of Valium; 200 vials of injectable morphine sulfate; and thousands of doses of other powerful drugs, such as Quaaludes, Vistaril (for management of anxiety and tension), Noludar (habit-forming sleeping aid) and Innovar Injection, a tranquilizer normally used for surgery and diagnosis.

These behavior-altering drugs can cause hallucinations, blurred vision, confusion and speech disturbances, involuntary movements, suicidal tendencies or other emotional upheavals. They were sometimes administered in dangerously high doses to ECU patients, though there is no indication they were given to the general Jonestown population through food or other means.

Jones seemed obsessed with the ECU. In "instructions" he read over the loudspeaker on October 20, 1978, he said he believed people were feigning mental illness so they could get into ECU and thus escape work. He vowed to put a stop to it. It was difficult to imagine why anyone would want to con his way into the ECU. As Jones specified: "They're going to get there and hear Russian and news and they're going to do push-ups and down. If they've got constipation, instead of taking a laxative, they can break it up their ass with their finger."

The instructions Jim Jones read over the loudspeaker on October 16 were neatly typed in capital letters, seven pages in all. for the hundredth time, Jones told his people about their many enemies among the defectors. He told them that the Russians had promised to protect Jonestown's people from any invasion by the Guyanese and would offer university scholarships in the Soviet Union. And he told them that the "little detective"—Joe Mazor—had revealed that class enemy Tim Stoen had been in the CIA for eight years.

Father issued other instructions: security was to roam constantly and no one was to talk to them. People were to drink lots of water because the full moon was coming. People, he explained, are 98 percent water. So they, like the tides, are affected by lunar motions.

This night, Jones again took a stand against "nonrevolutionary" suicide. A few nights earlier Ricky Johnson, eighteen years old, had run into the bush, distraught that his girl was sleeping with his best friend; the next night he tried to kill himself by drinking gasoline, and his guilt-consumed girl friend tried the same. The affair deeply offended Jones's concept of self-destruction; he did not want his people dying for selfish reasons, such as homesickness or "sick" love affairs. He himself wanted to choose the time, place and manner of their destruction.

Verging on incoherence, his digression covered everything from Tim Stoen to the girl who had allegedly left her panties on his desk in high school because he would not make love to her. "The next person I revive from suicide," Jones said, "I will see that medication will not be spent on you. . . . Think what you could do if you would not internalize that violence by self-destruction and [instead] think towards the enemy. Don't forget that Tim Stoen's still walking around."

As an alternative to suicide, Jones suggested that despondent people come to him to be sedated. "We can give you assistance that will enable you to walk about. But you will be for a while sleepy and drowsy."

Stephan Jones cringed when he heard his father talk like that. It also renewed a thin hope: maybe people soon would recognize his words as nonsensical orders from a madman and would stop dancing to his whims and fantasies. However, the growth of any rebellious seeds was retarded by mistrust and paranoia, the inner circle of protective aides and Jones's growing isolation.

Rarely did Jim Jones venture out of his own house and talk to people one to one. Rarely did he encounter anyone who would tell him anything he did not want to hear. His fears could run unchecked and unchallenged: there was danger everywhere. Danger from mercenaries in the bush. Even danger from the Guyanese government, which had shown itself ineffectual in handling Temple enemies. And most of all, it seemed, dangerous forces threatened him inside Jonestown, where people were displaying their unhappiness by trying to escape even from life itself. All it would take was one more talkative defector. . . .

The next day, October 17, Jim Jones warned his beloved people that the Guyanese had been instructed to shoot escapees in the heart and that Temple guards would not hesitate to use crossbows and guns to kill them. "If you try to cross that border you'll get shot from either side," Jones emphasized. "It is illegal to cross that border, so just face some facts and grow up."

Escape from Georgetown was portrayed as equally difficult. Jones falsely said the Guyana Tax Board promised to notify him of any Temple member who applied for a tax clearance. And runaways would need passports from the U.S. Embassy, where officials also had promised to tip off the Temple, he lied. One would-be escapee had come down with a rare disease, he added.

Jones also told the suicidal in vivid detail about the perils of drinking gasoline: "It causes instant death. The very eyeballs turn until you see the whites of their eyes and they die an agonizing death. The one who took gasoline [Ricky Johnson] shit fire and his mouth was on fire for six hours." If anyone realized that a person could not "shit fire" for six hours and "die instantly" at the same time, no one said so. People no longer responded to the content of Jones's messages, but to his emotional cues, key words and body language, and to their own fears.

As morale plunged, Jones tried to buoy up his people with an odd hard sell. People eschewing the move to the Soviet Union would be sent back to the USA, to rot in fascist concentration camps, he said. "Some of you don't hate that system enough. You're still in love with that goddamn system . . . you're always griping about some little old damn thing you don't have. I don't miss all those white faces I don't see. To me, if we never got further than this, it would be heaven."

And for people who worried that their chronically ill Dad might depart this earth in their time of travail, Jones added one last reassurance: "I will long outlive you. It is quite obvious that I have gone through the valley of the shadow and returned . . . I did not bring you to this point to leave you without a future, without someone who loves you, who will plan and care for you."

In his tyranny, Jones was turning more and more to his Extended Care Unit to throttle malcontents, and it was becoming obvious to many people. Anyone with eyes could see Vincent Lopez or Shanda James staggering around the compound after they had emerged from the ECU. Lopez had been drugged to unconsciousness because he ran into the bush; when he woke up, groggy, he told Stephan Jones, "I know I been drugged, but that food sure is good." He remained in ECU two weeks.

The drugging had begun with Barbara Walker, a tall volatile woman who kept attacking Stephan for resisting her advances. She thought people were telling Stephan not to go with her because she was black. After she jumped young Jones three times, once with a farm implement, his father decided to have her drugged on a more permanent basis, despite Stephan's objections.

Others joined Barbara Walker in ECU. One was attorney Gene Chaikin, who had two kids in Jonestown. He had made disloyal noises to Charles Garry during the six-day siege, and Chaikin's brother in the States had been threatening to get him out of the jungle. As the Temple's only remaining lawyer, Chaikin knew too much ever to be let go.

Another valuable settler, Mike Touchette's father Charlie, also found himself feeling woozy at times. Jones feared that his barely repressed negativity would become open defiance. Touchette really was no more negative than he had been for years, but Jim Jones had become more intolerant.

An October 6 report about Christine Lucientes—who had encountered Jones in night school in Ukiah and eventually became one of his lovers—made painfully clear the extent to which Jones was using the ECU.

"Christine Lucientes was at home changing her clothes and said that she just couldn't believe that she was being put on PSU because she refused to go to ECU and be drugged," a woman informed Jones.

"I told her if she were really grateful, there would be no reason for anyone to want to drug her. She then replied, 'Grateful for what? To go to PSU?' I said, 'No, grateful to Dad for being here.' She said, 'I'm grateful to be here. It's just that I don't want to be drugged.'

"She next said, 'I can't believe I've been lied to, I've been tricked.' . . . Her whole attitude was like some injustice had been done to her and the ECU thing had been previously planned. . . . She said, 'I refuse to be another Vincent and another Shanda,' and she named some other names I can't recall."

Treatment of Shanda James was not only tragic; it also ended the age of innocence for Stephan Jones's brothers, Jim Jones's elite bodyguards. For the first time, they faced up to their father's monstrous behavior.

Shanda James was nineteen and beautiful. She was married to Bruce Oliver, but Jones wanted her body. Soon he and Shanda were spending time at his cottage under the guise of counseling for her "suicidal" tendencies. People close to the scene began to suspect something more, especially when they saw her assisting Jones back to his cottage after meetings. Soon she had begun to take on airs, a telling sign. Like other mistresses, Shanda—already in charge of Jonestown entertainment —was given new responsibilities. But what was unusual about this mistress was her color. Stephan believed she was his father's first black lover. In fact, he thought that Jones felt threatened by black women, afraid he could not measure up to black men.

One day Stephan Jones was walking with his father near the medical clinic when Jones turned to him and said, "I'm having sex with Shanda." Stephen felt Jones was boasting about his success because so many men in Jonestown were attracted to her; all he muttered was, "I know."

"You *know?*" said Jones. "I can't pull anything over on you, can I?"

"No," said Stephan, coldly.

"I told your mother."

"You told Mom?!" Stephan was upset. When his father said something about how Marceline had tried to manipulate guilt, Stephan walked away.

As the affair became more public, others began to resent Shanda James. Tim Jones, like his brother Jimmy and some of their friends, still believed in Jim Jones. They blamed his excesses on others, on Carolyn Layton or Johnny Brown or Maria Katsaris. In the case of Shanda James, Tim Jones was so indignant that he came up to Stephan and snorted, "That bitch. She's making Dad fuck her."

"He doesn't mind it that much," said Stephan.

Fifteen minutes later, the radio blared, "Stephan Jones report to the radio room." Once there, he was handed the phone hot line to his father's house. "What the hell did you mean by that?" Jones demanded. "Saying I don't mind fucking Shanda?"

"Well, you don't," Stephan said.

"What do you mean," repeated Jones. "I go through hell every night for all of you."

"Yeah, yeah, yeah," Stephan agreed, to shut him up.

Though he silenced his son, Jones felt some guilt over the affair— and needed reassurance. He took the matter to his small circle of advisers, among them Harriet Tropp, Carolyn and Karen Layton, Maria Katsaris. Tim Carter happened to be hanging around when the subject came up.

"I thought I left this shit back in the States," Jones said. "What do you do? A black woman comes up, wants to make love to you. They've been oppressed all their lives because they're women and black. At first I said no, but she kept pressuring me. What should I do? Should I keep going to bed with her?"

Without exception, all the women told Jones to keep sleeping with Shanda James to make her a better worker, more loyal to the cause.

Carter was a little bothered by the affair, because he thought Jones had left behind his philandering in the States. But few of the rank and file knew much about Jones's sex life, other than that he did it "for the cause." They were not privy to all his partners.

One of those in the dark about Shanda James was Al Smart, a new arrival who immediately took a liking to her. When Jones spotted Al and Shanda chatting a bit too flirtatiously, he had Smart brought to the floor on another pretext. A few days later, Shanda sent Jones a note: "I care about you a lot, but I want to be with Al Smart." Apparently she did not anticipate the hazards of throwing over Jim Jones for a nineteen-year-old black kid.

That night, she was sent to ECU and drugged. Jones explained to others that she had tried to kill herself. But Johnny Cobb told Tim Jones about the contents of Shanda's note. The effect on the basketball team was electric; Jones's treatment of a girl they all knew and liked outraged them. Over the following few days, she would emerge from ECU so dazed that she needed to lean on someone as she staggered around. She was a zombie.

The Jones boys were not upset because Jones had a new mistress, or a young one, or even a black one. His sexual promiscuity was institutionalized. But this affair unmasked his sexual motives.

Now, as his sickness spread like a malignant tumor, his deeds got more despicable and mean-spirited—and his lies no longer could gloss over his sins and weaknesses. Even for the expert juggler, there were too many balls in the air. Jim Jones was about to lose control. At the height of his powers, he could have cleverly concealed his weaknesses or defused accidental revelations of them. But now he was tripping over his own base instincts, laying them bare for public view.

Sometimes, when there was a lot on Stephan Jones's mind, he liked to just sit alone in pavilion with the lights out and listen to the soft jungle sounds. Were it not for the thoughts racing through his mind, it would have been peaceful that night late in October when he heard his brother Tim walk by. He called him over.

Tim Jones still seethed with the anger of betrayal. He felt revulsion for the corruption and cruelty of his adopted father. "We gotta kill him," he exploded. "We gotta kill him. We gotta have a revolution. We gotta throw this son of a bitch out."

Stephan replied sarcastically. "This is funny. It's been almost ten years that I've been putting up with this shit." His words were biting, a touch bitter. "You've known about it for a month and you're going nuts. You want a revolution. Let me tell you something. You know what would happen if you killed Jim Jones now? . . . Some of these seniors think he's God and he's their only hope. And you're gonna go up there and kill Jim Jones? That won't work. The only way you can take care of Jim Jones is to hope he dies naturally or gradually phase him out. That's the only way you're gonna do it. I'm sorry. There have been things I've wanted to do . . ."

The next day, while Stephan encountered his father on the little path halfway to Jones's house, Jones said, "Come on, walk me up. My security isn't here." On the way, they began to argue. Jones hardly could stand up. Stephan propped him up. As Jones gazed up at Stephan, he looked like a frail and sick man of average size, not God.

"What's really wrong with Shanda?" Stephan demanded. "You put her in there because she wants to leave you, didn't you?"

Jones drew back, perhaps surprised that he had been so obvious. "I can't believe you're saying that, that I drugged Shanda." He pretended to be offended.

"You're a fucking liar!" his son shouted.

"You're a fucking liar!" Jones hollered back. He wheeled around and Stephan wheeled around, and they started in opposite directions. It was a rare burst of public disrespect. In his weakened condition, Jones could hardly walk away, but somehow he managed. Then he spotted Tim and Johnny observing the whole thing from the pavillion. In private, he ordered them to put Stephan under armed surveillance.

A few minutes later, the boys came up to Stephan. "We're supposed to be watching you," they laughed. Then they all walked back together to the kitchen. The others took strength in seeing Stephan stand up to Jones. And it was an important moment for Stephan, too. No longer was he isolated from his brothers in his hatred of his father. Soon word spread through the whole basketball team.

After the confrontation, Stephan began to suspect that he was being drugged. His stomach felt awful, his face broke out, and there were days when he could hardly drag his body out of bed in the morning. He did not complain to anyone, however, and he did not even tell his mother; it would upset her. But one day when Jim Jones, disbelief on his face, watched him work, Stephan was certain his father was behind his weakened condition and accused him to his face. Enraged, Jones denied it.

When Jones saw Stephan huddled with his brothers, he ordered a turn-in of all guns in the compound. They were locked in a warehouse. There were two keys. Jim Jones had one and Joe Wilson, now his most trusted security guard, had the other. On the sly, Stephan kept his rifle.

During a catharsis session soon thereafter, another of Jones's sons asserted himself. Going down a list of disciplinary infractions, Jones was criticizing Tim for playing music on guard duty, sleeping on the job and arrogance. Tim did not even try to defend himself:

"I ain't got nothin' else to say," he said, refusing to play the penitent son. "I don't wish to talk about it. Whatever you want to do with me, go ahead on. . . . Three-fourths of it is bullshit."

"Don't give me no stuff . . ." Jones said. "That's arrogant. If anyone else had done that to me, you'd have jumped off this platform. That's totally wrong."

"That's right!" came the cries from the crowd.

"You know what it sounds like to me?" Tim said defiantly. "Someone isn't getting his ass kissed. . . ."

In the meantime, another family member took a stand. The unspoken rivalry between Marceline Jones and Carolyn Layton generated an open altercation, the only one ever in Stephan Jones's memory. With old wounds still festering, the women argued in Marceline's house while Stephan eavesdropped from the porch. Layton wanted Marceline to sign twenty blank sheets of paper in her hand. Marceline refused.

Stephan figured his mother was worried that Layton would use her signature on blank pages to somehow get back $8,000 that Marceline had had her parents place in a bank account for him.

"If you don't want to sign these papers, you don't have to," Layton said indignantly. "I have better things to do [than to argue]. I'm not going to betray you. I'm not going to use these papers. I can't believe you don't trust me to do this."

Marceline was calm. "You have to understand my position. I don't know what I'm signing."

Stephan tried to comfort his mother afterward. She told him she was tired of signing so many blank pieces of paper over the years.

Even so, Stephan cautioned her. "Argue when you really feel strongly about something. But don't question everything, because then he'll quit even coming near you, and he'll quit listening to you. When you have something really strong to say, he'll disregard that like everything else."

Stephan and Marceline Jones could challenge Jones on occasion, but did not try to stop him. For the past year, every time Marceline left Jonestown, the last thing she told Stephan was, "Don't kill him. Something will work out." Stephan knew that physically it would be easy to remove Jones, but a blatant power grab or coup would never go over with the loyalists. It would take a dictatorship, he felt, to consolidate his revolution. But the teen-ager was not ready for that, nor equipped with the powers of persuasion and broad support it would take to depose his father.

Stephan could not succeed without the help of his mother—yet, for complicated reasons, the woman who had been compromised by three decades of collaboration with a tyrant could not or would not fight him.

Ultimately, Stephan Jones saw himself as the successor to Jones, the person who would take over, in conjunction with Marceline, if Jones became incapacitated or died. No doubt Marceline, too, longed for that eventuality. Carolyn Layton, Jones's most important assistant, had already sent Stephan a letter which said, "I want you to know if anything ever happens to your father, I'll be behind you 100 percent." Stephan interpreted that letter to mean an official blessing of sorts. Succession would be easier, and cleaner, than throwing Jones aside. But despite the many signals to the contrary, those closest to Jones had failed to realize he had no intention of permitting his movement to survive him.

As their days were numbered, the powerless in Jonestown could not hope to overthrow the madman; their only feasible act of rebellion was escape. Only someone or some group who already possessed some power —like the aristocratic German army officers who plotted to blow up Hitler with a briefcase bomb—could hope to succeed. But without Stephan and Marceline Jones, there would be no revolution. The madness would rage.

FORTY-NINE

The Congressman, and Others

Back in the United States, the state of affairs in Jonestown remained an agonizingly inconclusive issue. For more than a year, nearly a thousand Americans had lived in the South American jungle under a cloud of accusations that, if true, meant that their lives were in danger of being extinguished at the whim of Jim Jones. Because some visitors hailed Jonestown as a utopian paradise and because the situation could never come to a head in California courts, the central question never changed: What *really* is going on in Jonestown?

The search for someone to galvanize the issue had actually ended almost a year earlier, though that was not yet clear. My November 13, 1977, story about Bob Houston's life and death had ignited the interest of Leo Ryan, a U.S. representative from the suburbs south of San Francisco. Soon afterward, at his own initiation, the congressman visited Sammy Houston at his house, where the photographer was recovering from his throat cancer operation. Looking gaunt and grim, Houston wore a cloth bib around his neck to hide the breathing hole in his throat. The Houston family tragedy touched and shocked Ryan, arousing both the empathy and sentimentality of the sometimes blustery Irishman. He came as a friend to help the photographer he had roomed with almost twenty years earlier in Washington, D.C., at the Kennedy inauguration. The contrast was sad. In those days, when Ryan was a teacher, Sam was healthy, and Bob a member of the high school band.

Houston could not talk, so he pounded a typewriter: "Hello roommate," he began. "Welcome to our home. . . ." His briefing of Ryan touched all the points and emphasized the conflicting welter of facts and charges.

Over the next six to eight months, Ryan's interest was aroused further by new developments reported in the press—the custody fight over John Stoen (in which he wrote a letter on behalf of Stoen), the defection of Debbie Blakey, the emergence of the Concerned Relatives. Various constituents wrote the congressman voicing alarm over the deteriorating situation, especially Jones's veiled threats of mass suicide. He invited one of them, Burlingame schoolteacher Clare Bouquet, to come talk to him personally about her fears for her son Brian. Battered by bureaucratic indifference, she went to Ryan's office in the summer of 1978 with only a glimmer of hope. "We are desperate, Mr. Ryan," she said, expecting him to pass the buck.

"I'll tell you what, Clare," Ryan said. "I'll promise you right here and now . . . I'll go down there.

"I'm not going alone," he added. "I want a group."

In a short time, Ryan met with various members of the Concerned Relatives and told them he would make the trip only after the November general election, and would not try to capitalize on it for his reelection campaign. The relatives agreed to keep the trip confidential. In the meantime, Ryan directed his staff to begin exploring logistics and to compile information about Peoples Temple. After meeting with some high State Department officials, Ryan wrote on October 4 to Representative Clement J. Zablocki, chairman of the House Foreign Affairs Committee, seeking approval for a fact-finding mission to Jonestown.

Unfortunately for the Temple, Ryan sat not only on the Foreign Affairs Committee but also on the International Operations subcommittee, which concerned itself with protecting the lives and property of U.S. citizens abroad. Objective as he might try to be, Ryan in the eyes of the Temple carried built-in biases: his nephew's membership in the Church of Scientology, his friendship with Sam Houston, his letter regarding Tim Stoen's paternity claim, and the fact that the bulk of the pretrip research came from Temple detractors. Furthermore Ryan, as a rebellious Irish Catholic and political maverick, had little reverence for either churches or the Temple's friends in high places. Most important, he was a compassionate man, and he had been moved by the appeals made to him.

Independent, brash, tenacious, Ryan would be no easy mark for Jim Jones. Diversions and stall tactics would be wasted; if anything, the standard church games would awaken the same competitive spirit and sense of mission that had driven Ryan on other quests: to play schoolteacher in Watts after the riots there; to live behind bars in Folsom Prison to assess conditions; to hike over snowy wilderness in an effort to save baby seals.

The Temple, of course, tried to cast Ryan as a right-winger, but in fact he held many liberal and humanitarian beliefs. During his first term in office he had authored an amendment strengthening the congressional oversight on the CIA; on a trip to NATO nations, he had made contact with Italian Communist party leaders against the wishes of the U.S. Embassy there. Ryan disliked bureaucracy and all government authoritarianism, and had led a fight to cut aid to the Marcos regime in the Philippines for violating human rights.

Travel guidelines of the Foreign Affairs Committee compelled Ryan to try to find a colleague to join him for the Jonestown expedition. His letters to his colleagues interested only one committee member, Representative Ed Derwinski of Illinois—and he would bow out at the last moment. It was not particularly surprising that Ryan's cohorts passed up the invitation. On the face of it, the trip sounded crazy—who would volunteer to enter one of the most inaccessible jungles on earth to check on the welfare of someone else's constituents?

On November 1, 1978, a week after receiving committee permission for the congressional delegation, Ryan wrote Jones in Guyana, telling him politely of his concerns and his planned visit and asking for cooperation. In the meantime, Ryan and various members of his staff requested and received five briefings from the State Department, the last on November 13. At the initial meeting on September 15, Ryan expressed concern that people might be held against their will, and he asked about the mass suicide threats reported by Blakey. One department official characterized the report as "nonsense." The State Department evidently also did not accept Blakey's report that Jonestown residents were coached for Embassy visits.

At the September meeting, the State Department advised Ryan against including four or five Concerned Relatives whom Ryan had mentioned as possible companions. The same position was taken in November when the group had expanded to eighteen relatives and nine news media representatives, all unofficially traveling with Ryan's congressional delegation. In the interim the Temple, through an Embassy official, told Ryan that it wanted no press coverage; it already went without saying they did not want their avowed enemies, the Concerned Relatives. And at the same time, Guyanese Ambassador Mann, who had his own very personal tie to the Temple, informed the Embassy that Guyana would not and could not force Jonestown to open its gates to Ryan's group.

Ryan's congressional staff members felt that the U.S. government also was not cooperating sufficiently. They thought the State Department was being overly cautious in its interpretation of the Privacy Act, guarding too closely Embassy files about Temple members. Also, although Ambassador John Burke in Georgetown had recommended that a State Department lawyer travel with the Ryan party, the department said none was available. As a substitute, State Department legal officers briefed committee staffer Jim Schollaert and Ryan aide Jackie Speier to explain the negligible legal standing the delegation would have in Guyana. All would depend on the grace of the Guyanese government and the hospitality of Jim Jones.

After Ryan won reelection and the trip date drew close, some members of the Concerned Relatives—Grace Stoen, Debbie Blakey and

Steve Katsaris—flew to Washington to make final rounds briefing congressmen on the controversy. They also met with committee staffer Jim Schollaert, who would accompany Ryan. After hearing their stories for three or four hours, Schollaert became concerned about the volatility of the Jonestown situation.

On November 13, 1978, the day that Concerned Relatives and news media boarded a San Francisco jet to rendezvous with the Ryan delegation, Ryan arranged a final meeting with the State Department, so they could hear firsthand Debbie Blakey's allegations. This meeting provided State Department officials in Washington with their final opportunity to share with Ryan any information which might prove valuable on his trip, yet they did not avail themselves of it. They did not ever mention to Ryan the Leon Broussard escape, which would have partially confirmed Blakey's account and provided additional guidance. More important, though this session occurred six days after a U.S. Embassy official had visited Jonestown, the department failed to relate this very telling, new eyewitness account.

On November 7, McCoy's successor, Consul Douglas Ellice, Jr., had found Jones in a bizarre condition, slurring his speech, unable to spell simple words, wearing a gauze mask, claiming a 105-degree fever and complaining of a recent heart attack. Ellice later would say that he had tried to tell Ryan about Jones's condition when the congressman came through Georgetown, but that Ryan had brushed him off with the assurance of someone who already had done his homework.

Meanwhile, the State Department spent most of their time subtly discouraging Ryan by talking about transportation difficulties and so on, while neglecting to provide crucial information—the apparent psychological state of Jim Jones.

One morning in November attorney Charles Garry picked up the *San Francisco Chronicle* to read that Representative Leo Ryan was leading a fact-finding congressional delegation to Jonestown. It was the first Garry had heard of the Ryan trip, although Mark Lane and the Temple knew all about it. Garry was furious. Already he had threatened to quit when he heard that Lane was holding press conferences and that the Temple were violating his warnings to lie low. Once placated, Garry had agreed to handle the existing lawsuits but refused to work with Lane, whom he detested for butting into the case. Now, with the wounds to his pride scarcely healed, he was hit with the final indignity of learning that Lane was already acting as the Temple's chief attorney.[72]

In a November 6 letter urging Ryan to delay his trip, Lane said Jones wanted him, as legal counsel, present for any congressional visit. Lane noted that he had prior commitments in November before the House Select Committee on Assassinations. And he suggested that Ryan select a later date for a visit.

Lane's rather threatening letter to Ryan riled Garry all the more.

Page two was especially disastrous, he thought, because it provided ammunition for Temple enemies.

"You should be informed," Lane told Ryan, "that various agencies of the U.S. Government have somewhat consistently oppressed Peoples Temple. . . . Some of the members of the Peoples Temple have had to flee from the U.S. You should know that two different countries . . . have offered refuge to the 1,200 Americans now residing in Jonestown. Thus far, the Peoples Temple has not accepted either of those offers, but it is their position that if religious persecution . . . is furthered through a witch hunt, they will be constrained to consider accepting either of the offers. [It] might very well result in the creation of a most embarrassing situation for the U.S. Government."

Leo Ryan's November 10 response noted that he would resolve the scheduling conflict in favor of the House of Representatives. In other words, he was coming down.

"No 'persecution,' as you put it, is intended, Mr. Lane," Ryan wrote. "But your vague reference to 'the creation of the most embarrassing situation for the American government' does not impress me at all. If the comment is intended as a threat, I believe it reveals more than may have been intended. I presume Mr. Jones would not be supportive of such a statement."

Charles Garry was appalled by Lane's latest performance and made his objection absolutely clear in a November 11 telephone conversation with June Crym, a Temple secretary in San Francisco. He said Lane's letter was disastrous because it implied the Temple was unhappy in Guyana—and that church members were fugitives. "He's sticking his goddamn fucking nose into a situation where he doesn't know his ass from a hole in the ground. . . . If anyone's gonna protect the rights of the organization, it's my job. . . . I will call the shots or it's gonna be Mark Lane calling the shots. It's not gonna be both of us. . . . I'm not going to permit this kind of wishy-washy situation to run wild."

Unfortunately for Charles Garry and more than nine hundred residents of Jonestown, however, that is exactly what was about to happen.

The zealotry of the Temple stateside staff was turning into a sort of martyrdom. Many sensed that they were part of a dying organization. The Wednesday night and Sunday meetings still were held in San Francisco, with Marceline or other members presiding. But now that the Temple's drawing card, Jim Jones, was gone, attendance dropped off. By August, less than a hundred regulars were attending. Without the big healing donations, the church had to convert its assets into cash. Like a family going into hock, the Temple sold off pieces of property just to raise money for shipments to Guyana, some of which cost $30,000. The city staff generated the money, purchased the supplies, crated them and shipped them down. Since personnel was shrinking all the time, the few people left behind were overworked.

Temple loyalists in San Francisco were experiencing the same epidemic of frustrations as the staff at Lamaha Gardens and the people in Jonestown—conflicting demands and answerless questions from their leader, unbearable stress, physical exhaustion to the point of failing health. Internal division and racial bitterness tainted both California temples. Blacks were angry that whites alone controlled the pursestrings, made the day-to-day decisions and consulted most often with Jones on the radio. Some whites, in turn, thought blacks were themselves to blame for their isolation from the power positions because they refused tedious work such as radio room duty.

In addition to everything else, there was serious concern that the Temple would lose its lifeline to Guyana—the radio. Several times the FCC threatened to shut it down. But the Temple forestalled that while breaking amateur radio rules against using codes and conducting business, and while making contingency plans to move their radios to Mexico and transmit to Guyana from there.

Jones's degeneration dragged down everyone. For example, he ordered the skeletal stateside staff to produce immediately fifteen hundred letters to the Federal Communications Commission and fifteen hundred to the Internal Revenue Service to ward off governmental action. As the Temple's problems increased in number and its options were cut off, Jones could only react defensively. To protect his flanks, he brought to Jonestown any distrusted or wavering members or anyone in a position to embarrass the church. In the early years, he sent the problem children to his tropical Siberia, but now he began calling down trusted aides.

Because she worked efficiently out of the immediate presence of Jones, Sandy Bradshaw had been chosen to stay in the city, sharing Jones's former Temple apartment with Marceline when she was in town. Up by 7:30 A.M., Bradshaw would scan the local papers for news of Peoples Temple then clip articles and buy a broad range of papers and magazines to send Jones. By about 10:00 A.M., the radio band would be "up," meaning the Temple had fixed on its customary frequency. Bradshaw spend most of her time in a tiny nine-by-twelve-foot room deciphering words in a sea of static, often until the early morning.

Bradshaw kept at it, convinced the cause superseded her personal sacrifices. Sometimes she daydreamed about being in Jonestown, a field worker without any responsibility or worries. But the problems in the city kept popping up. Who should stay in San Francisco and who should leave for Guyana? Who was cracking under the pressure? Could they handle the new demands from Jonestown? When would the next media attack hit? What was Tim Stoen doing? And why could the church not regain its old momentum? For a change, the past looked better than the future. The present was miserable.

After renovating all of the Temple's Los Angeles property for sale, faithful Archie Ijames had moved back to San Francisco to help with the packing and crating of supplies for Jonestown. At one time, Ijames had wanted to bring his wife to Jonestown. But once Debbie Blakey had defected and told horror stories that rang of truth, he was glad to be in the United States. After several months in San Francisco, however, Ijames got a radio call. Jones told him a beautiful flower garden already was planted in paradise, for Archie and Rosie. Ijames's stomach cramped; he figured someone in San Francisco had reported him for a negative attitude. Ijames respectfully said no one else could perform his job, and Jones reluctantly let him stay.

The defection of key people always threw Jim Jones into fits of rage and self-pity. But for sheer bad timing, perhaps no defection could rival that of Teri Buford on October 27, 1978, a time when Jones already was balancing too many problems. Buford, the strategist who had accompanied Debbie Blakey on their international financial sleuthing, likely knew more about the complex Temple finances and bank accounts than anyone aside from Carolyn Layton.

At twenty-six, Buford was painfully thin, with deep-set eyes, shoulder-length brown hair, tireless energy and utter loyalty. After she had joined the Temple in the early seventies as a University of California student, Buford had risen rapidly in the Temple hierarchy. Her ability to quickly plot complicated strategy with Jones cemented her standing. But many other members thought she embodied the worst traits of Jones's staff—secretive, conspiratorial, often speaking in a whisper. Wearing a bunch of keys on a necklace like symbols of her dedication, Buford worked harder than just about everyone there.

The disenchantment of this true believer was not sudden. While in San Francisco during the six-day siege, Buford—like other staffers—felt Jonestown residents had the right to choose the time and manner of their death. But after six months in the Jonestown radio room, after seeing the effect of the Blakey defection on Jones in May, she realized that the man who had once inspired her loyalty and love had changed.

By early fall, she had wangled a transfer to San Francisco. She left Jonestown with the intention of never returning. Not only had Jim Jones become a sick tyrant but also his decisions were tactically weak. And there was a distasteful mission Jones had entrusted to her—that of gradually drugging Sandy Bradshaw, so she could be moved to Jonestown peacefully.

Sandy Bradshaw's health had deteriorated. Under constant stress, she experienced heart palpitations, other physical symptoms and depression. She yearned to move to carefree Guyana but was awaiting the results of various tests. Ever skeptical, Buford believed Bradshaw was faking illness to get out of the work in San Francisco. In a memo to Jones marked "For JJ's Eyes Only," Buford asked Jones how to handle "Lilly," the code name for Bradshaw. On the matter of drugging her, Buford wrote:

"As for the other thing, it is going to be extremely difficult to do because her eating is extremely odd (I mean it is hard to mix something with potato chips). I don't know. Also, your job may be done for you in that she already believes that she is dying."

Buford already had heard about the drugging of Shanda James. She probably knew about the drugging of Chaikin, too. His treachery indicated that Jones would bring to Jonestown, and drug if necessary, anyone who showed the slightest disloyalty. If Jones could order Buford to drug a peer and a rival, Buford must have wondered whether she might be next. Though she willingly had played informer, she was unwilling to become executioner as well.

Buford knew that Jones would discover her own disobedience soon enough, because Bradshaw was scheduled to leave for Jonestown within a week. More than ever she was convinced that regardless of how her defection was disguised, Jones would react hysterically. She thought they might try to kill her. She resolved to get her name off all the bank accounts so no one could accuse her of running off with Temple money.

Buford knew that every prominent defector eventually had teamed up with Tim Stoen and the Concerned Relatives. She would not take that route because she deplored Tim Stoen. Still, that past pattern provided her with a plausible reason for her sudden departure: she would say she had embarked on a mission to "get" Tim Stoen.

Buford needed help from an outsider—a trusted person who would advise her and, if necessary, provide a refuge. She remembered a spark of skepticism in Mark Lane's eye as they rode the truck from Jonestown to Matthews Ridge that September. Lane had asked her the familiar question: Why was the leadership white in a largely black movement?

Buford made final plans in San Francisco. She arranged to spend a few days with her sister, and slowly began mailing her belongings to her sister's house. And she phoned Mark Lane. "If I tell you some things, are you obligated to tell them to Jim Jones?" Buford asked tentatively.

"As you know," Lane replied, "I have been retained by Jim Jones to file applications under the Freedom of Information Act. The information that you are telling me, would it be related to that?"

"No, another matter."

"Then it may not be a conflict of interest if it is another matter. I am not the general counsel."

With detailed ground rules, they agreed to meet at the Gramercy Park Hotel in New York on Sunday, October 29. Buford bought an airline ticket with money her parents regularly sent her, money that usually ended up in the church coffers.

At 5:45 A.M. on Friday, October 27, Buford went to Charles Garry's office, picked up a small briefcase she had left the night before and headed for the airport. Five minutes prior to takeoff, she called Pat Richartz. Buford said she was going to the dentist and asked her to call Jean Brown in an hour and direct her to some messages.

The package for Brown contained a four-page "confidential" letter to Jim Jones, which was Teri Buford's carefully woven "cover." It said she had gone to play double agent and infiltrate "Tim Stoen's group" to learn its strategy.

She began by noting that she was extremely upset about the state of Jim Jones's health and frustrated by the Temple's failure to expose the other side. "I don't know how much longer you are going to live," she wrote. "I heard you on the phone patch the other night and you could barely get out the words."

Buford took great pains to explain why her "defection" would fool the other side into accepting her and divulging their anti-Jones strategy. For one thing, Buford noted, she had no blood ties to Jonestown so she could be embraced more readily than an infiltrator with kin in the jungle. "Frankly," the letter continued, "if I don't fuck up and get myself in a lot of trouble, there is a possibility that Stoen in particular would be quite interested in cultivating a working relationship. . . ."

The letter continued in that vein for several more pages and concluded: ". . . if you try to interfere, you will have a suicide. . . ."

When he later read this letter, Jim Jones was not put at ease. It looked to him as if Buford had gone on an ill-conceived "adventure," not a church "mission." He sent Sandy Bradshaw to look for her in feminist bars in Berkeley. But Buford was actually in hiding back east with Mark Lane, informing him, among other things, that Debbie Blakey had told the truth about nearly everything.

By early November, Buford had not surfaced anywhere. Jones was almost positive that she was merely buying time with her letter and had turned against him. Deciding to find out for sure, he sent a message to Tim Carter to infiltrate the Concerned Relatives and find out what Buford was doing. Carter had been traveling in the United States after delivering some of the affidavits Garry had prepared during his 1978 visit to Jonestown. He had gone to his father's home in Boise, Idaho, for some dental work—but Jones's orders sent him packing to the Bay Area. Soon Pat Richartz was being informed that Carter had infiltrated the relatives and would contact her with the code name "Jonathan." Within moments, the phone rang at Garry's office. "This is Jonathan," a voice said. "Hi, Tim," Richartz said. Taking the phone, Charles Garry told Carter that the plan was stupid. But Carter continued his mission, calling in a few more times to report on his progress. Once Jones heard about the Ryan trip, he asked Carter to find out about that as well as about Buford.

The night of the first newspaper article announcing the Ryan trip, Pat Richartz was awakened at her Berkeley home by a pebble bouncing off her window. She looked out. There was Tim Carter, dressed in black and wearing a knit cap. "Pat. Pat. Lemme in."

He was breathless and as nervous as a cat. He sat on the kitchen floor so that no one could see him from outside, and he asked her to keep the lights low and to close the shades, as Temple members always did when they came to her home for dinner. She brewed some herbal tea to calm him. Carter said that he had met with Stoen as well as the others: they said Ryan was going to Jonestown—with Stoen.

"Who else is going?" Richartz asked.

Carter named some of the relatives who had done the most screaming, and some reporters. Jones would never let in Reiterman, he commented. Since Buford was not among the defectors, Carter had managed to confirm her betrayal. So his mission was a double success.

Using a credit card, he called Lamaha Gardens and told Sharon Amos to relay everything to Jones and his aides. Though much of it had appeared in the newspaper, his information was reported as undercover intelligence. In great detail, Carter explained how he had met three times with various relatives and what they told him about the Ryan trip. He quoted himself saying to Stoen: "What a coup! What a coup! You've really done it." And he quoted Stoen as saying, "Wait until you see what happens once you get to Jonestown."

It was a long call to Guyana, maybe an hour. Carter was excited and happy with the information he had stolen from "the belly of the enemy." Richartz suggested he go back to his roominghouse, continue the cover and find out what Stoen meant by his tantalizing reference to Jonestown.

Carter presumed, however, that the call to Lamaha Gardens had blown his cover, since the Concerned Relatives were monitoring radio transmissions. He left hurriedly, seeming to think his life was in danger.

FIFTY

The Eye of the Storm

As October turned into November in Jonestown, events toppled onto Jones with head-spinning speed. He learned the specifics of the Ryan trip almost in the same breath as he got confirmation of Teri Buford's defection. At the same time, the Jonestown basketball team, including top security guards, prepared to leave for the basketball tournament in Georgetown. On November 7, the new American consul, Douglas Ellice, would arrive for his first visit to Jonestown and the first Embassy inspection in six months. And to add a surreal touch to the most critical month in the history of Peoples Temple, Marceline Jones had just returned from the States with her parents, the Baldwins, who had wanted to see Jonestown firsthand for a long time. It was hardly an opportune time for a folksy visit with the in-laws.

The Baldwins had first planned a September visit to Jonestown, but Jones delayed it. Then Marceline called her parents from New York in October and said she would visit Indiana, then fly down to Guyana with them. Marceline was proud of Jonestown, eager to have her parents see the progress and share her joy. But her Indiana stopover troubled the family.

Marceline told her sister, Sharon, that Jones was "very sick," raising her hopes that the family troubles might end with Jones's death. Marceline said Jim was feeling closed in, and stayed in his cabin most of the time. It was harmful emotionally, she said, because he had been accustomed to the road, organizing bus caravans, driving or flying between cities. Now he was afraid even to go into Georgetown.

Marceline still believed in the cause and in the people, but no longer in her husband. "He's like one of my children, now," she told her sister. Jones was both her scourge and her charge. She feared him and dreaded what he and his sometimes vicious mistresses might do, yet felt protective and motherly toward him at the same time.

In his mad fantasies and his deliberate cruelty toward his wife, Jones had bragged of seducing Sharon. Now Marceline needed to know for sure. She pulled her sister into the bathroom of their parents' house. The question was unbearably difficult.

"Did Jim ever ask you to sleep with him or touch you in any way?" Marceline asked.

"No."

Marceline's thoughts evidently leaped back to Guyana. "I can't bear the thought of any children being harmed."

Sharon picked up immediately on Marceline's multiple meanings: Jones had degenerated so far that Marceline could not be sure that he had not molested her own younger sister, nor that he would keep his hands off the children in Jonestown.

"Marceline, you've got to get out of there," Sharon pleaded. "You've got to get out of there."

In another conversation, Marceline admitted to her mother that she and Stephan were watched in Jonestown because they challenged unfair discipline. She said that Jim depended on drugs and saw enemies everywhere, that every time she tried to intervene, his aides derided her "emotionalism."

"I wish you'd gotten out of this years ago," Mrs. Baldwin said.

"Oh, mother," Marceline cried. "Please don't say that. I have suffered so much for so many years."

The Baldwins' grandson, Jimmy, Jr., met their plane when it landed at Timehri Airport on October 26. The group spent the weekend at Lamaha Gardens to allow Walter Baldwin, who had undergone surgery in May, to rest from the arduous flight. During the layover, they went sightseeing and heard Marceline speak at a church.

Monday, the thirtieth of October, the Baldwins flew into Port Kaituma on a government plane and rode into Jonestown by tractor. They had flown, unknowingly, into the eye of the storm. This Republican former city councilman from Richmond, Indiana, and his wife were about to be given the royal tour in the socialist sanctuary of Jim Jones, who within days would openly advocate the assassination of a congressman and make secret preparations for mass murder. For nearly thirty years, they had pushed aside their doubts about Jim Jones, unwilling to intrude in their daughter's marriage. This would be the final deception.

They received first-class treatment. Their guest cabin was well outfitted—a king-size bed with mosquito netting and bright-colored pillows, highly polished wooden floors with hand-woven throw rugs, a stereo, a sunny enclosed shower and bowls of fresh cut flowers and fruit.

In the musical program planned that first night, their grandson Lew sang his first solo with the band. Jim Jones made a special trip to the pavilion to greet his in-laws, but the sight of him appalled the Baldwins. His face and body were badly swollen with edema, his hands almost twice their normal size. He could barely walk. In the month Marceline was away, his health had worsened.

"Jim," his wife said. "Are they giving you any medication?"

"I don't know," he replied.

The Baldwins would not see their son-in-law for the next ten days, though they would hear his voice over the loudspeaker, his words tumbling out, almost garbled.

On their first full day in Jonestown, they received an upbeat tour. But Marceline talked to her parents in private. "Since I have arrived," she confided, "things have gotten out of hand, and I have to do something about it. I have come back to something that displeases me very much, and I won't get to spend as much time with you as I would like. But we'll eat our evening meals together and spend whatever time together we can."

The Baldwins told her not to worry. Just being near her was enough for them. Whenever they walked past her cottage, they saw her talking and counseling people on her porch. By the end of every day, she was exhausted. Finally, Marceline confided that while she was gone, Jones had put almost twenty people on tranquilizers for causing unrest. So far, she had gotten all but seven off the drugs and out of the Extended Care Unit.

The following Sunday night meeting, November 5, saw Jim Jones at his most bizarre. Raving incoherently at times, Jones opened the meeting by announcing that enemy infiltrators had made a third attempt to poison his food in Jonestown. But there was a much greater and more immediate danger, he said: "A congressman . . . who's close to the John Birch Society wants to drop in, and my opinion is to tell him to stick it."

This reference to Leo Ryan apparently brought Jones back to thoughts of security and defense, because the next subject was the six-day siege of September 1977. He spoke of it often, as the combat experience that proved the mettle of the Peoples Temple army. Now Jim Jones faced a new Leningrad where he would have to hold off "the fascists."

"One advantage we have," Jones said, "is we're not afraid, some of us, to die. I remember too well how four hundred of you stood up, and didn't flinch an eye, and honey, if you're afraid of death the first day, by the third day you aren't afraid no more."

Then the catharsis began. The first victims were two small children Jones bawled out for killing bugs; he threatened to put them on PSU as punishment. Then the basketball team was confronted. He addressed coach Lee Ingram: "I'm interested in socialist conduct. Twenty-nine years I've sweated to build a communist movement, and I didn't sweat to come over here and die in no fuckin' jungle."

That last comment came out of the blue. No one had suggested dying in the jungle, but Jones clearly was pondering responses to the Ryan visit. At the same time, he was thinking of ways to extract public relations mileage from the basketball team when they went to Georgetown the next day. Perhaps they could display socialist consciousness on the basketball court, he said, by clapping every time the other team made a basket. Taken with his brainstorm, he declared: "How many thousands you can lead to communism! If the fucking referee works against you, don't you dare show it. Go right on and, believe me, that superiority will communize some of those youth."

As Stephen got up to defend himself and the team, Jones suddenly flashed back to what was pure fantasy: his days of basketball greatness. He sounded as though he believed he had been something more than just a kid who occasionally sold soft drinks at the high school games.

"If I had my son's hands, I'd be a pro. I was a very good forward and played hard. But in the U.S., no one was kind. I quit basketball because I saw them treat one black man wrong. . . .

"So when they make a goal, clap for a few seconds. . . . Don't do it long," he warned, "cuz they'll be passing the fuckin' ball when you're under the post. Shit, I forgot the fuckin' names. . . . Look humble. Grab them between recesses and give them a hug."

"I don't know if they'll let me," said Stephan, whose mind was strictly on basketball. "I've done it before and I've been treated like I was some kind of fag."

"Well, then, shake hands," Jones replied. "And if they don't want to shake hands, that'll make them look like assholes. . . ."

"As soon as the ball is shot," said Stephan, "I'll be snatching it and throwing it as fast as I can. We're too small to be a slow team."

Jones told them to be careful in Georgetown, to get plenty of rest and to avoid urban temptations. There was an incurable venereal disease called "Z," he warned.

Then he ended the session by coaching residents once again on how to talk to strangers. The embassy man would be visiting on the next day, and Ryan on the eighteenth. There could be no mistakes. "It must be done on the eighteenth," he said, referring to proper conduct. "If we don't, we're foolish."

As the sun climbed over the treetops the next morning, all of Jonestown, except Jim Jones, turned out to send off its basketball team. Mike Touchette, who was driving the truck, never had seen such a spontaneous outpouring of emotion. Marceline ecstatically hurried the team into the truck, afraid Jones might change his mind. Just before they pulled out, she went over to Touchette and hugged him, tears streaming down her face. "No matter what happens," she said, "please take care of my sons for me." Touchette's mother cried, too. It was only the second time Mike had seen her shed tears. The whole town, it seemed, was crying in farewell. Did they expect something dreadful was going to happen?

Before the team had a chance to unpack its gear in Georgetown on November 7, Jones ordered them back. But Marceline pleaded their case so persuasively that Jones reluctantly reversed himself. Everyone on the team was overjoyed, and thanked Marceline over the radio.

By then, much of the team had turned dramatically against Jones, some with open derision. The players drove around the capital in a blue van ridiculing Jones's paranoia. Passing a telephone pole, they would make a wide swing because, they laughed, it could be part of the "conspiracy." Or someone would joke, "We can't stop at the next spotlight because it's bugged." Not all team members knew what was going on, but they took cues from leaders, such as the Jones brothers, and happily joined in the irreverent humor.

But then the contradictory orders bombarded them from Jonestown. As Ryan's Guyana arrival neared, the team was instructed to intimidate the group at the airport. They were relieved when the orders changed. Next, Sharon Amos told them, "He wants you out of the house. He wants you to go to Surinam or hide somewhere." Coach Lee Ingram pointed out the absurdity of the 180-degree reversal, to no avail. Then the team was told to guard the Jones boys, Johnny Cobb and Mike Touchette, because Ryan's party might try to kidnap them.

Finally, they went to the "snake man's" house to hide. It was easier than leaving the country for neighboring Surinam. The snake man was a stocky East Indian judo teacher and venom salesman. Six team members slept in the van outside while the rest slept on judo mats inside the house, where he kept illegal guns and a basement full of poisonous snakes. Meanwhile, the team continued to work out, practicing at the National Sports Hall, enjoying the luxury of glass backboards.

On November 7, U.S. Consul Douglas Ellice and his vice-consul— who were well briefed about the Temple case—left Georgetown for their first Jonestown visit. Because of a scarcity of airplanes, the pair shared a flight with Maria Katsaris and another church member. Upon arrival, the Embassy team interviewed many of the fifteen or so people on their "welfare and whereabouts" list, listened to a rendition of "America the Beautiful," dined on a lunch of pork chops and chicken and met Jim Jones, who had wobbled up to the table in a white gauze mask, a person on each side to steady him.

One of the people interviewed was Brian Bouquet, whose mother had inquired about his condition a few months earlier and was coming with Ryan. Ellice delivered a letter from Mrs. Bouquet. Brian opened it and read it with no apparent emotion. He said he was happy in Jonestown and would write his mother soon. Ellice also talked to Larry Layton, whose father in Berkeley wanted to know about the death of his wife, Lisa. Young Layton promised Ellice he would contact his relatives shortly to give them the details.

Overall, the new consul had thought the place primitive, though he understood how residents might be delighted with their accomplishments. If anything, the visit had merely confused Ellice. It had not helped him decide which side was telling him the truth about Jonestown.

In the week prior to Ryan's arrival, Jones warned graphically against escaping into the jungle.

"I want to remind you again," he said in a monologue, "that there are, within a half mile of East House, quicksand. I'd a gone up to my head if it hadn't been for a miracle. Stephan can verify we were out there scouting about. Now I can't imply to you what a tiger can do with one blow of his leg. One blow can break your whole spine and neck. Not to mention, of course, he can eat you. Caymen, larger than crocodiles, the most fierce in the world, can swallow you in one gulp. . . ."

The uncertainty of Ryan's visit heightened the tensions. Messages kept going among Georgetown, San Francisco and Jonestown. When was Ryan coming and how? Who was coming with him and what were their intentions?

On November 8, Jones projected a new fear. Ryan might approach by sea and enter at night. Jones believed that forty people were descending upon him, among them Wayne Pietila of the Eight Revolutionaries. If necessary, the Temple would meet the group by force, he said.

"There might be an attempt to enter the mouth of the river without legal permission," Jones declared in one of his periodic bulletins, "because it has been discussed by this disreputable fascist, Congressman O'Ryan, who has supported the murder of President Allende . . . Stoen also is in the number, naturally, and Grace. They are now as high in their salutation to fascism as they were in their devotion to socialism. They are traveling with an astrologer who is guiding them as to the right time to enter our premises. They are filled with hate. They tell the most horrible lies— people chained here to work spots twenty-four hours a day, and women forced to have intercourse with whoever wants them. They whip dreams of madness out of their own nightmares and evil souls. These are wicked people."

Jones assured his people that his information was absolutely reliable, because he had sent agents such as Tim Carter to infiltrate them. "We have trained infiltrators to be in every sense like them, to sound like them, to talk like them, to listen to their talk. Our infiltrators are inside their movement entirely. . . ."

Yet Jones wanted to know the identities of the rest of Ryan's fellow travelers. He asked his people for a list of potentially hostile relatives, saying the Guyanese foreign minister had requested them.

"Report any relative that may be hostile, because if any of them approach this community illegally, they will leave it dead . . ." he said in his most prophetic voice.

"No one enters our territory without our approval. . . . if they come in here by night, they are finished. Thank you. Much love."

There was no longer any doubt. Jim Jones would kill to protect his sanctuary.

Jones always had kept families divided to safeguard the loyalty of individual members. Divide and conquer. But Jonestown, the isolated setting which allowed him tremendous control over people, also put family members in close proximity to each other, some for the first time in years. Some of these people then discovered that their blood ties were stronger than loyalty to a man who had turned monstrous.

Dale Parks, the hard-working respiratory therapist, reckoned that Jones would snow Leo Ryan as he had snowed every other visitor. He thought any attempt to leave with Ryan or any other government official would reap catastrophe. But at the same time, neither Parks nor his family could take much more of Jim Jones and his pervasive voice.

Although the public perceived Parks as intensely loyal, his family knew about his disaffection. The Parks family had talked among themselves since arriving in Jonestown in January 1978. Although they pretended to play the good soldiers and criticized each other in catharsis sessions, they proceeded continuously with escape plans, terrified of what might happen if they got caught. Unknown to anyone else, the Parks family had begun to conceal belongings near the piggery, where Dale's father Gerry worked. They waited for the proper day to break away and hike a trail to the main road to Port Kaituma. They figured that Jones's sloppiness would provide the opportunity soon.

The Bogue family—with the exception of nineteen-year-old Marilee —wanted desperately to escape, too. Jim Bogue, one of the original 1974 settlers, had become disenchanted, as had his teen-age son Tommy, Teena, Juanita and their mother, Edith.

Whenever Jim Jones talked or held one of his increasingly frequent White Nights, Juanita Bogue had become extremely upset. She hated Jim Jones talking about violent death—beheadings with cutlasses or bodies blown to pieces—especially in front of the small children. It sickened her to hear the news, the praise given the Red Brigades for kidnapping and killing Italian Prime Minister Aldo Moro. She hated the regimentation.

She hated the moist climate that turned minor cuts and scratches into swelling sores.

She thought her weeding work in the cassava fields was pointless, designed to keep the crews busy. But working in the fields had afforded one advantage. She saw her family every day, and in the absence of security guards, they began the laborious process of rebuilding family bonds and trust.

Their escape plan was born while Teena and Juanita worked together in a field. While comparing notes, they realized that each had legitimate complaints about life in Jonestown. The next step was for the sisters to talk to their father. They were scared at first, thinking that even their own father might report them. But Jim Bogue agreed with his daughters and confided that, for years, he had hoped conditions would improve. Together, a few members of the Bogue family began to plot their escape.

Others, in some small corner of their minds, guarded the same notions. One of them, eighteen-year-old Monica Bagby, never had joined Peoples Temple voluntarily. When Monica graduated from Opportunity High with seemingly nothing better to do, her mother, an enthusiastic member, sent her down to Jonestown in the summer of 1978. Beset by health problems because of the poor diet and unfamiliar climate, the young woman hated the place immediately. Given an opportunity to leave, she would become the only black to take the dangerous step; she would team up with a young white man named Vern Gosney.

Even families without immediate plans to escape could not easily push aside their familial bonds. The Cobbs, for example, stuck together. When Christine, the mother, received a photograph of Jim Cobb's son, they were all as delighted as any family could be about the new addition and proudly displayed the photo—even though the father was considered a Temple traitor. Christine was called up before a meeting for doing so.

During their Jonestown stay, Charlotte and Walter Baldwin heard no one asking to leave Jonestown. Nor did they see their son-in-law again until November 9, when he called them to his house. They knew he was unpredictable. But they were far too cloistered, physically and emotionally, to foresee Jones's violent intentions from their guest accommodations.

Jones looked better than he had that first night at the pavilion, but he told them how concerned he was about the impending Ryan trip. The Baldwins tried to calm Jim and even suggested letting the congressman into Jonestown. "You have nothing to lose. It's a nice place," they told him. But they got nowhere. He was too distressed for reasoning. Mrs. Baldwin thought he was worried that he would lose John Victor Stoen.

After a few uneventful days, the Baldwins arose early on Monday the thirteenth, looking forward to the boat trip out, to seeing Amerindian villages and beautiful tropical wildlife. Their bags were packed and waiting behind Marceline's cabin for the truck ride to Port Kaituma. Then Jones suddenly announced over the public address system that he had canceled the boat trip. No one was allowed to leave, not even sick people scheduled for Georgetown hospital treatment.

"Jim won't let the boat leave," Marceline told her parents after investigating. "So you can get a plane out today. I'm going to order a Land Rover to take you to Matthews Ridge. . . ."

The Baldwins flew home on Wednesday—only hours after Ryan's party had landed in Georgetown. One of the last things their daughter had told them was: "I have lived, not just existed."

After his in-laws departed, Jones allowed the *Cudjo* to sail for Georgetown, anyway. There, it picked up its cargo and headed back to Port Kaituma on Wednesday, the fifteenth. Harold Cordell, the longtime church accountant and now Edith Bogue's paramour, was one of the dock workers waiting to meet it. Checking off the cargo list, Cordell suddenly spied a hundred-pound plastic drum wrapped in paper. The shipping manifest listed equipment, animal feed and bags of supplies for the settlement —but no drum of chemicals. No one seemed to know anything about it. The chemicals had been purchased in Georgetown outside normal church channels.

In Jonestown, the Temple agronomist, Russell Moton, examined the drum and said it was a very dangerous chemical that should not be stored in the central supply area. "That stuff is highly toxic," Moton said. "Mixed with water, it can be fatal to people." It was a cyanide compound.

Cordell wondered if Jones had some secret plan to poison the congressman. He also knew it could be easily slipped into the water supply, their few wells. Cordell already knew that a chemical engineer was researching explosives, and that Jones had said bombs were being built to blow up buildings—and themselves—in case of an invasion. But the discovery of the poison really shook Cordell: he was now convinced that Jones had gone completely insane. His thoughts turned to ways to leave.

With Ryan's party pushing for a visit, Jones dispatched an order to the basketball team at the snake man's house: he wanted them back in Jonestown immediately. Stephan Jones thought the order stupid, and the rest of the team implored him to dissuade his father. Using the Lamaha Gardens radio, he told his father: "You want to make good p.r.? Well, we're doing it. Every place we go, we talk to people. They're getting to like us. They razz us, see that we don't get mad, that we're good guys. . . . We've got a game tomorrow with the national team."

"I told you," his father broke in, "that I want you to come back."

Thinking his father might have called a White Night, another drill, Stephan insisted. "No. We're doing too much good here."

Jones put Marceline on the radio, hoping they would listen to her. But Stephan knew his mother always took the White Nights more seriously than he did, so he did not believe there was any real danger in Jonestown.

"Steve, I think you should come back," she said. "You don't know what's going on out here. We really need you."

That plea helped convince Stephan Jones not to return. He thought his father had put the words in his mother's mouth. Stephan had watched Jones before, standing over people in the radio room, telling them what to say, word by word. With his son, Jim Jones had cried wolf once too often.

The team wanted to stay not only to avoid the miserable experience of another White Night but also to have fun in Georgetown. Using money Stephan swiped from his father's house, they ate well and played basketball, having a great time, anticipating the tournament, even thinking ahead to a triumphal return to Jonestown.

Stephan had guessed correctly. Marceline had only repeated Jones's orders; she really wanted her son to stay away. But she was not trying to save the basketball tourney; she was warning him away from danger. In Mike Carter's presence, Jones yelled at her for being indifferent to what was happening and overprotective of her sons.

"Hell," Marceline snapped back, "I've been keeping this place together [recently], not you." With that, she turned and stormed back to her cottage.

A little while later, Stephan got back on the radio to repeat his earlier message: the basketball team was not returning. When Jones got that message, he wanted Marceline to take to the radio and fight her disobedient son. She refused. On the eve of a momentous visit, Jones's authority was shaken. His wife and son had disobeyed him; his security guards preferred to play basketball.

As Friday the seventeenth dawned, Jim Jones was resigned to another failure: he could not keep Leo Ryan out of Jonestown. He reacted predictably, by calling a White Night.

Marceline Jones was infuriated by his counterproductive actions. "Are you out of your mind?" she cried. "You want these people to stay in Jonestown, and you're talking about suicide right before this congressman comes in!"

Surprisingly, Jones accepted her logic. But before he relented, he commanded some people to ambush the Ryan party on the road to Jonestown—if the plane managed to land. "It looks like they're coming after all," he told the frightened crowd. "Maybe the plane will just fall out of the sky."

Jones had hoped Sharon Amos would board that plane; in fact, the Temple had told local police officials that she would be accompanying the Ryan party. But there had been no room for her. When she returned to Lamaha Gardens from the airport, she was near hysteria. Had Jim Jones ordered Amos on a kamikaze mission to shoot the pilot and bring down the plane? It was known that Amos would do anything Jim Jones ordered. In less than twenty-four hours, she would give her life for him.

FIFTY-ONE

En Route

At first, Ryan's staff and the Concerned Relatives had cloaked the Guyana trip in great secrecy. Even after a relative tipped me about "something big" in the air, Tim Stoen refused to supply any information. However, I called Ryan's office on an informed hunch and invited myself and the *Examiner* along. Ryan seemed to want news media to help force open the Jonestown gates, to publicize the findings and to afford a measure of protection. But he limited the number.

His total media complement consisted of the *Examiner;* Gordon Lindsay, who had written an unpublished exposé for *National Enquirer;* an NBC news team and the *Washington Post,* both of which had been put on the story by Lindsay. The *Examiner's* competitor and neighbor, the *Chronicle,* learned about the trip from a Ryan aide and decided to go along. So the congressman wound up with a national television network, the two major newspapers in his congressional district and the most prominent newspaper in the nation's capital.

After the congressional inquiry became public in November, I called Charles Garry to get a reading on my chances for entering Jonestown. Garry perfunctorily read me a Temple statement he had found on his desk. Essentially, it said that Ryan would not be admitted. As for me, the attorney warned that I was considered a Temple enemy and, given the church's paranoia, should expect to be barred from Jonestown, whether Ryan was admitted or not. According to Garry, I had written "prejudicial stories."

"You're entitled to your opinion, Charlie," I said. "But please put in a good word for me. Make a pitch." I assured him that I would be open-minded.

Despite my dim prospects, the *Examiner* decided to stick with me, a veteran of the Temple story, rather than send another reporter. After consulting with Garry, the *Chronicle,* however, decided to send someone other than Marshall Kilduff. They chose Ron Javers, a Philadelphian who had never written a word about the Temple.

On the night of November 13, while I was home packing and hoping to have time for a nap before the red-eye flight to New York, the *Examiner* phoned with an "urgent" message to call Al Mills at the Human Freedom Center in Berkeley. When I called, Mills expressed grave concern for the safety of Tim Carter. He was afraid the Temple might have kidnapped him. I then learned for the first time that Carter had come to former members seeking shelter, telling them he had escaped Jonestown on the pretense of getting dental work in the States. Because Carter spoke convincingly against the Temple, swore hatred for Jones and cried with longing for his baby in Guyana, the Millses and other defectors believed him. They treated him as one of their own and found him an apartment in Oakland. Now he had disappeared.

I asked Mills a series of questions:

"Did Carter's mouth appear to be swollen?"

"No," he replied.

"Was he seeing a dentist regularly here?"

"No."

"Did you tell him anything about Ryan's trip?"

"Yes," admitted Mills. "He asked about it Friday afternoon. We set up an appointment for him on Saturday [to have his oral surgery stitches removed] and he didn't show up. We checked his room, and he had left behind a half bottle of wine and a half loaf of bread."

"I think he's a plant," I said, and gave him my reasons: no one with two root canals would likely stray far from his dentist; he had disappeared immediately after securing information on Ryan's trip and right before a dentist could check him. "I'll bet gathering information was his mission."

Suddenly realizing he and his wife had been duped, and that security had been breached, Mills excitedly expressed fear for the Ryan party. The Temple might put a bomb aboard the plane, he said. Though I thought he was overreacting, he said he would call the FBI or Ryan's office.

On the way to San Francisco International Airport, Greg Robinson and I got better acquainted. It was our first assignment together in my nearly two years at the *Examiner*, and we were both charged with anticipation. For both of us, it was also a first overseas assignment, and for Greg, the subject was foreign as well. When the twenty-seven-year-old photographer had come by my desk a few days earlier, he had thought we were going to see Rev. Moon. But he had done his homework since then.

With his great zest for work, he was the sort of young photographer who would answer the photo department phone with a rapid-fire "Hello hello hello," then dash for the door with the cry, "I'm gone!"

Steering the photo car south on Highway 101, Greg said he loved travel assignments and spoke of one particular action photo he had taken recently of the salmon wars on the Klamath River. Greg was disappointed that *Life* magazine had rejected it. But he hoped with characteristic optimism, *Life* might be interested in Jonestown photos. It all depended, of course, on whether the story attracted national attention.

As the airport lights loomed, Greg told me that, after the Jonestown trip, he planned on spending Thanksgiving on Trinidad or another Caribbean island. There he could bake on the white sand beaches, swim and sample the local rum and the women. He smiled to himself at the thought of it. As he parked the photo car, he said, "In case you end up coming back first, I'll put this money here. Use it to pay for the parking, and take the car into town." He slipped $35 into the visor.

Neither of us had taken the assignment lightly. We were as well equipped and as mentally prepared as anyone could have been for the unknown and potentially hostile future. In preparation, Greg had consulted with a well traveled photographer friend who happened to be a doctor. In addition to giving advice about the proper shots and malaria medicine, he had warned Greg that Guyana was a dangerous part of the world. Though we discussed the Temple and the severity of the allegations, the major concern was not personal safety. We were most worried that, after traveling six thousand miles and spending thousands of dollars, our effort would fall short of Jonestown. As a contingency plan in case I was locked out, Greg would carry my tape recorder inside. No one even considered the possibility that I would have to use his camera.

In addition to clothes and toilet articles, we each had packed a poncho (on the chance that we would camp out in the rain forests), insect repellent, foot powder, candy, a pocket knife, water purification tablets and antimalaria pills. Greg must have stowed twenty-five pounds of cameras and equipment into his canvas shoulder bag. My rucksack was crammed with a half-dozen notebooks, a fistful of tapes, the recorder and a compact personal camera.

Though we carried passports and a "to whom it may concern" letter of introduction from the *Examiner*, we lacked entry visas. The Guyanese Embassy in Washington had given me incorrect information about visiting requirements, and absolutely no assurance that we would be allowed to enter the country at all. And, as for getting into Jonestown, Ryan's office promised only to do their best. An aide frankly admitted, "It's a game of chicken between us, the Temple, the State Department and Guyanese government." A State Department official had told me, "If the Temple doesn't want you in, you won't get in. It's that remote and inaccessible."

By the time Greg and I toted our bags to the boarding areas, a crowd had gathered. Not everyone was there to wish us bon voyage. Besides West Coast Ryan staffers and Concerned Relatives, we spotted a small contingent from the Temple, staring at us sullenly. Their pretext for being there was to return some belongings left behind by the NBC crew. Though I was unaware of it at the time, the Temple had invited NBC and Javers to the Geary Boulevard church for a chicken dinner and a chance to interview Temple members and Garry and Goodlett. I was excluded from this final bit of public relations, most likely because the Temple considered me a hopeless case.

Near the boarding ramp escalators, NBC reporter Don Harris greeted me like an old friend, though we had only talked briefly on the telephone. He was happy, he said, to see that I stood six feet four, in case we ran into trouble. The feelings were mutual. Just before the trip a fellow journalist had told me this about Harris and the burly producer accompanying him, Bob Flick: "I can't think of two better guys to be along on a dangerous assignment. Flick would take on a tank, and Harris, lean as he is, is a tough sonofabitch. Nothing will stop him."

Both Harris, a fortyish Clint Eastwood lookalike from Georgia, and Flick, a craggy and burly six feet three, were veterans of Vietnam war coverage.

Cameraman Bob Brown, a swarthy handsome man, seemed to have traveled everywhere and done everything. Brown, who also had logged time in Vietnam, oozed confidence yet had an underlying kindness. Sound-man Steve Sung, a muscular and compact Asian-American, was delightful company. He kept a cheery face but later would speak more bluntly about the assignment. When I would ask him whether NBC had balked at spending money for extra television equipment, camping gear and a $50 Smith and Wesson "survival knife," he would say, "What's a little money to NBC? This is a dangerous assignment."

Having a well seasoned network news team with many thousands of dollars in equipment provided comfort in this open-ended assignment. From the start, it was apparent that NBC provided our best alternative ticket to Jonestown, if Ryan failed to deliver. If necessary, the tight little network crew planned to hire a plane, then hike to Jonestown, possibly with an entrée from Carlton Goodlett. I offered to split the cost of any charter plane.

On board the eastbound airliner, I met the only other Temple "enemy" among the reporters. Gordon Lindsay served as NBC's unofficial guide, having gone through the frustration of gathering material in Guyana for an ill-fated *Enquirer* piece. The Britisher said he had been initiated as a reporter at age seventeen, while covering African uprisings. Now in his forties, he free-lanced, chasing stories around the world. Stalking the aisles impatiently, smoking, drinking and talking nonstop, he openly derided the Temple and Jones.

Javers dropped into a neighboring seat. "I'm the new kid on the block," he said. "I just spent three days reading your stories in our Temple clips. . . ." Slight and bearded, he looked younger than thirty-two, though he came across as a sharp, experienced reporter. Frankly, I would have preferred Marshall Kilduff instead of a recent arrival from the *Philadelphia Daily News;* I respected Kilduff's work and thought it only fair that he, if anyone from the *Chronicle,* should be there. The final press addition was Charles Krause, Buenos Aires correspondent of the *Washington Post.* Krause would join us on the last leg of the trip, even more poorly prepared than Javers. To him the Temple was, as he would later put it, "a kooky cult," and the assignment in large part an entrée to Guyana.

The flight from San Francisco to New York allowed us reporters to get acquainted. For me, it also was a reunion with Concerned Relatives whom I had used as story sources. As Greg and I roved the aisles, socializing and getting material for an in-flight story, the relatives immediately took to Greg. "You look like brothers," one commented, noting our brown hair and mustaches. Beyond his amiable personality, Greg seemed to be everywhere all at once, eagerly shooting every minute, without being obtrusive.

Tim Stoen had paired off with a mystery woman, a blonde with a beehive and makeup that made her appear older than her early thirties. Stoen introduced her as Bonnie Thielmann—a name that meant nothing to me. I did not realize that this woman, the daughter of Rev. Edward Malmin, represented yet another part of Jones's past converging on him. She said merely that she had lived with the Joneses in Brazil and still remained a close friend to Marceline. If the Joneses would see anyone, they would see her, she said. Stoen sounded determined, vowing that he would not stop until he got John or got killed. I was not aware until then that he had written the State Department a month earlier saying he would use "any means necessary" to get the boy.

Although Sam Houston's health had prevented him from going, his wife Nadyne and their daughter, Carol Houston Boyd, were aboard, hoping to find whether Bob's girls were happy in Jonestown. The Houstons were not particularly optimistic about retrieving Judy and Patty because they had learned that their mother had been summoned to Jonestown to block attempts to take them.

Jim Cobb and Mickey Touchette had about a dozen relatives between them in Jonestown. They hoped to determine whether their family members were alive and happy—and possibly to bring some back. For the third time, Howard and Beverly Oliver were making the arduous trip to get their sons, despite Oliver's failing health and the need to borrow money for the trip.

Wayne Pietila—who along with Cobb and Touchette had been branded a member of the Eight Revolutionaries—hoped to see his stepfather Tom Kice and his brother Tommy Kice. Pietila had picked up a report that Kice had tried to escape from Jonestown but had been turned in by his own son.

Clare Bouquet was convinced that her son Brian had been brainwashed and held against his will. Sherwin Harris, who had been rebuffed on the radio by his daughter Liane, said he was going to Lamaha Gardens where the girl lived with her mother, Temple public relations woman Sharon Amos.

The relatives—who would be joined in New York by Steve Katsaris with his son Anthony and by Grace Stoen—had not deluded themselves. Some had trimmed their expectations, pessimistically believing that

Jones's conditioning and coaching would defeat their efforts. But most considered this their last chance; some could not afford more trips, financially or emotionally; all other channels were exhausted. Some felt this trip could signal the end for Jim Jones—or might backfire and render Jones effectively untouchable.

During a layover of several hours in New York, I stayed awake preparing a story, consulted with our editors, and tried unsuccessfully to square away our visa problems with the Guyanese Embassy in Washington, D.C. At the airport, with our plane about to take off, a Guyanese official advised us not to take the Guyana flight because we would be turned back upon landing. "We'll have to take our chances," I said. "Please do your best to resolve the problem." *Examiner* city editor Jim Willse had told us to stay with Ryan.

Representative Ryan had also ignored warnings and plunged ahead, despite State Department advice that Jonestown was private property, despite the Temple's discouraging letters. On the plane out of New York on November 14, Ryan sat beside his aides Schollaert and Speier, absorbing briefing papers and their comments while holding court to an audience of press and relatives. Although neither the press nor the relatives were an official part of his delegation, he was counting on the news media to help him get into Jonestown and to bring out anyone who wanted to leave. If Jones stopped him from entering Jonestown, Ryan reasoned, he wanted it on film. In a way, he also viewed the press as a key element in forcing out the truth about Jonestown and as protection; the glare of publicity might inhibit any Temple inclinations to cause trouble. By the same token, the press looked upon Ryan as an entrée to a community that had turned down visit requests from me and others. With a United States congressman there, the public relations-conscious Temple would show its best behavior; everything was bound to remain civil, or so we thought.

My problem was avoiding exclusion. Even if the rest of the group rode into Jonestown, I could be stopped, perhaps at the last moment. More than once I had imagined myself standing in the mud at the Jonestown entrance, alone. Ryan had said that he would not turn back just because one reporter was barred.

As the jet banked toward Timehri Airport at midnight Tuesday, Georgetown stood out as a strand of lights between the moonlit Atlantic and the black jungle interior. A couple of us vowed not to use the adjective "steamy" to describe the place, and I made a mental note not to make any comparisons to Conrad's *Heart of Darkness*.

On the ground, the doors swung open with a rush of Guyana's hot, wet sticky air that clung to us as we filed in the near-darkness toward the terminal. Several men in powder- blue shirt-jackets swarmed around Leo Ryan and swept him off in another direction. So much for Ryan's help in getting through the immigration lines, I thought. As we approached the terminal, dozens of faces, mostly black, peered out of windows and from places around the building. I wondered how many were Temple greeters.

We reporters had decided to stick together going through the lines. Greg and I were uncertain whether our last-minute requests for visas really had reached Guyana itself. The immigration officers seemed cognizant of the entourage's mission. Flick reddened and nearly blew up when one asked him a few too many questions. When I went through the immigration station a moment later, however, a U.S. Embassy official was bringing Ryan's papers for VIP processing. I struck up a conversation with him, and things went smoothly for Greg and me.

After making it through a customs search, most of us quietly congratulated ourselves. Then two sobering things happened. Some relatives were whispering and gesturing fearfully toward a Mutt and Jeff pair across the room—stocky Sharon Amos and towering Jim McElvane, their arms folded, mouths in mean crescents, eyes hard as drill bits. When Grace Stoen confessed her discomfort, Tim Stoen told everyone to avoid looking at them. The intimidation technique would have worked better with greater numbers.

Next, Ron Javers appeared outside a nearby floor-length window, with a policeman guarding him. He had lagged behind, and now had been stopped. His eyes were wide, his face white, and he pounded the glass, frantically, helplessly. Since NBC had its visas in good order, they volunteered to stay to help Javers while those of us on shakier ground set off for Georgetown itself.

Feeling free and extremely fortunate to be in the country, Greg Robinson, Gordon Lindsay and I savored the ride on good two-lane pavement, through marshy flatlands, past silvery waterways, bungalows on stilts and some small industry. As we breezed along, Greg and I grinned to each other and shook hands; we had passed our first hurdle.

At the outskirts of Georgetown, the cab cut through the sweet smell of rum from a nearby distillery. In spite of the late hour, knots of young men conversed on street corners, and some young women and bicyclists plied the roadsides.

The Pegasus Hotel rose like a toy drum, resembling a truncated Miami Beach or Waikiki highrise. Piling out, we headed for the front desk. "I'm sorry, sir, but we have no reservations for you," said the clerk. "We are booked up." We raged and complained that our reservations had been confirmed. The clerk offered regrets, nothing more.

Soon the Concerned Relatives arrived to face a similar plight. "Did Jones deliberately book up the place?" they asked. The lobby became an encampment for a dozen of us, who decided to stay rather than search for another hotel. Since no beds were available, our most immediate need was cold beer.

Shortly before 4:00 A.M., after I had filed an arrival story by phone, the desk clerk came up with a room Greg and I could share. After two days without sleep, the bed sounded great. But no sooner did our heads hit the pillow than the phone jangled. Immigration had called: there was a problem with our passports.

Greg and I headed for the lobby to meet the officer, anxious that we would soon be sharing Javers's fate. Over two hours later, up strode a black man in an orange motorcycle helmet, blue T-shirt and jeans. Without his uniform, I barely recognized our immigration officer from the night before. He demanded the passports, then with his pen instantly reduced our authorized stay from five days to twenty-four hours. "I made a slight mistake," he explained. "You must go to the Home Ministry. It opens at eight o'clock."

It already was approaching seven o'clock, so that precluded sleep. That day, during gymnastics over our visa problems, we visited a number of ramshackle wood-frame government buildings with erratic electricity and poor ventilation. Lindsay, who had suffered the same grind on his previous trip, led the way, first to the security chief for home affairs. After questioning us about published allegations against the Temple, this black man with a bear-trap handshake observed: "There must be something to it. I have a feeling we will know more about this organization before this week is out."

On the cab ride back to the Pegasus, my two companions chided me for perhaps hurting our case by repeating too many negative accusations. But within hours, the government's treatment became markedly more cordial.

Our own Embassy's role was unclear. When I had asked for help, they displayed an infuriating laissez-faire attitude—and one official said, "We may or may not be able to influence things." Finally, the Embassy arranged for the press to see the chief information officer of Guyana. Soon, after a few more bureaucratic hurdles, our visas were extended to five days. And Ron Javers was released after twelve hours of airport detention for an unintentional currency violation.

Whether our passport problems were orchestrated or not, the government clearly wished to control our visit to some extent—they provided us with a press officer-escort and voluntarily arranged a press conference with a government official who had visited Jonestown. The session with Education Minister Vincent Teekah showed that the government wanted to go on record to dispel any notions that the Burnham regime was an unequivocal Temple ally. Teekah noted that the government did not even recognize the name Jonestown, just an agricultural experiment near Port Kaituma. He recounted his own ministry's conflicts over the Jonestown school system. And, without even being asked, he noted that he had observed no evidence of flogging during his visit. The government wanted it both ways, to come out unscathed regardless of the findings.

As Ryan and relatives worked at opening channels to Jonestown, none mistook the ponderous motion for progress. The Embassy introduced Ryan to Guyanese Foreign Minister Rashleigh Jackson, but their cordial discussion yielded nothing. The Embassy showed Ryan slides of Jonestown, revealing its physical conditions—but not psychological conditions. Embassy officials did not tell the congressman about Jones's bizarre behavior just a few days earlier—they remained silent even when the Temple invited Ryan to visit Jonestown without the press or relatives.

Ryan learned more about the condition of Jim Jones from the Temple itself than from the U.S. Embassy. That night, he made a spontaneous trip to Lamaha Gardens, taking *Post* reporter Charles Krause to wait outside as a precaution.

During the meeting—as Ryan later would tell us—only big Jim McElvane and Sharon Amos ventured to speak. When the congressman asked to negotiate the visit by radio with Jones, Amos refused. She said Jones was very ill but refused to elaborate.

The next day, Thursday, Embassy officials met privately with the relatives for an hour in the modern white embassy, but only at Ryan's insistence. None of the relatives was comforted by the Jonestown slides shown by Ambassador Burke. As the relatives told their stories in moving fashion, some broke down in tears of frustration. There was hardly a dry eye in the room. But Embassy officials refused to take sides.

When it was over, Burke was driven away quickly in a diplomatic car with little flags on the front fenders. As reporters hurled questions, he said only, "It was a useful meeting." When asked whether the relatives would see their loved ones at the mission, Burke replied, "It's too soon to say."

While Grace Stoen daubed at tears, and Beverly Oliver swore in frustration, Steve Katsaris, who had taken the leadership role, said, "The ambassador was polite and told us there was no way he legally could do anything. We told him we would go on our way without his help." Katsaris sounded grimly determined.

Strangely, in the midst of that dejection, Ryan seemed extremely confident. To reporters, he whispered "off the record" that an airplane was available to transport himself, the press and a few relatives. He was miffed about the State Department's hands-off attitude. In private, he swore, "I'm going to have something to say about this when I get back."

Ryan's tactics—keep moving forward and ignore resistance—paid off only modestly. Mark Lane, whose presence was supposed to be a condition for any Jonestown visit, was reported en route to Georgetown that night along with Charles Garry.

But the Temple, meanwhile, released a November 9 petition signed by about six hundred Jonestown residents and a November 13 statement essentially disinviting Ryan's group and accusing them of trying to generate adverse publicity, "hopefully by provoking some sort of incident."

Late Thursday, sensing the Temple's hardening resistance and some disenchantment within his own entourage, Ryan's language took a tougher turn. Thinking the Temple might plan to use the attorneys to stall him, he held out a threat, implying that he might stir up investigations of the Temple's tax-exempt status, as well as its handling of social security checks.

We reporters felt restless, too, and skeptical of Ryan's ability to break through the Temple's stone wall. His assurances had begun to ring hollow; the fact that he had chosen one reporter—Krause of the *Post*—to make an impromptu visit to Lamaha Gardens gave the lie to his promises that we all would stick together. In a frank confrontation, Don Harris told Ryan: "Leo, we don't know if we can trust you." Ryan flinched. He defended himself, trying to reassure everyone we were going in together. Moments later in the hallway, some of us discussed NBC's contingency plan for reaching Jonestown by chartered plane from Trinidad.

The truth session came at an awkward time; that night Ryan hosted a dinner for the entire party in the main Pegasus dining room. Just as we ordered rounds of drinks, some relatives burst in. Clare Bouquet told me that she, Grace Stoen and Steve Katsaris had encountered some Temple basketball team members, including Stephan Jones, on the seawall near the hotel. It seemed more than coincidence, but she insisted it was amicable. She was comforted because the team members seemed to want the relatives to see their families in Jonestown. Of course she had no way of knowing that the team's attitude was a distinctly minority view.

On Friday morning, Garry and Lane marched into the Pegasus with Sharon Amos, ready to parley with the weary-looking congressman. After some discussions in private, the two attorneys spoke with us reporters in the lobby. They accused Ryan of switching positions, of first saying he would go alone then pressing for the media and relatives.

Knowing he had a twenty-passenger plane reserved through the Embassy, Ryan stood firm. Within a couple of hours, the obstacles were plowed aside, surprisingly enough with the assistance of the two Temple attorneys. Garry, although furious with Lane, had teamed up with him to encourage Jones to allow a visit. Using the radio at Lamaha Gardens, the lawyers told him that Ryan probably would come with or without permission. If he were turned away, the media would record the insult, which would look bad for the church.

After Jones responded with a tirade and Lane tried to talk to him, Garry issued an ultimatum: "Jim . . . You can tell Congress to go fuck themselves, and if you do that, I can't live with it. . . . I am imploring you to open it to the world and let them come in."

Finally Jones agreed, "All right. Come on down."

In the poolside patio dining area, the relatives huddled around a table, all tense. Ryan had reluctantly made an announcement: with all nine newsmen and the two attorneys aboard the plane, there would be space for only four of the relatives who had come so far for reunions with loved ones. Clearly, Ryan's first priority was focusing the world's attention on Jonestown.

In making their selection, the relatives figured Grace and Tim Stoen almost certainly would be stopped at the gates. Jim Cobb was selected because he was resourceful, well informed, black and eager to see his large family. Out of a feeling that the contingent should be racially balanced—as the Temple had demanded of the congressional delegation

—the relatives also selected Beverly Oliver. The third member was musta-chioed Anthony Katsaris, who was tall and sharp-featured like his sister. If anyone could bring back Maria, her brother could. And if Maria could be persuaded to leave, her defection—and her inside information—might well break the Temple. Finally, relatives selected Carol Houston Boyd, as a Ryan constituent and as the daughter of Ryan's friend Sam Houston.

Those left out were disappointed but resigned. In Steve Katsaris's case, the flight limitations caused some last-minute adjustments in a highly tuned plan. He had hoped that both he and Anthony could make the trip. Katsaris, believing his daughter was disillusioned, was 90 per-cent certain that she would leave without resisting. But he also was prepared to abduct her, possibly using drugs to subdue her. He planned to commandeer a vehicle to rush Maria to Port Kaituma, where he had arranged to steal an airplane to fly to Trinidad and freedom. Now Leo Ryan's decision had ruined those fragile arrangements.

Upstairs in their hotel room, Anthony was stuffing things in his knapsack—cookies from Maria's mother and personal items Maria had requested. "What do I do now?" asked the young student teacher. Anthony had only an inkling of the original plan.

"Don't talk to Maria about leaving," Steve said. "Spend as much time as you can talking about memories and old ties." The psychologist had to hurry his instructions; he handed his son a wad of bills. "Look, Anthony. Here's some Guyanese money. You may need money. Spend as much time as possible with her. When you leave, I'm sure she'll want to spend as much time as possible with you. If she doesn't want to leave, take her by the arm and say, 'Pop loves you. . . . None of the things you said [about him] matter. He'll protect you if you want to leave.' "

Katsaris gave Anthony one last instruction. Handing his son the silver cross he kissed each morning, he said, "Maria always loved this cross. She said that when I die, she wanted it. If all else fails, give her this cross. . . ."

Like the relatives and Ryan's aides, we reporters rushed around gathering baggage and making transportation arrangements. Sam, our driver, leaned on his cab out front, ready to go. Once on the plane, there would be no way to call the *Examiner* again or to file another story until we came out of the jungle wilderness. So I called the city desk and said that if they did not hear from me, it meant that we had boarded the plane for Port Kaituma. The newspaper would have to rely on other sources to confirm that we indeed had reached Jonestown. Just prior to leaving the Pegasus, I filed a story quoting Ryan: "The matter is fluid, and is chang-ing from hour to hour."

A grim melancholy tinged a hopeful and excited airport farewell. Even those relatives feeling excruciating disappointment came to Timehri Airport to see us off, to give last-minute instructions and requests to Ryan, to hope again out loud that their people might come out with the party after all. The emotion of the moment overcame Grace Stoen. In her shorts, she moved away a few feet and, behind a pillar, cried in privacy. Ryan sadly embraced Clare Bouquet and Nadyne Houston. People who had come far yet could not travel the final distance murmured words of encouragement to the fortunate ones.

As the group waited alongside the runway, a twin prop DeHavilland Otter was readied for boarding. It turned out that the crew needed an extra seat. To make room, Carol Houston Boyd had to be bumped. She stood crying on the apron, among the other unlucky ones.

Inside, the pilot, earphones in place, checked his passenger list on a clipboard. Ryan evidently did not hear him yell, "Sir, do you want any more aboard?" But I yelled back, "Any more room?"

"Yes. One more. Hurry."

Urgently, I shouted toward the rear, "There's room for one more." An attendant sprang the rear door and beckoned Carol Boyd forward. After a moment of hesitation, she recognized the signal. Others pushed her. Tears flying, she sprinted for the gangway. For Sammy's sake, I was happy she had made it aboard.

FIFTY-TWO

Port Kaituma

From the twin-engine Otter, the hinterlands of Guyana unrolled beneath us like a great green carpet, cut into smooth contours by broad brown rivers that muddied the Caribbean to the east. The land appeared as magnificent as it was mysterious, as inviting as it was forbidding. The sheer boundlessness and inaccessibility were awesome.

"There's no way to walk through that," observed Jim Cobb.

After about an hour aloft, the red mud of Port Kaituma airstrip stood out like a rude gash in green felt. Everyone craned toward windows as the plane swooped downward. It was 3:30 P.M. The pilot shouted over his shoulder, "Georgetown said it is unserviceable. They said the strip is in pretty bad shape, but didn't say what it was. We'll have a look anyway."

As we dropped down for a closer view, we could see the yellow Temple dump truck obstructing the middle of the field—and the muddy tracks where it had plowed across the lightly graveled strip. As the plane climbed and word traveled to the rear seats, disappointment darkened our faces. The alternative was landing at Matthews Ridge, the mining town some thirty miles away. And that would delay our visit until the next morning, leaving us with only a single day to answer the question: Was Jonestown a paradise or a concentration camp?

For the benefit of those with cameras, the pilot made a pass over Jonestown and banked to afford a better view. Aluminum roofs threw the tropical sun back at us like tracer bullets. Here and there inhabitants shaded their eyes to watch us drone past. The militarylike uniformity of the buildings and the spartan setup impressed me immediately. The structures looked functional yet not primitive.

Instead of turning toward Matthews Ridge, the pilot doubled back to the Port Kaituma strip. "It looks okay to me," he said, anxious to land before our Temple transportation left. Eyes rolled at the prospect of landing. I looked beseechingly toward Neville Annibourne, the information officer assigned to us by the Guyana government. "Well," he shrugged. "He's the pilot." Dwyer, the U.S. Embassy's number-two man, did not seem to care either, though some in the group already were worried that the twenty-seater could not negotiate the tight 2,100-foot strip. The pilot confidently eased down the Otter and reversed the engines, throwing us forward against our seat belts. When we came to rest with a third of the runway to spare, applause broke out.

As we groped down the wire railing of a shaky gangway, a half dozen robust young men glared and postured by a heavy-duty dump truck. In T-shirts and tank tops, they menaced muscular arms and shoulders. Beneath bandannas and angry brows, their eyes pierced us with hostility. Their legs were spread and firmly planted in the muddy earth. Their earth.

Prominent among them were two black men—Jonestown security chief Joe Wilson with a corn-row hairdo, and six-foot-seven former head of security Jim McElvane, who seemed to turn up everywhere since our arrival in Georgetown. Mike Prokes, the public relations man, circulated with a tape recorder running and joined the huddle of Temple members and Temple attorneys.

Within minutes, we were confronted with disappointment: Garry and Lane would proceed on the Temple truck, but the rest of us would stay at the airstrip. Why? Corporal Emil Rudder, a portly black Guyanese policeman with sandals and not a single garment that could be construed as a uniform, announced: "I was informed by a superior officer that Peoples Temple do not request the parties present [to go] into the Peoples Temple. . . . I don't know the reasons. I was informed three days ago of this. . . . You can wait around."

"I'm Congressman Ryan," Ryan said extending his hand. "And we are a congressional delegation, and we are here to inquire into the health and welfare of the people here. We intend not to violate any laws." His voice took on a statesmanlike timbre as he added, "We have great respect for your country and its ruler."

At that point, another black man stepped forward and introduced himself as Herbert Thomas of the Ministry of Regional Development. He seemed embarrassed and confused as to why the Temple had sought to delay us. "We are neutralists because we don't know what is going on," he said, as though war had been declared. "You can't go to Jonestown, but I am an officer in charge of this port, and if you want to come to Port Kaituma, you are welcome."

A few minutes later word came from town, apparently from a superior official, that we could not even leave the airport. As we loitered in the parching sun, the Temple truck suddenly raced back, and Lane told Ryan, "You and Dwyer and your aides are invited. This is the first stage."

To the press, Garry added, "We'll try to get you in today or tomorrow if we can. But don't try to come on your own to Jonestown." Obviously, Jim Jones was having a change of heart about allowing us to visit.

The press and the relatives were left alone with Corporal Rudder, his sad-eyed young assistant cradling a 12-gauge shotgun and some barefoot children gnawing on sugarcane. As rain clouds blew past, the sun grew hot and we took shade beneath the airplane wing. The idea of beer sounded refreshing. After a lecture about the country's glass conservation program, Corporal Rudder allowed us to send two teen-age boys to town for two cases of Banks, the tart Guyanese beer.

During the wait, I wandered over to the pilot, Guy Spence, who was chewing a sugarcane stick from the children. To my compliments about his flying skill, he said, "If I can't make a decent landing after so many years, I'd better catch fish for a living." He went to say that he had landed on many fields in far worse condition. Why the hesitancy then? "Jonestown called the Georgetown tower and said it was unserviceable," he confided.

As we drank beer and killed time on the airstrip, some ominous bits of information came our way. Corporal Rudder confided that he feared violence in Jonestown if we went in uninvited. And a short time later, when Rudder and Don Harris went into town to talk with Rudder's superiors by radio, the slim constable with the shotgun engaged in an intense conversation with Beverly Oliver. Abruptly, she called me over. Whispering at first, he reported strange goings-on—airplanes landing in the middle of the night at the unlighted strip to pick up injured Temple members. "It was always, 'Accident, accident, accident.' But they were beaten, man.

"If someone asked me," he seethed quietly, his dark eyes showing fire, "I'd put a bullet in Jim Jones's head." His words electrified me; I shuddered. His animosity showed he was not under the sway of Jones, but also bespoke of Jones's power and perhaps his ruthlessness. Unsatisfied with his conclusion, I asked him more about the alleged beatings.

The constable recounted one man's escape from the mission and his tales of mistreatment there. "They forced him to work," he related. "Someone here helped hide this man. He said they beat him."

"How old was this man?" I asked.

"He was an older man, heavy," he said. "His name was Leon. He hurt inside, something bad."

"Was his name Leon Broussard?"

"Yes. That's him."

The exchange was chilling. Here on this airstrip in the middle of nowhere, thousands of miles from that home on Potrero Hill where months earlier I had interviewed Broussard, I was offered corroboration for his story.

At about 6:00 P.M., after a couple of hours of waiting, a red Temple high-wheeler farm tractor sped toward us, with a black man at the wheel, a burly weather-beaten white woman standing behind him with the abandon of a chariot rider. Without dismounting, she said, "Everyone who wants to come out to Jonestown can come, except Gordon Lindsay. The truck is coming now."

So the Temple had singled out him and not me, I thought. As the Temple truck lumbered up, Lindsay shrugged without protest. Instead, in his polite British accent, he asked me if he could file a story for me with the *Examiner*. In turn, Greg promised to take some photos for him. It miffed me that the Temple would deny entry to any of us: Why, I wondered, had they banned Lindsay but overlooked me?

At six-twenty the Otter lifted off with Lindsay aboard. Then the rest of us climbed into the Temple truck bed to begin the trip through the little river port then on to Jonestown. As the truck jounced along dirt roads in the rain, Greg and I smiled at each other and shook hands, just as we had after slipping through airport immigration.

On the way out of town, the truck stopped briefly at the Port Kaituma government guest house so McElvane could try to arrange our accommodations for later that night. Moments later, McElvane gracefully pulled his long frame back onto the truck. "There's room only for the women."

With the question of lodging unresolved, we resumed our journey in a moderate rain. McElvane and a white woman sat on the paint-bare truck cab roof, legs dangling. Easing over, I wanted to measure McElvane and get a reading about the situation in Jonestown. I was unaware that Jones had called him to Guyana just a few days earlier, because he feared McElvane would be indicted for property extortion in Los Angeles.

"Beautiful country," I commented as the clouds cracked and released a golden sunset.

"So's our project. A beautiful place with a lot of love," he replied in a baritone, gazing from under a sun visor.

Remote. That was it in a word. Every spin of the tires of that six-wheel drive reminded me of the isolation, of our dependence upon the Temple. How easily the big tires could bog down in that deep reddish mud. And it was not even the rainy season.

We passed a Peoples Temple greeting sign and a guard shack equipped with a radio. A chain across the road had been removed by two black men. Beverly Oliver hailed one of them, James Edwards, the tall elderly man whose relatives had told me he was disillusioned, emaciated and eager to escape. Yet he guarded the entrance.

As we moved on, I commented to McElvane, "Must have been a real job clearing this road." The dark jungle on both sides soared a hundred feet.

"Lots of hard work went into it," McElvane agreed. "It was done the hard way. Lots by hand, and tractors too."

"Cut and burn?"

"Yeah," he said, "And we plow the ashes into the soil. You can grow almost anything."

"Are those bananas?" I asked, gesturing at rows of broad-leafed fruit trees, which seemed to hold back the jungle some fifty feet from the roadside.

"No, they're plantain. And that's cassava along the road."

My mind traveled faster than the truck could. "Have you heard anything about how Ryan's talks with Jim Jones have gone?"

"No."

"When Ryan went to Lamaha Gardens, he was told that he couldn't come here because Rev. Jones was very ill. What's wrong with him?"

"Look," he said, summoning a little anger. "I've been around. Don't try to interview me on the sly." I had poked an inflamed nerve. Was Jones worse than we had imagined? Or was he not ill at all?

The truck slogged uphill through the last quarter mile of muck. By sunset's afterlight, we jumped one by one into the sloppy ground and helped NBC with their equipment. As we took tentative steps on the slippery boardwalk, someone made a five-point landing in the mud.

Jones was not among the cheery faces greeting us, but the two attorneys came out to the truck. While Lane helped with baggage, Garry escorted Ron Javers to a large open-air pavilion roughly a hundred yards away. I tagged along, through a playground area with swings and a jungle gym of timbers, then along a short pathway, past a pair of macaws on perches. Hundreds of people under the metal roof, reconnoitering around a stage in front or sitting at long wooden tables and on benches, looked up as we entered. Greeting everyone who met my eyes, I worked my way through gawkers and followed Garry to the center table.

For a moment, I did not see him. Then Garry was introducing Javers to the shrunken man in a pimiento-colored shirt. They exchanged pleasantries, with Javers expressing gratitude and Jones playing host. Garry went on for a minute extolling Javers's compassion as an investigator of poor prison conditions in Pennsylvania.

Without interrupting, I stepped in to introduce myself to Jones. As he stood, bracing himself against the table, his shoulders seemingly slumped under the weight of his oversized head of straight black hair that fell in a boyish sweep across his forehead. His glasses were not tinted enough to mask the glazed, almost gelatinous cast of his eyes; and they did not cover the hollowness of his sallow cheeks, nor the clamminess that seemed to drip from his body and terminate in an involuntarily feeble handshake. When he heard my name, he said with steady eyes, "I've read many of your stories." He implied his disapproval, but remained cordial. "I suppose you can only write what people tell you."

"We've tried without success to get your side of the story," I said. "I'm here to see the mission for myself."

"Good. Many others have found it to be beautiful, a paradise." He glanced Garry's way and unwound with words, one thought and one subject after another. In a way, it reassured me; no one would need to pry answers out of the man. But his shaky appearance bothered all three of us, and we encouraged him to sit down.

Jones took a chair at the head of a long table, about forty feet away from a raised stage spilling with musical instruments, amplifiers and loudspeakers. Musicians gathered beneath a black sign with white lettering: "Those who do not remember the past are condemned to repeat it." Jones faced the stage; on his immediate right sat Javers; on his left Garry took a bench seat. I sat between Garry and Karen Layton, the second Temple wife of Larry Layton. Jack Beam, Carolyn Layton, Harriet Tropp, Dick Tropp and Patty Cartmell chose places around us at the main table. At the far end, near the stage, Jim Cobb talked with members of his family, the only black members and nonleaders at the head table.

While other relatives seated themselves nearby with their family members, the smell of food filled the pavilion. The Temple served us a delicious meal of pork and gravy on homemade biscuits, with greens and potatoes, while most of their own people—presumably they ate earlier—stood around talking or waiting for the entertainment to begin. We washed down dinner with fruit-flavored punch and sweet well water.

Greg Robinson left the table to circulate, to capture on film the faces of Jonestown. From all appearances, the people seemed happy and healthy. Children horsed around, poking each other, tugging the tails of mongrel dogs, as the band warmed up. Among the many senior citizens, teen-agers and young adults stole glances our way. Everyone was dressed in his Sunday best.

In a few minutes, all Temple members stood at attention while a singer on the stage led them in a rendition of the Guyana national anthem. Then, led by the same bronze-lunged black woman, the congregation belted out, "God Bless America," with no less enthusiasm. The entertainment itself opened with a dance number from a snappy black-suited group called the Soul Steppers, who soon had the entire congregation—from wrinkled seniors to toddlers—clapping, bouncing and boogying to the disco routine.

The mock patriotism and the overall choreography struck me as strained, not to say phony. But where does one draw the line between a staged event and an honest attempt to put the best foot forward?

As the band jacked up the volume, the music drowned out Jones's ramblings about the project's achievements, and he stopped talking rather than shout himself hoarse. On my left, a pallid-looking blonde introduced herself as Karen Layton, shouting into my ear as I shouted into hers. "What are your politics?" she asked. "You've written negative things about us."

"I've got nothing against your politics. And nothing I've written reflects any political bias," I said.

"Don't you think we've been attacked because we're socialists and we've challenged the system?"

"I've taken pains to keep your politics out of my stories. Your politics weren't the issue. The accusations of former members transcend politics."

"You know they're all lying." She turned the attack on my sources of information. "They advocated violence and when that was rejected, they left and took money. . . . And now they're part of a sophisticated conspiracy. They want to destroy us."

The Conspiracy. With the warm reception and the toothsome victuals, I almost had forgotten that I was alleged to be part of some vicious conspiracy. Almost as though on cue, the band eased off enough that we could hear Jones rant softly about the conspirators—Tim and Grace Stoen, Jeannie and Al Mills, the gang of eight "violent revolutionaries," and other followers-turned-antagonists. To document his conspiracy claim, Jones ticked off incidents that made my head spin—arson fires, assassination attempts in the States, threats on his life, shots fired at Jonestown. Even Garry felt compelled to raise the question: "What I don't understand is, who is doing it and why? It baffles me."

"Charlie," Jones rasped, "it's the government. They will not let us live in peace because we're socialists."

As the band was playing, the print media reporters interviewed Jones in earnest while NBC shot film around the pavilion, interviewing relatives. Jones lost his thread of meaning several times. He would grope for a word or a sentiment, then jump to another subject. He attributed all that was humane to himself, and all that was evil to his enemies. His aides squirmed. Garry did not intrude. I felt embarrassment and pity for Jones, as he stumbled and sometimes almost slurred words. I wondered whether he was drugged by fever or by medication or was mentally ill. And an uneasy feeling came over me when he moaned, "Sometimes I feel like a dying man."

The child John Victor Stoen and Tim and Grace Stoen were obsessions that surfaced sporadically throughout a few hours of conversation that night. When asked why he did not honor the California court order or fight through legal channels for custody of the boy, Jones said helplessly, "What can I do? Could I kill a child? . . . He said he'd commit suicide if he was given back to his mother."

Behind the whole sickening affair was the life of an innocent child, but Jones obviously was most intent on vengeance. Tim Stoen was behind everything, even the false incriminating statements signed by members, Jones said. "I have no desire to hurt that man, though he would want to kill me."

At the conclusion of the meal, Marceline Jones introduced Ryan to a rousing cheer. He bounded onto the stage and took the microphone with aplomb. Graciously accepting the boisterous reception that he knew and we knew was standard procedure, Ryan waited until the applause died. "I'm glad to be here," he began, adding parenthetically, "And already I've met one of my former students."

Sounding as friendly as a political stumper, he said, "This is a congressional inquiry and ... from what I've seen, there are a lot of people here who think this is the best thing that happened in their whole life." An explosion of hand-clapping cut off his declaration as the entire nine hundred settlers, Jones included, took to their feet and sustained the applause for what seemed an eternity. The metal roof nearly shook, and those of us at the head table looked around in amazement.

When the clapping abruptly ceased, as though on an invisible cue, Ryan quipped, "I'm sorry you can't all vote in San Mateo County." Jones jumped up: "We can, by proxy." Then he added more quietly, "You have my vote." Again a roar of approval reverberated through the pavilion, a slightly intimidating roar.

After the congressman stepped down and the entertainment resumed, I leaned over to Jones and asked why he allowed us to visit now, a year after my first request. "What have we got to lose?" he said confidently. "There's no barbed wire here. We don't have three, let alone three hundred, who want to leave."

Interviews by Ryan and Jackie Speier since their late afternoon arrival tended to support that conclusion. Not a single relative of the Concerned Relatives in Georgetown had accepted an invitation to leave with the Ryan party.

When Ryan first strode into the pavilion that afternoon, a Temple member had asked, "Who do you want to see?"

"I want to see Brian Bouquet," he said, keeping his promise to Brian's mother. The Temple people chuckled, because Brian stood on stage just fifteen feet away, with his saxophone. When Harriet Tropp told the gaunt-looking musician to come over to talk to the congressman, Ryan objected, saying he wanted to meet in private. So they walked away together for a short interview, away from Temple eavesdroppers.

When the congressman returned to the pavilion, he told Dwyer of the Embassy that Brian did not want to take the time to visit his mother in Georgetown. "Well, what about your mother coming here?" Ryan had asked. "Would you be willing to see her?"

The response, Ryan reported, was something like: "The only way I want to see her is through the sights of a gun." Temple members who overheard the statement were pleased that Brian rebuffed his mother using the very language Jones had specified earlier.

Hours later, on Friday night, Brian took a far different tone as other Temple members listened to him talk directly to his mother on the radio. He did not try to discourage her when she said she planned to travel to Jonestown on Saturday aboard the plane coming to pick up the Ryan party. Proudly he told her how he had played for the congressman. "I wish you could have been here to see me."

"I wish I could have been there, too," she replied. "I'll be there tomorrow."

"I look forward to seeing you."

"I love you, Brian."

"I love you too, Mom."

Those few words set Clare Bouquet's hopes running high: tomorrow they would be reunited in Jonestown.

When Leo Ryan got on the radio, however, he put a damper on her plans. Dwyer opposed bringing more Americans out to Jonestown and complicating the situation, so Ryan told her that the Embassy wanted no relatives on the incoming flight because of some technicality. "I can't tell you what to do," he said, but he strongly discouraged her and the other Concerned Relatives from coming. Since Ryan seemed obviously upset, Mrs. Bouquet decided to wait until the congressman returned to Georgetown. She figured she could fly to Jonestown on Monday instead.

That night, another message reached Jonestown via the radio from Lamaha Gardens. It was rushed to the stage in the pavilion. Someone grabbed the microphone and announced proudly, "Our Jonestown basketball team just beat the national team by ten points." Above the thundering applause, Jones shouted toward Annibourne, the Guyanese information official, "That's a coup," and graciously shook his hand, claiming the triumph made the Temple team one of the best in the Caribbean. It seemed so improbable that the Temple could whip the national team that I made a mental note to check the score. Later, my hunch would be confirmed.

Repeatedly, with no prodding at all, Jones took the offensive, addressing allegations against the church before we could bring them up. He even pretended to want to know who was playing dirty tricks on the Temple's enemies. "We're not violent. We don't do violence to anyone." He said he wanted to know who hoaxed reporter Kathy Hunter into coming to Guyana, who made bomb threats and set small fires in her hotel.

While performers from thirteen years of age to their seventies did song and dance numbers on stage, Jones said piously, "Ageism, sexism and racism have been eliminated and elitism is almost eliminated. Each of us takes our turn in the fields." But Jones and the white leadership around him, I noted, had indoor complexions.

"I'm a little nervous," called out an elderly black woman billed as "Jonestown's Moms Mabley." Jones called back, "So am I."

As she spread laughter with a saucy down-and-outer's soul song, Jones turned to us. "When will this dialogue stop and we can have some peace?" he asked rhetorically. "I didn't speak [to the allegations before this] because I was advised not to."

Why, if nothing was amiss in the Temple, did his former followers turn against him? "The love-hate syndrome." He quoted Tim Stoen saying that destroying Jones was his mission in life, and he referred to the Eight Revolutionaries. "It was they [defectors] who advocated violence, blowing up bridges, cutting of telephone lines. If they don't want us in America, why not let us live in peace?"

With Lew Jones singing in a clear tenor voice, Rev. Jones spoke of his many children, still promoting the "rainbow family" concept. But in recent years, some had questioned whether the Temple was, in reality, a church. It is a church, Jones said, explaining that Jesus also had commanded his followers to sell their possessions.

When another reporter asked whether the Temple was Marxist, Jones's affirmative answer seemed vague, almost confused. So I asked him, "In what sense is it Marxist?" He paused. "That's a very perceptive question. . . . We're Marxist in the sense of sharing work, in the distribution of goods and services." His apparent difficulty in relating his avowed political philosophy to Jonestown's operations and structure caused me to ask whether the Temple embodied his personal philosophy, theology and priorities.

Jones replied, simply and curiously—and I believe accurately— "It's a reflection of what I thought was best."

His admission of ultimate control made it more distressing to see him suddenly lapse into moods of self-effacing self-pity, of near-surrender to his enemies. "I curse the day I was born," he lamented. "I don't know why these people hate me so. They can have me, but leave these people in peace.

"I don't want anything in life," he added sadly. "Some people say I wanted to be President, but I had no illusions of. . . ." After that ill-disguised grandiose notion, he apparently lost his thought for a moment then began rambling about Joe Mazor. "Mazor told us he was here [earlier] with rocket launchers ready to blow out our transmitters and radio," Jones confided with the voice of a vindicated man. So, I thought, Mazor had indeed switched his allegiance, and perhaps he had tried to set me up.

Though the gravity of the message was not transmitted at the time, Jones signaled us, telling those investigating him that he was feeling ill, trapped, despondent.

Would he ever return to the United States? The question that had caused him to collapse whenever it was broached in Brazil nearly twenty years earlier made him muse: "That's where I belong; though I love Guyana, I'm not Guyanese. We built a model here and [it's known] in every part of the world. People come in here every day. It's the easiest place in the world to get out of."

His answers proved what I had suspected: that jungle life—cut off from the world of social and political conflict, and power—did not appeal to him. His needs for stimulation and ego satisfaction were too great. "Power?" he scoffed in response to a question. "What kind of power have I got walking down a path talking to little old ladies? I hate power, just as I don't want money. I wish I never had been born, because [that way] I never would have made mistakes. I brought 1,200 people here."

He spoke of himself as a prisoner. He said he needed the medical treatment ordered by Dr. Goodlett, but could not leave Jonestown for fear John Victor would be kidnapped, for fear things would collapse in his absence. "In some ways, I feel like a dying man," he said. And again the child custody matter surfaced like a bloated body. "This is very painful," he said. "Now he doesn't know who his mother is. He forgets his mother. I haven't taught any hate to the child."

He denied outright that John Stoen had been turned systematically against his mother. "We teach love," he said as the seven-year-old in a brown and yellow striped T-shirt was brought to his left side. The handsome olive-complexioned child appeared bashful and a little uneasy, yet curious about the television equipment that suddenly appeared. He squinted into the lights.

"We have the same teeth and face," Jones said, baring his teeth and pulling off his tinted glasses for the first time. Taking the boy's chin between his thumb and fingers, Jones squeezed gently, making John show his teeth for comparison. The child was being treated like a show dog on parade. It was grotesque.

"He's very bright," Jones said, stroking and holding him. The passive child projected no warmth.

"John, do you want to go back to live with Grace?" Jones asked.

"No," the boy replied softly.

"See?" Jones said approvingly. "It's not right to play with children's lives."

As John was led away, Jones addressed all our questions about conditions in the settlement. He denied that sex was banned, pointing to the birth of thirty-three babies since 1977. He said social security recipients could choose to keep their checks, yet only one did. "I don't have a dime, or control over any money," he added, though he estimated several million dollars had been poured into the project. Jonestown workers, he maintained, were never subjected to sixteen-hour days under guard, nor corporal punishment; the only punishment was denial of sweets, of television time or of the privilege of working with other communards. As for the Temple's infamous thrashing sessions in the United States, the preacher said, "No more. We had our periods . . . I hated it so bad and said, 'You spank me first.' I told the kids to hit me hard. I said, 'I want you to realize you're hurting me by your behavior.'"

As the hour got late, and Temple aides milled around anxiously, Jones was asked about the alleged threats of mass suicide. Acting grossly misunderstood, he said, "I only said it is better that we commit suicide than kill. Why hurt social progress?" But he talked much of death, suicide and murder as he recited attacks on him and his church. It made me uncomfortable. He also railed against the "smear campaign" against him, declaring finally, "It would have been easier if someone had shot me as they did Malcolm X or Martin Luther King."

Given Jones's appearance and morbid talk, I was glad to already have conducted one interview; it seemed conceivable that he might plead illness Saturday and become unavailable to talk further.

Then, when Jones's aides made noises about terminating the interview, I told Jones, "On the way through town, your people checked for accommodations and found room only for the women. So we wonder whether we could spend the night here."

The request startled Jones. "We don't have accommodations for you. So it's not possible. There's no place for you."

"We don't need rooms," I said. "We could sleep here on the tables and benches or on the stacks of tin out by the road."

"No. No. We couldn't have you do that." Jones looked pleadingly to McElvane and Johnny Brown Jones, who had hovered over us since the first talk of departure.

"You can find them a place to stay in town," Jones told his aides. But why, I asked myself, did Jones prefer the inconvenience of trucking us into town? I had expected him to view our willingness to stay as a hopeful sign of trust. Was he afraid, I wondered, that we would snoop around during the night or that shabby accommodations would prejudice our visit? I did not expect anyone to come to us reporters during the night, asking to be taken out.

As we bade good night to Jones and the rest, a clean-cut young man appeared at my elbow wearing a broadly striped sports shirt. I had seen the same man with a thin wavering mouth standing near Jones during dinner, watching us. "Can I help you with your bags?" he said introducing himself. He was Tim Carter, the infiltrator Al Mills had told me about.

"It's only a backpack," I said, shouldering it. "Quite a place you've built here. I'm really happy to be seeing it finally."

He responded with enthusiasm. "I hope you'll see through all the lies about us."

"What lies?"

"The lies being put out by the people at the Human Freedom Center, by people who hate Jim. I've heard them with my own ears, saying this place was a concentration camp. You can see for yourself that it isn't."

"I heard you were at the Human Freedom Center last week. Were you spying on them?"

"I was at the Center," he said coyly, as we crossed the darkened playground area, approached the truck and parted company.

As the truck bounced and slid along the moonlit road, we hugged the sideboards. Although my skepticism ran high about the truthfulness of Jones in some matters, the people appeared happy, the camp well run. Only in retrospect could I see special tensions in the adolescent faces of Sam Houston's two granddaughters at dinner, skittishness on the faces of elderly women, the burning concern of Jones's aides as he forged foolish statements, the duties of those silent and brooding young men watching the reporters.

That night, two things tempered my generally favorable impressions of the settlement. While making every effort to pass the most difficult trial of his life, Jones appeared unhealthy and obsessed with death. He had cried for peace and to be left alone, yet, in his eyes, we were hounding him in his faraway refuge. The second problem really was a feeling of inadequacy. Knowing that politicians and other reporters had been duped in the States with similar demonstrations of brotherhood and talent, I feared that we might be waltzed through another day's visit without uncovering the truth. Given the isolated setting and Jones's demonstrated ability to condition and intimidate people, it seemed probable that we would fly out of the jungle Saturday afternoon without conclusive answers. As things stood, I could not be convinced the place was either a concentration camp or a humane social experiment. Jones's answers did not dispel the accusations by dozens of former members.

During the forty-five-minute truck ride, we reporters talked quietly. Javers and Krause shared my misgivings about Jones and agreed he seemed paranoid, if not crazy. Yet they were more favorably impressed with the encampment. Javers suggested the Temple might have been assailed, as Jones said, for its socialist politics, and its need for an authoritarian system to keep ex-convicts and former street denizens in line. Krause said wistfully that the people appeared to be happy. Javers seemed perturbed that I repeatedly led Jones into the sordid paternity fight over John Victor Stoen—an issue which, whether it was a smoke screen or not, had assumed dire importance. And the three of us agreed that most likely no one would defect and that none of the Concerned Relatives would be satisfied their loved ones really were happy in Jonestown.

As we neared the town, both Jim Cobb and Beverly Oliver tried to speak to Johnny Brown Jones, who rode at the front of the truck bed. When they appealed to his memory of their years together in the Temple, he clipped off their sentimentality: "I got nuthin' to say to you."

The truck soon rumbled past the cheery lights of houses at the outskirts of Port Kaituma. Inside some lighted windows and open doors entire families moved about, with children getting ready for bed or doing homework, parents sitting at tables. A dog yapped as the truck squeezed onto a side road, went a short distance, then stopped alongside a garden fence.

Johnny Brown Jones jumped down, entered a building and returned a minute later with a black man in a white dress shirt, our host. "You can stay here," Johnny said. "We'll come and pick you up in the morning, eight thirty." When the Temple truck groaned and rumbled away, the proprietor of Mike and Son's Weekend and Disco—whom we knew only as Mike—gestured toward the white two-story house next to the ground-level little disco bar. "You can stay in my house."

From the dirt roadway, we filed up rickety wooden stairs. After pulling off our muddy footwear, we dumped our gear in an anteroom and stepped into a sparely furnished living room with immaculate dark hardwood floors that would serve as our bed. The women would sleep in a small bedroom behind a curtain.

That settled, we gathered next door at the disco, where Mike's teen-age son served up drinks from behind a kitchen counter to one side of the dance floor. The black-painted walls glowed and pulsed with phosphorescent figures—voluptuous nude women reminiscent of Tijuana black velvet paintings. The heat and heavy decibels from Bob Marley and the Wailers drove us onto the patio area, where the plant leaves were highlighted with Day-Glo paint.

At low tables, we downed bottles of Banks beer, Pepsi and rum, drowning our tensions in laughing, razzing and story telling. Then Bob Flick, his safari shirt over his "God Rides a Harley" T-shirt, pulled up a chair and said to me privately, "You know Jim Cobb pretty well, don't you?"

"Just as a reporter," I said.

"Well, he may be in need of a friend." He jerked his head in the direction of the road.

I found Cobb alone, his arms hanging over the top of the whitewashed fence, staring into the darkness, letting his emotions pour out. Though I did not know it then, he had just suffered a flash of cognition: after talking warmly with his family, he knew they would not leave Jonestown with us.

"Jim," I said quietly. "Is there anything I can do?"

"No," he murmured. His voice sounded fragile, ready to crack.

"Well," I said, touching his shoulder. "If you want to talk, or if there's anything else, I'll be over there. When you're up to it, come over and have a drink with us."

"Thanks, Tim."

Around the tables the mood stayed light and relaxed. For the most part, we steered clear of conversation about Peoples Temple. "It sure seems quiet here," I said. We were the only customers.

"There's a dance cross the town," Mike, the owner, explained unruffled.

"Do you know the Temple very well?" I asked.

"They have been very good to me," said the tall man. "They helped me haul some things. They are very friendly people. Sometimes they come here to dance, but they drink only Pepsi." Mike was the first Guyanese I had met who spoke entirely favorably about the Temple.

While I chatted with the innkeeper, Javers and Krause put their heads together with a young Afro-Guyanese who had wandered in. It took me a few moments to recognize the constable without his shotgun. Soon I joined them. The constable, ill at ease under the gaze of the innkeeper, whispered, "Meet me on the road." The three of us reporters bade him good night, then drifted off, one by one, pretending to head for bed.

Following the policeman up the road, along railroad tracks, over a tiny footbridge, up a grassy hillside, we entered an adobelike windowless building. A match was struck and a candle flickered to life, throwing yellowish light on a couple of tables, some chairs, a bench along one wall and a small safe plastered into the structure. It was the police station.

In hushed voices, we resumed the conversation about the Temple. No one asked the constable's name, fearing it might curtail our discussion. The constable was a slender man of about twenty-five, about six feet tall, who spoke with those Caribbean soft *a*'s and *r*'s. He acted as though he risked his position by informing on an organization which had the blessing of some powerful Guyanese.

The officer recounted his story of Leon Broussard, confirming many parts of Leon's account, including the hole. "We went to the mission to investigate," the officer said. "We found the hole where this man said people were held. It was several hundred meters behind the kitchen and to one side. It was deep, with a cover. I asked what it was, and they said it was for storing beans." He smirked.

Did he see anything suspicious? No, he said, but there were reports of guns there, and the Temple had acquired permits for several weapons, apparently semiautomatics.

Then he spoke of the mysterious nighttime flights, of two or three times that the townspeople were frightened by flares fired to light up the local airstrip. But what, we asked, had led the constable to conclude that "accident" victims being flown out really had been beaten? "They said tractors fell on these people, things like that. They had broken arms and legs and hands." He grimaced, then went to the safe, removed a ledger and pulled the candle near as he read the names of three people flown to Georgetown the previous Wednesday. One was eighty-four and was simply ill; one man had a broken leg, another a broken arm. The evidence was not conclusive and probably was colored by the constable's contact with Leon Broussard.

Abruptly the officer stopped talking and hushed us. A crunch of footsteps caused him to shut the ledger. Someone outside hailed, and the constable helloed back. "It's the electrical plant engineer," he whispered. We all assumed relaxed positions.

In walked a black man with a silver hard hat. Regarding us cautiously, he dropped without invitation to a bench. The constable introduced us. "These chaps are here to visit Peoples Temple."

"Ah, yes," said the engineer, seeming familiar with the mission.

The talkative fellow first explained that he shut town power generators each night at about 2:00 A.M. to conserve energy, a national policy.

Then talk turned to Jonestown. While blaming the Temple's socialist politics for its troubles with the press, he scoffed at all the local rumors —about cannibalism and ghoulish tortures. We gathered that the jungle mission had become a subject of exaggerated local gossip.

After the engineer excused himself to go shut down the power, the constable promised to try to arrange to visit the mission while we toured it, to help us find the hole and to provide protection in case of any confrontation. We thanked him and said good night.

Back at the disco, our fellow journalists whooped it up, exchanging war stories and anecdotes. On the patio, Greg Robinson rocked back his chair, busting a gut, and Jim Cobb grinned. "Come on, Tim," he called. "Have some rum."

Our group intact again, we drank and talked and laughed. I bought a tray of beers, causing Brown to crow, "My God, I don't believe it. Reiterman bought a round." Everyone laughed. In Georgetown, I had to write and file stories during the evening drinking sessions.

A short time later, I turned in. Stepping over a sleeping form or two on the floor, I curled up on the wood, put my head on my pack and pulled a nylon poncho over myself for warmth.

FIFTY-THREE

Last Chance

Around seven o'clock, the sound of someone showering awakened me. With the sun up, the morning air already had turned sweet and balmy; songbirds flitted among the coleus along the whitewashed fence. Javers and I encountered each other on the road outside, then we took a stroll along the same route used the night before. We soon discovered that we had walked with the constable just a few yards from a finger of the deep green river and from the moored Temple fishing boat, the *Cudjo*. Someone stirred in the pilothouse, so we moved on, still comparing notes about last night's events.

For the first time, I realized why Kaituma was called a port. Train tracks from Matthews Ridge paralleled the river on a low cliff, so close to the water that boys had wedged a sturdy plank into the tracks for a diving board. On the other side of the tracks, several metal buildings with conveyor belts probably served as freight warehouses. It was easy to imagine small rivergoing boats and trains loading and unloading, and local laborers sweating on the docks. Though airplanes might have ferried American visitors and officials back and forth, the languid river and those rusty tracks were the lifelines of that drowsy town. These, and the dirt road to the Ridge, provided the most accessible escape routes for anyone trying to flee Jonestown.

In spite of our long conversations with Jones, in spite of the revelations and suspicions of the constable, the critical question remained: Were the settlers free to come and go? If they willingly subjected themselves to Temple discipline, rules and diet, willingly surrendered their material possessions to live in the jungle and work in the blistering sun and mosquito-infested forests, that was their right. It was conceivable to me that some people would find a pioneering alternative lifestyle and extended family extremely attractive. But it seemed unlikely that virtually *all* wished to stay, as Jones had claimed.

At that time, Javers and I had no inkling that anyone wanted to accept safe passage out with the Ryan party. And frankly I doubted that anyone would choose that time to leave, because most likely the relatives of the Concerned Relatives had been briefed and coached and because we were insulated from the rank and file.

But on the way back to the disco, Javers shared his belief that Don Harris had learned something of importance or had planned something significant. Steve Sung, he said, had made a slip and had begun to tell Javers something. Whatever it was, I wanted to know in advance because we soon would reenter Jonestown and might not be free to talk there.

"Why not make a deal with Don?" I suggested. "We can bargain with what we learned last night."

On the disco patio, Harris agreed to trade. Smiling his tallest whitest smile and taking a confident drag on his cigarette, he knelt down, pulled off a boot and removed a piece of paper. "I was slipped this last night." The paper said, "Vernon Gosney and Monica Bagby. Please help us get out of Jonestown."

Though neither name meant anything to me, my spine tingled. Not only did some people want to leave, but also they feared coming forward openly. Coupled with our information about the hole, the message tended to confirm our worst suspicions.

The Temple truck had not showed up at eight thirty as scheduled. As ten o'clock neared, we really worried about the delay. Corporal Rudder, looking a little sleepy, padded toward us from the direction of the police station. Harris took him aside and explained that some people wanted to leave Jonestown with us. In essence, Harris was asking for protection. Rudder nodded solemnly as the reporter spoke; sweat glistened on his forehead and worry saucered his eyes. His simple life was being complicated. Pressured, he seemed willing to help. Though he was supposed to travel to Matthews Ridge that day, he said he would try to come to Jonestown instead, to oversee matters.

After we rounded up some coffee and Pepsi and drank it leisurely in the sun, I wandered down the road.

"Have you seen a dump truck this morning?" I asked a woman in a print dress. She pointed toward the river moorings. As I turned the corner, the parked Temple truck came into view; seeing me, a few people started peering under the hood and engine. "What's the matter?" I called.

"Steering problems," one of them called. "We'll be right there."

In a few minutes, we piled aboard. On the way out of town, as Corporal Rudder waved at us, I focused hard on his round face and thought I saw a sign of confirmation. We passed the town's communications center with its shortwave radio antenna and low roofline, then were swallowed by the bush.

As we exited the main road, the Temple greeting sign loomed on a lodgepole framework. The tallest of us ducked. Again, a few people stood guard at the sentry shack. Ahead, the road narrowed and the truck strayed near the rutted edges.

Standing and clinging to the wooden side slats, I asked Carol Boyd, "How are you doing?"

"Okay," she said. Then she told me the first night in Jonestown really had been frustrating for her, as well as for all the Concerned Relatives. As she dined with her nieces and their mother, they all had smiled for Greg Robinson's camera. But she had not been allowed a minute alone with the girls, and they had mouthed the same meaningless praise of Jonestown that went into their letters.

As the settlement road turned slushier, the truck shimmied and the six drive wheels whirred and sideslipped. On a long downgrade, the right wheels foundered into a roadside trench and carried us straight into a brown, three-foot-deep moatlike wash, tipping violently, throwing us around. The driver backed up, then took another run at the muddy wash, but we bogged down again. Had the driver deliberately steered us into the morass, as a stall?

As we prepared for a third run, along came a red farm tractor, its tall rear wheels throwing mud clods as it squirmed through the wet spot. "The steering," shouted one of the Temple members when we demanded to know the problem. Because the tractor was equipped with a crescent wrench and steering fluid, I wondered whether the breakdown was prearranged.

In any case, we went on our way within ten minutes. As the large Jonestown clearing spread before us, I snapped a photo of Greg Robinson in full camera regalia and safari shirt, and of Bob Flick in his white stevedore's hat with a "Bell" motorcycle helmet patch. The aluminum roofs of Jonestown lay across the background, today as gray as the thickening clouds. A young woman of twenty or so smiled and waved enthusiastically as she hiked toward the settlement on the raised road shoulder. In pants and sandals and sunblouse, she floated happily along, a quarter mile from the compound. I could not help thinking that she could have escaped, if she had wanted, just by ducking into the jungle and working her way along the edge of the roadside cassava. Soon we would learn that she was planning exactly that—with us. Her name was Juanita Bogue.

As the truck sloshed to a halt, Marceline Jones appeared below us with her characteristic thin smile, seeming more rested and buoyant than the night before. It seemed doubtful that she knew of any defectors. "We'll serve you breakfast, then we'll show you around," Marceline said in a den-motherly welcome. But the invitation dangled there awkwardly, out of place like the many keys hung around her neck on a chain. Too much time had been wasted already. Though Krause wanted to eat, I said, speaking for Greg and me, "I think we'll pass. We're behind schedule." Don Harris said more diplomatically, "We have a great deal to do today and want to see as much as we can. But coffee sounds great." He pulled back the sleeve of his powder-blue denim jacket to see his watch. "Shall we start, say, at ten forty-five?"

After Marceline accepted the adjustment gracefully, we meandered toward the pavilion. Along the way, I stopped Greg and gestured toward two boys with baseball gloves tossing a ball around, awkwardly and unenthusiastically. I had guessed, correctly, that they were props.

To the other side of the path, away from the playground, Mr. Muggs reigned as camp mascot from his tall cage of wooden poles. Once bottle-fed, diapered and pampered by Joyce Touchette, Muggs had since matured into a hairy, hulking adult. Though he looked pensive and innocent this morning, I had heard nearly as much about his antics as those of the more notorious Temple members—his escape and raid on Port Kaituma natives, his spitting, his attempt to urinate on the Guyana Supreme Court marshal. And some former members had alleged that Jones used to threaten to throw interlopers to the cantankerous chimp.

Between the kitchen area and pavilion, two macaws of blue, orange and yellow preened on their perches and nibbled fruit. The magnificent mascots seemed to proclaim like so many feathered road signs: welcome to the tropics.

Jones was nowhere to be seen, but that was because he had stayed awake until at least 3:00 A.M. talking with Garry. The attorney would say later that he had given Jones an ultimatum: "Lane goes or I go." And if Garry went, most likely Garry's friend Carlton Goodlett would withdraw his important support too. Another self-generated problem was heaped on Jim Jones's back.

Though not speaking to each other this day, the two attorneys still would not let each other out of sight. Ryan, the relatives and the rest of us milled and talked in the shade of the pavilion while Temple aides moved with purpose. Several dozen children gathered around the stage, staring raptly at a television videotape showing of *Willie Wonka and the Chocolate Factory*. So incongruous was this jungle television scene that I took photos.

Soon our coffee arrived. When I caught Don Harris alone, I asked about the defectors.

"There could well be more, so we'd better stick close to the pavilion," Harris replied.

"The tour's about to start," I noted. "I'd like to look around after coming so far. And Greg has to get pictures."

"Try not to stray too far," he said in a very quiet voice. "I'll whistle when something happens." He sent his crew off to film the mission.

A moment later, I passed the word to Greg: if the number of defections increased, we would need to converge quickly on the pavilion to serve as a deterrent to possible harassment, as well as to record any defections. Then Jack Beam eased over to me and struck up a conversation beneath a sign on one post: LOVE ONE ANOTHER. Beam—always described by defectors as a villainous henchman—impressed me as a jovial sort. He looked like a weekend golfer with his cheeky smile, a crushable hat and potbelly. He proudly described the lumber mill operation, and when I complimented him on the handmade furniture, he introduced the carpentry instructor. As though prearranged, someone marched out to us with a thick photo album illustrating the slow development of the sawmill.

A few minutes later, Marceline gathered us around her, took a deep breath and summarized our tour stops: the hospital, nursery, kitchen, library, wood shop, lumber mill, machine shop, the piggery, the chickery, fields, citrus orchards, living quarters.... It sounded as if the tour would consume the entire day—right up to the moment we would reboard the dump truck and rush to the airport to meet our return flight. Time for locating the pit in the ground, for questioning residents about their living conditions, for putting difficult questions to Jones would be soaked up.

Don Harris asked Marceline to pare down the tour to a half-hour or so. When Mrs. Jones obliged us, I felt a twinge of guilt: my opportunity to see Jonestown—after over a year of trying—was being whittled down. However, the stakes had been raised. With evidence that fearful people wanted to leave, questions about programs and living conditions—even the hole—became secondary.

With Marceline and other Temple aides leading the way, we took a short path to the nursery, the pride and joy of Mrs. Jones. This nursery, with flowers painted on its sign, rough-sawn wooden walls and a shiny metal roof had functioned as the first home for the thirty-three babies born in Jonestown. Inside, the nursery, named Cuffy Memorial after a Guyana national hero, reflected tender care, cleanliness and attention to detail, with colorful print coverings and rags braided into rugs. In the one room, the tour director showed us tiny cribs equipped with mesh to keep out snakes and insects. Pointing to an incubator, Marceline noted, "We haven't had to use it, or the aspirator." Introducing us to the nursing staff, she estimated that about three hundred children lived in Jonestown, a figure that always would stick in my mind.

Outside, under a veranda on the left side of the building, several women knelt on pillows leafing through books for little children no older than eighteen months, giving them sensory stimulation. Looking closer, I thought it odd that one of the infants, Lew Jones's son Chioke, was being introduced to a book about dinosaurs, with small print. Again, it caused me to wonder how much of the tour had been choreographed for our benefit. The props—the books, the boys playing baseball, some children taking dance classes under an awning nearby—were superfluous. The place was impressive enough without all that.

Clearly, specific Temple aides had been attached to each of us. Marceline and Jack Beam led the way, while Johnny Brown Jones stood in reserve, making no pretenses of cordiality. When I shook his hand to introduce myself, he glared at me and said, "I'm not sure I should." The rank and file seemed to respect—or perhaps fear—this young man who had so frightened Leon Broussard. In either case, they kept their distance and keyed to him. Some were shooed away with subtle body language or a flash of displeasure.

For the most part, the common people remained just a collection of faces to me, seen only fleetingly moving down paths, or positioned as props along our tour route. There was not the slightest spontaneity of behavior—and the people seemed to grow even more tense during the tour because word was spreading: some brothers and sisters were deserting. At the pavilion, people had come forward asking for safe passage out.

As the tour group traveled along a path away from the gathering storm of people and emotions in the pavilion, a Temple member whispered something to Marceline. Her expression tightened. Now she knew. Yet we all went ahead, as though nothing had changed, first past the Harriet Tubman Place, a barnlike building with "apartments" for singles, then to the Sojourner Truth Apartments, which Marceline said housed children with learning disabilities. As we entered, I noticed other reporters had drifted off to see what was happening. The tour disintegrated around me; I was left practically alone with Marceline, whose face had grown taut to the cracking point. As she introduced me to the staff members, who told of their work with two dozen troubled youngsters, my attention was fragmented—What was happening in the pavilion? Where was Greg? Where were the other reporters? In a few moments, I excused myself, trying not to be rude.

On that long path with sickly plantings on one side and buildings on both sides, the bulk of the settlement unfolded like a military boot camp. But I turned my back on it. With Jack Beam spouting off about the agricultural enterprises and trying in vain to keep up, I headed toward the pavilion. On the way, I encountered Javers and Krause, who pointed out a wooden building with tightly shuttered windows. In contrast to the shower house, which sounded alive with chatter and splashing water, not a sound emanated from Jane Pitman Gardens. The concern among the other reporters was that some people wanting to leave might be locked inside. Seeing Javers and Krause heading for the front door, I double-timed around the back of the building. Johnny Brown Jones caught up with me. "What's the matter?" he said.

"I'd like to see what's inside that building."

"There are seniors in there, and they don't want to be disturbed. They're afraid of you. In the States, they've had burglars, the police and everyone else break down their doors. They want their privacy."

"I'd like to hear that from them. The shuttered windows make us wonder." The air was hot by now.

We stood eye to eye for a moment, then he said, "All right. . . ." At the back door, he knocked and called, "This is John. Don't be afraid. Open up."

The door unlatched and swung inward several inches. A shriveled black woman in a cotton print housecoat peered out, her leathery mouth in a frown, her eyes cowed.

"There are reporters here and they want to come in and look around," Johnny Brown said. "I told him you want your privacy."

"We don't want our pictures taken," she said, probably taking his cue. "You can't come in."

"No one will take any pictures of anyone if they don't want it," I assured her. "Would you ask the others if they're willing to talk to me?"

The question only terrified her further. She looked to Johnny, and he nodded permission. She stepped behind the door for no more than thirty seconds, peeked out and said, "We need our privacy. All of us is getting dressed. We don't have our clothes on. Nobody wants to be interviewed."

"See?" Johnny said, as the door shut and latched.

On the path out front, I saw Garry and Lane and explained my concern. When Garry insisted the women had a right to privacy, I proposed, "How 'bout you and Mark going in there and asking each and every one whether they would agree to speak with me?"

While the attorneys mounted the porch decorated with potted plants, I waited outside with Johnny Brown Jones. "We have nothing to hide," he said, and I replied, "You can understand why I want to be sure." He glared. "No, I can't."

Garry emerged to say the women "unequivocally" did not want news media in there and did not want to talk to the press. Accepting the answer for the moment, I headed for the pavilion where Javers, Krause and Harris continued to press for access to the same dorm, apparently unaware of my efforts. A refusal would indicate secrecy and cast a pall of suspicion over the entire visit, so Lane was trapped. To clear the air, he finally admitted, "You know the problem? It's crowded. It's to be expected. Jonestown went from eighty to twelve hundred people." He said the Temple had feared the reporters would misinterpret the crowding. While I joined in the request to see the dorm and the attorneys tried to convince Temple aides to open it up, a man arrived with a platter of hot grilled cheese sandwiches. With the coffee eating away at my empty stomach, I welcomed the sandwich, and Garry took one too; Lane declined.

Finally, the lawyers announced that we could see Jane Pitman Gardens. We found the barracks as crowded and stifling as a prisoner of war camp. Under the metal roof and behind locked shutters rose two tiers of bunk beds. In the rafters, just a foot or so above the top bunks, sleeping bags, suitcases and boxes of belongings were stacked on planks. Harsh light rushed inside with us as the elderly residents, fully dressed, filed out, squinting like moles, scattering.

"The plan calls for one hundred more cottages," commented one of our young escorts. "We'll move people out as we build cottages."

Despite the touches of individuality—clothing on nails, small throw rugs, embroidered pillows, colorful quilts—the dormitory for elderly women appeared seriously overcrowded. "The place is very neat and clean," I commented. "How many people live in here?" My escort shrugged.

Though a head count was impossible, the numbers on the bunks, which were lined up head to foot in several rows just a few feet apart, went at least into the sixties. Whether such crowding was inhumane or adequate would hinge to a great extent on the attitudes and self-determination of the residents. But I asked myself why the elderly—those who were to be revered and afforded dignity—were herded together in what seemed to be the least desirable housing in the settlement.

"Thank you for letting us see your house," I said to a woman near the door. "I'm sorry to have disturbed your privacy." She nodded yet held her tongue like the others.

As a last resort, I asked my escort, Prokes, to invite someone to speak with me. Stopping a bony and very short black woman of about seventy, he said, "This man would like to ask a few questions. He's a reporter."

On the porch, with her back against the wall, she looked up at me, eyes like eggs, lips drawn thin. In answer to my questions, she said that she hailed from Los Angeles and had resided in Jane Pitman Gardens for her entire two years in Jonestown. She said she liked the accommodations just fine and intended neither to leave nor to seek better quarters. Even after I asked Prokes to move out of earshot, she maintained, "I'm happy as can be."

When Prokes rejoined us, he said, "She's one of our chief gardeners. She worked on this beautiful garden here." Not a negative syllable escaped the woman's mouth, yet her voice was bereft of enthusiasm. She actually leaned away, hoping to leave, consumed by anxiety either because of me or because of the aides hovering around us.

For me, the masquerade ended there. We had seen what we were not supposed to see, enough to write negative reports if we were as biased and antagonistic as Jones believed. And we had dashed the illusion of trust by insisting on seeing the dorm.

When I returned to the pavilion, I was unsure how many people were defecting and how much the Temple knew. However, I could tell from the expressions on the Concerned Relatives that none of their people would be riding out with us. Anthony Katsaris, on a bench with his sister, looked absolutely wrung out emotionally. For two days, his sister had kept him at arm's length. The previous night, he had lured her away from the pavilion by asking her to show him to the bathroom. All he wanted was to talk with his sister alone, at least so he could be sure she really wanted to stay. When she refused, he had grabbed her arm—and she had called for a guard to protect her against her own brother. When NBC had interviewed them that night, he tried to hold her hand; she was cold; he blinked back tears. "Maria accused me of using words out of my father's mouth," he said.

When I introduced myself to Maria early Saturday afternoon and asked whether she was enjoying the reunion, she said grudgingly, "There's never been any problem with my brother visiting. But I have no intention of seeing my father until he drops that lawsuit. The suit's based on the fact that he says he didn't molest me; he knows he's lying." With a pained expression, Anthony listened to his sister castigate their father.

In the sunny sheltered spot between the pavilion and the school, flanked by plantain trees, Ryan posed with Carol Houston Boyd, her nieces and their mother, Phyllis Houston, as though the future seemed rosy. Spreading magnanimous arms, Ryan framed the entire group, and they all smiled as I took photos for Carol and myself. When the camera fell, so did the corners of their mouths. I remembered Ryan's voice booming in his Georgetown hotel room, "Sure, plenty of work has been done at Jonestown, but I want to find out how much of that work was done by Patricia and Judy Houston."

When I introduced myself, the girls smiled courteously, a little mindful of their mother's dour expression. The girls, one year apart, in their mid-teens, appeared well fed and healthy. In their rubber zori sandals, they looked like average California girls entering their high school years.

"How long have you been down here?" I asked their mother, a tall, well proportioned brunette.

"About two weeks," Phyllis said. "I had some vacation time and thought I'd come down. I'm an insurance risk inspector."

"Have you been here before?"

"It's my first time down," she said. "But we have constant communications by radio and letter."

Her answers confirmed Sammy Houston's suspicions that she had come to Jonestown solely because the Temple had heard that the Houston family would be represented on the Ryan trip.

The girls responded very cautiously to my questions. They stuck to safe subjects and canned answers, with no spontaneity. They gave little spiels about their routines—school, sports, drill team, work. "Nothing is wrong with the States," volunteered Judy, who hoped to become a veterinarian someday. "I just prefer it here."

Nearby, Beverly Oliver and her two sons, handsome and sturdy young men named Bruce and William, reclined on a bench together. Mrs. Oliver, her skin a creamy coffee color, radiated a thin, confident, knowing smile. Her boys had warned her earlier not to say anything negative against the Temple during the visit. Her boys tried to protect her; they loved her and perhaps even wanted to leave soon. They were still her boys, not Jim Jones's. For their NBC interview, however, Bruce and Billy recited the party line.

Jim Cobb, who had taken movies and still photos of his attractive family, listened as his mother and siblings told Don Harris about the wonders of Jonestown—the beauty of the birds, the compassionate work done by the free clinic. "We have nothing against the States," said Mrs. Cobb, echoing the Houston girls almost word for word.

Just several yards away, in the shade of the pavilion, all eyes turned in one direction. Jim Jones had emerged, once again in his red short-sleeved shirt, khaki pants and black military-type shoes. With his face ashen, his dry lips plastered together, his frame wilting in the damp heat, he avoided the sun like an amphibian whose skin would dry and split in direct light. He looked ill—and this day he had a good reason. He had been told a short time earlier that some of the "children" of Jonestown had opted to leave with Ryan. A group of about eight people—including his aides, his attorneys, Ryan and Embassy official Dick Dwyer—clustered around him. No one smiled. Pride and reputations, politics and propaganda, people's loves and lives were at stake.

Ryan, though clearly pleased, refrained from openly gloating. The tall congressman almost dwarfed Jones as they conferred, standing, then sitting at a far corner of the pavilion. Ryan did most of the talking, though the remarks were not audible from my range. Both he and the attorneys, I would learn later, tried to comfort Jones, to assure him that a few departures would not besmirch the beauty of the settlement.

In small knots, Temple members whispered worried asides to each other, sometimes blatantly hiding their mouths with their hands. Certainly, legal aide Harriet Tropp, propagandist and professor Dick Tropp, longtime follower Jack Beam, public relations man Mike Prokes, former security chief Jim McElvane, portly staffer Patty Cartmell and mistress Carolyn Layton knew by then that traitors had stepped forward. And several dozen others, with their haunches on tables or benches, with their eyes strafing us, had read the crisis through the face of Jim Jones.

The cautious optimism from the previous night's successes—Ryan's positive statement, the polished entertainment, the basketball victory—faded into the past like a cloud over the horizon. A group of people whose names I did not know had decided to leave with us. In addition to the first two—a black teen-ager named Monica Bagby and a white curly-haired man named Vern Gosney—two families had come forward. To make matters worse for the Temple, they were large families who had followed Jones for many years—and who secretly had been plotting their escape.

Over the next hour or so, Jones huddled repeatedly with both families, to test their resolve, to question them quietly, to try to mediate their problems. Reporters were ordered to keep our distance, but the expressions told the story. Jones eased onto a bench with the matriarch of the Parks family, wizened white-haired Edith Parks, speaking intently with her and her relatives—Gerald, a balding man in a striped tank top; his wife Patricia, who strongly resembled Marceline Jones; their son Dale, who looked twenty-eight going on forty; teen-ager Brenda, and Tracy, a pink-faced preteen blonde bewildered by it all.

During the tense minutes of conversation, the Parks family remained the most visible, though Jim and Marceline Jones devoted much time trying to dissuade the Bogues and Harold Cordell, who was with Jim Bogue's estranged wife Edith. "We're gonna go back," Edith Bogue told Jones with great difficulty. "I've got my whole family back there. . . . It's not that I don't think what you're doing here is wonderful, cuz I do."

In a low, resigned voice, Jones told the Bogue family, privately, "There's always a place, just know there's always a place for you. Always a place." He managed a slight smile, as he fell back to his secondary position of accommodation. He did not want them to leave feeling threatened; that would make them more likely to talk. And, if he already had made his momentous decision, he certainly did not wish to tip them by being hostile. "Even some of those who have lied [against the Temple after defecting] have come back," he added. "So many people have lied."

Disappointment was a mild word for Jones's facial contortions. In his emotion and pain, he sucked in his cheeks then inflated them, then licked his dry lips, repeating the actions again and again. This once-eloquent man appeared lost for words, his lips seemingly cemented together even as he spoke. The once-charismatic minister could not muster the animation to turn around followers who had believed in him and loved him. No doubt, the presence of outsiders constrained Jones: he could not harangue over loudspeakers, summon up hostile peer pressure or threaten with his security detail. He could rely only on the bond, the personal bond between Jim Jones the man and these important members; he could only try to stimulate guilt in them for leaving a good cause and good people.

The scene collapsed into a quiet chaos, with too many things for one person to observe, too many unknown people huddling or rushing in and out of the pavilion, too many worried faces overlooking, overhearing, murmuring. As more defectors came forward, Ryan's aide Jackie Speier added them to a list and took oral affidavits. Still dressed in platform shoes and a black and white polka-dot sundress, she talked into a tape recorder, "I am Jackie Speier, an attorney on the staff of Leo Ryan. What is your wish today?" And they would reply, "To go back to the United States." Because the defectors feared harassment, they were accompanied by Speier and others when they went to their quarters for belongings.

At one point, Leo Ryan stood back as the Temple leadership and their attorneys pulled close together to parley in low tones. "How are things going, Leo?" I asked. "Are many leaving with us?"

He cocked back his head, then dropped his chin to his chest and out of the corner of his mouth said with a touch of bravado: "Looks like about a dozen. There are more every minute. They're coming out of the woodwork." Ryan was vindicated and he knew it; no one could say any longer that he was on a political witch hunt, or chasing headlines. So many people had come forward that an additional plane, a six-seater Cessna, had to be ordered via the Temple radio—and it appeared that might not suffice.

The gloom in the other camp was oppressive. From the rank and file to the higher-ups, not a soul could summon a smile. Only the very small children obliviously played on or watched television. All other eyes remained riveted on Jones as pressures built inside him. Stepping away from his attorneys and his legal aide Harriet Tropp, he motioned Marceline to come over. One hand to his chest as though it hurt, he rasped: "A pill." Lovingly, his wife resisted his entreaty.

In that degenerating scene, hope vanished from the faces of the Temple inner circle and the Concerned Relatives alike. Neither group would come away from the test with their desired results, and they knew it.

As Jones wearily tried to persuade the defectors to stay, Jim McElvane stood, pillar stiff, his arms folded, looking more unapproachable than ever. "How do you feel about these people leaving?" I asked. With genuine sadness, he said, "It brings almost tears to my eyes." Then he caught himself and tried to minimize the impact of the desertions: "They were never really in it completely. . . . We try to make them feel very much at home. It's their choice. If they had expressed a desire to leave earlier, they could have." Appearing hurt, the big man stared off, his brain adrift, probably wondering what crisis strategy his leader would adopt now, with so much on the scales.

"How many people are leaving?" I asked.

"I don't know," he replied, as though it did not matter whether one or a hundred left.

In her floral muumuu, rotund Patty Cartmell had not given up; she pleaded with me to understand. "No one else has ever left. Jim Jones has never expressed anything but love—and I've been with him twenty-one years. I've been here eighteen months. Before I came here, I had hypertension. This is the whole world to me. He represents all that is kind and loving. He has one fault—his heart is too big."

A young white man in his late twenties chimed in, "If people had really wanted to leave, peer pressure couldn't keep them. People travel to Port Kaituma, Matthews Ridge and Georgetown every day. And what's to stop them from leaving?" It was a compelling question.

Attorney Charles Garry appraised the situation, implying that some members of the Parks family might reverse their decision. "If the Parkses decide to leave, I've got five thousand dollars Guyanese for their transportation. That's from the Temple." In his hand, an envelope bulged with currency, which would not go very far toward repatriating a half-dozen people and resettling them in California.

"It was expected that someone would leave, but Jim Jones is a perfectionist," Garry said. "If one leaves, he has failed." For the second time, someone was saying the number of deserters did not matter, that Jones could be devastated by even one.

When the clouds boiled together in swirls of gray and black, and departure time raced nearer, NBC set up for their finale. In the news media, it is known as a confrontation interview, usually done at the conclusion of an investigation, with the prime target. The print media had pitched questions at Jones the night before, but the television people wanted the drama and daylight of a Saturday afternoon session, after their tour and inquiries. At the rear edge of the pavilion, where the cloud-filtered light was brightest and the bodyguards thickest, Jones took a straight-backed chair, crossed one leg, sipped a glass of water and awaited the barrage. With hostility as subtle as it was deep, he watched Bob Brown meter the light on his gray face. His back stiffened, Jones sat as motionless as the macaws, yet poised. At the outset, the interview struck me as ominous, faintly climactic.

For Javers, Krause and me, these few minutes were nearly as important as they were to NBC, because of the defections, because of the constable's information. We had held off on some of the thornier questions until now. We gathered closely around Jones, standing or squatting out of the camera line, taking notes and awaiting our turn with him.

In response to soft opening questions from Harris, Jones described his utopia, the Temple's escape there from U.S. racism, and its attempts to eradicate racism, classism and elitism in the jungle. "You never accomplish what you set out," he added. "I am a perfectionist."

To another, he said with weariness, "We want to fade out of the whole arena of public attention but obviously we haven't, because of lies. I never understood how people could *lie* with such total freedom and conviction."

Were the stories of beatings and corporal punishment true? "No." He acted misunderstood and repeated his earlier explanation of abuses that had been stopped.

Asked about the report of the underground enclosure, Jones showed slight surprise. "We don't have an underground enclosure here." Then he changed the subject.

What about allegations of armed guards around the perimeter? "There are no armed guards," he said.

Harris told Jones that police records show the Temple bought an automatic weapon with a twenty-round clip—he probably was referring to one of the few semiautomatic rifles under government permits. Arguing that the Temple had only a few guns licensed for hunting and insisting correctly that no "automatic" guns were delivered to the compound, a baffled-looking Jones swore, "That's a lie. . . ."

Why do these terrible things happen to the Temple and why are allegations made? "Obviously, there is a conspiracy. Someone shot at me and missed me by a couple of inches. We went through a week of hell."

But who would do such a thing? "Who conspired to kill Dr. Martin Luther King, Malcolm X and John Kennedy? Every agency of the whole government is giving us a hard time. Somebody doesn't like socialism."

Was he dying, as some had speculated, and as he more than implied? "I don't want to be one of those people in their golden years," he said from behind his sunglasses. "I have no knowledge. I don't know. I haven't had a diagnostician. Our doctor is competent, but he can only see shadows."

Harris said he had heard that security guards with guns had gone to the houses at night and warned people not to cause trouble during the Ryan visit. Jones denied it with little outrage. "No one came to see people with guns. I have strictly prohibited guns.

"You don't have to shoot me," he added excitedly. "The media smear does it." Again, he had placed a figurative gun in our hands; the casual talk of violent death bothered me.

Jones gave an epitaph, telling us how he wanted to be remembered: "I've given my life for people, serving people."

As the clouds blackened and groped toward us, Harris produced a piece of paper, and said, "Last night someone came and passed me this note."

Jones took the note and read in silence. The words—"Vernon Gosney, Monica Bagby. Help us get out of Jonestown"—clouded over his face. His nose was being rubbed in his humiliation, his failure, his catastrophe. "Friend, people lie and play games. . . . Please leave us. People can go out of here when they want." He showed the note to Prokes, who leaned over his shoulder. Rev. Jones had been put on the run, but it was to be no stampede. He kept most of his composure.

What was his response to the defections? "I only feel that every time people leave up until now, they chose to lie. . . ." For the second time, he expressed fear that those leaving would expose him.

When the questions ceased, he shrank visibly, his water glass dangling in his hand. He sat there, as wooden as a marionette, while Bob Brown shot cutaways to be spliced into the footage. Taking the opportunity to approach him, I asked, "Reverend Jones, what are your feelings now that it's apparent some of your followers want to leave?" Wounded to the point of numbness, he said in an even voice, "I must have failed if people can't talk to you and be up front with you."

He excused himself as the belongings of the defectors were being carried along the boardwalks. As he rose and walked away, almost transfixed, black clouds collided in the skies overhead, and a sudden wind tore through the pavilion, riffling the pages of my notebook. "That's the biggest blow I've seen in a month," Jones shuddered. Then, without even a preliminary thunderclap, the skies dumped a violent rain that bent the plantain fronds and sent people scooting for cover. Something so freakish had to carry some meaning, I thought.

The last good-byes were painful. Jones did not seem so wooden as he bent to hug little blond Tracy Parks and took her twenty-eight-year-old brother Dale by the shoulders, attempting to whisper something or kiss him on the cheek as the young man recoiled. Harold Cordell exchanged an embrace with fellow old-timer Jack Beam. One was going, one staying. Each shed a tear.

When Jones turned away from that sadness and headed toward the truck, I placed myself in his path. I needed more answers. Had he tried and failed to talk them out of going? "No." He shook his head. "I wanted to be sure what I heard was true." Would he take greater pains in the future to assure members they were free to leave? With a stare, he said in a roundabout way that he would. "If they want, I'll let them leave." It was a curious, self-incriminating statement for a man who had maintained his followers' freedom to leave at will.

As I asked further questions in a conciliatory and tactful way, Jones answered vaguely that he would allow other Concerned Relatives to see Jonestown and their people. His mind seemed divorced from his words, his eyes detached from his body. Yet his voice stayed steady, sluggish as though each sentence had been diagramed in advance. With Javers and Krause looking on, Jones told me, "I feel sorry that we are being destroyed from within. All we want is to be left in peace."

His talk of failure and perfectionism was a disturbing echo: if one person leaves, I have failed. But he reversed himself, not wishing to leave a final impression that all was lost. "I will continue to try," he said vacantly. "Time will tell whether I will succeed."

My thanks rolled off him as I shook his hand and our gazes met. His chin was low, his eyes angled upward through the tinted glasses, chilly as the wet wind. We parted.

For the first time, propagandist Dick Tropp was sitting down on the job, his lean rump on a nearby table. I joined him, watching the procession of Temple members shouldering the trunks and suitcases of defectors and hurrying along the rain-slickened boardwalks. Thirsty, I lifted a glass of water but put it down again; it was cloudy for a change. Did Tropp believe this day proved that Jonestown was an open society? "I hope so," he answered gently, with a hint of agitation. "I don't know what happened to these people. I hope people can see this is not a closed community—media, Congressmen and relatives can come in. The truth will out. We don't have anything to hide."

Before venturing from the shelter, I pulled my poncho from my backpack. A loudspeaker blared, "Bonny Simon. Bonny Simon. Please come to the radio room!" Then, barely able to keep my footing on the wet walkway, I headed toward Mr. Muggs's cage and the truck. All at once, I heard pounding feet behind me, and a woman screaming, "I'll kill you. I'll kill you! You bring those kids back here. Don't touch my kids." A husky white woman in her thirties came to a skidding stop just short of a stocky American Indian in a T-shirt. He had two children in tow, and she wanted them. She lunged, then there was a frenzied instant of tug-of-war over a little boy. Temple members reassured Bonny Simon that her husband Al would not be allowed to take her children. Then the attorneys stepped in. Garry took a stand: the father had no right to remove the children from their mother's custody, even if he wanted to leave with Ryan. The attorneys agreed the matter should be settled in court. But in the meantime the children would not be stripped from their mother, who wanted to stay in Jonestown. Simon, nearly mute during the brief exchange, sulked back toward the pavilion, muttering that he would remain with his kids even if it meant being harassed.

Hearing Simon's statement, Garry turned to Jones inquiringly; the minister quickly assured him there would be no harassment. Nonetheless Ryan volunteered to stay behind with Simon and others who might wish to repatriate yet could not get space aboard the two planes. The noble gesture probably was necessary. The emotional climate darkened noticeably after the incident. The threat to kill—whether in a fit of temper or not—had charged the air. Child-stealing accusations had been introduced. The time for warm good-byes had ended. Departure time had drawn upon us. We streamed toward the truck.

Off in the playground, Jones took up a vantage point, with an aide holding an umbrella over his head. In his red shirt and khaki pants, mud creeping up the sides of his shoes, he looked little like the minister who had charmed politicians in his pastel and white leisure suits. He held an eerie directionless gaze until one of his aides whispered to him. Then he waved, like the mayor of a big city bidding farewell to visiting dignitaries.

Yet there was nothing final about the gesture. The community seemed poised. Dozens stood stiff as cane stalks around the playground perimeter, their attention fixed on Jones and some aides—Jack Beam, Maria Katsaris, Harriet Tropp, Jim McElvane, Mike Prokes among them. The rank-and-file members by the truck had turned their backs to us to watch and wait. They all looked as though there had been a death in the family.

Mounting the big truck was an acrobatic feat until a ladder was propped at the back of the bed. The defectors were surprisingly agile. As I held Patricia Parks's hand, her muddy feet took the aluminum rungs one by one. We had heard the fiftyish woman had been the last holdout in the Parks family. But she chose her family over Jones. Edith Parks, her snowy-haired mother-in-law, looked comical in her baseball cap and sneakers, with a sheet of clear plastic to keep her dry. She was as frail as her son Gerald was youthful-looking. Dale had his father's dark hair and receding hairline. Brenda Parks, the teen-ager, boarded with her boy friend, Chris O'Neill, a scraggly-haired white youth. Tracy Parks, the towheaded preteener, clung to her mother. With Jim Bogue, who looked like a farmer in a tractor cap, were his children—Tommy, Teena and

Juanita, whom I recognized as the friendly stroller that morning. Bogue's estranged wife Edith, her hair pulled back, glasses low on her nose, boarded with Harold Cordell. The original defectors, Vern Gosney and Monica Bagby, stood together in the truckbed crowded with people in the rear and baggage in the front.

One of the last to clamber aboard the truck was a sharp-featured man my age, thirty or so. About five feet six with a wiry body and a nearly emaciated face, he stood next to me in the right rear of the truck bed. When this man boarded, Dale Parks angrily hushed up some of the relatives. With their hair stringy in the rain, their expressions grim, some looked over at the newcomer. I introduced myself and, though he kept his hands locked on the sideboards, he gave the name Larry Layton. Was he leaving with us? "Yeah, and I'm happy to be getting out of here."

"Why are you leaving?" I asked.

He hesitated. "I'll talk to you about it later." His eyes shifted straight ahead, aimed at the blank side of a building with fuel drums on the porch. His stare did not seem to meet the eyes of dozens of members loitering on dry porches or looking out of windows.

There were sixteen defectors aboard, and Ryan was still back at the pavilion. He planned to stay overnight to complete the paperwork and to safeguard, if necessary, any more defectors.

When the truck engine cranked over, Maria Katsaris, waif-thin and sunken-eyed, appeared below me in the mud, toting a huge purse. "Here," she called, throwing a small metal object overhand. "Tell Steve I don't believe in God." With those harsh and cold words, she turned heel and went back to Jones, her first and last lover. In my hand was a silver cross and chain. Though Maria's brother stood just across the truck, she had thrown it to me. Perhaps she had not located him in the crowded bed; perhaps she wanted to spare him further pain. Already, Anthony was dejected, looking off at the wet fields of crops, seeing nothing.

My initial impulse was to return the cross directly to his father and spare Anthony's emotions. But I decided it would only mean a delayed trauma, and I was not entirely certain what would happen in the coming minutes. Placing the cross in Anthony's hand, I repeated his sister's message, having no idea of the cross's importance. Anthony collapsed against the side of the truck and wept. Holding back my own emotions, I gave his shoulder a parting pat and stepped back to the other side of the truck.

The truck revved in reverse, but we went nowhere. Though just a few yards from a gentle downgrade, the worn truck tires would not grip in several inches of mud. Our driver leaped out. Moments later a yellow Caterpillar tractor was pulling us to the edge of the grade. But my relief lasted only an instant.

What sounded like a cheer rumbled from the pavilion. Scores of people stampeded toward the far end of the structure. The noise stopped both Greg, who had been shooting from the truck roof, and Bob Brown, who was spread-legged on the hood taking footage of the fields. "I'll wave if it amounts to anything," barked Don Harris, hitting the mud with a squish of boots, then jagging a course through the crops. A moment later, he whistled and flailed both arms like a madman. We other reporters hit the muck and ran through tall beans to the pavilion. There, Harris held up one hand, halting us near the stage, calming us. His breath came in fast rushes, but he deliberately controlled his normally unexcitable voice. He said, slowly, so there would be no misunderstanding, "Some guy tried to kill Leo. Leo's all right. The guy grabbed Leo around the neck. Put a knife to his throat. Said, 'I'm gonna cut your throat, you motherfucker.' Leo and the rest took it away. The guy was cut in the scuffle."

My neck muscles swelled with adrenalin. I felt an overwhelming need to see for myself, to be there to support Ryan. At that moment, we were as one—the outsiders, the enemy. Distinctions among reporters, the congressman, the relatives fell away. Our only hope in a crisis was sticking together.

But Johnny Brown, backed by a group of husky young men, instructed us to turn back. When we did not budge, he said, as had Harris, that the congressman was all right. "Please go back to the truck," he said firmly, over and over. The situation was volatile, he said, and our presence might touch off more trouble. "People are uptight."

His impassioned pleas and the mass of glaring faces behind him finally convinced us to go back. Once we reporters, including Harris, had scaled the truck sides again, the vehicle began to lumber down the road.

In the distance, a long-legged white boy came flying out of the pavilion, hollering for all he was worth. He hurdled crops in the field and charged toward us pell-mell along the roadbank. He quickly overtook us and stopped the driver. As usual, those of us in the back could not hear above the rapping diesel exhaust pipe.

Then, like an apparition through the exhaust, Leo Ryan came down the road, his blood-spattered shirt torn open to his beltline, his pants soiled around the knees, his briefcase in one hand. Jim Cobb hurried up the road to greet him, as the congressman was escorted toward us by a Temple security guard, Tim Carter and a worried-looking Mark Lane, with Embassy official Dick Dwyer bringing up the rear. Ryan's normally ruddy face was as white as his untanned belly, his brow deeply furrowed, his thatch of gray hair matted. After trudging to the truck, Lane helped him into the cab. To an apparent apology, Ryan said, "No problem." His face taut, Ryan seemed greatly relieved to be there, to be alive. Yet he looked, in a pitiful way, victorious, like a boy who had taken some licks yet won the fight.

Back at the pavilion just a few minutes earlier, the departure preparations had been proceeding uneventfully. Charles Garry and some of Jones's aides had been standing around the minister as the Ryan party finished boarding the truck. Under the metal pavilion roof, Larry Layton had come forward to join the congressman's group of defectors. His wife

Karen was hysterical. "I don't understand this," she cried. "I don't understand. Larry, what is this all about?" Layton, sullen and silent, ignored her and hugged Jones good-bye. After Ryan straightened out his paperwork for him, he headed for the truck.

All seemed to be going smoothly and amicably. Ryan thanked the Temple lawyers for their help, said it was a pleasant visit and assured Jones that his report to Congress would show fairness. Then, after Ryan asked Jones to make it easier for people to leave on their own, a husky man named Don Sly walked up behind him without warning. Sly threw his arms around Ryan and said, "Congressman Ryan, you motherfucker. . . ." Ryan felt a point pushing at his throat, and at first believed that it was a pin and that someone was joking. But Sly's left hand was prodding the congressman's jugular with a homemade knife.

As Lane went for the weapon, Garry grabbed Sly's neck and Ryan pitched backward with his assailant. Tim Carter joined the scuffle on the ground, and eventually the knife was wrested away. When the men disengaged themselves, they found that Ryan, whose shirt was dotted with blood, was unhurt. But Sly accidentally had been cut between the thumb and index finger on one hand.

When Ryan picked himself up, he was angry. Then he composed himself. Jones stood to one side, silently, as if in a trance; he had not lifted a hand or protested in any way, and did not apologize now. He only listened as Ryan promised that his recommendation and report to Congress would remain unchanged, providing the attacker was arrested. Jones agreed to call the police only after the lawyers instructed him to do it.

Drawn to the area by the commotion and gathering crowd, Dwyer evaluated the situation and thought Ryan's continued presence might be unwise. The diplomat urged the congressman to abandon his plan to stay overnight to process more potential defectors. Volunteering to stay in his place, Dwyer said he would take Ryan to Port Kaituma, then come right back. With Lane as an escort, both Ryan and Dwyer left the pavilion, hurrying to overtake the departing truck.

In a light rain, with Ryan and Dwyer aboard, the truck rolled again, with a belch of black smoke. There was some comfort in heading away from Jonestown—though the defectors privately believed that we would be ambushed and killed before reaching Kaituma. We outsiders, though ignorant of those fears, still could hardly take comfort in the fact that someone had tried to slit the throat of a U.S. congressman, the man we had considered our shield.

The severe bouncing and slippery footing forced us to flex our knees to absorb the shock and to keep balance. As the tiresome position became numbing, Jim Cobb grabbed my shoulder and took my head to whisper, "Larry Layton's in front of you. There's no way he's a defector; he's too close to Jones. These people say that Layton's been desperate, depressed, since his mother died a few months ago. They think he's got a gun and is going to try something. Watch him." I nodded my thanks.

At that moment, Jim Cobb was as earnest as a human being can be. His manner and voice said: our lives might depend on it.

He repeated a similar message to Bob Flick, and the two of us held positions behind and to either side of Layton, with Flick on the left, me on the right and Cobb behind us. With all of us well over six feet tall and 200 pounds, it seemed we could overcome the diminutive Layton if his hand dipped under his poncho for a weapon.

Next to Layton, up on the tailgate, perched a Temple escort named Wesley Breidenbach; he had stayed close to Jones in the final hour or two of our visit, seemingly acting as a security guard. This bushy-haired handsome man in his early twenties, a former pitcher at Opportunity High, probably could be overcome too, I thought. He was a thin six feet one, but his rubber raincoat broke over something at the back of his waistband. When he bent forward to look around the side of the truck, I tried to brush it with my hand to see if it was a gun. But he straightened up.

While keeping one eye on the taciturn Layton, I struck up a conversation with Breidenbach. Like Tropp and McElvane, he said with sadness that the defectors could have left Jonestown at any time. But my comments about the beauty of the terrain, the openness and freedom of the land, seemed to relax him. And when he talked of the spectacular sunsets, the land full of wildlife and fertility, I wondered momentarily whether perhaps some of Jones's paranoia had not rubbed off on us.

But Breidenbach, though very likable, betrayed a nervousness that kept me uneasy. He seemed to know my eyes were trained on Layton, the silent one. Layton's right hand had inched down the boards, lower than chest level. If it went much lower and disappeared under his poncho, I would have to act.

FIFTY-FOUR

Holocaust

When Stephan Jones awoke Saturday morning, November 18, the Lamaha Gardens house was quieter than it had been for the past week. The Ryan party, the Temple attorneys, the press were all in Jonestown, and there was little to do in the Temple house but wait.

As he walked down the narrow hallway to the living room area, Stephan felt better than he had for a long, long time. He was happy about the positive radio reports from Jonestown the previous night. Leo Ryan had announced that many people told him that Peoples Temple was the best thing in their lives. And Stephan thought that once Jonestown had weathered the visit, the openly rebellious basketball team-security squad could return to Jonestown and perhaps do something about Jim Jones. Perhaps they could move him aside gently, or somehow contain his madness.

Stephan also was keyed up from the basketball game the night before. He had lied when he radioed the score to Jonestown. In fact, the team had lost—not won—by ten points. Still, it had felt good to hear the ovation from the crowd in the pavilion.

Once the players were up and dressed, they took team photos, then the day was theirs. Stephan and Lee Ingram went over to the gym for some one-on-one basketball. When they got back to Lamaha Gardens, Sharon Amos's ex-husband Sherwin Harris was there, visiting his twenty-one-year-old daughter, Liane. Stephan did not want Harris to think the team had come to intimidate him—which Harris did—so he suggested the ballplayers take in a Georgetown matinee, a John Saxon movie about hit men.

Harris, after trying to see his daughter for several days, finally had been invited to the Temple house at two o'clock that day. He wound up spending the afternoon and early evening with her. At about four thirty, as Harris and Liane were strolling outside, he noticed something strange: Mike Touchette went storming out of the house shouting, "Bullshit!" Harris wondered what had upset him so much.

Sharon Amos had been hunched over the radio downstairs when the bad news started coming from Jonestown. Richard Dwyer earlier had radioed, asking her to call the U.S. Embassy: there were so many defectors that another airplane was needed to bring them out of the jungle. Amos knew as well as anyone the critical meaning of even one defection. When Mike Carter, the Jonestown operator, got back on the radio, Amos asked him, "Is this for real?" Carter told her it very definitely was.

"Who are they?" she wanted to know, tension edging her voice. Carter told her the names of the traitors.

"Oh, my God," she uttered. Then she put out a call for the Temple security squad members in town.

Stephan Jones never saw the end of the John Saxon movie. His brother Tim was tapping on his shoulder: Stephan and the others were wanted back at the house, urgently. As they responded to the emergency order, none knew what had happened in Jonestown. When their car pulled up in front of the house, Stephan jumped out and raced into the radio room. Sharon still was bent over the radio receiver. Since she wore headphones, Stephan could not hear the Jonestown end of the conversation. Suddenly she turned to him, trembling. "He wants us to go out and get revenge." The coded message began to spell out the weapons—KNI. . . . Jones wanted them to use knives; there were no guns in Georgetown.

Stephan's stomach did a reverse. Every muscle jerked taut. The message meant: go out and kill Temple enemies. Something catastrophic was about to happen in Jonestown. But what?

"Hold it," said Stephan, trying to slow his racing mind. "We've got to talk." He needed to take stock of the situation, to stall for time. Had the day finally come? Was Jim Jones really calling on the Jonestown security squad to avenge the death of a movement? If so, it was hardly a crack unit. Torn by doubts and disillusionment, Stephan, his brothers and friends were no longer ready to carry out such extreme orders unquestioningly.

He had to consult his brother Tim. As they walked outside to the iron gate at the front of the house, Debbie Touchette followed. "I know how you guys feel, and I know what you're thinking," she said. "But you better get back in the house or Sharon will go out of her mind."

Stephan's head still spun. He did not know exactly what to avenge, though he was fairly certain it involved the Ryan party. While no one had identified any targets, Tim Stoen at the Hotel Pegasus had to rank high on the list. Stephan knew Jones was given to issuing irrational orders or falsely creating life-and-death situations, but somehow this had the feel of a more authentic crisis. If another White Night really had been called in Jonestown, what were the implications? Did it mean his mother, Marceline, would die? His girl friend, Michelle? His best friend, Albert? How could he know whether his people had been attacked by real enemies, or whether his father had gone irretrievably mad, or whether this was another elaborate hoax? As things stood now, his instructions were ludicrous.

"Look, we're not just going out there," Stephan said, finally. "We've got to get some weapons. We've got to have a plan or we won't get anything done. And what are we supposed to use, butter knives?"

Tim Jones and Johnny Cobb were no less confused. They decided to head for the Pegasus Hotel—but not to take revenge on the Concerned Relatives there. They wanted to see whether the relatives had any more information than they did. By that act alone, they would be disobeying the orders of Jim Jones.

In San Francisco, meanwhile, everyone was gathered around the radio on the second floor of the temple waiting anxiously for news from Jonestown. Sandy Bradshaw, Jean Brown and Tom Adams had been ecstatic the night before when they heard about Ryan's positive appraisal. Bradshaw reasoned that if Ryan came home saying good things about Jonestown, their troubles would disappear. Then they could get back to the work of socialism, helping people and building the mission. Bradshaw knew that enough lumber had arrived on the dock in Port Kaituma that week to erect one hundred new cottages. She did not know the poison had arrived too.

When San Francisco reached Jonestown on the radio Saturday morning, Jonestown was reluctant to talk openly because the Ryan party was still there. The radio room was next to the pavilion, and they were afraid of being overheard. Mike Carter, the Jonestown operator, finally tapped out a message in Morse code: Carolyn Layton wanted to talk to Sandy Bradshaw. As they tried to get both parties on the line, Jonestown said San Francisco should move to the top of its radio frequency. That meant an urgent message was coming. San Francisco moved to fifteen meters, the band it normally used for Morse code, and tuned it to the top frequency. After a wait, San Francisco moved to the twenty-meter band. Still, there was no answer. It was noon, San Francisco, 5:00 P.M. Guyana.

As we rode out from Jonestown, I pondered the shape my story would take. My mental review of the visit told me to describe the place as physically impressive and the people as generally appearing happy and healthy. The accusations of the policeman and people like Leon Broussard would be balanced with the denials and assertions of Jim Jones himself. Jones's words would speak for themselves. Though the attack on Ryan had marred the visit, it sounded like a freak incident, perhaps the act of an unbalanced individual.

The sun burst through the clouds as we neared the Temple gate. Six or eight persons were posted in and around the guard shack, far more than for either of our trips in. They halted the truck, and two men came around to the rear. One was James Edwards, the other Joe Wilson, the mean-faced head of security. Edwards stood with his legs apart, one hand fingering something in his pocket. Wilson demanded that we crowd to the sides of the truck bed. "Let me see who you got in there," he snapped impatiently. Supposedly he was looking for his wife and baby, who had walked away from Jonestown that morning. That escape by the security chief's wife was not a good omen, and some people had seen a gun in Wilson's waistband. As the two men stood there, I had a momentary fear —and so did the defectors—that they would open fire, and we would be trapped in the tall-sided truck bed, like cattle in a corral. If the suspicious defector—Layton—and the tailgate escort—Breidenbach—jumped down and joined them, we could be mowed down by bullets as we scrambled over each other to escape.

After what seemed an eon, the truck begin to move. Wilson was hanging on the side, just behind the cab. A wave of relief passed over me as I watched the Peoples Temple welcoming sign shrink in the distance and disappear.

As usual in sleepy Port Kaituma, a few children and nondescript dogs wandered along the roadside. A few adults waved out of habit, but no one waved back. Our faces were taut. After splashing and bouncing through a few more puddles and over rocky stretches, the vehicle turned onto the airstrip. Several soldiers who were lolling around the disabled Guyanese airplane looked up as we passed and continued a few hundred yards to a metal passenger shack.

After helping each other and the defectors off the truck, we reporters accompanied Ryan to the corrugated metal waiting shack. It was
about four thirty. Though he still looked sapped, he had pulled himself
together somewhat on the ride. His silvery hair was tousled, as if he had
been running his fingers through it. His bloodied shirt was buttoned. He
squatted on a piece of luggage and tried to rub the weariness from his
eyes. Veins bulged in his hands as he clasped them, loosely but nervously.
Dispassionately, but with sweeping arm gestures and graphic language,
he described the attempt on his life.

Greg Robinson snapped off frame after frame as Ryan hunkered
there in the shack, his thick hands folding and unfolding. At the end of
his story, Ryan announced he was finished, stood up, then went to the
back half-wall of the shack where he leaned out, looking into the jungle
for a moment of reflection.

A while later, Ryan did an airstrip interview with Don Harris that
covered not only the knife attack but also his impressions of Jonestown,
which he summed up, saying, "It was very different from what I thought
I'd find, in both positive and negative ways."

By then, a six-seater Cessna had landed, followed a moment later
by the larger Guyana Airways Otter. Both were ready for boarding, but
we were several seats short. It was decided—logically so—that the defectors would be the first to go.

But Jackie Speier announced that some of us newsmen would have
to remain behind for another plane. We reporters huddled to discuss who
would stay, and it was decided generally that those of us with daily
deadlines and stories to file would fly out first. Before we had resolved our
seating problems entirely, I noticed the Temple dump truck and the red
tractor with a trailer, pulled side by side about 150 to 200 yards down the
airstrip. Puffing anxiously on a cigarette pinched between thumb and
forefinger, Don Harris stood stiff-legged watching them, like a field general. As I sidled up to Harris, he said with finality, "I think we've got
trouble."

Almost a dozen men stood in and around the two Temple vehicles.
It seemed unlikely that Jones would send such a large group simply to say
good-bye. There was a possibility, I thought, that they might attempt to
harass the traitors, try to retrieve their people from our midst or even
take a few swipes at them and us.

Edith Bogue said, hands on her hips, "They've got a trap there."

Wilson and two other Temple loyalists wandered over from their
group to the plane boarding area. When they asked Steve Sung which
people were assigned to each plane, the NBC soundman pleaded igno-
rance. The two looked around and asked the same of Jim Cobb and some
defectors.

Meanwhile Layton asked emphatically to be assigned to the first
airplane, the Cessna—and he lined up with several other defectors at the

right plane door. Ryan positioned himself there to frisk each for weapons. Like the rest of us, he was aware of rumors that someone among the defectors conceivably might bring down or hijack one of the planes.

At the end of the line, his curly hair snarled by the rain, stood Layton. Quickly, I positioned myself behind him in a shallow puddle out of his line of vision. As the line into the Cessna shortened, he slipped around to the opposite side, entered the aircraft and climbed into a back seat behind the pilot's seat. Was he simply anxious to get aboard and reach safety, or were his intentions more sinister? I informed Ryan that Layton had skirted the inspection, and Ryan confronted him. "I was frisked already," Layton said. When I contradicted him, he reluctantly climbed back out and submitted to a search by Ryan. Not even a knife was found on him, but I escorted him back to his seat anyway. As we passed the tail section, he scooted ahead and climbed inside.

A black man from the tractor had appeared near the plane as Layton was frisked, then had gone to join Wilson and the two others questioning the defectors. One of the loyalists looked up, apparently saw the tractor highwheeling across the airstrip, and said to the others, "Come on. Come on." They hurried toward the Temple vehicles.

As belongings—trunks, suitcases and packs which represented the defectors' earthly possessions—were lugged to the larger plane for loading, the red farm tractor-trailer moved slowly toward us. About a half dozen men stood in its high-sided trailer. Their faces, young to middle-age, black and white, stared in cold hostility. The driver waved away the knot of a dozen or two Guyanese. Obediently the onlookers dispersed toward the apron in and around the metal shack, as though that thin steel would protect them from whatever was going to happen.

Catching up with Greg Robinson directly in front of the tractor, I said, "Be careful. I think we've got trouble." He looked me squarely in the eyes for an instant, as though gauging my seriousness. Then he glanced past me at the tractor-trailer. He nodded, but there was nothing more to say.

The proximity of the tractor, the stillness of the damp air, the uneasiness of the defectors who knew that some men there were security personnel—all these accelerated the loading of the larger Otter, which until then had been almost leisurely. Jackie Speier, still in her sundress and wedge-heeled shoes, urged everyone, "Come on. Get on the plane. Get on the plane." With clipboard in hand, she strutted to the foot of the Otter's stairway; a bunch of people followed, looking over their shoulders toward the tractor.

In that hurried moment, she asked me to help her frisk the defectors. As a reporter, I did not relish the idea of searching anyone for hidden weapons, but Ryan was not available at the moment, and haste seemed important. Speier searched the women in a sloppy and tentative manner, and I checked the men with about the same thoroughness. Gerald Parks and Harold Cordell volunteered pocket knives, which surprised me: I had assumed Temple members—unless on security—were prohibited from carrying weapons of any sort.

A second truck—not from Peoples Temple—pulled up dramatically. Dick Dwyer of the Embassy was in the front seat. Several blacks piled out, the young Guyanese constable among them, with his trusty shotgun. He was a welcome sight. It appeared that Dwyer had rounded up the constable and some friendly locals, perhaps also constables, to safeguard our final moments in Kaituma. Ryan embraced Dwyer and patted his shoulder, then Dwyer shook hands with the pilot near the cockpit while Greg Robinson looked on.

As the frisking went on, the young constable stood at port arms. The next moment, a burly dark man with a round head was cradling the constable's shotgun. I assumed that the man was an assistant. While I was occupied with searches, another hefty dark man, dressed like the constable's assistant in light shirt and dark trousers, came around the tail of the plane with a rifle or shotgun. Shortly thereafter, the constable and his assistant disappeared. Jim Cobb had recognized the second gunman as a Temple member and had told the constable trouble was going to start: we needed help.

It was almost 5:00 P.M. The sun was plunging toward the jungle horizons and softening the light. The forest was turning a dusty verdigris: the tall grass at the edge of the airstrip was gilded; the air was cooling off a few degrees at a time, as splotches of overcast passed. Patricia Parks, wearing striped blouse and slacks, had just boarded with her family. Most of the defectors were inside, and so were Guyana information officer Neville Annibourne and Concerned Relatives Beverly Oliver and Carol Houston Boyd. My back was to the tractor and I was about to frisk someone when the unmistakable sound of gunshots pierced the quiet. "Hit the dirt," yelled someone. "Hit the dirt." The opening few shots were distinct, then booms and pops and cracks overlapped, peppering the plane and the ground around us.

At the first shots, I spun around, crouched and scrambled for the far side of the plane, bending at the waist to clear the low-hanging belly. Bullets kicked up dirt and gravel; bodies were airborne and crawling and running in a frenzy of evasive, panicked motions that were more instinctual than rational. Out of the corner of my eye, I caught a one-frame image of what I mistakenly thought was the constable's assistant—aiming his shotgun at us and firing! "My God," I thought. "The police are shooting at us!"

Not knowing how I got there, I found myself midair, diving headlong to the other side of the plane, trying desperately to tuck my head behind the right airplane wheel—the only real protection on the ground. With my body extended above the ground and my arms ready to break my fall, I could hear screams of pain and fear and shouts and guttural losses of air. People were being hit all around me.

Just as I made a four-point landing, with my head low, I saw red explode from my left forearm just below the elbow. The slug ripped through my arm and apparently passed under my still partially airborne body. Before the pain could burn the message to my brain, a second round punched my wrist with such force that my left arm nearly crumpled beneath me and my watch was blown off. Simultaneously, what seemed like particles of gravel sprayed my upper body. At the sight of my own blood and in pain, I seethed, spitting out a curse of terror and disgust. In the next microseconds, I grasped that the shooters—government police, Temple members, whoever they were—were not simply trying to cripple the plane or kidnap the defectors or frighten us. They were killing us.

While bodies rolled and tumbled about me, some tripping, some scattering, I immediately pushed to my feet and in one motion took flight. Head down and legs pumping, I lengthened my stride, pursued by the cacophony of bullets and shotgun slugs. I saw no one else; I looked for no one else. I sprinted those forty yards with my eyes fixed straight ahead on one thing only—that tall, golden grass. From several yards away I dived headlong, as low and yet as far as my momentum would carry me.

Crashing into the brush, my arms and legs kept churning. Crawling as fast as I normally run, I mowed down the tall, brittle weeds, hardly glancing at my bloody arm. There was no looking back. I could not outrun, let alone outcrawl, a bullet. I fully expected someone to be following close behind me with a gun. Without so much as lifting my head, I bellied on all fours through thirty to forty yards of grass, then clawed a tunnel into a clump of dense bushes just at the edge of the jungle.

My head drummed as I curled up in a nest of foliage and knelt, completely still but for thumping heart and aching lungs. My pants quickly became drenched with blood to the knees, my wounds gushed. Perking my ears to every sound, every shot, I heard the rough beating of the Otter's engine. I tore off my wide leather belt. My first impulse was to make a tourniquet to keep from bleeding to unconsciousness or worse. Passing the belt end through the brass harness buckle, I instead cinched down the leather over the two long gouges in my forearm, hoping to stop the bleeding with directly applied pressure. But the loop of leather was not stemming the flow. On my second try I wrapped the leather over the wounds several more times, but the stiff leather kept slipping in my blood, refusing to be tightened. Finally, I positioned the belt correctly and pulled the loops tight with my teeth. My own blood tasted sickeningly salty.

The throbbing in my wrist caused me more pain but less concern and less bleeding. A glancing bullet or shrapnel had hit my wrist bone, splattered and embedded fragments in me.

The shooting sounded like shotguns and rifles rather than bursts from automatic weapons. The pops seemed relentless at first, then they faded and died. Silence. Then a few more shots—isolated, deliberate shots, booming, echoing. Final shots, accompanied by not a single, audible cry. Those last blasts made me sink deeper into my lair, hoping that my red shirt and white skin would not be spotted in the glossy green undergrowth. Did those solitary shots mean that gunmen were stalking survivors in the bush?

Thoughts buzzed in my head like hungry mosquitoes. The fear was raw yet dreamlike. My mind rebounded from one extreme to another—one instant I was the lone survivor, the next I was the only one wounded. Bleeding to death or being gunned down was merely the final manifestation of the terror. Being left behind in that jungle alone with nothing but my wounds and my hunters was the greatest dread, and so the steady beat of that airplane comforted me.

When the engine noise of the Temple tractor and truck had faded away, I realized that a Temple death squad had done the shooting. It was time to move. I hoped there would be an opening to dash for the plane, get aboard and fly out of hell.

In a low crouch, I pulled my way through the brush and grass, as stealthily as possible, until I could stand on my toes and see through the brittle foliage. I was about thirty yards from the apron, ready to drop again to the ground and retreat if any remaining gunmen should turn upon me. Walking alongside the plane was a heavyset black man in a green and yellow sweat shirt. My heart fell and my muscles tensed. Was he one of *them?*

When Bob Flick came into view, it dawned on me: the black man was Neville Annibourne in an unfamiliar outfit. Surveying the field, I took cautious steps forward. Bob, looking flushed and strangely subdued, turned to meet me. His eyes were dulled by emotion, his face a mask of shock. I asked him about Ryan, who was the closest figure, and most easily identified with his light bluish clothing and bushy gray hair. "He's dead," Bob said. It was then I noticed that the congressman's head was bloodied and a piece of flesh lay on the ground next to his face.

"Don?" I asked, seeing that the NBC reporter was on his back, boot toes straight up, his face a mess. I did not look closely. The answer was apparent before Bob said it.

At that moment I felt the reality of death—unmistakable, irreversible, senseless. I looked around and asked, "Where's Greg?"

Near the bullet-flattened left plane tire was a crumpled form in khaki and brown. Greg, my roommate, companion, photographer and new friend, lay face down, one cheek pressed to the gravel, his glasses askew. His left shoulder was tucked under his body as though he had fallen violently on it. A large but seemingly bloodless crater behind his shoulder looked like an exit wound. His cameras still hung around his neck, or were pinned under his body. "Greg, Greg," I called softly, shaking him lightly. I touched the side of his neck to feel for a pulse. Nothing.

Behind and beyond the tail of the plane, Bob Brown's body was sprawled, his brains blown out over his camera and the ground. But for his clothes and camera, he would have been unrecognizable. He too had been cut down working. Just prior to the gunfire, Don Harris had warned the NBC crew to spread out, and Bob Brown and Steve Sung had taken up a position out of the main line of fire. Brown had filmed the opening volleys, then one of the guns turned on him with a puff of smoke. He went down with a leg wound, while Steve Sung, attached to him by an electronic umbilical cord, was hit in one arm. Sung lay motionless, fighting pain as the seconds passed. A gunman had finished Brown, then someone fired from close range at Sung. The blast, partially deflected by his inch-thick leather shoulder harness, blew away part of his shoulder, throwing so much blood and flesh against his head that he appeared dead. His life rode on the knife edge of his capacity for pain. He endured it silently, without stirring. Once the death squad had left, he managed to stagger to the bush and collapse.

At the gangway, near Greg's body, I came upon Anthony Katsaris, flat on his back. Blood seeping from one nostril, his chest bloodied, a lung collapsed, he looked up at me with dazed and entreating eyes and gasped my name. He was fighting for breath. "Anthony," I said. "Stay still. You'll be all right. Just stay still. Be calm." Others, mainly defectors, carried him to the edge of the bush, where he would be less visible.

As a first priority, the injured were cleared from the airstrip so that they would not be exposed targets, even though this was an imperfect precaution. If the Temple death squad had raced back down the field, they could have killed all the nonambulatory and probably some of the rest, particularly those of us bleeding. In my head I calculated roughly how long it would take the Temple truck to cover several hundred yards of airstrip, then compared that to the time it would take us to thrash through thirty to forty yards of tall grass to the cover of jungle vines and trees. Those of us who could run and walk could probably make it, but there was another problem: after emerging from the airplane and from sections of nearby jungle we had congregated in such a way that the killers, returning for a final assault, could sweep down and corral us that much easier. My initial sense of relief, my elation at finding living comrades, turned into a probing uneasiness.

Some defectors were tending Steve and Jackie at an open spot in the tall grass about fifteen yards from Anthony. In excruciating pain, Steve was lapsing into delirium. He cried about losing his arm and rolled from side to side, digging his heels ever deeper into the moist earth. Jackie appeared more calm, almost sedate; she was probably in severe shock. Tears welled in her eyes but never seemed to fall. Several of us stood around the two, not really knowing the extent of their wounds, nor how to treat them. The defectors were the most helpful; all but a few had escaped injury and some knew first aid or had worked in the Temple clinic.

They had been the first to board the planes. Though I was not aware of it at the time, some on the Cessna had been wounded—and the small plane did not get off the ground. It sat far down the airstrip.

When the shooting had started, those on the large Otter had taken cover inside. Some of the children had had the presence of mind to pull up the gangway and lock the door. The one fatality on the plane was

Dale's mother, Patricia Parks, who was sitting near a window. She lay near the gangway now, on her back, her skull blown open, her face a death mask. Her youngest daughter Tracy had witnessed her sudden death. It seemed cruelly ironic that perhaps the most ambivalent of the defectors had been eliminated so ruthlessly.

The magnitude of Jackie Speier's wounds left me feeling helpless and nauseated. A slab the size of a frying pan had been gouged out of her thigh, and the flesh above and below the vicious gunshot wound was bridged only by an inch-wide strand of skin. The torn muscles quivered loosely. There were other wounds—to her arm and her pelvic area—though the blood on her dress and underwear obscured the damage. Her life seemed to be hanging by little more than that band of skin.

The extreme wounds around me made me all but forget my own. I stood by holding my belt bandage and watching the able-bodied make Jackie more comfortable with a headrest of rolled-up clothing.

"We've got to get out of here," I said to Bob Flick at one point.

"How are we going to do that?" he said, pointing at the flattened left wheel of the Otter.

"I'd be willing to take the risk," I said.

"With only one engine? One's shot out."

Carol Boyd found me and hugged me tearfully. We were happy to see each other alive. Then someone came up and pointed out that she was an excellent target with her white blouse and pants, and pale face. "Cover that up," she was told. But she had no other clothes, she said, rather frantically. Everything was back at the plane. It was only a short distance across the no-man's-land between the grassland and the Otter where the dead lay scattered like pieces of luggage. But walking out there seemed an invitation to any attackers who might be in hiding.

Moments later, the concern did not seem unwarranted. Carol and I were standing around Anthony Katsaris in the tall grass where he lay with helpless dark, wide eyes. Anthony, who like me had tried to hide under the Otter's right wheel, had been hit by one bullet, then had been shot in the back while trying to play dead. Despite his serious wounds and the drying blood chilling his body, he had enough character to ask about Greg.

"They're coming back," someone shouted. At the far end of the strip, Guyanese men, women and children scattered to both sides of the clearing, a flurry of white clothing and black limbs. Certainly they must have seen something alarming, maybe the Temple vehicles, we thought. Defectors and others in our party lit out for the undergrowth, expecting a truck or tractor bristling with guns to bear down on us. Panic-stricken, I looked at Carol, snatched her hand and said, "Let's go."

Leaving Anthony behind in the faint hope that he would not be found, we bounded into the tall grass. For a few seconds I thought of dragging Anthony with us, but moving him might kill him and us too. For the second time in minutes, survival was all.

Scurrying along in our path was a frightened native boy wearing nothing but knee shorts. "Can you lead us into the bush, to safety?" I said, stopping him: "We are Americans. We were attacked. We were unarmed. We won't harm you." With luck, this dark-skinned Amerindian boy would know every foot of the undergrowth within a mile or two of his home.

The urchin beckoned us to follow him into a deep shade that approached total darkness. At first the bush was simply thick, with tangled vines, fallen logs and a confusion of brush and brambles. The boy knifed easily through openings that thwarted us and sent us looking for easier paths. Soon he had pulled five to ten yards ahead of us.

"Slow down," I called out in a hoarse whisper. "Come here." He stopped and I pleaded, "Please take it slower." He was expressionless, out of physical reach. In a few moments the distance grew wider.

The leafy floor had dropped to soggier ground. Old stumps and logs lay rotting in blackwater bogs. The moldy stench of decomposing vegetable matter pressed downward, trapped to the ground by an umbrella of branches that allowed not a ray of sunlight to warm the forest floor. Our shoes sank ankle-deep. As we pulled them free with loud sucking sounds, the boy scooted ahead, then vanished. We stopped. We were alone. We listened. Voices—men's voices—rang out, but dozens of yards of greenery filtered out the accents and meaning. There was no telling if they were American or Guyanese, friend or executioner.

We crept a little deeper into the jungle, then squatted on a soggy log, listening. We needed to talk to each other, say anything, reassure one another. But the fear of missing the slightest noise caused us to hush, then fear of pursuers pushed us onward.

When the belt slipped off my wounds and the blood started flowing again, we were forced to stop. Once or twice Carol tried to help me fasten the belt, but the leather was saturated and too slick to work as a cinch any longer. The warm blood soaked through my corduroy pants and reached my skin. It turned surprisingly cold.

"Shhh." I cocked my head to one side. "Listen." We perked up our ears. For an instant, it sounded as if small airplanes, far off, were approaching. Then I looked at my arm and saw squadrons of mosquitoes homing in on my blood.

We had no handkerchief or bandanna, so Carol helped me wrap my arm with my shirt, then tie down the wad with a few turns of the belt. "Your dad asked me to help you out, and here you are helping me," I said.

Inches above the muck, we huddled together on a stump. Carol's pants were muddied and her shoes were soaked, and so were mine. The chill would cut to the bone once total darkness forced us to freeze our position. We had probably been in the jungle only a quarter hour, maybe not even that, yet it was too much already. It was entirely possible to become lost in there, permanently.

"I don't know about you," I said. "But I'd rather take my chances of getting shot. . . ."

"I know what you mean," Carol said.

We planned to work our way to a remote corner of the airstrip, then sneak out for a peek. Our slow steps, careful as they were, produced loud splashes. Snapping branches sent echoes far across the watery land. Each step deepened my fear that we might already have become lost and disoriented, or that we might be plunging once again into the gun barrels of our hunters.

Then suddenly a violent sound broke through the bush. An airplane engine! The engine of a small plane on the ground was revving. The pilot poured on throttle until it seemed the buzz would tear directly into us. Then white metal flashed overhead.

We looked at each other, terror-stricken. We had been left behind. "Let's go," I said. "Maybe it will circle back and we can wave it down."

We ran for the strip. Tripping and half crawling, we pawed through vines and thorny growth along a twisting, random path. All at once we saw a bright spot ahead like an opening in a storm front. We burst toward it. The forest was breaking. The leaves turned from black to emerald to pale green in the space of a hundred feet. A short embankment, a four to five foot rise of grassy brush, blocked our path. We scaled it, digging knees and toes and fingers. We bounded across the last thirty to forty yards of brush.

At the edge of the strip, gasping and wheezing, I looked to my right. The Cessna was gaining altitude as it soared toward Georgetown. Breathless, sweaty, my bare back and shoulders scratched, the frustration welled inside me. We were stuck. Stepping out from the brush, I took a gander to the left. Guyanese natives had gathered around the Otter and the bodies sprawled nearby. Some of our people stood at the edge of the strip. We were not alone after all—and the Temple gunmen had not returned.

As we approached, however, I could make out Larry Layton amid Dwyer, Dale Parks and some Guyanese men. They looked deadly serious and were pointing fingers. The last person I wanted to encounter now was Larry Layton, someone who still might be scouting for the killers.

My first inclination was to hang back, but my curiosity drew me forward. Dale Parks was accusing Layton of having tried to kill him, the pilot and several defectors in the small Cessna which had just taken off. A .38-caliber Smith and Wesson revolver with one unspent bullet was being shown around. Parks, a mild man, contended that Layton had started shooting as the death squad opened fire. He maintained that Layton had hit Monica Bagby and Vern Gosney—wounding them seriously—then missed the pilot, after which he turned his gun on Parks with a bang but no bullet. Surprised to be alive Parks had then struggled for the gun. Though an admittedly ineffectual fighter, he was twenty or thirty pounds heavier and a few inches taller than the weasellike Layton, and had managed to disarm him as they tumbled out of the plane. Parks then had tried to shoot his attacker, but the weapon would not fire, so he slugged him instead.

After a moment of discussion, a few Guyanese said, "We know how to take care of him," and they led Layton off, presumably to the police station. The gun was entrusted to Dwyer after the diplomat had made a pronouncement about bringing Layton to American justice. Dwyer's vow was pathetic under the circumstances: it was a long way to the nearest U.S. courtroom.

Nearby, Jackie Speier and Steve Sung were a few feet apart on the ground, calling to each other, entreating each other to hang on, to live. Steve was crying pitifully for his daughter and wife. "I love you," he would moan. "I didn't mean to do this to you. It was stupid. Stupid. Stupid." He was no longer talking about losing his arm but digging in his heels for a bout against death. Two fist-sized chunks of flesh were missing from his arm and shoulder. He was cold and trembling and, with each onslaught of pain, his boot heels cut deeper trenches in the ground. "Hang on, Steve," Jackie would call, and Steve would call back, "Hang on, Jackie baby. We're gonna make it."

"I'm cold," Jackie cried, so I fished a pair of pants from my pack and draped them over her. Flies and mosquitos had discovered the raw flesh, so we tried to fan them away. Local people stood by, offering suggestions, sending children for water and rum.

A wave of dizziness caused me to drop to my back for a minute. My pack under my head, I stared at the sky. Through the grass to one side I could see the bodies scattered round the plane; to the other side I could see the agonies of the wounded. My own wounds were paltry by comparison; I regained my feet.

A tape recorder—my tape recorder—was on the ground near Jackie. Krause said something about recording her in case something happened to us. "No," I said. "We've got better things to do." There seemed to be no point in demoralizing ourselves by preparing to die. A little later, however, Jackie did tape a message to her parents, to be delivered if she perished, along with the will she had prepared just before leaving the United States.

Two Guyanese men—one with a gallon cooler of water and one with a bottle of rum—came up to me. A long draft of water settled my bilious stomach and spinning head a little. The loss of blood and sweating had drained my body fluids. My thirst was overwhelming. "Take a big drink of this too," said the other Guyanese, handing out the golden rum. "Then we'll disinfect your arm."

The amber liquor went down like honey. I loosened my bindings, and they doused my wounds with rum. The burning had stopped by the time Carol found some bandages and taped my arm.

Dwyer, wounded in the buttock but ambulatory, soon was taking down a list of the casualties on a clipboard. Javers, Krause and I helped him account for the various people. We counted five dead, five severely injured, five ambulatory injured, including Krause with what looked like a gravel scratch on one hip. A half-dozen people were missing, in unknown condition.

By virtue of his title and experience in Guyana, Dwyer was gradually assuming the role of battlefield commander. He was the United States for all of us. A tall, graying fellow with lead now in his behind, he moved ponderously. A clipboard and khaki clothing were his only symbols of authority. He peered through his glasses, his brow wrinkling in worry. We asked: Had word reached Georgetown yet? When would help arrive? Dwyer said that the Otter pilot had sent a message during the shooting, but that did not console me; it seemed unlikely that a grounded plane could communicate through such jungle over such a long distance. Most upsetting was that the two pilots, for some reason, had taken only one of the seriously injured with them—Monica Bagby. We cursed them.

Apparently, the commotion at the other end of the strip had been a false alarm; the Temple gunmen had not returned to finish us. But, I found out, they had behaved curiously as they fled the strip, taking the time to circle the Cessna once with the tractor. Although they had shot out one of the Otter's engines, they did not touch the Cessna, nor harm its pilot, who foolishly stood by his plane asking what on earth was happening. They probably had ignored the pilot because Jones did not wish to harm any Guyanese. But why had the plane remained untouched? Did they hope to use it later? Would they come back?

As Dwyer spoke, I glanced over my shoulder at the Otter, which was listing toward its flattened left wheel. There was blood on the top boarding step; the luggage compartment where Krause and Jackie Speier had hidden after the initial assault was wide open. "Actually," Dwyer said, "I wouldn't count on anyone getting in here tonight for us." Our quizzical looks caused him to add, "I know the country well enough."

While Dwyer left to speak with local officials and soldiers, I stood alone for a moment, smoking a borrowed cigarette, in a cloud of disbelief. A dozen or more Guyanese moved about the plane, horrified, shaking their heads, bending over to look at the dead. A group of them came over to me. All were black or Amerindian men; most were in their twenties and thirties except for a hoary little man in a watch cap. Clearly, he was a respected elder.

A man in his mid-thirties, a stout-boned Afro of six feet one or so, asked me about the condition of my arm. "It'll be all right," I said. "The photographer with me was not so lucky."

They nodded sadly. They had seen Greg's body, and their sympathetic murmurings were extended to me. "Why? Why?" the elder cried. "What happened to you?"

It was the first of many times I would be asked to recount the attack, to reexperience the suddenness, the fear, the helplessness and ruthlessness. My breath was short, my emotions swelling in my chest, pushing the air from my lungs. "The Peoples Temple attacked us," I told him. "We were unarmed. We were here because of allegations about conditions at the Peoples Temple mission. We had been told there were beatings and that people were not free to leave."

My audience nodded, some quite solemnly as though they had heard or suspected the same.

"It's horrible," said the little man, throwing up his arms. "Why would they do this to you?"

"I don't know," I said. "I don't know." The frustration of not understanding clenched my fists, but curiously, I felt no bitterness or anger, just incomprehension.

"We were told that you, the group with the congressman, were CIA and were heavily armed," said one of the men.

So, Temple members had apparently told townspeople that we were an armed force of U.S. imperialists. Rather than scoff at this ridiculous notion, I took pains to project my sincerity. This was not a time to be silent, misidentified or misunderstood.

"I am a reporter," I explained. "I write stories. I don't carry a gun. I came here to find out whether the accusations about beatings and imprisonment and other inhumane practices at the mission were true. I am not CIA.

"And look at these people with me. Some are Temple members who wanted to escape. Others are relatives of Temple members. They simply came to assure themselves and their families that their loved ones were alive and well. Wouldn't you do the same for your brothers and sisters, and parents and children?"

These men in tired sandals and high-topped sneakers nodded understanding. Then, however, the tall, outspoken one—a certain Patrick McDonald Luke—pulled from his pocket a worn paperback about foreign intrigue and the CIA. Though my recollection of the conversation is imperfect, the exchange took on surreal and somewhat discomfiting overtones.

"Your government has not spoken out adequately against the governments of South Africa and Rhodesia," Luke said.

The request to justify U.S. foreign policy made my head swim all the more. "This is true," I agreed. "And not all of us agree with all of our government's positions and actions. In my short time in your country, I've seen that the same holds true here."

Luke, as he called himself, went on to a new topic, but I stopped him, not wanting to leave the wrong impression. Some of their questions were probing at the issue of racism. Again, I wondered whether the Temple had planted some accusations.

"Wait," I said, rising to my feet. "You asked me about South Africa and Rhodesia. I can't speak for all of the U.S. or the government or these people with me. But I can speak for myself. Those governments should be condemned. They shouldn't be allowed to stand on white minority rule. I believe in democracy. Regardless of color, a man should be free to go where he pleases and do what he pleases. His vote should be as valuable as the next man's. We are all human beings."

At that, the little man spoke his emotions. "We are with you. We will protect you. My God . . . how can they do this? We are all human beings." He was speaking on behalf of these compassionate men with barefoot children.

"Anything we can do, anything, will be done," he declared, jabbing with his index finger. "We can't stand by and do nothing when they have done this to you. We are in this together. Our families live so near." He pointed toward the simple houses on stilts dotting the jungle near the strip. "They are frightened of Peoples Temple."

At this offer, I felt as though I had just negotiated a Middle East peace treaty. We still were wounded, defenseless and frightened in the hinterlands, but we had allies, people who empathized with us enough to say, "We will fight to protect you if necessary."

His eyes flashing with fiery commitment, the elder offered his hand and I grasped it with both of mine and thanked him profusely. The others shook hands on our pact too. These people could have taken to the road for Matthews Ridge with their families; they could have huddled in relative safety in their houses. Brave or foolhardy as it may have been, they had chosen to stay and fight.

"Do you have any weapons?" I asked, not wanting to be caught defenseless again.

Their faces dropped. "There are a couple of shotguns," the elder said. "We will hide you. We must get you away from here. If the Peoples Temple returns, they will find you. Each one of you can be concealed in a different house."

"I think we'd prefer to stay together," I said, knowing we would feel even less secure in separate locations.

Pondering a moment, the elder said, "I see your point." Then he suggested that "the rum shop," a disco like Mike and Son's, would be the most suitable place. Lights and voices would arouse no suspicions there, and there would be plenty of refreshments and space.

Darkness cloaked the airfield, hiding us from snipers—and snipers from us. We had only one flashlight, and Dwyer had taken it. I joined a group at the metal shack where locals and others had moved most of our belongings. Ron Javers and I sat with our backs against the metal front wall, our butts on piles of gear. We wondered aloud why no help had arrived. At least a couple of hours had elapsed since the ambush; Dwyer had reported that the pilots had radioed ahead. And a local who called himself airport manager and closely guarded our rum supply told us repeatedly that he had radioed for help too. Assuming even the slowest scenario—that our rescuers had not been mobilized until after the Cessna reached Georgetown—some relief, some reinforcements, some message should have reached us by now.

We sadly lapsed into talk about Greg, the injustice of his death, the wastefulness. We still were mired in incredulity. "Hey, that won't help things," Bob Flick said. We changed the subject.

Rock-jawed and boulder-shouldered, Flick smoked feverishly. His forehead was knit even tighter than usual. He had lost two members of his crew—two friends—and the third was seriously wounded. He paced alone, a numb, sorrowful expression on his face. He was pessimistic about our chances of getting help in time.

Within fifteen uneasy minutes, Dwyer returned with a plan. The most severely injured would spend the night in the army tent with the four soldiers, near the disabled military plane. Since the soldiers were unwilling to defend the rest of us, we would hide at the rum shop, the nearby disco at the edge of town.

Using metal bedsprings as litters, some of our Guyanese friends carried the severely wounded toward the tent. Others hefted our gear. In the dark, I located Greg's camera bag beneath some baggage alongside the shed. I resolved to take out his equipment even if I could not bring out his body; his family would want it.

At a careful pace, we dragged ourselves down the field in darkness. Our local friends guided us, saying, "Come this way. This way," to keep us from straying into puddles. Suddenly from our right came a feline snarl and a creature—somewhat larger than a house cat—catapulted through our midst. No doubt, we had interrupted its nocturnal wanderings toward the nearby river.

We paused at the tent to watch the badly wounded eased inside on their litters. "No light," a soldier whispered. "No light." The soldiers did not want to become illuminated targets. They had also not wanted to be caught in the middle during the afternoon ambush. I felt some disdain for them; they had refused Bob Flick when he barreled down to them during the shooting and pleaded for help, then for the loan of a gun.

I asked myself: Why hadn't they helped us earlier? Apparently, in their elementary thinking, their orders to guard a disabled military airplane on a remote landing strip meant exactly that and nothing else. To exceed those orders, particularly when it involved leaving their posts and firing upon foreigners, would be inviting harsh discipline. Also, as they later said in their defense, how could they have sorted out the sides in those few minutes of confusion?

Their excuses left me unsatisfied. It seemed they at least could have fired a few bursts of automatic weapons into the air that might have prevented the gunmen from walking around and blasting heads and faces in cold blood.

Despite all my misgivings, the assortment of automatic weapons held by the soldiers created an air of security around the tent. I was not particularly happy to leave the soldiers, because we had no idea where the Temple gunmen had gone, nor what had transpired after we departed from Jonestown.

Just a few minutes after the knife attack on Congressman Ryan, Jim Jones had reflected on it with Charles Garry at the rear of the pavilion while Mark Lane escorted Ryan to the departing truck. Jones showed little remorse over the ugly incident. Had he, in fact, ordered the attack? If so, the outcome of the scuffle suggested that Sly either had been instructed to stop short of hurting Ryan or had disobeyed orders to kill him. Sly, a big and very strong man, easily could have cut Ryan ear to ear in the congressman's momentary confusion, but instead he had uttered threats, giving Ryan and others time to take defensive action. Did Jones really stage the incident to get the congressman on the truck with the rest of us marked for death? Did he want the congressman out of the way during the next climactic hours in Jonestown?

"The goddamn fool," Jones said. "Why did he come out here without security?"

Garry looked at the minister, shocked. "That would have been an affront to you," the attorney said.

From Garry's perspective at that moment, Sly's attack had marred what was otherwise a very successful two days. Garry was no closer than he ever had been to seeing through Jones. "This is the act of an agent provocateur," he told his client.

"No," Jones said. "People were just angry." Again, Jones was attributing the attack to some mystical collective will. This hardly jibed with Garry's impressions—the people milling around the pavilion had appeared bewildered, not angered. They had remained disciplined, obedient. Given their conditioning, chances were remote that anyone would have initiated an independent attack on Ryan—and Jones's subsequent treatment of Sly would tend to corroborate that.

Meantime, Marceline Jones came on the public address system and asked everyone to retire to their cottages and dormitories, to rest. Obediently, people dispersed toward their housing, not knowing what lay in store. Something in the wind—and Jones's peculiar statements—heightened Garry's apprehensions and caused him to turn to his rival, Lane, who had just returned from seeing off Ryan. "Let's you and I go for a walk," Garry said. The lawyers—the only nonmembers in the settlement—strolled toward the basketball court and cottages. On the way, Lane said, "I'll tell you something I don't want repeated." He too had seen disturbing signs; he revealed that Gerry Parks had asked for his protection while collecting his belongings. When alone with Lane, Parks had said that if people had felt free to choose, many more would have joined the Ryan party. The defector said that everyone was working long hours, conditions were terrible, and Jones was a tyrant.

As the two lawyers talked, Jack Beam and Jim McElvane came directly to them, apparently to check out their reaction to the situation. "What do you think of this?" McElvane asked. Garry did not yet understand the gravity of the situation. "I think you've got a beautiful place," he said. "But it seems to me there should be more open discussion so people can express opposition."

"There's a suggestion box," said McElvane.

They were interrupted by another announcement over the loud-speakers: "Everyone report to the pavilion immediately." People who were ordered to quarters just a few minutes earlier reemerged from buildings and streamed in droves toward the central structure. As Beam and McElvane brought the lawyers to the school building on orders from Jones, the group converged with this procession of rank-and-file members. The people who knew the attorneys smiled; some quipped, making light of the defections, "Yeah, we're all defecting."

In the school building, the lawyers found Jones seated on a bench, with Tim Carter and Harriet Tropp nearby. Flanked by their escorts, Lane and Garry stood before the minister. Things had changed; the counselors were being moved and ordered about, though in firmly polite fashion. The emperor had reascended his throne.

"All is lost," he told the attorneys. "Every gun in this place is gone." Jones indicated that some members—supposedly unprompted—had taken Temple guns and gone after the Ryan party. He also announced that three of those who had left with Ryan—Joe Wilson, Gerald Parks and Larry Layton—were not defectors after all. They had gone to kill. Even now, Jones manipulated the facts: security chief Joe Wilson had not left with Ryan but had boarded at the gates, a fact Jones somehow knew; and Gerald Parks's negative comments to Lane had made it quite clear that he was truly a defector. Violating Lane's confidence, Garry called Jones on one part of his lie; he revealed what Parks had said to Lane.

Jones shrugged off the new information and went on trying to convince the lawyers of Layton's violent intentions. Again Jones spoke as though misguided loyalty and uncontrollable dismay had provoked his followers. It was his "intuition" that told him of the violence ahead: "When Larry hugged me, he said, 'You'll be proud of me.' "

By this point, hundreds of people had thronged to the pavilion. Just a few yards from the school building, they awaited further orders. They had nothing to do, no one to address or entertain them. This was a rare vacuum in such a highly structured community. Taking note of them, Garry asked Jones, "Shouldn't someone say something to all those people?"

"Let them think," said Jones.

Maria Katsaris entered the school and called to Jones, "I want to talk to you a second." Jones went over to her for just a moment, then came back to the attorneys. He did not share her message with them; they were pawns now, not advisers.

"Charles, you and Mark will have to leave. People are angry with you. Your lives will not be safe. You have to go to East House." The impassively expectant people in the pavilion did not appear upset with the lawyers for bringing Ryan; perhaps Jones was. Even now he had to make an excuse to send the attorneys away from his staging area. He did not wish to be inhibited by outsiders; he did not want them to witness his final sermon; he probably wanted to spare them.

Behaving queerly, Jones walked a dozen feet or so away and stooped over to pick up an empty cigarette package. Then he dropped it into the trash, as though litter control remained important.

A few minutes later, the attorneys arrived at East House as ordered. Their escort McElvane split off toward the basketball court. "Jim," Garry called after him. "Let me know what they are gonna do." Garry was disturbed.

"I will," McElvane promised.

To their surprise, the lawyers found that Don Sly, of all people, had been dispatched to watch over them. With his cut hand bandaged, he sat on the steps to East House. It was a curious turn of events; the man whom Jones had agreed to turn over to the local police now was guarding the lawyers.

"What happened to you, Don? Flip out?" asked Garry, referring to the attack on Ryan.

"In all deference to you, Mr. Garry, I don't want to discuss it."

Time passed. The lawyers saw about eight men file out of a nearby building lugging numerous guns and a couple of heavy ammunition boxes. Sly called to them as they headed toward the pavilion. "When do you want me to come up there?"

Garry and Lane looked at each other, petrified by the sight of guns and the dark mood. Outside, moments later, their fear became immediate at the approach of two shirtless gunmen named Johnson—Poncho from San Francisco, and another from Los Angeles, both known to Garry because they had attended the San Quentin Six trial. The pair halted at East House, rifles ready, then sent Sly to the pavilion.

"We're gonna commit revolutionary suicide," the gunmen announced.

Lane asked if there was not some alternative.

One Johnson replied, "We'll die to expose this racist and fascist society."

That "we" hung ambiguously in the air. Lane thought fast. "Well, Charles and I will write your story."

That appealed to the gunmen; someone needed to stay behind to tell "the truth" about Jonestown. Either the men had not come to execute the two lawyers or had been dissuaded from doing so. Happily they embraced Garry and Lane.

In the background, Lane and Garry could hear Jones's voice and sporadic yelling from the pavilion. There was talk of death; periodically, one woman's voice rose above the rest. She was arguing against whatever Jim Jones wanted to do. Others were shouting her down. In this climate, the lawyers were not safe.

"How do we get out?" Lane asked the two gunmen.

"Go through the bush," the gunmen said. Apparently it would be dangerous to walk out to the main road to Port Kaituma. The two Johnsons explained how the lawyers could work their way along the perimeter of the camp. Minutes later, Garry and Lane bade the two a final farewell then headed toward the jungle, running and panting. Over rough terrain, through gullies and brush, they went as fast as their stamina could take them. It was hundreds of yards up a hill toward the edge of the dense jungle. With his heavy briefcase, Garry struggled to keep up with the younger lawyer, who also had a lighter tote bag. They heard Jones's voice cry, "Mother mother mother mother!" This was followed by what sounded to Garry like three shots. The lawyers did not even comment, they were running so hard. Garry was completely out of breath.

At approximately six o'clock in Georgetown, Sharon Amos—apparently unable or unwilling to make contact with the San Francisco temple over the radio—rushed frantically up the outside stairs of Lamaha Gardens on her way to the telephone inside. It was, she knew, the most critical message she would ever deliver. The White Night was on, this time for real. If Peoples Temple was not to be allowed to live in its own fashion, it would nevertheless choose its own way of dying. The time had come. It was 1:00 P.M. San Francisco time when Sandy Bradshaw answered the phone at the Geary Street temple. Amos told her to get out the code books.

"There's been an incident," Amos said. "Some people have gone to see Mrs. Frazier. Others will be going to see Mrs. Frazier."

Bradshaw did not need to consult the code book to know that "Mrs. Frazier" meant death.

Amos continued: "Do what you can to even the score. I'm going out to find George." "George" was the Temple name for Tim Stoen, the traitor of traitors.

The always intense Sharon Amos was almost beside herself. The choice of Bradshaw was not accidental: the former probation officer not only had bought several weapons, she also knew how to use them.

In San Francisco, Bradshaw staggered back to the radio room, looking as if she had seen a ghost. She told Jean Brown and Tom Adams what she had heard. There was no longer any doubt that the worst must have happened. Had the CIA or some other equally malevolent force finally achieved its goal of destroying the best man and the best movement they had ever known? Was there any hope of saving Jonestown? As bleak as Amos's call had been, she had relayed no details or explanations, just word of an incident that warranted deaths in the settlement and revenge outside. The situation was still too foggy to be acted on immediately. They needed more information.

Earlier, Stephan Jones had been present in the Lamaha Gardens radio room when his father's voice came over the airwaves, shouting, pleading, imploring. "Please, please, take care of everyone there." Jones not only wanted Stoen and the enemies dead; he wanted every member in San Francisco and Georgetown—maybe two hundred or more people —to kill themselves. Stunned, Stephan asked Paula Adams and Debbie

Touchette, the regular Lamaha radio operators, if Jones had demanded such things on the radio before. They nodded yes. "Did he call it off?" Stephan pressed. Again the answer was yes. "Then wait," he ordered. "We'll see what happens." Stephan was stalling. Again, doubts and uncertainties swirled in his consciousness. Was this the real thing or more of his father's tricks? Had Jones gone too far now to pull back? If so, could Stephan resist the pressure to follow his father over the edge? Could the nineteen-year-old afford to sit tight and hope for a way out? Hold on, he told himself. Keep hoping.

Upstairs, Sherwin Harris had just sat down to dinner with his daughter Liane and with Sharon's two other children, Christa and Martin. Harris and his daughter were discussing how they would spend the following day together. When Sharon came upstairs in the middle of dinner, about six thirty, Harris noticed that she appeared very distracted. And he was surprised that his ex-wife readily agreed to his request to see Jonestown. His daughter Liane had been resisting the idea.

After Sharon Amos disappeared for a while, she came back again to tell Liane to take a call in another room. Harris had not heard the phone ring, so he presumed it must be a radio call. Liane followed her mother downstairs to the radio room, where Stephan and the others were standing around, still shaking from Jones's final message.

"Liane, we may have to die," Sharon said.

"Okay, fine," Liane said, without hesitating. To Stephan, it appeared that Liane was putting up a dedicated front. Sharon told her to go back upstairs and send her father away from the house. Somehow composing herself, Liane returned to the dinner table and resumed her conversation with her father. It tapered off quickly. About 7:00 P.M., she announced that she was tired and excused herself to go to bed. Though this abrupt end to their reunion dinner seemed odd, Harris went downstairs to call for a cab back to the Pegasus.

Meanwhile, Stephan Jones became more desperate than ever for information on what had happened in Jonestown. He decided to go over to the Pegasus. First, he wanted to find out what Tim Jones and Johnny Cobb had discovered there; second, he simply needed to get out of that house. He was scared to the bottom of his soul.

Before leaving, he said to Sharon, "Don't tell anyone in the house what's going on." To Lee Ingram he said privately, "Keep an eye on Sharon," though Ingram did not have to be told. Stephan got into a rented car with Mike Touchette and Mark Cordell, ignoring Sherwin Harris, who was standing by the rain gutter waiting for his cab.

Harris was peeved that they had not offered him a ride to the hotel. Soon, however, his thoughts turned to pleasant things. He was excited that he would be able to spend the entire next day with Liane, comforted that Sharon had given permission for a Jonestown visit.

It was nearly eight o'clock and already dark as Stephan Jones pulled up to the Pegasus. Johnny Cobb and Tim Jones had been talking in a friendly fashion to the Concerned Relatives. As Stephan walked into the airy lobby, he spotted Tim Stoen, sitting on a bench outside the small bar. Seated next to him were Grace, and Steve Katsaris. Stoen looked up at the tall young man, and they greeted each other nervously. Stoen knew nothing about any trouble. Their conversation quickly heated up:

"Do you know what you're doing?" Stephan asked him. "Do you know what could happen?"

"I want my son," Stoen replied, thinking he was hearing the same old Temple warnings. "I don't care what they tell you. I drive a Volkswagen. I don't have much money. I don't work for the CIA. I work hard."

Stephan was insistent. "Do you know what could happen?" he repeated.

Stoen was equally firm. "I want my boy. I'll do anything to get him. I want my son. I have a court order. If the congressman doesn't get him, I'll be out there in a few days with the GDF."

"Why are you going to cause all those deaths?" Stephan demanded, incredulous that Stoen could be so stubborn that he would risk everything for one child.

"Do you mean he'll kill everybody?" Stoen asked in a shocked voice. "He's a madman."

"I know that," Stephan said, taking a chance.

"I didn't know you felt that way," said Stoen, amazed that Jones's own son would make such an admission.

A tearful Bonnie Thielmann interrupted, telling Stephan she was worried about him and his mother. "I'm fine," he replied, trying to brush her off. "I can't stay. I gotta go."

On his way out of the lobby, Stephan shouldered past journalist Gordon Lindsay, too, then joined the other basketball team members in their car.

While Stephan was at the Pegasus, the Guyana police drove up to the Lamaha Gardens house. They had heard—probably by radio message from the northwest—of a shooting involving Peoples Temple, so they wanted to check the Georgetown house. When the police drove up, Ingram left Sharon Amos alone and went out to talk to them.

The sight of the police panicked Amos. She immediately assumed that her hated ex-husband had called them, that Jim Jones's dire prediction finally had come to pass: they were after her children. The time had come for her to carry out her part of the White Night.

Sharon went back upstairs with Liane and found her two other youngsters seated in the living room playing cards with Stephanie Jones, a nine-year-old girl. Christa, eleven, and Martin, eight—Sharon's children by another father—were Georgetown fixtures, frequently seen trailing after their determined mother as she made her public relations rounds. Martin was the precocious boy who had resisted taking the punch during a suicide rehearsal.

With characteristic determination, Sharon Amos crossed through the living room to the kitchen, where she searched the drawers for a large, sharp butcher knife. Clutching it to her bosom, she walked back through the living room and motioned for Christa and Stephanie to follow her. "Come here, Martin," she added. The kids followed her to the white-tiled bathroom at the end of the long corridor. Just before she turned into the hallway she motioned to Chuck Beikman, Becky's husband, to follow her. As the person in charge at Lamaha, Amos spoke with the authority of Jim Jones; Beikman obeyed her.

As she led her three children into the shower, Amos was shaking and uncontrollably nervous. She turned to Beikman, saying she was going to kill the children before the police took them. She pulled Christa to her, and holding her by the face, she slit her throat. Christa fell screaming to the floor, her legs kicking up spasmodically. Beikman watched helplessly. He could not, or would not, interfere. Sharon then reached for Martin, who began to slink away from her, but she caught up with him, held him by his nose and mouth, and slit his throat, too. Beikman froze as she ordered him to kill Stephanie; he administered only a superficial cut and let her drop to the floor. Amos, meanwhile, turned to her daughter Liane and handed her the knife. "Here," she cried, "you've got to do me," and as Liane cut, Sharon urged, "Harder, harder." She took Liane's hands, and with her own hands guiding them, managed to complete her own suicide, murmuring, "Thank you, Father," as she collapsed to the floor. Liane then turned the knife on herself. With some difficulty she slashed her own throat, before she fell convulsing to the floor.

People in the living room first heard Christa say, "Oh, Mama." Then came the screams. Calvin Douglas, the forward on the basketball team, bolted from the card table and raced down the hall. When he threw open the bathroom door, Calvin found three bodies in a deep pool of blood. Amos's oldest daughter was still barely alive; her body twitched, the knife still in her hand. There was hope for little Stephanie, with a relatively minor cut on her neck. So Douglas snatched her up and whisked her to the living room, where someone attended to her. The whole slaughter had taken just a couple of minutes.

During this time, close to 9:00 P.M., Stephan Jones was driving back to Lamaha Gardens from the Pegasus. He was crying. As he got out of the car, he heard an airplane pass overhead. "Please, let that be the Congressman," he prayed to himself. There was no reason for optimism any longer, but Stephan was grasping for hope, trying to push back the awful inevitability. As he stepped inside the front door at Lamaha, he knew all hope was gone. He heard the news: "Sharon has just killed herself and her children."

"What?" Stephan cried, incredulously. His mind raced as he ran to the bathroom. "Oh, oh, God," he moaned as he saw Christa, cut from ear to ear, her blood mingled with her family's on the white tile of the shower. He could not bear to look at little Martin's lifeless body. Sharon was curled up, out of her misery, behind the door. Liane, up on her elbows, shaking violently, collapsed as he looked in. "God, call an ambulance," he cried. But he knew it was over. People in the rest of the house were becoming hysterical.

Stephan went into shock. He wanted to fall asleep. His eyelids were closing involuntarily. After a moment of complete denial, of blacking out the horrifying bloody image in his mind, a wave of total hopelessness passed over him. Every other crisis lacked finality; something always had provided a way out. But these people were dead.

Fortunately, Lee Ingram had the presence of mind to call the San Francisco temple, twice to be sure, to tell them not to heed Sharon Amos's White Night message.

Archie Ijames happened to be in the temple parking lot in San Francisco that Saturday afternoon when the temple custodian rushed up to him and declared, "They've shot Ryan." As they sat stunned in the parking lot and listened to the news on a portable radio. Archie knew immediately that Peoples Temple was finished. There was no point in spinning fantasy scenarios of how to recoup from this disaster. For him, it was the final betrayal by Jim Jones. It was the end of everything.

The top leadership frantically gathered in the financial room upstairs. For hours, they tried futilely to reach Georgetown for more news. They could not know that Guyana police had already sealed off the Lamaha Gardens house and seized control of the telephone there, permitting only Lee Ingram's call to San Francisco to cancel the White Night message.

The night dragged on with horrifying suspense. Every one of them had relatives in Jonestown. Were they dead or alive? If they were alive, why didn't they call or somehow get in touch with their loved ones? The San Franciscans knew there might be a massive reaction, maybe a mass suicide. They could only hope some people would be able to escape.

At mid-afternoon Saturday, congressional committee staffer Jim Schollaert took a cab with Howard Oliver to Timehri Airport to greet the Ryan party. Although the planes were running late, Oliver had wanted to come along to be there when his wife—and possibly his two sons—disembarked. While the two men bided their time at an auxiliary terminal, an Otter landed. But it was the wrong plane.

Around 5:00 P.M., curious as to whether airport officials had heard anything of the Ryan party's flights, Schollaert and Oliver went into a control room. The Chinese man who headed the airport was on the radio, saying excitedly to someone, "Stay calm. Stay calm! Close the door! Close the door!" Schollaert did not realize immediately that he was overhearing the airport official talking with the Otter's pilot during the ambush at Kaituma. When he learned there had been trouble, Schollaert sent Oliver back to the Pegasus by cab to wait there with the rest. He spared Oliver the news, because he was not in the best of health.

Soon, airport officials notified Prime Minister Forbes Burnham. U.S. Ambassador John Burke was summoned immediately to the prime minister's residence. By 6:15 P.M. Embassy officials knew there had been a shooting at the airstrip. They told Schollaert, who tried without success to contact the congressional committee chief of staff in Washington, D.C. But no one at the Embassy contacted the Concerned Relatives staying at the Pegasus Hotel, to warn them that their lives might have been in danger. Over two hours later, at about 8:30 P.M., Sherwin Harris bounded into the spacious hotel lobby, bubbling with hope after his visit with his daughter at Lamaha Gardens. The relatives there were, in general, expectant, happy to hear that some defectors were coming out with Ryan, hopeful that someone could corroborate Debbie Blakey's story.

Within fifteen minutes, however, the mood dissolved. The hotel manager began calling the Concerned Relatives in to talk to him, one by one. With two police inspectors present, the manager told the relatives that he could not divulge what had happened, but that the relatives, for their own safety, could not leave their rooms. If they needed to leave the hotel for something important, they were to notify the management. After Grace Stoen and several others were called in, the process collapsed; the relatives spread the word among themselves, and their anxiety climbed to new heights. In their worst nightmares, they could not have visualized what was happening at that very moment in the jungle.

A few minutes later, Sherwin Harris was called to talk with the manager and the police; it was a special message. His ex-wife and her children—including his daughter Liane—had been found murdered, their throats slit. It hit him with the force of megatons; within an hour, his mood had traveled from elation to horrified despair. Now these mingled suddenly with fear. Madness had been unleashed. He quickly made two phone calls to the States to his family: he ordered his daughter to leave their house immediately and to hide; he asked his brother to protect his surviving children. There was no way to know who might be next, who might be targeted for revenge.

The Concerned Relatives gathered in Steve Katsaris's room to await further news. They had been deliberately trying to keep calm since 6:00 P.M. when they heard that the Ryan party might be staying overnight in the jungle; they had thought all along the situation might be explosive, and now they knew something was amiss. Bit by bit, they learned of the terrible events, each revelation worse than the last. No one really broke down; they held each other up, braved it together.

From Schollaert and from a California relative of Katsaris, they heard Leo Ryan had been shot. By phone, reporter Gordon Lindsay exchanged information with reporters in the United States. When they heard that Ryan and others had been killed, they were stunned and frightened, helpless to do anything to save their loved ones. They were tortured through the night with uncertainty, wondering, "What is happening in Jonestown?" That morning Howard Oliver suffered a stroke.

It was a normal slow, Saturday afternoon at the *San Francisco Examiner*. Weekend editor Dexter Waugh had just hung up the phone when another one rang. Assistant city editor Fran Dauth was typing a memo while waiting for a story from Tim Reiterman in Guyana. There was plenty of time to make the last deadline for Sunday's paper. Waugh motioned Dauth to the phone.

It was Joe Holsinger, Leo Ryan's administrative assistant. There had been a shooting at the airstrip near Jonestown, he said. Ryan and others, possibly nine or ten, were dead. Dauth felt an electric bolt shoot through her. By coincidence, city editor Jim Willse called in at that moment from the Cal-Stanford football game in Berkeley; Tim Reiterman's parents were attending the Big Game too, oblivious to the trouble.

Reporters from all over the country immediately began calling for information. A long—agonizingly long—night of waiting had started. Nancy Dooley, Reiterman's collaborator on some Temple stories, raced to the office to write the main story. Dauth had already begun writing trip background: "The doomed trip began Monday." Reporter John Jacobs said he had a bad cold and a car that would not start. Then the impact of Dauth's call hit him. He took a cab to the office, not knowing this was the first night of a story he would work on for the next three years.

Unlike some other big stories, this one was no fun. Everyone hoped against hope that neither Reiterman nor Greg Robinson would be listed among the dead or injured.

By 8:00 P.M., Jim Willse and photo editor Eric Mescauskas left for Guyana. As official representatives of the *Examiner*, they could claim bodies, if need be. At 1:00 A.M. Sammy Houston called the paper with a tape he had just made of a phone conversation with his wife, Nadyne, who was at the Pegasus. Radio and television were carrying the news of Ryan's death to millions, and the *Examiner* replated its front page as often as necessary, three times for the final edition. The *Washington Post* called the *Examiner* for help. Their man Krause was incommunicado with the Ryan party, and there was nothing in their clippings about Peoples Temple. There was still no news about Reiterman or Robinson. Around 3:00 A.M. word came that the last unidentified victim had been wearing three cameras. The real chill set in. The final deadline passed, and still people clustered in the news room.

Shortly after 5:00 A.M., 10:00 A.M. Guyana time, reporter Pete King rolled a sheet of paper into his typewriter and called the Guyanese Ministry of Information, for what was perhaps the hundredth time in the past twelve hours. "I'm afraid I have some bad news for the *Examiner*," said Minister Shirley Field-Ridley. "Greg Robinson is dead."

King's mind stopped. He could not think of the next question. People gathered around his typewriter. He had spelled "dead" as "died."

People began to cry. Greg's friend, Bob McLeod, went into the darkroom to develop an obituary photo of Greg. Managing editor Dave Halvorsen called Greg's parents, and Mr. Robinson broke down on the phone.

It was only a few minutes' walk from the massacre site to the Port Kaituma "rum shop." The dirt roadway around the building was dark. We straggled along a short walkway, then took a few steps up and passed through a doorway. I carried my gear and Greg's camera bags down a short corridor that opened into a small dance floor. White wooden tables ran along two black-painted walls like those at "Mike's disco" crosstown. The phosphorescent graffiti took on the ghoulish cast of Halloween decorations. Oddly, someone had painted two-foot-tall phone numbers as decorations, though there were no phone lines stretching to the town. Behind the bar climbed several rather bare shelves of local rum and whiskey and imported British gin. There were no stools at the counter, no brass railing, no gut-sprung bartender, only a dark-haired, olive-complexioned little woman who had just stepped out of the kitchen to the left.

After taking drink orders, Bob Flick and I bellied up to the counter for beer and rum and Pepsi. Our Guyanese friends sat down to drink among us, and for the first time we could talk in relative comfort and with a measure of security.

Dwyer came in and posted himself in the middle of the room. With a clipboard tucked under his arm, he announced that help was on the way but might not reach us until morning. Either this announcement or a later one included mention of helicopters, troops and evacuation planes; it was impossible to be sure what was arriving or when. Taking a relatively strong leadership role for the first time, the low-keyed diplomat stated that the uninjured would care for the nonambulatory in shifts, two per shift.

Bob Flick seemed to me the most resourceful of the survivors, so I was happy when we took the second watch together. A local man escorted us back to the wounded via an overgrown path. As we set foot on the strip, lights from a truck bathed us momentarily, then went out. We were recognized before we had a chance to use the password.

We dropped to the ground near the tent so we could hear our charges if they called for us. Among the clouds, stars stood out in sharp swirls. The soldiers loitered in the dark a few paces behind us, between the tent and the airplane. One was fiddling a little too frantically with the jammed action of his automatic rifle. The others offered advice. The scene was not comforting.

Nursing a Banks beer, I folded my arms against the slight chill of my water- and blood-dampened clothes. We speculated quietly about our immediate future, wondering aloud whether we would survive the night. I felt more secure with modern weapons close at hand, but Bob had little confidence in the Guyanese crew guarding us; he thought they would probably run into the bush at the first sign of attack.

A moaning brought us to our feet. "I'll go," I said. Once inside the cramped tent, I could not see my patients, so I had to borrow a flashlight from a soldier. The insanity of our situation struck home at that moment. Four persons in serious and perhaps critical condition lay before me, someone with virtually no first-aid experience. Soldiers in war zones received better care, I thought. All were in pain, if not shock. Our stock of medicine consisted of a few aspirin, an undefined "pain-killer" or two, rum and water from rain barrels or the river.

In that rank-smelling air of rotting flesh and sweaty canvas, the four slept or stared into the darkness. When they heard me groping around, new requests were whispered out loud. Anthony Katsaris, bathed in sweat, felt chilled and thirsty. I pulled his clothes and blankets more tightly around him and brought him a drink of water, managing to spill much of it on him. Steve Sung was sleeping soundly, thanks to the rum he had quaffed right after the shooting. For a moment he looked to be dead, but his breathing became audible when I nudged him. Vern Gosney, the one Temple defector among the group, had been wounded in the back; he needed water and a change of position; I helped him sit up for a moment so he could breathe easier.

Near the front of the tent, Jackie Speier called my name. As I knelt to feel her clammy forehead, she murmured, "It's hurting. My arm is hurting." Her black hair was tangled and matted with sweat. She was in bad shape and knew it.

"There's one pain pill here at your head," I said. "Just one. Do you really need it now? There's just one."

Her breath seething with pain, she sighed, "No. I'd better hold off. There's some rum." A bottle was on its side next to her litter. Propping up her head with one hand, I poured as she gulped. I stopped pouring when it started dribbling down her neck.

Back outside, Bob and I folded our legs and talked in low voices while keeping watch. Any time a truck bounced down the road toward us, the soldiers snapped to the ready. Fortunately, each time the intruder was only a local resident. The natives were taking Dwyer back and forth from the town communications center to the rum shop, and patrolling the village.

After a bit—I could not tell exactly how long, having no watch— I was relieved from my post. My escort back to the disco was the curly-haired young man who claimed to be airstrip manager, the one who assured us that the Guyanese Defense Forces would drop from the sky with rescue planes and helicopters within minutes. After calling for rum to treat the wounded, he had appointed himself guardian of the liquor.

After he and another Guyanese with the same thick booze-garbled accent tried to steer me across town for a party at the other disco—the one run by a Temple sympathizer—I demanded that we turn around. Within a few minutes, we barged into the "safe" disco. A few handfuls of Guyanese occupied the tables. Without Americans, the crowd might have been a crew of Saturday night regulars, except that music was not wailing and not a smile broke in laughter. Under one cocktail table sat Greg's gear, which I had asked my companions to watch closely. Irritated and a little worried that something might have been lifted, I put the bag on my shoulder, ordered a bottle of rum for my escorts, then struck up a conversation with a few locals.

One man, of East Indian or Amerindian extraction, told me he had served in the country's army as a colonel until two years ago. "When the army gets here, I may have to put on my old uniform again," he joked.

"Do you have any guns?" I asked again.

"One shotgun is on the way," someone said. "Maybe two."

In the kitchen, I found Krause and Javers sitting pensively, elbows on the table. The lady of the house, the petite woman who tended bar, was heating water on a burner near the back door. The door was equipped with a small slide lock. Still, at least there was a rear exit.

The defectors and the Concerned Relatives, strangers thrust together, were sprawled together on mattresses and bare floors in two rooms decorated simply with a mobile and print fabrics. In the dark, some peered out at us expectantly, others pretended to sleep.

As we talked in the kitchen, some locals entered with a pounding of feet that put everyone on alert. One carried a shotgun, one a machete. The woman loaned them a couple of knives, including an eighteen-incher probably used to whack off coconut husks. It was the kind of arsenal a worried homeowner would keep to ward off an occasional burglar, not what you would want to battle a small army. If it came down to fighting, our only hope was that the sound of gunfire and our shelter—flimsy though it was—would buy us time to scatter into the jungle.

Once Javers, Krause and I had got some of the fretting out of our systems, we took our notebooks and with help from the defectors compiled a list of the casualties, missing and uninjured. As things stood, one out of every six people in the party was dead. One out of three was wounded. A half-dozen people were missing somewhere in the bush, condition unknown.

Jim Cobb and several of the defecting children were among them. Of Cobb, Bob Flick had said, "If anyone will make it, he will." Sixteen-year-old Tommy Bogue was also missing, wounded in the leg it turned out. His father was not worried: "He knows the bush. He'll lead out those other kids who ran with him." I was not so sure that terrified children or adults, possibly wounded, could withstand much exposure and keep their wits about them in the dark jungle, but I said nothing to deflate anyone's optimism.[73]

When the list was done, we reporters made a pact—no one would interview anyone for the time being. Keeping quiet was important, and none of us was in the mood to debrief the fearful, tired and grieving bodies in the adjoining rooms. Our own exhaustion was warded off by coffee which the lady of the house, Elaine, made Guyana-style—strong with a generous pour of milk. She also served us Pepsi and ice water from a long freezer used as a cooler.

This petite hospitable woman with a wispy, dark-eyed daughter who hid shyly behind her apron expressed sympathy for our plight. Apparently Amerindian or East Indian, she maintained an aura of peace and quiet determination. She survived the night gracefully, unfazed by the American strangers packed in her bedrooms and lounging around her kitchen, smoking, drinking and talking.

Again I was moved by the generosity of these rural people, who had exposed themselves to possible revenge for strangers. We did not have to ask them for the things we obviously needed, and they responded with ungrudging willingness when we asked for less apparent things. On the table before us was a large bottle of aspirin, the sum of our medical stash. Wounds caused Javers and me some discomfort, and we were not sure how seriously hurt we were or whether infection had set in.

"Is there a doctor in the town?" someone asked.

"There's a dispensary," Elaine said apologetically. "The woman there is afraid to come."

Dale Parks, short hair and long sideburns aging him a few years, leaned around the room partition, then came in. Explaining that he had worked as a medical therapist at University of California Medical Center in San Francisco, and as an assistant to Larry Schacht in Jonestown, Parks inquired about our wounds.

Setting to work, he bandaged Javers's shoulder, which was pierced by a single bullet wound—a small clean hole with no sign of an exit. The bullet would have to come out eventually. Parks turned to Elaine. "Do you have any merthiolate, iodine, alcohol?"

"No," she said.

"There's rum," someone said.

"How 'bout vodka?" Parks said. "It's almost straight alcohol."

Elaine shook her head. "We have gin."

"That'll have to do."

After bandaging Javers, Parks cut and pulled the crude wrappings from my arm. It was a strange feeling—one Temple member treating wounds inflicted by another. There was no more gauze, so he asked for sheets, cloth, anything. Elaine went into the next room and brought back filmy white curtains that she no doubt prized. When my arm was bandaged and the time was right, I took Elaine aside and slipped another twenty-dollar bill into her hand. She attempted to give it back, but I insisted. She tried again. "Please," I said.

"But water costs nothing," she protested.

One of our guards, the one with the military training, joined us at the kitchen table. Cigarettes were passed around. Puffing deeply, he related a little about his military career, the various weapons he had learned to use. And, loyal to his old employer, he expressed confidence that the Guyanese Defense Forces would reach us in the nick of time. "It won't be much longer."

The few times that a truck engine ripped away the silence, an alert was called. Our hearts leaped. Each time the rumble conjured up images of that Temple dump truck with a dozen or more armed fanatics. Each time Elaine or one of the men recognized the vehicle by the timbre of the engine and identified the owner. That relieved me every time, except once, when they said, "Oh, that's Mike's truck."

With an exchange of greetings and loud footsteps on the hardwood floors Mike, the owner of the other disco, appeared in the doorway of the kitchen. He said hello to Javers, Krause and me, putting all of us on edge. He stayed for only a few moments, then walked into the main part of the disco. When we asked whether it was not true that he was a Temple sympathizer, our hostess said, "He was afraid to go home because Peoples Temple might come there and find him." Sensing our suspicions, she assured us, "He's all right. He's scared too."

Most reassuring was the tapping of rain on the roof. The sound insulated us from the outside world, making it impossible to key on footsteps and other relatively subtle noises. Perhaps eventually it would conceal the approach of assailants; for the moment, it meant we could shed a little tension.

Occasionally, a defector would step into the kitchen and announce the need to relieve his or her bladder. As the person slipped outside, he or she would quickly close the back door so the rest of us would not be open sniper targets. This routine was repeated several times before I went out with some others.

The worn ground was slick as wet marble, and household junk was stacked randomly among the glistening trees. The pungent smell of wet earth cleared my head; again it occurred to me that my chances might be better on my own. A night in the rain was tolerable, and certainly I would be more inconspicuous alone at the edge of the bush. But I needed the camaraderie, and the illusion of strength in numbers.

Back inside at the table with my two colleagues, that tradeoff between comfort and security became even clearer to me. Of all the members of our reporting crew, I had wound up with the two least physically formidable. Under normal circumstances, that would not have been a consideration. Tonight it was: all of us foresaw violent scenarios.

Krause—nicknamed "Ralph" by the NBC crew because of his Ralph Lauren jeans—stood about five feet seven, smoked heavily and spoke with the confident, nasal tones of one who told officials he had journeyed to Guyana to report on a picture larger than the Peoples Temple story.

Javers, a self-described Philadelphia kid with a scraggly beard and an enterprising spirit, had impressed me as a talented reporter. But he seemed to believe that we could defend ourselves if a band of gunmen kicked open the doors and blazed away. We would pick up the table before us and hurl it at our attackers, he suggested, though both of us had only one usable arm.

"What time is it?" I asked. Midnight passed, but the other time-posts inched by. I yawned again and again, exhausted, yet too wired to sleep. Conversation was a therapeutic, time-passing device.

Subconsciously, as the squalls picked up, we keyed our senses on the sounds outside. We listened to the metallic tapping of rain on the roof. Minutes dragged on, and the conversation lagged. Then it happened. A boom like the ones on the airstrip reverberated through the house. Out front, where the guards were posted, there was a scramble of feet on hardwood and urgent shouts. With a collective gasp, we all hit the floor or froze. I crouched against an interior wall, reaching for a knife in my pocket. Javers took shelter, and Krause darted into a small bedroom occupied by the little girl.

An eternity later, one of our protectors came back to inform us that the "shotgun blast" was a rotted branch that had plunged to the roof after absorbing enough rain to snap off. After a general release of tension, we went back to our posts and marked time.

After a while, chills rippled through my body. My clothing was damp, and I had been sitting still too long. Javers asked Elaine for a blanket. With the wool around my shoulders, my shivers stopped.

Soon, another boom shook the house with a percussion that could only have been caused by gunpowder. "Christ," someone cried. Like the first time, the defectors hit the floors and pressed themselves to walls. Javers and Krause bolted out the back door into the rain. Another wet branch.

After a while, I went into the darkened rooms with the defectors. Krause was already asleep. I shared a mattress on the floor with Javers, but was unable to doze off. Even when I shut my eyes, events replayed themselves. Sleep was impossible. Rest was less important to me than being ready for whatever might happen, so after an hour or so of tossing I returned to the kitchen.

As morning slowly approached, Dwyer paid us one of his periodic visits. He said that Guyanese troops would be coming by train from Matthews Ridge, thirty miles to the north. Apparently the government had not wanted to risk ambush by flying airplanes to an unsecured airfield at night. We had heard reports of imminent rescue before and were not relieved.

Before daybreak, a barely audible whistle wended its way to us, shrill and soulful. "What was that?"

"The train," said Harold Cordell, his back against a wall in the darkened room, his knees drawn up.

My heart quickened. "Are you sure?"

"I heard it every day in Jonestown," he said. "That's it."

Nevertheless, we were not home safe yet. The next reports took the edge off our tired elation. The troops were not taking the train all the way to town; apparently concerned that the cars might be dynamited or otherwise sabotaged, the Guyanese forces were marching the last several miles, very warily and slowly.

Some of the defectors joined us in the kitchen. We chatted casually for a while, then the notebooks came out. With Cordell doing most of the talking, the defectors told us which members had done the shooting at the airport. There was disagreement about some identities.

"You're gonna see the worst carnage of your life at Jonestown," Cordell interjected without warning. "It's called 'revolutionary suicide.'"

In the cover of night, as the train slowly made its way toward Port Kaituma, Stanley Clayton, a cousin of Black Panther Huey Newton, fearfully made his way along the muddy road from Jonestown to the tiny river port.

Clayton had lacked the gumption to step forward and accept passage out with Congressman Ryan, but he had had the street smarts and survival instincts to escape on his own. He had been standing around in the kitchen after the Ryan party left, getting ready to fix the evening meal.

Then, like the blanket of black clouds overhead, a strange mood fell over Jonestown. People were quiet, expectant. No more cries of children nor buzzing machinery; no scurrying feet along the boardwalks. The music had stopped. Everything was suspended, in shock. The banter and loud talk ceased; whispers took over. What did they feel? What did they think would happen? Were they upset that some—mostly white people—had abandoned them? Did they regret not having left themselves? Did they believe the trouble would blow away in time like the storm clouds?

Clayton heard Marceline Jones's amplified voice, shrill and worried, ordering everyone to quarters. About twenty minutes later he heard the command for assembly in the pavilion. He had picked up the news that Don Sly had tried to kill the congressman. He had seen someone come into the kitchen and haul away a large metal vat. Then Lew Jones came to tell him to report to the pavilion, along with everyone else. And Clayton obeyed.

At about 5:00 P.M., Maria Katsaris ran up to Mike Prokes on one of the pathways. A group of armed members had gone after Ryan, she said. "It's out of control." She told him to meet her at Jones's cabin, West House. He took off as instructed.

In the pavilion, hundreds of people waited on the benches or stood around, still in their finest clothes. An eerie silence hung over them. Tim Carter was struck by the blank stares on the faces of many. On stage, a young woman freaked out. She danced and screamed uncontrollably. "I'm going to be a freedom fighter!" Paralyzed by apprehension and the absolute quiet, no one moved a hand to stop her. For five minutes or so, she babbled incomprehensible slogans. Finally, someone subdued her.

A short distance away, Maria Katsaris encountered Tim and Mike Carter near Mr. Muggs's cage. She asked Tim to lend a hand to Mike Prokes—he would need help lugging out a big suitcase. First she wanted Tim to change his clothes, then report to West House.

In the pavilion on an elevated section of stage, in his prison-green chair, with the sign above his head—THOSE WHO DO NOT REMEMBER THE PAST ARE CONDEMNED TO REPEAT IT—Jones sat above his people. There in front of him, their faces upturned, were his "children," over nine hundred who had followed him for many miles and many years. The time-wrinkled and weathered faces of the elderly, some who in reaches of memory could call up images of a fresh-faced boy-man spouting with the best evangelists in Indiana. The old ladies from Watts and the Fillmore, who struggled down the steps of Temple buses with puffy ankles and felt the glow in the services, the warmth of family. The former millhands, nurses, clerks, teachers, truck drivers and longshoremen. Those who chose the South American bush over the slow death of urban jungle. Those who came needing help, and those who came to give it. The idealists. The true socialists. The teen-agers, such as Judy and Patricia Houston, at the threshold of adulthood. The professionals, such as Gene Chaikin, and the students, such as Johnny Brown Jones and Harriet Tropp, ready to begin careers. The smaller children, growing and learning, several hundred of them. The three dozen babies who had been born in Jonestown.

"How much I have loved you," Jim Jones began. "How much I have tried to give you a good life."

As the applause died down, he went on. "In spite of all I have tried, a handful of people . . . have made our life impossible. There's no way to detach ourselves from what's happened today. . . . We are sitting here waiting on a powder keg," he said, fear tinging his voice.

The man whose voice had slurred and whose thoughts had faltered during the Ryan visit was alone again with his family. No outsiders were present; only the tape recorder monitored what he said. He was in his loft, with his audience captive. His pliant voice almost whined in sadness, hopelessness. Gently he lifted them and carried them along, bending and choosing his words, breaking it to them slowly.

He declared: "It is said by the greatest prophets from time immemorial, 'No man takes my life from me; I am laying my life down.'" His people shouted, "Right! Right!" as they had so many times before when he spoke of dying for the cause. Yes, this was what he wanted to hear. "As Jack Beam often said, 'If this only worked one day, it was worthwhile,'" he told them to cheers.

Speaking of impending violence, of catastrophe on Ryan's airplane, he reminded them, "It almost happened here. The congressman was almost killed here. You can't steal other people's children without expecting a violent reaction."

As the clapping and supportive shouts faded, Jones's voice turned intently earnest and he talked of betrayal by the defectors and the response. "Now what's gonna happen here in a matter of a few minutes is that one of those people on that plane is gonna shoot that pilot. I know that. I didn't plan that but I know that's gonna happen. They're gonna shoot that pilot and down comes that plane into the jungle.

"And we had better not have any of our children left when it's over because, I'm telling you, they'll parachute in here on us. . . .

"So my opinion is that we be kind to children and be kind to seniors and take the potion like they used to take in ancient Greece, and step over quietly because we are not committing suicide. It is a revolutionary act."

Although a woman cried "yes" when he asked for dissenting opinions, Jones plowed ahead at first: the children would be butchered if they were not killed first, he said. Some people should go to Georgetown and get Tim Stoen, he suggested. "He brought these people to us, he and Deanna Mertle. The people in San Francisco will not be idle over this. They'll not take our death in vain, you know."

Christine Miller, as usual, stood in dissent, to ask Jones whether it was too late to go to Russia, as they had planned earlier. Jones assured her, "It's too late. I can't control these people; they're out there. They've gone with the guns. And once they kill anybody. . . ." There was another obstacle: Jones would never surrender Don Sly to the authorities. "You think I am going to deliver them Ujara [Sly]?" he asked rhetorically, raising his voice. "Not on your life . . . I've lived for all. I'll die for all."

Despite the supportive cries and applause for Jones, Christine Miller—the one always mocked for her objections, the one whose materialism had been merely tolerated by Jones—was not finished. It did not make sense to her, this casting aside of all hope, this surrender of life, all dying for one, all going over to the "other side." Could they not emigrate to Russia, where they would be among other communists, where they would be a living reminder of American oppression?

Finally, the woman's persistence and logic forced Jones to turn to a radio operator. "You can check with Russia to see if they'll take us immediately; otherwise we die."

Breaking into the cheers, Christine Miller argued again for life. "I think there were too few who left for one thousand two hundred people to give them their lives."

"Do you know how many left?" Jones asked.

"Oh, twenty-odd," she said. "That's a small amount compared to what's here."

"Twenty-odd," Jones repeated, mocking her. "But what's gonna happen when they don't leave [safely]?

"There's one man there who blames, and rightfully so, Debbie [Layton] Blakey for the murder of his mother, and he'll stop that pilot by any means necessary."

"I wasn't speaking of that plane," Miller said. "I was speaking about a plane for us to go to Russia."

"To Russia . . . it's . . . it's. . . ." Jones, flustered, was stammering. "You think Russia is gonna want us with this stigma?"

"I don't see it like that," she said. "I mean, I feel that as long as there's life, there's hope."

"I am talking about what we have—no other road," he explained. That was it—no other road. That was what he had been trying to explain since those first words, "How much I have loved you." He had to persuade his people that all their options had been stolen by forces beyond his control: Larry Layton was acting on his own, the gunmen heading for the airstrip were acting on their own, and what they were doing with their guns precluded a migration to Russia.

Miller gallantly protested that the children deserved to live; no one could hold the children responsible for what happened. Jones agreed that the children deserved to live, but added, "What's more, they deserve peace." No protest issued from the nine hundred people before him— many with children on their laps or cradled in their arms.

Miller could not be muffled, however. The woman many Jonestown residents thought crazy or selfish was the only one to keep her wits. Her lone sane voice rang out in a sea of silence. She would not surrender the microphone. Big Jim McElvane, who had arrived in Jonestown less than two days earlier and perhaps wanted to prove his loyalty, broke into the exchange. Patronizing her, disparaging her and ridiculing her arguments, he told her that she had been nothing before she met Jim Jones, that Jim Jones had given her everything she had. "It's over, sister," he added resolutely, in his barrel-echo voice. "It's over. We've made a beautiful day. . . ."

Jones broke into the applause to say, "We win when we go down. Tim Stoen has nobody else to hate. Then he'll destroy himself." Switching tempos, Jones spoke almost biblically for a time, talked of laying down his "burden by the riverside," then screeched about GDF paratroopers shooting innocent babies. "I'm not letting them take my child," he shouted. "Can you let them take your child?"

"No," the people shouted back. And with that, it was decided that the children would go first.

Once again Miller broke in. "You mean you want to see little John die?" she asked Jones in disbelief.

Subduing the hostile shouts directed at her, Jones said, "Peace . . . Peace. . . .

"Do you think I'd put John's life above others?" he asked her. "He's just one of my children. I don't prefer one above the other."

Suddenly, a man shouted loudly, "Everybody hold it." The gunmen had returned from the airstrip.

Jones, calming the crowd, said, "Stay. Peace. . . . Take Dwyer on down to the East House." Jones evidently assumed that Dwyer (who really was in Kaituma) had returned with the truck as he had planned to do. Jones wanted him held with the attorneys, at the guesthouse.

Jones conferred with his aides and received a whispered report of what had occurred at the strip. Then he interrupted a woman speaker. "Stop talking," he cried. "The congressman has been murdered!"

"We're ready," a woman called out. "It's all over," shouted another.

"It's all over," Jones agreed, almost as if satisfied. "What a legacy. What a legacy," he marveled.

"Please get the medication before it's too late," he commanded. "The GDF will be here. . . . Don't be afraid to die." His voice rose urgently; his words flowed in powerful rushes, like a flood of water. The man was mad, and the madman was tired, but he summoned his energy for one last push of his people.

"I don't know who shot him," he cried. "How many are dead?" He received a report from the shooters, then told the crowd, "Oh, God almighty. Patty Parks is dead." There was remorse in his voice, for Patty had been popular in Jonestown.

A woman asked, looking for a way out, some delay. "Can the others endure long enough in a safe place to write about the goodness of Jim Jones?"

"It's too late," he replied, and he urged them to come forward for their last drink.

Along one side of the building on a wooden table was a vat with the potion. Grape Flavor Aid, a Kool Aid–like drink, colored it purplish. Potassium cyanide was the poison. Liquid Valium and other drugs stood alongside it in vials. Dr. Schacht supervised about a dozen members of the Jonestown medical staff. Hypodermic needles were filled. Potion was poured into paper cups from metal and plastic tubs. Large syringes and small squeeze bottles were loaded.

Around the pavilion, security people and some who returned from the airstrip patrolled with guns. No one was to run. No one would pass through alive.

Odell Rhodes, a former drug user from Detroit, saw the first to die—a woman in her twenties with her month-old daughter. The children were brought forward first. A nurse directed the crowd and addressed them in a taut voice: "There's nothing to worry about. So everybody keep calm and try to keep your children calm. They aren't crying out in pain. It's just a little bitter-tasting."

Youngsters were bawling and screaming. Some were fighting, pulling away from their elders. Some had the potion shot to the back of their throats with syringes, where the swallowing reflex would bring it home. Parents and grandparents cried hysterically as their children died—not quickly and not painlessly. The doomed convulsed and gagged as the poison took effect. For several minutes, they vomited and screamed, they bled.

McElvane, validator of Jones to the end, spoke of his days as a therapist and of his study of metaphysics. Hoping to console the dying and the condemned, he raised his voice to inform them that dying people are often comforted by thoughts of reincarnation. "Everybody was so happy when they stepped to 'the other side,' " he promised them.

While others cried in anguish, a woman took the microphone. "This is nothing to cry about," she chided. "This is something we could all rejoice about. . . . Jim Jones has suffered and suffered. . . . He is our only God."

Telling them he loved them, Jones moved among the dying. His followers stood in groups, hugging each other, saying good-bye to old friends. People wept and cried in anguish; Jones begged them to die with dignity.

McElvane and other security people strode up to people, coaxing them ahead. "Come on, brother, let's go." McElvane almost carried one man along to the vat. The guards brought people forward, then went off to find others.

Tim Carter had been waiting at West House with Annie Moore and two children. She was looking for further instructions from Maria about what to do with the children. Frightened and apprehensive, Carter went back to the pavilion to see what was happening there. Ten to fifteen bodies were on the ground. Mothers were kneeling down with their children. His wife was kneeling too, bent over their child, tears streaming down her cheeks. He hugged her. She was cold. "I love you," he said. She convulsed; she had taken the poison.

Survival instincts took over. Carter, who was trusted enough to play double agent, was seized by one thought: if he stayed, he too would die. He headed back toward West House.

The testimonials to Jim Jones began as they always did, even as other people wailed in contortions of pain, mouths foaming and nostrils bloody. Said one woman, "I'd like to thank Dad because he's the only one who stood up for me."

A man spoke of his love of children as he looked out over the bodies of dozens of them. "I'd rather see them lay like that than to see them die like the Jews did," he said. "I'd like to thank God for giving us life and also death."

Proclaimed Jones: "Anyone who wants to go with their child has a right to go with their child. I think it's humane.

"I want to see you go [to your deaths]. They can take me and do whatever they want, but I don't want to see you through this hell no more. No more. No more. . . ."

He jumped from one subject to the next, much as he had during Ryan's visit. He urged people to calm themselves. He talked about people rotting twenty years in nursing homes, people locking others in chains, stealing their land away from them. Then, back to the congressman's murder:

"I don't know who fired the shot, but as far as I'm concerned, I killed him," he said. "He had no business coming. I told him not to come."

As the crying mingled with the voices of adults, Jones's words reached a powerful timbre: "Die with respect. Die with a degree of dignity."

He addressed himself to the children, saying the sweetened potion was merely something to put them to rest. Still, an outburst of crying caused him to exclaim, "Oh, God." Then he thundered, "Mother mother mother mother mother mother! Please, mother, please, please, please, don't do this! Lay down your life with your child, but don't do this. . . ." His wish evidently was fulfilled; she took the final drink. "Free at last!" Jones proclaimed.

Repeatedly, he called on his followers to keep down their emotions. He urged children and young adults to hurry for their potion so that seniors, the last to die, could get theirs. "Quickly. Quickly. Quickly. Quickly."

The testimonials went on. A man said, "You people should think about how your relatives was, and be thankful the children would be laid to rest." An elderly woman said, "I'd like to go for socialism and communism. I thank Dad very much." Another thanked Jones for his "love, goodness and kindness to bring us to this land."

And Jones, just before the reel-to-reel tape ran out, assessed the sight before him: "We've set an example for others. One thousand people who say: we don't like the way the world is.

"Take our life from us. . . . We didn't commit suicide. We committed an act of revolutionary suicide protesting the conditions of an inhumane world."

The cries of children rose as a haunting counterpoint. The sequence of death would be children, young adults, adults, the elderly. Such a clever way to make sure all died: What would the adults have to live for after they watched the next generations die?

Despite the guns and guards all around, some people chose to rebel, to survive. When a nurse sent Odell Rhodes to fetch a stethoscope to check the bodies, Rhodes left the pavilion. He crawled under a building, cut through a garden, and slipped into the jungle. He kept on going, until he reached the police station in Port Kaituma at around 2:00 A.M.

Stanley Clayton saw his girl friend in the crowd, but did not dare tell her that he was going to break for it. He saw adults being forcibly injected with poison—murdered. It seemed there were about sixty of them. Christine Miller met her end with a needle, resisting. At one point, before nightfall, he had seen Annie Moore leaving the pavilion area with John Stoen. The boy had been crying, sniffing, and saying, "I don't want to die. I don't want to die." Jones saw him and said, "Is that my son doing all that crying? My son shouldn't be crying." John did not fully stop; he tried to jerk away from Annie Moore as they walked toward Jones's house.

During the ritual of suicide and murder, Clayton floated around the edge of the pavilion. But he knew he would be dead if he did not make a decisive move soon. After the security guards were ordered to turn in their guns at the radio room and were instead outfitted with crossbows, he felt his chances of escape were better. He counted about twenty persons with crossbows surrounding the pavilion. The only two persons carrying firearms were Billy Oliver and Lew Jones, who had told Billy that he had been specially selected to remain alive until the end, to make sure everyone was dead. Clayton judged himself a fairly speedy runner, and crossbows and pistols were not the most accurate of weapons.

As nightfall began to work in his favor, Clayton headed out toward Muggs's cage and the road. Being shot seemed preferable to death by poison. He walked down the path, positioning himself several steps behind a security guard, Amondo Griffith, and started quickening his pace.

"Where are you going?" Griffith asked as Clayton passed him.

Clayton had planned to run as soon as he was fifteen or twenty yards beyond the guard. He said he was going to see Ed Crenshaw on security at the guns warehouse. Griffith said Crenshaw already had "gone over," but Clayton kept walking.

Near the exit road, he came upon a group of about a dozen people with crossbows. "Hey, brother, what's happening?" one called. Another, Marie Lawrence, held her crossbow at the ready.

Clayton had been hoping to just walk by them to see how they would react. Marie Lawrence's response caused him to dig for another excuse: "I was instructed to count security heads." It was the first thing that came into his mind. It worked.

As Clayton counted heads, he came to the last bowman between him and the open field. He told the man he was ready to die. The man hugged him, saying, "I'll see you in your next life."

Clayton then went into the school tent, telling the guard that he was going to say good-bye to more people. Instead, he dashed out the other side into the bush. After sprinting fifty yards or so, a short distance into the jungle, he paused to catch his breath and listen for pursuers. It was pitch black. The lightning bugs scared him; he thought he heard voices calling.

A short time after Tim Carter returned to West House, Maria Katsaris stepped out of the cabin with a suitcase and two .38-caliber revolvers. She was frantic. "There's a lot of money in here and a letter," she told Prokes and the two Carter brothers. "Give it to the Embassy." She handed Prokes and Mike Carter the two guns with the instruction, "If you get caught, shoot yourselves."

She did not say which embassy, but the three assumed that she meant the Soviet Embassy. It was a correct assumption. In the last hours, the Temple's financial secretary had been busy making hasty arrangements to transfer some $7.3 million to the Soviet Union government from

Venezuelan and Panamanian bank accounts. The funds were held in fixed time deposits in the name of Annie Jean McGowen, a jovial and loyal seventy-year-old black woman born in Mississippi.

Two letters, signed by McGowan, instructed the Union Bank of Switzerland and the Union Banking Corporation, both of Panama City, to turn over the deposits as they became due to Feodor Timofeyev, the Soviet consul in Georgetown. "I am doing this," a letter explained, "on behalf of Peoples Temple because we, as communists, want our money to be administered for help to oppressed peoples all over the world, or in any way that your decision-making body sees fit. . . . Cooperatively yours, Annie McGowan."

Another letter with the suitcase was handwritten in blue ballpoint pen on lined paper: "I, Maria Katsaris, leave all the money in Banco de Venezuela, in Caracas, to the Communist Party, Soviet Union. . . . This is my final wish before I die." It was witnessed by Jim McElvane and Marilee Bogue, who had refused to leave with her family. A letter directed the Swiss Bank Corporation (overseas) S.A. in Panama to transfer one sum of $577,000 and another of $1,486,000 to a new account in the bank, closing an old account.

The three couriers also were given two passports, which turned out to be those of Maria Katsaris and Annie McGowan. Apparently they were meant to provide signature comparison, since neither woman would live to verity their instructions.

The suitcase itself contained about $550,000 in United States currency and about $130,000 in Guyanese currency.

The three men would say later that they tired quickly as they lugged the money toward the main road. After a mile, they opened the suitcase, and removed and buried part of the money. Later, they hid the suitcase and more of the money in a chicken coop. They continued toward Port Kaituma, with $48,000 in their pockets, the two guns, the letters and the two extra passports. They were arrested by Port Kaituma authorities. At the time, they were heading toward the *Cudjo* mooring place, though the boat had been sent away earlier in the day by Jonestown officials.

Charles Garry and Mark Lane had run and stumbled in the dark until they reached a point about one hundred yards into the jungle, near the spot where the main road entered the compound clearing. Garry saw two people—Lane saw three—walking out of Jonestown. They were carrying what looked like a box on their shoulders. By Garry's reckoning, it was about 6:45 P.M. The lawyers dropped to their knees; they were afraid, and it was too dark to tell who the people were. The pair plunged into the jungle, fearing for their lives.

The two lawyers—though they had not really been speaking to one another up to that point—them spent the night huddled together in the cold, wet rain. They called a temporary truce. In the course of the night, according to Garry, Lane disclosed that Teri Buford had been staying with him since her defection some three weeks earlier. Among other things, Lane said that she had told him that Gene Chaikin was a prisoner in Jonestown and wanted to leave. Garry suddenly realized why Lane had told him on Saturday morning when he asked to see Chaikin, "Don't ask. You'll never see him." There was no doubt about it: Chaikin had been drugged.

And, though Lane later denied it, Garry would insist the conspiracy theorist had told him during the night that he turned down the cheese sandwiches that day because he thought they were drugged or poisoned. "You sonofabitch, why didn't you tell me?" Garry asked him during the night. Lane laughed and said, "We weren't speaking."[74]

After a long time in the bush, Stanley Clayton heard the sound of voices, then a cheer. Three cheers. It was many people yelling. His first thought was that the poison was not real, that the people who keeled over really were not dead after all—and if that were true, he would be in big trouble for taking off. Then he recalled how an acquaintance had gone into the pavilion and had fallen into convulsions, gasping for breath, his eyes rolling. It was real; it was death. Maybe, he thought, the cheer had come from a small group close to Jones, going out with dignity as he had entreated them all to do, cheering before the final step.

After sitting for about thirty minutes in complete silence, Clayton ventured out of the bush. He would need his passport if he wanted to slip past Guyanese and U.S. authorities. The passport was inside Jonestown. About twenty-five yards from the edge of the clearing, he heard what sounded like handgun fire. Not four, not three, but five shots: he was sure of that. After one of the shots, he heard Muggs screaming. Another shot. Silence.

When Clayton ran back into the bush and hid, he heard what sounded like a male voice out in the field, someone looking for him. He went deeper into the undergrowth. After a long time, he came out of the bush.

He felt that he should head for the main road. Keeping low and moving cautiously, he worked his way back into Jonestown's housing areas. He was sweaty and muddy, having stumbled into swampy spots along the way. He went to his house and changed into dry clothes, and exchanged his tennis shoes for boots. He noticed the time: about ten forty-five.

As he skirted the compound, he tried to get a clear view of the pavilion. He could tell the lights were on but could not see the bodies.

He went through the kitchen. All was quiet. He opened the door to the room where the passports were stored. He waited five minutes motionlessly to make sure he was alone. He had never been in the passport box before, but fortunately it had been left unlocked. The passports, over nine hundred of them, were in alphabetical order, so he found his quickly. Just as he shut the box, he heard one more shot.

He froze. He could tell it had come from inside a building. It was closer and louder than the other five, and might have come from the pavilion or from West House. Jim Jones's house.

Clayton watched in both directions, thinking someone might be coming. He closed the door and turned off the light, and waited. After a few minutes of silence, he emerged from the building and padded slowly, his eyes toward Jones's house. Then he took off down the road, running. Behind him, the only sound was the barking of dogs.

In the pavilion, Jim Jones lay dead, a bullet hole in his temple, a gaping exit wound where his brains and skull were blown away. The bullet had traveled at an upward angle through his head and into oblivion. A gun was resting, mysteriously, some twenty feet away. His body lay in repose on a cleared space near his throne, between two other bodies. His head of raven hair was cushioned by a pillow, as though someone had made him comfortable before—or perhaps after—the squeeze of a trigger removed him from his misery. Marceline had taken final rest among the people, poisoned.

In Jones's house, thirteen people died. Among them were the two small boys Jones claimed to have sired—John Stoen and Kimo Prokes. Maria Katsaris, Carolyn Layton, Jim McElvane were among the others. A man, a woman and a baby—believed to be Lew Jones and his family—died on a bunk. There were still others, all poisoned except for one. Annie Moore's body was sprawled near a filing cabinet. Next to her lay a bloody gun, a .357 magnum said to be Jim Jones's personal weapon. A massive bullet wound to the head had ended her life.

Next to her body on the blood-splattered floor was a spiral notebook with a red cover. Annie Moore had written her own suicide note.

"I am twenty-four years of age right now, and I don't expect to live to the end of this book. I thought I should make some attempt to let the world know what Jim Jones and Peoples Temple is—or was all about.

"It seems that some people—and perhaps the majority of people—would like to destroy the best thing that ever happened to the one thousand two hundred or so of us who have followed Jim. I am at a point now so embittered against the world that I don't know why I am writing this."

She wrote in praise of Jonestown, saying, "It seems that everything good that happens in the world is under constant attack." And she spoke with love of the man whom she nursed and comforted: "His love for humans was unsurmountable and it was many whom he put his love and trust in, and they left him and spit in his face."

The final line was added in a different color ink and at a different angle:

"We died because you would not let us live."

The Ryan party had probably left Jonestown around 3:30 or 3:45 P.M. The Port Kaituma ambush started between 4:45 and 5:00 P.M., the same time Jones was beginning to address his people. The suicide-murder ritual was well under way by 6:00 P.M., and the two attorneys already were on the run. Perhaps forty-five minutes later, at about 6:45, the attorneys evidently saw the Carter brothers and Prokes carrying the heavy suitcase of money out of Jonestown. Around the same time, Clayton fled into the darkened jungle at the Jonestown perimeter, where he hid for perhaps an hour or two, maybe until 9:00 P.M., when he apparently heard the final cheer of Jones's inner circle before they took the potion. After another half-hour, Clayton started out but was driven back by the sound of shots, so he hid for a long time, probably almost an hour. When he came out, it was 10:45 P.M.—almost everyone was dead. He heard a shot, a final shot, which the authors believe—in part because of the positioning of Jones's body—was Annie Moore shooting herself. Since there are no known living eyewitnesses to the death of Jim Jones by a "contact wound" to the head, the evidence suggests that either he shot himself or he was shot by a close aide, probably Annie Moore.[75] Sources among survivors have said that Jones long had planned to have someone kill him when the final White Night arrived.

At around 6:00 A.M., the last of our people had roused themselves and sat up, marking time. Dwyer showed up at the rum shop and without smiling announced, "I think we're pretty much out of the woods. The first twenty soldiers arrived and staked out the airstrip. There will be eighty more, then some by train. . . . They're mobilizing everyone in the country. Washington is aware of what happened."

He then blurted, "Sharon Amos has killed herself and her two children in Georgetown." Soft exclamations traveled through the room. "Rumors of Jonestown are bad. It looks like there are killings and suicide. I'm sure that once this triggered it, the world collapsed."

Some of the defectors stiffened with new fear. They predicted that Jones's avenging angels, members of the basketball team, would come to slay us and others.

When asked about the mass suicide, Gerry Parks, eyes dark and receding in anguish, said, "This is what always was planned. If you go there now, you might find they are all dead, unless they could overcome the leadership. We never figured we'd make it out the gates. When you came, Jones said that you would come in to attack us with guns."

What in the world was revolutionary suicide? "The theory," Dale said, "is that you can go down in history, saying you chose your way to go, and it is your commitment to refuse capitalism and in support of socialism."

At about eight-thirty a couple of Guyanese soldiers showed up and stood in the kitchen doorway. They were in green battle fatigues and carrying automatic rifles. We showered them with warm smiles. "It's been a long night," I said.

Dwyer returned to give passports and other personal effects to the survivors. He handed me my watch, with a broken band, and a couple of muddy cameras that had weathered the night on the rainy strip. I stowed Greg's cameras with the rest of his gear.

Word spread fast that the soldiers had arrived, and more Guyanese descended on the disco. Some sipped coffee at the front entry corridor, which converted into a porch when storm boards were removed. I walked out for fresh air and a look at the roadway. The town looked friendlier by daylight.

A man asked whether I was one of the Americans. I nodded. "A damn shame, man," he said. Agreeing, I left and was accosted by the self-proclaimed airport manager. Though his speech had grown sloppier with each bottle of rum, he seemed to take credit for the arrival of the troops and reminded me of his assurances that we would be safe. Soon we were sharing a table with Carol and a soldier. With an experienced hand, the airport manager poured a couple of fingers of rum, then a couple of fingers of cool condensed milk into paper cups. The soldier turned down a drink with a contemptuous head shake.

The breakfast concoction went down smoothly, the milk cutting the fiery sweetness of the rum. We saluted our survival. The drink lightened my head and put something in my queasy stomach. My only food for the past thirty-six hours had been a cheese sandwich at the mission and a banana at the disco. We were running on adrenalin alone.

Carrying my second rum toward the back room, I walked into the kitchen and found Gerry Parks crying into his fists. "The goddamn dirty bastard. The bastard. I've never done anything in my life to hurt anyone. He never had the guts to do anything on his own. He would sit there and laugh when twelve beat the hell out of one person." His hatred for Jones wrenched his body and contorted his face.

Embarrassed to have intruded, I went into a rear room where Jim Bogue, a bespectacled forty-six-year-old man with a tractor cap, sat in a corner with his twenty-one-year-old daughter Juanita. They wondered how to reconstruct their devastated lives.

"When you came in, we knew there would be mass suicide if anyone, even one, wanted to leave," Juanita said. "He's threatened it a lot, but . . ." Guilt apparently set in. "I knew we'd get it before we got to the front gate. We would have got it right there at the gate on the truck, but they couldn't get the tractor there on time."

Her father slumped noticeably when I asked if they would be leaving with us. "I just can't leave without my kids," he said. "There are two in the bush . . . and my youngest daughter, Marilee, nineteen, wouldn't go. She wouldn't even answer me [when we went to leave]. She knew what was going to happen. She'd take the poison without a gun to her head."

When word arrived that the medical evacuation planes had landed, I walked down the strip to survey the scene. A couple dozen soldiers rimmed the field, firearms at the ready, some facing the surrounding jungle. One yellow med-evac plane of uncertain vintage and Guyanese origins was parked near the crippled plane the soldiers had been guarding. Far down the strip, I could make out several lumps on the ground around the Otter. The bodies had not yet been moved.

Near the first plane, Guyanese soldiers and a woman medic hooked up intravenous tubes and did what they could to patch up the injured as they were rushed aboard the aircraft. Remarkably, Steve Sung was walking under his own power. His straight black hair in disarray, he grinned and called my name. We shook hands and I embraced him, accidentally jostling his sore arm. His joy and strength attested to his resilience. He had weathered a night of delirium, hot and cold sweats, and was going to make it. Incredibly, the rest had survived, too, though Anthony was in particularly serious shape with breathing difficulties, and Jackie had gangrene in her leg.

There was some outside chance—with the five-hour time difference —that I could make the final deadline for Sunday's paper if I left on the first plane, if the editors could stretch production schedules, if I could make a quick phone call from Georgetown, if I could dictate fast and clean. There were many uncertainties, but it was worth a try. I knew it was a big story, though I was not certain how big because the events in Jonestown were hazy unknowns.

Javers and I discussed the situation, and each of us decided against staying behind in Kaituma to cover the story. We were really not sure of the seriousness of our wounds and the possibility of infection. And after being out of touch with our offices for almost forty-eight hours, we were anxious to get to a phone rather than risk being out of touch for another newspaper cycle or more.

Dwyer said we could take the first plane, because we were among the half-dozen most severely wounded. "Do I have time to get my gear?" I said. "Hurry," he said. Though I had Greg's camera gear, his pack and my pack were back at the disco.

When I bolted through the front door, Carol Boyd looked up and came over to me. "The first plane is ready to leave," I reported. "And they're taking out the injured. I'm going out."

Her mouth dropped and she grabbed my arm. "I don't want to stay with these people, no matter what." Carol did not trust the defectors and did not want to be left alone with them. "Come on," I said. "Maybe there's room."

On the way out, I paused to shake hands or clasp the shoulders of the men and women who had shared that horrendous night. We wished each other luck and exchanged tight smiles. They were good people, I thought, good people like those who had left the Temple long ago and spoken against Jones. Good people like those at Jonestown.

At the side of the evacuation plane, Dwyer told me there was no extra room for Carol since she was uninjured. So I gave her my seat, and Javers gave his seat to Beverly Oliver, who had foot wounds. Fortunately, a second med-evac plane soon landed across the runway, and we were told that it would get us to Georgetown at about the same time because of its superior speed. We both agreed to wait for it.

Leaning in the door of the first plane, I bade good-bye to our companions. "We'll see you in Georgetown." Some of them waved weakly as the plane started its engines. Javers and I carried our baggage to the second plane, skirting puddles and knots of natives gathered to witness local history. We placed our packs against a wall across from the door, and rested for a moment. "Where's your camera?" I asked.

"It's lost," he said. He had tossed it off while scrambling through the bush.

"Someone's got to take a picture of this, or people will never really see what happened here," I said. Rummaging through my canvas pack, I was unable to find my Olympus compact. I figured it was with my tape recorder, sitting in a mud puddle alongside the strip somewhere.

Unflapping Greg's bag, I pulled out a Canon motordrive, but it was crusted with mud. The second Canon's lens was cloudy with moisture. An old Nikon rangefinder camera in a front compartment was clean and more to my liking. The frame counter showed Greg had taken about twenty-one or twenty-two shots, meaning the balance of a thirty-six-shot roll was available without reloading or risking the film inside.

Stepping outside, I framed a couple of photos of the soldiers and the tent where our injured had spent the night. The difficult part still faced me. The few hundred yards to the Otter passed slowly. Dizzy and slightly nauseated, I stopped fifty yards away and took a head-on photo of the plane. The range was too long for that lens. The plane looked like a toy through the viewfinder, the bodies like baggage. I would have to walk closer.

Holding the camera in my right hand, I strode resolutely to the plane and swung to the right. A group of soldiers near the waiting shack watched me, their guns poised. It was eerie, stifling, ghoulish. But it had to be done.

For the final time, I approached Greg's body. Someone had rolled him over, apparently when he was stripped of personal effects and perhaps looted. His shirt had pulled open to the waist. My eyes could not focus on his muddied face, but I noticed his glasses were not there. Examining his wounds seemed pointless. I picked up a couple of articles around him—a key to his room at the Pegasus and a severed piece of camera strap.

Nothing on earth could have made me take close-ups of Greg and the others. Without snapping the shutter, I backed off and circled the plane, past the remains of Patricia Parks and Bob Brown. Taking several more paces away from the plane, I filled the frame with the scene and took a couple of photos. Then my path went full circle, past the Otter's nose and a little to the right. Finally, I had found an angle showing all the dead, the plane, the open cargo door and the extended boarding stairway—the mute horror of the massacre. My left arm was not much help, so, holding a deep breath, I squeezed off a one-handed shot with my right hand. As the shutter slammed closed, I realized that the camera was aimed along the death squad's line of fire.

When I tried to cock the shutter again, the film jammed. Several shots were still left. Just then, a jeep with Bob Flick and others drove down to pick me up.

Within a few minutes, our plane lifted off and left behind that muddy strip where bodies still sprawled around the Otter. Then gray turbulent clouds soon screened the meandering rivers and deep green jungle.

Neville Annibourne, the government man, was sitting across the aisle, just behind an army officer. He was in a reflective mood. Leaning across the aisle, I asked, "Is this the end of the Peoples Temple mission?"

He started to say something about others having to make such decisions, but stopped abruptly. "I can think of no better way to put it than that," he said. "It's ended."

Epilogue

As Jim Jones had prophesied, the Guyanese army descended upon Jonestown. But they came not to kill and maim and to steal children, but to assess Jones's carnage. They found the bodies of Jim Jones and Annie Moore, each with a single bullet wound to the head. John Victor Stoen and Kimo Prokes were dead. The poison also had killed Marceline Jones, the Jones's adopted daughter Agnes, their adopted sons Lew and Johnny Brown. It claimed Jones's closest aides too: Carolyn Layton, Karen Layton, Maria Katsaris, Jack Beam, Patty Cartmell, Dick and Harriet Tropp, Jim McElvane, Dr. Larry Schacht. Drugged attorney Gene Chaikin and dissenter Christine Miller died, as did the loyalist Marilee Bogue. Rebellious schoolteacher Tom Grubbs died, as did students Patricia and Judy Houston and their mother Phyllis. Those who made the trip to the airstrip to attack the Ryan party—Tom Kice, Joe Wilson, Wesley Breidenbach, Albert Touchette and others—took the potion. Old friends Le Flora Townes and James and Irene Edwards died, and so did Billy and Bruce Oliver, Brian and Claudia Bouquet, and Christine Cobb and several of her children. Shaun Baker, the singer who had entertained San Francisco politicians, was dead. Carolyn Looman, whose family believed she wanted to leave, was dead. Jane Mutschman, who expressed her doubts and dedication so sincerely, was dead. Shanda James, whose drugging helped turn Jim Jones's own sons against him, was dead. In all, 913 Temple members had perished in his final White Night. Very few people in Jonestown escaped death; very few outside the reach of Jones's voice followed his orders.

All but one of the defectors who fled with Ryan were white, as

Jones had so pointedly reminded his flock. Most who fled on their own, either before or during the suicide ritual, were black. When Jones gave everyone the day off that Saturday, nine members—including security chief Joe Wilson's wife and baby—made their exits before the climax of the Ryan visit. Some pretended to go on jungle "picnics," but most simply walked off, believing that Jones had gone mad, perverted their common dream and started the death march.

Once the death ritual began, only the savvy and the lucky survived. Street-smart and independent young blacks such as Stanley Clayton and Odell Rhodes saved themselves through cunning when all seemed doomed, as did Grover Davis, a seventy-eight-year-old black man who slipped into the jungle. Finally, there was one survivor who actually remained in Jonestown while the nine hundred died. An elderly Los Angeles–area black woman named Hyacinth Thrash slept through the entire night; she awoke in her cabin to find her sister and everyone else dead.

On that horrible Saturday, no one, save Christine Miller, took on Jones; no one kicked over the vat of poison or turned guns on their leader to stop him. No one could stop him, not after he had manipulated his people into believing their fortunes lay only in a grandiose final statement, not after he had sealed their compact with the airstrip murders and the command: bring the children first. The executioner had initiated an act of such enormity and tragedy that Jonestown—the life-sustaining symbol and dream for his followers—would become a degraded international synonym for unspeakable evil and waste. The worldwide perception alone would prove the last gesture a failure, Jones's closing act a fraud.

From the day of the holocaust, outsiders refused to accept the interpretation Jones sought to place on the self-destruction of his movement. They viewed it as madness, cruelty and later as deception by a Satanic leader, not as a political or social statement; even committed socialists and communists and the USSR disassociated themselves from this bastardization of Huey Newton's concept of "revolutionary suicide." The terrible images of poison being squirted down the tiny throats of babies, of screaming adults twisting on the ground in death throes or being forcibly injected with poison, of entire families dying inside a perimeter of guns, crossbows and jungle—the incomprehensibility of all this caused the world to shudder in revulsion and disbelief.

The horror of Jonestown, however, did not end in a muddy jungle clearing. The state of mind lingered and traveled like the stench of death. Paralyzing fear grabbed the church enemies as the first reports of Temple "hit squads" were transmitted. For once, law enforcement agencies took seriously the stories of the defectors: public officials, reporters and ex-members all were potential targets of those Jones called his "avenging angels." But the supposed "hit squad"—the basketball team and the public relations team—was held under virtual house arrest at Lamaha Gardens.

In the San Francisco Bay Area, as elected officials, law agencies and mental health professionals took steps to avert the spread of violence and death, ex-members gathered under police protection at the Human Freedom Center in Berkeley to await word about the identities of survivors.

Unbeknownst to the "traitors" and enemies, the same sorts of fears permeated the camp of the loyalists. The troops at the San Francisco temple expected to be attacked in a backlash against the church. They were so afraid of McCarthy-era types of prosecutions and official harassment, and perhaps of their own legal vulnerability, that some smuggled church documents and records past police cars stationed outside, then burned them in a nighttime beach bonfire. Others surrendered perfectly legal weapons to police through an attorney, fearing they might be shot if found armed.

Meantime, the temple building itself was besieged by the nation's news media and by angry and distraught relatives of the Jonestown dead looking for someone to blame. Day after day, the relatives hung around the temple's chain-link security fence, crying and shouting at equally grief-stricken but more sober-faced loyalists such as Archie Ijames.

As it turned out, no one attacked the temple, or rounded up large numbers of Temple members. And no Temple hit squad stalked back to the United States with guns and millions of dollars to buy death contracts. Jones was not coordinating his elite security squad trained in martial arts; Jim Jones was dead. And the most logical candidate to succeed him or to carry the banner, Stephan Jones, had publicly condemned his father's actions and said he hated him.

Among the church's influential friends, especially the politicians, this was a time for nauseating self-examination—or strategic retreat. For some a painful, sometimes slow realization pulled at their insides as they asked themselves how they were fooled, what went wrong, or whether they should not share responsibility for the rise of Jim Jones and all it had wrought. Some, Carlton Goodlett and Willie Brown among them, continued to defend the Temple and showed no remorse at first. Lieutenant Governor Mervyn Dymally successfully hid from reporters' questions. The White House quickly sought to minimize contacts between Jones and First Lady Rosalynn Carter. When Mayor George Moscone heard about Jonestown, he vomited and cried. And he called the families of the dead and injured in the Ryan party, including mine, to express his sympathies. While that climate of terror endured, Moscone himself was assassinated, along with another Jones supporter, Supervisor Harvey Milk, by right-wing supervisor Dan White in a dispute unrelated to the Jonestown holocaust.

Though many people suffered—thousands personally felt the losses in the San Francisco and Los Angeles areas alone—in some ways it was the loyalists who were devastated most. At least some of the hundred or two hundred active members in the United States gladly would have swallowed the potion if chance had placed them in Guyana

November 18, 1978. Instead circumstances doomed them to live with one of the greatest human tragedies in history, sentenced to a kind of living death for an indeterminate time. In addition to losing their loved ones overnight, they awakened to an unending nightmare, without their religion, their political organization, their leader, their self-image, their past and their future. Like many nonmembers who lost loved ones, they hovered near mental collapse. Their present held nothing, for they had lost everything, even their sense of identity. Scorned, isolated, directionless, they could only wait for the initial publicity, scrutiny, hostility and pain to subside, then try to begin new lives.

In the next two years, some would put the Temple behind them, with difficulty, sometimes with help from friends and family they had cut off for years. In resuming their lives, they found jobs and assimilated without fully forgetting who they were. A number would cling to other survivors—and in a few cases, would marry other survivors. They gravitated toward the few people who could understand them, who shared a common experience. Some survivors even reestablished friendships with ex-members once marked as traitors by Jones. And some families split by Jones reunited.

Other people suffered—not just on each year's anniversary of the holocaust—but each day, unable to escape or cope effectively with the past or to venture into the present, let alone shape a future. Some endured almost incessant depression, turning deeper within themselves or turning toward drugs. Many felt classic survivor's guilt, longing for the Temple and Jones, aching to die, to join their comrades, inwardly cursing fate for sparing them, yet not quite tormented enough to end it all too. Only one did so deliberately.

Several months after Jonestown died, Michael Prokes, Jones's press aide for almost a decade, called a news conference in his hometown of Modesto, California. To convince reporters to attend, the former television newsman promised front-page news. He kept his promise. After he issued a statement praising Jones and attempting to explain the deaths of his comrades, he stepped a few feet away into the bathroom and, with reporters outside the door, fired a bullet into his brain. His suicide brought the headlines he promised and sent new spasms of terror through survivors, defectors and others.

Before his last news conference, the Temple public relations man had told relatives and friends that he hoped to write a book, to tell the truth about the Temple. But he also wondered aloud whether he would need to reveal the negative things as well, such as the sexual practices of Jones. He left behind a partial manuscript that made some effort at being even-handed; but he also claimed that he had joined Peoples Temple originally as a government agent. In his death, Prokes sought to prove Jones's old conspiracy thesis. But he left behind not a shred of traceable evidence to prove or disprove his statement. He wrote, finally, "If my death doesn't prompt another book, it wasn't worth living." To date, it has not.

Amid an initial whirlwind of checkbook journalism, many publishers bought and commissioned books on the tragedy. Jonestown was not a fleeting news event; public opinion polls ranked it only behind Pearl Harbor and the John Kennedy assassination in terms of public recognition. Magazines, newspapers and tabloids scrambled for stories, some offering money to survivors for exclusive rights. There were instant books by the *San Francisco Chronicle* and the *Washington Post*. A number of ex-members and previously uninvolved writers turned out books, several by small religious publishing houses. The family of Debbie Blakey and Larry Layton, and escapee Odell Rhodes, wrote accounts with the help of professional writers. And an estimated two dozen other members began drafting manuscripts that to date have not been published. At least one commissioned book by a free-lance writer never was completed.

Immediately after Jonestown, the bidding by publishers probably was most intense for a nearly completed book by Jeannie Mills, formerly Deanna Mertle, one of the major sources for earlier exposés and co-founder of the Human Freedom Center in Berkeley. Mills aroused the ire of antimaterialist defectors and survivors alike when she used her $30,000 advance to buy a Mercedes Benz. Then, fifteen months after the tragedy, she and her husband Al were shot to death, execution-style, in their Berkeley home. Initially the murders resurrected the climate of fear, but police found no evidence of a Temple hit squad, and instead focused their attention on Eddie Mills, the dead couple's teen-age son.

Other media sought to capitalize on the Temple tragedy, sometimes with incredibly poor taste, distortions and blatant exploitation. The Jonestown affair was immortalized in several calypso records, including one with the refrain, "Who Shot Jimmy Jones?" A film made in Mexico and called *Guyana, Cult of the Damned* drew the scorn of critics and was repulsive to anyone familiar with church history. CBS followed with a highly rated two-part "docudrama" depicting Jones as a good man victimized and corrupted by others, mainly by women and a black man named Father Divine. Unfortunately, such partially fictionalized and sensationalized accounts reinforced myths about the Temple and created new ones, and they retarded public understanding of Peoples Temple.

At the same time, the public never received anything better than a disjointed accounting of government conduct and culpability in the tragedy, which was in part the fault of news media. In the aftermath, a number of government agencies tried to shelter themselves from any blame. But since jurisdictions at all levels of government had investigations into Temple activities, since advance warnings came through news media and private citizens, it became gratuitous for public guardians to claim that Jim Jones had "slipped between jurisdictions," that nothing could have been done to prevent the deaths of nine hundred Americans overseas, including a congressman.[76] Whether they could have stopped Jones or not in Guyana is debatable, but it is undeniable that they squandered opportunities in the United States, and made little attempt to check him abroad.

Both the House Committee on Foreign Affairs and the State Department itself criticized the State Department's handling of Peoples Temple. But neither provided a full airing of the government's role in the affair. State Department officials who dealt extensively with the Temple and who appear compromised in the Temple's internal reports never testified in public, nor were they subjected to public cross examination. And thousands of pages of documents—some reportedly indicating the depth of the government's knowledge about the Temple and the scope of the complaints brought to government attention—were classified. Many documents, especially those concerning the CIA and its knowledge of the Temple, have been exempted from disclosure. However, the House Committee on Intelligence, after months of study, found no evidence to suggest that the CIA knew about mistreatment of Jonestown residents, nor that the agency conducted mind-control experiments there, as some alleged, nor that it used Jones for its own purposes. Although Concerned Relatives said they asked the FBI for help, FBI Director William Webster maintained the bureau had opened no investigative file on Peoples Temple.

Larry Layton and Chuck Beikman were the only two Temple members ever charged in connection with the Guyana deaths; Beikman pleaded guilty in Guyana and was sentenced to prison for his role in the throat slashings of Sharon Amos and her children in Lamaha Gardens. Layton was acquitted there of attempting to murder defectors on the small airplane, then he was returned to the United States for prosecution in the murder of Ryan and the wounding of U.S. diplomat Richard Dwyer. Layton was not accused of actually having fired the shots, but of aiding and conspiring with others. After one mistrial, Layton was convicted in 1987 and was paroled in 2002.

Hundreds of millions of dollars in claims were placed against the assets of Peoples Temple by the families of the slain Ryan party members, by defectors and survivors. The federal government wanted $4 million to cover the cost of shipping the bodies back to the United States. A total of about $7 million was retrieved by a court-appointed receiver for disposition.

In Guyana, where the political opposition seized on the tragedy to embarrass the regime of Prime Minister Forbes Burnham, the government conducted an almost laughable inquest. A five-man jury concluded—at the government's direction—that all Jonestown residents were murdered by Jones. Later, the government appointed a high-level commission to study the Temple in Guyana, but the commission had yet to meet three years afterward. The affair exacted no political costs on the ruling party. In fact, in December 1980, Burnham was elected to another five-year term, in what an impartial British observation team concluded was another rigged election.

In California, the state attorney general's office, which declined to probe Temple matters in both 1972 and 1977 for jurisdictional reasons, finally investigated after the November 1978 episode. Investigators concluded that state health and welfare officials failed to handle properly serious complaints not only bearing on the treatment of foster children and children under guardianships, but also on the well-being of every child in Jonestown. It found no evidence of criminal wrongdoing by Tim Stoen, nor of any Temple welfare fraud conspiracy.

Virtually all local and state politicians associated with Jones have rebounded nicely. The lone exception was Stoen's former boss, District Attorney Joseph Freitas, who was defeated for reelection. Former California Lieutenant Governor Mervyn Dymally was elected congressman in a Los Angeles district in 1980. Assemblyman Willie Brown of San Francisco was elected by his peers as Speaker of the California State Assembly, considered the second most powerful office in the state. San Francisco voters elected former Sheriff Richard Hongisto to the county Board of Supervisors. Republican State Senator Milton Marks ran successfully for reelection, after winning the nomination of *both* major parties.

But despite any culpability of government bureaucrats, investigators or politicians, blame for the Jonestown tragedy must ultimately come to rest in the deranged person of Jim Jones. His ends-justify-the-means philosophy, paranoia, megalomania and charismatic personality must weigh much more heavily in the balance than any oversight, ineptitude, weakness or political exploitation by those outside the church. It was not the Temple's enemies that brought down the Temple, but Jones's destructive personality. The prophecy of doom had become an end in itself.

Despite his movement's collapse, some people continue to see the world through his eyes. Three years after his death, some still read his prophecies into world events and accept his world view. Though their leader is gone and their dream dashed, time has borne out some of Jones's social and political predictions. Most strikingly, his followers have seen a right-wing resurgence with the election of Ronald Reagan to the presidency, the growing boldness of the Ku Klux Klan and neo-Nazis. But now they face the troubled times alone, no longer with Jim Jones or the hierarchy of the Temple to guide their lives or to interpret history. Instead they have begun reestablishing their identities and making decisions about their lives as autonomous human beings. They have chosen life over death —and even chosen to bring children onto this wretched earth.

Contrary to the predictions of Jim Jones, the relationship of Grace Stoen and Walter Jones survived the years. They married and continued to live in San Francisco, Grace doing clerical work, and Walt working as a builder. In the Jonestown aftermath, they opened their home to survivors and tried to help them.

Tim Stoen weathered an attorney general's investigation, then migrated down the California coast to a small town to work on a book about the Temple and practice law. After the murder of the Millses, Stoen, deeply resented by some survivors, moved to parts unknown.

Teri Buford cooperated with attorney Mark Lane on his book about the church and continued to believe the church fell victim to government conspirators as well as to Jones.

Jim Cobb returned to dental school, intending to practice children's dentistry someday. He and his brother Johnny established a relationship and kept in touch with other members of the Temple basketball squad, including Stephan Jones.

Debbie and Mike Touchette lived in northern California. They became parents of a son and renewed ties with some defectors. After running the Temple boat in the Caribbean, Touchette's father Charlie joined him.

Sandy Bradshaw worked as a legal aide in San Francisco. Almost single-handedly she tried to present the positive side of the Temple experience—and she provided the authors with the perspective of a Jim Jones loyalist.

Archie Ijames reestablished friendships with some Temple defectors and former Temple critics, and cooperated with the authors. He remained a self-styled universalist—committed to the concept of helping his fellowman and to Temple-style communalism. He harbored deep bitterness for the man who betrayed Temple ideals, Jim Jones. Archie and Rosie Ijames were blessed with a new grandchild in California, but when they moved to Florida to help their adult son Norman with a business venture, tragedy struck the family once again: Norman died in a Venezuelan plane crash.

Dale Parks found work as an inhalation therapist in the Bay Area. The rest of his family moved back to the Ukiah area, and the Bogues did likewise. Juanita Bogue gave birth to a child conceived in Guyana.

Tim and Mike Carter escaped prosecution and were living in Idaho.

Stephan Jones started a new life for himself in the Bay Area.

Some outsiders were permanently affected, and sometimes more adversely so than the survivors. Others readjusted quickly and a few profited from the experience.

Sam Houston, despite more surgery and continuing health problems, not only fought back and resumed working at Associated Press but he also won an award as sports photographer of the year in the Bay Area. The family and Bob's widow Joyce reached an out-of-court settlement with Southern Pacific railroad in connection with Bob's still-mysterious death.

Leo Ryan's family—particularly his mother and one sister—pressed for full disclosure of government culpability and blamed the government for negligence in the congressman's death. About two years after Jonestown, it was reported that one of Ryan's daughters had joined an India-based cult; she insisted it was nothing like the Temple.

Anthony Katsaris recovered from severe wounds and went on to a teaching career in northern California. His father Steve Katsaris buried his daughter near Ukiah and resumed his life as a private school administrator. The story of Peoples Temple, he told the authors, is how Jim Jones could turn a close and loving child like Anthony into someone like Maria.

Howard Oliver survived his stroke, but was left in ill health; Beverly Oliver's wounds healed. Since their sons were gone, they took a smaller apartment.

Freddy Lewis, who lost twenty-seven relatives including his wife and seven children, kept working as a butcher at the same San Francisco supermarket. Each year on the anniversary of Jonestown, he returned to Oakland to the hillside mass grave of the unclaimed Jonestown dead, many of them children.

Clare Bouquet, the mother who tried so tirelessly to rescue her son from the Temple, finally met her daughter-in-law's family at Brian's funeral. She returned to her teaching job but found time to push for government inquiries into its own responsibility for the affair and to campaign for candidates who supported that goal.

Jackie Speier, who survived her terrible wounds, believed that Ryan in his dying breaths asked her to run for his congressional seat. She and a longtime Ryan aide, Joe Holsinger, ran against each other and lost to a third Democrat in the primary; a Republican took Ryan's place. Speier eventually landed a seat on the San Mateo County Board of Supervisors. Both she and Holsinger have called for public hearings into the tragedy and have blamed the U.S. government.

Like the Ryan family, Greg Robinson's family sued for Temple assets, hoping to make some memorial to their son. Greg's father also sued the State Department. With over $60,000 from the sale of Guyana photos, the *San Francisco Examiner* started a scholarship in Greg's memory at San Francisco State University.

Attorney Charles Garry resumed his law practice in San Francisco and tried to asist a number of survivors in readjusting, giving at least two of them jobs, and helping others. Garry still is haunted by the tragedy.

Attorney Mark Lane wrote an unheralded book called *The Strongest Poison* and went on a tour of college campuses in 1979, delivering at least thirty lectures at $2,750 each. *Esquire* and *Mother Jones* magazines published articles portraying him as a publicity-hungry opportunist. He later turned up in New York, defending pro-Khomeini students during the Iranian hostage crisis.

Despite the finality of the epitaph Annie Moore left beside Jim Jones's body, tell-tale signs point to the possibility that Jones had in fact made a plan for escaping the fate of his followers. Jones had always felt that a mass suicide might be subject to misinterpretation, that someone —he—would be needed to explain it to the press and authorities. On November 18, 1978, Jones spoke of being the last to die, which would have allowed him to flee after his people had killed themselves. The means for a last-minute escape were at hand and partially mobilized: the Port Kaituma airstrip assassins had left untouched the small plane, the Cessna, although they had disabled the larger plane. Did Jones make plans to escape by air with some of his aides?[77]

Jones apparently was alive when the Carter brothers and Prokes left the encampment with money and guns: Prokes, a onetime licensed pilot, certainly could have flown the Cessna on the Kaituma strip, and for that matter, so could Maria Katsaris, likely one of the last to die in Jonestown. Assuming that Prokes was designated pilot, the Carter brothers could have served two other functions: Mike was a radio man; Tim was a Vietnam vet with some knowledge of weapons and was Jones's most recent double agent. What did happen? The Carters and Prokes were apprehended in Kaituma, where they said they were sent to board the *Cudjo*, which is curious because the boat had been sent upriver that day.

If such an escape plan was readied for execution, or as a backup measure, we can only speculate as to whether Jones aborted it or whether someone else made sure that he did not survive the death of his movement. Unless new, documented information comes forward, the mystery will always remain: who shot Jim Jones?

Notes

1. Several of Lynetta Jones's literary efforts used in this book as epigraphs show at least a subconscious understanding and need to capture her son's personality problems and strengths. His grandiosity and her half-belief in his "godlike nature" are expressed by her poem about shaping a young child like clay; it was almost certainly *her* child. The foreboding tenor of her essay, *The Poisoner*, is undeniable. Though the effort was prompted by the poisoning of Temple dogs in Ukiah, it seems likely Lynetta was cognizant of the poisoning of the Joneses' chimpanzee in Indianapolis—and the atmosphere of paranoia and persecution which led to the mass poisoning after her death. Her "Ode to Liars" stands as a morality tale; one can almost imagine her showing it to her son, so that the unsubtle message might reach him without a direct confrontation. Whether intentionally or not, it tells the story of Jim Jones's lies, growing ever larger until they overtook and consumed him.

2. Mother-child scene related by Alicia Heck of Crete. Events in Lynetta's early life and marriage are based largely on her taped recollections and writings, mainly those designated 10B and 0761 by the FBI.

3. Boyhood friends said there was no indication that Jim's father belonged to the Klan, though Jim himself wore a sheet for religious reasons, and for theatrical reasons in the loft. The Lynn area was not considered Klan country; blacks were very scarce in the entire county. And just a few miles from Lynn, Levi Coffin had operated a way station for the underground railroad in Fountain City. What emerges is that Jim Jones blamed his father for the pain of his youth—and cast him later in a villainous role at times. Lynetta in her writings makes reference to bigotry in her husband's background, but does not venture any allegations about the Klan or overt racism.

4. As Lynetta Jones wrote about herself in 1974, in her lofty rhetorical style, "I had read the signs correctly in the early years of our marriage; economically, this marriage was and never could be greater than my ability to endorse it with whatever worldly goods were required to make it. I was of limited strength,

but according to my philosophy, nothing was impossible and my ambition for my son knew no bounds. I had chosen what I had considered a favorable time to bring him into the world, and my judgment had been at its lowest ebb at that moment. My son was born right in the midst of the Depression and all he had seen of this world since had been the grinding aftermath of depression."

5. Lynetta evidently sensed that neighbors disapproved of her motherly conduct. She wrote in 1974, in a manuscript obtained from the FBI under FOIA, that some people resented "something about my attitude toward my son. These I assumed to be close associates of my husband's sister-in-law, who held that one's character of a housewife was dwarfed by working outside the home. . . ."

6. The train incident is based on a July 30, 1976, letter from Mrs. Kennedy to Lynetta.

7. Lynetta Jones, in a narrative called "Skid Row," written evidently in 1974, ventured the opinion that Uncle Bill was murdered by some men who were angry with him over a $36 debt. In the course of her narrative, she also indicated that she and her husband did not sleep together, confirming information by George Fudge. The reason for separate beds was not explained, but perhaps it was related to Mr. Jones's coughing spells.

8. Lynetta apparently was conscious of her own eccentricity. Whether she was fantasizing or recounting, she revealed some of that attitude in a short narrative called "Jim Babe's adventures on the long walk." She said that she used to talk to two stuffed animals she made for Jim—Ms. Bear and Ms. Samantha. "I often discussed with them the vexations of our times and the trials and tribulations of my days. I missed them when they were absent from the big crib when dusk came, just as I missed young Jim at that hour when he was overdue from his wanderings. A psychiatrist would dub such conduct on my part as a departure from the norm, no doubt just as I, on the other hand, have always entertained a deep conviction that the theory advanced by the doctors of psychiatry is merely the outward manifestation of deep seated disturbance of the mind. There is no verification of the claim that psychiatry ever 'cured' anything or anybody."

9. In a Sept. 1977 tape made in Jonestown, Jones admitted great feelings of hostility and inferiority as a child. A partial transcript was published in the *Guyana Chronicle*, Dec. 6, 1978. The tape itself (Q134) was obtained under FOIA from the FBI.

10. These perceptions reflect Temple tapes of Jim and Lynetta, and Lynetta's written accounts. Pentecostal churches are organizations that seek fulfillment by absorbing the Holy Ghost or Holy Spirit. The members strive to emulate the early disciples of Christ who, on the first Pentecost, received the "gift of tongues."

11. In a 1974 account, Lynetta confirms Jim's urinary expertise, as related by boyhood friends Don Foreman and George Fudge. She said that after he was circumcised, apparently late in childhood, he could "piss over the chicken coop." Most likely, he won the contests because he developed a technique and because he called for contests when his bladder was full. Throughout his life, he would drink tremendous amounts of fluids, and in later life, he had minor urinary tract problems.

12. Lynetta Jones, in a tape recovered at Jonestown, confirmed Jim's hatred of the pool hall–card parlor, and of his father's routine. She also said he once gathered up rat poison to save the rodents riddling the building. Jones himself in the aforementioned tapes confirmed his hostility and lack of respect for his father.

13. Late in his life, Jim tried to recast his own youth. He wanted to be remembered as a great rogue in Lynn, courageously challenging the Middle American norms. He claimed in the Sept. 1977 Jonestown interview that he had

dated the school "whore," the girl whom no one took out in public but whom everyone took to bed. He claimed that he brought her to his prom and they danced by themselves, with all the sneaky hypocrites looking on. Actually, he dated the nice girls, the popular ones—and had moved out of Lynn before the prom.

14. Richmond preaching scene was described by Don Foreman, who witnessed this after giving Jim a ride there.

15. In a Temple tape recording made in 1977, Jones related the following:
Once as they washed dishes, Marceline told her husband, "I love you, but don't say anything about the Lord anymore."
"Fuck the Lord," Jim snapped—and they argued again. Out of frustration, Marceline threw a glass at him and cried. There were other rows, too.

16. Jones viewed his mother, the union organizer, as a potential target of the "Red" hunters at this time, when the FBI was snooping around factories.

17. The tendency to keep running, changing jobs and homes, etc. is one of the classic traits of paranoia.

18. If it was vitamin B_{12}, the shots likely either were useless or were used as a placebo. As an experienced nurse, Marceline would have known that someone with secondary anemia—after a disease, for instance—would not benefit from B_{12} except as psychological support. And Dr. Wayne Ritter, an internal medicine specialist on call to the Temple nursing homes, would have told her that anemia most likely would not have caused a collapse unless there was hemorrhage. Most likely, Jones was faking collapses in an effort to gain the sympathy of those around him, or a combination of drugs and fatigue had caused a physical reaction in a stressful time. Whether he was abusing drugs at this time is not known—but he certainly had access to prescription drugs. He once offered Winberg some Darvon for headache.

19. On Dec. 4, 1962, Lynetta Jones wrote a friend and mentioned her concern for Jim's health. "It is imperative that I have my birth certificate acceptable to immigration authorities at once as my son is ill in South America and I must go there as early as possible."

20. In a passage of a biography being prepared by the church, Jones apparently referred to the incident, with some changes and embellishment. "I . . . [took] him by the nape of the neck and [threatened] to throw him out of the second story window."

21. In a Nov. 1978 *Indianapolis Star News* story, Thomas Dickson of Tampa, Florida, a former assistant minister, said that Jones had started a church interrogation committee in the late 1950s after visiting Father Divine. Dickson said Jones believed people in the church were plotting against him, so he squelched dissent.

22. In preparation for the journey to California, Jones incorporated Wings of Deliverance in Indiana as a nonprofit tax-exempt religious corporation to receive properties donated by church members and to manage church business. Though Jones tightly guarded his personal and church finances, he most likely planned to use Wings to hold property donated by California pioneers; their homes and real estate could be held indefinitely tax-free, then sold as needed or when the real estate market was favorable. The procedure—which the Temple also would employ in a later exodus—provided another benefit: tying members financially to the Temple.

Although there were separate corporations, the distinction between church property and Jones's personal property had blurred. For years, Jones never took a salary, and he gave a great deal to the church; later he would give everything to the church in exchange for financial security for himself and his family.

The exact activities and revenue of the corporations never were recorded, and there is no indication that more than a handful of properties were donated to the Temple in Indiana. Indiana tax officials would revoke the charters of both entities on the same day in 1970 for failure to file any returns. In 1972, Wings would be reincorporated and a church member signing for Jones would liquidate a house, a nursing home, another property and the church building itself.

23. The Hindus believed in deities of many forms, in reincarnation and in liberation from earthly evils—a precept that jibed nicely with the personal sacrifice required of Temple members. Buddhism also emphasized self-sacrifice, teaching that extinction of the self and of the senses can transcend suffering and even existence. To Jones, there was great appeal in these concepts.

24. Christine Lucientes's conversion is taken from her account as described in a Temple chronicle called "No Haloes Please. . . ."

25. A Temple account said that Jones wanted nothing less than the position of assistant senior elder in Golden Rule.

26. Vitamin B_{12} is a placebo, something a physician might have suggested for hypochondria, which Jones later and earlier showed symptoms of having. An overdose of insulin, according to physicians, might well have made him incoherent. Among his physicians, there was some disagreement about whether Jones was diabetic or not.

27. This account, confirmed in part by Grace Stoen, is taken from a handwritten document to Jones from Tim Stoen.

28. As one 1970 leaflet put it: "Notice! Some in San Francisco have tried to hinder us from coming. In order to get a hall, we must pay $500 to rent the facilities, not including other items such as chairs, a P.A. system, organ, etc. . . ."

29. It probably was wise to maintain a Republican image in a county with a Republican district attorney, and a 37 percent Republican registration that converted into victories for Ronald Reagan in the gubernatorial race and for Richard Nixon in the presidential contest.

30. The Temple had laid the organizational groundwork for the new church some time earlier. After donations to the Southern California Disciples of Christ organization and on the recommendation of the northern California leadership, the Temple was accepted for affiliation with the Southern California region, as well. Dual affiliation was unusual, but Disciples considered the generous and large congregation a boon to the denomination. The Temple's large crusades and bus caravans even caused some officials to wonder whether Jim Jones planned to establish a nationwide church.

31. This account of John Stoen's escapades comes from undated prose by Lynetta Jones in Temple files.

32. Kinsolving later criticized the *Examiner* for bowing to pressure from the Temple. Yet on Oct. 5, 1972, he wrote a memo to a San Francisco journalism review in response to its inquiry: "I have been assured by men whom I trust . . . that the Examiner is by no means abandoning this subject because of extended picketing and threats from three attorneys. What we are waiting for now are further developments of a legal nature and which involve more legal than ecclesiastical . . . coverage."

Kinsolving said in a 1981 interview that he tried subsequently to get the *Examiner* to run the rest of his stories, but failed in that effort and in one to convince *Time* magazine, the *Los Angeles Times*, the Associated Press and others to pursue the story. In 1975, though no longer with the *Examiner*, Kinsolving picked up the chase again and lined up several Bay Area newspapers to publish a column on the Temple. But the Temple got wind of it and drew up a suit that probably scared off Kinsolving's publishers.

33. Marchesano disputed MacIntosh's recollection. In a 1979 interview, he told Reiterman he recalled no such meeting nor such a veiled bribe. Though

Kagele was not present for the meeting with Jones, the vice officer recalled that he had heard about the bribe offer at the time it allegedly was tendered. There is disagreement about the timing of the Temple donation offer too. Kagele believes it occurred after dismissal of the lewd conduct charges; MacIntosh thought it preceded dismissal.

34. Judge Stromwall declined to answer questions directly from the *San Francisco Examiner* in March 1979, but he answered some written questions from the Los Angeles press corps. He defended all his actions in the case, including his right to order Jones's records sealed and destroyed. He was asked whether he had any discussions with Kwan other than in the presence of a representative of the city attorney's office. "It's not my practice to discuss any case without both sides being present," he replied, according to the March 29, 1979, *San Francisco Examiner.*

35. In 1950 whites had comprised 89 percent of the population, blacks 5.6 and Asians 3.9. By 1960, blacks, many of whom came from the South seeking work, increased their percentage to 10.1. By 1972, the racial breakdown was 69.4 percent white, 14.1 black and 14.3 Asian, according to Frederick M. Wirt's *Power in the City*, p. 33. And the "minority" population would continue to grow.

36. The power-acquiring techniques of the Temple were neither unique nor inventive. Other close-knit organizations—for example, the Black Panther party in Oakland and Delancey Street Foundation in San Francisco—had won favor with Establishment figures and in some ways became partners through use of bodies available to them. In San Francisco, when issues of concern to left and liberal communities arose, Delancey Street and Peoples Temple either were involved themselves or were consulted. Jones and Maher, while not bosom friends, discussed matters of mutual interest such as protecting Indian leader Dennis Banks from extradition.

37. Hongisto later became police chief of Cleveland, Ohio, and was nominated to become head of New York State prisons. He returned to San Francisco and was elected to the Board of Supervisors.

38. Population breakdowns are estimates from Guyanese and American officials. The black minority government for obvious reasons does not like to distribute official statistics.

39. Though Jones added to the eclectic creed and made adjustments almost daily, the Temple's principles were no more jumbled than earlier pioneer communal societies. And some Temple lifestyles bore remarkable similarities to earlier communities, and their sexual, psychological and economic features. Their effect, if not intent, was to create great dependency and a psychological wall around the community.

In political respects, the Kaweah Cooperative Commonwealth, founded in the Sierra Nevadas in the 1880s, blazed a trail much like the Temple's. Its founders hoped to promote a kind of Christian anarchy—a mixture of Marxism and utopian socialism.

Another California utopia, Icaria Speranza, founded in 1881 by two Frenchmen near Cloverdale, about 25 miles south of Ukiah, espoused a community property concept resembling the Temple's. The community creed—that brotherhood among men was contingent upon complete equality of social rights—was consistent with Jones's concept of social justice, as were other guiding principles —the authority of the majority and control of the individual by the society. However, the Temple's supposed "authority of the majority"—or participatory democracy—was perverted by Jones's personal magnetism and conniving.

Templelike criticism or catharsis sessions were not new inventions in history. The Oneida Community, founded by John Humphrey Noyes in the mid-1800s in New York, conducted mutual-criticism sessions that, unlike the Temple's, incorporated safeguards against authoritarian tendencies. However, Jones, Noyes and a number of other communal leaders recognized the tremendous potential for control through sex and through relative isolation from outside morality. Noyes's closed community was perhaps ahead of its time in carrying on sexual experiments and selective breeding. While Jones arranged marriages, broke down sexual barriers and used sex to elevate and humiliate, his practices were not scientific enough to be labeled experiments.

Probably inadvertently, Jones almost duplicated some techniques of Thomas Lake Harris, a famous nineteenth-century mystic. One hundred and ten years before Jones had visions of an Indianapolis holocaust and a sanctuary among the California redwoods, Harris had envisioned himself "dwelling in the vicinage of the great forests of Sequoia near the Pacific." He moved seventy-five people from Brockton, New York, to establish a Santa Rosa area community called Fountaingrove. Harris separated husbands and wives and split children from their families, to train them to endure hard times, just as the Temple did with its "survival training." And as with Jones, a scandal eventually brought his downfall. In Harris's case, a San Francisco newspaper carried allegations of communal baths and mate-swapping. Harris—who had also adopted the title "Father"—was accused of having relations with five women in a single day (a feat Jones boasted to have tripled).

40. According to most definitions, Jones qualified as a cult leader. Cults are distinguished by charismatic leaders, and are based on a personality, not a creed. In his arrogance, the cult leader sets himself up as the fountain of all truth. Usually his most powerful truths are prophecies and revelations that cannot be tested. And he often creates the illusion of giving more to his people than he takes for himself.

Because commitment can be stronger than fear of death, cult leaders have a tremendous responsibility toward their members. As history has proved, they can exploit that commitment for good or evil.

However, in the universe of cults, Peoples Temple, with a claimed membership of 20,000 and a maximum of 3,000 to 5,000 regularly attending members, was a small planet. Jones's church was basically a one-state organization with satellite congregations. The Rev. Sun Myung Moon's Unification Church, on the other hand, claims 30,000 members in the United States alone, and has a worldwide following. The Church of Scientology, which maintains it is not a cult, claimed 5.5 million members worldwide in 1972. But as Jones reminded his people again and again, he was seeking quality rather than quantity.

41. Reiterman called Dawsey's house in Macon, Georgia, and the homes of some of Dawsey's relatives, but attempts to get Dawsey's comment were unsuccessful. A woman answering the phone May 12, 1980, at his home said Dawsey had nothing to say, then hung up.

42. Although Carlton Goodlett volunteered the existence of the company in a 1979 interview with Reiterman, he declined to name the company, list the partners or provide details about its activities. He said he would not discuss the details because the other partners were embarrassed about having been involved with Jim Jones. However, he insisted that the Temple had invested no money in the company. Goodlett gave the name, California Import Export Co., to author James Reston, Jr., yet the California Secretary of State's Office showed no record of incorporation.

43. There are some hints that John realized his paternity was a confused matter. In an undated letter, a friend of Lynetta's named Lois wrote her, "Dear Lynetta, please excuse my delay in answering your most interesting letters. Certainly enjoyed hearing of John Stoen and his discussion of his fathers. Where did he learn that type of language? He sounds like a very mature and interesting child." Ex-members confirmed that John spoke of his "two fathers."

44. Stoen would claim in a 1979 interview with Reiterman that he consented

to sending John to Guyana only to allay the church's fears that he was becoming disloyal, too. He said he really was planning to get John out of the church prior to departure, but Jones moved the boy sooner than expected.

45. In an Oct. 10, 1978, affidavit, Carolyn Layton said that the papers shown to Joyce Shaw stated that the church had esteem for Bob Houston and urged Shaw not to pressure the Houstons into removing their grandchildren from the church.

46. Others have reported that Jones collapsed at the Housing Authority when he heard about a Treasury Department investigation of the Temple. Yet, by best recollections, the collapse occurred March 23—the day of Stoen's disappearance. Furthermore, it is unlikely Jones knew of the Treasury investigation at that time. An affidavit by Dennis Banks, who tipped the Temple to it, says that he himself did not learn of the probe until May 1977. As for the validity of Jones's collapse, Sandy Bradshaw believed it might have been faked, simply to allow Jones to disappear from public life temporarily.

47. The Temple's Grenada visit went so well that Prime Minister Eric Gairy stopped off in San Francisco less than a month later, on June 2, before leaving for London for an award from Queen Elizabeth. He was welcomed at a Peoples Temple reception by Lieutenant Governor Mervyn Dymally, Mayor Moscone and other dignitaries. Less than two weeks later, Gairy opened the Organization of American States general assembly by repeating his call for an international inquiry into flying saucers. Such calls went over about as well as his oppressive government in Grenada. In March 1979, his government was overthrown by rebels, and a Marxist government installed.

48. Although the Temple never responded directly to the allegations one by one, their defense was printed by *San Francisco Chronicle* columnist Herb Caen, probably the church's most widely read media acquaintance. His lead item on Aug. 18, 1977, said: "The Rev. Jim Jones, target of a ceaseless media barrage these days, wants to come home and answer the charges being leveled at him and his Peoples Temple, but his lawyer, Charles Garry, is advising against it. 'Garry thinks Jim would be chewed up by the media,' says Jones's aide, Mike Prokes. . . . 'This campaign against Jim,' suggests Prokes, 'is orchestrated at the highest level, perhaps FBI or CIA. . . .'"

49. In a resignation letter prepared in mid-July on Housing Authority stationery, Jones said he was resigning because he received an appointment to the California State Board of Corrections and he noted that the City Charter prohibits anyone from belonging simultaneously to state and city commissions. (Governor Brown's office later would say that Jones's name had been submitted for the position and he was being considered at one time, but he never was appointed.) Although the church publicly denied it, drafts of Jones's resignation letters indicated that the Temple's troubles with the news media actually prompted his resignation.

50. According to documents seized by the Los Angeles district attorney's office in 1979, 50 pieces of property deeded to the Temple since Aug. 31, 1976, had been sold for a total of almost $1.5 million. That figure included only eight pieces of property in San Francisco, where the Temple had a few dozen communes, and only eight pieces in Ukiah, where the *San Francisco Examiner* located some 30 Temple properties, at least $1 million worth. So it appears that the Temple's total real estate holdings were worth well in excess of $2.5 million.

51. The $10 million figure is an estimate shared by Stoen and financial officer Debbie Blakey; it is consistent with assets recovered after the holocaust of 1978. Jones had told Stoen in 1970 that the church goal was to accumulate $10 million, and within five years, he told the attorney, "We've reached our goal." Former members, church members and law enforcement sources said the Temple kept numerous bank accounts all over California. There were better than a half

dozen accounts in various San Francisco banks alone, in the names of the Temple, Apostolic Corp., the Joneses and prominent members.

Even the search for the highest interest rates was a learning process for the Temple's plodding financiers. Although millions of dollars were available for investment, they struggled to obtain a mere 10 percent return on their money. For instance, in 1974–75, the Temple investors were guided largely by a San Francisco newspaper article which noted the high interest rates available through Canadian banks on short-term prime certificates of deposit.

Jones made various members trustees for his personal wealth, which Stoen believed exceeded $1 million when the minister came from Indiana in 1965. In return, the church paid Jones a salary of $20,000 and agreed to meet all his financial needs, including legal defense. In another trust arrangement, the children of Jim Jones were to receive $23,000 on their twenty-first birthdays, a protection not accorded other children in the Temple. From a technical standpoint, this arrangement allowed Jones to publicly plead personal poverty, and it constituted another bond between the man and his church, a financial one.

52. Six weeks after the holocaust, when Mike Touchette heard about the Temple's multimillion-dollar accounts, he was too angry to speak.

53. Associacion Evangelica de las Americas, formed ostensibly for church-related purposes, began operating in late 1975 with a bank account in Union Bank of Switzerland, Panama. The lawyers formed a dummy corporation, called Bridget, S.A., in case of lawsuits, and in Dec. 1975 opened an account with Swiss Banking Corp., Panama. Although the initial deposits were under $5,000, the Temple soon wired larger amounts—$20,000, $100,000, $200,000 or more. Wire transfers were used on the assumption that the money could not be traced that way.

For purposes of security, convenience and maximizing income, the money was spread around the world—in accounts in Switzerland, Panama, Venezuela, Guyana, Trinidad and the United States. As the exodus began in the late 1970s, the accounts in the U.S. became temporary repositories for operating expenses and for funds ultimately transferred to foreign accounts. Because of ease of withdrawal and concealment, the Temple placed the bulk of its money in Panama and Swiss banks, often in numbered accounts, or in the names of longtime but low-ranking members who almost certainly never would quit.

An example of how the church sought to disguise its assets and to keep money moving: the Panama account under Associacion Evangelica de las Americas first was transferred to Associacion Religosa por San Pedro, another front religious corporation. Then the funds were shifted to a numbered account, and later under the name of Esther Mueller, Jones's longtime housekeeper. In Oct. 1978, seven time deposits ranging from $200,000 to $1.6 million would be transferred to the name of Annie McGowan, another elderly Temple member. Similarly, even the dummy corporation Bridget was made into a numbered account.

The amounts in various accounts varied from nearly nothing to millions of dollars. The church reportedly kept up to $2 million in Union Bank of Switzerland in Zurich, but usually no more than $1 million, and even these funds were later transferred to Panama. The funds kept in Caracas, where the Temple frequently did business, were limited too; in fact, the final balance would be $33,757 in Maria Katsaris's name. For a time, the church maintained an account with the Banco Mercantile in Panama City, as well as a separate account operating Temple boats. In Trinidad, an account contained funds for purchasing equipment and supplies for Jonestown. The balance in the Guyana banks seldom dipped below $1 million —most of it in external accounts in U.S. dollars. Although Jones had promised to deposit millions of dollars in Guyanese banks, he kept most Guyana funds out of the official Guyana bank, the National Cooperative Bank of Guyana, because he feared money would be frozen there if the Temple were forced to flee the country.

Also, Jones did not want to lose money on reconversion from the weak Guyanese dollars to U.S. dollars.

54. Freitas was defeated in his 1979 reelection bid in part because of his office's handling of the Peoples Temple case and the Dan White murder prosecution. His opponent, Arlo Smith of the state attorney general's office, hit very hard on Freitas's Temple probe and the conduct of the Stoen voter fraud investigation. Ironically, the state attorney general's office itself could come up with no evidence of wrongdoing, though its voter fraud reinvestigation, it should be noted, was hamstrung by the destruction of old voter records.

55. A World Airways spokesman later told Reiterman that although there were no negotiations about a plane at the time, there may possibly have been a call to World by Mazor. However, there was no record of such a call, no discussion with Daly nor with senior vice-president Brian Cook, the spokesman said.

56. According to a Banks affidavit in Sept. 1977, the Indian leader met with David Conn in May 1977 at the El Cerrito home of another Indian activist, Lehman Brightman. There, after reading him some disparaging material about Jones, Conn asked Banks, then a fugitive, to do two things—one, make a public denunciation of Jones; two, meet with a Treasury agent. All this, claimed Conn, would help Banks's chances at avoiding extradition to South Dakota. Conn later would say that he respected Banks and was only trying to spare him embarrassment. For his part, Banks—benefactor of a $20,000 Temple donation and never a great fan of government agents—logically considered Conn's approach a blackmail attempt, so he informed the Temple. Soon Temple members began eavesdropping under the home of Conn's former wife, and were able to confirm the existence of the Treasury investigation—*before* many of the guns had been shipped.

57. Traces by the Federal Bureau of Alcohol, Tobacco, and Firearms after the November 1978 holocaust determined that several guns recovered in Jonestown were purchased legally at the San Francisco Gun Exchange.

58. On Sept. 29, the Temple learned about the search from its shipping agent in Miami, who told them that seven customs men held up the cargo, then pulled and searched one crate at random. In reaction, the Temple alerted Charles Garry, who asked customs for an explanation, but the agency refused to explain the search, and would neither confirm nor deny the investigation.

Assistant Guyanese Police Commissioner C. A. "Skip" Roberts shared the Aug. 26, 1977, customs report with Temple women public relations workers. (Roberts told the authors in 1981 that he did so after the Temple demanded to know why Guyanese authorities were checking incoming cargo so closely.) The Temple memo on the contents said Interpol had sent the customs report to Guyana "because [the] investigation disclosed allegations that Jones intends to establish a political power base in Guyana and that he may currently have several hundred firearms in that country."

59. With troubles mounting throughout the period, the demands on Garry's law firm probably consumed a tremendous amount of time beyond the $37,000 worth which they billed.

60. Stoen had asked Grace to sign it, he said, but she thought it was ridiculous and refused. She later would deny even having seen it during her Temple days. As stated earlier, Stoen did not tell Grace that *he* signed it.

61. Perhaps Jones was reacting to the April 11 press conference called by "concerned relatives" in San Francisco.

62. Amos and Debbie Touchette also discussed the Stoen case with Fred Wills and Home Affairs Minister Mingo on at least several occasions.

63. "When we told him, Mingo, about Barker's negative reactions to us," Amos reported to Jones, "he told us he'd have a talk with Barker and explain the official government position toward us. The next time . . . Barker . . . was extremely nice, making a very pointed effort to say hello and smile . . . "

64. A month after Kathy Hunter's ordeal, free-lance reporter Gordon Lindsay came to Georgetown while doing a story on the Temple for the *National Enquirer.* After immigration officials inexplicably ordered him out of the country, he and his photographer chartered a plane in Trinidad and made eleven sweeps over Jonestown. They spotted not a single person in the camp until the plane climbed and banked away; then people poured out of the cabins to watch the intruders leave. The Temple complained to U.S. Consul Richard McCoy, wrote an informational memo on the violation of Jonestown "air space" and later claimed that the plane buzzed the camp, causing an elderly resident to have a heart attack.

65. No one in the Embassy felt it was worth several days to take a boat trip in, though little else should have been more compelling in a country of such small size and minor strategic importance. Ambassador Burke, who later would say he was too busy administering a $6 million aid program and tending to other duties, chose never to visit in person because he was afraid Jones might somehow exploit the trip, claiming it as proof of the Embassy's approval.

66. If the agency were searching for the perfect coercive drug, it would not have left other coercive techniques—sensory deprivation boxes, beating and humiliation—in plain sight of everyone which would have defeated the purpose of the drug. And by all accounts, the CIA had abandoned the program before 1970 at the latest.

Joe Holsinger, former aide to Leo Ryan, is the chief proponent of the MK-ULTRA theory, based partly on a speculative and unpublicized paper by an unnamed Berkeley psychiatrist and based on circumstantial arranging of certain facts—including an apparent mistake by Jones on the last tape in Jonestown. Proponents of the theory allege that Embassy official Richard Dwyer was a CIA agent and was in fact present at the murder-suicides—and their proof is Jones's command, "Get Dwyer out of here." Most likely Jones had incorrectly assumed that Dwyer was in the camp, and not at the airstrip with the Ryan party. Dwyer had planned to accompany Ryan to the airstrip, then return to Jonestown to process any additional defectors. But the airstrip shooting intervened, and he was wounded there.

The first apparent mention of the CIA and MK-ULTRA was in a Black Panther newspaper. The paper also said that the Jonestown killings were caused by the American government with a neutron bomb, since black people tend not to commit suicide.

When asked by House Foreign Affairs Committee investigators about CIA infiltration of Peoples Temple or a government conspiracy against it, Temple insider Teri Buford and her lawyer, Mark Lane, perhaps the foremost conspiracy theorist in the world, could offer only scant evidence. Buford, in secret testimony, said she had suspected Edith Roller of being a CIA agent because of the voluminous diary she kept, day by day, for years. Roller, who died in Jonestown, was sixty-three. Lane could refer for evidence only to Tim Stoen and Joe Mazor. And when asked if anyone connected to the Embassy could have been part of a government-CIA conspiracy against the Temple, Lane did not mention Dwyer—his only contact and the man most commonly linked in other conspiracy theories—but said McCoy's conduct was "almost unexplainable." Dwyer later was asked by reporters, including Jacobs, if he worked for the CIA. He said his terms of employment with the foreign service forbade him either to confirm or deny it.

As a reporter for the *Washington Post,* John Jacobs spent three months investigating the CIA's MK-ULTRA program, wrote several dozen articles on the subject for the *Post* in the summer and early fall of 1977, and personally reviewed thousands of pages of CIA MK-ULTRA documents released under the Freedom of Information Act.

67. Temple recipients of Supplemental Securities Income (SSI) for the aged, blind and disabled of limited means were not permitted by law to receive those benefits while living overseas. Yet Temple records showed that more than 100 checks were received incorrectly at Jonestown between July and Dec. 1977. Later, Social Security officials tried to stop the forwarding of such checks, but postal officials, apparently erroneously, stopped all social security checks, even those receivable overseas. Rep. Phil Burton and actress Jane Fonda came to the Temple's aid. When the regular social security payments resumed, so did some of the illegal SSI payments. About 102 more SSI checks worth $18,691 reached Jonestown, and after the holocaust the church returned them. A later agency investigation showed that 23 of the 160 Jonestown residents who ever had collected SSI were overpaid a total of 93 checks worth $17,549. Officials found that 17 percent of the Jonestown residents had been on SSI, compared with a 2 percent national average.

A November 1979 "Investigation Report on Peoples Temple," prepared by the California Department of Social Services, found that of 992 Temple members checked, 550—about 55 percent—had a history of receiving public assistance of some sort. According to the report, 109 of the 550 continued to receive assistance in Guyana, and 51 of those cases were "potentially fraudulent." Fifteen cases involved forgeries on checks and 36 cases involved parents, spouses or grandparents fraudulently signing public assistance checks after the rest of the family had migrated to Guyana.

Twenty children in Guyana had a history of receiving foster care payments from California, but the report said all but one payment was discontinued and returned to the natural or adoptive parent or legal guardian before the child migrated. The one exception, payment for a nine-year-old, was discontinued in September 1977.

68. Goodlett insisted that Jones go to a hospital in New York, Cuba or even the Soviet Union, for a better diagnosis. But Jones refused to budge from the jungle, instead sending Goodlett sputum samples by overseas courier.

69. The truth behind all this is something else altogether: odds are there was never more than one mercenary—Joe Mazor—and that he did his stalking from San Francisco, not the Venezuelan jungle. Perhaps, inspired by the prospect of a $25,000 movie consultancy fee, Mazor was gilding and padding his "movie role." His stories—in Jonestown and later to reporters—were far-fetched and contradictory. Mazor was careful to avoid saying directly that, among other things, he had fired on Jonestown, or that the supposed expeditionary force had intended to assassinate Jim Jones, though he said as much by implication.

Later, Mazor would claim that he had accepted the Temple's invitation in 1978 not because he was working for them, but just to "see the place," hardly an explanation if he had spent two days spying on it a year earlier. And, if he had seen shotguns during those two days, as he claimed, why did he now tell Jones the camp needed better security, and why did he offer to come back to train members in security and volunteer to send Jones a bulletproof vest?

70. In a Feb. 4, 1979, article in the *New York Times*, reporter John Crewdson quoted Bob Levering as saying Mark Lane expressed an interest in the *Enquirer* article during lunch. Levering told Crewdson that Hal Jacques of the *Enquirer* had responded that the newspaper "had canned it, or words to that effect." Both Lane and Jacques deny that. If it were true, that would mean that Lane already knew that the *National Enquirer* article was dead when he accepted Temple money to counter it.

Lane told *Los Angeles Times* reporters Henry Weinstein and Robert Scheer that he never accepted money to get an article killed but did not see anything wrong with such an act. In their Dec. 4, 1978, *Los Angeles Times* story, Lane is quoted as saying that he met with Temple members in Los Angeles "about refuting or investigating statements that were made in various articles," including the *Enquirer*. The Los Angeles district attorney's office investigated the matter but did not find grounds to prosecute Lane.

71. On February 24, 1978, only seven months before the Jones letter was sent, State Department spokesman Hodding Carter III had written to Jones thanking him for sending his views on United States–Guyana relations. "While it is impossible for President Carter to respond personally to all of the correspondence . . . every communication is carefully read and noted, and the contents are reported to the Secretary of State. . . ."

72. Temple lawyer Gene Chaikin described the problem of Garry's continuing representation in a November memo to Jones: "Charles is a liberal. If he had any intimate knowledge of the situation here, or to some extent in the USA, he would not approve . . ."

73. All those missing did in fact survive.

74. Lane later would deny both publicly and in a Feb. 2, 1978, letter to Jackie Speier that he had any knowledge about the cheese sandwiches being drugged. In a Nov. 24, 1978, article, Charles Krause of the *Washington Post* wrote, "Lane says now that he knew strong depressants and tranquilizers were used to keep the people at Jonestown against their will. . . . Lane also says that he was warned beforehand that the grilled cheese sandwiches served out Saturday by the Peoples Temple to Ryan and others in his party may have been laced with tranquilizers or other drugs. 'I brought along some cough drops, which have a lot of sugar in them,' Lane said. 'I sure as hell wasn't going to eat the cheese sandwiches.' " In an interview with Reiterman, however, Stanley Clayton, who worked in the kitchen that day, said he never had prepared grilled cheese sandwiches at Jonestown and did not believe the sandwiches were drugged.

75. John Russell, spokesman for the U.S. Justice Department, told Reiterman in 1979 that Jones's death was caused by a gunshot wound to the head, a contact wound, meaning the gun barrel was pressed against his skull. Annie Moore, he said, was killed by a shot to the head too. Only one other Jonestown resident was reported killed by gunfire, an unidentified man found on a path.

A U.S. Air Force autopsy on Dec. 15, 1978, concluded that Jones died of a gunshot wound to the left temple but could not determine the manner of death. The autopsy report stated, however, "The manner of death is consistent with suicide because of the finding of a hard contact gunshot wound to the head. The possibility of homicide cannot be entirely ruled out because of the lack of specific and reliable information."

The autopsy found no evidence of prior disease. Although concentrations of pentobarbital in the liver and kidneys were within "the generally accepted lethal range," the drug level within the brain—the most critical indicator—was *not* within the lethal range. The cause of death was not thought to be barbiturate intoxication because the brain level was low; tolerance can be developed for barbiturates and the lethal levels vary from individual to individual.

76. The authors had intended to include a complete list of the Jonestown dead but discovered that no such roster had been compiled. A list supplied by the court-appointed Peoples Temple receiver in February 1982 contained only 883 names—those 660 people whose bodies were positively identified and 223 who were presumed to have died at Jonestown. Receiver Robert Fabian said there was no way to account for the other 30 bodies found at Jonestown but suggested that many were children who had been born there. The authors decided against using the list, however, because it contained many omissions, some inaccurate entries, and other errors in the case of adult membership.

77. Additionally, there was an unconfirmed report of a radio message to

Temple members elsewhere in the Caribbean that six people from Jonestown soon would be flying to meet them. Who would the six have been? The Carters and Prokes, plus Jones. Was Larry Layton the fifth? Would Jones have added Maria Katsaris as a copilot, Annie Moore as nurse, or Carolyn Layton as his most valued mistress and adviser? If so, would he have brought along John Stoen or Kimo Prokes?

Sources

PROLOGUE

INTERVIEWS

Sam and Nadyne Houston; Joyce Shaw; James Berdahl, U.C. band director; Tom Tuttle; Garry Lambrev.

MATERIALS

Peoples Forum newspapers, 1976–77; San Francisco police and coroner's reports on Bob Houston's death; the Houston family photo album.

1. A SCRUFFY START

INTERVIEWS

Two residents of Crete, including Alicia Heck; Donald Foreman; George Fudge; Thelma Kennedy Manning; three of Jones's former schoolteachers in Lynn; Frank Beverly; Stephan Jones; several Lynn residents, including Bill Townscend and Oliver Thornberg; Dick Reynolds, *Richmond Palladium Item* reporter-columnist who provided background on the region.

MATERIALS

Lynetta Jones's poem, entitled "The Molder," and dated Jan. 23, 1977, from *Peoples Forum* newspaper and document HH6A obtained from FBI under Freedom of Information Act (FOIA); Lynn School records and Jones's report cards; assorted *Richmond Palladium Item* articles about Crete, Lynn and Jim's background; historical information from *The Glory and the Dream*, by William Manchester (Little, Brown, 1973); Lynetta Jones's personal papers from Peoples Temple files in San Francisco; Nov. 1978 wire service stories quoting Lynn residents Wallace Fields and Vera Price on Jones's boyhood; Lynetta Jones's family background from her personal papers and from Nov. 1978 stories by the *Indianapolis Star News;* Lynetta's tape-recorded reflections on her background and on Jim's childhood, from Peoples Temple files recovered at Jonestown and released by the FBI under FOIA; school photos of Jones from Don Foreman; Jones childhood photos from the family photo collection; and Jim Jones's own reflections on his childhood, from tapes in Sept. 1977 in Jonestown, obtained under FOIA from the FBI.

2. BREAKING AWAY

INTERVIEWS

Don Foreman; Bill Townscend; Thelma Manning; Violet Myers; George Fudge; several unnamed teachers and classmates; Frank Beverly.

MATERIALS

Lynn School records and class photos; accounts of Jim and Lynetta in tapes and written documents obtained from the FBI under FOIA; William Manchester's *Glory and the Dream.*

3. MARCELINE

INTERVIEWS

Walter and Charlotte Baldwin; Marceline's sister's, Sharon Mills and Eloise Klingman; Marceline's cousin Ronnie Baldwin; Evelyn Eadler and a few unnamed fellow nursing students at Reid; Dick Reynolds of the Richmond newspaper; Tom Lowry, Reid Memorial Hospital spokesman; a Richmond High School spokesman; Kenneth Lemmons; Jim Green, Indiana University spokesman; I.U. Alumni Association; a Methodist Church information center spokesman; Russell and Wilma Winberg; Don Foreman; George Fudge.

MATERIALS

Marceline Jones's accounts of their courtship and early marriage, some dated May 20, 1975, and some undated, though probably written in the late 1970s, in document HH-61 obtained from FBI under FOIA; Reid Memorial Hospital records on Jim and Marceline; photos of Marceline's nursing class; Indiana University records of Jones's attendance and curriculum; Richmond High School yearbook; Methodist Social Creed; wedding photos.

4. THE CALLING

INTERVIEWS

Russell and Wilma Winberg; Archie Ijames; Rev. Ross Case; Jim Cobb; various people attending a Winberg revival meeting December 1979; Stephan Jones; Charlotte and Walter Baldwin; Rev. Edwin and Audrey Wilson; Rev. R. T. Bosler and Mercer Mance, who recommended Jones for the Indianapolis Human Rights post.

MATERIALS

Richmond Palladium Item, March 1953 article on Jones; Butler University school paper's article on Jones; Marceline Jones's undated account of their early marriage obtained from the FBI under FOIA; Jim's account of early marriage from the Sept. 1977 tape recovered at Jonestown, from FBI document called "Letters from Jim Jones" and from the Dec. 6, 1978, transcript printed in the *Guyana Chronicle;* accounts of then-Temple members Rick Cordell, Rheaviana Beam and Esther Mueller regarding early Temple obtained from the FBI under FOIA (document HH-6); May 1956 *Herald of Faith* article by Jones; Temple photos of the free restaurant, with captions, obtained under FOIA from FBI; Loretta (Stewart) Cordell's account of her conversion, called "No Haloes Please," from church files in San Francisco; April 10, 1954, *Indianapolis Star* and Jan. 4, 1957, *Indianapolis News* stories on Jones.

5. NEW DIRECTIONS

INTERVIEWS

Russell and Wilma Winberg; Edwin and Audrey Wilson; Mother Divine and several followers by *San Francisco Examiner* for a story by Tim Reiterman and Ken Kelley, 1979; Charlotte and Walter Baldwin; Archie Ijames; Bonnie Thielmann; Ross Case.

MATERIALS

Philadelphia Inquirer stories on Divine, including Dec. 6, 1979; numerous stories from *San Francisco Examiner* clipping file on Divine including Reiterman–Ken Kelley story April 18, 1979; tape of Jones's 1959 sermon obtained under FOIA from FBI; March 25, 1979, story about Carlos Foster and Cuban recruitment written by Joseph B. Treaster, *New York Times*, appeared in *San Francisco Chronicle*, March 27, 1979; Tim Stoen letter of Jan. 24, 1977, to Castro regarding Jones's first visit; accounts of the auto accident were based on an AP story May 11, 1959, Audrey Wilson's recollections, and Jones's account (document SO-1) obtained under FOIA; the song "Black Baby" from Peoples Temple song book, courtesy Ross Case; written releases from the Peace Mission regarding its contacts with Jones.

6. THE CRUSADER COLLAPSES

INTERVIEWS

Ross Case; Disciples of Christ officials, including A. Dale Fiers; Indianapolis civil rights pioneers, including Mercer Mance and Rev. R. T. Bosler; former Mayor Charles Boswell; Archie Ijames; Russell Winberg; Charlotte and Walter Baldwin; Rev. Edwin and Audrey Wilson; Dr. E. Paul Thomas; Dr. Wayne Ritter; Stephan Jones.

MATERIALS

Various reports of Jones's civil rights work from Indiana newspapers including the *Indianapolis Star*, the *Indianapolis Times* and the Butler University student newspaper; the *Indianapolis Record*, Oct. 7, 1961, "Jones Integrates Hospital"; *Guyana Graphic*, Oct. 25, 1961, "Church Blamed for Reds' Rise"; undated Marceline Jones account of early ministry obtained under FOIA (FBI document HH-6) and from Temple files; Jones's power of attorney document to Lynetta from church files; January 1962 *Esquire* magazine article; Jones résumé from church files; Indiana University school records of Jones.

7. ASYLUM

INTERVIEWS

Rev. Edward Malmin; Bonnie Thielmann; Stephan Jones; Ross Case; Archie Ijames; Walter and Charlotte Baldwin; Russell Winberg.

MATERIALS

Article on Jones's Brazil stay, from *Manchete*, Nov. 1978; a Temple tape of Stephan Jones, undated but apparently made in 1978 for an official Jones biography; Lynetta Jones letter, Dec. 4, 1962; various *San Francisco Examiner* clippings on Brazil politics in the 1960s; *Standard American Encyclopedia*, Vol. 3, 1940, on Brazil; *A Broken God*, by Bonnie Thielmann with Dean Merrill (David C. Cook Publishing Co., 1979); *Post Report*, 1966, U.S. Embassy in Rio; Rheaviana Beam account of Brazil stay obtained under FOIA from FBI; *Macumba*, by Serge Bramley (St. Martin's Press, 1977); *Golden Book Picture Atlas*, 1960, Book 2, Margaret Bevans; Lynetta Jones correspondence during the period; Jones's own account of the period, taped by the Temple and reprinted in *Guyana Chronicle*, Dec. 6, 1978.

8. THE PROPHET

INTERVIEWS

Rev. Russell Winberg; Rev. Edward Malmin; Archie Ijames; Ross Case; ex-member of the Indiana temple who declined use of her name; Sandy Bradshaw; the Baldwins; Mickey Touchette; former *Ukiah Daily Journal* editor George Hunter; several tax officials from the state of Indiana and the IRS.

MATERIALS

Poem by Judy Houston from a Temple newsletter, 1973; a Temple pamphlet, "The Letter Killeth. . ."; *Indianapolis News,* April 17, 1965; correspondence with the IRS in 1977–78; *San Francisco Examiner* stories by Reiterman, Sept. 1977, regarding real estate acquisition and Indiana corporations; *Esquire,* Jan. 1962; Mendocino County background from *Historic Spots in California,* by Mildred Hoover, Hero Rensch and Ethel Rensch (Stanford University Press, 1966); Rheaviana Beam account of Brazil period and westward move obtained under FOIA; Harold Cordell letter, Feb. 18, 1965, to Ross Case; Indiana corporations records obtained from State of Indiana and Temple files.

9. RURAL EDEN

INTERVIEWS

Stephan Jones; Jim Cobb; George Hunter; Archie Ijames; Wanda Kice; Golden Rule official who asked anonymity; Ross Case; Mike Touchette; various Redwood Valley and Potter Valley residents.

MATERIALS

Esther Mueller, Rheaviana Beam and Richard Cordell accounts of move west, obtained under FOIA; *Ukiah Daily Journal* article, July 26, 1965; unpublished *San Francisco Examiner* stories by Lester Kinsolving, 1972; chronicle of Golden Rule takeover bid from Temple files; list of alleged attacks on the church, compiled in 1977–78 by the church.

10. A DREAM OF LOVE

INTERVIEWS

Grace Grech Stoen; Tim Stoen; Jim Cobb; Jeanette Kerns; attorneys Jeff Haas and Margaret Ryan; a former teacher of Grace Grech.

DOCUMENTS

Tim Stoen résumés and other papers in Temple files; June 1970 article in the *Ukiah Daily Journal* reporting the marriage; copies of vows, from church files.

11. CHILDREN OF THE SIXTIES

INTERVIEWS

Debbie Layton Blakey; John Finn, a Larry Layton schoolmate at Davis and Berkeley; Rev. and Mrs. John Moore; a Potter Valley schools source; Joyce Shaw; Sam and Nadyne Houston; Tom Tuttle, the brother of Phyllis Houston; John Pizzo, Layton's supervisor at St. Mary's Hospital, San Francisco, and several church members who knew the Laytons and Houstons.

MATERIALS

Berkeley Tribe, Aug. 22, 1969; *Glory and the Dream,* by William Manchester; Reiterman's masters of journalism thesis "Alternative Institutions," 1972, University of California, Berkeley; Robert Lindsey's *New York Times* story on the Laytons, Dec. 3, 1978.

12. FAMILY AFFAIR

INTERVIEWS

Stephan Jones; Marceline's sister, Sharon Mills; Rev. and Mrs. John Moore; the Baldwins; Archie Ijames; Ruby Bogner; Sandy Bradshaw and several other former Temple members on Jones's drug use and sexual activity.

MATERIALS

Stephan Jones's poem about his mother, 1971, courtesy Stephan Jones.

13. GOLDEN BOY

INTERVIEWS

Grace Stoen; Tim Stoen; Disciples of Christ officials including Karl Irvin and A. Dale Fiers; Republican official Marge Boynton; District Attorney Duncan James; Supervisor Al Barbero; social services chief Dennis Denny; U.S. Department of Agriculture officials; the Baldwins; Stephan Jones; Sandy Bradshaw; Jeanette Kerns; State Assemblyman Willie Brown; former San Francisco Supervisor Dianne Feinstein; former San Francisco Chief Administrative Officer Tom Mellon; the physician attending the birth of John Stoen (the doctor requested anonymity); Reiterman's radio-telephone interview with Jim Jones from Guyana, Feb. 1978.

MATERIALS

USDA investigation report on the alleged theft of agricultural commodities by the Temple; Temple documents requesting the ordination of Tim Stoen and Guy Young; various Stoen documents in Temple files; birth records of John Stoen from Santa Rosa Memorial Hospital; Feb. 6, 1972, statement of Stoen regarding John's paternity.

14. ON THE ROAD

INTERVIEWS

Joyce Shaw; Garry Lambrev; Sandy Bradshaw; Stephan Jones; Tim Stoen; Rev. George L. Bedford and his wife Estelle; Rev. Amos Brown; Rev. Cecil Williams; Carlton Goodlett; former Supervisor Terry Francois, and others in the San Francisco black community; Council of Churches sources; Democratic Central Committee sources; Agar Jaicks; Mother Divine; Birdie Marable; Elmer and Deanna Mertle (Jeannie and Al Mills); Archie Ijames.

MATERIALS

Temple newsletters and newspapers from Joyce Shaw and Temple files; police reports of death threats against Hannibal Williams; *San Francisco Examiner* library files on Father Divine, with dozens of newspaper and magazine stories.

15. THE HAIR OF THE RAVEN

This chapter is based on a Peoples Temple videotape of the service in Ukiah. The quotes are taken verbatim from the tapes, with editing for length; the description comes from observing the tape and from numerous interviews with Temple members. The analysis is our own.

16. WIRING THE TOWN

INTERVIEWS

Sandy Bradshaw; Tim Stoen; Grace Stoen; Jim Cobb; George Hunter; Marge Boynton; Garry Lambrev; owners of the local answering service and former owners; Jim Adameski and other local Redwood Valley residents who worked with Temple members; Walter Heady; Dr. S. R. Boynton; Dennis Denny; former Supervisor Al Barbero.

MATERIALS
Temple correspondence with politicians from Temple files and from the FBI under FOIA; *San Francisco Examiner* checks with Mendocino sheriff's office to obtain names of Temple members given gun permits and status as reserve deputies; Temple tapes of conversations between Jones and Denny, and between Jones and Sheriff Tom Jondahi; USDA investigation report on alleged Temple theft of agricultural commodities.

17. THE SYSTEM AT WORK

INTERVIEWS
Grace Stoen, Sandy Bradshaw; Tim Stoen; Wayne Pietila; Jim Cobb; Mike Touchette; Archie Ijames; Stephan Jones; Linda Dunn by the *San Francisco Examiner*'s Nancy Dooley, 1977.

18. LOURDES ON WHEELS

INTERVIEWS
Disciples of Christ officials; Stephan Jones; Tim Stoen; Sandy Bradshaw; Tim Carter; Joyce Shaw; Grace Stoen; Jeanette Kerns; Laura Cornelious by the *San Francisco Examiner*'s Nancy Dooley, 1977; Richard Cordell on the mailers; Jeannie and Al Mills on fund raising; Mickey Touchette on collections; Don Foreman; Thelma Manning.

MATERIALS
Temple newsletters and newspapers; printed announcements of the Los Angeles temple opening from church files; Disciples of Christ annual donation reports; *Congressional Record* item on the Temple, June 1973; *Washington Post* editorial about the Temple, Aug. 18, 1973; sampling of Temple leaflets from church files; June 29, 1976 *Richmond Palladium Item* account of Jones's return home, and July 9, 1976, Temple press release about bus trip by 600, covering 10,000 miles over three weeks; prose by Lynetta Jones found in Temple files.

19. SEX IN THE TEMPLE

INTERVIEWS
Archie Ijames; Sandy Bradshaw; Grace Stoen; Mike Touchette; Tim Stoen; Jeannie and Al Mills; Tim Carter; Rev. and Mrs. John Moore; Stephan Jones; Jeanette Kerns; a boyhood friend of Mike Prokes.

MATERIALS
Articles on Karen Tow Layton in *Chico* [Calif.] *Enterprise Record,* Jan. 30, 1979, and in *New York Times,* Nov. 1978; Temple records of undated sexual confessions from church files.

20. TRAINING YOUNG MINDS

INTERVIEWS
Stephan Jones; Ruby Bogner; a Potter Valley teacher and an administrator there, both of whom requested anonymity; Redwood Valley parents; Mike Touchette; Jim Cobb; Jeanette Kerns; Wayne Pietila; Mickey Touchette; Sandy Bradshaw; then-San Francisco Police Chief Charles Gain, and other police officials and San Francisco Community College District officials on the gun training received by Temple members.

DOCUMENTS
Jones family photo album; school records, athletic and scholastic awards and poetry of Stephan Jones; newspaper clippings of Jones boys' athletic achievements; Temple records and questionnaire by Eddie Mills; trunks full of testimonies from Jones by his followers, including children; a certificate showing that Jim Cobb completed the gun training course from July through Sept. 1972.

21. HER FATHER'S DAUGHTER

INTERVIEWS
Steve Katsaris; Jeanette Kerns; Stephan Jones; Sandy Bradshaw; Tim Stoen; Jeannie and Al Mills; Grace Stoen; Mike Touchette.

DOCUMENTS
Los Angeles Times story by Bella Stumbo; Katsaris family photos and correspondence; newspaper articles about Katsaris in Salt Lake City and California; background check on Katsaris by a private investigator hired by the Temple; Temple tapes of Katsaris visit to the church, Aug. 1, 1972, obtained under FOIA from the FBI; description of the seduction of Maria largely from *Six Years with God*, by Jeannie Mills (A&W Publishers, Inc., 1979).

22. THE ARMS OF GOD

INTERVIEWS
Marvin Swinney; Wayne Pietila; Jim Cobb; Sandy Bradshaw; Stephan Jones; Archie Ijames; Teddy Ballard; local merchants, Fire Chief Delbert Phelps and volunteer firemen in Redwood Valley; Jeanette Kerns; Tim Stoen; George Hunter.

DOCUMENTS
Ukiah Daily Journal article by Kathy Hunter, "Terror in the Night," 1975; *The Poisoner*, essay by Lynetta Jones from Temple files; Temple photos of picnics in the church parking lot.

23. FIRST CRACKS

INTERVIEWS
Officials of the Indiana State Psychology Board; Indiana tax officials and IRS officials there; Carolyn Pickering in 1977; Rev. Lester Kinsolving; *Examiner* photographer Fran Ortiz; John Todd; former *Examiner* publisher Charles Gould; former *Examiner* editor Ed Dooley; Tim Stoen; Mike Touchette; Sandy Bradshaw; Karl Irvin and A. Dale Fiers of Disciples of Christ; Ross Case; Archie Ijames; George Hunter; Sheriff Tom Jondahl; former Sheriff Reno Bartolomie; District Attorney Duncan James, in 1977.

DOCUMENTS
October 14, 1971, *Indianapolis Star* article on Jones; Dec. 1971 stories in the *Star*; Jan. 1, 1971, *Time* magazine profile of Kinsolving; Carolyn Pickering notes to Kinsolving regarding their joint investigation; Kinsolving's unpublished stories on the Temple; Tim Stoen's Sept. 12, 1972, letter to Kinsolving; Kinsolving's 1972 series in the *Examiner*; a Sept. 27, 1972, legal memo from Temple files; Disciples of Christ annual reports and other records on Temple contacts and donations; the story based on John Burke's Sept. 20, 1972, interview with Jones; a tape of conversation between Ross Case and Leo W. on Aug. 24, 1973.

24. THE EIGHT REVOLUTIONARIES

INTERVIEWS

Jim Cobb; Wayne Pietila; Mike Touchette; John Biddulph in 1977; Jeanette Kerns; Mickey Touchette in 1977; Grace Stoen; Jim Jones in Nov. 1978.

MATERIALS

Defection letter obtained from Temple files; tapes of Jones's emergency meetings following the defection, obtained under FOIA from the FBI.

25. PLAYING WITH FIRE

Both Reiterman and Jacobs have covered the left in the Bay Area for years and reported on the bank robbery trial of Patricia Hearst. This chapter reflects that background. as well as numerous interviews, some with confidential sources.
The San Francisco section:

INTERVIEWS

Friends and relatives of Chris Lewis; Neva Sly; Jeannie and Al Mills; Sandy Bradshaw; Jim Cobb; Grace Stoen; Tim Stoen; former district attorney's investigator Dave Reuben; Gene Suttle at San Francisco Redevelopment Agency, and Federal Housing Officials; Ivory Collins; Sam Houston.

MATERIALS

Miscellaneous *San Francisco Examiner* clippings on WAPAC and Chris Lewis, The SLA and the Slaying of Rory Hithe; the Symbionese Declaration printed in the *San Francisco Chronicle*, Feb. 13, 1974; *Peoples Forum;* Tapes of Jones's speeches on terrorism and the SLA in fall of 1975 obtained under FOIA; police intelligence files on the Temple and the SLA; Chris Lewis testimonials in the *Living Word;* an undated Temple organizational blueprint for migration to the Caribbean.
The Los Angeles section:

INTERVIEWS

Tim Stoen; officials of the Los Angeles City Attorney's office; police sources in Los Angeles; former Lieutenant Bob MacIntosh; then-Captain Joe Marchesano; Officer Arthur Kagele; the Los Angeles press corps' written interview with Judge Clarence Stromwall; *San Francisco Examiner* interview with Deputy State Attorney General Mike Franchetti; spokesman for then-Chief Ed Davis and future Chief Daryl Gates.

MATERIALS

Police reports on both the riot and lewd conduct incidents; the unreleased and undated Temple defense statement, and the Temple's medical excuse; the city attorney's investigation report on the lewd conduct case handling; and legal documents filed in 1977 and 1978 over the state's attempt to unseal Jones's lewd conduct records.

26. ESCAPE VALVE

INTERVIEWS

Emerson Mitchell, a Guyanese government official who requested that his name be changed in the account; Archie Ijames; Stephan Jones; Mike Touchette, Father Andrew Morrison, Tim Stoen.

MATERIALS

Silent color video footage of December 1974 settlers trip to Guyana, plus footage of Sacred Heart healing service from Peoples Temple files. Also copy of Peoples Temple advertisement in Dec. 1974 *Guyana Chronicle*.

27. COMMUNALISTS

INTERVIEWS

Nadyne and Sam Houston; Joyce Shaw; Sandy Bradshaw; Garry Lambrev; Thomas J. Sammon; Jeannie and Al Mills; Grace Stoen; sources familiar with the medical treatment of Jim Jones.

MATERIALS

Various essays and poems by Temple children, including the Houston girls; Bob Houston résumés and Houston family scrapbook; Temple newsletters 1972–76; San Francisco Fire Department arson report on Temple fire; tape of Redwood Valley beating obtained under FOIA from FBI (Q454), with name of the teen-age victim changed to protect his identity.

28. SAN FRANCISCO IN THRALL

INTERVIEWS

Carlton Goodlett; Tom Fleming; Rev. George Bedford; Rev. Cecil Williams; various former Peoples Temple members including Sandy Bradshaw, Grace Stoen and Tim Stoen; Assemblyman Willie Brown; aides and political consultants to the late Mayor George Moscone, including Corey Busch and Don Bradley; John Maher of Delancey Street Foundation; Agar Jaicks and two other members of the Democratic Central Committee; Robert Mendelsohn; Milton Marks; Dianne Feinstein; Joseph Freitas; Richard Hongisto; Jack Morrison; Marshall Kilduff; former Mendocino Supervisor Al Barbero; Quentin Kopp; Rep. Phil Burton; Doris Thomas; H. Welton Flynn of the Black Leadership Forum; Grandvel Jackson and Joe Hall of the NAACP; Terry Francois and Rev. Amos Brown.

MATERIALS

Numerous clippings from the *San Francisco Examiner* library; tape of the Cecil Williams anniversary celebration in 1975 obtained under FOIA from the FBI; San Francisco voter records; *Peoples Forum*, 1976–77.

29. BACKWATER

INTERVIEWS

Dozens of Guyanese officials, former officials, journalists and members of the political opposition; foreign diplomats including those from the American Embassy in Georgetown; Father Andrew Morrison; Rev. Paul Tideman; Mike Touchette.

MATERIALS

Guyanese history and contemporary politics based on booklets prepared by Guyana's Ministry of Information and on a November 1974 *New Yorker* article, "Letter from Georgetown," by Jane Kramer; *CIA Diary*, by Philip Agee (Stonehill, N.Y., 1975); *White Night*, by John Peer Nugent (Rawson Wade Publishers Inc., 1979); Peoples Temple lease of the Jonestown tract, and Guyana's incorporation papers for the church.

30. RADICALS

INTERVIEWS

Al Mills; Sandy Bradshaw; Jim Cobb; Joe Freitas; Carlton Goodlett; Richard Hongisto campaign sources; Huey Newton in 1977 regarding his Cuba stay; Tim Stoen; Grace Stoen; Charles Garry.

MATERIALS

Temple files, *Peoples Forum* articles and *San Francisco Examiner* clippings on Angela Davis, Dennis Banks and Jane Fonda; Temple video tape of

Jubilee in Los Angeles; many *Examiner* clippings of International Hotel protests; Peoples Temple files and *Peoples Forum,* 1977, on the alleged spying incident; Temple correspondence with Rep. Phil Burton and the Air Force and Congress; Tim Stoen's letter to Fidel Castro Jan. 24, 1977; *Peoples Forum,* March and April 1977, on Jones's Cuba trip; Oct. 1976 letter from Mike Prokes to Forbes Burnham; *Guyana Chronicle* articles about Dymally visit in 1976; Charles Garry correspondence with Sir Lionel Luckhoo; Dec. 23, 1976, tapes of Jones's speeches to the Housing Authority regarding the International Hotel.

The interviews, documents and observations that led to our conclusions at the start of this chapter are too numerous to list, but here are some important materials used in the analysis: *New World Utopias,* by Paul Kagan (Penguin, 1975); March 1979 speech by C. Eric Lincoln, professor of sociology and religion at Duke University, while in San Francisco; *Los Angeles Times* article on cults by Dr. Louis Jolyon West and Richard Delgado, Nov. 26, 1978; House Foreign Relations Committee Report on the Assassination of Rep. Leo Ryan; *Los Angeles Daily Journal,* Dec. 1, 1978, article by Richard Delgado on "Religious Totalism...."

31. FLIGHT OF THE PRINCESS

INTERVIEWS

Grace and Tim Stoen; Joyce Shaw; Walt Jones; Mike Touchette; Stephan Jones.

MATERIALS

Temple tapes of conversations between Grace Stoen and Jim Jones, from church files; Lynetta Jones's written accounts of John Stoen from church files; various legal documents signed by Grace and Tim Stoen, from church files.

32. ONE GALLANT, GLORIOUS END?

INTERVIEWS

Marvin Swinney; Jeannie and Al Mills; Walter Jones; Joyce Shaw; Sam and Nadyne Houston; Garry Lambrev in 1977; Sandy Bradshaw; Stephan Jones; Grace Stoen; Fresno Four member George Gruner; *Fresno Bee* City Editor Ray Steele; Associated Press co-workers of Sam Houston who attended Bob Houston's funeral.

MATERIALS

Introductory quote from Jim Jones from Temple tape of Redwood Valley meeting, obtained under FOIA from FBI (Q454); police and coroner reports on Bob Houston's death; affidavits from Carolyn Layton and Harriett Tropp on the church attempts to silence Joyce Shaw, dated Oct. 10, 1978.

33. PRESIDENTIAL EMBRACE

INTERVIEWS

Agar Jaicks and other members of the Democratic Central Committee; Cecil Williams; *Examiner* reporter Lon Daniels; sources on Mrs. Carter's advance team; Charles Gain, Robert Mendelsohn, Milton Marks, Willie Brown, Carlton Goodlett, Charles Garry, Marge Boynton, Walter Heady, George Hunter and some members of the Fresno Four who attended the Jones testimonial.

MATERIALS

Fall 1976 issues of *Peoples Forum* on Jones-Mondale; tape of the Jones-Rosalynn Carter conversation obtained under FOIA after recovery in Jonestown; correspondence between Jones and Mrs. Carter from Temple files; *Peoples Forum* stories, Temple film and other files on the Sept. 1976 testimonial; *White Night,* by John Peer Nugent (Rawson Wade Publishers, Inc., 1979).

34. THE WRITING ON THE WALL

INTERVIEWS

Stephan Jones; Mike Touchette; Grace Stoen; Tim Stoen; Walter and Charlotte Baldwin; Marshall Kilduff; Joseph Freitas on the Julie Smith article and church inquiries about it; district attorney's investigators, including Dave Reuben; Sandy Bradshaw; Steve Katsaris; William Hunter by the *San Francisco Examiner*'s James A. Finefrock, and in January 1982 by Reiterman; Don Canter; John Egan. David Jenkins; Steve Gavin; Katy Butler.

MATERIALS

San Francisco Examiner library stories on Yvonne Golden; and article about Opportunity High School by Nancy Dooley in the *San Francisco Examiner*, Dec. 12, 1978; Summer 1977 Temple tapes of conversations between Grace Stoen and Jim Jones and between Grace Stoen and Tim Stoen; transcripts of the same; Jan.–March 1977 *Peoples Forum; New West* magazine of Aug. 1977 on Kilduff's earlier attempts at publication; documents regarding the guardianship and power of attorney over John Stoen from church files; copy of Tim Stoen diary and postcard to Chaikin from church files; the Temple's organizational blueprint, undated but calling for migration to Caribbean; Temple documents and the results of church FOIA requests to the FCC, Treasury Department, FBI and others; Oct. 10, 1978, affidavit of Harriet Tropp regarding the Georgetown legal conferences, and a similar one from Gene Chaikin; memos marked "To JJ, from TB," from Temple files; memos from Debbie Touchette and others from Temple files; accounts of suicide protest published in Nov. 1978 in San Francisco and Indianapolis; church files on Stoen defection.

35. SCANDAL

INTERVIEWS

Marshall Kilduff; Phil Tracy in 1977; Cecil Williams; Bill Barnes regarding his story in the *Examiner;* Carlton Goodlett; political figures including three Democratic Central Committee members; State Assemblyman Art Agnos; over 18 defectors including Mickey Touchette, Jim Cobb, Wayne Pietila, Grace Stoen and the Millses; George Moscone, Willie Brown, Mervyn Dymally and other politicians interviewed by the *Examiner* in 1977; Dave Reuben and Bob Graham of the district attorney's office.

MATERIALS

April 1977 *Peoples Forum;* Aug. 1977 *New West;* Bill Barnes's June 11, 1977, story on Temple anti-*New West* campaign; police reports on "break-in" at *New West;* Temple transcript of July 31, 1977, rally, and *Peoples Forum* accounts of it; Aug. 7, 1977, *Examiner* and other issues; Peoples Temple files on the Housing Authority; Herb Caen column Aug. 18, 1977; district attorney's investigative report on Peoples Temple, Sept. 1977.

36. EXODUS

INTERVIEWS

Marshall Kilduff; Harold Turley; mutual friends and relatives of the Edwardses; immigration sources; Sandy Bradshaw; Archie Ijames; Debbie Blakey; Los Angeles district attorney's investigator Steve Ramirez; Sam Houston, Veronica Perry, Freddy Lewis interview from Peter H. King of *San Francisco Examiner;* Mike Prokes with Reiterman, 1977; Mike Touchette and Stephan Jones on early Jonestown; Dave Reuben and other sources within San Francisco district attorney's office. Information on Temple bank accounts from interviews with former members, including Tim Stoen and Debbie Blakey, and an *Examiner* interview with Teri Buford; also, Buford's interview with House Foreign Affairs Committee investigators.

MATERIALS

Temple travel records on Le Flora Townes; Temple exodus forms and records; 1979 reports from both State Department and the House Foreign Affairs Committee on assassination of Rep. Leo Ryan; Jonestown skills forms; radio communications intercepted by ham radio operator "R. V. Peacock" listening to Jonestown transmissions for the *Examiner*.

37. HEAVEN ON EARTH?

INTERVIEWS

Stephan Jones; Mike Touchette; Charlotte and Walter Baldwin; Mike Carter; Dale Parks; Mrs. B. who requested anonymity.

MATERIALS

Marceline's letters home to her parents, provided by the Baldwins; Peoples Temple tape recording of Jones and Jerry obtained under FOIA from FBI, dated Oct. 21, 1976, labeled Q735; Jonestown progress report to the government, summer 1977; Temple death list compiled Nov. 1978.

38. CLOSE ENCOUNTERS

INTERVIEWS

Joe Mazor; district attorney's sources and federal sources; Charles Garry and Pat Richartz; Grace Stoen and Walt Jones; World Airways spokesmen; Jeannie and Al Mills; Duncan James; Marvin and Jackie Swinney; Mendocino County Sheriff Tom Jondahl; Sandy Bradshaw; Tim Stoen; Archie Ijames; Treasury Department sources; Amos, a streetperson; Leon Broussard; Mr. and Mrs. B.; Stephan Jones; "Skip" Roberts; State Department officials familiar with the Broussard affair.

MATERIALS

San Francisco Examiner clippings (April 11 and May 11, 1971) on Joe Mazor's prison term; Mazor's criminal record and June 8, 1965, probation report from Temple files; Temple files on the customs investigation; Temple radio transmissions intercepted by *Examiner* ham; Temple correspondence with U.S. Customs; Temple notes on intercepted customs report routed through Interpol to Guyanese police; Sept. 1977 affidavit of Dennis Banks; Mendocino County property records obtained by the *Examiner* and property information obtained by Reiterman from Joyce Shaw and others; church files on care homes and children's homes; the Sharon Amos documents found by AP's Peter Arnett; House assassination report; documents obtained from customs under FOIA on Temple gun purchases and smuggling; inventory of guns recovered at Jonestown Nov. 1978.

39. SIEGE

INTERVIEWS

State Department officials familiar with the Broussard affair; Stephan Jones; Leon Broussard; Sandy Bradshaw; Jeff Haas; Clarence Hughes; Sir Lionel Luckhoo; Mike Carter, Pat Richartz; Charles Garry; Dr. Carlton Goodlett; Juanita Bogue; a Guyanese constable.

MATERIALS
Peoples Temple tapes of the siege from church files; a two-week written chronology of the period written by Carolyn Layton; testimony of Teri Buford and Mark Lane to the House Committee on Foreign Affairs; documents on the Stoen case from the legal file of Clarence Hughes; copies of letters furnished by Guyanese sources; Federal Communications Commission cable transcripts obtained by the Temple under FOIA, and now in church files; Temple tape recording recovered at Jonestown, by the FBI.

40. ON THE DEFENSIVE

INTERVIEWS
Charles Garry; Pat Richartz; Marshall Bentzman; Stephan Jones; Sam and Nadyne Houston; Tom Tuttle; Joyce Shaw; Leo Ryan; Phyllis Houston; interviews with Concerned Relatives.

MATERIALS
Streetfighter in the Courtroom, by Charles Garry and Art Goldberg (E. P. Dutton, 1977); Teri Buford letter; tapes of Charles Garry recorded by the Temple and obtained from FBI under FOIA (Q708); Temple records on lewd conduct case and David Kwan letter; Reiterman's Nov. 18, 1977, story on the Houston family; the Temple's legal files.

41. SINS OF THE FATHER

INTERVIEWS
Grace Stoen, Tim Stoen, Jeff Haas; Debbie Blakey; Jim Jones by Reiterman; Jean Brown; political figures in San Francisco, including Willie Brown, and Agar Jaicks and John Maher of Delancey Street Foundation; Steve Katsaris; Richard McCoy; Howard and Beverly Oliver.

MATERIALS
California court documents on Stoen custody case; Temple files and notes about the San Francisco hearing; Nov. 25, 1977, Tim Stoen letter to Jones; radio transmissions obtained by the Temple from the FCC under FOIA; affidavits of Bruce and Billy Oliver from Temple files (interviews done by Charles Garry).

42. WHITE NIGHTS

INTERVIEWS
Stephan Jones; Mike Touchette; the Bogue family, especially Juanita Bogue; the Parks family, especially Dale Parks; Mike Carter; Tim Carter; Mike Prokes; Sandy Bradshaw; Charlotte and Walter Baldwin; Sharon Mills; Richard Dwyer and State Department officials who declined use of their names.

MATERIALS
DeeDee Lawrence school book recovered at Jonestown by *San Francisco Examiner* reporter Peter H. King in Dec. 1978; Temple tape obtained under FOIA from FBI, dated Dec. 12, 1977, and labeled Q938; inventory of Jones quarters from Jacobs's visit Nov. 1979; Internal Revenue Service documents obtained under FOIA by the Temple; Temple tapes obtained under FOIA, dated April 12–13, 1978, and labeled Q635–40 and Q588–94; letters from Marceline Jones to her parents, spring 1978; appendix to House Foreign Affairs Committee report, p. 137.

43. SECESSIONS AND SKIRMISHES

INTERVIEWS

Debbie Blakey; various State Department sources; Jeff Haas; Stephan Jones; Mike Touchette; Mike Carter; Sandy Bradshaw; Dr. Laurence Layton; Steve Katsaris; Jeannie and Al Mills; Sam Houston; Clare Bouquet; Sherwin Harris; George Hunter; Howard and Beverly Oliver; Tim Stoen; Charles Garry; Tim Carter; Pat Richartz; Jim Cobb on Stoen lawsuits.

MATERIALS

The Amos documents, about 150 pages of Temple documents and memos recovered at Jonestown in Nov. 1978 by AP reporter Peter Arnett; a May 12, 1978, memo from Karen Layton to Jones; a Debbie Touchette memo on May 13, 1978, to Jones; a May 13, 1978, Terry Carter memo to Jones, and a July 15, 1978, memo from Karen Layton to Jones regarding Lisa Layton; the Temple's "decision to die" statement in a letter by Pam Moton to the U.S. House of Representatives; news accounts of the Concerned Relatives protest April 1978; Concerned Relatives petitions and briefs; Temple files on Brian Bouquet letters; Clare Bouquet correspondence with officials.

44. 41 LAMAHA GARDENS

INTERVIEWS

Stephan Jones, Mike Touchette, Mike Carter, Tim Carter, Mike Prokes, "Skip" Roberts (Guyana police assistant commissioner); Paula Adams; Sandy Bradshaw; Dale Parks; Brindley Benn; several State Department officials, including Richard Dwyer and Douglas Ellice; Tim Stoen; Sir Lionel Luckhoo; Clarence Hughes; Jose Louis DeSilva; Cecil Griffith; Paul Persaud; Father Andrew Morrison; Mrs. Harold Bollers; a number of other Guyanese officials; former officials and journalists; diplomats from other countries.

MATERIALS

The "Amos documents," obtained by AP's Peter Arnett, specifically March 3, 1978, memo by Sharon Amos, a March 22, 1978, memo from Amos, an undated unsigned memo to Jones; March 1978, May 19, 1978, March 9, March 7, Feb. 27 memos from Amos to Jones; an Aug. 25, 1978, Marceline Jones memo to Jones; Guyana purchase orders from Temple files; copies of Benn's newspaper articles on the Temple.

45. NO NEWS IS GOOD NEWS

INTERVIEWS

George Hunter; Tim Carter; C. A. "Skip" Roberts of the Guyana police; Richard Dwyer and State Department officials familiar with these events; Gordon Lindsay; Mike Prokes; Reiterman's numerous interviews with Social Security Administration officials for 1979 stories in the *San Francisco Examiner*, including Fred Adams, Fred Young, Ed Kramer, Howard Rolland and Al Bartoli.

MATERIALS

The May 1979 House Foreign Affairs Committee and the State Department reports on the Ryan assassination; Kathy Hunter's journal, published in the *Guyana Chronicle* in a special Jonestown edition, Dec. 1978; Gordon Lindsay's unpublished account of his Temple coverage, "Legacy of Fear"; Social Security Administration documents obtained under FOIA by the *San Francisco Examiner*, copies of Ambassador Burke's cable to Washington and the State Department reply.

46. THE DOWNWARD SPIRAL

INTERVIEWS

Tim Carter; Mike Carter; Mike Touchette; Stephan Jones; Sandy Bradshaw; Dale Parks.

MATERIALS

Nearly 300 "Dear Dad" letters recovered from Jonestown by various news correspondents, including Jacobs; Temple tape recording obtained under FOIA, dated April 17, 1978, labeled Q736.

47. CON GAMES AND HIJINKS

INTERVIEWS

Don Freed; Pat Richartz; Charles Garry; Joe Mazor; Stephan Jones; Carlton Goodlett; Paul Jarrico; Jeff Haas; Gordon Lindsay.

MATERIALS

Tape of Don Freed's speech at Jonestown and comments on the Temple's Georgetown, Guyana, radio show; Mark Lane's speeches in Jonestown and San Francisco, and transcripts of news conferences following his Jonestown visit; tape and transcript of St. Francis Hotel meeting; miscellaneous newspaper and magazine articles about Lane, including Feb. 13, 1979, *Esquire* and Aug. 1979 *Mother Jones;* testimony of Lane and Teri Buford before the House Foreign Affairs Committee investigators; undated letter of intent for film on Jonestown; St. Francis Hotel bills for Lane and Freed, Sept. 5, 1978; Jim Jones letter to Jarrico, Aug. 2, 1978; Sept. 5, 1978, note on hotel meeting, signed by Freed; tape of Garry and Mazor after their Jonestown visit; transcript of Lane's Sept. 20, 1978, news conference, Georgetown; the legal counteroffensive documents; Temple transcripts of Lane's statements, as reported on San Francisco radio stations; newspaper clippings from San Francisco radio stations; newspaper clippings from *San Francisco Examiner* of Lane's Oct. 3, 1978, San Francisco news conference; Temple notes on negotiations with Lane and various Gene Chaikin legal memos; Jonestown tape on Oct. 2, 1978, regarding *Enquirer* article; Jean Brown Dec. 3, 1978, affidavit regarding payments to Lane.

48. IN THE HANDS OF A MADMAN

INTERVIEWS

Stephan Jones; Mike Touchette; Lee Ingram; Dale Parks; Mike Carter; Tim Carter.

MATERIALS

Temple tape recordings recovered by FBI from Jonestown and obtained under FOIA—Oct. 1, 1978, Q352, Oct. 2, Q401, undated labeled Q271; records of punishments recovered from typed "Instructions" of Oct. 16, 17 and 20, 1978, found by *San Jose Mercury* reporter Peter Carey; inventory of Jonestown drugs from *San Francisco Examiner* article of Dec. 28, 1978, by reporters James A. Finefrock, Peter H. King and Nancy Dooley; undated Temple recording after Timofeyev visit of Oct. 1, labeled Q393 by the FBI.

49. THE CONGRESSMAN, AND OTHERS

INTERVIEWS

Sam Houston; Leo Ryan; Clare Bouquet; Clement Zablocki; congressional staffers of House Foreign Affairs Committee; the Ryan family; backgrounders with various State Department officials; Charles Garry; Steve Katsaris; Debbie Blakey; Douglas Ellice, Jr.; Pat Richartz; Sandy Bradshaw; Dr. Carlton Goodlett; Marshall Bentzman; Archie Ijames; Paula Adams; Tim Carter.

MATERIALS
    The State Department and House Foreign Affairs Committee reports in
May 1979; tape recording recovered from Jonestown and obtained under FOIA,
dated Nov. 11, 1978, and labeled Q708; Dec. 9, 1978, article by Joseph B. Treaster,
New York Times; Mark Lane and Teri Buford testimony to House Foreign Affairs
Committee investigators.

50. THE EYE OF THE STORM

INTERVIEWS
    Charlotte and Walter Baldwin; Sharon Mills; Stephan Jones; Mike Tou-
chette; Douglas Ellice; Dale Parks; Teena Bogue; Juanita Bogue; Jim Bogue;
Monica Bagby; Jim Cobb; Harold Cordell and Mike Carter.

MATERIALS
    Temple tape recordings obtained under FOIA, dated Nov. 5, 1978, and
labeled Q161; tape undated but most likely late Oct. or early Nov., labeled Q341;
tape dated Nov. 8, 1978, and labeled Q175; Ellice's Dec. 1978 cable to the State
Department.

51. EN ROUTE

INTERVIEWS
    Sam Houston; Gordon Lindsay; Joe Holsinger; Jackie Speier; Charles
Garry; various individuals at the *Chronicle;* Jeannie and Al Mills, and management at the rooming house where Carter stayed; Tim Carter; free-lance photogra-
pher Terry Schmidt; Fran Ortiz and other colleagues of Greg Robinson; several
State Department officials; Don Harris and Steve Sung; Temple transcripts of
interviews conducted at the send-off chicken dinner Nov. 13, 1978; Sandy Brad-
shaw; Carlton Goodlett; Concerned Relatives, including Tim Stoen, Jim Cobb,
Mickey Touchette, Steve Katsaris, the Houstons, Clare Bouquet, the Olivers,
Bonnie Thielmann; Leo Ryan; Bob Flick; Guyana officials at Washington Embassy;
Guyana and State Department officials in Georgetown.

52. PORT KAITUMA

INTERVIEWS
    Neville Annibourne, Richard Dwyer; federal sources; Corp. Emil Rudder;
the local constable; Charles Garry; Herbert Thomas; Beverly Oliver; Steve Sung
and Bob Flick; Gordon Lindsay; Jim McElvane; Jim Jones; Karen Layton; Clare
Bouquet; Tim Carter; Jim Cobb.

MATERIALS
    Port Kaituma police logs of plane travel and injured Temple members; NBC
film of the visit; State Department and Foreign Affairs Committee reports in May
1979.

53. LAST CHANCE

INTERVIEWS
    Ron Javers; Don Harris; Charles Garry; Marceline Jones; Stephan Jones;
Mike Touchette; Anthony Katsaris; Steve Katsaris; Maria Katsaris; Patricia and
Judy Houston; Phyllis Houston; Carol Houston Boyd; Beverly Oliver and her sons;
Jim Jones; Jim Cobb; Dick Tropp; Richard Dwyer; Leo Ryan; Patty Cartmell;
Wesley Breidenbach; Tim Carter.

MATERIALS

Several hundred photographs by Greg Robinson; Reiterman photos; NBC film; State Department and Foreign Affairs Committee reports; Temple agricultural operations files; Temple files on the Steve Katsaris defamation case and Maria's polygraph; NBC film of the Cobb and Oliver families.

54. HOLOCAUST

INTERVIEWS

Stephan Jones; Mike Touchette; Sherwin Harris; Richard Dwyer; Mike Carter; Lee Ingram; Sandy Bradshaw; Grace Stoen; Tim Stoen; Gordon Lindsay; Thomas Beikman; Archie Ijames; Jim Cobb; federal sources; Steve Sung and Bob Flick; Ron Javers; Harold Cordell; the Bogues and the Parkses; Anthony and Steve Katsaris; Carol Boyd; Sam Houston; Patrick McDonald Luke; Charles Garry; Tim Carter; congressional staffer Jim Schollaert; ten *Examiner* staffers; Clare Bouquet; Stanley Clayton; Odell Rhodes to reporters in the aftermath; Skip Roberts, eyewitness to positioning of the bodies after the holocaust; Jackie Speier.

MATERIALS

A deposition Chuck Beikman gave to his Guyanese lawyers; State Department and Foreign Affairs Committee reports in May 1979; Mark Lane's press statements and testimony to the House Foreign Affairs Committee investigators; testimony of Mike Prokes and the Carter brothers at the Matthews Ridge inquest into the holocaust; autopsy reports on Jim Jones and Annie Moore; Mark Lane's *The Strongest Poison* (Hawthorn, 1980).

INDEX

ABOUT THE AUTHORS

Tim Reiterman has specialized in investigative projects as a reporter and editor for most of his four decades in journalism. He was awarded his undergraduate degree and his master's in journalism at UC Berkeley, where he began his reporting career covering the tumultuous 1960s and early 1970s for major publications. While attending college, Reiterman began working for the Associated Press, where his coverage included the Patty Hearst kidnapping and the Hells Angels. He moved to the *San Francisco Examiner*, where he investigated Jim Jones and the Peoples Temple before covering Congressman Leo Ryan's trip to Jonestown in Guyana in 1978.

Reiterman was wounded in the jungle airstrip attack that killed Rep. Ryan—the first congressman to die in the line of duty—and three newsmen and a temple defector. He spent eighteen months investigating abuses within the temple before the tragedy and years following it unraveling why and how it occurred.

After stints on the *Examiner*'s investigative team and as city editor, Reiterman moved to the *Los Angeles Times*, where he led the investigative team and helped supervise Pulitzer Prize–winning coverage of the 1992 Los Angeles riots and the 1994 Northridge earthquake. Projects Reiterman directed and edited were nominated for several Pulitzer Prizes, won top awards from Sigma Delta Chi and Investigative Reporters and Editors in 1997, and won the Associated Press's top sports enterprise award in 2000.

Reiterman lives in San Francisco, where he serves as the Associated Press news editor for northern California. He has taught at the UC Berkeley Graduate School of Journalism for nearly a decade.

John Jacobs, Reiterman's collaborator, was a widely respected journalist who died in 2000. Jacobs earned a bachelor's and master's degree at UC Berkeley, as well as a master's degree at the State University of New York at Stony Brook. He worked at *The Washington Post* from 1977 to 1978 before moving to the *San Francisco Examiner.* When Reiterman was hospitalized after the Port Kaituma shootings, Jacobs traveled to Guyana and largely took over responsibility for *Examiner* coverage of the Jones story there.

    After fifteen years at the *Examiner,* Jacobs moved to *The Sacramento Bee,* where he wrote a political column and served as political editor for the *Bee* and other McClatchy newspapers. He is the author of *A Rage for Justice: The Passion and Politics of Phillip Burton* (1995), a highly praised biography of the late California congressman who had shaped landmark legislation. It won the D.B. Hardeman Prize for the best book on Congress from the Lyndon B. Johnson Foundation.